The Power of Total Perspective

R.E. McMaster, Jr.

CONTENTS

SECTION III: SCIENCE AND TECHNOLOGY
Chapter

SECTION IV: ECONOMICS

SECTION V: WHERE WE STAND

SECTION VI: SOLUTIONS

SECTION VII: LOVE AND MONEY

SECTION VII: HEALTH

CONCLUSION

INTRODUCTION

THEY LIVE...BUT WHAT ABOUT US?

June 29, 1989

A brief personal history: During the Vietnam War, I was a USAF pilot, a T-38 and T-41 instructor pilot and a VIP pilot at NORAD HQ, Colorado Springs. Remember the movie "Top Gun"? The aircraft flown to simulate the Soviet MiGs in that movie were T-38s. It's the same airplane the astronauts fly when they accompany a space shuttle during landing.

I turned down a law school deferment to become an AF pilot because I thought it was important to spend some time serving my country. Knowing what I know now about this government and the way the military is run, would I do that again? I think not.

There are a number of serious threats to our freedom which we may want to carefully consider. If we're not free politically, what good is it to be rich? Freedom always walks on the legs of both law and economics. Both circumscribe our territory. Our freedom is limited by, defined by, and exercised within the law and economics of our society; increasingly influenced by political and scientific change. New technology often challenges old customs and laws, necessitating new ones; shifting power, influencing politics, and reshaping society.

History - Two Views

There are two views of history: (1) History happens by accident or, (2) it is planned. The general public is taught that history happens by accident. However, the upper echelons of our religious, governmental, economic, military, educational institutions, etc. know that history is planned. For example, RAND Corporation was planning the future, and consequently, the history of the Pacific Basin as far back as 1954. Was this planning in line with the will of the people who live in the Pacific Basin? I doubt it.

If future planning is not in the best interest of the vast majority of the people, then it is kept hidden. Otherwise, the enlightened public would see to it that the plan was scrapped. The definition of a hidden plan contrary to the general interests is a *"conspiracy."* But *"conspiracy"* is not a word which Americans like to use, because we have been conditioned to think of the word *"conspiracy"* in the same vein as the words *"radical," "redneck," "revolutionary," "bigot,"* etc., all very negative.

Up until recently, the very best movie out of Hollywood on how the world really works was the 1976 MGM blockbuster, *Network.* Faye Dunaway, William Holden, Peter Finch and Robert Duvall brought the work of Paddy Chayefsky four Academy Awards — best actor, best actress, best supporting actress and best screenplay. More than just a novel, a work of fiction, it was, in fact, the truth. I discussed this movie in some detail in *The Reaper* a few years back.

Network focused on how television is used to program and control the masses for the benefit of the multinational corporations. The television networks condition the masses to react emotionally, without thinking, contrary to their own interests. *"We, the people,"* are pawns in the money game.

In the most brilliant monologue of the entire movie, a multinational corporate chairman, Mr. Jensen, declares,

"You are an old man who thinks in terms of nations and peoples. There are no Russians. There are no nations. There are no peoples... There is only one holistic system of systems, one vast, interwoven, interacting, multi-variant, multinational dominion of dollars....That is the atomic, subatomic and galactic structure of things today....you get up on your little 21-inch screen and howl about America and democracy.... There is no America, there is no democracy. There is only IBM and ITT and AT&T and DuPont and Dow and Union Carbide and Exxon. Those are the nations of the world today. What do you think the Russians talk about in their counsels of state? Karl Marx? They get out their linear programming charts, statistical decision theories, mini-max solutions, and compute the price/cost probabilities of their transactions and investments just like we do. We no longer live in a world of nations and ideologies,.... The world is a collage of corporations, inexorably determined by the immutable bylaws of business. The world is a business,... and it has been so since man crawled out of the slime...

"Our children will live,...to see that perfect world...one vast ecumenical holding company for whom all men will work to serve a common profit, in which all men will hold a share of stock, all necessities provided, all anxieties tranquilized, all boredom amused. And I have chosen you,...to preach this evangel."

In other words, *Network* forecast the victory of money over the human spirit.

Freedom in Perspective

Because we are effectively brainwashed by the distracting entertainment (sic) of television today, *"we, the people,"* of the United States have forgotten that 99% of the human race, until the United States was founded, lived under the tyranny of kings. Many Americans today have no sense of time or history, demonstrated by the fact that there is a movement to put the actor Ronald Reagan on Mount Rushmore. Too many Americans today are no longer willing to bear the burden and responsibility (pain) of freedom. Freedom requires men to assume the painful responsibility for their own lives, and also perform appropriate duties for their fellow man. Freedom requires men to covenant and contract with each other, rather than prey or depend upon others. Freedom demands principles for which men will fight and die. No man is free until he has decided for what he's willing to fight and die. Freedom requires keeping one's governmental, religious and economic power close to home, where it can be nurtured, watched over and husbanded. Freedom means that individuals are held accountable.

In early American history, ignorance of the law was no excuse, because all men were self-governing according to the common law and the Ten Commandments, which formed the basis of the legal system. Further, there was honest money, and men controlled their own finances. They didn't trust banks, and if they did, only local banks. They dared not ship their money off to distant places where it would be stolen, squandered or ultimately used to finance their own unemployment. But, this is history. Today, the United States is filled with timid, weak men who prefer the calm seas of bureaucratic tyranny and irresponsibility to the tumultuous seas and risks of liberty. Americans have sold out for bread crumbs, and I mean bread crumbs. *The Wall Street Journal* reports that only three out of ten families in the United States have any discretionary income at all after necessities and taxes are paid. And of the remaining 30%, the total discretionary income amounts to a whopping $12,300. So, the spread between the few rich and the many poor in this country is widening dramatically, making the country increasingly unstable, politically and socially.

With debt-bloated lifestyles and dehydrated spirits, the deification of greed and the legislation of envy have marked the Eighties. Seething hatred has followed. The great Soviet freedom fighter, Alexander Solzhenitsyn, had harsh words for those whose god is materialism: *"It is enough if you don't freeze in the cold, and thirst and hunger don't claw at your sides. If your back isn't broken, if your feet can walk, if both arms can bend, if both eyes can see, and if both ears hear, then whom should you envy? And why? Our envy of others devours us most of all. Rub your eyes and purify your heart and prize above all else in the world those who love you and who wish you well. Do not hurt or scold them, and never part from any of them in anger. After all, you simply don't know; it might be your last act."*

The Socialization of Envy

There is no sense of community in this nation any more. There is no social consensus, because there is no moral consensus. Juvenile drug gangs have spread out from New York and Los Angeles into smaller cities across the United States. Small towns are also affected. The cities are degenerating into crime-ridden war zones. The cities killed the countryside, and so committed suicide in the process. Cities depend upon the countryside for people and resources. They are essentially parasitic.

The prospering development of community is being undermined by the divisiveness of envy and the destructiveness of drugs and crime. The occultism which has also captured this country is a throwback to paganism. All Third World undeveloped countries are marked by envy, magic, drugs, and resistance to change. Third World people are generally desperately poor, except for the elite few, and live in miserable conditions. The environment is plundered just to survive.

The appeal of socialism/communism is the appeal of envy; the urge to destroy those who are, or have it, better than you do. Socialism and communism are the great leveling political systems. But so is democracy. Democracy is mob rule, a transitory step between republicanism and socialism/communism. Democracy also focuses on the transfer of wealth, the leveling of people economically through the progressive income tax and welfare, as our federal budget's butter programs so clearly demonstrate.

Socialism/communism and democracy take from those who have (forcibly) and give to those who do not have. This is legalized theft. It usurps from the church and family their biblically mandated charitable roles. It is the politics of envy and legislated gangsterism. It is criminal. Small wonder that Americans say that one out of three members of Congress is corrupt, and only 12% of Americans have a great deal of confidence in the men and women running the U.S. government. This is a pre-revolutionary attitude. But, rather than having any sense of local community, Americans today feel alienated and autonomous. Anomie is prevalent.

Unsocial

Once when I was in Houston, I got caught up in rush hour traffic. I was appalled at how empty the separate carpooling lane was. As long as Americans continue to maintain their radical autonomy, isolation and insulation, we won't come close to having a sense of local community, much less national unity. Today the media emphasis is on *"do your own thing," "every man for himself," "get what you can while the getting's good," "me first."* With no common moral/social consensus and the likes of 80 languages alone being spoken in the Los Angeles public school system, there is no basis for peaceful democracy, only bureaucratic tyranny. Moreover, when men are uneducated and without vocabulary, the only way they have left to express themselves is emotionally and violently. This makes them easier to control, too. Television has homogenized us, and computers can now track our every move.

The destructive force of envy has reached such a pre-revolutionary intensity, that the media is now destroying many who have power, are successful or even look or act like a hero. Despite their Achilles heels, across the board, in nearly all occupations, the destructive thrust of envy in this country has either destroyed or undercut Jimmy Carter, AT&T, Pete Rose, Dr. James Dobson, Oliver North, Michael Milken, Jim Wright, Robert Prechter, and Dan Quayle. Our courts are revolutionary and used for the radical, envious redistribution of wealth. Fully 96% of the civil lawsuits in the world take place in this country.

TV the Opiate

The public schools and network television instill and then reinforce the gospel of envy. Was the Ayatollah Khomeini correct when he commented in his will that Iran has no greater source of pride *"than the fact that the U.S. with all of its huge military arsenal and string of puppet regimes, and the interna-*

tional mass media at its service, has been so disgraced and humbled against Iran that it does not know to whom it should resort." Notice the key phrase in our context, *"...the international mass media at its service...."*

Americans watch over seven hours of television a day. They are habitually addicted to TV. John Muller, professor of political science at the University of Rochester, wrote in *The Wall Street Journal* of May 23, 1989, *"Western television has already proved itself a highly successful opiate for the masses. That's exactly what the Soviets need right now."* That says it all! Television is a drug for the masses, an escape from reality and involvement in life. (The Soviets spent $250 million annually on disinformation in the U.S. filtered through their plants in the media.) Add professional sports to TV and Americans live in never-never land. So, why shouldn't our youth flip-out on drugs also? Their parents set the pattern of escapism.

People Programming

A far more evil practice, in the tradition of *The Manchurian Candidate*, is afoot. Called *"red termites"* by Jaspar Riggins, a former civilian specialist for the U.S. Army's Electronic Counter-Measures Intelligence (Search) branch, some poor folks in the U.S. are being programmed by these *"red termites"* to kill. These assassins respond to post-hypnotic commands, possibly triggered by tiny electronic implants. The methodologies of A.R. Luria, L.B. Beria, K. Platanov, W. Wundty, L. Rohklin and W.H. Gantt have proven successful in setting off the compulsive behavior. Certain lethal and debilitating neuro-toxic poisons facilitate receptivity. The possibility that Patrick Purdy, who shot several students at Cleveland Elementary School, Stockton, California, was programmed is being investigated.

Little by Little

Leonard Peikoff's book, *The Ominous Parallels: The End of Freedom in America,* has been uncannily accurate in predicting precisely how the United States would follow the same path as Nazi Germany. In fact, the United States is fast becoming a combination of fascist Nazi Germany and/or Argentina. In Argentina, martial law was declared and civil rights were suspended. Ditto South Africa, Red China, Venezuela, and the U.S.S.R. Is this what we have to look forward to here in the United States in the *"Nasty Nineties"*? By the year 2012? I am concerned - the movement to confiscate guns is certainly a bold step in that direction. Only 1,649 Americans died from gunshot wounds in 1985. Compare that to the fact that 1,663 died from choking to death while eating, 3,612 as a result of drugs or medication, 4,407 drowned, 4,938 died in fires, 12,001 died from falls, and 45,901 Americans met their end in automobile accidents. Do we outlaw the automobile? Do automobiles kill or do drivers of automobiles kill? Do guns kill people, or do people kill people? When a nation eliminates risk and personal responsibility, it sheds freedom and dons the cloak of tyranny.

The world is getting tense. The effort to lock up this country and tie the world down tight under a totalitarian global one world political order will occur by 2012. Such is the logical extension of an integrated global economic marketplace. The magic show concocted to woo the masses will be straight out of ZARDOZ (The Wizard of Oz). But the next immediate grab could be to replace the U.S. Constitution.

There is dissent across this land as well as across the globe. Minorities are unhappy. Some Blacks want to be compensated for slavery and returned to Africa. Americans who have leveraged their credit cards to the hilt, who have mortgaged and re-mortgaged their homes, and who have sold their wives to the workforce, are fast approaching the point of physical and financial exhaustion. Climatic aberrations are aggravating the situation. Meanwhile, the total tax burden is between 44%-46% (1989), double what the slaves of the ancient world paid. But an IRS survey of 12,000 foreign-owned corporations, operating inside the United States, revealed that foreign-owned companies are paying an effective tax rate of just 1% on their U.S. profits. The American people are increasingly economically disenfranchised, while the U.S. is a cozy tax haven for the corporate elite. The Federal Reserve notes in the denominations of $10, $20, $50 and $100 now have magnetic ink patterns that make each of them unique, and can set off metal detectors.

The Ozone Hoax

In pursuit of a One World Order, scare tactics and fraud are being used with regard to the ozone hole at the South Pole. This climatic crisis is partially a ruse to seize at least one-third of the world's prime land and place it under the umbrella of the World Wilderness Fund and the United Nations, so that the multinational banks can control it. It's part and parcel of the move toward a global order.

In 1983, Soviet academician N.N. Moiseyev announced the discovery that a nuclear winter would wipe out all of life on earth in the aftermath of a nuclear war. This radical concept has now been totally discredited. But - surprise, surprise - in 1989, this same N.N. Moiseyev announced his discovery that the greenhouse effect is caused by industrial emissions threatening the biosphere. Kremlin leaders and the Trilateralists of Europe, the United States and Japan are using the environmental emergency as a pretext for destroying the sovereignty of nations and establishing one world rule. Just think how effectively the network media masters and mind-benders will be able to use all the nasty natural climatological phenomena which will be occurring in the next two to three years to their diabolical benefit.

The claim that the ozone hole (described by a British Antarctic expedition in 1985) was generated by the use of chlorofluorocarbons (CFCs) is a scientific fraud. This ozone hole in the Antarctic was first discovered in 1956 by another British scientist, the late professor Sir Gordon Dobson, who is known as the

"Messiah of Ozone Research." A U.S. geologist specializing in ozone research, Rogelio Maduro, has confirmed that the atmospheric readings in the Antarctic are being distorted by recent volcanic activity there.

The world's volcanoes contribute 36 million tons of chlorine gas each year to the atmosphere, compared to only 750,000 tons attributed to CFCs. Upwind from the Antarctic observation post is a volcano named Mt. Erebus. Mt. Erebus has been erupting since 1982. It contributes 1,000 tons of chlorine gas to the atmosphere every single day. It is Mt. Erebus that is contributing on average 360,000 tons of chlorine gas or half the amount produced by CFCs. It is Mt. Erebus which is causing the ozone hole in the Antarctic. Further, if it were true that chlorine is destroying the ozone layer, the ozone layer would have been totally depleted by now.

Mr. Maduro has aligned with 30 leading environmental scientists in the United States who have disputed the correlation between the ozone depletion and the use of CFCs. Maduro, like Dobson before him, knows the ozone hole in the Antarctic is a natural phenomenon. Mr. Marcel Nicolet, a Belgian scientist, also disputes this ozone hoax.

Incidentally, if the volcanoes all over the world blow as expected in this upcoming time frame (until 2012), then the ozone layer will have many more holes than just those in Antarctica. We could all need some type of earth-sheltered housing.

"Global warming is an outright invention. It is absolutely unproven and in my view is a lie, a lie that will cost billions of dollars annually. ...It's the same thing with CFCs, the chlorofluorocarbons. There is no danger from the CFCs to the ozone layer. Nor is there any danger from CO_2, no greenhouse effect, nor any risk of any kind of global warming. It is, to me, a pure falsehood," states Haroun Taxieff, 77-year-old Polish-born Frenchman, a world famous volcanologist, who has taught at many universities and worked for UNESCO. He was also recently a French Secretary of State.

Trouble Brewing

We should make no mistake about it. There is natural trouble coming. Climatic upset, coupled with financial and economic upset, results in political crises. This is why the One Worlders are having to move so quickly. They know they risk losing control. The concept of allowing Third World countries to make interest payments to foreign creditors in their own currencies will inescapably lead to hyperinflation and ultimately revolution in those Third World countries. A form of international corporate fascism is the tyrannical order planned for the world. But first, controlled anarchy is being planned so that people will in turn demand *"law and order"* at any price. The Hegelian dialectic is at work. The world cities will hold the countryside hostage.

Is Anybody Home?

Meanwhile, Americans sit back and do nothing. They feel powerless against the system. Bureaucracy is the worst form of tyranny because there is no one person to hold responsible. Occasionally we get the equivalent of people raising their windows and hollering as they did in the movie, *Network "I'm mad as hell and I'm not going to take it anymore!"* But such is a rare, empty, lonely cry. Americans, who see themselves as radical, autonomous individualists, may actually be cultural conformists, with no sense of common bond or community. They are like dominoes stacked up in a row, ready to fall one by one. As Protestant clergyman Martin Niemoller stated, *"In Germany, the Nazis came for the Communists, and I didn't speak up, because I was not a Communist. Then they came for the Jews, and I did not speak up, because I was not a Jew. Then they came for the trade unionists, and I did not speak up because I wasn't a trade unionist. Then they came for the Catholics, and I was a Protestant, so I didn't speak up. Then they came for me... By that time there was no one left to speak up for anyone."* Today in Augusta, Georgia a full platoon of Vietnam war vets, who dealt in drugs on behalf of the U.S. government, are being held and treated with drugs and electroshock therapy. Americans who believe in the *"Right to Life"* are being railroaded in kangaroo courts and thrown into jail. Tax protestors and believers in the common law are being rounded up and harassed, some jailed. The Amish are leaving this country because of religious persecution. When the economy turns sour in the 1990s, the media power will harness the masses with the incendiary of envy and then assault investors. I seriously doubt if the concept of investing as we know it today will be with us by the turn of the century....If you boil a frog slowly in water....put your finger in the water. Is the temperature rising?

As discussed above, the United States is following the path of Nazi Germany. Remember that Hitler ended up relishing the destruction of his own people. Such destruction could also occur in this country by 2012. Many of the military bases being closed down around the United States are being transformed into prisons and holding camps for Americans. How long until the United States looks like a map of the former Soviet Union, where the camps there which hold political prisoners are so numerous that a map looks like a bad case of chicken pox? Sports arenas in major U.S. cities were designed as holding tanks, and as locations where men could turn in their firearms for food. The plans of FEMA, the Federal Emergency Management Agency, are massive.

A lot is happening around the world, about which the networks never tell us anything. Former U.S. Federal Reserve Board chairman Paul Volcker is being retained by the murderous Chinese Communist government to help devise a plan for combating uncontrolled inflation. Volcker has his fingers in other pies as well. The Wall Street banking firm of James D. Wofensohn, which is headed by Paul Volcker, has announced a partnership with Fuji Bank.

The purpose of this cozy relationship is to facilitate Japanese acquisition of businesses and assets in the United States. Of course, all the top employees are either CFR or Trilateral members.

How many Americans know that Argentina is already a year behind on its foreign debt, or that more than half of U.S. cities are expected to seek emergency tax hikes or cut services in the 1990s? Peace and quiet in the cities? Hardly.

Has the network evening news told Americans that the Japanese have again become so militant that they want their Samurai swords back?

Seeing Red

Have Americans been told by the network news anchors that CIA director William Webster is working with special prosecutors Walsh and Kekar to eliminate any remaining anti-communists in the CIA? What about the fact that the U.S. CIA is being told to cooperate with the Soviet KGB? Or the absurdity that Soviet generals are being asked to testify before the U.S. Congress to make recommendations for U.S. military disarmament! (1989)

Between 1995 and 2000 there will be a dangerous period in which the Soviet Union will not possess necessary currency to even buy oil on world markets, much less produce it. Every ruble the Soviets print will be needed for scarce food at that time.

Who has been told that the Soviet Union has signed a mutual trade pact with South Africa, and that in order to prevent an internal revolution instigated by the Soviet Union, and in order to avoid internal terrorism, South Africa has effectively sold out to the Soviet empire.

Why have the Soviets stepped up their massive tank production to 5,000 units per annum? Why have our advantageous Landsat 4 and Landsat 5 satellites been sold to private interests when they only cost a meager $18 million a year to operate? Eighteen million dollars is only a drop in the ocean of the federal budget. Don't we want to monitor Soviet troop movement? Or are we being set up for a surprise Soviet surgical strike, which will in turn allow the U.S. federal government to declare a state of emergency. The U.S. government would welcome a state of emergency. It can then be ruthless with no accountability. South Africa has used its three-year state of emergency to suspend civil rights, limit freedom of the press, freedom of speech and freedom of assembly, and also to round up 30,000 dissidents without charging them. FEMA is ready and waiting in this country.

Golden Financial Reality

Fredrick Lips, a former director with Rothschild in Zurich, declared, *"We may not be too far away from an expected emergency situation. Even before the debt-laden 20th century reaches its end, you will all experience a gold market where people are no longer concerned about supply and demand, but on the contrary, will want to own gold at any price... Gold today is going over from weak hands into strong ones, mainly into the hands of the richest and the most liquid investors in the world, the central banks of the Far East. This is not any secret, but for the moment, the enormous meaning of it is being completely ignored. Sooner or later we will experience fireworks in the gold market, which hardly anyone would dare believe today... Forget the reports about climbing gold production. It is nothing compared to climbing paper money production."*

Isn't the next century the century of the Far East? Absolutely. Do Americans generally have any concept of what they are up against? By no means. Will food be more important than gold in the late 1990s? Most probably.

They Live

I began this introduction with the discussion of the movie, *Network*. I said until recently it was the most important movie made in revealing exactly how the world system works. But now, a little over a decade later, there is another movie which does as good, and in some areas, a better job than *Network*. It is John Carpenter's little-discussed flick, *They Live*. I have seen it twice. I have bought it for my permanent library. I have made it mandatory viewing for my children before they go out on their own in this world. I recommend you see it also, despite the rough language, violence and brief unnecessary sex.

Based on a short story, Carpenter's *They Live* probes to a depth not reached by *Network*. *They Live* was sold to the American public as science fiction. It is anything but. *They Live* is the closest to present-day reality of any movie I have ever seen. It's all there - the effectiveness of mass conditioning accomplished by subliminal advertising; the break-up of matter by altering electromagnetic fields, first accomplished by the U.S. Navy in the Philadelphia experiment of 1943; the ability to spy on people at any time in any place with satellites which can pick up a golf ball or read a license plate from hundreds of miles above the earth; the reality that the world's people are viewed by the elitists as nothing more than *"livestock"*; the sell-out by the media and their role in perpetrating this human exploitation; the love of money as the root of all evil and as the god of this world; the odious campaign of disinformation and people planted in key TV positions to reinforce the lies; the abuse of dissidents and the unfortunate, which is seldom reported; the trusting, mindless nature of the masses; and finally, the global elite's selling of their souls for money, linked up with the demonic occult.

This is the United States today. *They Live* has absolutely nothing to do with science fiction. Every situation or piece of technology portrayed in *They Live* has crossed my desk many times. The fact that the American public (the few who saw this film after it was spiked) think this movie is science fiction shows how truly deceived *"we, the people,"* are, and how tragically far we are removed from reality. How many Americans know the U.S. government has had UFOs for 40 years?

In one of the most powerful (if overdone) scenes of *They Live*, a fight occurs. This fistfight took place between two friends as one man tried to force his buddy to put on a specially-made pair of sunglasses. When these special sunglasses are worn, anyone can see the world as it really is, rather than as it appears to be. So great was this one man's resistance to the truth, that he fought with every ounce of strength to keep from putting the sunglasses on. So, too, it is with the American public today. The ostriches prefer their heads buried in the sand, and will fight, kick, bite, scratch, and maybe even kill, to keep from knowing the truth. Slaves grow accustomed to their chains. They don't want to see or know what is really going on. The 4th of July means firecrackers and an extra day off, not freedom.

Reflections

The fact that I can publish this essay is testimony to the fact that we've lost. Freedom, as our Founding Fathers intended, is dead in this country. The masses are so far gone and so under control that nothing moves them anymore except bread and circuses. The powers that be know my words are effectively falling on the ears of a very small minority, and so they leave me alone.

By stark contrast, Dan Smoot, in the 1950s was severely persecuted for revealing the CFR and the plans of the insiders. Smoot saw clearly that things did not happen "*by accident.*" They happened because they were planned that way, secretly so, by "*conspiracy.*" Those who plan and execute, lead. All others follow. And planners plan in their own self-interest, not in the best interest of the masses.

If by this time, dear reader, you have any lingering doubts about what's coming down, then secure a copy of *The Shadows of Power*, by James Perloff. Its subtitle is *The Council on Foreign Relations and the American Decline.*

A subscriber once admonished me, "*Why waste your time with all your words on One Worldism? All that's left prior to One Worldism is a mop-up operation. They're coming for us next, investors, those few who have financial freedom. The movie, "Wall Street," and the likes of Milken set us up for that. At the very least we'll have to turn in our guns for food, or surrender for medical care, or whatever. Or the envy of the frightened bankrupt masses could just as easily be turned against us. The public schools and TV have ensured that. What happens when bank accounts are frozen or confiscated, muni-bonds are defaulted upon, or home mortgages are canceled and everyone immediately lives in government housing? Either way, we're trapped coming or going. Plus, there's nowhere to run. Want to live like a gypsy? For what price will you sell out, or for what will you fight and die?*" ...Grim words from a thinking subscriber. And you thought I was grim.

I think I'll reread the Declaration of Independence. That treasured document is foreign to the mindset of most Americans today. THEY LIVE...BUT WHAT ABOUT US?

June 29, 1989

* * * *

Francis Fukuwama, in his book *The End of History?*, basically said that communism has lost and that Western liberal democracy has won. Now we are moving toward a *"universal homogeneous state."* Translated, that means a one world, fascist, debt capitalistic, multinational order.

* * * * *

"The entire Federal Reserve System and the fiat currency on which it is based is a scheme founded on deception and dishonesty on a scale so massive that its premises are seldom challenged." — Howard Phillips

* * * * *

"All governments, of course, are against liberty. " — H.L. Mencken — American Writer

* * * * *

"There is indeed a plot against the people, and probably always will be, for Government has always been hostile toward the governed...this has nothing to do with an 'ideology' or form of government...nor with races or religions, for the conspirators are beyond what they call 'such trivialities'... This is probably the last hour for mankind as a rational species, before it becomes the slave of a planned society...." — Taylor Caldwell, from her novel — *Captains and the Kings*

* * * * *

"Cameras the size of a pinhead can provide a continuous visual record of your most intimate activities. They are being hidden by the government in sprinkler heads. Your behavior and buying patterns are being monitored continuously by credit card bureaus and direct marketers. The federal government already has the equivalent of a 100-page dossier on every living American and computer power available is increasing tenfold every five years for such activities. In the future, electronic surveillance will be mind-reading devices and machines that can see through solid walls." — Source: Mark Nestmann

* * * * *

American business today turns down approximately half of all job applicants because prospective employees cannot fill out the required employment forms. This should be no surprise since 40% of the American public is functionally illiterate. Nearly 60% of American adults never read a single book once they're out of school, and most of the rest of Americans read only one book a year, mostly fiction, usually romance novels. Television dominates our lives today. The revered philosopher, Malcolm Muggeridge, expressed the TV problem succinctly: *"From the first moment I was in the studio, I felt that it was far from being a good thing. I felt that television would ultimately be inimical to what I most appreciate, which is the expression of truth, expressing your reactions to life in words. I think you'll live to see the time when literature will be quite a rarity because, more and more, the presentation of images is preoccupying.*

"I don't think people are going to be preoccupied with ideas. I think they are going to live in a fantasy world where you don't need any ideas. The one thing that television can't do is express ideas...There is a danger in translating life into an image, and that is what television is doing. In doing it, it is falsifying life. Far from the camera's being an accurate recorder of what is going on, it is the exact opposite, It cannot convey reality nor does it even want to."
— Source: *Imprimis* (Hillsdale College)

...Meanwhile, the Federal Register (in small type) enters the new regulations of the federal alphabet bureaucracies. These regulations now total 68,000 pages per year. Who reads them? Only the bureaucrats.

* * * * *

On TV, businessmen commit a third of television murders and violent crimes and a fifth of overall crime, depicting only 8% of the characters. Only 30% of businessmen have positive roles on TV. In real life, blacks commit 50% of the murders in the United States, while on television blacks commit only 3%. Ninety percent of the killings on TV are done by whites. One out of four televised Hispanics commits a crime. Feminist arguments are supported in 71% of television shows, and criticized in only 7% of them.

SECTION I

Politics, War and the New World Order

THE USSR: MADE BY USA, INC.

April 24, 1986

Why We Built the Soviet Union

At the end of WWII, the United States was the world's undisputed supreme military power. Every other challenging country on the face of the earth had been devastated economically, militarily and/or by loss of life during the carnage of WWII. The ally of the United States at that time, the USSR, was exhausted, militarily and economically. The loss of Soviet life was also enormous. Thus, at that time, the United States had every opportunity to put an end to communism once and for all, as Patton and other leading U.S. generals recommended.

The elimination of communism, however, would not have been in keeping with the international plan to move the world toward a One World Order, allowing the eventual merging of the atheistic Soviet Union's socialistic bureaucracy with the USA's bureaucratic socialism; exemplifying the thesis (monopolistic debt capitalism) versus antithesis (communism) equaling the synthesis of Hegel's dialectic. For this reason, Patton's army was told to stop its advance. The Soviets were allowed to capture Berlin, with all the horror, rape and pillage that followed. Berlin ended up a divided city. Next, to buttress the Soviet economy, when the victors divided the spoils at Yalta, the United States gave Eastern Europe to the Soviet Union. Meanwhile, trainloads of Soviet freedom fighters and refugees were sent back to Russian by allied troops in sealed boxcars for certain execution by the Soviet communists. Some of these poor souls tried to slit their own throats on rusty nails, rather than face the brutality of the communists.

The CIA Connection

Finally, so that the U.S. military-industrial complex and its bankers would have the continued capability to reap huge profits at the expense of the U.S. taxpayers, FDR allowed the Soviet Union to steal the plans on how to construct the atomic bomb. For this reason, among others, President Eisenhower bitterly warned against the military-industrial complex during his farewell address. President Eisenhower's *"Crusade For Peace"* had been smashed when the CIA, against Ike's orders, sent up Gary Powers' U-2 spy plane, which was allegedly shot down. Powers declared that he was not shot down at all, but that there had been a bomb put on board his U-2. Gary Powers later died in a mysterious accident. Intelligence expert Colonel L. Fletcher Prouty, who worked for the CIA for nine years and authored THE SECRET TEAM, stated, *"There is ample evidence to show President Kennedy was killed because he was moving to end the Cold War. The Cold War was basic and essential to the support of the CIA as well as the Pentagon; it was also a necessary part of the continually expanding military-industrial complex."*

Former New Orleans District Attorney Jim Garrison told *Freedom* magazine (April, 1986) that President Kennedy was killed by CIA agents and operatives. The April 25, 1966 *New York Times* stated that JFK blamed the CIA for the Bay of Pigs disaster and that he (JFK) wanted *"to splinter the CIA into a thousand pieces and scatter it to the winds."*

Presently over 150 Soviet weapons systems are based on U.S. technology, which has been begged, borrowed, stolen or bought. Dr. Antony Sutton, formerly of the Hoover War Institute, has documented that 95% of Soviet technology has come from the West.

To reiterate, at the end of WWII, an enemy of the United States had to be created to sustain the master socialistic, CIA, banking, State Department, military-industrial complex game plan. The U.S. ally, at that time, the U.S.S.R., became the natural candidate to be transformed from a friend (?) into an enemy. The Soviet Union, a country possessed by an army, doing the bidding of its own bureaucratic elite, increased its efforts to bring about bureaucratic socialism. Meanwhile in the U.S., the population was slowly but peacefully being conditioned through the public school system, universities, seminaries, churches and the mass media to accept bureaucratic socialism. Small wonder then that we do not have perimeter defenses, a militia or a civil defense system in this country. Such is against the interests of the international planners.

Communism — A Western Idea

Too often we forget (or were never taught) that Soviet communism is a product of monopolistic Western debt capitalism. Karl Marx wrote *Das Kapital* in London. The communist revolution in 1917 was financed by New York and German banking interests. Lenin was reportedly a redheaded, washed-up Hollywood actor. Since 1921, Armand Hammer, chairman of the board of Occidental Petroleum Company, had free access to top communist leaders and traded consistently with the Soviet Union. General Electric, Dresser Industries and Caterpillar provided nearly all the technology for the Trans-Siberian pipeline. American banks which have branch offices in the former Soviet Union include Chase Manhattan and Bank of America. Loans are also regularly made to Eastern Bloc countries.

The sad truth is that the Soviet Union would have fallen flat on its face economically and militarily long before it did if it had not been for the support given it both militarily and economically by the United States.

Capitalism's Support of Communism

Roger W. Robinson, Jr. wrote the informative book, *Financing the Soviet Union.* Mr. Robinson is president of RWR, Inc., a Washington based consulting firm. He is former senior director for International Economic Affairs of the National Security Council.

Mr. Robinson wrote, *"United and unobserved Western financial flows to the Warsaw Pact countries are, in my view, a principal avenue by which the West contributes to the Soviet Union's ability to maintain and expand its costly global commitments."* Put simply, we are financing communism!

Malcolm Baldridge, our U.S. Secretary of Commerce, wrote in an unpublicized letter, *"The President (Reagan) is seeking to build a more constructive working relationship with the Soviet Union, and he favors an expansion of peaceful trade with the U.S.S.R. as part of this effort. After a seven-year hiatus, the United States agreed to a joint commercial commission meeting this year."* No wonder then, that in 1985, over 435 U.S. businessmen rushed to the Soviet Union to see how much rope they could sell the Soviets, so the Russians could make nooses (with slave labor) with which to hang amoral Western debt capitalists.

The huge Kama River truck assembly plant in the former Soviet Union builds more military vehicles than any truck factory in the world. Some of the trucks produced there were used in Vietnam, and to transport Soviet troops into Afghanistan. Thank you, Ford. An alarming 45% of this project was financed by the U.S. taxpayer subsidized Export-Import bank, which at that time was headed by William J. Casey, who is now head of our CIA. Chase Manhattan Bank was the other major financier. Freedom fighters in Central America claim that the CIA is the socialistic secret police arm of the multinational banking community, operating contrary to traditional American interests there. Contra freedom fighters in Central America don't want U.S. aid. They say it goes to the wrong people. Also in this regard, it is alarming that then-Vice President Bush was CIA director after he was ambassador to Red China. David Rockefeller has long said that George Bush was his man.

General Electric played the key role in providing electrical power for the former Soviet Union. General Electric supplied large quantities of electrical power station equipment to the U.S.S.R. GE also sent products and technical assistance that enabled the Soviets to build their oil, coal, gold, paper, aluminum, steel construction and railroad industries. Gleason Corporation trained more than 300 Soviet engineers after providing the communists with machine tools. U.S. industry even provided the Soviets with the technology and ball bearings to make their missiles more accurate.

Military Sell-Outs

As the U.S. military has retreated globally, the former Soviet Union obligingly picked up the pieces. For example, Wheelus Air Force Base in Libya, was once the largest U.S. Air Force base outside of the United States. The Libyans, naturally, have turned it over to the former Soviet Union. In Iraq, the Habbaniyiah Air Force Base was once the second largest base outside of the

United States. It too has been turned over to the Russians. In Vietnam, Da Nang and Cam Rahn Bay were conveniently left intact when we fled. The Soviets made these facilities major communist military bases. What about the Soviets long sought after warm water port? Chah Bahar and a second base in the Persian Gulf in Iran were once effectively operated by the U.S. military. It just seems like after we went into an area, and built it up with American men and money, we then regularly turned it over to the Soviets. Is it planned that way?

Political Sell-Outs

We do have a regular policy of selling out our friends to our communist *"enemies"* (?). We sold out Chiang Kai-shek for Mao Tse-Tung in China. We gave up Batista for Castro in Cuba. Is Iran better off without the Shah? Was Vietnam well served by our withdrawal? Somoza was traded for the Sandinistas in Nicaragua. The U.S. State Department knew while Somoza was still in power that Daniel Ortega was a hard-core communist. Central American freedom fighters swear that Ortega then and now is working for the CIA. Makes sense, if the CIA is indeed the policeman for the multinationals. Presently, over 35 U.S. firms still operate in Nicaragua. These include IBM, Nabisco, Tenneco, Colgate-Palmolive, General Mills and United Brands. Exxon refines all of Nicaragua's oil.

We sold out Rhodesia. Marcos was traded for Aquino. We are presently selling out our ally, South Africa. The January, 1986 Heritage Foundation report, *"How the State Department Betrays the Reagan Vision"* detailed how the U.S. State Department frustrates traditional American causes and supports the communists. Senator Jesse Helms is correct. We don't have a U.S. desk at the State Department. Is this why former Secretary of State George Schultz refused to take a loyalty lie detector test?

U.S. Multinational Support of Communism

In the January and April 1986 issue of THE PHOENIX LETTER, Dr. Antony Sutton (#216C - 1517 14th Street W, Billings, MT 59102) exposes the U.S. - U.S.S.R. Trade and Economic Council, Inc. (TEC). Dr. Sutton flatly accuses TEC of treason. In fact, he headlined his January 1986 PHOENIX LETTER, *"Secret U.S.-Soviet Group Plots Treason."* Dr. Sutton argues that it is insane to spend over $300 billion a year on military defense against the former Soviet Union when we were in turn economically, politically, financially and technologically supporting the Soviet Union. Dr. Sutton is correct, of course, unless the master plan is to really merge these two superpowers. The emerging evidence indicates such is overwhelmingly the case. Both are bankrupt philosophically. Communism has not led to the withering away of the state. It has degenerated into an elitist bureaucratic socialism. The same is true for the U.S. The principle upon which this country was founded, *"that the government which governs least governs best,''* has been smothered by bureaucratic socialism. History does not happen by accident. It is planned.

TEC has 30 Soviet directors and 20 U.S. directors. TEC has eight full-time Soviet engineers living in New York to assess U.S. technology. Permanent directors of TEC are Alexander Trowbridge, President of the National Association of Manufacturers, and Richard Lesher, President of the U.S. Chamber of Commerce. TEC is headed by Vladimir N. Sushkow (Co-Chairman), a Soviet citizen, and Yuri V. Legeev (Vice-President), also a Soviet citizen. President of TEC is James H. Giffen, while Dwayne O. Andreus is Co-Chairman, both U.S. citizens.

Dr. Sutton also produced a key partial membership list of TEC, as well as advertisements by U.S. multi-national debt capitalists, which American citizens are never supposed to see.

PARTIAL LIST OF MEMBERSHIP

U.S.-U.S.S.R. TRADE & ECONOMIC COUNCIL INC.

Abbot Laboratories	Allen Bradley	Alliance Tool Corp.
Allied Analytical Systems	Allis Chalmers	American Cyanamid
American Express	Archer Daniels Midland	Armco Steel
Bunge Corporation	Cargill	Caterpillar
Chase Manhattan	Chemical Bank	Clark Equipment
Coca Cola	Con Agra	Continental Grain
Corning Glass	Deere & Company	Dow Chemical
Dresser Industries	E.I. DuPont	FMC Corporation
Garnac Grain	Gleason Corporation	Hope Industries
Ingersoll Rand	Intrn'l Harvestor	Kodak
Marine Midland	Millipore Inc.	Minnesota Mining
Monsanto	Occidental Petroleum	Owens Illinois
Pepsi Co.	Phibro-Salomon	Phillip Morris
Ralston Purina	Rohm & Haas	Seagram
Stauffer Chemical	Tendler-Beretz Assoc	Tenneco Inc.
Union Carbide	Unit Rig & Equip Co.	Xerox

Dr. Sutton concludes, *"The real enemy of free enterprise societies is not world communism - it is the multinational corporation which gives technological and financial subsidy to non-viable socialist economies.*

"World communism is a political threat as we see in Nicaragua, Angola, Afghanistan and Ethiopia—it generates subversion and totalitarian revolution. Communism is not an economic threat. Socialism does not work, period. Socialism can only advance through injections of free enterprise technology. Lenin knew that.

"The danger is from financial monopoly capitalism—the corporate empires built by Rockefeller, Morgan, Armand Hammer and others. They want financial MONOPOLY. Why? Because monopoly guarantees profit.

"The New World Order generated by financial capitalists is WORLD MONOPOLY.

"Old John D. Rockefeller once said, 'Competition is a sin.' That credo is supported by the monopolists in New York and the monopolists in Moscow. That's why David Rockefeller and Armand Hammer get along so well with Brezhnev and Gorbachev. They all think power. They all plan for power."

The Love of Money

Government is always religion applied to economics. The God-given order is God first, government (self-government primarily) second, and business/economics third. Today, it is flipped upside down. Money rules this world. The Golden Rule has become, *"Whoever has the gold makes the rules."* Big business calls the shots. Government does the bidding of the monopolistic multinational debt capitalists, and God is dismissed. The borrower is the slave of the lender. Thus, in the United States today, effectively a modern Babylon, we see truly that *"the love of money is the root of all evil,"* as financial gain supersedes the rightful economic, governmental and religious stand against the atheistic, murderous slavery of communism. As Founding Father William Penn declared, *"Men must be governed by God, or they will be ruled by tyrants."* Long-term, if this trend continues, all of us lose. It will make little difference what we make in our investments or pass on to our children if we lose our freedom or our lives. The present trend is toward a One World Order, run by high tech bureaucrats for the benefit of a small, privileged elite. Terrorism in the U.S. will accelerate centralized control. We will be unnecessary, expendable. Therefore, we had better become involved. It's all too true that if we don't hang together, we'll all hang separately. Trouble is, we've also financed and sold them the rope to hang us. And the opposition has its act together. Who is financing this opposition?

"For there is nothing hid, which shall not be manifested; neither was anything kept secret, but that it should come abroad." — Mark 4:22

"AMERIKA" TODAY: THE REALITY

March 4, 1987

ABC's fictional *Amerika* is closer to reality than most Americans realize. Here's the latest compilation of data which confirms just how close we have moved toward becoming "*Amerika.*" My thanks to Johnny Johnson, editor of *Daily News Digest*, and Dr. Antony Sutton, editor of *The Phoenix Letter*, for much of this excellent though distressing information.

Source: *U.S. Chamber of Commerce sponsored Journal of the U.S.-U.S.S.R. Trade and Economic Council.* This is David Rockefeller speaking: *"...it is of interest to recall that at the Chase Manhattan Bank we can look back to an unbroken relationship with Russian financial institutions that straddles well over 50 years... When in the early 1920s, the Soviet Union set about to rebuild its textile industry, representatives of the all-Russian Textile Syndicate approached Chase, then known as Chase National Bank, and obtained the credits necessary to pay for their first imports of U.S. cotton. And in 1924, when the Amtorg Trading Corporation was incorporated as the Soviet Union's sole export-import agency in New York, Chase National agreed to handle its promissory notes as the 'paying agent' for the Soviet Foreign Trade Bank... It was at the seventh session of the Dartmouth Conference in Hanover in 1972 that the idea of forming a joint high-level Trade and Economic Council was first proposed. This in turn led me to think that we ought to be doing something more at Chase to establish a unit specifically to deal with the Soviet Union. The Chase representative office in Moscow, the first to be opened by a U.S. banking institution after World War II, grew out of this as did our first major post-war credit to the Soviet Union. This credit opportunity developed out of the giant undertaking by the Soviet Union to build the world's largest truck plant on the Kama River and the Naberzhnye Chelny or Kamaz. The $86.5 million dollar credit Chase agreed to extend for this project was matched by the U.S. Export-Import Bank which was finally allowed to open its doors to the Soviet Union under the 1972 Trade Agreement...Through participation in international banking consortia Chase has also participated in all three branches of the credits raised by the International Investment Bank in Moscow to finance purchases in the U.S. and elsewhere of equipment for the joint CNEA project of a natural gas pipeline connecting the Orenburg Fields with terminals in eastern and western Europe...Beyond my involvement in Chase's banking relations with the Soviet Union, I have continued to participate in the work of the Dartmouth Conference."*

The U.S.-U.S.S.R. Trade and Economic Council was a secret corporation between the Reagan Administration and the Evil Empire. It was revived by Shultz and Baldridge in 1983. The U.S. kicked out 25 U.N. spies but supported eight full-time Soviet engineers in New York. Secretary Shultz would not let the FBI put an agent in U.S.T.E.C.

The Soviet Foreign Trade Bank became the first Soviet financial institution to participate in underwriting a bond issue in the international capital markets. The lead manager of the issue is CitiCorp.

The 8/15/86 *Wall Street Journal* reported, *"The Soviet Union is contemplating joining the International Monetary Fund and the World Bank, as well as other international financial agencies, to give it further reach into the world economy."*

The Soviet Union ranks first in the world in loans subsidized by Western governments.

In 1972 the Export-Import Bank, headed by William J. Casey, who until just recently was CIA director, financed the construction of the U.S.S.R.'s infamous Kama river truck plant. This was a $2 billion project. The Export-Import Bank gave the Soviets 16.5 years to repay their debt at low interest rates. The loan was funded through David Rockefeller's Chase Manhattan Bank. Military trucks and armored personnel carriers are produced at this mammoth facility.

NSC-68 (National Security Council - 68) was a document that laid down the rule that we should never win a war, never *"challenge Soviet prestige"* in international activities. We must permit the U.S.S.R. to *"select whatever means are expedient in seeking to carry out its fundamental design...We have no such freedom of choice, and least of all in the use of force."* NSC-68 explains why we were not allowed to win wars in Korea and Vietnam and why any future war must be a no-win war.

Over a single generation Washington lost over half the world to the Soviet Union.

The *"Rules of Engagement"* in Vietnam guaranteed a no-win war.

In September 1961 State Department document 7277, *"The Total Elimination of All Armed Forces and Armaments Except Those Needed to Maintain Internal Order Within States and to Furnish the United Nations with Peace Forces,"* projected that the United Nations global government would be so strong no nation could challenge it. The three men involved in disarming the United States were Robert Strange McNamara, then Secretary of Defense who became president of the World Bank, Paul Hilken Nitze who is now part of the U.S. arms negotiation delegation, and Henry Kissinger who became NSC Director, then Secretary of State under Nixon, and was a foreign policy advisor to President Reagan. All are CFR members.

Every head of the U.N.'s *"peace keeping"* forces has always been a Soviet general.

General Daniel Graham, former head of the U.S. Defense Intelligence Agency, said there is a strong possibility that Soviet KGB agents secretly sabotaged the Space Shuttle Challenger, four other American rockets and a French rocket. All four American rockets plus the French ARIANE rocket carried American reconnaissance satellites. America has only one *"spy in the sky"* satellite. For the first time in history Soviet electronic spy ships, normally off Cape Canaveral for every shuttle launch, mysteriously left the area at high speed only four hours before the Challenger blew up. The KGB had a major celebration of *"perfect active measure"* (their term for dirty work) at KGB headquarters on the night of the Challenger explosion. Soviet condolences of the Challenger tragedy came only two hours after the explosion. In the past the Soviets have waited days or weeks. Dr. Peter Beckman and Dr. Harry Schultz, after researching the subject, think the Challenger was brought down by the U.S.S.R., but U.S. officials won't admit it because to do so would mean we have to declare war on the Soviet Union...Call it KAL 007, part two.

We lost a key Star Wars expert, Capt. William Hughes. He mysteriously disappeared in the Netherlands three years ago.

A Heritage Foundation report, Back-grounder #84, 1/31/86 was entitled, *"Rhetoric Versus Reality: How the State Department Betrays the Reagan Vision."*

U.S. taxpayers actually built the Soviet Union through multinational bank loans.

President Nixon in an Executive Order canceled $10.3 billion of an $11 billion Soviet debt owed to the United States, originating from World War II. This loan allowed the Soviets to buy U.S. wheat at 4% interest from American farmers. When the Soviets bought the wheat, their timing was precise. Their agents in Europe had reduced wheat futures to their lowest levels in years. And Chicago used closing European wheat prices for its opening figures. The Soviets manipulated an immense international bargain, and then the great wheat deal began to roll.

We're selling subsidized wheat to Russia and undercutting our good friends Canada and Australia today.

On August 4, 1986 the United States and the Soviet Union signed 13 agreements for a variety of new exchange programs with 19 more to be worked out later. The exchange involved high school students and teachers for ten months, with Communist teachers coming to instruct American students and the assignment of a Soviet specialist to the United States to advise on the teaching of Russian, etc. Also involved was the creation of new textbooks for the study of the Soviet system.

Now the U.S. is injecting Soviet ideas, philosophy and history into our educational system. The Reagan administration made an agreement with the Soviet Union to develop computer software for a common curriculum for Soviet and American schools. But Soviet schools have no computers. These programs are under contract to the Carnegie Foundation.

Radio Moscow will now be beamed from Des Moines, Los Angeles, New York and Miami on A.M. and F.M. stations. Charles Wick, director of the U.S. Information Agency, said there are only tentative plans to beam Voice of America broadcasts over Soviet stations in return...Welcome to *"Amerika!"*

RED DAWN AND DUSK
August 28, 1991

Red dawn and dusk

And conquer we must

When our cause

It is just.

But this one ain't

'Cause we aren't saints.

Here comes the judge,

Here comes the judge,

The judge of the New World Order.

King George Bush certainly looked worried and weary during the harrowing three days of coup and no coup in the Soviet Union. After all, his and Gorbachev's dream of a New World Order, complete with super-bureaucracy, world court, world central bank, world currency, ad nauseam, almost went up in smoke, literally. The hardliners who held Mikhail Gorbachev captive in his vacation home for three days had seized the Soviet President's briefcase which contained the codes needed to activate the U.S.S.R.'s nuclear arsenal. As I discussed in the August 14, 1991 REAPER, the *"Ides of August"* were *"Death Week"*: *"...the total Soviet gold reserves now amount to only $4.4 billion, the equivalent of four days of U.S. deficits. The Soviets are also selling 40 year-old platinum bars. The Soviets shipped 730,000 ounces of platinum to Switzerland in the last six months. That's more platinum than the Soviets shipped globally in all of 1990. This means Soviet selling in platinum should be about exhausted. The Soviets are scraping bottom financially in their attempt to raise foreign exchange by selling their precious metals. Plus, the Soviet oil reserves are rapidly being depleted. And the Soviet empire is politically breaking up into regional factions. Starvation of the masses is a real threat this winter. This increases the probability of a civil war there. Undoubtedly many of the Soviet Military hardliners are reckoning their best bet is to exercise their global strategic nuclear option...*

"...Then there's Chairman of the Joint Chiefs of Staff General Colin Powell's August 8 statement regarding the Soviets: 'Even with the START treaty, you will have the capability to destroy us in 30 minutes'."

Small wonder that the Insiders' equivalent of 007, Robert Strauss, was quickly dispatched to the Soviet Union as the new U.S. ambassador. Strauss was to coordinate getting the U.S.S.R. back on track toward its merger with the U.S.A. in the New World Order. Amerika. The Hegelian dialectic had too close a call for comfort in its movement of the thesis (the evolutionary, human-istic individualism and democratic debt capitalism of the U.S.A.) versus the antithesis (the evolutionary, humanistic, radical, communistic collectivism of the Soviet Union), into its new evolutionary, humanistic synthesis of global socialism in the New World Order.

Perhaps for some time we will never know just how close we came to having the 20,000 Soviet warheads aimed at the U.S. launched. It may be a while, too, before we are told what the 400,000 Soviet troops still in former East Germany were ordered to do. Further, what were Castro's instructions regarding its Soviet SS-22 nuclear missiles? These SS-22s were confirmed to be installed in Cuba on April 25, 1991 by U.S. spy satellite photos. Addition-ally, the Soviets had just installed 18 new rail-mobile nuclear missile launchers for the SS-24 missile. Plus, over the previous six years, the U.S.S.R. had pro-duced 400 new strategic bombers compared to 104 by the U.S., 715 ICBMs compared to the 63 by the U.S., 54 nuclear submarines compared to the U.S.' 24; and the U.S.S.R. long-range bomber production in 1989 and 1990 hit a whopping 140, compared to one by the U.S. This is what 50% of Soviet GNP went for, military spending. And it could have cost us dearly, irretrievably, irreparably, eternally.

The *"Death Star's"* close call shook its commander-in-chief down to his *"Skull and Bones."* After all, how could things turn so quickly, and catch the Old World Order (which is in its metamorphosis of becoming the New World Order) so totally off guard? It was only last month that Commander George Herbert Walker Bush told the President of Greece, *"You are welcome to be part of my new world order"* (7/18/91).

The early 1970 Trilateral plan was to divide the world into three regions (thus the name "Trilateral"). Such is just about completed. The North Ameri-can common market between Canada, the U.S. and Mexico is all but in place. The second leg of the Trilateral scheme, the European Economic Community, came on stream in 1992. All but lost are Margaret Thatcher's comments con-cerning Britain's political merger with western Europe: *"It would be the great-est abdication of national and political sovereignty in our history."* Japan has been slow to come through with the third leg, the western Pacific segment of the Trilateralist agenda. But the Soviet coup was a not-so-gentle reminder that the U.S. pays $50 billion a year to defend Japan.

Japan is having to rethink its own long-term strategy of controlling the world economically. Michael Crichton's new novel, RISING SUN, now a movie, stated, *"Japan insidiously has taken over every important aspect of American business and technology, infiltrated the police, the newspapers, and the government, and literally gotten away with murder."*

Anyway, once all three segments of the Trilateral plan are in place, then abracadabra, out pops the New World Order. The Red Dawn to Red Dusk scenario resulted in a quantum leap forward for the New World Order. Now they're just like us, except poorer. Democracy has always been a prelude to socialism. Gorbachev once stated, *"I am convinced that socialism is correct, I'm an adherent of socialism..."* U.S.A. democracy to socialism. U.S.S.R. socialism to democracy. Presto! Merger. They're as broke in fact as we are technically. The break up of the U.S.S.R. into republics, plus the Baltics and Eastern Europe, is the equivalent of states in the U.S.A. Both the U.S.A. and the former U.S.S.R. have a strong central government and military. We're all the same. ...The next financial and economic crisis could level the U.S. democracy economically to allow for a more comfortable merger.

U.S. military dog tags are being replaced with microchips embedded in molars. Scanners will read the bar code off the tooth such as blood type, allergies, medical history, etc.

In the skies above U.S. cities, soon there will be tiny pilotless aircraft, which look much like model airplanes. Inside these planes will be high-resolution cameras which can pick up the smallest objects and details from hundreds of yards up. These tiny spy aircraft will also be armed with infrared detectors that can see in the dark, and chemical sensors which can pinpoint drugs in any area. Called Unmanned Aerial Vehicles (UAV), these *"spies in the sky"* will be used for government surveillance. ...Shades of the movie *They Live*.

In June, 1991, new identity cards were issued to every citizen in Singapore over 18 years of age. This way the Singaporean government's bureaucracies can keep electronic track of most of Singapore's 2.7 million people. The so-called *"smart cards"* have a machine-readable bar code that keeps the owner's number and personal information ready for any official who demands it for inspection. A photograph, a thumbprint, and comprehensive personal data are recorded electronically on this *"smart card"*, which is the size of an ordinary credit card. ...The New World Order coming...rapidly! How about an invisible infrared tattoo on the hand?

SCORPIONS IN A BOTTLE
December 6, 1990

Political Deception

The more I research this Middle East mess, the more serpentine the situation becomes. Whether we're talking about Iraq, Kuwait, Saudi Arabia, Israel, China, the former U.S.S.R., or the Bushwhacker administration, all are/were scorpions in a bottle. And we, the people, are the recipients of their stingers. The stormtroopers, the bureaucrats who rule over us on behalf of the politicians, remind me of the henchmen who mindlessly obeyed Darth Vader in the *Star Wars* series. You remember them - the faceless soldiers all decked out identically in sterile white plastic uniforms - bureaucrats! Bureaucracy is always the greatest collective manifestation of human evil.

Let's not forget what government really is - an economic parasite which plays the role of God. Intellectual H.L. Mencken wrote, *"No government is ever in favor of the freedom of the individual. It invariably seeks to limit that freedom, if not by overt denial, then by seeking constantly to widen its own functions."* Mencken also commented, *"The kind of man who wants the government to adopt and enforce his ideas is always the kind of man whose ideas are idiotic."* He additionally called elections, *"sort of an advance auction of stolen goods."* Centuries earlier, Machiavelli correctly identified why the masses are such easy marks for the politicians: *"But the great majority of mankind is satisfied with appearances, as though they were realities...and they're often more influenced by things unseen, than by those that are."* Politicians are in the business of selling illusions, of fostering false expectations, of putting on pompous appearances rather than causing people to focus on the difficult responsibilities of reality.

Respected biblical law scholar R.J. Rushdoony noted that up until the time of Napoleon (1803-1873), power was seized and held by kings under the concept of *"divine right."* This approach was increasingly at odds with the Magna Carta and the likes of the Cromwellian revolution in England in 1640. But Napoleon was clever. (Indeed, Saddam Hussein has stolen a page from Napoleon's book.) Napoleon used the umbrella of humanitarian democracy to cover his dictatorship. Power was seized in the name of the people, supposedly for their welfare. This is what exists today. Rushdoony comments, *"Politics for the most part now means promising more and more to the people, while taking more power and wealth from them to concentrate power in the state. Wars are fought in the name of the people. Modern tyrannies rule in the name of the people."*

The Swiss Exception

Switzerland has been a notable exception in this statist rule. Switzerland has not fought a war since 1833. Why? Because free enterprise and depoliticizing the Swiss economy has resulted in peace and prosperity for that country. It is the worn out concepts of collectivist economies and centralization of political power that leads to war, particularly as the state's credibility breaks down. Wars, after all, are a continuation of political policy by other means. *"Wars happen because certain people want them to take place for their own profit, and to further a cause that they have embraced,"* according to David J. Meyer, editor of Last Trumpet Newsletter. Specifically regarding the Middle East, one only has to look at where the financial vested interests lie, with the multinational banks and oil companies, to see that every decision George Bush made he made as though he were the president of a big international bank. It was George Bush who once put his hand on David Rockefeller's shoulder and said, *"All that I am I owe to this man."*

The Luciferian Conspiracy

We must also recall that government is always religion applied to economics. Every government takes abstract religious concepts about morality and good and evil, and codifies them into law. These laws in turn both frame and dictate human action, or in other words, economics. Meyer, for example, also brought to light the writings of Dr. Albert Pike, a Luciferian and author of *The Degrees of the Scottish Rite of Freemasonary.* A Luciferian, for those of you unfamiliar with the term, is a worshipper of Lucifer, another name for Satan. Luciferians hold that Lucifer/Satan was the rightful firstborn son of God and that God the Father was deceived when Jesus Christ, in a conspiracy, wrongfully displaced his older brother, Lucifer, at the right hand of the throne of the Father. So Luciferians are working to replace Lucifer/Satan in the throne room of God and displace Jesus Christ. It's all very moral this way, you see.

Dr. Albert Pike, a Luciferian, wrote to his co-conspirator, Giuseppe Mazzini, on August 15, 1871, describing what would be the nature of the third world war. Pike said World War III *"would be fomented by political strife as stirred up by the agents of the Illuminati between the Zionists and the leaders of the Moslem world. The third great world war's purpose is to cause the nations to fight themselves into a state of complete exhaustion physically, spiritually, mentally and economically."*

Interesting that this letter was written on August 15, the same date of the Harmonic Convergence of 1987, and in the same general time frame when World War II started, about when the U.S. dropped the atom bomb on Hiroshima and Nagasaki, and approximately when Hitler appeared on the cover of *US News & World Report* in 1989 and 1990, and Saddam Hussein was being called the new Hitler.

Pike accurately projected the direction which the New World Order and New Age of Light would take. Lucifer, after all, means *"Light Bringer."* Pike wrote this on August 15, 1871: *"We shall unleash the nihilists and the athe-*

ists, and we shall provoke a great social cataclysm, which in all its horror will show clearly to all nations the effects of absolute atheism, the origin of savagery and of most bloody turmoil. Then everywhere, the people forced to defend themselves against the world minority of revolutionaries, will exterminate those destroyers of civilization; and the multitudes, disillusioned with Christianity, whose deistic spirits will be from that moment on without direction and leadership; and anxious for an ideal but without knowledge where to send its adoration, will receive the true light through the universal manifestation of the pure doctrine of Lucifer, brought finally out into public view. A manifestation, which will result from a general reactionary movement, which will follow the destruction of Christianity and atheism, both conquered and exterminated at the same time."

Bushwhacking Scorpion

Now, let's turn and look at each of the scorpions individually: First, let's nail down how the American people were being Bushwhacked by their own president. The November 19, 1990 *US News & World Report*, in its feature editorial, declared, *"Election Hangover: If you liked Washington's last show, you'll love the next one. The maneuvering of George Bush and the next Congress will be more politicized, less productive and more focused on penny ante politics than the one that just ended."* George Bush traveled to Turkey in the first quarter of 1991. ...Birds of a feather. George Bush was a globetrotter, letting the domestic scene degenerate while he worked on his assigned internationalist agenda.

How did Americans feel about the 1990 election? *Business Week*, in its feature editorial of November 19, 1990, declared, *"The painful truth is that the U.S. political system offers the voter little real choice. Incumbents nearly always win - 97% of them did this time around - because they have no effective opposition....But most of the time, the sheer power of incumbency is enough to scare the best qualified challengers out of the race. An unhealthy result is the scandalously low voter turn out - about 36% this year."* ...The U.S. political system is frozen, locked up by special interests - politicians, bureaucrats and big money power brokers. *"We the people"* have dropped out, or rather, have been squeezed out.

Presently, a majority of Americans believe the federal government is ruled by a few big interests looking after themselves. Just how locked up is this country politically? Just how frozen and unresponsive is our political process? Despite grassroots outrage, only one of 32 senators who ran for office in 1990 was dumped, and only fifteen of the 406 House members up for reelection were thrown out. The system is now totally unresponsive.

The majority of Americans also feel the U.S. is in a state of economic decline. The tax hike of 1990 was an offense to any thinking American. But Americans need to remember ultimately what tax policy is all about.

It's not about generating revenue. In the January, 1946 issue of *American Affairs*, Beardsley Ruml penned an article entitled, *"Taxes for Revenue Are Obsolete."* Beardsley Ruml was at that time chairman of the Federal Reserve Bank of New York, the key bank in the Federal Reserve system. Ruml stated: *"Federal taxes can be made to serve four principal purposes of a social and economic character. These purposes are: (1) As an instrument of fiscal policy to help stabilize the purchasing power of the dollar; (2) to express public policy in the distribution of wealth and of income, as in the case of the progressive income and estate taxes; (3) to express public policy in subsidizing or in penalizing various industries and economic groups; (4) to isolate and assess directly the costs of certain national benefits, such as highways and social security."*

It is no accident that George Bush signed a Clean Air Act which punishes American industry and aggravates this country's financial problems. This Clean Air Act will cost American businesses $50 billion. It is no fluke that George Bush wanted a common market with Mexico, to the detriment of thousands of American businesses and workers. As commander-in-chief of the U.S. military, George Bush wouldn't even let American soldiers carry Bibles into Saudi Arabia or hold Christian religious services there. And his former Secretary of Labor, Elizabeth Dole, had her bureaucrats sue the Salvation Army for not paying the minimum wage. But what else should we expect from old *"Skull & Bones"*? George Bush has always been an Eastern Establishment elitist. He was at one time a member of David Rockefeller's executive committee of The Trilateral Commission. His Zapata Oil Company was originally funded by the Rockefeller family. Zapata reportedly has long and questionable ties to the CIA, which George Bush later headed.

Iraq has neither borrowed from nor made deposits with Rockefeller's Chase Manhattan Bank and Citicorp. Kuwait, on the other hand, was heavily indebted to these major multinational banks. Kuwait's Sabah family had substantial deposits at both Chase and Citibank, too. The only Americans who wanted our young men to invade Kuwait and die in the process were George Bush, his henchman Jim Baker, Eastern elitists, those who stood to benefit financially, and those who still buy U.S. media propaganda.

This was not a war the U.S. could win, even if it did win militarily. Forty-five Democrats filed suit to force George Bush to deal with Congress' constitutional right to declare war. The families of the hostages, assured that Saddam Hussein would release their loved ones between Christmas and March, certainly didn't want the invasion, which could have resulted in the assassination of up to 2,500 Americans. Gorbachev, the Soviet Union and Mubarak of Egypt asked George Bush to wait three months before considering an invasion of Iraq. Anti-war protests in the U.S. were held; Vietnam veteran groups warned against any offensive action by the Bush-led U.N. one-world military force. There was no U.S. resolution authorizing U.S. ground forces or military force to retake Kuwait.

Some federal officials in the Bush administration discussed needing U.S. troops in Saudi Arabia for years. U.S. forces are in Saudi Arabia based upon secret agreements signed by Secretary of Defense Dick Cheney and Saudi officials. What are the terms of these secret agreements? The U.S. does not have any treaties with Saudi Arabia, Kuwait, or with any other Persian Gulf states that obliges our military to be there, either. Oil is certainly not the reason we're there. Oil prices would have dropped as a result of increasing Iraqi production from both Iraqi and Kuwaiti oil interests as a result of Saddam Hussein's consolidation of those two countries. Saddam Hussein would have loved to sell oil to the United States. He was/is a ready and willing seller. He needs the cash. Furthermore, our ambassador gave Saddam Hussein the green light to invade Kuwait the week before he did so, when April Glaspie told him we had no interest in his domestic border dispute with Kuwait. Saddam Hussein only wanted $21-a-barrel oil. But thanks to George Bush, oil hit as high as $40 a barrel. George Bush's oil buddies had T-shirts in Texas which read, *"God Bless Saddam Hussein."*

The Reagan administration (where George Bush was V.P.) made loans and provided military equipment to Iraq's Saddam Hussein in his war against Iran. During the Reagan administration also, Kuwaiti oil tankers were reflagged with U.S. flags and thus were protected by U.S. warships. Why? Because Kuwait would not allow the U.S. to protect Kuwaiti ships. Why? Because Kuwait did not want to be publicly associated with the United States.

The U.S. won a quick war against Iraq, but the aftermath of such a victory is certainly a fusion of Arab terrorists and the uniting of the Arab Muslim world against U.S. interests and citizens globally. There is literally a bounty on the head of every American who travels abroad. Head hunters are seeking American scalps. A holy war, a jihad, has been declared.

U.S. taxpayers are paying for the reconstruction of Kuwait. Any American administrators (bureaucrats) in Saudi Arabia, Kuwait or Iraq are subject to continuous assassination attempts. Arab nationalism is closely tied to Islamic pride and the feeling that the U.S. is the *"infidel"* and the *"Great Satan."* Meanwhile, the U.S. has made an ally out of Assad of Syria, who has a chemical weapons stockpile at least equal to that of Saddam Hussein. And the U.S., in exchange for Syria's support, allowed Syria to massacre in a horrible conventional military onslaught over 700 Lebanese Christians. This received maybe a paragraph stuck in some remote column of some obscure newspaper somewhere.

So in summary, George Bush blew it. It's lose-lose now, and the situation only gets worse, long term. The American people lost regardless of how you cut it. And remember, these are not the words of some peacenik. I gave up a law school deferment to become an Air Force pilot during the Vietnam War.

Big Red Scorpion

Let's look at the next scorpion: the former Soviet Union. The Soviet Union proved it's bankrupt. If Gorbachev were not a part of the One World Order power clique, he would have been ridden out of town on a rail, tarred and feathered there by the locals. When a country can't feed its own people, it has demonstrated to the world its dismal religious, political and economic bankruptcy. On November 14, 1990, Gorbachev announced that he feared bloody social upheaval in the Soviet Union. The Soviet people were literally starving. As a result, the Supreme Soviet stated that the Soviet Union was on the verge of famine, political anarchy and civil disorder. Question: How much gold and platinum could the Soviet Union export under such conditions?

US News & World Report in its November 19, 1990 cover story headlined, *"Death of a Nation,"* and featured a tombstone with the words U.S.S.R. inscribed on it. *US News* went on to declare: *"The Last Hurrah: The largest country on earth is disintegrating and so far there's no one who can save it."*

Nor should anyone save it. The November 9 *Intelligence Digest* reported: *"Both the Soviet Union and China are supplying arms, chemical weapons, food, and other essential supplies to Iraq by way of Afghanistan and Iran. Both Moscow and Beijing have assured Saddam Hussein of uninterrupted supply."* So the Soviets are being two-faced as usual throughout their bloody 73-year history. It is now apparent it was no accident that there were over 7,000 Soviet troops, advisors and technicians in Iraq, along with the Soviets' top tactical military general, prior to Iraq's invasion of Kuwait.

The Soviet Union's deception and intrigue get even dirtier. The November 2 *Intelligence Digest* declared: *"For many years there has been a growing body of evidence concerning the role played by the Soviet Union and other communist countries in the narcotics trade."* Dr. Joseph D. Douglass, Jr., in his book *Red Cocaine: The Drugging of America*, reported how the Soviet Union (along with Cuban and Latin American leftists and the Red Chinese) had been instrumental in the drug trade and distribution effort here in the United States.

Little Red Scorpion

And then there is the scorpion George Bush so comfortable with his multimillion dollar investment there - the bloody Red Chinese. The Red Chinese still regularly drown baby girls and ruthlessly slaughter their own citizens (Tianemen Square). And George Bush secured Most Favored Nation trade status for the Red Chinese and invited them to Washington. Why didn't he instead encourage them to behave like the freedom loving, happy and prosperous people of Taiwan?

Red China in mid-November 1990 arrested fourteen Buddhist nuns as they protested *"forcible blood extractions"* from Tibetan prisoners. This loss of blood, combined with a starvation diet, killed these Tibetan prisoners. Why aren't American troops invading Tibet to free the Tibetans from the bloody Red Chinese? Never mind, the U.S.-subsidized World Bank removed all restrictions on further lending to Red China.

Steven Mosher's books, *China Misperceived: American Illusions of Chinese Reality, Broken Earth,* and *Journey to a Forbidden China,* present a bleak and alarming picture of rural China and the Chinese Communists. Red China is ugly.

Kosher Scorpion

Then there's the United Nations creation, Israel. Two pro-Israel Christian missionaries with whom I once visited independently stated that the only word to describe Israel today is *"butcher."* An Israeli lawyer and human rights activist, Felicia Langer, after years of battling the inequities of the Israeli system of justice as applied to the Palestinians, called it quits and closed down her law practice in Jerusalem. She also left Israel. She stated, *"I no longer believe in my country's justice."* Felicia Langer called Israeli justice *"a travesty."* But there's more. A book (which has been spiked in this country) was written by a former Mossad agent, Victor Ostrovosky. It is entitled *By Way of Deception.* Ostrovosky's book reveals that the Israelis were ultimately responsible for the 241 U.S. Marine deaths in Beirut on October 23, 1983. Israeli intelligence knew ahead of time that this event was going to happen, but did not tell the U.S. Nevertheless, U.S. taxpayers are shelling out $400 million to provide housing for Soviet Jews in Israel.

Israel loses either way in this Middle East mess. Even though the U.S. was successful in the brief Gulf war, Israel is faced with a well-armed and united Egypt, Syria, Saudi Arabia and like-minded powers against it. Thanks to up-to-date American arms given these Islamic countries for the purpose of fighting Saddam Hussein, these same countries will turn and use them eventually against Israel. On the other hand, if Saddam Hussein is allowed to continue to rule Iraq, Iraq could become fully nuclear and unite the Islamic community and the PLO in future years for a critical strike against Israel. It's lose-lose for Israel.

It seems that anything the U.N. touches or creates, such as Israel or Korea, ends up a scorpion. Any U.S. ally ends up betrayed or destitute. It is the way of scorpions, after all.

Oil Scorpions

Saudi Arabia? In the back pocket of the One Worlders. As early as World War II, the king of Saudi Arabia granted an oil monopoly concession to Aramco. More than $30 million in payments for this concession was made by U.S. taxpayers. The U.S. Export-Import Bank gave another $25 million to provide a pleasure railroad from the main palace to the summer palace of Saudi King Ibin Saud. FDR secretly appropriated $165 million out of war funds to Aramco for pipeline construction across Saudi Arabia. The U.S. Army built an airfield and military base at Dhabran, near the Aramco oil fields. Mobil Oil has joint ventures with the Saudi government. An oil refining and petrochemical complex there has a price tag of over $1 billion. Standard Oil of California and Bechtel have multibillion dollar projects in Saudi Arabia. And how do the Saudis stand with regard to human rights and democracy? Neither exists there.

The Kuwaitis are no better. Kuwait ended civil liberties in 1986. Many Kuwaitis did not want the Sabah family to return to power, so punishing were they to their own people.

Persian Stinger

Finally we come to the last scorpion, Saddam Hussein, the *"beast of Baghdad,"* the *"butcher of Baghdad."* Iraq has 200 of the mighty G-5 155 mm Howitzers, which can fire a shell 25 miles. This super gun, which was built in South Africa, outshoots anything U.S.-led forces could muster in the Persian Gulf. This gun was fully combat tested in Iraq's war with Iran. Can it carry chemical or biological weapons? Plus, Saddam Hussein may have missiles which can hit U.S. warships.

Saddam Hussein is a ruthless street fighter. Not to worry, the World Bank, which made loans to Iraq in its war against Iran, is now making loans to Iran, to the tune of $300 million, subsidized of course by U.S. taxpayers, you and me.

Scorpion Bait

The Bush administration making deals with the devil is what got us into the Middle East mess in the first place. All of these countries are *"scorpions in a bottle."* All of them treat their citizens as *"pawns in the game."* But alas, a war is a convenient distraction from economic recession. It allows the federal governments to further centralize power. War further allows an acceleration of the process of creating a One World Order, exhausting the remnants of nationalism. Old Luciferian Albert Pike must be laughing in hell.

Scorpions in a Bottle: Late Thoughts

I used to be pro-Israel. Now I am neutral. I evaluate her according to her works. The writings and thoughts of respected scholars such as religious historian Dr. Stuart Crane, economic historian Dr. Gary North, political historian Otto Scott, and archaeologist Dr. Barry Fell have modified my thinking. Also, most influential have been the writings of orthodox Jewish historian, Dr. Arthur Koestler, in his important book, *The Thirteenth Tribe.* According to this Jewish scholar, the Jews presently in Israel have no consistent bloodline ties to the Hebrew nation of the Old Testament of the Bible. (There were only twelve tribes in Israel.) Plus, the hostility of modern Israel to Christianity is becoming more apparent.

A major reason the Palestinian question in Israel is heating up is that since January, 1989, over 200,000 Soviet Jews have entered Israel. The immigration of Soviet Jews has now reached a thousand per day. Further, over one million Soviet Jews hold confirmed invitations to emigrate. This is squeezing the Palestinians. The Israeli military has cut back medical care to Palestinians to such a degree that suffering Arabs in some cases have died. Dying Arabs have been turned away from hospital doors. Horrified Israeli doctors have begun to give Palestinians the names of dead Jewish patients. Moreover, Israel's refusal to withdraw from the West Bank is both military and economic, including a desire to control the water resources which originate as rainfall in the West Bank mountains and seep in underground streams and aquifers to the coastal region of Israel. Israel's invasion of Lebanon and its refusal to withdraw from that region is also motivated in part by its plan to tap the water resources of Lebanon's Litani River. Israel will need additional water for its 2.5-3 million new immigrants who are expected in the next couple of years. This means Israel's water supply will need to increase by 25% before the end of this decade. As I've written in previous REAPERs, to Israel, water is more crucial than oil.

The September 23, 1985 issue of *USA Today* featured an interview with ex-hostage Rev. Benjamin Weir. Weir told *USA Today, "Israel is an 'oppressive, aggressive, militaristic' country whose foreign policy won't lead to peace; the Israeli lobby in the U.S.A. 'pretty much creates U.S. foreign policy' in the Mideast. The State Department declined comment. "* This is effectively what Senator Patrick Leahy (D,VT) declared in early December 1990 when he stated the U.S.S.R. should be made eligible for USDA export credit guarantees since every other country in the world is provided this type of assistance. However, in the United States, the Jewish lobby prevented this from occurring because the Soviet Union did not put down in writing its policy with regard to the emigration of Soviet Jews.

The real reason the U.S. had to push Saddam Hussein out of Kuwait was to fulfill the secret deal made between the U.S. government on behalf of U.S. multinational corporations, banks and London international banks regarding substantial Kuwaiti deposits and loans. When the Kuwaiti ruling family got its country back, the loans and deposits stayed on line with these banks.

If the former U.S. ally, Iraq, was really a threat to United States' interests long term, all George Bush had to do was bomb specific areas of Iraq, not invade Kuwait or Iraq, and then continue the economic sanctions. With our sophisticated technology and air superiority, it would take next to no effort, and cost very little in war material or manpower, to bomb Iraq's chemical, biological and nuclear capabilities, etc. out of existence. At the same time, we could continue the economic blockade. This would have gone a long way toward resolving any threat Iraq would be to the U.S. military or oil interests short-term, intermediate term, or long term. Iraq never intended to invade Saudi Arabia. The real issue here is that an armed, united and dedicated Islamic world is the only real threat to the multinational banking One World Order. We witnessed what happened to Margaret Thatcher when she opposed the British pound entering the EMS on the grounds it undercut British sovereignty. She was terminated. What was the first thing her replacement, John Major, said? He endorsed the British pound joining the EMS!

For what the U.S. military build-up in Saudi Arabia cost U.S. taxpayers, the U.S. could have converted all the cars in the United States (for $1,500 a piece) to natural gas and dramatically reduced our dependence on foreign oil. Journalist Helga Graham penned, *"The U.S. administration actively encouraged President Saddam Hussein to pursue an aggressive policy of higher oil prices seven months before the invasion of Kuwait."* Why? To benefit Bush's banking and oil buddies.

James Webb, the Navy Secretary during the Reagan administration, called George Bush's 430,000 troop build-up in the Persian Gulf a mistake. Retired Admiral William Crowe, former chairman of the Joint Chiefs of Staff, stated, *"We may be on the horns of a no-win dilemma,"* regarding the Persian Gulf. *"Even if we win, we lose ground in the Arab world and further injure our ability to deal with the labyrinth of the Middle East."* Dr. Gary North wrote, *"Technically and strategically, we may be at the maximum military risk in U.S. history."*

THE BUILDING STORM
February 2, 1991

THE BUILDING STORM

GEORGE BUSH
(Former Member TC)

The U.S. government and private money system are *not* "out of control". They are scientifically controlled by the CFR/TC!

NATIONAL SECURITY COUNCIL

Brent Scowcroft	Dan Quayle	James Baker	Richard B. Cheney	Colin L. Powell	William Webster
CFR/TC	(Non-Member)	(Non-Member)	CFR	CFR	CFR
NATIONAL SECURITY ADVISOR	VICE PRESIDENT	SECRETARY OF STATE	SECRETARY OF DEFENSE	CHAIRMAN JOINT CHIEFS OF STAFF	DIRECTOR CENTRAL INTELLIGENCE AGENCY

Dick Thornburgh	Nicholas F. Brady	Richard G. Darman	James B. Williams	Horace G. Dawson, Jr.
CFR	CFR	CFR	CFR	CFR
ATTORNEY GENERAL	SECRETARY OF THE TREASURY	DIRECTOR, OFFICE OF MANAGEMENT OF BUDGET (OMB)	DEPARTMENT OF EDUCATION (Asst. Sec. Post Secondary)	U.S. INFORMATION AGENCY Director, Office of Equal Opportunity and Civil Rights

FEDERAL RESERVE SYSTEM

Alan Greenspan, FED Chairman	CFR/TC	John R. Opel	CFR
Andrew R. Brimmer	CFR	Donald C. Platten	CFR
E. Gerald Corrigan	CFR/TC	Emmett J. Rice	CFR
Sam Y. Cross	CFR	Anthony M. Solomon	CFR/TC
Robert F. Erburu	CFR	Edwin M. Truman	CFR
Robert P. Forrestal	CFR	Cyrus R. Vance	CFR
Gerald D. Hines	CFR	Paul Volcker	CFR/TC
Bobby R. Inman	CFR/TC	Henry Wallach	CFR
John V. James	CFR	George Weyerhaeuser	CFR/TC
Robert H. Knight, Esq.	CFR	Henry Woodbridge, Jr.	CFR/TC
Steven Muller	CFR		

ENERGY COMPANIES

EXXON CORPORATION
Lawrence G. Rawl, Chmn.	CFR
Lee R. Raymond, Pres.	CFR
Jack F. Bennett, Sr. VP	CFR
Jack G. Clarke, Sr. VP	CFR

TEXACO
Alfred C. DeCrane, Jr.,Chmn.	CFR

ATLANTIC RICHFIELD-ARCO
Philip M. Hawley	CFR
Hannah H. Gray	CFR
Donald M. Kendall	CFR/TC

SHELL OIL
John F. Bookout	CFR

MOBIL CORP.
Allan E. Murray, Chmn.	CFR
Richard F. Tucker, V. Chmn.	CFR

CHASE MANHATTAN CORP.
Willard C. Butcher,Chmn.& CEO	CFR
Thomas G. Labrecque,Pres.& COO	CFR
Robert R. Douglass, V.Chmn.	CFR
William T. Coleman, Jr. Dir.	CFR
James L. Ferguson, Dir.	CFR
Richard W. Lyman, Dir.	CFR

CHASE MANHATTAN CORP. cont'd
Joan Ganz Cooney, Dir.	CFR
David T. Kearns, Dir.	
David T. McLaughlin, Dir.	CFR
Edmund T. Pratt, Jr. Dir.	CFR
Henry B. Schacht	CFR

CHEMICAL BANK
Walter V. Shipley, Chmn.	CFR
Thomas S. Johnson, Pres.	CFR
Robert J. Callander,V.Chmn.	CFR
Richard S. Simmons,V.Chmn.	CFR
Donald C. Platten, Dir.	CFR
Rawleigh Warner, Jr., Dir.	CFR
Richard D. Wood, Dir.	CFR
Franklin H. Williams, Dir.	CFR
Martha Redfield Wallace, Dir.	CFR
W. Michael Blumental, Dir.	CFR
Michael L. Sovern, Dir.	CFR
Lawrence G. Rawl, Dir.	CFR
George V. Grune, Dir.	CFR
Charles W. Duncan, Jr., Dir.	CFR

CITICORP
John S. Reed, Chmn.	CFR
Hans H. Augermueller, V.Chmn.	CFR
John M. Deutch, Dir.	CFR
Juanita M. Kreps, Dir.	CFR
CITICORP cont'd	

C. Peter McColough, Dir.	CFR
Charles M. Pigott, Dir.	CFR

MORGAN GUARANTY
Lewis T. Preston, Chmn.	CFR

BANKERS TRUST NEW YORK CORPORATION
Charles S. Stanford, Jr., Chmn.	CFR
Alfred Brittain III, Dir.	CFR
Vernon E. Jordan, Jr., Dir.	CFR
Richard L. Gelb, Dir.	CFR
Patricia Carry Stewart, Dir.	CFR

FIRST NATIONAL BANK OF CHICAGO
Barry F. Sullivan	TC

EXPORT-IMPORT BANK
Hart Fessenden, General Council	CFR

MANUFACTURERS HANOVER DIRECTORS
Cyrus Vance	CFR
G. Robert Durham	CFR
George B. Munroe	CFR
Marina V. N. Whitman	CFR
Charles J. Pilliod, Jr.	CFR

26

MEDIA

Past & Present CFR/TC Members (partial listing)

CBS		ASSOCIATED PRESS		TIME,INC.	
William Paley	CFR	Keith Fuller	CFR	Ralph Davidson	CFR
William Burden	CFR	Stanley Swinton	CFR	Donald M. Wilson	CFR
Roswell Gilpatric	CFR	Louis Boccardi	CFR	Louis Banks	
James Houghton	CFT/TC	Harold Anderson	CFR		CFR
Henry Schacht	CFR/TC	Katharine Graham	CFR/TC	Henry Grunwald	CFR
Marietta Tree	CFR			Alexander Heard	CFR
C.C. Collingwood	CFR	**U.P.I.**		Sol Linowitz	
Lawrence LeSueur	CFR	H.L. Stevenson	CFR		CFR/TC
Dan Rather	CFR			Rawleigh Warner, Jr.	CFR
Harry Reasoner	CFR	**REUTERS**		Thomas Watson, Jr.	CFR
Richard Hottelet	CFR	Michael Posner	CFR		
Frank Stanton	CFR			**NEWSWEEK/WASHINGTON POST**	
Bill Moyers	CFR	**BOSTON GLOBE**		Katharine Graham	CFR/TC
		David Rogers	CFR	Philip Graham	CFR
NBC/RCA				Arjay Miller	TC
Jane Pfeiffer	CFR	**L.A. TIMES CHRONICLE**		N. deB. Katzenback	CFR
Lester Crystal	CFR	Joseph Kraft	CFR	Frederick Beebe	CFR
R.W. Sonnenfeldt	CFR			Robert Christopher	CFR
T.F. Bradshaw	CFR	**BALTIMORE SUN**		Osborne Elliot	CFR
John Petty	CFR	Henry Trewhitt	CFR	Phillip Geyelin	CFR
David Brinkley	CFR			Kermit Lausner	CFR
John Chancellor	CFR	**WASHINGTON TIMES**		Marry Marder	CFR
Marvin Kalb		Arnaud de Borchgrave	CFR	Malcolm Muir	CFR
CFR				Maynard Parker	CFR
Irving Levine	CFR	**NEW YORK TIMES CO.**		George Will	
H. Schlosser	CFR	Richard Gelb	CFR		CFR
P.G. Peterson	CFR/TC	James Reston	CFR	Robert Kaiser	CFR
John Sawhill	CFR/TC	William Scranton	CFR	Meg Greenfield	CFR
		A.M. Rosenthal	CFR	Walter Pincus	CFR
ABC		Seymour Topping	CFR	Murray Gart	
Ray Adam	CFR	James Greenfield	CFR		CFR
Frank Cary	CFR	Max Frankel	CFR	Peter Osnos	
John Connor	CFR		CFR		CFR
T.M. Macioce	CFR	Jack Rosenthal	CFR	Don Oberdorfer	CFR
Ted Koppel	CFR	Harding Bancroft	CFR		
John Scali	CFR	Amory Bradford	CFR	**DOW JONES & CO.**	
Barbara Walters	CFR	Orvil Dryfoos	CFR	**(Wall Street Journal)**	
		David Halberstram	CFR	William Agee	CFR
CABLE NEWS NETWORK		Walter Lippmann	CFR	J. Paul Austin	TC
Daniel Schorr	CFR	L.E. Markel	CFR	Charles Mayer	CFR
		H.L. Matthews	CFR	Robert Potter	CFR
PUBLIC BROADCAST SERVICE		John Oakes	CFR	Richard Wood	CFR
Hartford Gunn	CFR		CFR	Robert Bartley	CFR
Robert McNeil	CFR	Adolph Ochs	CFR	Karen House	CFR/TC
Jim Lehrer	CFR	Harrison Salisbury	CFR		
C. Hunter-Gault	CFR	A. Haye Sulzberger	CFR	**NATIONAL REVIEW**	
Hodding Carter III	CFR	A. Oche Sulzberger	CFR	William F. Buckley, Jr.	CFR
Daniel Schorr	CFR	C.L. Sulzberger	CFR	Richard Brookhiser	CFR
		H.L. Smith	CFR		
		Steven Rattner	CFR		
		Richard Burt			
		CFR			

The U.S. government and private money system are *not* "out of control". They are scientifically controlled by the CFR/TCI

If there is one regret I have about writing THE REAPER during the Bush administration, it is that I did not prepare you well enough for the realities of that administration. I needed to more forcefully hammer home the point that George Bush's perspective is that of a bureaucratic internationalist. The Bush administration could be easily understood, and its actions forecast, once this perspective was understood. Moreover, every decision George Bush made was from the viewpoint of a multinational banker. Did the Bush administration do anything beneficial for the domestic economy, for ordinary U.S. taxpayers?

Above is a layout of this nation's *"elite,"* the Establishment. It explains why nothing changes in the federal government regardless of who is elected. The Council on Foreign Relations (CFR) and the Trilateral Commission (TC) cross party lines. (For the complete CFR/TC list write F.R.E.E., P.O. Box 33339, Kerrville, TX 78029. A donation would be appreciated.)

If you want to make an omelet, you have to break some eggs. Creating a national crisis is the preferred way to activate the thesis of debt capitalism versus the antithesis of communism to bring about the synthesis of a new world order of mercantilistic fascism. We are definitely in a national economic and military crisis. The Bush promise to the American people of a *"kinder and gentler"* America has yielded to the fulfillment of George Orwell's *1984* prophecy, *"Perpetual war for perpetual peace."* Said George Bush to the Religious Broadcasters on January 28, 1991, *"No one is more determined to see from this battle a real peace, a new world order."* The warriors of the New World Order, George Bush and James Baker, are about their sponsors' business.

Poor Boy You're Bound to Die

Disillusionment among America's grassroots is becoming more widespread. Of course, the Far Left, who protest against any and all wars, as well as for welfare spending, were hostile to the Bush administration. But the Far Right, too, was disillusioned, as represented by the John Birch Society's full page ads taken out against the Bush administration's involvement in the U.N.-sponsored Persian Gulf war. The minorities, too, were put out. Congressman Henry B. Gonzalez's January 16, 1991 *"Resolution of Impeachment of President George Bush"* was issued largely on behalf of Hispanics and blacks, who were bearing the brunt of this war with their lives. As Gonzalez wrote, *"Our soldiers in the Middle East are overwhelmingly poor white, black, and Mexican-American. They may be volunteers, technically, but their volunteerism is based on the coercion of a system that has denied viable economic opportunities to these classes of citizens."* Gonzalez maintains many of today's volunteer army joined to pay for a college education.

The continued depreciation of the U.S. dollar, brought about by a spendthrift Congress, coupled with the encouragement by the Bush administration for U.S. business to go offshore (like Mexico), truly undercut the lower income echelon of American society. This is why, according to a CNN January 27 poll, only 55% of blacks approved of this war, and less than half, 49%, of blacks thought the U.S. had a right to go to war in the Persian Gulf in the first place.

The potential for civil unrest in our cities on a scale not seen since the 1960s exists. Civil unrest in the United States, coupled with terrorism, would give the current administration just the excuse it needs to declare martial law in this country; a national emergency complete with executive orders, and then strictly limit and control Americans' freedom and movement of assets. Three of my sources have stated the executive orders are already being quietly implemented.

Fly Away

Free Americans who desire to travel abroad, and have the wherewithal to invest offshore, are having trouble exercising their preferences. The Persian Gulf war made Americans unwanted, persona non grata, all over the globe. Just as I warned, Americans are no longer welcome, and in fact are targets for terrorism, throughout the entire Arab world.   In Jordan, 412 newborn babies were named Saddam in honor of Iraqi President Saddam Hussein.   On February 4, 1991, the State Department warned all American citizens to leave Jordan. On February 1, 1991, the U.S. embassy in Peru was struck by mortar fire. India is off limits, too.   On January 25, 1991, the U.S. advised its citizens to leave India temporarily and even postpone travel to India because of terrorist threats from Iraqi or Palestinian agents there.   Hmm.   India has nuclear weapons.   Why not attack India?

Iraq won't have a functional nuclear weapon for 5-10 years, if then, according to the March 1991 *Bulletin of the Atomic Scientists*:   *"After a month-long investigation of the requirements any country would need to build nuclear weapons, and an assessment of Iraq's ability to meet those requirements, we conclude that Saddam Hussein was many years away from developing usable nuclear weapons."*   Iraq has no plutonium.   Besides, Iraq would have had only one crude atomic bomb, compared to Israel's 85 and the U.S.' 8,000.   To use it would have been suicidal.   No matter, Iraq's nuclear facilities have been bombed into oblivion.   None other than Vice President Quayle declared the nuclear option for the U.S. still exists in the Gulf.

Same song, second verse for Pakistan.   Americans are not welcome there. Seventy-seven percent of Pakistanis oppose the U.S. presence in the Persian Gulf.   The U.S. State Department gave its embassy personnel in Pakistan the option of leaving that country and returning to the U.S.   Pakistan could make a nuclear weapon in a week.   Should the U.S. bomb Pakistan?   Filipinos in Manila on January 25 and 28, 1991 burned the U.S. flag to protest the war.

The Third World has gotten its back up against what it considers to be *"the ugly American."*   Even the normally affable Mexicans are protesting and turning hostile against their *"Neighbor to the North."*   As a result, Mexican politicians are being forced to rethink their oil policy of readily supplying the United States.   Many Mexicans view the U.S. *"aggression"* in the Persian Gulf as just another case where the American superpower has bullied a poor Third World country, a situation with which the Mexican people thoroughly identify.   Thus, both George Washington's and Thomas Jefferson's warnings that the proper choice for a nation is to conduct free trade with all and war with none, except in the actual physical defense of the country, came home to haunt the United States under George Bush.

Green, Green

Environmentalists are also turning hostile.   The devastating Persian Gulf oil spill (now two of them), which the Iraqis blamed upon the U.S. and the U.S. on the Iraqis, is a natural disaster of monumental proportions, two and one half times bigger than the Exxon Valdez oil spill.   *Oil Spill Intelligence Report* estimated the slick to contain 24-40 million gallons of crude.   This 50-mile-long, 12-mile-wide oil slick was intended to be a threat to an allied amphibious landing. It was definitely a threat to the critical major water desalination plants in Saudi Arabia. The slick moved to within 60 miles of Jubail, site of the world's largest desalination plant. (You may recall that in an issue of THE REAPER I pointed out that desalination plants were targeted by Saddam Hussein.)

Environmentalists are beginning to bring up the reality that environmental abuse and international mercantilistic fascism go hand in hand.

Red Money

The Persian Gulf war was about *"blood for money,"* not primarily *"blood for oil."* This is why the Saudis and Kuwaitis viewed American soldiers there as *"mercenaries,"* as *"white slaves."* Recall that it was London and New York, England and the United States, who were the only two powers who rejected the reasonable last-minute French peace proposal. There was too much money at stake. Sheik Al Ahmad al Sabah, the thirteenth Emir of Kuwait, has approximately $200 billion of his assets managed by his mysterious London firm, K10. That's a lot of dough. It can buy a lot of political influence, maybe even a war. So, it was no surprise that both the Saudis and Kuwaitis each pledged to cough up $13.5 billion the weekend of January 27, 1991 to fight this war, since both the U.S. budget and dollar were gasping for air. The combined contribution of Japan and Germany did not cover the cost of the Persian Gulf war for even one day. Plus, neither country had any troops in the Gulf. Finally, on January 29, 1991 Germany pledged $5.5 billion. The WSJ reported the Pentagon received only $6.26 billion in actual cash and supplies; only $2.5 billion in cash from Kuwait's exiled government and only $760 million in cash and $854 million in goods and services from Saudi Arabia.

U.S. Comptroller General Charles Bowsher (head of the GAO) stated that the Persian Gulf war was wiping out the deficit reduction envisioned in the budget plan approved after the long, contentious discussion between the Bush administration and Congress. Senator William Cohen (R, Maine) declared, *"Germany is a country I feel is getting a free ride."* Senator Carl Levin (D, Michigan) stated, *"I think it would be a very bitter irony if, after all the American blood and treasure goes into this effort, we emerge as an exhausted superpower."* Representative Byron Dorgan (D, North Dakota) said, *"This country is already running on empty. We don't have the resources to pursue significant new agenda items."* Friend and editor of *Dow Theory Letters*, Richard Russell, also warned about the high cost of this war: *"World War II was fought at a time when the U.S. had very little federal debt. That war was financed with bonds and the debt rose mightily. Korea was no major financing problem, but then came Vietnam. President Johnson wanted guns and butter and he never financed the war. The result: the succeeding generation was saddled with chronic inflation and a massive rise in federal debt.*

"Now comes the Persian Gulf war, and Mr. Bush has mmm, neglected to talk about financing. We'll fight the war, and finance it later (like Vietnam, maybe). But this time, unlike Vietnam, we're starting the war when we already have a $3 trillion deficit. How will it all work out? I'm not sure, but keep your eye on the dollar." ...Sounds just like what I had been writing in THE REAPER as a primary reason the United States should not have been involved in the Persian Gulf war. The United States is financially exhausted and could not afford it. On February 4, 1991, the March U.S. dollar index hit new lows, falling below 82. The Federal Reserve and Bundesbank, along with other central banks, had to intervene in the currency markets and buy up dollars to prevent panic selling.

Right Face

Disillusionment over the Bush administration as a result of the Persian Gulf war increased among traditional American conservatives. Howard Phillips of The Conservative Caucus formed a third political party, called the U.S. Taxpayers Party. (If you are interested, you may contact the U.S. Taxpayers Alliance at 450 Maple Avenue East, Vienna, VA 22180.) Highly respected, longtime Washington conservative fixture Howard Phillips wrote in his January 21, 1991 *Issues and Strategy Bulletin*, *"Regardless of one's own views of Saddam Hussein and the appropriate role of the United States in the Gulf, the correct constitutional vote in this issue was 'no.' It is an outrage that members of Congress would commit American men and women to battle with the United Nations cited as a source of authority and conceded the right to set up the terms of engagement.*

"President Bush's policy in Iraq does much to advance his 'new world order'...It does little to safeguard or strengthen our republic.

"The proximate threat of the United States prior to Mr. Bush's overcommitment of our prestige and our resources, emanated not from Baghdad, but from Moscow and, closer to home, from Havana. If we wish to stop aggression, why not begin in Lithuania?"

Poll Pop

President Bush's popularity continued to ride high on the shoulders of middle America, whose sons and daughters were *not* fighting the war, who did *not* understand the internationalist plan and purposes of this war, nor the reality that Americans were slowly but surely being plucked like a Thanksgiving turkey. Americans should have been reminded that only 10% of their fellow countrymen cast a positive vote for George Bush for president of the United States. The rest either did not vote, voted for Michael Dukakis, or voted against Michael Dukakis. Plus, under the distraction of this Persian Gulf war, the Bush administration took actions which, if known, would literally outrage middle America.

To the AIDS of Our Country

On January 26, 1991, the Associated Press reported, *"The Bush administration served notice Friday that it intends to lift rules that prohibit foreigners with AIDS, leprosy, or any of five venereal diseases - including gonorrhea and syphilis - from entering the United States."* Beyond question, the average American will concede that this action by the Bush administration clearly violated the general welfare clause of the U.S. Constitution. It amounts to a double whammy - killing our sons and daughters on foreign battlefields while killing them through bankrupt political public health practices at home.

In 1990, I had two separate White House sources tell me the Bush administration was adamantly pro-gay. The evangelical Christian community had been harping about this for some time. Members of the White House staff who took a stand against this pro-gay stance were fired. The actions by the Bush administration in an age of promiscuity amounts to nothing more or less than biological warfare against the American people at home. And it came at a time when AIDS deaths in the United States were soaring. Why didn't the Bush administration fund more free market research dedicated to curing AIDs? The Persian Gulf war cost $1-$2 billion a day. Isn't the *"War on AIDS"* likewise worthy of funding?

Rev Up

The federal bureaucratic dictatorship, as represented by the legislation written by the alphabet agencies, the EPA, IRS, FDA, etc., hummed right along. The Federal Register, the daily government publication of rules and regulations, ran a whopping 238 single-spaced pages on Wednesday, January 23, 1991. This is the law of the land. No congressman or senator even reads it, and yet it rules over us all.

I agree with historian Otto Scott that we are in a pre-revolutionary stage in this country presently, not unlike the pre-French revolutionary era. Not that revolutions do any good, mind you. They nearly always simply replace the old corrupt order with a new corrupt order. As long as the federal government is the ultimate source of law, and therefore the god of the society, there are effectively no checks and balances against its tomfoolery, corruption, madness or mistakes. After all, who can challenge a god? The reason why the American system of checks and balances worked is because there was always considered to be a higher law, God's law, to which not only the federal government, but all other human institutions, including the church, were accountable. All civil government entities were considered limited entities under this higher law. But now higher law, God's law, has been thrown out and there are no checks against the government's ruthlessness. So Americans shouldn't blink too hard to find that the U.S. is aligned with Syria, who recruited the Libyan intelligence agent who blew up Pan Am Flight 103 over Lockerbie, Scotland in late 1988. *"Scorpions in a bottle"* are all these governments are.

When there is no *"higher law,"* men revert to power and money as their gods. This war is a power play between Saddam Hussein and George Bush, and it's about big money - the Emir of Kuwait's $200 billion in his London firm, K10, for example. It's about Kuwait's Sabah clan owning a large chunk of British Petroleum and keeping enormous deposits at Chase Manhattan Bank and Citibank. It's about Iraq refusing to patronize these big banks.

Money Rules

Let's now take a closer look at just how big the money issue is in this war. The U.N. vote to approve the use of military force in the Persian Gulf against Saddam Hussein was bought and paid for by the Bush administration. Congressman Henry B. Gonzalez, who for thirty years has sat on the House Banking and Finance Committee wrote: *"It is clear that the President paid off members of the U.N. Security Council in return for their votes in support of war against Iraq. The debt of Egypt [$7 billion] was forgiven; a $140 million loan to China was agreed to; the Soviet Union was promised $7 billion in aid; Colombia was promised assistance to its armed forces; Zaire was promised military assistance and partial forgiveness of its debt; Saudi Arabia was promised $12 billion in arms; Yemen was threatened with the termination of support; and the U.S. finally paid off $187 million of its debt to the United Nations after the vote President Bush sought was made."* When Yemen voted *"no"* at the U.N., voting not to approve the use of force against Saddam Hussein, U.S. Secretary of State James Baker told Yemen it would be *"the most expensive 'no' vote you ever cast."* On January 28, 1991, U.S. aid to Yemen dropped to $2.9 million from $23 million.

Well, we were always told as children that money rules this world. The U.S. effort to restore the Emir of Kuwait to power shows just how far this country has sold itself out for money in compromise of its moral heritage. This is a clear demonstration of the moral bankruptcy of the pragmatic power politics of money.

Slimeballs

I am indebted to German-speaking Charlie Walters, editor of the respected publication, *Acres, U.S.A.*, for bringing to my attention an exposé on Sheik Al Ahmad al Sabah, the thirteenth Emir of Kuwait, which appeared in a recent issue of the German magazine, *Bunte. Bunte* disclosed there are 1,200 princes in the Sabah clan. Counting their wives and children, this royal family has 5,000 members. They are Kuwait. Period. Each of the 5,000 is a millionaire. Each has a special passport. In Paris, their spendthrift ways are legendary. Further, in Kuwait's prewar population of two million, only 750,000 were native Kuwaitis. The rest were Palestinians, Egyptians and other non-Kuwaitis. The Kuwaiti military was made up of mercenaries. The 5,000 members of the Sabah clan basically considered these people peasants. They called them - hold your breath - *"sand niggers."* (Wonder what the Kuwaitis in private call our fine black fighting forces who are risking their lives to restore this Sabah clan to power?)

And how about the granddaddy of the Kuwaiti Sabah clan - Sheik Sabah? For starters he has gold-plated seatbelts in one of his private Boeing jets, a 200-room palace, a falcon (bird) which cost $1 million, three water fountains costing $14 million each, fourteen private jets, one a jumbo jet with marble baths, ten Rolls Royces, fifteen Cadillacs, five Lambourghini Jeeps, and a secret fleet of bulletproof Mercedes limos. His meals are pre-tasted for poison, so unpopular is he with the common people. Up until 1988, he rented a year-round $3,333-a-night suite at the Carlton Hotel in Cannes. He has a 50,000 square foot palace built near luxury fortresses owned by King Hussein, King Fahd and others of the same caste. His wives have been numbered between 40 and 80, although he claims to have only three regular wives. He has at least 700 children. But despite all this opulence, to which the average American can't relate, Sheik Al Ahmad al Sabah also gets married once a week, always on Thursday evening. At that time his bodyguards bring him a beautiful Bedouin maiden from the desert. She is always a virgin. Before the marriage is contracted, she is bathed in marble chambers, sprayed with perfumes and powdered. Then the next day, after spoiling her the night before, the Sheik simply utters three times the following words, *"I repudiate you."* Under Muslim law, he is thereby divorced. ...Yes, Martha, we sent our sons and daughters to fight and die to support the alleged return to power of such decadence - all with your tax money. That's not all. The January 24, 1991 *Wall Street Journal*, in an article by Jane Meyer, declared, *"For some Kuwaitis, war is just reason for another party..."*

"When allied bombs first hit Baghdad, many young Kuwaitis here had their own unique response: They hit the dance floors." (This was in Cairo, Egypt.)

Red Oil

Then there's the money and power that comes from the control of oil in the Middle East after this nasty war was over. After all, Iraq was at war with fellow OPEC members Saudi Arabia, Kuwait, and the United Arab Emirates, after being at war with Iran for eight years. (Iran is supposedly neutral in this conflict. Not likely.) According to Sheik Ahmed Zaki Yamani, *"Immediately after the war, OPEC will not be in a position to protect the price of oil. It will be very difficult to ask Iraq and Kuwait to restrain their production at a time when they want to reconstruct their countries. It will also be very difficult to ask the Saudis to considerably reduce their production at a time when they have a heavy financial burden; financing the war is very tough."*

Urban Renewal

The Persian Gulf war smacked throughout of a CIA operation. The CIA, headed previously by George Bush, is considered to be the U.S. taxpayers' contribution to the multinational bankers' private army. Just ask Oliver North. The U.S. multinational industrial and banking complex were already gearing up for the reconstruction of Saudi Arabia, Iraq and Kuwait even before the termination of the war. Don't believe it? Ask anyone who tried to find some good new or used equipment in the U.S. at the right price. It was being gobbled up all over the country by the multinationals, who were licking their chops at the huge profits which would come from this latest military misadventure. After all, to many multinational banks and corporations, war is nothing more than a form of *"urban renewal."*

"Read my lips - no new taxes," George Bush spoke on January 28, 1991 to the annual Convention of Religious Broadcasters: *"No one wanted this war less than I did...When this war is over, the United States...will have a key role in restoration of peace in the Middle East...We will seek nothing for ourselves...."*

Red Dawn Over Baghdad

But then there were the Soviets. After all, Moscow still has a Treaty of Friendship and Cooperation with Iraq. If Israel entered the fray, the entire Arab Islamic world would probably have united against Israel and the U.S. The Soviets would have won huge *"brownie points"* by coming in on behalf of the Iraqis, supporting the Islamic Arab world, enforcing their Treaty of Friendship and Cooperation with Iraq. The Soviet Union told the United States in no uncertain terms not to enter Iraq. Recall that Soviet Colonel-General Albert Mikhaylovich, who was the Soviet tactical military genius, was in Iraq along with 7,000 Soviet advisors three weeks before Iraq's invasion of Kuwait. Another Soviet general, whose name escapes me, stated that basically 80% of the targets the U.S. and allied forces bombed were not hit, that many of them were cardboard and wooden decoys. Soviet Lt. Gen. Evgeny Shaposhnikov told the *Red Star* defense newspaper that Saddam Hussein had successfully concealed most of his sophisticated war planes. Major General Viktor Filatov, editor of the *Soviet Military Historical Journal*, predicted on February 1, 1991 that Iraq would win the Persian Gulf war, that the war would be worse for the U.S. than Vietnam. *"There has been no real action in the Gulf yet. Iraq has all its forces hidden under the Earth. They will appear when the foreign occupation forces arrive - when the first American soldier appears on Iraqi soil."*

International geopolitical analyst Don McAlvany told me his reliable sources claim that from August 9, 1990 until January 14, 1991, each and every day 12 Soviet transports flew in and landed at an airport outside of Baghdad. These planes were the 89-ton capacity AN-22s (the equivalent of the USAF's C-141) as well an AN-124s (similar to the USAF's C-5A). The AN-124 carries a 165-ton payload. By any measure, this was a massive build-up of Iraq by the Soviet Union over a five-month period. Further, always reliable *Intelligence Digest* of London reported, *"According to reports reaching 'Intelligence Digest' from India, both the Soviet Union and China are supplying arms, chemical weapons, food and other essential supplies to Iraq by way of both Afghanistan and Iran. Both Moscow and Beijing have assured Saddam Hussein of uninterrupted supply."*

Incredible insanity was additionally demonstrated by the fact that the Kuwaiti government (Sabah) in exile lent the former Soviet Union $1 billion, when it was the Soviets who built up the Iraqi military machine which took over Kuwait!

On January 28, the *"Read my lips - no new taxes"* White House declared that the Soviet Union was not aiding Iraq in the Gulf war.

Down to Earth

If we stop and think about it, everything Saddam Hussein said he was going to do, he did - attack Israel and Saudi Arabia with missiles, create an environmental/ecological disaster in the Persian Gulf, etc. The truthfulness of Saddam Hussein concerning this war was also noted by senior Western diplomats in Baghdad. Saddam Hussein said he had a number of surprise weapons waiting for the U.S. forces. The respected June 1988 issue of *Weapons and Tactics of the Soviet Army* stated that fifteen of the Soviet SS-12 missiles were sent to Iraq. Additionally, analysis of Iraqi tactical radio communications confirmed that Soviet advisors were manning Iraqi tank regiments and battalions. There were 150,000 literate, mostly college graduates who made up Saddam Hussein's elite and seasoned Republican Guard. Saddam warned in the future his Scud missiles could carry chemical and biological warheads. Iraq had a squadron of kamikaze pilots armed with incendiary bombs to strike Israel and Saudi Arabian oil fields. Suicide runs were also scheduled for Iraqi SU-24 bombers, equipped with chemical bomb tanks.

Soviet Lt. Gen. Stanislave Petrov told *Izvestia* that Iraqi nuclear reactors are not destroyed, that Iraq has 2,000-4,000 tons of toxic chemical agents including mustard gas, anthrax and prussic acid. Additionally, the January 28, 1991 *Washington Post* reported that 65% of Iraqi airfields were still in operation, 20% of Iraq's air radar were on line, and that only eight of Iraq's 30 fixed Scud missile launchers were disabled. (*Time Magazine* declared that 100% of Iraq's nuclear manufacturing capability and more than 50% of Iraq's chemical manufacturing capability were destroyed.) The United States wrote checks in the Persian Gulf it doesn't have the spiritual bank account to cash. This country is no longer Daniel of the Old Testament.

Rattlesnake Round-Up

Make no mistake about it, Saddam Hussein is a rattlesnake, but he's a rattlesnake the U.S. and former U.S.S.R. fed, watered and nurtured. Now the U.S. desires to kill its pet rattlesnake. But Saddam Hussein, being the rattlesnake he is, doesn't want to die. He intends on striking back, any way he can, whether that means using Scud missiles, environmental devastation, chemical and biological warfare, terrorism, and any and all other weapons at his disposal. Those horrible weapons will be used to *"save face"* and destroy the *"infidels."* Also, Saddam has fifty African magicians, soothsayers and fortune-tellers giving him daily advice, according to the January 11, 1991 *Jerusalem Post*. Thus, U.S. troops are up against a hideous darkness. Do our troops have the spiritual maturity to ward off such evil? U.S. pilots were being shown pornographic movies before they take off to fly their sorties. Saddam's black art specialists were telling him a major Alliance leader would be assassinated, resulting in an upheaval in the Alliance.

Throw out all war conventions. Throw out all morality. This was war, Saddam Hussein style, to the death, and anything goes. This rattlesnake was attempting to lure the United States into its den where the U.S. could sustain more snakebites than it could handle. The additional danger was the very real possibility there was a hungry Soviet bear also hiding in the rattlesnake's den, waiting to maul the U.S.

Moral Bankruptcy

Any time any nation decides to resort to the use of force, it is effectively admitting its philosophical bankruptcy. The very act of the use of force means that a nation has failed to persuade through logic, evidence, or moral persuasion. Such is the nature of military aggression. This is why the purpose of the U.S. militia, as envisioned by our Founding Fathers through the U.S. Constitution, was to protect and defend the United States against those foreign powers who transgressed our shores.

Saddam Hussein earlier proclaimed himself to be a secularist Islamic Arab, but he has seen now it's in his own self-interest to proclaim himself a savior of the Palestinians. Immigrating Soviet Jews taking Palestinian jobs in Israel strengthen Saddam's hand. The high number of Iraqi civilian casualties reported in the Arab and European press (spiked in the U.S. press) lit the fire for a holy war against America. Being $80-$100 billion in debt, Saddam Hussein's Iraq had little to live for peacefully, much to fight for religiously.

No Pain

The American lifestyle is one of immediate gratification, with no sense of deferred gratification. It is a lifestyle of all gain with no pain. This was reflected in the January 25, 1991 *Wall Street Journal* poll which revealed that 91% of Americans felt that the U.S. and allied forces should force Iraq to withdraw from Kuwait, and 87% felt the U.S. should destroy Iraq's offensive military capability. However, only 56% wanted the war to continue if the war would cost thousands of American casualties. Poll after poll showed that if the war continued beyond 60-90 days, or there were stiff American casualties, support for this war would evaporate.

Support

It's been encouraging to see highly respected American thinkers echo my thoughts concerning this war. Remember my comments regarding this country's probable *"exhaustion"* resulting from this war? The U.S. Congress' chief auditor warned on Wednesday, January 23, 1991 that the Iraqi armed forces threatened the U.S. economy as well as American troops, as minimal allied contributions to the Persian Gulf war made matters worse. Douglas Bandow, a Senior Fellow at Cato Institute of Washington, D.C., wrote, *"Washington's paramount goal should be ending the U.S.A.'s unnecessary involvement in this unnecessary war."* Dr. Paul Kennedy, historian and professor at Yale University, author of *The Rise and Fall of Great Powers*, wrote in the January 24, 1991 *Wall Street Journal*: *"We have come a long way since the Founding Fathers warned their countrymen against overseas entanglements, but whatever reasons were given for American interventions in earlier wars of the century - protecting freedom of the seas, responding to Pearl Harbor, stopping North Korean aggression - I do not think that recovery of America's lost self-esteem was one of them.*

"To the historian of international politics, however, this reasoning has a very familiar and disturbing ring to it.

"...But the point of this historical analogy is to remind readers what the theory of 'imperial overstretch' is really about. Essentially, it rests upon a truism, that a power that wants to remain number one for generation after generation requires not just military capability, not just national will, but also a flourishing and efficient economic base, strong finances and a healthy social fabric, for it is upon such foundations that the country's military strength rests in the long term...

"I do not want the U.S. to follow the path of imperial Spain and Edwardian Britain; but it is no use claiming that America is completely different from those earlier great powers when we are imitating so many of their habits - possessing garrisons and bases and fleets in all parts of the globe and acting as the world's policeman on one hand, running up debts and neglecting the country's internal needs on the other.

"The dilemma that the U.S. faces during the next decade in achieving a proper balance between ends and means - thus avoiding 'imperial overstretch' - is awkward enough. But the last thing that is needed is for its people to be encouraged to seek its self-esteem on the battlefield. If the U.S. wishes to recover its 'reputation,' it must begin by repairing its inner cities, public education, crumbling infrastructure and multiple social needs, at the same time resisting the temptation to follow the path of Spanish grandees. The 'sense of self-confidence and self-esteem' that Americans desire to see restored would be more appropriately felt in a democracy like this one if it rested upon evidence of the nation's health and strength rather than upon reported distant glories in war."

U.S. Secretary of the Navy under Ronald Reagan, James H. Webb, Jr., wrote in the January 31, 1991 WSJ, *"The Bush administration...has relentlessly maneuvered our nation into a war...*

"...One must go even further, perhaps to the Mexican War, to find a president so avidly desirous of putting the nation at risk when it has not been attacked. In fact, if the president's ever-vague war aims continue to escalate as they have over the past two weeks, he might even fulfill The Wall Street Journal's *desire to see a 'MacArthurian regency in Baghdad.'...*

"...Support for President Bush's desire to send Americans out to die was reed-thin before the first shot was fired, and will remain only as long as casualties are extremely low. George Bush believes he has taken us to war over 'the greatest moral issue since World War II,' but he has not convinced the country of this..."

Former President Jimmy Carter, a true Middle East expert, criticized the Bush administration for *"not leaving any possibility of a negotiated settlement."*

"When we prohibited any sort of resolution of the issue in a peaceful fashion, then we made it inevitable that Saddam would not yield at all..."

"My own preference would have been that the U.S. support the U.N. resolution but that we encourage the Saudis and the Algerians and the Yemenis to try to negotiate the differences between Saddam and Kuwait," said Carter. ...Ten Moslem states have accepted Iraq's call for an emergency Islamic summit to end the war.

Dr. Edward N. Luttwak, who holds the Arleigh Burke Chair of Strategy at the Center for Strategic and International Studies, argued that the Iraqi army needed to remain intact. Why? Because Luttwak says the Iraqi army is a very important checkmate against the Syrians and the Iranians. Iran cannot be unconstrained and allowed to be the strongest power in the Persian Gulf, and Syria must be restrained from its own natural aggressiveness. Dr. Luttwak concludes, *"Thus a U.S. ground offensive would not only be intermediately costly in lives, but would also be strategically counterproductive."*

When the U.S. government does not tell its people the truth, it has stolen power from them and the constitutional right to make sound decisions.

A MISSING PIECE
January 24, 1991

Bombs Away

Beyond question, both the Iraqi people and the world would be better off without the barbaric Iraqi military machine and Saddam Hussein. Could we have let Israel lead the air strikes for us without U.S. military forces becoming involved? After all, that's in part what we pay Israel billions of dollars of U.S. taxpayer money to do, to act as our surrogate in the Middle East. But this way, Bush hoped to wind up with the leaders of Kuwait and Saudi Arabia (and their billions and oil) in his back pocket. On the other hand, if we had let well enough alone, U.S. ally Saddam Hussein would have sold us all the oil we wanted at cheap prices. It would have been just a matter of time before he was overthrown or assassinated. We could, even now, wait him out. Contrary to popular press, the economic sanctions are working. And with the massive air strikes, all the allied forces had to do was to sit back and wait, let the air strikes continue and the sanctions work, to bring Saddam Hussein and his military henchmen to their knees.

Division At Home

The Congress and the country were deeply split over this war until the bombs started to fall. Then, as is typically the case with modern Americans, nearly everyone rallied around President George Bush. His approval rating in one poll reportedly shot up to 87%, an all-time high for any president. This is a reflection of the effectiveness of the government (public) schools and the mass media, of modern Americans' *"Patton"* mentality, *"My country - right or wrong."* Within 24 hours of the outbreak of war, I received a call from an elderly gentleman who reads THE REAPER. This man told me in no uncertain terms that now that the war was started I should quit writing negative things about President George Bush and get solidly behind the President. I asked this gentleman if he had been a German under the Nazi regime if he would have supported Hitler. His immediate answer was, *"Yes."* Hmm.

The Chain Gang

Americans did not always feel this way. This country was carved out of history by a group of tax protestors (Boston tea party). Now, most Americans view tax protestors as kooks. The Declaration of Independence was an open rebellion against authorized government and the ruling political authority. The U.S. Declaration of Independence made the case for the overthrow of a government which operated for its own interest, contrary to the will of the people. The primary purpose of the U.S. Constitution was to put chains on the federal government to maximize the freedom of the states and particularly individuals. But most Americans thought the original U.S. Constitution did not go far enough to restrict the federal government. This is why the Bill of Rights was added, to protect individuals against the central government in Washington. The U.S. Civil War was fought for much the same reason, individual freedom and states' rights. (Every other nation on earth ended slavery non-violently.) And even at the time of the outbreak of World War I, Americans were strongly against becoming involved in a foreign war. Up until World War I, it was widely held to be unconstitutional for American soldiers to fight on foreign soil unless they volunteered to do so. Over 20,000 court cases were filed in the U.S. court system at the beginning of World War I to protest the unconstitutional nature of that action.

A Fallen Star

We have fallen a long way since the time that Americans viewed *"government"* as primarily the self-government of the individual under God, the federal government chained by both God's laws and limited by the U.S. Constitution, and the concept of the superiority of states' rights. By contrast, today Americans are enslaved by debt, considered by Europeans to be the most obedient people in the world, are the most heavily regulated, and on a per capita basis are the most imprisoned by their federal government of any nation on the face of the earth. Americans today quietly adhere to the tyrannical rules and regulations of bureaucracies which make the law, administer the law, and judge the law. America's founding fathers, and indeed, Americans up until 1913, would be rising up in protest and indignation against what we have today. But perhaps the ultimate insult is that the Saudis saw no reason to fight in their own defense because as they state, they have American soldiers, their *'white slaves,'* to do that for them. In the finest tradition of the Roman Empire, Americans have let a professional army fight for privileged special interests while the people are distracted by bread and circuses (welfare and football).

What it all adds up to is that Americans have lost the distinction between being patriotic and loyal to one's country, one's constitution, one's people, and one's way of life; and supporting the central government in Washington even when it is out of line. This lesson is not lost on politicians. What is to keep some future president from implementing another Machiavellian military policy and taking us to war for whatever reason, particularly if he knows it will bring him almost total overnight support?

Our forefathers would have risen up in protest against George Bush following his September 11, 1990 comments: *"Out of these troubled times, our fifth objective - a new world order - can emerge...We are now in sight of a United Nations that performs as envisioned by its founders."* Oh? Did the American people vote in favor of joining a New World Order? By no means! We are now seeing the fulfillment of Leonard Piekoff's 1982 book, *The Ominous Parallels: The End of Freedom in America.* Also, the 1983 work of Rael Jean Isaac and Erich Isaac, *The Coercive Utopians: Social Deception by America's Power Players,* has been realized. Roland Huntford's *The New Totalitarians*

(1972) are alive and well in America. Freedom in America died several years ago when compliant Americans, without a whimper, gave up their ultimate expression of freedom, the right to self-destruct without harming anyone else. This was when Americans acquiesced passively to automobile seatbelt laws. Will the federal bureaucrats next require us to strap into bed at night? Like the imperial Roman Empire, in the short span of just a few years, mighty Grenada has been conquered, Panama invaded (much like Iraq invaded Kuwait), and now the Iraq attack by the U.S. military forces. The empire does indeed strike back. These words of the freedom loving American president, Theodore Roosevelt, are lost on modern day Americans.

Patriotism means to stand by the country.

It does not mean to stand by the President or any other public official save exactly to the degree in which he himself stands by the country.

It is patriotic to support him insofar as he efficiently serves the country. It is unpatriotic not to oppose him to the exact extent that by inefficiency or otherwise he fails in his duty to stand by the country.

In either event, it is unpatriotic not to tell the truth - whether about the President or anyone else - save in the rare cases where this would make known to the enemy information of military value which would otherwise be unknown to him. — Theodore Roosevelt

Out of Sight, Out of Mind

Americans truly do not understand the mindset or the culture of the Mideast. (This incidentally is why Americans do not understand Christianity and particularly why Western Christianity is so far afield today. Christianity is, after all, a Middle Eastern religion, the balance between the religions of the East and West.) A primary reason most Americans thought that all Americans should back President Bush is because we no longer, as a people, really like or respect those among us who are different. And somehow, some way, Americans believed presenting a united front to the Iraqis would help save American lives in battle. Unfortunately, this is simply not true. Once you have offended a Middle Eastern Islamic Arab, like an Iraqi, or an Iranian, or a Libyan, once they have been bombed, embarrassed and/or *"lost face,"* it doesn't make any difference what you do, united or divided. They will get even at any and all cost. If not them, then their sons. If not their sons, then vengeance will be exacted by their sons' sons. Now that we have bombed them, expect terrorists to keep charging, relentlessly, like Arnold Schwarzenegger's Terminator. They don't care a whit for our view of life as being precious. Nor do they care how long it takes to bag the U.S. They have all the time in the world, plus the promise of eternal reward for their efforts.

This intractable vindictiveness is foreign to the American mentality. So is this long-term view of the grudge/offense. Islamic Arabs believe they have generations to make Americans pay for this war. This is a major reason why we should not have gotten involved. Let Israel fight its own battles. After all, Israel is backed by U.S. weapons and money for such purposes. Kuwait doesn't deserve to be freed. It was an oppressive, undemocratic, stingy dynasty which persecuted Christians, Jews, and women, and did not allow freedom of the press or human/civil rights. Saudi Arabia wasn't threatened, either. It was not consistent with our historical values to fight to restore the Sabah family of Kuwait to power.

Left and Right

Most Americans would expect the Far Left, who are commonly viewed as *"soft heads and soft hearts,"* the protestors from San Francisco, *"the land of fruit and nuts,"* to protest any and all wars engaged in by the U.S. government. But here is an interesting and very important twist. The Far Right, represented by the John Birch Society, took out full page ads against the Persian Gulf war, against *"Operation Desert Storm."* The John Birch Society has always been seen as ultra-patriotic, as following the *"America, Right or Wrong"* philosophy. So it was startling to see what the John Birch Society was saying in their ad:

1. The UN's "founders" from our nation, led by a secret communist named Alger Hiss, included 15 other communists and more than 40 members of the world-government-promoting Council on Foreign Relations. What they "envisioned" was an end to the independence of the United States.

2. Incredibly, you, Mr. President, went to the UN to gain its approval for initiating a war against Iraq. You then told the U.S. Congress that you neither needed nor intended to seek its approval.

3. You demand that Iraq be punished because its troops "raped, pillaged and brutalized" a neighbor nation (Kuwait). But you delight in welcoming as an ally against Iraq the Soviet Union, whose troops during the 1980s "raped, pillage and brutalized" a neighbor nation (Afghanistan).

4. You and Secretary of State Baker insist that UN resolutions must be implemented. Why? Your oath was to support the U.S. Constitution, not the UN Charter. When did it become the responsibility of America's military to implement resolutions passed by the United Nations?

5. War, or the threat of war, has always been big government's best friend. in this case, are you not using war, or the threat of war, as world government's best friend?

JBS: *Ahead of its time!*

The vast majority of Americans just have great difficulty comprehending that its federal government could have an agenda, which includes war, which is contrary to the U.S. Constitution, the best of American tradition, and harmful to the welfare of ordinary Americans and the American way of life long term. From the founding of the United States up until 1920, Americans understood that their federal government was potentially their greatest enemy. Now that concept is foreign to the typical American mind.

Stop and reflect for a minute how negatively Americans viewed atheistic communism up until the 1980s. And yet George Bush's father and grandfather, and Secretary of State James Baker's father and grandfather, worked on developing oil in the Soviet Union as early as the 1920s. So it's not strange the former U.S.S.R. became our ally, given the perspective of the Bush administration. The mercantilistic multinational corporation and banking one world view has always been at war with the U.S. Constitution and the best interest of the common American people long term. Don't Americans know that the tremendous wealth accrued by the Saudis and Kuwaitis in the 1970s allowed them to buy significant interests in what were formerly U.S. multinational oil companies and Aramco, that the so-called big American oil companies are now substantially Arab oil companies? If someone wants a painless way to review this situation, just go rent the movies *Tucker*, *Network*, and *They Live*.

George Bush is simply the epitome of this internationalist mindset. How else did he become the U.S. envoy to Red China, effectively our United Nations ambassador, and head of the CIA? Why would George Bush, who over his entire career has been a bureaucrat's bureaucrat, trust anything else? George Bush views the free market as *"voodoo economics."*

My Job

Every writer who's worth his salt has a strong philosophical base from which he writes. I view government as religion (philosophy) applied to economics. My job is to research, think, and write in such a way to help you understand the world in which we live so that you can best protect your family, freedom, assets, and multiply your talents and worth, for the purpose of making this a better world in which we live by serving your fellow man in your God-given calling, with your God-given freedom.

You will recall it was the July 26, 1990 REAPER which forecast the probability of war the first week of August 1990, when Iraq could invade Kuwait. War has always indeed been big government's best friend, the means by which big government dons the cloak of legitimacy for the purpose of limiting human freedom and confiscating assets under the guise of endless nationalism. Americans just don't have a clue that Kuwait is a banking system without a country, while the United States is a country without a banking system. Kuwait is America's banker in effect. Further, most Americans cannot even conceive of the reality that the Eastern Elitist, CFR and TC, those who really call the shots (even from behind the scenes) at the major U.S. multinational banks and corporations and in the Bush administration, have far more in common philosophically (and in vested interests) with the ruling elite of Saudi Arabia and Kuwait than they do with the common American. Neither Saudi Arabia nor Kuwait stand for anything Americans hold dear.

We were not informed that former Secretary of Defense Cap Weinberger and former Secretary of State George Shultz, who served under Ronald Reagan when George Bush was Vice President, were top executives with San Francisco-based Bechtel. Bechtel has a tradition of billions of dollars of contracts with Saudi Arabia. George Bush personally traveled to Saudi Arabia in 1986 to urge the Saudis to increase oil production. Americans have never thought about questioning whether there should be an investigation regarding George Bush's alleged family interest in a Marriott Hotel in Panama or in a multimillion-dollar resort in Red China. Nor have there been any questions raised about alleged Bush family oil concessions off Bahrain or about George Bush's old oil company, Zapata Oil, having drilling rights in Kuwait. It is just beyond the comprehension of most Americans that many of these people put their own self-interest first, or that they view the good, honest, hard-working, typical American as a *"maggot in a flour sack,"* as it was disdainfully put by one Eastern intellectual. As an actor quipped recently on the TV show *Dallas*, *"You know, the nice thing about this country is that if you are rich enough, you are above the law."* Viewed this way, why wouldn't young U.S. soldiers be seen as *"cannon fodder?"*

War Sell

The war-torn Lebanese have an old proverb which has long served them well: *"Truth kills those who hide from it."* Now with the foregoing perspective to ground us, let's look at the reasons (excuses) Americans were given for buying into this war. We'll also analyze the strategy of the Bush administration, and finally, the important *"missing piece."*

First, let's review the reasons for which Americans were hooked into this war, and think each reason through, point by point.

1. *"We must free Kuwait and punish Saddam Hussein for his aggression against a sovereign power."* ...Why? Why not instead let these old pirates fight it out among themselves? The families which are the ruling elitists of these Middle East kingdoms/fiefdoms have been squabbling with each other for centuries. Why did we need to get involved? Besides, Iraq has a legitimate claim against Kuwait going back to the arbitrary British partitioning of that country. Iraq has additional legitimate grievances with Kuwait. Kuwait stole Iraq's oil, denied Iraq access to the sea, and broke its contract with Iraq by producing too much oil, depriving Iraq of $14 billion a year. Iraq gave due notice to Kuwait that it would take military action if Kuwait didn't stop its thievery. Isn't the use of force legitimate to stop theft? Moreover, as Orthodox Jewish writer George N. Spitz pointed out on the editorial page of the January 15, 1991 *USA Today*, Iraq allows far more human rights than Kuwait, Saudi Arabia, Iran, Egypt or any of the other Middle East countries. *"Iraqi women experience rights equal to if not superior to women of other Islamic states. Freedom of religion prevails; Christians such as Foreign Minister Tariq Aziz hold high posts. Despite persistent hostility from Israel and the U.S. Jewish community...Saddam never scapegoats Iraqi Jews; they enjoy university admission, government employment and unrestricted travel and emigration..."*

Previously Kuwait had effectively spit in the face of the U.S. when it refused to allow its tankers sailing under the Kuwaiti flag to be escorted by U.S.
naval vessels, so offended were the Kuwaitis to be associated with the United
States. The ruling elite of Kuwait hold in scorn everything the average American holds dear. And we must remember, too, Saddam Hussein asked permission of the U.S. for him to *"take care"* of his border dispute with Kuwait,
permission the U.S. government granted!

If we're going to spend American blood, money and machinery to free Kuwait
and stop aggression there, then let's do it up right. Why don't we also pick a cause
more consistent with the American tradition, and fight the Red Chinese on behalf
of the Tibetans, or fight the former Soviets on behalf of the people of Lithuania,
Estonia and Latvia, or send the Marines in to overthrow all the human-rights-vio-
lating Marxist tribal leaders who are committing atrocities in Africa? Why not
fight Turkey to free North Cyprus, or attack Syria to free Lebanon, or assault Israel
to free the Palestinians of the West Bank, East Jerusalem and South Lebanon, or
return to Vietnam to free the Vietnamese people and the Cambodians? It becomes
ludicrous to think we can right all the wrongs in the world.

2. *"We must protect Israel."* Oh? Can't Israel protect itself? Hasn't Israel always been more than able to protect itself in the past? Hasn't Israel
already attacked Iraq once to protect its national interests when it bombed
Iraq's Osiraq plant? Didn't then Vice President Bush *"deplore"* this action?
Of course. Wouldn't Israel attack Iraq again in a New York minute if it
thought it necessary, without U.S. involvement? Surely. Didn't the majority of
the Jewish members of the U.S. Congress vote against the resolution authorizing President Bush to use military force in the Middle East? Yes, indeed.
Weren't these Jewish members of Congress looking after what they perceived
to be, at least in part, the best interests of Israel? Most certainly. Moreover,
there is nothing constitutionally that requires the U.S. people to spend the time,
money, energy and lives of their sons and daughters to come to the defense of
Israel. The government of Israel today persecutes nearly everything which the
average American holds dear, including Christianity and basic human rights,
according to Americans who live there. Israel's government today is a brutal
regime, particularly when it comes to the Palestinians.

3. *"We must defend the U.S. ally, Saudi Arabia."* Really? From whom?
On what basis? The United States government has no treaty to come to the
defense of Saudi Arabia. Besides, even the most casual observer knows by this
time that Saddam Hussein never in his wildest dreams ever intended to invade
Saudi Arabia. He told us that from the outset. King Hussein of Jordan has
stated this to be the case repeatedly, too. Iraq simply camped its troops on the
Saudi Arabian border as a way of effectively telling Saudi Arabia to *"butt out"*
of Iraq's dispute with Kuwait. In fact, the Saudis were not at all concerned
about being invaded by Iraq until envoys from George Bush flew to Saudi
Arabia and convinced them otherwise. Also, are we to believe that an old
cunning fox like Saddam Hussein is so inept that he is just going to sit there,

when he has overwhelming military advantage, and let the Saudis and the U.S. build up their defenses so he will have a more difficult time of invading later? Fat chance! Saddam Hussein never intended to violate his non-aggression pact with Saudi Arabia.

4. *"The United States is defending its economic interest in the Middle East."* Hold the ponies! The amount of oil the United States gets from the Middle East, from Iraq, Kuwait, Saudi Arabia and all the rest is relatively insignificant. The United States has Venezuela and Mexico, in addition to Alaska, as reliable oil suppliers. Not so for Japan and the EEC. The Middle East oil is crucial to them. So why not let them (Japan and the EEC) fight for their economic interests? Besides, is it moral to fight for oil? Would God approve of Americans spilling blood for oil? Is such consistent with our American heritage? Moreover, if energy is so critical to our national interest, why did the Bush State Department secretly give away five oil-rich Alaskan islands, including Wrangell Island, to the Soviet Union without disclosing this fact to the American people? Why have tremendous reserves of additional Alaskan oil been put off limits and producing wells there capped? Why did the Bush administration discourage domestic exploration and development of oil resources, while using the EPA and other environmental bureaucracies to harass the domestic U.S. oil industry? Why did the Bush administration shut down lucrative offshore oil production for ten years under the pretense of environmental considerations which have proven to be unfounded concerns? Why have all the new *"free energy"* technologies which are now becoming cost efficient - including wind and solar power, as well as new Tesla/quantum physics free energy devices - been either canned or nominally supported, and in some cases suppressed or harassed by the Bush administration? The United States is swimming in energy. The U.S. has no general economic welfare interests to defend in the Middle East.

5. *"Iraq is a threat to the New World Order."* This certainly is true. George Bush used Saddam Hussein to televise a message to the rest of the world not to cross the New World Order. In this sense, is God on Saddam Hussein's side? God has always preferred individual nations to empires or the Tower of Babel, which was the first *"New World Order."* Iraq is most definitely a threat to the New World Order, particularly under Saddam Hussein. But the New World Order is a threat to everything the average American stands for and believes in. The average American should be fighting tooth and nail against the New World Order, not for it. The New World Order means a drastically lower standard of living for Americans and a terrible loss of freedom. It is a ticket to slavery.

6. .*"If we don't stop Saddam Hussein now, we'll have to stop him later and then it will be far more difficult."* ...Why would the United States need to stop its own ally? Saddam Hussein was an ally of the United States until George Bush decided otherwise in August of 1990. The Reagan and Bush administrations helped build Saddam Hussein's Iraq. The Bush administration through its ambassador, April Glaspie, tacitly okayed Iraq's invasion of Kuwait, stating it

had no interest in the Iraq/Kuwait border dispute. One of Iraq's purposes in invading Kuwait was so Iraq could produce and sell more oil. Iraq was willing to sell the United States all the oil it wanted to buy. This would have driven the price of oil down, to the benefit of the U.S. consumers and the U.S. economy. Who knows? Saddam Hussein might have sold the U.S. oil at even lower (subsidized) prices.

Where was Saddam Hussein going after he took over Iraq? Nowhere. That was abundantly clear. So we had to stop him from what? Was Saddam Hussein really a threat to Israel? Saddam Hussein never really made Israel an issue until the United States first threatened Iraq, planted troops in Saudi Arabia, and turned the world against Iraq. Then as a purely defensive measure, Saddam Hussein threatened to attack Israel if the U.S. attacked Iraq. This was a means for Iraq to garner Arab support and weaken the U.S.-led alliance. Would any other power, under the same threatening conditions, have done otherwise? The truth is, Saddam Hussein's Iraq has treated Jews more fairly than have any of the other Islamic Arab powers prior to this war.

Bushwhacked

All the reasons the Bush administration sold the American public for instigating a war in the Persian Gulf have crumbled into illegitimacy. So just why did U.S. troops pay the ultimate tax (their lives) and fight in the Persian Gulf? Despite all I've written about this military misadventure, there is still a *"missing piece."*

In order to fully comprehend an important missing piece of this war puzzle, and a very important reason why the Bush administration long ago planned and then orchestrated this war against Iraq as part of a long-term strategy, let's review the evidence. We will find clearly that the Reagan and Bush administrations: (1) built Iraq as a military power; (2) endorsed Iraq's invasion of Kuwait; (3) refused to undertake any reasonable or legitimate face-saving negotiations necessary to prevent this war; for the purpose of (4) defeated Iraq militarily to protect favored special interests and preserving elitist powers.

Regarding point 1, I strongly recommend Rachel Flick's important article, *"How We Appeased a Tyrant"* in the January, 1991 issue of *Reader's Digest*. Flick's carefully documented piece makes apparent that both the Reagan and Bush administrations were primary contributors to Saddam Hussein's military build-up and also paved the way for his invasion of Kuwait. Flick comments, *"The West made Saddam Hussein. The Soviet arms mill gave Iraq its artillery and air defense. But, by handing him everything from chemical weapons to ballistic missiles and the makings of a nuclear bomb, America and Europe transformed a two-bit dictator into a world-class threat."*

Back in 1981, after Israeli war planes had bombed Saddam Hussein's Osiraq nuclear plant, Saudi Arabia offered to finance the rebuilding of this nuclear reactor, built for the purpose of making nuclear weapons. Then Vice President Bush *"de-*

plored" this Israeli strike. In 1982, the U.S. State Department removed Iraq from its list of terrorist nations, despite ongoing terrorist activities. This allowed Saddam Hussein to buy American computers, commercial aircraft and other important goods. It also made Iraq eligible for U.S. taxpayer guaranteed loans, including guarantees by the Commodity Credit Corporation. In 1984, despite Saddam Hussein's battlefield use of mustard gas against Iranian forces, after the November election the Reagan-Bush administration restored full diplomatic relations with Iraq.

In 1985, Marshall W. Wiley, former U.S. ambassador to Oman, founded the U.S.-Iraq Business Forum that promoted American investments in Iraq. Seventy U.S. multinational corporations joined, including Westinghouse and Caterpillar. The U.S. Commerce and State Departments approved the shipment of a computer similar to the one used by America's White Sands missile range to Iraq. The computer was produced by New Jersey-based Electronic Associates, Inc. Iraqi agents moved ahead with plans to acquire the Condor II nuclear missile from Consen. Also in 1985, the Reagan/Bush administration ignored the terrorist activities of Abul Abbas, who traveled on an Iraqi passport and later found refuge in Iraq after he murdered wheelchair-bound American Leon Klinghoffer on the cruise ship *Achille Lauro* in the Mediterranean. On May 17, 1987, a French-built Iraqi war plane accidentally attacked the frigate U.S.S. Stark with an Exocet missile. Thirty-seven Americans were killed. The Reagan/Bush State Department incredibly blamed the attack on Iran and later emphasized that Iraq has apologized and offered compensation for the dead Americans as well as the ship. Also in 1987, Americans signed a trade agreement to increase commerce with Iraq. On March 16-17, 1988, when Saddam Hussein used poison gas to murder over 5,000 Kurds in Iraq, in the town of Halabjah, the Reagan-Bush administration spurned calls by two U.S. senators (one Republican, one Democratic) for sanctions against Iraq. After all, the U.S. Export-Import Bank had insured Iraqi purchases of American pesticides.

In 1989, total loans made to Iraq which were guaranteed by U.S. taxpayers through the Commodity Credit Corporation exceeded $750 million. Iraq further requested and secured over $1 billion in guarantees in 1989 and 1990. Then in January 1990, President Bush waived Congress' ban on Iraq's use of Export-Import Bank funds, citing America's *"national interest"* regarding Iraq. When in February 1990 a U.S. Voice of America radio broadcast included Iraq in its list of police states, Secretary of State James Baker instructed U.S. Ambassador April Glaspie to apologize.

Also in 1990, from the Bush administration's Commerce Department, Iraq obtained permission to buy state-of-the-art imaging and photographic equipment from International Imaging Systems of Milpitas, California. On July 25, 1990, in addition to providing tacit approval for Iraq to invade Kuwait to resolve its border dispute in which the U.S. said it had no interest, U.S. Ambassador April Glaspie also praised Saddam Hussein's *"extraordinary efforts"* to rebuild Iraq, despite the fact that at that meeting Saddam Hussein threatened to unleash terrorists on America as a protest against the joint U.S. naval exercise with the United Arab Emirates.

On July 27 and 28, 1990, U.S. intelligence sources warned the Bush administration that Iraq might invade Kuwait, and that on July 30, Iraqi strength near the Kuwaiti border was above 100,000. Representative Lee Hamilton (D.-Ind.) then asked Assistant Secretary of State John Kelly what U.S. forces would do if Iraq invaded Kuwait. Kelly replied that *"the United States has no commitment to Kuwait."* And Americans are asked to believe the Bush administration acted in the best interest of this country. Source: *The Howard Phillips Issues and Strategy Bulletin,* and Rachel Flick's article, *"How We Appeased a Tyrant,"* published in the January, 1991 *Reader's Digest.*

Later, CIA Director William Webster met with the head of Kuwait's Internal Security Bureau for the purpose of plotting how the United States and Kuwait could both benefit by exploiting the deteriorating economic situation in Iraq. Shades of the movie, *Three Days of the Condor.* The split congressional vote in the U.S. Congress on Saturday, January 12, 1991, which barely authorized President Bush to use military force against Iraq, was for the most part a farce. President Bush had already decided to use military force against Iraq, and had even decided the date (January 17) following the dark of the new moon, January 15, 1991 U.N. deadline.

From the very start of the August U.S. military build-up in the Persian Gulf, President Bush never had any intention of doing anything other than using military force against Iraq. But this Persian Gulf war was totally unnecessary. The United States, by compromising only a little in negotiations, or by allowing Saddam Hussein even a modicum of face saving, could have prevented this war. But George Bush knew exactly what he was doing when he took the hard line, the intractable position that the only solution possible was for Saddam Hussein to withdraw unconditionally from Kuwait. From his advisors, George Bush knew that without any way for Saddam Hussein to save face, without any discussion of the legitimate border dispute of Palestinian question, without any way for Saddam Hussein to withdraw from Kuwait except under conditions of total humiliation, that Saddam Hussein played into George Bush's hands. The President of the United States did not want Saddam Hussein to withdraw from Kuwait. He instead wanted to destroy him militarily. Did the world suffer, did American troops die, in part because of the out-of-control egos and pride of two men - Saddam Hussein and George Bush?

Deals With the Devil

Both the United States and Israel negotiated with Anwar Sadat of Egypt and rewarded him for his aggression with land and substantial aid as a way of buying peace. It was Anwar Sadat who started the Yom Kippur War, which resulted in the most Jewish deaths since World War II. It was Anwar Sadat who ordered Hitler to *"return and finish the job"* on the Jews. The U.S. has also directly or indirectly rewarded the aggression of China, the U.S.S.R., Israel and Syria. Why then not negotiate with Saddam Hussein over the Palestinians, allowing him to keep the two islands and access to the sea, and the Ruaila oil field? These would have been minor, insignificant concessions on the part of Kuwait, concessions to which Iraq had legitimate rights. Otherwise, economic sanctions were working and had the unqualified support of the world community. Further, the U.S. could have substantially increased its standing in the Islamic Arab world by calling a conference to discuss the Palestinian issue. This alone would have given Saddam Hussein a face-saving out.

Why were none of these reasonable actions taken? Because George Bush's objective, as part of a Machiavellian long-term strategy, included the necessary destruction of Saddam Hussein's military and Iraq to establish U.S. hegemony over the oil-rich Middle East. It should be absolutely unconscionable to Americans that the U.S. was allied with Syria and Iran at that point. Both of these nations' actions and governments have been far more damaging to their own people and American interest than was that of Saddam Hussein's Iraq. Syria, Iran, the Sabah family of Kuwait, the royal family of Saudi Arabia, Egypt, Turkey, Israel, the former Soviet Union, radical Islamic terrorists, the major London and U.S. multinational banks, the multinational oil companies, the U.S. military/industrial complex, the U.S. Treasury, George Bush and the New World Order were the big winners in this war. But there is still a missing piece.

A Missing Piece

Two types of imperialism have vied for superiority in the twentieth century. Imperialism has been effected through military power, as demonstrated in this century by Germany, Japan, the United States, the Soviet Union, and Red China. But since World War II, economic imperialism has also proven to be quite effective. The two World War II foes defeated by the United States, Germany and Japan, have won the economic war in the post-World War II era. Japan's hegemony over the Far East and the western Pacific Basin, and Germany's leadership in the EEC, have left the U.S. out in the cold so to speak, despite the fact the U.S. financially rebuilt both Japan and West Germany and bore the expense of militarily protecting these two old foes over the past 45 years. Now the U.S. economy (and inescapably with it the U.S. government) is on the ropes. Japan and West Germany, who up until 1990 were willing to buy U.S. Treasury debt, have withdrawn their financial support.

War has always been a convenient distraction during desperate times to deflect the people's attention from their legitimate economic concerns and their government's failure. War instead gathers the support of the people behind the central government against a created Hitlerian-type enemy who is then viewed as a common threat. Saddam Hussein was perfectly typecast for the part. War in the Persian Gulf and the threat of terrorism in the United States turned the trick for the Bush administration.

New World Order

From the perspective of the internationalists, who are moving quickly toward the New World Order, the former Soviet Union has long been an ally.

The former Soviet Union has been the international military arm, complementing the international U.S. debt arm, of the move toward a New World Order. This is why freedom-loving U.S. allies all over the world have fallen like flies and claim with a friend like the U.S., who needs enemies. The Hegelian dialectic is being fulfilled through the thesis (the collectivism of communism) versus the antithesis (the radical individualism of debt capitalism), merged into the mercantilistic fascism of the new world order. (I unwillingly tasted this bitter union back in 1983, when I was a consultant to President Efrain Rios-Montt of Guatemala. Rios-Montt declared it was the U.S.S.R. who suggested to the U.S. State Department that the U.S. overthrow the government of Guatemala. General Paul Gormann, who at that time was head of Southern Command, formulated the conspiracy for the overthrow of the Guatemalan Rios-Montt government on the U.S.S. Enterprise one week before the coup took place the first week of August 1983. What was Rios-Montt attempting to accomplish in Guatemala? Nothing more or less than establish a debt-free, honest money, Christian government, economy and society, much like existed in early U.S. history.)

As Dr. Antony Sutton at Hoover War Institute of Stanford University has comprehensively documented, the U.S.S.R. was a product of the United States. The United States multinational debt capitalists built the Soviet Union and bailed the U.S.S.R. out at least a half a dozen times since the 1917 communist revolution. Gorbachev and the KGB were a different side of the same coin of George Bush and the CIA. Did Mikhail Gorbachev wear his Nobel Peace Prize when his military henchmen and black berets went in and killed the freedom-loving people of Lithuania and Latvia, while the attention of the world was conveniently distracted by George Bush on the Persian Gulf war? Wouldn't the U.S. taxpayer-subsidized development of the Soviet oil industry, now made justifiable by the Persian Gulf war, prevent the bloody Soviet Union from collapsing and ensure its ongoing viability? Wouldn't this economic joint venture between the U.S. and the U.S.S.R., who both built Saddam Hussein, coming on the heels of all their other merging activities (the U.S.-U.S.S.R. Trade and Economic Council, art exchanges, the U.S. military academy exchanges, Boy Scout and Little League exchanges) allow an effective merging of the U.S.A. with the U.S.S.R., as in the movie *Amerika*? Certainly, the global events which are unfolding will drop the living standard of the United States to such a low level that it will be comfortably able to merge with the rest of the world. The U.S. middle class is being destroyed, leaving only a few rich and many poor, as is the case throughout most of the world, and particularly in Third World countries.

A New World Order, brought about by this economic/military alliance between the U.S. and the former U.S.S.R., would then make it rather simple to merge the three Trilateral regions - the Japanese-dominated Far East, the German-dominated EEC, and the American-dominated All-Americas common market - into a New World Order. Then the slavery of a global bureaucratic dictatorship could be soft-sold as *"the greatest good for the greatest number,"* to the *"citizens of Mother Earth."*

It's a frightening scenario. Power corrupts, and absolute power corrupts absolutely. We're talking about the approaching manifestation of the greatest comprehensive evil ever seen on the face of the earth, buttressed by that hideous strength of quantum-based technology and the revival of the feminine and environmental occult paganism of old empires manifested anew as Luciferianism (the ultimate Skull & Bones).

Fini

In light of all the foregoing, was the war in the Persian Gulf in the best interests of the Bush administration, its long-term strategy, and its narrow special interests? The evidence strongly suggests that it was. Was the war in the Persian Gulf, given all of the above, in the best interests of the American people, their tradition, their way of life, heritage and the U.S. constitution? The evidence clearly suggests that it is not.

Every country, just like every family and every individual, must have the humility to know its limits to prevent catastrophe from overtaking it. At this time, the United States is fighting too many battles on too many fronts. The domestic scene is coming unglued in at least a dozen ways. Internationally, the U.S. is on the ropes, too. The U.S. could not afford the psychological, physical or financial stress, or cost, of the Gulf War. The nation is already too close to exhaustion.

The United States is in a state approaching comprehensive exhaustion, running the risk of activating the self-destruct syndrome, taking on more than it can handle at one time. Unlike the end of World War II, the U.S. is no longer omnipotent. Will it take another devastating war to learn the hard way what the U.S. dollar has already learned economically? Are we really able at this time to deal with the ongoing threat of terrorism? Do we really want to destabilize the Middle East for at least a decade? Do we really want to expose our sons and daughters to the horrors of chemical/biological weapons in this war? For what?

Accordingly, what is the correct thing for honest, hard working, courageous, God-fearing, country-loving Americans to do? That is the sobering question that must be wrestled out in the thoughtful minds, hearts and souls of every freedom-loving American. Will the Bush administration be rightfully held accountable? Will our elected representatives ask the hard questions? All it takes for evil to triumph is for good men to do nothing. God bless America.

Persian Gulf
February 27, 1991

Games, Barbarians and Savages

The U.S. public thundered, *"Let George do it."* And by George, George did it. And so *"Saddam the Savage"* was routed and the world lived happily ever after.... The world also got the message loud and clear not to cross the New World Order. The one stumbling block to it, Islamic fundamentalism, was broken on the wheel of high tech weaponry. The United States finally was allowed to win another military Super Bowl, too, after politically being forced to play to a draw in Korea, and after suffering a humiliating political defeat in Vietnam while winning on the battlefield. Denver Broncos take note, there is hope. Try, try again is the American way. The U.S. military executed this war in brilliant fashion.

I remember how startled I was when respected climatologist Dr. Iben Browning told me that in surveying the world's nations, the Soviets and the U.S. were effectively the modern barbarians. Not savages like Saddam Hussein, mind you, but barbarians. Definition: Barbarians prefer to settle their differences by conflict (war, lawsuits, domestic violence, win-lose games). Dr. Browning's perspective was that WASPs, when they get their backs up, are the most dangerously violent people on the face of the earth. This is why even the disciplined Roman legions were so shaken when they went into battle against the Anglo-Saxons/Celts. Our distant forefathers waded into battle stark naked (except for some well-placed paint).

Modern thoughtful observers have remarked that the U.S. win-at-all-costs emphasis on team sports is effective preparation for war. Football, basketball, and perhaps even baseball, qualify for team sport-addicted Americans. True enough, the losing team isn't beheaded, as was the case in the Mayan team games, but knowing the history of team sports played with a ball, Thomas Jefferson remarked, *"Games played with a ball and others of that nature are too violent for the body and stamp no character on the mind."* From this perspective, team sports are good training and not all that different from war.

The protesters of the Persian Gulf war took to the phrase, *"Blacks fighting Browns for Whites."* Blacks were, for the most part, against this war, while whites were overwhelmingly for it. Whites cheered for black soldiers fighting Iraq, just as whites cheer for black football and basketball players.

Violence/conflict has always been an important characteristic of the American psyche. It's inbred. Just ask the American Indian. The United States was the only country that didn't end black slavery peacefully, but instead settled the slave issue with a civil war that decimated 600,000 of its *"best and brightest"* young white men. Today, the United States remains the nation leading the world with the most violent crime per capita, blacks accounting for one third of it. The U.S. also aborts 1.6-1.8 million of its young annually. So, the blacks who make it alive through the birth canal, the inner city war zone and the drug mines, are primed for the likes of the Persian Gulf. And the United States enjoys (sic) 96% of the civil lawsuits in the world. So, for such a frustrated population, which had not been allowed to taste victory in the last two wars, a disgruntled people who had been kicked around economically the past decade or so, kicking the hell out of the Iraqis was just what the doctor ordered.

The United Nations is a catalyst for war. Since its inception, 157 wars have actually been induced by the U.N. But chaos has long been viewed as necessary to produce what the New Age has now termed the *"New World Order,"* or *"Novus Ordo Seclorum,"* as it has appeared on the back of the U.S. one dollar bill since the 1930s.

Slip Sliding Away

The Bush administration gave lip service to, and effectively ran roughshod over, the mid-January 1991 French peace proposal and the February 23, 1991 Soviet peace proposal. Both peace proposals appeared rational. Both had the support of the world-at-large, including the Secretary General of the United Nations, Javier Perez de Ceuellar, who publicly praised the Soviet peace plan. But the die was already cast, and the French and Soviet peace proposals were irritating distractions from a Bush plan already long established and implemented. Saddam Hussein was set up to be sacked.

Real insight into what the Bush administration was thinking in mid-February 1991 came in the form of statements made by Alton Frye, a senior fellow for national security for the Council on Foreign Relations (CFR). Frye's comments were strategically placed on the February 15, 1991 editorial pages of *USA Today.* CFR mouthpiece Frye there wrote that for the Bush administration to be satisfied with an Iraqi withdrawal from Kuwait, such a withdrawal had to be made subject to adequate supervision, and that Saddam Hussein had to leave his military equipment behind. This is precisely what we are seeing in the ground war. Said Frye, *"When the Iraqis leave Kuwait, they should do so with only their small arms. The armor and artillery that made them a menace to their neighbors should be left in place, to be destroyed as a first step toward a stable military balance in the gulf."* ...Israel was also worried about any peace plan that would leave Saddam Hussein and his military machine (and face) intact. No one should ever underestimate the power of the CFR or the Jewish lobby, as exercised through U.S. politicians and the American media.

Groundhogs Surface

My Islamic Middle East contacts finally surfaced. They stated that unfortunately, they felt only the U.S. was capable of stopping *"Saddam the Savage."* They stated that Saddam is as bad as they come. But they were very dismayed over the fact that the U.S. did so under the guise of a *"just war,"* when the real reasons were political and economic: to appease Israel; to take advantage of the opportunity to break the back of Islamic fundamentalism; to control Middle East oil; and to secure Saudi Arabia and Kuwait as ongoing U.S. bankers. They bemoaned the fact that the U.S. role as an idealistic world policeman has now been replaced by U.S. forces acting as mercenaries for powerful multinational banks and corporations, as well as foreign powers, all at the expense of the Arab culture and religion and the American taxpayer.

This should not be surprising to us. Government is always religion applied to economics. Every government takes the moral ideas about right and wrong and good and evil from its culture's religious realm, and then legislates those religious ideas into laws which frame the arena of human action (economics). (Separation of church and state means only that the men who run the church and the men who run the state are different.) A civilization on the rise has its priorities based in the spiritual nature of man, which in turn determines political action and finally economic and financial reality. By contrast, a civilization in decline focuses on the natural man, with his emphasis on economic matters - money and materialism. This in turn dictates to the political realm with religious morality yielding to pragmatism. This explains why the U.S. both bought the U.N. war vote and formed an ungodly alliance with terrorists such as Assad of Syria in this war.

These moderate Arabs were also dismayed that the Middle East countries that experience a measure of democracy were all either neutral or aligned with Saddam Hussein in this war. They were concerned, too, that the New World Order was simply putting a new face on the Old World Order, that effectively the more things change, the more they remain the same. But, as the founder of communism, Karl Marx, identified: *"The first step in revolution"* is to *"win the battle of democracy."* That's right, Martha, communists have long held *"democracy"* to be a halfway house between a *"republic"* and *"socialism,"* as in the Union of Soviet Socialist Republics. This is why up until 1930 the concept of *"democracy"* was despised in the United States, which was originally founded as a *"republic."* Until recently, the United Nations was also held in contempt by most Americans. The founders of the United Nations were 16 communists led by Alger Hiss, and 43 members of the Council on Foreign Relations (CFR).

The Council on Foreign Relations (CFR), in a 1959 study entitled, *"Basic Aims of U.S. Foreign Policy,"* urged the United States to *"build a new international order."* A 1974 CFR journal, *"Foreign Affairs,"* carried an article written by Richard Gardner entitled, *"The Hard Road to World Order."* We are effectively seeing the fulfillment of Gardner's perspective, an end run around national sovereignty, eroding it piece by piece. This is why Margaret Thatcher was axed. She saw that the EEC, and particularly the British pound becoming part of the EMS, would erode Britain's national sovereignty. So she had to go in the faces of the one worlders. The political puppet strings were pulled, and Margaret Thatcher was gone, just like that.

Where the Buck Stops

On February 25, 1991, the Office of Foreign Assets Control (OFAC) of the Department of the Treasury announced that at the request of the Central Bank of Kuwait, it had licensed seven blocked Kuwaiti banks to settle directly most types of obligations arising prior to the August 2, 1990 Iraqi invasion of Kuwait. In other words, the banks were back in business. The Bank of England, also on February 25, 1991, granted approval in the United Kingdom for implementation of the seven banks' settlement programs in coordination with the Central Bank of Kuwait. *"The Central Bank of Kuwait has added its payment guarantee for all valid obligations covered by the OFAC licenses"* (Source: FWN/UPI). So Kuwait, a banking system without a country, and the U.S., a country without a banking system, were back in business together. Money does indeed run today's world. It was only the U.S. and England who balked at the mid-January 1991 French peace proposal.

FWN/UPI also reported on February 25, 1991, *"Reports indicated the Kuwaiti government-in-exile already has awarded several contracts to U.S. firms for everything from putting out the burning oil fields...to other rebuilding efforts."* Again, war as a form of *"urban renewal"* has been realized. Bechtel can now officially sign its $50 billion contract for the reconstruction of Kuwait, this contract being effectively in place before the ground war even started. Contracts overall could hit as high as $100 billion. But with the Emir of Kuwait having over $200 billion on deposit in his London firm, KIO, there should be, as they put it, *"no problem."* UPI stated the situation clearly: *"With few facilities of its own to undertake such a massive rebuilding, Kuwait must rely on outside help to carry out the task."* In other words, the ground war had to be fought so U.S. multinational corporations could be financed by U.S. multinational banks to rebuild Kuwait. Islamic Arab nationalism was broken up in the process. Plus, there will certainly be funds left over for Saudi Arabia and Kuwait to continue to be the two primary financiers of U.S. Treasury debt. What a coup!

Will British Petroleum (BP) also go back and continue its process of draining 50% of the oil from the Rumaila oil field, which sits on the Iraqi/Kuwaiti border, despite the fact that only 10% of the oil deposits are on Kuwait's side of the border? This was the economic sore spot which led to the dispute between Iraq and Kuwait in the first place.

Not to be denied either is Citicorp, which is being bailed out by a Saudi prince who magnanimously purchased $590 million of Citicorp's convertible preferred stock. Alwaleed Bin Talal already held 4.9% of Citicorp's common stock. Now he will hold close to 15%, according to *The Wall Street Journal*. What a nice thing for this Saudi prince to do, help Citicorp raise capital. Certainly this couldn't have anything to do with the war, could it?

Seeing Red

The desperate Soviet attempt to help Saddam Hussein save face and extricate himself from Kuwait gracefully, with his military intact, minus humiliation, should come as no surprise to REAPER readers. As I have documented all along, the Soviets were up to their eyeballs in helping Iraq since three weeks prior to the Kuwaiti invasion. This is why the Soviet leaders howled in anguish, scorning *"adulation of anything American,"* when Iraq was routed on the ground. *The Wall Street Journal* finally reported what I had also been declaring all along, that *"Gorbachev now relies heavily on the Communist Party, the KGB, and the military - institutions (dubbed the 'neo-Stalinists') that are comfortable with the coercive methods used to enforce law and order."* And despite the rightful pride which Americans felt over the professional performance of our troops in the Persian Gulf, we should also seriously question why President Bush's response to Gorbachev's heavy-handed treatment of the Baltics was muted. These New World Order leaders stick together. Amerika.

Slam Dunk

Ever since the July 26, 1990 REAPER predicted Iraq's invasion of Kuwait, we tracked this war. The one big surprise was how easily the ground war was fought and won. Incessant bombing by allied forces in the Nintendo war obviously took its toll. Both the speed and effectiveness of the U.S. military precluded Iraq's use of its most dangerous weapons. The Iraqis were caught flatfooted. But why did not Saddam Hussein use his chemical weapons and his superior heavy artillery, where he had the advantage? There are several reasons: Despite propaganda claims of Saddam Hussein's madness, he is a practical savage. He wants to live to fight another day. And in the Arab mind, Saddam won by losing.

Know News

With every bit of war news being cleared by either Israeli, U.S., British, or Iraqi censors, it was some time before we got to the truth of the matter of the casualties. We expected the Iraqi government to lie to its people. It did so marvelously and predictably. But what is not widely known is that the U.S. government has become adept at lying to its people also, another reason why civil governments worldwide today are *"scorpions in a bottle."*

When you control the microphone and the stage, and can orchestrate all the cast and props, you can create your own reality. (The U.S. government today plays god anyway, so it should come as no surprise that it creates its own reality.) People respond to their perception of reality. Washington, D.C. today is still Hollywood East.

In this regard, Panama was a trial run for the U.S. military. In Panama, the war news was manipulated; the public was told what the U.S. military and U.S.

government wanted it to hear; a lie was passed on as the truth; the American general public bought the lie; the U.S. government got away with it. There is precedence for this. We were warned. Back on December 6, 1962, then United States Assistant Secretary of Defense for Public Information, Arthur Sylvester, proclaimed, *"The government has the right to lie."* Panamanian sources, statements by U.S. soldiers who fought there, and Jonathan Franklin, writing in *The Los Angeles Times*, confirm this. The Pentagon reported that the Panamanian invasion resulted in only 23 American deaths. Verified statements by U.S. soldiers, however, are that dozens of U.S. paratroopers died, many from *"friendly fire."* The Orwellian named *"Operation Just Cause"* just had a false face put on it. The real truth is at least 60 U.S. soldiers died in the Panamanian invasion, not 23. Further, at least 314 Panamanians, not 50, were killed also. Thus, from the hard evidence gained after filtering the disinformation put out by the Pentagon regarding American casualties in Panama, we must at least maintain our concern over the statistics publicly released regarding American casualties in the Persian Gulf war. Our suspicion is heightened by the fact that on January 17, 1991, Dover Air Force Base was closed to the press and the public for the first time ever. Dover Air Force Base is the largest entry point of return for military personnel killed in the Persian Gulf. My moderate Arab sources reported that Iraqi civilian losses were at least two to three times the number reported by the American media. Indeed, eternal vigilance is ever the price to be paid to safeguard freedom.

OUR COMING WAR WITH IRAN
July 20, 1993

Muslim Abuse

Muslims are being kicked around in key parts of the world these days. *"Greater Serbia"* is on the march. It won't be long before they kick back. Muslims are taking it on the chin in Bosnia and Herzegovina. There is a stronghold on Sarajevo. Muslims have also been beaten up by Indians in India. Christian Armenians have socked it to the Muslims in mostly Islamic Azerbaijan in an acceleration of the five-year civil war over Nagorno-Karabakh.

The Shining Light

Where do these beaten, battered, abused, raped and economically destitute Muslims look for hope and help? To the shining light of Islamic fundamentalism - Iran. Iran is paying huge sums to Muslim groups all over the world, not just to terrorist groups. The accompanying message from Iran is that the holy war (jihad) against the West, and particularly the United States, *"The Great Satan,"* is accelerating.

West Disconnect

I can remember when we used to teach Iranians how to fly right along side U.S. Air Force officers. In fact, I went through my initial undergraduate pilot training in Laredo, Texas with Iranian students. (This was during the Vietnam War.) In the late 1970s, I became a consultant to the minister counselor for political affairs to the Shah of Iran. I was one of the few Western market economists who understood the link that the Shah of Iran and Islam had with the West, that Mohammed took his economics from Moses. But when the Shah was overthrown, the Ayatollah came to power, and the war between Iran and the U.S. began in earnest.

The War on the West

Most Americans only faintly remember Iran, the hostages, Jimmy Carter, Ross Perot and the supporting cast. Lest we forget, Iran has reason to despise the U.S. The Shah's secret police brutalized the Iranian people. The Shah, who sat on the Peacock throne, was considered to be a *"puppet"* of the United States. It's also important to remember that the United States was an active military participant on the side of Saddam Hussein and the Iraqis while they were fighting the Iranians all those years. The U.S. was, in fact, engaged in a covert war against Iran and actively cooperated with Iraq on bombing missions against Iran. As late as 1987 and 1988, U.S. military officials were operating out of Baghdad. (How quickly things change.)

In 1988, John Walcott of the U.S. State Department warned, *"Iran may be preparing for terrorist attacks on Americans."* Certainly such was the case. Initially the targets were American embassies, military bases and businesses owned and held by Americans in Europe, the Middle East and Southeast Asia. Of course, the latest Islamic terrorist attack in 1993 on the New York World Trade Center brought events much closer to home. We should expect more of the same, much more, by no later than the 1994-1996 time frame.

Terrorist attacks were instigated by Iran against the United States because the U.S. humiliated Iran. Understand the mindset of the Middle East Islamic community. Humiliation is something you simply do not do. It is the ultimate *"no-no"* in the Middle East, *"losing face."* In May of 1989, a West German magazine first broke the story that Iran had ordered the bombing of Pan Am Flight 103 and had paid Palestinian terrorist Ahmad Gibrel $1.3 million for his effort. Iran had been calling for the killing of Americans in a worldwide campaign of terror publicly in May of 1989. Syria was also implicated in the bombing of this Pam Am jet over Lockerbie, Scotland. The key countries to watch in the Middle East which are aligned with Iran in its war against the United States are Syria, Libya, Sudan, and North Yemen.

When the U.S.S. Vincennes shot down an Air Iran airliner and killed all 290 passengers aboard, it was serving on pro-Iraq duty. There was an initial coverup by the Reagan administration of the shooting down of this Iranian airliner by the U.S.S. Vincennes. Nevertheless, Retired Admiral William Crowe stated on an ABC interview with Ted Koppel that the Vincennes was in Iranian waters when the shoot down occurred, not in international waters as was earlier declared. (Admiral Crowe was Chairman of the Joint Chiefs of Staff at the time of the incident.) Then there was the fact that the U.S. State Department blocked the U.N. denunciation of Iraq's chemical warfare against Iran. And when Iraq sent an Exocet missile into the U.S.S. Stark by mistake, killing 37 American seamen, the Reagan administration incredibly blamed Iran. In November, 1992, the U.S. offered a $2 million reward for the capture of at least four Iranian-backed terrorists who are charged with taking and killing U.S. hostages in Lebanon, and the bombing of a TWA jet over Greece. ...The point of all this apparently disjointed history is to show how the upcoming U.S./Iranian war should not be an unanticipated event, but rather one which has been building for some time.

Sitting Duck

From Iran's perspective, the United States is a sitting duck, an easy target for terrorism. The overwhelming majority of Americans live in cities which can be easily penetrated, compromised and sabotaged. Americans are vulnerable because of a very complex technological support system in their cities. Urbanites' power systems, water supplies and the like are all but unprotected. A backpack nuclear weapon and/or chemical/biological warfare is a relatively easy way for competently trained terrorists to exact a huge payback. Once a backpack nuclear weapon, or chemical and biological warfare, is unleashed on just one American city, the world will never be the same. The bombing of the World Trade Center is just the start.

From Iran's perspective, the purpose of terrorism is payback, to destabilize and intimidate, to keep the West off balance, and leave no one with a sense of security. To this end, Iran is becoming successful. Moreover, the return on terrorism for every dollar invested is $100,000 to $1 million, not counting the loss of human life. Terrorist networks and training camps exist in Iran, Syria, Libya, Sudan, North Korea, Cuba, Nicaragua, and Northern Ireland. What most Americans do not know is that as early as 1985 Islamic terrorists began appearing in Texas and other border states, having entered the U.S. from Mexico. Furthermore, Iran as early as 1985, was training 300 white women from Ireland, Britain, Canada and the United States as suicide commandos. Latin Americans have also been recruited. These suicide terrorist commandos don't appear any different than ordinary Americans.

Time is on their side, too. Just when Americans are relaxed and least expecting it, terrorism will strike. It's important to remember that Muslims are historically very patient. An old vindictive Muslim phrase goes something like this, *"If I don't get you, then my son will get you, and if he doesn't get you, then my son's son."* And so it goes.

The Middle East Strategy

Iran is intent on increasing it's hold on the Middle East. Islamic fundamentalists in Egypt have caused disruptions by attacks on busloads of tourists in which several foreigners have died. This is an attempt by the Islamic extremists to bring down the Egyptian government by hamstringing Egypt's tourist-supported economy. Recently, 32 Egyptian disciples of a Muslim cleric were convicted of trying to topple the Egyptian government by attacking tourists. On May 21, 1993 Islamic extremists killed a police officer and were responsible for a car bomb which killed 4 and injured 16 in Cairo. Iran also has contingency plans to assassinate Mubarek of Egypt and in the resulting chaos, bring forth a fundamental Islamic republic in Egypt aligned with Iran.

One of the primary reasons, if not the main reason, the U.S. moved into Somalia was to respond to the increasing challenge Iran poses to Egypt and the Red Sea. Somalia, a Moslem nation, is also strategically located on the Horn of Africa, and could close the sea lanes in the Red Sea and the Indian Ocean if it falls into the hands of Muslim extremists.

In Sudan, civil war rages between the Islamic north, which controls the government, and the Christian south, which wants to secede, and also has the oil. The Islamic Sudanese are backed by Iran, who desire to create a Shi'ite Islamic empire. In January 1992, the Islamic government of Sudan adopted the Islamic law code, called the Sharia. This gave Iran its long sought after foothold in Africa. The Sudanese made a deal with the Somalian warlords to install

the Islamic law code in Somalia as well. This widened the beachhead of fundamental Islam in Africa. American troops were sent there as a counter-balance.

Of late, tensions have been high between Egypt and the Islamic government in Sudan over a border dispute. Sudan announced it would mobilize its
armed forces. Egypt is really getting squeezed. On March 27, 1993, Algeria
announced it was severing diplomatic relations with Iran and recalling its ambassador from Sudan. Algeria accused both Iran and Sudan of backing Islamic
extremists who are fighting the Algerian government. Algeria openly accused
both Iran and Sudan of supporting terrorism. The fundamentalists in Algeria
did so well in the preliminary round of parliamentary elections there, the Algerian government suspended constitutional rule and canceled the second round.

Saudi Arabia is also under pressure. A group of Saudi Arabian scholars in
late May 1993 attempted to establish a human rights organization based on
Islamic law. Within 10 days it attracted 10,000 followers. The House of Saud
squashed it.

The four Muslim republics in the former Soviet central Asia - Kazakhstan,
Tadzhikistan, Kirghizia and Uzbekistan - have fallen under the influence of
Iran, even though they are primarily Sunni Moslems. Iran recently bought four
nuclear warheads from Kazakhstan. In so doing, Kazakhstan broke its pledge
to safeguard nuclear weapons. Moreover, an Islamic economic common market
has been formed which includes Afghanistan, Iran, Pakistan and Turkey. It
encompasses 300 million people. It's called the Economic Cooperation Organization (ECO). The four former Soviet Muslim republics in Soviet central Asia
have joined the Islamic economic bloc, along with one other former Asian central Soviet republic. (Kyrgyzstan's parliament just voted to issue its own currency, the som, backed by hard-currency reserves.)

The Force of War

Iran eventually wants to attack Israel, and specifically regain control of
Jerusalem. In order to do this, it needs to take over both Somalia and Egypt,
controlling Egypt at one end of the Red Sea, and Somalia at the other. The
U.S., of course, defends Israel, with both military arms, high tech weaponry,
and U.S. taxpayer funds. So any Iranian military assault on Israel would inescapably bring the U.S. into the fray. Israel has nuclear weapons, and when
push comes to shove, will unmercifully use them without hesitation. The irony
of this is, back in 1985, Israel was smuggling arms to Iran to protect the 40,000
member Jewish community in Tehran.

Arab sources in Washington, D.C. say Iran is behind the relatively recent
guerrilla attacks on Israel from southern Lebanon, seeking to disrupt what
seemed to be a growing detente between Israel and Syria, suspect to say the
least in my opinion. In Israel, the radical Islamic group, Hamas, has increased
the violence and resistance against the Israeli government, killing dozens of
Israelis. The Israeli government has, in typical fashion, responded harshly with

mass killings of Arabs, the destruction of homes of suspected terrorists, and a general martial-law declaration of a state of emergency. Thus for security reasons, Israel closed off both the West Bank and the Gaza Strip on March 30, 1993. This means 75,000 Gazans are not allowed to come to Israel every day to keep their jobs. Unemployment in Gaza is 74%. The Palestinians question waxes ever worse. Increasingly the Palestinians look to Iran to liberate them and establish a Palestinian homeland. In Jordan recently, radical Palestinian leaders warned of more violence in Israel's occupied territories if the peace process continues.

Iran's War Machine

Iran's current military budget is placed at between $850 million and $2 billion annually. This is very small when compared to Saudi Arabia's $15.5 billion budget. (Saudi Arabia's arms purchases annually have run twenty times that of Iran.) But what David and his sling-shot were to Goliath, Iran and terrorism are to Saudi Arabia, Egypt, Algeria and Kuwait. High tech terrorism is an effective leveler of the military giants.

On April 13, 1993, an Iranian ground forces commander said at a news conference that the reconstruction of the Iranian military was *"taking place at all levels."* He further commented that it involved all aspects of the Iranian armed forces, including manpower, equipment, facilities and installations. This Iranian military commander stated that Iran, *"has no need for assistance from foreign countries in training its personnel."* He further stated, *"We have been able to make some good changes,"* regarding the rebuilding of the Iranian military.

Militarily, Iran now has nuclear weapons which can be dropped from a MiG-27. Red China has supplied Iran with over $1 billion worth of arms. The former Soviet Union has supplied Iran with nuclear technology and arms also. Iran had a real military windfall, buying up Soviet weaponry, high technology, and former Soviet scientists. Iran has been developing long-range missiles capable of carrying nuclear or chemical warheads. Iran and Syria have continued to assemble poison gas. Indeed, nuclear weapons have been smuggled out of the former Soviet Union to Iran. Iran has been one of the main employers of many of Russia's 15,000 nuclear scientists. Russia itself sold diesel submarines to Iran despite U.S. protests. Iran has also taken delivery on the first of three Russian "Kilo" class submarines. Iran plans to station them outside the Straits of Hormuz, the crucial bottleneck through which 12 million barrels of oil pass daily, upon which the West is dependent.

There have been a series of secret deals cut between Iran and North Korea which is the reason North Korea pulled out of the Nuclear Nonproliferation Treaty for awhile. Iran is reportedly paying North Korea $500 million *"to help it develop a ballistic-missile system that could deliver nuclear and chemical warheads to targets as far away as Japan."* North Korea is selling an unspecified number of nuclear bombs to the Iranians and providing them with designs for nuclear weapons reprocessing plants. By 1995, North Korea will possess sufficient weapons-grade plutonium to manufacture as many as seven bombs, according to the March 29, 1993, *U.S. News & World Report.*

Mother Blows Up

The ungrounded New Age goddesses are going to have Mother Earth's head handed to them when Israel starts using it's 100 or so nuclear devices, India its 60 and Pakistan its 10. Who knows how many nukes will be unleashed by a combination of Libya, Sudan, Iran, and Syria? (The religious inspiration for the feminine New Age, the Hindus of India, are never going to get along peacefully with the brutal male-chauvinist Muslims of Pakistan. They've always fought.) In short, Iran is buying up weapons left and right and will force Israel to respond militarily. Moreover, when the ANC gains control of South Africa, it will link with Russia and radical Islam, boycotting oil and strategic minerals to the West, particularly the U.S. The *"kinder and gentler"* Billary New Age movement will come to an abrupt end at that time. The U.S. will go to war. Recall in late October 1992, a North Korean ship carrying as many as 100 Scud missiles left North Korea for Iran and Syria. This was the second such shipment from North Korea to the Middle East. The first shipment reached Iran in March of 1992 after eluding a U.S. naval blockade. The War Clock is ticking down to the equivalent of Armageddon.

Subsidizing the Enemy

Once again, the U.S. and its Western allies are building up its enemy, Iran, just like it did with Suddam Hussein and Iraq. (Cynically, one would suspect it was planned that way; finance both sides to create chaos for the New World Order.) South Korean and Japanese investors have invested over $1 billion in industrial projects in Iran. The U.S. taxpayer-subsidized World Bank has loaned Iran $460 million even while the Clintonistas' Secretary of State, Warren Christopher, has called Iran an *"international outlaw."* U.S. oil companies are presently aiding Iran in making a comeback in its oil production by helping to build offshore rigs and to ship oil. The U.S. Department of Commerce has released reports showing the U.S. imported $1.75 billion worth of goods from Iran while exporting only $54 million to Iran (1988), leaving the U.S. with a huge trade deficit with Iran. In short, the U.S. buys more from Iran than from Egypt, Bahrain, Iraq, Jordan, Kuwait, Lebanon, Qatar, Syria, Yemen and Morocco combined.

That's not the end of it. Hundreds of pages of still highly classified documents provide increasing evidence that former President George Bush was directly involved almost from the beginning in the decision to sell missiles to Iran in exchange for the release of the hostages. This was reported in the November 2, 1992 issue of *U.S. News & World Report.* Egyptian General Abdel

Satter Amin, speaking in late October, 1992 to a NATO conference at Knokke-Heist, Belgium, declared, *"Definitely Iran is preparing for a war in the Gulf as phase one to control the Middle East under the cover of Islamic revolution through extremist groups."*

Why should this come as a surprise? Iranian officials declared war on the United States May 20, 1988!

Idle Chatter

What are the feminist New Age Clintonistas doing about all this? What they do best, talk. Stated the Center for Security Policy on April 2, 1993, *"Hurling invectives at terrorists and despots may deceive the American public into believing that the Clinton administration is dealing effectively with 'international outlaws.' Unless backed with the credible threat of military action - and where necessary, its utilization - however, such empty rhetoric will do nothing to check these dangerous forces. If anything, evidence of American impotence will stimulate intensified anti-Western activity."* In other words, the Clintonistas are only making things worse, both by their empty rhetoric, and by cutting the U.S. military. Our enemies abroad have no respect for a former pot-smoking, draft-dodging president who is weaker than his wife.

War Date

So when's our next war? When do the ungrounded Clintonistas' get to purge more of our children from *"Mother Earth"* and use our progeny as cannon fodder? After all, these liberal, Eastern Establishment, Yale elitists often refer to us common folk as *"maggots in a flour sack."* The feminazi environmental movement is just a facade to cover how they really feel toward us inhabiting the earth. They want us gone. The countdown? Radical Islam would like to attack Israel within three years. The director of the U.S. CIA recently stated that Iran and its allies would pose a military threat to the United States within three to five years. Lawrence H. Berg of Omaha, Nebraska, writing in the July/August 1992 issue of *Cycles* Magazine, stated *"The Astral Indicator bottoms in 1992 and peaks in 1995, making for an increased probability for war, peaking stock markets, and low temperatures in 1995."* Solar Cycle 22 (sunspots) bottom in 1995-1996, the same time the 18-1/3-year real estate cycle in the United States bottoms. So, my war cycle work, which projects our next significant U.S. war for 1995-1996 is right on the button. The year 1995 is when Harry E. Figgie predicts the U.S. will default on its debt (*Bankruptcy 1995*). To be cynical, what better way for the Clintonistas to attempt to stay in power than to declare a national emergency, canceling the 1996 elections because of war and a bankrupt currency.

Fire Away

What to do? I say again, we're moving into a Nazi-like bureaucratic police state, a state of martial-law with a loss of civil liberties and freedom. War and

a bankrupt currency ensure it. Good old-fashioned, hard-working, family oriented, religious Americans, particularly white American males, will bear the
brunt of a disintegrating government turning on its people. It's thus best to live
outside this country, or at least out of the major cities. Investment wise, for-
eign-held gold and off-shore investments/currencies are looking better all the
time. Stateside, long-term buy and hold blue chips in key military stocks, domestic petroleum and natural gas stocks (particularly Canadian and U.S. natural
gas issues), mining stocks, crude oil, gold, silver and platinum, short the U.S.
dollar, and short the U.S. stock market - all make a lot of sense. The time is
short, when you stop and think about it. Let's work to get our own estates in
order.

SECTION II

The Environment

THE WORLD
CONSERVATION BANK

February 10, 1988

On September 11-18, 1987, with limited local media fanfare and absolutely zero national publicity, the seemingly benign World Wilderness Congress met in Denver, Colorado. How wonderful. Let's all vow to plant a tree and picket all the industrial polluters in our hometowns.

Wilderness Congress

Who could complain about a bunch of well-meaning environmentalists getting together and trying to improve the environment for all of us? The Greenies with all their nuts and berries are well-meaning and harmless, correct?

Why didn't we, the people-at-large, hear about this Fourth World Wilderness Congress? In fact, who had heard of the first three congresses?

We might raise an eyebrow when we study the title of this congress - WORLD Wilderness Congress. Why wasn't this a United States Wilderness Congress? We couldn't be seeing a move toward one world land ownership as part of the New World Order, could we? Nah. There are only a few wild environmentalists in the Earth First group who are nailing spikes in the trees in order to blow up the chain saws of loggers.

We didn't really believe that we the common people were going to benefit, when 10 percent of the attendees for this congress were multinational bankers, and 30 percent of the attendees were U.N. and federal government bureaucrats! Mr. James MacNeill, the Secretary General, U.N. Commission on Environment and Development from Geneva, didn't travel all that way just to placate some sweet environmentalists, did he?

What's this? The official hosts of this congress were the Findhorn Group of Loveland, Colorado. Hey, they're a big New Age group aren't they? And wait a minute, what were Baron Edmund D. Rothschild of England, the Secretary of the United States Treasury, James Baker, and the kingpin of the U.S. multinational banking himself, David Rockefeller, all doing there? There's more here than meets the eye!

What is going on? The bottom line of this conference, the scheming in the smoke-filled back rooms, was to establish a World Conservation Bank (WCB). Good old Michael Sweatman of the Royal Bank of Canada was there to ramrod this effort.

It seems that the scheme underway is to eventually transfer title of a large portion of the wilderness lands, owned by the various countries around the world, into this World Conservation Bank. We are not talking small acreages, either. These heavyweights don't mess around. We're talking big time - in fact, 30 percent of the earth's land surface!

Interesting idea. Have the whole globe as your fiefdom. Too bad it's not just an idea, but an emerging reality! Just picture, if you will, the United States and Brazil alone deeding a large chunk of their wilderness areas to this World Conservation Bank. Thirty percent of the world's land surface is 50 million kilometers square! Of course, the land would be put in a trust first, and then the trust would deal with the Bank, all on our behalf, naturally.

This is really a scheme to get the multinational bankers off the hook with their deadbeat Third World loans, and then further consolidate their power in a One World Order. The United Nations would, of course, approve and supervise this World Wilderness Land Inventory Trust. You can just see all the propaganda supporting it - save the San Quentin quail and the last of Rudolph the reindeer, etc.

The Bank would issue a soft currency, which would eventually turn into an international currency and then a hard currency. The Bank would issue loans to the likes of Brazil, and Brazil would, in turn, put let's say the Amazon Basin up for collateral, against which Brazil could draw down its loan money. But, of course, when Brazil could not repay its loans and defaulted on them, then the Bank would own the Amazon Basin. Previously, there would be a loan for equity swap taking Brazil out of its overdue loans to the likes of Chase Manhattan Bank. Chase Manhattan would then have a viable loan on its balance sheet.

What a neat deal! A great debt-for-equity swap. Bad loans are made good by collateralizing them with land, laundering it all through the World Conservation Bank. John Law is still alive and well. Long live the assignats!

Mother Earth gets to be owned by the international bankers, too, who I'm sure all good environmentalists would argue have been excellent stewards of this oscillating 7.83-Hertz planet.

Needless to say, Brazil's finance minister, Juan de Ovieras, didn't sleep all that well at this conference. He knew the handwriting was on the wall, that Brazil would never be able to pay its loans back. Score another blow for rapacious multinational debt capitalism! So, in addition to the World Bank, the International Monetary Fund and the Bank of International Settlements funding global monetary schemes, we will now have a global central bank controlling land.

On a trip to Canada, I was startled to learn that a pair of handcuffs worn on one's wrist was the latest in punk jewelry fads. What a subtle statement of recognition of slavery. The next step will be for the middle class to take off its wrist watches and bracelets and join the punks with some stainless steel handcuff jewelry. (Maybe add a diamond or two for class.) By becoming accustomed to handcuffs now, it won't seem so foreign to us when we literally start wearing chains (stainless steel, please).

Impossible, you say? Just think this through one more time. The nations of the world, including the socialistic U.S. congressional members, set aside more and more land for wilderness areas. This wilderness area is then given by the United States government to a World Wilderness Land Inventory Trust which is owned and operated by the United Nations. The United Nations then cuts a deal whereby this land is made available to the World Conservation Bank. The World Conservation Bank issues a currency and makes loans available based upon the value of this land. The likes of Brazil comes in and borrows money from the World Conservation Bank and puts up as collateral the Amazon Basin. After awhile, Brazil defaults on its loan. The World Conservation Bank forecloses on the Amazon Basin. Another part of Brazil is then owned by the World Conservation Bank. The swap arrangements between the World Conservation Bank are settled with the World Wilderness Land Inventory Trust. Now, throw in the present debt owed by Brazil to the likes of Chase Manhattan Bank, which is swapped for equity or land ownership, and before long you end up with the international banks owning most of the land in the world.

But, maybe you're right. Perhaps slavery is too harsh a word. Maybe it's more accurate to simply call us serfs.

DROUGHT -
AND MUCH, MUCH MORE
June 16, 1988

Shake and Bake

In late spring of 1988, a primary focus of investor interest was on the soybean market. Drought triggered a roaring bull market in soybeans and the grains, igniting fears of inflation. Reports that there could be no soybeans left within the next two years fueled the buying fever. Summer weather during springtime in the soybean belt, and disclosures that elevators in Iowa were having difficulty buying soybeans, led to limit-up sessions. Subsoil moisture in Iowa was reported to be sharply below 1987 levels, with dry conditions in the western one-third of the corn and soybean belt becoming exacerbated as the land baked under 90-100 degree temperatures. Reports of *"Water woes,"* and *"Water wars"* made headlines in the nation's press.

The Drought Clock

Long term, the dramatic climatic changes underway probably make the 1988 drought scare in soybeans the tip of the iceberg. Remember the cover of my first book, written back in 1978, *Cycles of War*? On that cover I reproduced a copy of Raymond H. Wheeler's 1945 *"Drought Clock."* Chapter 4 of *Cycles of War*, *"Planets, Cycles, Climate, and War,"* was one of the most important chapters in that book. I discussed not only Wheeler's work, which called for global cold weather conditions, civil wars and drought beginning in 1980, but also the latest scientific evidence which demonstrated how solar activity affects our climate, weather, economy and human action. Droughts are accompanied by economic recession approximately 70 percent of the time!

In my 1982 book, *Wealth For All: Religion, Politics and War*, I again featured Raymond H. Wheeler's 1945 Drought Clock. In that book, Chapter 43 discussed, *"The 510-Year Cycle."*

With regard to this 510-year transition period, Raymond H. Wheeler wrote (over 40 years ago): *"It seems highly certain that the initiative is again passing from the West to the East for a 500-year period. The present 500-year cycle is due to end around 1980."*

Bingo! Japan, South Korea, Taiwan, Hong Kong, Singapore and China confirm that Raymond H. Wheeler was right on target.

With regard to climatic and civilization shifts, I further quoted Raymond H. Wheeler: *"The fifth 500-year cycle since the sixth century B.C. is just now terminating. The end of the cycle is due around 1975 or 1980, in the center of an expected cold-dry period corresponding to the one in the first century A.D. and the one in the tenth century.*

"Profound revolutions over the whole known world of humanity, regardless of race or culture, have occurred during each of these centuries, often amounting to cultural convulsions."

Despite the urbanization, demineralization and despiritualization of mankind, there is still a faint touch of intuition left in the human species. Put differently, man has a way of sensing trouble. And trouble from the *climate and land* side of the economic *land and labor* economic equation has a way of rearing its ugly head when the foolishness of man gets too far out of line, as it has today.

A 1988 study completed by the National Wildlife Federation found that fully 50 percent of us think the environment would be much worse five years in the future (now). The General Accounting Office (GAO) reported the amount of toxic wastes generated has risen from 9 million metric tons in 1970 to 247-400 million metric tons in 1984. Plus, the Pentagon's research budget for infectious diseases and toxins increased over ten times 1981 to 1988. And that's just for starters. Permit me to share with you some more not so cheery evidence.

Ninety percent of the tree covering of India has been destroyed. Over a third of India's land has been turned into deserts or semiarid regions. In 1988, India experienced the worst heat wave in 20 years. The groundwater level there is dropping 4 meters a year.

The forest cover of the Himalayas is down now to less than 25 percent. When we include the deforestation of Latin America, fully 119 square miles of the earth each and every day is being stripped and denuded.

Back in 1872, only 14 percent of the land areas of the earth were considered desert or severely degraded soil, which were incapable of supporting plant life. (This percentage excluded tundra, icecaps, high mountain ranges and urban areas.) Now, only 115 years later, 66 percent of the earth's land areas have been turned into desert or severely degraded/toxic soil, which is incapable of supporting plant life. This is an area equivalent to ten times the size of the United States. The Environmental Policy Institute has warned that up to one billion people will starve to death in the tropics as a result of deforestation of the world's rain forests. These rain forests will be gone within the next 30 years if the present rate of destruction continues.

When mankind knocks out plant life, he increases atmospheric carbon dioxide and decreases oxygen. Plants consume carbon dioxide and give off oxygen. For every ton of timber/trees, 1-1/2 tons of carbon dioxide is absorbed and one ton of oxygen is released. Since 1950, the earth has lost more than half of its trees. Trees are critical for oxygen, timber, paper, water cycle control and soil conservation. NASA scientists report that oxygen is falling in our air environment from 15 percent volume percentage in November 1982 to 7.8 percent volume percentage as of December 1986. Suffocation occurs at 6-7 percent volume percentage! Accordingly, the oxygen pressure in mankind's blood has dropped from 120 Torr. to 70 Torr. This accounts in part for the weakness of our immune systems and diseases such as AIDS.

The Man-Environment Link

There is a direct correlation between the deoxygenation and demineralization, acid levels and climate extremes of the earth with that of mankind. Put differently, as goes the earth, so goes mankind. We turn the earth into a desert and pollute the air, and we reduce the oxygen available in the atmosphere, while dramatically increasing the CO_2 level (the Greenhouse Effect). We simultaneously find the oxygen pressure of mankind's blood dramatically reduced to the detriment of his immune system.

We strip mine the earth of its minerals through our failure to let the land rest (every seven years), and we fail to practice organic agriculture because we seek greedy short-term profits through intensive agriculture and the application of toxic fertilizers, herbicides and pesticides. The result is we eat less nutritious food and more dead food, resulting in the demineralization of our bodies.

Ever spend a day and a night in the desert? The desert is noted for its temperature extremes. It is *hot as hell* in the daytime and *cold as hell* at night in the desert. This is exactly what is happening to our climate globally. It's getting increasingly *hotter than hell* in the summer and *colder than hell* in the winter. We are seeing temperature extremes. Accordingly, mankind is also exhibiting these extremes in behavior and wild and degenerative health patterns as more and more people *flip out.*

Acid rain, a terrible environmental problem, is matched by the acid pH condition predominant in our bodies. A sign of the death cycle of the earth is the tilt of the alkalinity-acidic balance of the earth. It is due, in part, to demineralization. So too in mankind is the excessive acid condition due to demineralization. (For a more complete explanation of the demineralization of the earth, see Chapter 9 of my last book, *No Time For Slaves, "The Climate Crisis."*

The Water Cycle

Trees are antennae. Trees, when they cover the earth in a garden-like fashion, balance out the flow of atmospheric, surface and subsurface water. Trees, by maintaining moisture circulation, cleanse the environment, the air above the earth and on the surface of the earth. When trees and other vegetation are removed from the earth, the CO_2 level increases, creating the *Greenhouse Effect*. This is why plus or minus 20 degrees latitude from the equator, temperatures are becoming much warmer. This is excess CO_2 around the equator.

This heat engine at the equator leads to increasing cloud formation. This equatorial moisture is sucked up into clouds and transported to the polar regions where it is dropped as snow. Cloud cover globally increases. Ice builds up, leading to glaciation. Presently, over 50 glaciers are expanding worldwide. So, we're simultaneously getting *"hotter than hell"* at the equator and *"colder than hell"* at the poles. We are seeing these temperature extremes in our country now almost year round. We are recording record highs and record lows, sometimes on the same day in different parts of the nation.

These temperature extremes between the poles and the equator have caused the circumpolar winds to waver and dip down. A result is that the formerly stable west to east flowing *jet stream* has become unstable and is more frequently spiking down in areas, causing unreasonable weather, often in the extreme. The jet stream has also generally dropped lower at places on the earth than it has in recent recorded history. So, wind extremes are picking up. In places such as Texas, the jet stream has literally strafed the earth.

Add to this equation the increasing earthquake and volcanic activity which pumps more dust into the atmosphere, cooling the earth and creating a more unstable environment, and the result is even more variable weather. Meteorologists in southern Florida are picking up considerable amounts of dust particles transported by upper atmosphere winds from the parched sub-Sahara.

The Nineties - Acceleration

We have moved into the acceleration phase of temperature extremes, high winds, increasing earthquake and volcanic activity, high acid levels, deoxygenation and demineralization of the earth.

Dr. Iben Browning predicted severe drought for North American beginning in the early or mid-1990s. Dr. Browning is expecting much worse conditions than in the 1930s. In fact, Dr. Browning confirms Dr. Raymond H. Wheeler's work when he states we could see the worst drought in 500 years. (This timetable unfortunately dovetails with my projections made in the U.S. War Clock in 1982.)

In many previous REAPERS I've presented the scientific evidence confirming how changes in sunspot activity affect our weather. This in turn affects the human body's electrical field, bringing on all types of illnesses as formerly latent bacteria and viruses are activated. Due to increased acidity, deoxygenation and demineralization of both our environment and our bodies, we are ill-prepared to face what we will be required to confront in this decade.

Establishment science is finally catching on to this reality. Mr. John Eddie of the Department of Commerce's Center for Atmospheric Research in Boulder, Colorado, in a speech to the American Association for the Advancement of Science, reported that scientists now know for sure what they've long suspected—that sunspots affect the earth's weather. We have warmer weather when the sun is more active. The sun is definitely entering an active period, when sunspots, solar winds and harmful cosmic rays are increasingly bombarding the earth.

The May/June 1988 issue of *Cycles* magazine, in its Climatology section, featured an article by James H. Shirley, *"When the Sun Goes Backward: Solar Motion, Volcanic Activity, and Climate, 1990-2000."* Shirley effectively confirms my research and projections as presented in this chapter.

Quoting from Shirley: *"The present study highlights an unusual 'solar event' that will take place in the years 1989-1991. During the period this Sun's motion relative to the solar system mass center will be retrograde. This condition has occurred twice previously in the last millennium, in the 1630s and in the second decade of the 19th century. Both periods were characterized by climatic extremes, and by remarkable outburst of explosive volcanic activity. A statistical evaluation suggests that the correlation in time of episodes of solar retrograde motion and major volcanic eruptions is unlikely to arise by chance.*

"There is reason to believe that the decade of the 1990s will be characterized by unusually persistent climatic extremes. Major explosive volcanic eruptions may occur...."

Shirley is projecting both the onset of global drought as well as possibly a little Ice Age. Also, extreme variability in temperatures is projected with the enlarged polar ice cap, accompanied by a weaker jet stream being displaced much farther south than it is today. We can only imagine the climatic turmoil and temperature and weather extremes resulting from this extremely cold air clashing with the CO_2 *Greenhouse Engine* at the equator. We could be entering a prolonged minima of solar activity when we could experience a cold period similar to the little Ice Age of 1250-1850 A.D. Shirley recounts the *"year without a summer"* (1816), when in the northeastern United States and Western Europe it froze every month of the year. *"The years 1812-1817 introduced three decades of economic pause punctuated by recurring crises, distress, social upheaval, international migration, political rebellion and pandemic disease."* Sounds just like Wheeler's, Browning's and my work.

Shirley concludes, *"The simplest statement that can be made is, if conditions in the 1990s are similar to those of the two previous episodes of solar retrograde motion, then societies will experience climatological extremes of a magnitude and persistence unprecedented thus far in this century."* Shirley further concludes that we should expect *"[i]ncreased frequency and duration of meridional circulation patterns, with associated climatic extremes of drought, flood, and other severe and unusual weather; along with, possibly,...*

"Major explosive volcanic eruptions...these should occur principally between 1993-1999...

"The mid-to-late 1990s also represent the next expected episode of severe drought in the western U.S."

Why the government has been increasing its choke hold on American agriculture and food supplies in this country should come as no surprise to long-time REAPER readers. Control of food is control of people, as the former Soviet Union has long demonstrated. This aggressive move toward total control of agriculture and food by the United States government dates back to an early 1970s CIA report, which broadly predicted what we are now seeing emerge. The problem is, when civil government anywhere controls agriculture, shortages result. Mother Russia used to not only feed herself, but also export food. Today Russia is the world's largest food importer.

Conclusions and Recommendations

What conclusions and recommendations do I draw from all of this? Move off of the volcanic islands. Get out of the cities, particularly the cities which are located in the cold north, as well as those which are subject to earthquake and volcanic activity. (Cities themselves alter the climate. Paramagnetic, human-built structures [buildings] should not be taller than trees. Schumann energy is dramatically reduced in cities. The U.S. is the third most vulnerable volcanic nation on earth.) The acceleration of the demineralization process of man, higher acidic pH levels, the reduced oxygen content of both the atmosphere and man, dead food, and increasing food and water shortages means the cities could be turned into *"hell holes"* as depicted by the movie, *"Escape From New York."* AIDS epidemics and other plagues will be prevalent too. Social unrest and pervasive violence will lead to oppressive bureaucratic government tyranny in metropolitan areas.

It's beginning to appear as though extreme survivalists like Kurt Saxon were correct, only too soon. Their timing was off. Living in the rural, remote areas of the southern states, where water and plant life are plentiful (ever notice how the two go together?), where families, churches and communities are close-knit, and food can be grown with relative ease for most of the year, are strong recommendations. Living outside of this country, and preferably in the southern hemisphere, is also recommended.

If this harsh climatic scenario comes to pass, then both Canada and Russia will lose the ability to grow food. Food prices will skyrocket. Today's normal run-of-the-mill urban-oriented investments will become high risk. Owning stock in typical urban companies, urban real estate, municipal, corporate and government bonds, T-bills and the like will require a different mind set. Instead, owning *reality*, basic commodities, in water and agriculturally rich safe rural areas is probably the best bet. (When was the last time anyone you knew bought survival food, or grew their own?)

Stock investments in water companies, agricultural companies and oil companies in the 1990s should be good investments. Oil stocks (Chevron, Texaco, Exxon, Tenneco) and agriculture stocks (Deer, Navistar, Vanity Corp., Caterpillar, Archer Daniels Midland Co., Dekalb Corp.) are widely known and traded. (Your stockbroker should be able to help you in this regard.)

Water stocks which investors might look into include United Water Resources, Southwest Water Company, Southern California Water Company, San Jose Water Company, American Water Works, Consumer Water, SJW Corporation and California Water Service. (I am not personally recommending any of these water stocks, or agriculture or oil stocks for that matter. The water stocks are just some that Dick Russell of *Dow Theory Letters* has mentioned from time to time over the years.)

Each of us should do what we do best. For survival food, there are a couple of firms you should investigate. Permapak, 3999 South Main St., #52, Salt Lake City, Utah 84107. Phone (801) 268-4381. Ask them about their minimum one-year food supply in bulk.

Also, Liberty Enterprises, 651 Columbia Lane, Provo, Utah 84604. Phone (800) 345-6468. This is a firm Howard Ruff recommended, and has an interest in.

I don't want you to panic. I have self-consciously written this essay according to a *worst case* scenario to hopefully motivate you to take some action. At least buy some survival food or plant a garden. You do have time, but the clock is ticking. In fact, it started ticking in 1980, and the acceleration process began in 1987. We have to become prepared for dramatic changes in our way of life. These alterations are already upon us. This is one of those times when I truly think, *"He who hesitates is lost."*

CLIMATE ON THE RAMPAGE
May 11, 1989

It's important that we keep in mind that economics is really very simple. It all boils down to two factors: land and labor, or put differently, people and things produced from the land. Because we live in an urban culture, literally a time of world cities, the overwhelming economic emphasis today is on people. True enough, people determine the use, consumption and abuse of things produced from the land side of the economic equation. But people need and are influenced by nature. People as of yet do not control the climate or the weather. Sure, we have the ability to partially control the weather. My two-part *"Rainmaker"* series in 1988 made this abundantly clear. And we can alter the climate also with long-term planning. But the point is, we're not doing either. And so we are still vulnerable to climatic change and weather upset. And this is what is coming.

Overall, I've written a great deal about the influence of climate on the affairs of men during the many years I've been writing THE REAPER. Chapters on this subject have also appeared in my book, *Wealth For All.* I have discussed the work of Dr. Iben Browning, Joseph Goodavage, Dr. Raymond H. Wheeler and others. So, I was delighted to see that the March/April 1989 issue of *Cycles* magazine did a feature issue on this subject.

Now, let's look at the exciting and somber evidence which *Cycles* magazine brought to bear on the *"time of trouble"* which we have just entered (1987). (The Mayans pegged the year 1987 as the beginning of the *"hell"* period of our civilization.)

This March/April issue of *Cycles* magazine ran the award-winning essay by James H. Shirley. I have featured the work of James H. Shirley in THE REAPER on how the sun went retrograde, beginning in October 1989. This retrograde motion carried into 1991. (The sun's motion relative to the solar system's mass center was retrograde.) I pointed out that Shirley's projections are that the decade of the 1990s may be characterized by climatic extremes and major volcanic eruptions.

Two times previously in recent history the sun has gone retrograde. What happened then? Will we experience weather in the 1990s similar to what occurred when the sun went retrograde twice before? If so, we will be living in interesting and trying times for which we are presently ill-prepared. Here is what James H. Shirley wrote about the climatic conditions of 1633-1643 and 1812-1822, the eras following the two previous times the sun went retrograde. Long-time REAPER readers and students of *No Time For Slaves* will find remarkable how closely Shirley's insights dovetail with the works of climatologist Dr. Iben Browning, Dr. Raymond H. Wheeler, Joseph Goodavage and your editor's writings.

Weather and Climate Records

for 1633-1643 and 1812-1822

The climate of the 1630s and 1640s was comparable to that of the subsequent Maunder Minimum period, if not somewhat colder (Robock 1979). It was not uncommon for the river Thames to freeze solid in this latter period, permitting the populace to hold "frost fairs" on the ice. This has not occurred during the present century. Lamb (1972, 1977) comments on the short growing seasons and growth of glaciers in the 1630s and 1640s. And, Ludlim (1968) describes the "landmark" winter of 1641 as one of the three worst of the entire century in the American colonies. Our records are not particularly complete for these times; nevertheless, it appears that this period included one of the most intensive burst of explosive volcanic eruptions of the past 500 years. Important eruptions included those of Hekla (1636), Roung (1638), Komagatake (1640), Awu (1641), and Gunung Adiksa (1641) (Lamb 1970).

Weather and climate conditions in the period subsequent to 1810 were more extreme than anything ever experienced by anyone living today. This was the period of the "year without a summer" (1816) in the northeastern U.S. and western Europe, when it reportedly froze during every month of the year. The cold winter that stopped Napoleon's advance in Russia took place during this period. The period was remarkable not only for single extreme years, but for a succession of these; cold summers and short growing seasons triggered major famines in places like Switzerland and the Ukraine. Post (1973) provides a succinct summary: "The years 1812-1817 introduced three decades of economic pause punctuated by recurring crises, distress, social upheaval, international migration, political rebellion and pandemic disease."

The cold interval was worldwide; it can be identified in ice cores from southern hemisphere glaciers (Thompson et al 1986). And, as with the earlier period, major volcanic eruptions took place. The 1815 eruption of Tambora is probably the largest eruption since the end of the last ice age (Stothers 1984), and a number of others (Sabrina in 1811, Soufriere in 1812, Awu in 1812, Mayon in 1814, and Roung in 1817) that occurred around this time injected large amounts of material into the stratosphere.

Climatic conditions during these two periods were arguably more extreme than anything experienced in this century. If the decade of the 1990s is similar, modern societies may be subjected to severe environmental stresses. Caution is needed here, however; other times during the past 500 years had conditions comparable to these episodes, and the correspondence in time of severe climates and episodes of solar retrograde motion might be a coincidence. Volcanic activity occurred in both periods, for instance; it has been shown that some eruptions cause climatic cooling, and this might independently account for the climate conditions (Porter 1981; Kelly and Sear 1984).

The simplest statement that can be made is, if conditions in the 1990s are similar to those of the two previous episodes of solar retrograde motion, then societies will experience climatological extremes of a magnitude and persistence unprecedented thus far in this century. The scenario can be developed in a little more detail. We can expect to encounter:

Increased frequency and duration of meridional circulation patterns, with associated climatic extremes of drought, flood, and other severe and unusual weather; along with, possibly,

Major explosive volcanic eruptions. Based on analog periods, these should occur principally between 1993-1999. Some may be of immediate climatological significance, cooling the northern hemisphere after the manner of Tambora (Stothers 1984; Kelly et al 1984).

The mid-to-late 1990s also represents the next expected episode of severe drought in the western U.S. Source: James H. Shirley, *Cycles* magazine.

What about the all-important agricultural sector of the economy? The decades following the sun going retrograde in 1632-1633 and in 1810-1812 were characterized by reduced solar activity, major clusters of volcanic activity and the climatic extremes of drought, flood and severely cold weather. If history repeats, U.S. agriculture will be devastated.

Zahorchak's work projects generally poor business conditions (due to dry climate and cold weather) through the mid-1990s. This cold/dry time period is projected to be a time of social unrest, civil war, of revolution and anarchy, according to Dr. Raymond H. Wheeler's work.

Isn't this precisely the trend we have been seeing emerge globally, one of civil unrest and revolution? Of course. Iran, Poland, Lebanon, Russia, etc. Civil wars nearly always occur during cold periods, and particularly cold, dry periods. Furthermore, with the sun going retrograde, commensurate with the peak of the most significant sunspot cycle in over 350 years, and poor business conditions, not to mention the debt debacle and AIDS epidemic, we could see society literally ripped to shreds. Plus, if there are global food shortages, as increasingly it appears will be the case, we could see a period of anarchy, matched by federal government tyranny. And this is just around the corner.

The conclusion we draw from all of this is that all hell is about to break loose with the climate and the weather; in the sun, with its explosive record peak in sunspots coming between late 1989 and 1991; with record high tidal forces triggering explosive volcanic and earthquake activity; and with the sun going retrograde, spinning us off into a decade marked by drought, cold conditions and climatic extremes. Further, all of this is coming at a time when the earth is totally unprepared for this type of challenge. The fraudulent fractional reserve debt banking system is on the verge of collapse. The incestuous U.S. Congress (99% reelection of members, financed by special interest groups, aligned with civil service bureaucrats) is totally ineffective. The social fabric of the nation is torn asunder. There is no cultural consensus when it comes to morals, ethics or values. People's immune systems across the nation are exhausted by stress, with the AIDS epidemic moving toward plague proportions.

We are in a period of great tribulation. It began in 1987. I expect it to continue until the year 2012, with episodic ebbs and flows. Between now and the year 2000, for sure, we will be forced to make major readjustments.

The following conclusions are drawn by *Cycles*...

Conclusions

Will there be drought, or inflation, or their opposites? A cyclic drought is expected, as stated in several other articles in this issue of *Cycles*. The following dates are given by the commentators:

Wheeler:1991

Thompson:1991-1992

Shirley:1992-1993

In addition, a cyclic El Nino condition is expected in the next year. This condition is a precursor of drought.

The cycles in grain forecast higher prices in late 1991. Then lower prices are expected. Gold and silver have higher prices projected into late 1990. In the last issue of *Cycles*, interest rates were forecast higher into the same period.

The conclusion would be drought and inflation until 1991, or 1992 at the latest. After this, a period of deflation and better growing conditions should begin as grains and metals fall in price. How extreme these conditions will be, is not known. Other economic cycles, such as the business-failure cycle, indicate the severest conditions will take place between 1998 and 2000. — Source: Cycles - Richard Mogey

As you can see, *Cycles* magazine focuses heavily on the 1991-1993 time period. Doesn't this coincide with my U.S. War Clock, first published back in 1982? It sure does! Isn't this also the time frame I've long projected when we should again see the massive reemergence of UFOs? It is.

Sometimes I tend to get frustrated. This is one of those times. I first started writing about climate back in 1977, in my first book, *Cycles of War*. I further wrote about it in my 1982 two-volume series, *Wealth For All: Religion, Politics and War* and *Wealth For All: Economics*. I followed those two books up with my fourth hardback book, *No Time For Slaves*, in 1986. And yet, despite the time, effort and money I put into trying to wake up a slumbering public (and its leaders), to my own financial and physical detriment, nothing has changed. It's as if the human race is drugged - mankind's computer chips are fried, the circuits are blown. Perhaps it's just gridlock. Individuals are oppressed economically, medically, and educationally, by the media, by the financial and legal institutions; and they are exhausted physically, mentally, emotionally and spiritually. My concern is that we no longer have the reserves or the will to fight the immense challenge we face.

And finally, mankind just seems to rock merrily along, paddling their canoe of life, headed for the rapids, only panicking and trying to turn things around once the crisis is upon them. Men just continue doing what their habits and traditions have taught them to do, until what they have been doing no longer works, cannot be fixed, and the pain of change is less painful than continuing on the present bankrupt path.

We are about to experience the pain of change for squandering our heritage, failing to plan, anticipate and provide for the future. Dr. Iben Browning does not think that at the end of the next 20 years any of the present forms of government which exist in the world today will still be with us. I agree. Given what I see coming, I don't think any major government in its present bureaucratic form will still be around 20 years hence.

So much for the destructive part of what we face between now and 2012. If we can just make it through the 25-year period from 1987 to 2012, we will see a world transformed in a way that today most minds can't even fathom. The challenge will be to endure the next couple of decades. Given this, how people can continue on their present mindless paths, performing insignificant and petty tasks, is totally beyond me. Everything that can be shaken will be shaken between now and the year 2012. It's time to get down to rock-bottom basics.

The weather/food/climate crisis (which we could solve with present technology) will instead develop into a full-fledged crisis - thesis. The antithesis will develop between now and 2012, as food shortages lead to civil unrest and total government control as civil liberties are suspended. National sovereignty will be sacrificed *"for the good of mankind"* so that a unified global effort can be made to fight a common enemy - a hostile nature reacting to human abuse. The World Wilderness Bank and World Wilderness Trust will be seen as the bright and shining hope - the synthesis. One third of the earth's prime land will be seized. Food will be strictly controlled and distributed as firearms are turned in for food. The religious worship of *"Mother Earth"* has already emerged, based in witchcraft. The *"purification"* (translated termination) will begin, eliminating those people unfit for the approaching golden New Age of One World currency, religion and all-powerful occult bureaucratic government. It won't be pretty for believers in God, freedom, free enterprise and classic American values.

In April of 1990, an asteroid a half-mile wide, traveling at a speed of 46,000 miles per hour, with a detonation potential equal to 20,000 1-megaton hydrogen bombs, passed within a couple of million miles of earth. This *"rock of doom"* nearly hit us in 1989, and was only discovered a week after the near miss. There may be 1,000 more such asteroids around undetected.

West Germany has three times as many registered witches as Christian clergy, 90,000 to 30,000. The *"Greens"* of West Germany are politically notorious. Worship of the earth is basic to witchcraft. April 22 of each year is celebrated as *"Earth Day."*

EARTHQUAKES...U.S.A.

March 8, 1990

The L.A. Quake

On Saturday, February 24, 1990, I was in L.A. to speak for the Foundation for the Study of Cycles. A significant portion of my talk there covered the nature of earthquakes, their causes and probability of future occurrence. After looking over the contemporary data with Jim Berkland, the famous Santa Clara County geologist, we concluded that an earthquake would most likely hit Los Angeles on Wednesday, February 28, 1990. The quake would be in the mid-5s. That projection hit the center of the bull's-eye.

"A strong earthquake Wednesday rattled Southern California from the Mexican border to the Nevada state line, setting off rock slides and a fire, rattling nerves but injuring only a few residents.

"The quake, measuring 5.5 on the Richter scale, rocked a 200-mile radius from its epicenter here [Upland, California], 35 miles northeast of downtown Los Angeles. The quake, which struck at 3:43 p.m., frightened thousands...

"It was the strongest earthquake in California since a 7.1-magnitude quake struck the San Francisco Bay region October 17, killing 67." — USA Today

Structural damage was suffered by many downtown buildings in Ontario. Disneyland shut down. Power and telephone outages were widespread, and the San Clemente nuclear power station was closed.

Two Quake Causes

After years of studying this earth-shaking phenomenon (pun intended), I have concluded that the primary causes of earthquakes are planetary gravitational pull resulting in high tidal forces, and disruptions in the electromagnetic/geomagnetic environment of the earth.

The causative factors which trigger earthquakes have only burst into the public's informational domain in recent years. Specifically, it has been disclosed that when the moon moves between the sun and the earth, causing the gravitational pull on the earth to come from one direction, high tidal forces occur. Then pressure on the tectonic plates increases. This in turn triggers earthquakes.

In addition to the planetary alignment/gravitational pull/high tidal force/tectonic plate/earthquake connection, other changes in the earth's geomagnetic field can trigger earthquakes. The sun is basically a large fusion ball, a gas sphere, which emits both solar flares and sunspots. Sunspots and solar flares each have a positive and negative magnetic polarity. Various planetary alignments determine the intensity of the sun's solar activity, as well as the frequency (wavelength) of the solar particles which are discharged by the sun toward the earth. These magnetically charged solar particles have long been linked to electromagnetic disturbances on the earth, coinciding statistically with shifts in wind patterns that affect weather.

Discharged solar particles collect at the earth's poles, which we see as the northern lights (aurora borealis). These particles literally bombard this big electromagnet we call planet earth, affecting the ionosphere and magnetosphere as well. As these solar-charged magnetic particles bathe the earth, flowing down from the magnetic poles, and falling from the atmosphere, the earth's electromagnetic environment is affected, resulting in changes in the earth's geomagnetic field. These disturbances do trigger earthquakes.

Scientists at Stanford disclosed they have been able to detect unusual electromagnetic waves prior to California earthquakes. Magnetometers detect unusually strong electromagnetic signals as early as two weeks in advance of a significant quake. The electromagnetic waves become quite intense in the hours just prior to a quake as the magnetic field intensifies.

Cats and Dogs

It is these intense changes in the earth's geomagnetic environment, in the earth's electromagnetic field, which animals (cats and dogs) sense. It causes them to go berserk. Their fine-tuned instinct tells them trouble is on the way, and so they attempt to escape it. This is why the number of lost and found cats and dogs listed in the classified ads of the *L.A. Times* increases sharply just prior to an earthquake.

Jim Berkland has tracked this *"cat and dog"* classified ad index for years. He says it is 80% reliable. (The Chinese have been doing this for centuries.) Berkland's *"cat and dog"* index showed a sharp rise the weekend of February 24, 1990. The following L.A. earthquake was therefore almost a given.

Electromagnetic Influences

Ancient history has a great deal to teach us about the sensitive electromagnetic energies of not only the earth, but also of the human body. Back in a time when men were less toxic, and their electromagnetic fields/countenances/auras more uniform and sensitive, astute men were not only aware of these energies, but also worked with them. Specifically, in ancient Egyptian medicine, the various angles of specific triangles were known to emit exact frequencies which oscillated in harmony with the ideal resonant frequency of a particular organ of the human body, say, for example, the pancreas. So the angles of triangles were used by the Egyptians to heal. (The angles of the triangle in the infrared range impacted the infrared countenance of the human body and channeled through to the dis-eased organs.)

In the seventh century, the Irish monks built paramagnetic round stone towers on the ground which matched the constellations of the night sky. These round towers were literally solar collectors which served to provide inorganic energy to help fertilize the organic monastery gardens.

In the Middle Ages, the monks of Europe used to strum a specific pitch of a note for hours on end while sitting alongside the bed of one of their ill brothers. The monks knew exactly which note vibrated the correct resonant frequency for healing the primary dis-ease in the fallen monk's out-of-tune organ.

Soviet Chicanery

There is a joker in this earthquake deck. Since 1938, the Russians have been hoarding the Tesla scientific literature and developing electromagnetic weaponry. The Russians have literally cornered the market on Tesla and Moray physics. In this regard, physicist Tom Bearden's work has tracked scalar interferometry in Russian weaponry. Using this offshoot of Tesla physics, the Russians are at least theoretically able to electromagnetically trigger earthquakes along fault lines, either at will, or when the geomagnetic field is primed. The Russians have for some time been able to wage weather warfare and direct electromagnetic warfare (Salem, Oregon, 1978; Afghanistan). Earthquake warfare would be an insidious new niche.

Infrared

NASA discovered an entirely new universe within our universe using infrared cameras. Literally, a new world has opened up to the NASA scientists as the infrared range of our universe is explored.

In the infrared range, frequency, form and substance are all interrelated. The shape or form of a substance determines the infrared frequency which it attracts or emits. Further, the material of which an infrared antenna is composed determines whether it is primarily a receiver or broadcaster of infrared energy. So, when planets align in various geometric and geomagnetic configurations around the sun, in the infrared range, these angles determine the angle and therefore the frequency which is bombarding our boiling ball of gas we call the sun. In turn, in cause-and-effect fashion, the sun emits specifically charged wavelengths of magnetic solar particles which bombard the earth.

Dr. Bob Beck, with his graduate students at Stanford, has further demonstrated there is a direct one-to-one correlation between the nature of the solar discharge and the outbreak of viral or bacterial diseases on earth. Is this why the Aztec leaders used to shield their people in underground caves during times of astronomical and solar upset? Apparently, specific wavelengths of solar-charged magnetic particles act as a battery which energize latent bacteria or viruses in the human electromagnetic field.

Arc of Fire

Back to earthquakes. The United States is part of the arc-of-fire/ring-of-fire which runs up along the west coasts of South America, Central America, and North America, down eastern Russia, through Japan, into eastern Southeast Asia and the South Pacific islands, and down through New Zealand.

Along the U.S. West Coast in this arc of fire, Mount St. Helens has already blown its top. There is an old Indian legend which states that when Little Sister (Mount St. Helens) blows her top, it won't be long until Big Brother (Mount Rainier) follows.

Significant mountains and geophysically active areas along the U.S. and southern Canadian West Coasts include Mammoth Lake, California, Mount Lassen, the lava beds of northern California, Crater Lake in Oregon, Mount Hood in northern Oregon, Mount St. Helens, Mount Rainier in Washington, Glacier Peak, Mount Baker, and Mount Garibaldi in British Columbia. Since the jet stream journeys from west to east, any significant earthquake or volcanic disruptions on the West Coast inescapably affect the electromagnetic and geo-magnetic environment of the rest of the nation, as does the fallout of volcanic dust.

I was in northwest Montana when Mount St. Helens blew her top. It was an awesome, ominous spectacle, watching that gray-brown, dirty cloud roll in. A perfect blue-sky, sunshiny day turned to dusk in a matter of minutes, with sparkling silver particles raining from the sky.

Trilateral Quakes

Significant earth changes historically have dramatically altered the eco-nomic and political systems of countries. As it turns out, two of the world's three Trilateral countries - the U.S. and Japan - are prime candidates for signifi-cant earthquake and volcanic activity. In fact, Japan and the United States are two of the top three most geophysically at-risk nations on the face of the earth!

The Weak Link

Geophysically, the earth's weakest link runs from the 27th to the 38th par-allel north. Here, a major band of unstable energy bisects the earth. This weakest collective line is the most dangerous on planet earth and the most sus-ceptible to physical eruption - earthquakes fall in this range. Geophysical dis-turbances within this area radiate out hundreds to thousands of miles. The dis-tance these shock waves travel depends on the density of the earth at the point of disturbance.

Within this vulnerable band are located the cities of San Francisco, Los Angeles and San Diego, and all points east. Lining up on the East Coast are Washington, D.C., Richmond, Raleigh, Wilmington, Charleston, Savannah, Jacksonville, Daytona Beach, Orlando, West Palm Beach and Ft. Lauderdale. In addition to all the major West Coast cities being earthquake prone, Salt Lake City, Kansas City, Memphis, St. Louis, Atlanta and New York City are at ma-jor risk.

Nuclear Implications

As the San Francisco quake taught us, earthquakes in and of themselves can do comprehensive damage to the areas struck. But we have created additional risks, unnecessary risks, which could prove to be long term even more devastating. The U.S. military establishment and the Department of Energy have located key nuclear weapon facilities, defense sites, nuclear power plants and dams in areas of the country which are subject to *"strong chance of damage."* It doesn't take much imagination to realize that the result of a *"China Syndrome"* at any of these facilities would produce a far worse situation both short and long term than the earthquake or volcanic eruption. Specifically vulnerable are the Hanford Reservation in Washington state, the Idaho National Engineering Lab, the Lawrence Livermore National Lab in California, the Sandia National Labs and the Los Alamos National Lab in New Mexico, the Bendix plant in Missouri, the Oak Ridge Reservation in Tennessee, the Savannah River plant in South Carolina, the Mound Lab, Reactive Metals, Inc. and Portsmouth Uranium Enrichment Complex in Ohio, and the Feed Materials Production Center in Ohio. Nuclear power plants and dams built elsewhere around the country in earthquake and volcanically sensitive areas are located on fault lines or epicenters!

To 2012

Looking down the road, the earth will again become vulnerable to significant earth changes between 1998-2002, and between 2008-2012. These two time frames could be even more severe than the 1989-1993 era. The earth has reportedly lost 25% of its magnetic field since the late 1800s. Further, according to Dr. Robert Beck, Peter Kelly, and Isaac Asimov, between the years 2000 and 2012, we could cross the zero point and lose all of the earth's magnetic field. Or the field could flip. The earth could reverse polarity. A polar shift is possible then as well. Imagine the earthquakes if a polar shift occurs.

Safety Zones

Where are the safest places to live in the U.S.A. today, from this perspective? Central, south and southeast Texas are the best places. The South overall generally is good. However, cities along the Gulf of Mexico will be increasingly subject to more severe hurricanes and high tidal waves, also generated by earthquakes along the Caribbean island chain, an earthquake/volcanic fault line. The Midwest generally and the Plains states particularly are subject to only minor earthquakes or none at all. But then again, these areas are vulnerable to high winds and tornadoes.

"Tornado Alley" will experience more severe weather in the upcoming years as the meridional flow of air from north to south increases. Colder temperatures at the poles and hotter temperatures plus or minus 20 degrees latitude

from the equator, will result in the extremes of weather rushing from north to south and back again, spawning numerous tornadoes. Dallas particularly is at risk.

Conclusion

What do we conclude from all this? If we live in earthquake-prone areas, we most definitely should pay the extra premium for earthquake insurance on our commercial and personal real estate. If possible, and if we have the flexibility, we should consider relocating out of these highest-risk earthquake and volcanic areas, particularly if they are in major cities. Stocking up on basic supplies, such as water, food, clothing, blankets, tents, fuel, lanterns, stoves, flashlights, batteries, heaters and the like - camping gear - is recommended. Self-defense should be a consideration also, as should an emergency supply of cash. Fallout shelters, tornado shelters and root cellars should be pondered. Just view any such preparations as a type of emergency insurance. Of course, banks, other financial institutions, and the financial system itself, could be threatened if the geophysical changes become as intense and widespread as some experts expect between now and 2012. So the safety of a financial institution, as well as its location, may become increasingly a prime investment consideration.

Finally, such physical upsets and changes in the earth's electromagnetic field and physical environment severely impact the human body's electromagnetic field and immune system. So, a solid religious philosophy, a sound people network, a good diet, fresh air, clean water, plenty of sunshine, nutritious alive food, and exercise, while minimizing stress, are critical during the upcoming era. We need to be grounded. After all, *"we're not wealthy unless we're healthy."*

Being grounded spiritually, mentally, physically and emotionally during the *"Nasty Nineties"* may provide us with the edge necessary to take advantage of the opportunities presented to us in the volatile financial markets. We have entered the decade of *"protein gold."* The United States has long been the world's bread basket. With the upcoming geophysical upsets - earthquakes...U.S.A. - we'll see the grain and soybean complex become *"protein gold."*

I really hope this chapter doesn't scare anyone. We just need to understand that we are living in a dangerous era. We must act. Remember the old Lebanese proverb: *"Truth kills those who hide from it."* The other side of this risk is opportunity, if we are first prepared. By becoming aware of the risk and making provision for same, we can make the most of the opportunity, and better serve our fellow men.

HELL WEEK
September 21, 1989

"I will show wonders in heaven above and signs in the earth beneath..." - Acts 2:19

Yes, Martha, Hell Week normally comes at the <u>end</u> of the college semester. The poor pledges endure Hell Week just prior to their initiation into their fraternity. The great *"rush"* takes place for the wide-eyed innocents in early fall. But this time, Hell Week also rolled in in early September 1989.

Pluto, the *"Lord of Hell,"* *rolled into place the first week of September 1989. I quoted Robert Cole in the August 9, 1989 REAPER, "Official word has finally arrived from the scientists at the Naval Observatory in Washington, D.C.: Planet Pluto will reach its perihelion...on September 4, 1989. This is the major astrological event of the century, possibly even more significant than the harmonic Convergence....September 4, 1989 is the midpoint of the Aquarian Renaissance which began in 1979 and will be complete in 1999. This present month of August...Planet Pluto, named after the Lord of Hell, is as close as it can get."*

Luciferian doctrines are expressed in witchcraft. A most important aspect of witchcraft is astrology. Astrology is the timing mechanism for all of the occult's plans and activities. Astrology also provides geometric structure for the occult's agenda.

Government is always religion applied to economics. For example, Nancy Reagan's astrology influenced former President Reagan's political decisions, which in turn affected the economy. Because we have an evolutionary, humanistic government, and a cryptic, death-based economic/financial system, I was very intent on documenting the events that transpired during the week of the *"Lord of Hell's"* arrival, stemming from this astrological event. Labor Day itself, which kicks off September, has its roots in pagan antiquity.

(In the ancient world, individual *"nations"* were groups of people who were like-minded religiously, or unified by race. Pagan, occult *"empires"* on the other hand, were characterized by a smorgasbord of people and religions, marked by the supreme, lawmaking authority resting in the political power, the state, which effectively played the role of God. Debt money, fraudulent money, and money characterized by unjust weights and measures, rather than gold and silver, were also characteristic of these ancient empires. Their pagan, cryptic, occult religions went hand-in-hand with the all-powerful humanistic state and dishonest money. This is the case today, too.)

At Issue

Hell Week 1989 was a black week for Christianity. As soon as the *"Lord of Hell"* rolled in, the global symbol of Christian selflessness, service and charity, Mother Teresa, suffered a heart attack. This former Nobel Peace Prize winner was admitted to Woodlands Nursing Home on September 5, 1989.

With the rare exception of the likes of Mother Teresa, what passes for Christianity today has little resemblance to Christianity's practical historical applications. Few Christians and non-Christians alike understand a major benefit of living under a Christian governmental, political and religious system. In this regard, I found it more than of passing interest that the Jews and Moslems in England cheered Margaret Thatcher when she made England officially a Christian country and required Christianity to be taught in the public schools there. The English Jews and Moslems believe their country will be better off when Christians begin behaving like Christians again.

Government Is Religion Applied To Economics

The essence of what I am referring to is that Christianity, which comprises 88% of the U.S. population, is at its base a covenantal religion. In other words, it is a contract-based religion and can provide the basis for individual self-governance. (Another word for covenant/contract is constitution, as with the U.S. Constitution, the covenant/contract between *"we the people"* and our civil (sic) federal government.)

With a covenant/contract-based religion, the centralization of power and the building of bureaucracies are minimized. Instead, decentralization is maximized and the locus of power is in the individual. Why? Because a covenant/contract is an individual governmental, religious and economic instrument.

A covenant/contract is governmental because it defines the legal rights of the voluntary (not coerced) parties to an agreement. A covenant/contract is religious because it is no better than the morality/ethics/religious values of the parties to an agreement. And finally, a covenant/contract is economic, because it defines both the economic duties required and benefits derived from the parties to an agreement.

So, a covenant/contract-based religion results in a covenant/contract-based government, and a covenant/contract-based economic system. This means individuals are held responsible and accountable for their own representations and actions, and power is localized. Therefore, every individual operates as a priest, king/ambassador and steward. This maximizes freedom and prosperity. Maximum prosperity follows maximum human freedom. Indeed, freedom walks on this earth on two legs: one leg is law, the other is economics. When the legal power in a society is vested in the individual because of his covenantal/contractual responsibilities - and the economic power in a society is vested in the individual's economic covenantal/contractual arrangements, because the underlying religion is covenantal/contractual - well then, the result is the maximization of peace, freedom and prosperity.

Every man is a priest! Every man is an ambassador/king! Every man is a steward! Government is religion applied to economics. Power is dispersed and maximized in the individual.

At this point, it should be obvious why the empires of today rage against a covenantal/contractual, religious-based political and economic order. Such a system guts today's political and economic power-oriented, bureaucracy-running predators and parasites, who run roughshod with their bureaucracies over the masses. Bureaucracies are always the greatest institutional manifestation of human evil, whether they are religious, political or economic. Bureaucracies centralize power and promote selfishness, corruption, insensitivity, inefficiency, irresponsibility and a lack of moral accountability. So it should come as no surprise that individual political freedom, economic freedom, and the religious freedom all came under heavy assault during Hell Week 1989. Hell Week was anything but a week of *"power to the people."*

Religious Hell

To reiterate, Hell Week was indeed a black week for Christianity, led off by the heart attack which felled Mother Teresa. Christianity took other big hits, too, as would be expected when the *"Lord of Hell"* arrived. Stateside, the materialistic/religious soap opera, the headline-grabbing Jim Bakker trial, dominated the press. The collapse of a prosecution witness, Bakker's emotional breakdown and curling up into the fetal position, his ball-and-chain psychiatric examination, Tammy Bakker's boo-hooing with eye make-up running - it was pitiful and disgusting.

Secondarily grabbing the headlines was the trial of two Seventh Day Adventists, who were in court for letting their son starve to death for religious reasons. It was reported that this family had the money to feed themselves, but the money was their tithe, and so they wouldn't touch it. ...Didn't Jesus's disciples pick heads of grain and eat it on the Sabbath? Didn't David eat the shewbread in the temple? Small wonder that the general public rejects Christianity when they see it showcased by the likes of these Bakker and Seventh Day Adventist trials.

Even the Establishment's evangelist, Billy Graham, was on network TV coast to coast, all wet, in raincoat, during Hell Week, live from London. Graham's newspaper ads thundered, *"You can feel it all over the world...in Eastern Europe, in China, in Africa...something is about to happen!"* You're right, Dr. Billy, it was Hell Week!

Far less conspicuous in the press was the uproar over the vulgar photographic exhibit of a crucified Christ put in a bottle, submerged in the artist's urine. This work of art (sic) was supported by a federal grant of $15,000 awarded to photographer Andres Serrano by the Southeastern Endowment for Contemporary Arts. Yes, Martha, this was your tax money again hard at work. *USA Today*, on September 9, 1989, in its "Debate" section, featured federally funded art, including this sacrilege.

What also crossed my desk religiously during Hell Week was the ruling by the Rhode Island State Division of Taxation which established witchcraft as a legitimate religion. In Rhode Island now, witch covens are entitled to the same tax break as those allowed *"established"* religions. The great global land grab underway for one third of the earth's surface, environmentalism and witchcraft are all linked up with the move toward a One World Order. Here, too, government is religion applied to economics.

Additionally during Hell Week, the Moral Majority disbanded after ten years of lobbying for conservative Christian causes. The September 4, 1989 issue of *Insight* magazine headlined, *"Swindlers cash in on religious beliefs."* Then the following week *The Wall Street Journal* took a potshot at Christian financial planners. And, oh yes, Oral Roberts' medical center needed a $50 million transfusion. The *"Lord of Hell"* had a field day.

I also found it extremely pertinent that it was announced during Hell Week that President Hussein of Iraq was rebuilding King Nebuchadnezzar's Babylon. The Great Ishtar (goddess) gates, the entrance gates to Babylon, were being slowly reconstructed. The 500-room Southern Palace was also rising from the archeological ruins. And even the fabled hanging Gardens of Babylon were to be reconstructed. Hussein is offering a $1.5 million reward to anyone who can figure out how these Hanging Gardens were watered. Of course, it was Nebuchadnezzar who destroyed Jerusalem and enslaved the Hebrews of the Bible. All in all, it was a very depressing Hell Week for the Christian religion.

Political Hell

Hell Week was a black week for individual political freedom, civil rights and the Bill of Rights, with the unveiling of the Bush-whacking version of the *"War on Drugs"* on September 5, 1989.

Let's get down to basics. All law is legislated morality, because all law is the enactment of ideas about right or wrong, good and evil, ethics - all of which are religious concerns. And yet, morality cannot be legislated in the sense that legislated morality does not work long term. Prohibition in the 1920s taught us this. When men are good and self-governing, laws (legislated morality) are unnecessary. On the other hand, when men are evil and corrupt, or men think laws are unjust, then laws (legislated morality) are a Catch-22. They break down long term. Criminals stay criminals, and good men are turned into criminals by unjust laws. So the refurbished *"War on Drugs"* by the Bush administration was a Machiavellian approach used to disguise the moral bankruptcy of both the federal government and an increasing percentage of the American people, particularly the black population of the inner cities which are drug-infested. Blacks are only 12% of the U.S. population, but account for 50% of emergency room treatment for heroin, 55% of those treated for cocaine abuse, and 60% for PCP. (As Black economists Walter Williams and Thomas Sowell have long pointed out, it is the federal government which has decimated both the black family and its ethnic educational/economic system through various federally funded *"butter"* programs.   See Williams' book, THE STATE AGAINST BLACKS.) Oh yes, 76% of those who use illegal drugs are white.

The Bush anti-drug campaign of punishing users and middlemen, rather than primarily the narcotics cartels, suppliers and their banks was treating the symptoms rather than the cause. Bush's czar, William Bennett, a true believer, is chopping off the leaves and branches rather than attacking the root. As Lynn Scarlett, research director of Reason Foundation, pointed out in the September 6, 1989 issue of *USA Today, "The real moral horrors Americans face are the abuses of civil liberties increasingly incorporated in the drug war; a parlaying of a health problem into a criminal one; and the condemnation of our inner cities to a world of violence that drug legalization could greatly reduce."* Further, Chuck Bowden, guest columnist for *USA Today*, also on September 6, 1989 commented, *"So I wish the president and his czar well. But I still wonder how they plan to wage war against their own people who live in this nation and find that experience so barren that they must blot it out with drugs. Perhaps we should bring the gunships home and settle this matter on native ground."* International observers have also commented on the moral bankruptcy of U.S. cities. The *London Daily Mail* wrote, *"Many of America's inner cities are now so ravaged by the cancer of crime and violence that civilized life is teetering on the edge of anarchy. Forget the Russians destroying the citadels of capitalism - there is now the very real threat that much of urban America could destroy itself."* (Foreign observers have also commented critically on the studies showing black violence to be 35 times greater than white violence; the running of an increasing number of America's major cities by corrupt black mayors; and the likely financial exodus out of these cities by both whites and foreign investors.)

Even former Republican President Ford attacked fellow Republican George Bush's drug program. Ford correctly pointed out that alcohol abuse is more damaging to society than cocaine and other drugs. Four times more people were killed in 1987 in alcohol-related accidents than in accidents involving drugs. Overall, alcohol kills 27 times as many people as do illegal drugs. Additionally, alcohol abuse costs society $120 billion a year, compared with $60 billion from drug abuse. Federal drug war expenditures tripled from 1981 to 1988 with no success. And the Bush administration's *"drug-busting"* $7.8 billion could do little good. It just wasn't enough.

So what gives? Why all the uproar and focus on drugs, and particularly the attack on the small fry, the little fish, the user/consumer and middleman? Such a focus obviously is ineffective. But if we refocus and recognize that this *"War on Drugs"* is primarily geared to further centralize power in the hands of the federal government and strip the Bill of Rights, then it all makes sense. Also, for years, the intelligence gathering branch of the federal government has enjoyed a cozy relationship with organized crime (in Cuba, the Kennedy assassination). But now with the rise to power of the Medellin cartel and their U.S. distribution network, the old power base is threatened.

The September 7, 1989 *Wall Street Journal* pointed out, *"Bush's get-tough drug plan shares a philosophy that didn't work for Rockefeller 20 years ago."* Aren't the Republicans smart enough to know that the same program which failed 20 years ago cannot be dusted off and succeed a second time around, particularly with today's far more sophisticated and pervasive drug underworld? Of course! But then again, who was George Bush working for?...

Two of the foremost liberal Democrats in Congress at that time, Geraldine Ferraro and Senator Daniel Patrick Moynihan, gave George Bush a B- and an A, respectively. After all, the Bush administration knew all too well that financing of the federal deficit is hostage to foreign investors, the Japanese and the international drug lords. (See THE REAPER of March 23, 1989, *"Hostage to the Drug Lords".*) George Bush once quipped regarding David Rockefeller, *"All that I am I owe to this man."* David Rockefeller has declared, *"International business is apolitical."* Back to the drug lords.

"The rise of $US78 billion in the U.S. banks' liabilities to the Bahamas and to the British West Indies between 1985 and 1988 represents about three years' worth of drugs profits from the U.S. drug business...

"Drug financiers, like all businessmen, don't want to invest their money in a wasting asset. But their financial clout is so immense that if they decided to make substantial transfers of money from U.S. banks to, say, Swiss banks or British banks or German banks, they have the power to bring the dollar to ruin. Such is the immensity of the sums involved."

So, it is no small surprise that the Bush administration did not go after the banks involved at all, and only targeted carefully selected major drug cartels. The purpose of this whole operation may have been to create a monopoly of U.S.-*"endorsed"* drug dealers who deal with accredited banks, that in turn gladly finance the federal deficit. So much for the world of international finance and economics. Plus, back at home, the purpose served by the drug war is to minimize freedom.

Hell is the loss of freedom. Bush's unveiling of his drug czar's bureaucracy (the greatest institutional manifestation of human evil) appropriately happened on September 5, 1989, just after the *"Lord of Hell"* arrived. The paint of freedom in this country is being stripped at record speed. Even the newspaper headlines speak of it.

The assault on personal freedom commensurate with the arrival of the *"Lord of Hell"* on September 4, 1989 and the unveiling of the new *"War on Drugs"* on September 5, 1989 was backed up by a media and legislative assault on freedom heretofore unequaled. The September 4, 1989 *Business Week* headlined its cover story, *"IS NOTHING PRIVATE? Computers know more about you than you realize - and now anyone can tap in."* *Business Week* disclosed that credit bureau computers are crammed with 400 million records on 160 million individuals. Most people can get data on any individual without the targeted subject's consent. And what about the files in federal computers, the IRS, NSA and the like?

Another way freedom was ruthlessly attacked during Hell Week came in the form of a proposal by liberal Democratic Senator Kerry, who offered up a series of laws to control and prohibit wire transfers of capital outside of the United States! This was a ploy to prevent flight capital from exiting the United States, to prevent a stampede out of the U.S. dollar. Perhaps a set percentage of one's assets should be kept offshore at all times, out of U.S. dollars. Then the September 7, 1989 *USA Today* reported, *"Area post offices stopped accepting $100 bills due to 93 counterfeit bills passed in south Florida during three days last week. Officials say drug traffickers frequently use bogus bills."* In other words, if you use cash to maintain your privacy, you are now put in the same box as drug dealers. *Washington Post* columnist William Raspberry called for legislation to outlaw all cash, bills and coins, which he called, *'the mother's milk of the spy, the terrorist, the thief, the drug pusher, the drug user, tax evaders, and embezzlers."* Raspberry called for a computer-readable debit card, encoded with an individual's bank balance, credit limits, medical records, passport, driver's license, photograph, thumb print and welfare eligibility.

Next, the Bush administration went on record as reconsidering whether to ban the sale of assault weapons produced in the United States. Earlier, assault weapons manufactured abroad were banned by Bush and Co.

What was the message delivered by the Chinese students after their insurrection was brutally crushed? *"Tell Americans not to give up their guns!"* Gun control paved the way for Castro's rise to power in Cuba, too, The Bush Justice Department pushed for a national I.D. card, which would double as a national gun registration card. This card would include fingerprints and retina scans, and would effectively be a biometric I.D. card.

Additionally, further emphasis was put during Hell Week on the transformation of the closed military bases in the United States into prisons. The U.S. prison population jumped by a record 46,004 inmates in the first six months of 1989, bringing the total to 673,565 men and women behind bars, according to the Bureau of Justice. The United States was requiring 1,800 new prison beds a week. The U.S. prison population has risen 90% since 1981 due to the incarceration of drug law offenders. The cost to the U.S. taxpayer was at least $15,000 per inmate per year. One out of every two men sent to prison was black.

Before it's over, the *"War on Drugs"* will have every excuse necessary to lock up any American for any reason. Political prisoners should be expected to become a way of life. And appropriately, the first book discussing one of the most highly publicized political prisoner, Lyndon LaRouche, crossed my desk during Hell Week. The book, entitled *Railroad: USA vs. Lyndon LaRouche*, provided documentation of how LaRouche's civil rights and First Amendment rights were so overwhelmingly violated by the Feds in their frame of

LaRouche, that over 500 lawyers in the United States, most of who do not agree with LaRouche on most things, signed an amicus brief. I was amazed at the number of respected conservative attorneys, who I either know or have heard of, who signed this petition. And despite the fact that I agree with Lyndon LaRouche on very little, the evidence leaves no question that he is a political prisoner who was railroaded by the federal government, locked up for 15 years. Indeed, Hell Week was a black week for individual freedom.

Black Hell

Hell Week was also a black week for blacks. *Insight* magazine headlined in its September 4, 1989 issue, *"In film, plays, books, music and other avenues of cultural and political expression, the image of Malcolm X is resurging. Young blacks are drawn to the angry rhetoric of the slain Muslim nationalist leader in the face of deep social and political problems."*

Violence characterized the black community during Hell Week, reminiscent of the 1960s. The black-white confrontations in New York over Joseph Fama's alleged slaying of Yusef Hawkins, one of four blacks attacked by a gang of 30 whites in Bensonhurst, captured the headlines. Hawkins was dating a white neighborhood girl.

Then, down in Virginia Beach, Virginia, during two nights of black college student rioting, 100 stores were looted and millions of dollars of damage occurred, resulting in 260 arrests and in 13 youths and 10 police officers being injured.

Black South Africa also captured the headlines. *USA Today* reported on September 5, 1989, *"South Africa unrest at boiling point: Black's anger focused on white-only election."* Rev. Tutu declared, *"We are on the brink of catastrophe."* White South Africans voted in the most important parliamentary elections held there in 41 years. More than 2 million black, Indian and mixed race workers staged a general strike to protest the black majority's exclusion from voting. The strike severely disrupted South Africa's industrialized economy, crippled transportation, idled dozens of factories, affected gold and coal mining operations, and forced white managers into jobs that are generally reserved for blacks. Tens of thousands of black workers and students joined the two-day general strike in Johannesburg on September 5, 1989. Transportation in the cities of Durban and Port Elizabeth was stalled. There were scattered bombings, stone throwing, and 39% of the black workforce did not report for work.

But perhaps topping things off, the September 4, 1989 issue of *USA Today*, the day the *"Lord of Hell"* arrived, featured an article by Barbara Reynolds, the *USA Today* Inquiry editor. She proposed a *"National Hate Week, because hate is in the air again."* Iran confirmed. Iranian Parliament speaker Mahdi Karrubi said, *"U.S. leaders will take the wish of overthrowing the Islamic Republic to their graves."* The Iranian parliament condemned 186 U.S. congressmen for endorsing Iranian resistance groups.

Economic Hell

The economic news released during Hell Week was long term black. Corporate debt was 39% of GNP. *Business Week* featured, *"With so many companies so deep in debt, the leverage binge winds down."* When leverage and borrowing winds down, a debt-based economy winds down into recession. Further, *"...the bias in the U.S. tax code favors debt over equity financing - interest payments are deductible while dividend payments are not - is bad."* U.S. consumer debt was 63% of GNP, compared to German consumer debt of only 11% of GNP. U.S. government debt was 52% of GNP. The last two recessions it was only (sic) 34% of GNP.

The Baby Boom generation will crimp home prices in the 1990s, because the number of first-time home buyers will drop off dramatically, most noticeably in California and the Northeast, where most of the Baby Boomers live. Real estate prices are expected to drop 37% in real terms by 2007, according to N. Gregory Mankin, economics professor at Harvard. Home prices could fall 3% a year over the next 18 years (54%). Some 75% of Americans' net worth is in their homes, and American consumers make up 70% of the economy. When home prices break, so will consumer borrowing and spending. Housing affordability in the U.S. dropped to its lowest level since September, 1985. Rising home prices offset increasing purchasing power. The August 29, 1989 WSJ reported, *"...California's housing market is showing signs of slowing down."* June 1989 sales of California homes fell 13.9% in the peak selling season. I have consistently written that when it was over for California residential real estate, it was over for the consumer and the economy. The demise of California real estate and the drop off in airline traffic were a 1-2 knockout punch for the economy.

Richard Maloney projected that interest expense alone will swallow up all federal government revenues by the year 2004. Dr. Jay W. Forrester of MIT released his calculations that show complete economic collapse of the United States is a 98% mathematical probability within the next ten years, based upon his differential equations. By the year 2000, the draw on Social Security will require a 100% tax, based on current income, too. U.S. oil imports had climbed to 50% after the oil price crash in 1985, exceeding domestic production for only the second time in history. This has left the U.S. at the mercy of OPEC in the mid-1990s. *"The balance of power in the energy industry is clearly tipping. Without incentives to stabilize prices and increased domestic drilling, America's ripe for an energy crisis of staggering proportions,"* according to Kent Hance, Texas Railroad Commission Chairman.

The U.S. recorded its first trade deficit in 31 years in the service sector of the economy. This dishonor was due to interest and dividends being paid to foreigners. Sounds just like Latin America. Speaking of Latin America, Ashby Bladen wrote in *Forbes*, *"...[T]he worst risk we face is that another bout of inflation will destroy the habit of personal savings here and create the same total reliance on hyperinflationary government borrowings that it has produced already in Latin America."*

The takeover activity we saw in airlines in the stock market is the type of activity that's expected at an economic peak. It speaks of a blowoff in the discretionary spending sector of the economy. Furthermore, it was the excitement in airline stocks which nearly exclusively propelled the U.S. stock market higher during Hell Week 1989.

The Conference Board reported that the global economy was signaling a slowdown, with the leading indicators in Europe, the United States and Canada being increasingly sluggish. The only economic vigor was in the Pacific Basin.

Moody's declared that debt conditions in developing countries were further unraveling. New York financial institutions increased their loan loss provisions. Argentina, Brazil, Peru and Venezuela are financial basket cases. Water was becoming so precious in the eastern United States that it was being compared to gold. The nation's infrastructure was falling apart, particularly in the cities, with no money to repair. It was reported that the statistics being spit out by the federal government were increasingly revised and were becoming more and more unreliable, so that no one really knew where the economy was. The Congressional Budget Committee announced that the 1990 federal budget would be at least 20% over the Gramm-Rudman targets. The S&L bailout cost every man, woman and child of the United States $1,000.

Inflation was projected to rise in fourth quarter 1989. The International Monetary Fund saw inflation as the greatest threat to the world economy. The world money supply doubled in the seven years prior to 1989, while the U.S. money supply increased 55% over the six prior years. The National Purchasing Managers Report fell to 45.2% from 46%, which was the lowest rate since December 1982. Below 50% is recessionary. Factory overtime was down. Factory orders fell 1.7% to their lowest level in eight months. The Conference Board said that hiring was slowing. Leading department stores declared their newspaper advertising spending would be flat in the fall of 1989, due to decreased expectations of sales. Capital goods were off and inventories were up. Consumer confidence dropped in August, 1989, according to the Conference Board.

Only 10% of the Leading Economic Indicators were expanding. Debt growth was the slowest it had been in 14 years, while liquidity reached a 20-year low. The U.S. was servicing $12 trillion of debt. And the September 5, 1989 *Wall Street Journal* announced, *"The Fed isn't likely to push interest rates down further unless there are major signs of economic weakness, policy makers suggested."* Nearly all of this was black economic news which flowed across my desk during Hell Week.

Russian Hell

Warnings of the imminent collapse of the Soviet empire were issued during Hell Week.

The U.S.-U.S.S.R. merger was already underway. The Boy Scouts were integrating with the Soviets, as was the Little League. Admiral William J. Crowe, Jr., Chairman of the Joint Chiefs of Staff, made an official visit to the Soviet Union that summer. Mike Wallace of TV's *60 Minutes* gave us a full report. In the summer of 1988, Marshall Sergei Akhromeyev, chief of the Soviet General Staff, visited the United States. During Hell Week, 17 lawyers from the Soviet Union came to the United States to gain hands-on experience in the U.S. legal system as part of a work-study program sponsored by the American Bar Association. If anything gave credibility to Hell Week it was these lawyers getting together. Soviet physicians were in the country doing the same things as their lawyers during Hell Week. And a defense scandal broke out over a contractor's (Retired Army Major Fred Westerman) disclosure of corruption in the COG (Continuation of Government) project. COG Is FEMA's contingency plan for the reconstitution and implementation of the federal government following a nuclear first strike on the United States. Westerman asserted his offices were burglarized by FEMA as he was working on the "Doomsday Project." Nice topic for the press to chew on during Hell Week.

And what were *"we, the people"* told about the U.S.S.R. during Hell Week? *The Wall Street Journal* reported, *"U.S. officials grow more pessimistic about Soviet reforms." US News & World Report* reported, *"Perestroika in the twilight zone...The Baltics want freedom, but Gorbachev cannot afford to let them go. "* Yeltsin was in the United States, declaring that the Soviet Union could be enveloped in strikes unless Gorbachev resolved the U.S.S.R.'s economic and nationalistic problems. This maverick Soviet politician declared that the Kremlin had only six months to a year to achieve definitive progress or face possible *"revolution"* and ouster. Echoing this, *The Wall Street Journal* declared that Gorbachev warned of *"dangerous consequences"* from internal conflict. *The Wall Street Journal* did a follow-up article headlining, *"Red Square Scare: As Coup Talk Sweeps Moscow, How Firm is Gorbachev's Grip?"* The *Wall Street Journal* reported on *"the possibility of impending political disaster. "* The Soviet army couldn't be counted on either. The officers in the Soviet army who supported perestroika were discharged. *"The growing estrangement of the army is a striking feature of contemporary communism, "* according to Stephen Sestanovich, director of Soviet Studies Center for Strategic and International Studies.

"Suddenly, the prospect of Mikhail Gorbachev's great reform experiment collapsing, perhaps in a river of blood, no longer seems beyond question. Over the past two months, the nation's mood has turned very dark as dozens of long-standing problems have spiraled, apparently out of control.

"For the first time, the Soviet media are openly speculating about the prospects of a Kremlin coup." Gorbachev himself even had to deny *'the threat of a coup or even civil war.'*

"In almost every republic, latent ethnic tensions have exploded into the open, and hundreds have been killed in race riots in the south. Moldavia, Azerbaijan and the runaway Baltic republics have put themselves on a collision course with Moscow." — WSJ

The U.S. government response? Butter up the Soviets. The United States government bought butter from American dairy farmers for $1.32 a pound and sold it to the Soviet Union for 73.3 cents a pound. In other words, U.S. taxpayers subsidized the selling of 110 million pounds of surplus U.S. butter to the Soviet Union. Then on September 13, 1989, Montana's ultraliberal Democratic Senator Max Baucus called for the Soviet Union to be granted Most Favored Nation status (MFN).

Birds of a feather do flock together. Both the United States and Russia are atheistic, evolutionary, humanistic, bureaucratic empires. The former Soviet Union, a creation of the West (Karl Marx wrote out of London), and an ally of the West in World War II, is now being merged back into the West, perhaps achieved by the appropriate military scare tactic to motivate the U.S. masses into surrender. This would be the fulfillment of Hegel's dialectic - thesis, antithesis, synthesis.

The Pentagon had better call out its psychics. Pentagon psychics are meditating for a peace shield around the U.S. The Pentagon Meditation Club meets weekly to generate powers to shield America from attack. This activity is dubbed the *"Spiritual Defense Initiative."*

Nazi Hell - U.S. Bureaucratic Style

What did I write in the August 24, 1989 REAPER, *"Reflections on Autumn "*?

"Well, on September 4, 1989, right in time for the Labor Day fall rush, the 'Lord of Hell' arrives. On that date, planet Pluto, named after the 'Lord of Hell', gets as close as it can get, reaching perihelion...

"It brings to mind Leonard Piekoff's important 1977 book, THE OMINOUS PARALLELS: THE END OF FREEDOM IN AMERICA. *In this important work, Piekoff put forth the thesis that the United States is paralleling the path taken by Germany which led to Adolf Hitler and Nazi Germany. The direction the United States has in fact taken over the past ten years has followed Piekoff's scenario with disturbing accuracy.*

"Hitler's Nazi bureaucracy was a satanic occult one to the core. Again, bureaucracy is always the greatest institutional manifestation of human evil.

"This is uncomfortable in its parallels. Further, consider this quote:

'Trust your feelings, your instincts, or whatever you like to call them. Never trust your knowledge. The experts never have the true instinct. You must never seek it in them, but only in yourself.' Sounds just like the words of a New Age leader of today, right? Wrong! These were the words of the first wave's New Age leader, Adolf Hitler! The second New Age wave is with us now in spades.

"The signs are in the heavens: the 'Lord of Hell' is here. We are entering the peak time period of the most dynamic sunspot cycle in at least 250 years. Plus, the time of the highest tidal force in nearly 200 years is upon us. And the sun is about to run and hide from it all, going retrograde. Light running from darkness? The 'Lord of Hell' is here and the sun goes backward."

How did it work out? What was the cover story of the *US News & World Report* of September 4, 1989? *"HITLER'S WAR AGAINST THE WORLD."* The 50-year cycle came back around to completion when the *"Lord of Hell"* arrived, marking the 50-year anniversary of Adolf Hitler and the plunge into World War II.

Hitler's empire was an occult, astrological, bureaucratic Machiavellian master of efficiency. It terrorized Germany and the world. Other than the U.S. becoming Amerika, what direction will be taken by the emerging New Age global One World Order to bring the world under the rule of a One World Bureaucracy?

Environmental Hell - Out on a Limb

There is nothing quite like a common scare and a common enemy for bringing people together. All these natural upcoming climatic eruptions will be used in a Machiavellian manner by the elite global controlling occult religious, political and economic/financial powers to panic mankind into surrendering its national sovereignty and remaining freedoms to a One World Order, probably under the U.S. The argument will go something like this: *"We all must work together to solve the global environmental crisis. And the only way we can do that is to have a 'One World Effort,' which means a 'One World Order.'"* Everybody sing!

So, *"we, the people"* are being prepped to accept the blame for all these upcoming naturally occurring catastrophic global climatic events. We are not told that ozone depletion is caused by radiation. Nor are we told that acid rain is formed often by rain water hitting acid soil on the earth which lacks sufficient mineralization.

Think it through. Anyone who controls the environment controls the earth and therefore controls all economic activity, and ultimately, all human activity. Control of the environment is control of everything, total control! This all fits in very nicely with the global, environmental, feminist, political agenda, which is increasingly emerging as the revival of witchcraft. Wicca, or witchcraft, basic to Luciferianism, is based in the lie of *"Mother Earth,"* or *"Mother Na-*

ture." (The earth on its own, without the efforts of redeemed man, operates according to the death-based second law of thermodynamics, which results in conflict, chance, cycles, poverty and death. None of these characteristics of the earth are naturally *"motherly."*)

Historically, a female dominated society is a security-oriented society. This means more government programs, more bureaucracy, and less opportunity and freedom. The August 14, 1989 *US News & World Report* stated, *"Women now vote in greater numbers than men, about 9 million more in the last election. And women have consistently favored candidates who advocate a greater government role in domestic social issues."*

Witchcraft, associated with astrology, feminism, Mother Earth and Big Government, are all linking up. So, during Hell Week, lo and behold, what appears as the cover stories of two of the avant garde magazines, moving us toward the union of occult religion with science? The cover story of the September, 1989 *Omni* was an *"Environmental Special," "SAVE THE PLANET: A 16-Page Activist's Primer to Healing an Ailing Earth."* So much for the religious/political side of the equation. Then *Scientific American* featured on its September, 1989, cover a *"Special Issue."* The cover story was, *"Managing Planet Earth."* So much for the evolutionary scientific link-up.

The *"Lord of Hell"* could not have been more pleased. Celebrating his arrival, *"the"* New Age magazine issued an *"Environmental Special,"* dovetailing with a *"Special issue"* by *"the"* magazine of evolutionary science. The alarm was sounded to *"Save the Planet"* by *"Managing Planet Earth."* It was all a coincidence of course, this simultaneous clarion call for a One World Environmental Effort, just as the *"Lord of Hell"* arrived.

All this was enough to send me off into the wilderness for a hike. As I drove up into the mountains on a steep one lane gravel road, I suddenly came head-to-head with a loaded Pack & Co. gravel truck, pulling a full piggyback trailer. I instantly pulled over to the edge of the road (which overlooked a deep ravine) and stopped. The dump truck was skidding off the gravel and could not stop. I immediately threw my Blazer into reverse and backed up while throwing gravel. All this transpired within a fraction of a second. The dump truck skidded to a stop a few feet from my vehicle. Hell Week almost did me and my oldest son in for good.

So, next I checked my fishing calendar. The *"Lord of Hell"* even messed up the fishing. According to Wright's Fishing Calendar, from August 28 through September 9, 1989, fishing was projected to be *"poor"* every day but two, September 5 and 6, when it was forecast to be *"good."* So, surrounding the arrival of the *"Lord of Hell,"*, even fishing was projected to be *"poor"* for 11 of 13 days. (The Wright fishing categories are *"best," "good," "fair"* and *"poor."*)

So next I check NOAA's *Forecast of Solar and Geomagnetic Activity* for the 30th of August, 1989 to the 25th of September, 1989. *"Solar activity is expected to be moderate to high for the 30th of August through the 10th of September due to the return on old Region 5629...*

"The geomagnetic field is expected to be mostly unsettled to active throughout the forecast period... There is a possibility for isolated periods of storm conditions in response to major solar flare activity."

In other words, both the solar environment and earth's geomagnetic field were in an uproar during the time of the arrival of the *"Lord of Hell." No wonder the fish signed off from biting the hook and dove down deep into the dark waters to hide.*

The *"Lord of Hell"* also drove honest money, gold and silver, to new contract lows during the week of his arrival. And what did the *"Don't worry, be happy"* American people focus on during this critical week? Bread and circuses, or rather beer and football! It was the advent of the new NFL football season.

It was all enough to cause one to throw in the towel and leave the country. And this is exactly what one of the United States's leading historians phoned to tell me for the first time ever he was considering doing, *"leaving the country"* during *"Hell Week."* **COLUMBUS AND THE NEW WORLD...ORDER**

Columbus and the New World Order
(A Wolf in Sheep's Clothing)

April 3, 1991

Buffaloed

We memorized it as children: *"In 1492, Columbus sailed the ocean blue"*...and discovered the New World. Now little more than 500 years later, with the EEC on stream, and U.S. banks required to meet the Basel accords, we are primed for the grand finale which began with Columbus' discovery of the New World - the bigger and better New World Order.

Before Columbus discovered the New World, America was a vast wilderness, inhabited by tribes of Indians numbering about 10 million, or so we're told. The Indians lived in harmony with nature, with each tribe supporting all its members, or so we're told. *"Oh, give me a home where the buffalo roam and the deer and the antelope play"*...where a rigid, dirty, disillusioned, white Army soldier can be converted into a *"noble savage"* who *"dances with wolves."*

First it was *"Earth Day."* Then in 1991, the folks bringing us the New World Order successfully sponsored *"Dances With Wolves."* Both *"Earth Day"* and *"Dances with Wolves"* are profoundly religious statements.

Wolfing It Down

"Dances With Wolves" was nominated for 12 Academy Awards and won 7, including best picture and best director. The Writers Guild of America named *"Dances With Wolves"* as best screenplay of 1990.

The social ramifications of this extremely slick reel of Hollywood propaganda continue to roll as the reshaping of American opinion accelerates in dramatic fashion. The March 25, 1991 *Wall Street Journal* in the center front column featured: *"A Century Later, Sioux Still Struggle, And Still Are Losing. But 'Dances With Wolves' Has Brought New Pride - And Maybe Some Tourists."* The March 25, 1991 issue of *USA Today* featured a major editorial page essay by Patricia Nelson Limerick which headlined: *"Hollywood's chance to get beyond the cliches of Western myth."* Said Limerick, *"For most of the 20th century, when Indians attacked the cavalry, the audience thought, 'Oh, no!' In Dances With Wolves, when Indians attack the cavalry, the audience thinks, 'Thank heavens!'"*

This 180-degree flip of American public opinion is a doublethink which boggles the mind. It is nothing less than revolutionary in nature. It marks the successful discrediting of the basis upon which Western civilization in the

United States stood. A civilization cannot stand for long when its historical roots and values are undercut. *"Dances With Wolves"* accomplished this in one fell swoop of Costner's film clipping tomahawk. No longer can John Wayne shoot once and four Indians fall.

Limerick went on to write, *"The shift limbers up the thoughts and emotions. That flexibility, in turn, permits Americans to face the fact that this nation originated in invasion and conquest, and that shock waves from those events still rattle our world today."* Actor/director Kevin Costner is called a *"Western historian."* ...Limerick really gets into it: *"Virtually every scene in Dances With Wolves reawakens us, as well, to the power of nature in the West..."* The blue and gold clad Western U.S. Cavalry are referred to as *"white wretches."*

Another piece which appeared in *USA Today*, penned by Susan Wloszczyna, headlined, *"Wolves, the new leaders of the pack."* *"The Big Bad Wolf is extinct. Good wolves, start howling...Thanks to Kevin Costner - who put the endangered animal in star's clothing with his Oscar-winning Dances With Wolves - the formerly reviled predator is getting its due."*

Air Conditioning

As an investor, sensitive to the impact of social trends on an emotional, mob-based democracy, which in turn affects our political and financial matters, I urge you to see *"Dances With Wolves."* It ranks right up there as a *"social conditioner"* with *"Patton,"* *"Close Encounters,"* and *"E.T."* The cinematic capturing of the landscapes is breathtaking. The Sioux Indian tribe is depicted as clean, wise, considerate, compassionate, *"noble savages,"* who live in harmony with the earth in sophisticated sensitivity. By sharp contrast, the U.S. Army cavalry soldiers are clearly vile, crass, brutal, stupid, filthy, wretched excuses for humanity, unjustly violent toward both their fellow white man and the Indians, and totally insensitive to their environment. No yellow ribbons for these guys. The buffalo hunters' greed and wanton slaughter of innocent buffalo just for their valuable hides left the audience solemn. A wolf is pictured as a smart, sensitive and shy creature, curious when it comes to man, an animal that is loyal and in the end sacrifices its life as an expression of this loyalty. ...Werewolves take note... All in all, it's a wonderfully spun story. But it's just that, a story, a movie, a myth marked by half truths.

Blowing Smoke...Signals

Yes, there were greedy, butchering buffalo hunters who slaughtered animals mindlessly just for their hides. But there were also responsible buffalo hunters who were aghast at this practice by their fellow white men and railed against it. Yes, there were too many incidents of brutalization of the Indians by the white U.S. Cavalry, but these were not in the majority. The Indians initiated more than their fair share of massacres and often rightfully earned their reputation as *"savages,"* as they were viewed by the majority of peaceful fron-tiersmen and pioneers who settled the West. How many wagon trains went out and attacked Indians unprovoked? Few. Were the Indians' massacres and war-ring against peaceful, westward traveling settlers any more justified than would be Americans today warring against and massacring Hispanics who come up from Mexico, or Vietnamese who immigrated to this country from Vietnam? Of course not.

A main myth had to do with wolves. I promise you, Little Red Riding Hood would never be one who *"Dances With Wolves."* Nor would anyone else in their right mind. Having lived in Montana, I have had the opportu-nity to visit with old ranchers who remember what it was like when wolves used to roam there. To a man, they hate them and want them exterminated. Wolves can be quite mean, and kill not for food, but just for the fun of it. Wolves, these ranchers say, delight in preying on innocent livestock, often just for the joy of killing. The spirit of wolves was/is also part and parcel of the Indian medicine man's black arts, particularly when he was involved with mind-altering drugs. Even the European legend of the *"werewolf"* has its basis in fact, depicting the uncivilized insane who roamed madly through the countryside at the time of the full moon, crying out like the bone-chilling howl of a wolf.

Of the approximately 10 million American Indians who lived on this vast con-tinent prior to the arrival of the settlers, many regularly starved to death. There was no love or compassion shown for widows, orphans or strangers in the land of the American Indian either. Such unfortunates were either appropriated as slaves, or in case of the old, including members of one's own family, often put out to die. What else could be done when tribes live off the land, which is exactly what *"living in harmony with nature"* is. There are unexpected food shortages, and someone has to be eliminated. *"Survival of the fittest"* is the natural evolutionary law of supply and demand. One accurate Hollywood depiction of this was Richard Harris' movie, *"A Man Called Horse."* Today, however, with man as a steward of nature and a Christian ethic brought by the settlers, 250 million Americans are able to live in this country and none have any reason to starve to death, providing the local churches and charities do their job, and the civil government gets out of the picture.

Lewis and Clark's journals describe traveling through northwestern moun-tain valleys where the smoke was so thick due to Indian campfires (air pollu-tion) that they could not even see the mountains on either side of the valley. Further, it was not unusual for the Indians to burn entire forests or set fire to grass prairies to drive out game that were slaughtered as they fled the fire. Clouds of dust from the buffalo in the plains at times rose ten miles in the air. The now fertile fields of Iowa, which feed the world, were once mosquito and vermin-infested swamps, effectively good for nothing, until they were terraced, drained, and the ground beneath tilled to handle runoff so the fertility of the soil could be utilized. Finally, Indian tribes did regularly massacre one another. This was not the case among white settlers.

Evergreen

It's important to keep in mind a basic economic principle, one proven evidentially, both in the present day and historically. People who live off the land live tribally, socialistically. Socialism results in human poverty, environmental abuse, envy and a squelching of individual initiative and creativity. (See Colin Turnbull's *The Mountain People.)* It also results in the lowest common denominator, tradition over innovation, and the lack of a work ethic. Both the people and the environment in such sad situations lose long term. This is true whether we investigate the advance tribal socialism of the Soviet Union and Eastern Europe, where basic human material needs go unmet, where civil rights do not exist, where millions have been murdered and abused, and where the environment has been devastated. It's also true in tribal Africa, Latin America, in the South Pacific and in Indian America.

Living *"in harmony with nature"* really means living in subjugation to nature. If nature turns niggardly, then both people and the environment suffer. Either there has to be a benevolent natural growing season, in which case the population expands beyond its natural limits (the limits of the land) or the limits of a tribe's land have to be expanded to take care of the population increase. This leads to tribal warfare. If expansion of tribal lands is not possible, then it's back to *"survival of the fittest."* The weak die, and the environment is savaged. Not very human, or pretty. The lack of savings, the lack of a long-term, future orientation, the lack of capital formation, the lack of technological development which goes with *"living in harmony with nature,"* inescapably time and time again results in abuse of either the environment and/or man.

This does not even consider the fact that military history has repeatedly demonstrated that a people with a superior technology inevitably conquer and rule over those with an inferior technology. The development of technology is a function of savings, capital, creativity and a long-term view; of men being stewards of the earth and taking dominion, rather than living in subjection to nature...rather than so-called *"living in harmony with nature."* Environmental preservation is a consistent product of excess capital and a long-term view, just like art.

Natural Religious Tales

Let's now get down to the crux of this movie matter, which is at its base religious. First of all, there is no such thing as *"living in harmony with nature."* Nature on its own operates according to the *"survival of the fittest."* *"Survival of the fittest"* is conflict, the opposite of *"harmony."* Nor is *"Mother Nature"* motherly. The characteristics of the natural earth are conflict, chance, cycles, scarcity and shortages resulting in poverty and death. None of these are motherly characteristics. Thus, peoples who live consistently under this tyranny of nature are subjected to this undesirable lifestyle.

Did the tribal American Indians live in continuous conflict or fear of conflict, whether it be from the white man or his fellow red man? Most certainly. Did the tribal American Indian live a chancy existence, dependent upon the whims of nature? In the case of *"Dances With Wolves,"* wasn't the tribe's very survival dependent upon the *"chance"* that *"where the buffalo roam"* would be close to them? Yes, of course. Were the tribal American Indians subject to the cycles of nature, so much so that even their homes had to be relocated with the seasons? Most certainly, in many cases. Did shortages, scarcity and poverty, which were inescapably part of living under the tyranny of nature, continually threaten the American Indian? Of course. And was death a constant threat also, a result of nature's cruel *"survival of the fittest"* methodology? Unfortunately, it was so.

There is yet another important religious tie. The myth of *"Mother Earth"* is basic to wicca, witchcraft, witches and their feministic spirit of the earth, Gaia. The wood used by witches in making their magic wands and the like is the wood of the holly tree, in other words, *"Hollywood."* Further, natural, pagan, feminine deities ruled over the empires of old, the original *"new world orders."* Egypt and Babylon, for example, both were ruled by female goddesses. The *East-West Journal* of December 1990 featured a key article, *"Return of the Goddess."* To the point, this New World Order is in the process of taking us full circle back to the slavery of ancient Egypt and Babylon, complete with their pagan rituals and religions, and demonic feminine goddesses, ruled by a Luciferian elite who manage an army of bureaucrats. It is thus no accident that the radical feminist movement is finding its grounding in witchcraft and pagan goddesses. It is also no surprise that when we read the literature of these hardcore *"Mother Earth"* environmentalists, that we find they think the earth's population needs to be reduced from its present 5 billion-plus level, down to less than one billion. In other words, 80% of us have to be eliminated in order for man to again be able to *"live in harmony with nature."* It's ugly.

One Fell Swoop

Now for the *"Fell"* swoop to the Hollywood root of *"Dances With Wolves."* We were all taught in the public schools that before Columbus came to America, there were only tribes of Indians living scattered across this continent. The only disturbance for centuries was by a few wayward Vikings who stumbled onto the place about 1000 A.D., regrouped, and sailed back home. Correct? But that too is an insidious lie. We were taught wrong. Would Americans believe the careful work of an emeritus professor of Harvard University, a man who was President of the Epigraphic Society, a man who is editor and co-author of eight volumes of decipherments of ancient manuscripts, a man whose book was presented to the White House in 1977 by the American Booksellers Association as one of the best 250 books published between 1973 and 1977 in the United States, a man whose work was published by none other than the prestigious Times Books - in other words, an impeccable establishment figure? Would Americans believe such a man? Such a man is Dr. Barry Fell of Harvard University, who has authored three important books about the true history of early America. Dr. Fell's three books are *Saga America* (ISBN 0-8129-0847-3), *America B.C.* (ISBN 0-671-67974-0), and *Bronze Age America* (ISBN 0-316-27771-1). Well, here's Dr. Fell's chronological listing of dates and events which occurred in ancient and medieval American history, as it appears in *Saga America*. Columbus was a Johnny-come-lately, and American Indians, too, stand back in line when it comes to American settlers.

Between 325 B.C. and 250 B.C. the Carthaginians and Phoenicians traded in America; Roman traders, mainly Iberians, were active in America between 100 and 400 B.C. Jews settled in Kentucky and Tennessee in 69 A.D., followed by a second wave of Hebrew refugees in 132 A.D. North African Christians came to America in 450 A.D., and Libyan science and mathematics flourished in the western portion of North America after 500 A.D. Christian Celts were found in the West, along with Islamic inscriptions, from 700 A.D. onward. Finally, in 1492, Columbus reached the Caribbean and *"discovered"* America. And as Dr. Fell notes, many of the early American so-called Indians were not red men, but white men, with blonde hair and blue eyes.

There are no wild assertions in Dr. Barry Fell's work. There are academic documentation and photographic illustrations of physical evidence presenting the history of America pre-Columbus. Dr. Barry Fell also documents how Old World ocean travelers settled in California and Nevada beginning in the third century B.C. He links the Pueblo Indian culture with the North African cultures. He plots the Norsemen's travels as far west as Colorado and British Columbia. Dr. Fell describes how Thomas Jefferson had suspected a relationship between some American Indian and North African languages. All this is in *Saga America*.

In *America B.C.*, Dr. Fell examines European temple inscriptions from New England and the Midwest that date as far back as 800 B.C. In *Bronze Age America*, Dr. Fell shows Bronze Age Norsemen reached North America thousands of years before the voyage of Columbus and built civilizations along the St. Lawrence River. Records were left behind by these Norsemen of their visits, their religious beliefs, a standard of measure for cloth and cordage, and an astronomical observatory for determining the Nordic calendar year. *"Dances With Wolves"* fans, get this: *"Their [the Norsemen] presence in Canada also seems to explain the later appearance of Nordic peoples on the North American Plains. On the evidence of inscriptions and artifacts found there, some Nordics migrated west and intermarried with the Dakota tribes to form the Sioux nation."* ...Well, well, well. In other words, the Sioux Indian nation so exalted and glorified in the movie *"Dances With Wolves"* was really a descendent of the ancient Nordic peoples! So much for the myth of native Americans.

I heartily endorse all three of Dr. Barry Fell's books. They should be available in libraries and from used book dealers.

Cross Up

Yes, clear evidence of Christianity was found, too, in early America. In *America B.C.*, on pages 326-328, in the epilogue, Dr. Barry Fell presents epigraphs of the birth of Christ and their deciphering. The Ogam inscription found in West Virginia is the work of Irish monks of the sixth century A.D.

Another useful book on the subject, but one which I endorse less enthusiastically, is Orville L. Hope's work, *6000 Years of Seafaring*. Hope includes in his documentation the work of Dr. Cyclone Covey of the Department of History at Wake Forest University. Professor Covey is author of *Calalus*, an account of a Jewish colony that existed at the site of Tucson, Arizona, some 700 years before Columbus. (Dr. Covey is also the author of *Homeric Troy* and *The Sea Peoples*.)

Hope, in *6000 Years of Seafaring*, provides photographic evidence of the Old Stone Tower located in Newport, Rhode Island, which was probably built by Irish monks many years before the Norsemen came to America.

On page 17, Hope comments, *"Practically every world map published in medieval Europe, showing North America, had a passage to the north around the continent. There was a good reason: Norsemen sailed the Northwest Passage before 1350, when it was ice-free for a short time in mid-summer. They left artifacts and housing foundations along the northern coasts of Canada, White Eskimos on Victoria Island, followed whales down the Pacific coast, hunted them in the gulf of California, and left blue-eyed descendants on the coast of Mexico among the Mayo and Yaqui Indians."*

On page 103, Hope writes, *"Brendan the Bold found the Promised Land in 550 A.D. He enjoyed a pleasant visit with monks already there, then returned to Ireland."* On page 202 writes Hope, *"Capt. Peter Wynne, a Welshman, was appointed to the Council of Jamestown by the London Company. In 1608, Capt. Wynne wrote a letter to his patron Sir John Egerton, York House, London. He stated that, 'Gentlemen have been up James River to the Falls. Near the Falls they met Indians who spoke Welsh. These Gentlemen desire me to accompany them on their next journey up stream, so that I may act as their interpreter.'"* On page 204, *"On May 15, 1819, the Public Advertiser, a newspaper in Louisville, Kentucky printed a story of Lieu. Joseph Roberts meeting a Welsh speaking Indian in Washington, D.C."* On page 207, *"In 1804, the Lewis & Clark Expedition was sent up the Missouri River and then on to the Pacific by President Thomas Jefferson. They spent the first winter at a Mandan village which was farther up stream than the Mandan villages visited by Varrenes. William Clark was much impressed by some Mandan women's blue eyes and blonde hair."* Also on page 207, Hope writes how the Welsh under Owen ap Zuinch, in the 12th century, found their way up the Mississippi as far as the Ohio. On page 209, *"Both legends and facts show that white people lived in the mountains of West Virginia long before Columbus. There are religious messages and astronomical information carved on stones in Irish Ogam and Tifinag scripts."*

No Dancing Around

I know I have presented here a plethora of *"truth shock."* But there's no good reason to dance around the issue. All this will take some time to settle out. It makes us wonder, that if the purpose of education is the search for truth, just what have we been taught in the public schools? Is there really a difference in what students are taught in the state schools in the United States and the former Soviet Union? Are both effectively State Indoctrination Networks (SINs)? We know we and our children have been propagandized in American public schools and universities when it comes to democracy, socialism, big government, money and economics. Now we know we've even been lied to about our own early history. What about science, health and religion? Our educators are howling like wolves while pretending to bleat like sheep as they sail us into the New World Order. Goodbye Columbus.

EASTER/EARTH DAY UPON US
April 12, 1990

Darkness and Scattered Light

A major conflict in the heavenlies, worked out in the spirit of man and in creation, is dynamically underway. At issue is power and freedom.

Easter is about true *"power to the people"* - individual power. Easter is about God through Jesus restoring to man individually (and ultimately collectively) the full spectrum of electromagnetic power, spiritual and material power, supernatural and natural power, spirit and law, so that each man is a self-governing priest, ambassador and steward. Government (ambassador) is religion (priest) applied to economics (steward). Easter is about the initial and ongoing establishment of the counterclockwise unwinding of darkness into light.

Socialism - In the Back Door

The deception of Earth Day is just the opposite. Earth Day is about power to the elite in a clockwise spiral back down into the darkness of paganism. And the deception is oh, so smooth. After all, who in their right mind would argue against what's good for the environment? Everyone's for the environment. After all, *"we're all in this together."* And there's the snag. The *"we're all in this together"* argument is the back-door route to globalism, a one world order, to comprehensive socialism. Environmentalism/Earth Day is the *"land"* argument for socialism. It is the other half of the communist/socialist approach to the *"labor"* side of the *"land"* and *"labor"* economic equation.

The argument for global communism was just as smooth. After all, who could argue against the idea of human equality, rulership of the proletariat, power to the people, and universal cooperation that communism promised? But it didn't work out in the real world. So the *"people/labor"* approach to global socialism has been canned in favor of the *"land"* approach, using environmentalism, beginning with Earth Day.

The bait's been taken - hook, line and sinker. Americans have changed their shopping and living habits to help protect the environment, including recycling newspapers, glass, aluminum, motor oil and other items. This, of course, is truly wonderful. But over the next twenty years it's going to come down to a few Spirit-guided men who are self-governing according to God's supernatural law versus a spirit-guided elite who globally rule over the masses through bureaucracy in socialistic slavery. (Islam is an economic wildcard. The New Age unifies science with spirits.)

Controlling people directly, as in socialism/communism, is not subtle. As a result, it brings about both active and passive - direct and indirect - resistance. On the other hand, controlling people indirectly through environmentalism is very effective. It is very subtle. When the environment is controlled, the means of production are controlled, and so people are totally controlled. It is the other half of the one-two punch - *"labor"* socialism plus *"land"* socialism. And actually, labor socialism is already in place. The West is moving toward Russia as Russia moves toward the West in the synthesis of Hegel's dialectic. Debt slavery, the legal system, the public schools, mass media, the AMA, ABA, the Federal Reserve, RICO, the IRS, EPA and OSHA are already in place to assure compliance.

The April 9, 1990 *New American* focused on the socialistic nature of this environmental power grab.

Socialist Environmentalists

The lead essay in the February 1990 edition of the socialist journal *Monthly Review* should put aside any doubt that the international left plans to rely increasingly on environmental issues in its attacks on free enterprise. The article, by Jack Weston, a retired professor of English literature and an old lefty, also suggests that many of those currently leading the environmental movement are closet socialists.

"At present only a few of the ecological writers who know that capitalism is the cause and enemy will be explicit," Weston writes. *"Authors fear that if they name capitalism they will be red-baited or at least not treated as respectable by ordinary readers conditioned during the Cold War to suspect critics of the system they are taught is natural and best. Socialist commentators on ecology must discard these old fears and adjust to an urgent time of life-saving social change. We must be open with our non-sectarian, new, and enlarged socialist politics and name the enemy: capitalism as a mode of production."*

Weston also urges old-line socialists to put their knee-jerk atheism aside and be open to an alliance with New Age mystics who share their notions about big government solutions to environmental problems. He has particular praise for a manifesto called *"The Dream of the Earth,"* written by Thomas Berry and published by the Sierra Club.

"The future he describes is attractive to socialists, although there's some ritual, shamanism, and dream vision that will take some getting used to," writes the ecumenically-minded Weston. — Source: The New American

How extensively are the earth's people being duped? Said David Brower, president of the Sierra Club, *"But this Earth Day [1990] has the potential to capture the world's concern for the planet and truly change the course of history."* Absolutely. Slaves of the New World Order get to unite under a common global bureaucratic monster which created this environmental problem in the first place.

Descent Into Witchcraft

I was invited to attend the 9th Annual Fourth World Assembly in 1990. The theme was *"Community Empowerment for the Ecological Age."* Scheduled to speak was Judith Plant, an editor of *The New Catalyst Quarterly*. Ms. Plant discussed her book *Healing the Wounds: The Promise of Ecofeminism*. She made a presentation *"...on the intimate relationship between the ecological and the feminist transformations of our society."*

Longtime *Reaper* readers will recall that I have oft stated that the political and economic roots of radical feminism will eventually be grounded in witchcraft. Actually, the link-up has already been established. Environmentalism and the concept of *"Mother Earth"* are rooted in feministic witchcraft. (Religion always comes down to economics.) The unrecognized lie, however, is that the earth is no mother. Without the stewardship of law-abiding, long-term oriented, peaceful men and women, she (Mother Earth) is instead a first class witch. The natural characteristics of the earth are conflict, chance, cycles, poverty and death, the result of the earth's natural *"survival of the fittest"* modus operandi. Who would want a *"mother"* possessed of such natural characteristics?

Plucking the Pigeons

It is we, dear readers, who are targeted in this global environmental power grab. Investors are the capitalists and free enterprise entrepreneurs who are seen as the enemy of the environment.

Lies and More Lies

Paul Ehrlich, who long ago should have been discredited as a population expert, told a Pittsburgh conference in 1990 that each rich person in the United States does a thousand times more damage than an individual born in a poor Third World country. So now we in the West are being blamed for damaging the planet twenty to a hundred times more in our lifetimes than a poverty-stricken Third World individual. Horsefeathers! The greatest pollution and environmental degradations are found where bureaucracies reign supreme (former East Germany and all of Eastern Europe, including the former U.S.S.R.), and in the Third World. In first quarter, 1990, the U.N. Conference on Trade and Development began talking about a new class of displaced persons in Third World countries. The U.N. called them *"environmental refugees."* The U.N. report declared, *"Growing human pressure on the natural environment has either rendered ecosystems more vulnerable or triggered off a self-reinforcing process of natural degradation, or both."* As it turns out, none of these 42 poor countries are Christian. None practice free enterprise. None have a republican democracy.

The fact that Paul Ehrlich still has credibility is a credit to Joseph Campbell's *The Power of Myth*. For it was Ehrlich, in his best seller, *The Population*

Bomb, who helped plant the environmental seeds for *"this present darkness."* Never mind that Ehrlich's projections have not come to pass. He still has a faithful audience. It was in 1968 that Stanford University professor Paul Ehrlich published *The Population Bomb.* Declared Ehrlich, *"In the 1970s the world will undergo famines; hundreds of millions of people are going to starve to death in spite of any crash programs embarked upon now."* Ehrlich further wrote, *"In 1984, the United States will quite literally be dying of thirst."*

In the September 1969 issue of *Ramparts* Magazine, Paul Ehrlich predicted what the world would be like in 1979: *"By September 1979, all important animal life in the sea will be extinct. Large areas of coastline had to be evacuated, as windrows of dead fish created a monumental stench."* Wrong!

The Real Skinny

In his February 1990 *Insider Report,* Larry Abraham skillfully presented how the elite were manipulating and pulling the strings of the masses in this *"Earth Day"* power grab. Abraham confirmed what socialist Jack Weston wrote in *The Monthly Review.* Environmentalists are often like watermelons, green on the outside, but red on the inside. It's a concealed socialistic movement. Abraham revealed how the environmental movement has replaced war as a means of maintaining cohesiveness in society and justifying big government. This plot was hatched 20 years ago, when on April 22, 1970, President Richard M. Nixon declared the first Earth Day. During the same year, 1970, Nixon also established the Environmental Protection Agency.

Abraham further discussed Harvard professor John Kenneth Galbraith's work, *The Report From Iron Mountain.* In that treatise it was affirmed that economic surrogates for war must meet two principal criteria: (1) They must be wasteful in the common sense of the word; and (2) they must operate outside of the normal supply-demand system. War, after all, is the principal organizing force in most societies. Without war, no government is able to obtain acquiescence to its legitimacy or maintain its right to rule its society. If war is discarded, new political machinery is needed to serve this vital function. *"It may be, for instance, that gross pollution of the environment could eventually replace the possibility of mass destruction by nuclear weapons as a principal apparent threat to the survival of the species. Poisoning of the air, and of the principal sources of food and water supplies, is already well-advanced, and at first glance would seem promising in this respect; it constitutes a threat that can be dealt with only through social organization and political power. But from present indications it will be a generation to a generation and a half before environmental pollution, however severe, will be sufficiently menacing, on a global scale, to offer a possible basis for a solution."*

The Report From Iron Mountain was written in 1967. So here we are, 25-plus years later, and the contrived environmental crisis is upon us, just as predicted. The threat of war is receding. So, this long-term plan of substituting the environment for the threat of war as a means of maintaining big bureaucratic government is being implemented. *"It is more probable, in our judgment, that such a threat will have to be <u>invented</u> rather than developed from unknown sources"* [emphasis added].

Those who are now accruing power to supposedly solve the environmental crisis are the ones who caused it in the first place, and who are using outright lies and doctored facts to frighten the masses. Putting government bureaucratic puppets, whose strings are pulled by multinational debt capitalists, in charge of caring for the environment is the equivalent of putting the fox in charge of the hen house. Big government and big multinational debt capitalism - who have raped the environment and are also partially responsible for devastating Third World countries - are the drug addicts in charge of the pharmacy.

Real Answers for Real People

The solutions to the environmental problems on a decentralized power basis have been with us for some time. I agree, the 1990s are the *"decade of the environment."* Actually, the earth is about to massively burp earthquakes and volcanoes which will cleanse the planet on its own, regardless of what man does.

Thank goodness key leaders of the environmental movement, with whom I share much common ground, are beginning to recognize that their issues are being taken away from them by the establishment. But right now, it's a divide and conquer issue, just like it has been for years with the Far Left and Far Right politically. If the Far Left and the Far Right in this country ever got together and seriously talked, they would realize that they are looking at the same problem from a different angle, and that their common enemy is big bureaucratic government/business, manipulated by multinational debt capitalism.

Starlight Connections

The 1990 *"Earth Day"* extravaganza was not chosen randomly. It was chosen astrologically. As astrologist Robert Cole wrote, *"Unity is the Key to 1990."* The problem is that astrology has always been used by the elite as a method of timing their plots to build global empires and enslave the masses. For reference see my last book, *No Time For Slaves*, chapter 12, *"Star Light - Astrological Slavery."* Here's what Robert Cole had to say regarding 1990. It goes a long way in explaining why this global Earth Day celebration was targeted for this year.

The year 1990 is blessed with a phenomenal astrological event. It's a very rare event that happens once every 682.9 years. This is a close alignment of three planets: Saturn, Uranus and Neptune. This alignment is a signal point which describes the opportunities we have for realizing unity. We can use this alignment and trace it back through history and see what previous generations have done to create unity in times of crisis. The last time there was a Saturn, Neptune, Uranus alignment was 1307. In that year Edward II reigned in England; France was ruled by Philip VI. The Swiss confederation was formed during this period. Politics and economics were unified under these flamboyant European leaders and we see an era of urban renewal beginning. The previous alignment was in 626 A.D. The Chang dynasty unified all of China and a great golden era in China began. In Persia the empire was restored under Darius the First and Byzantium declared peace with Persia. The true cross on which Jesus was crucified was returned to Jerusalem. In Arabia, Mohammed unified the nation under the new Muslim religion. In Japan we see the various tribes unified under Fujiwara Kamatari. In India, Harasha unified all of northern India and converted the whole nation to Buddhism. If we go back one more cycle we find ourselves in 55 B.C. The high point in the Roman Empire is 55 B.C. We have the official announcement of the Great Triumvirate which unified the Roman empire. Julius Caesar ruled Italy and Gaul. Pompeii ruled Spain and England. Crassus ruled Egypt and Byzantium. In 54 B.C. Crassus destroyed the temple at Jerusalem so you can see how unity does not just blossom in a great golden age but these are times of a lot of chauvinistic fascism where there is a strong urgency to create unity throughout the world and unity is forced on people rather than shown to them as an enlightening awareness. **Mantra Magic?**

This war in the heavenlies comes down to economics, finance and markets. Religion always comes down to economics, just as faith boils down to works. *"Ectopia," as Otto Scott named it, was first a war in the heavenlies, but now comes down to earth, as confirmed by other religious activities. Specifically, the April 5, 1990 issue of The Wall Street Journal,* pages A14 and A15, presented a two-page spread on *"Unified Field: Programs to Bring Perfection to Every Area of National Life."* This incredibly expensive two-page WSJ advertisement was paid for by the folks who follow *"His Holiness, Maharishi Mahesh Yogi,"* who is based at the *"Maharishi Capital of Heaven on Earth,"* Maharishi Najar 201 304 U.P. India.

The thrust of this advertisement by the Transcendental Meditation (T.M.) folks was how, due to the Unified Field, it is possible to eliminate century-old problems of administration of society through the application of the Unified Field in all areas of national life - education, health, economy, rehabilitation, agriculture, government and defense. *"What is fortunate is that only the square root of one percent of the population of a country practicing the Maharishi Technology of the Unified Field in any one place is sufficient to fully enliven the evolutionary qualities of collective consciousness of the nation, resulting in positive, evolutionary trends throughout society."* In other words, one can put to flight a thousand, two can put to flight ten thousand.

From April 8 through April 15, 1990, a large number of people who follow Maharishi Mahesh Yogi's method of Transcendental Meditation assembled in Fairfield, Iowa to attempt to prove their point. The goal of these T.M. folks was to prove that when people meditate in large groups, sociological changes take place which can be measured by standard statistical techniques. Arch Crawford declares that stock markets worldwide tend to rise during such periods.

Points of Light

What about George Bush's political *"thousand points of light,"* linked up to the Comet Austin, which was also projected to give the earth *"a thousand points of light"* as it became most visible April 18, 1990, streaking through our solar system until May 7, 1990. On April 1, 1990 (April Fools' Day), during the halftime break at the NCAA basketball finals, George Bush appeared on national TV to declare the NCAA as *"a point of light."* This linked George Bush with his campaign slogan, *"a thousand points of light,"* the Comet Austin (*"a thousand points of light"*), in the April 1990 time frame, when he referred nationally to *"a point of light."* To quote the March 29, 1990 REAPER, *"Austin is also the political center of Texas, from whence George Bush's political career sprung. Finally, in the ancient world, comets were viewed by rulers with fear and trembling, as they signaled their downfall. Is George Bush riding the tail of a falling star?"* There is a rattling at Skull & Bones.

TIGER BY THE TAIL

April 19, 1990

Reflection on Reality

You know, some days I long for the simple times of 20 years ago when all I did was look at markets and analyze them technically. But I discovered that fundamental events, particularly politics, have a significant effect upon economics and markets. So I began delving into the political realm of contemporary and historical literature and experience. This led to such experiences as interaction with the White House and consulting for the president of Guatemala in the early 1980s. Next, I found that science, and particularly solar, planetary, geomagnetic and electromagnetic influences, dramatically and consistently affect the markets and the economy. My turning point work kept demonstrating this truth time and time again, often calling market turning points to the day months in advance. So the study of the data issued by the likes of NOAA (National Oceanic and Atmospheric Administration), the research of Dr. Iben Browning, Dr. Raymond H. Wheeler and others became very important. Also Tesla physics and its later developments became increasingly relevant. But one thing kept leading to another. Behind money, behind markets, behind economics, behind politics, behind science and energy was always the spiritual realm. The evidence led to the conclusion that *"government is always religion applied to economics."*

If we know any one of the three (government, religion or economics) in any nation or social system, we can project accurately the status of the other two. Government is dependent upon both the abstract, unseen world of religion and the concrete, factual realm of economics. Government draws from both. Abstract religious ideas about right and wrong, ethics and morality, always form the concrete basis for legislation. Taxes paid from the economic arena support government financially. Therefore, every civil government is nothing more than the concrete enactment, the legislation of abstract religious ideas about right or wrong, good and evil. These legislated laws in turn frame and determine the rules (and therefore the behavior) of the human action arena of economics. So the holographic religious concepts held by a people determine the type of government and economic system they will enjoy - or suffer under.

Bureaucracies and the Environment

M. Scott Peck, author of *The Road Less Traveled* and the very important work, *People of the Lie*, was influential in my thinking. Peck effectively dubbed bureaucracies and bureaucrats *"people of the lie."* This helped form my conclusion, *"Bureaucracy is always the greatest collective manifestation of human evil."* In both economics and politics, on both the *"land"* and *"labor"* side of the economic equation, this concept has proven out (religion, too).

Eastern Europe and the former Soviet Union had the most comprehensive, all-powerful bureaucracies on the face of the earth. They have proven to be the greatest murderers and oppressors of mankind (labor), and also the greatest polluters of the environment (land). In the former Soviet Union specifically, 102 cities with 50 million people were exposed to industrial pollution ten times greater than safe health norms. Some rivers of the former Soviet Union are so polluted that when a worker tossed a lighted cigarette into one, that river exploded into fire for miles.

The former East Germany's biggest nuclear power plant at Greifsweld consistently exposed workers to lethal doses of radiation. This facility was called a Baltic Sea time bomb by the West German magazine, *Der Spiegal*, due to hundreds of accidents and near disasters at that plant. Further, the March 1, 1990 *Wall Street Journal* reported that one of the results of Eastern Europe's opening up was the shocking revelation that Eastern Europe is probably the most polluted area on the face of the earth. Ten percent of the deaths in Hungary were directly related to pollution. But it was worse in parts of Czechoslovakia, Poland and the former East Germany. Eastern European countries spewed out more than 17 million tons of sulfur into the air each year. That's the equivalent of five million loaded dump trucks. Emission levels in Eastern Europe per square mile were almost seven times those of the U.S. Huge quantities of nitrogen oxide and heavy metals - lead, mercury, cadmium, zinc and copper - have been linked to the decline of forests there, genetic defects and cancers. And yet most of these countries had strict environmental laws. The former East Germany was specifically called an *"ecological disaster area"* and *"a cauldron of poison."*

Business Week in 1990 reported that 85% of the river water was unfit for human consumption in former East Germany. In Hungary, 40% of the population lived in areas where air pollution was above international standards. And 54% of the sewage discharge there was untreated. More than 770 towns and villages had water unfit for consumption, too. In Bulgaria, experts estimate the Black Sea will be dead within 10 years. In Poland, five regions are ecological disasters, and 60% of the food grown in the capital area of Krakow was unfit for human consumption because of heavy metals in the soil. Fully 3.7 million acres of forest are threatened. Ninety-five percent of the water in Polish Rivers was unfit for human consumption, and 50% was unfit even for industrial use. In Czechoslovakia, mining wastes, nitrates, liquid manure and oil polluted 70% of the rivers. Also in Czechoslovakia, 40% of the sewage was untreated and 50% of the forests were dying or damaged.

Now, who has run, and still runs, the former Soviet Union and Eastern Europe? Who is responsible for these ecological and environmental disasters? BUREAUCRACIES! Omnipotent, omnipresent bureaucracies. So it logically follows that it is total insanity to turn the environmental problem over to an even bigger bureaucracy under the auspices of the U.N. or worse, a cooperative one-world bureaucratic global order. It is the ultimate manifestation of evil and a major source of degradation to the environment. It is a descent into darkness, not a golden dawn.

Of course, bureaucracies by their vary nature limit human freedom. When and where bureaucracies make the laws, administer the laws, and execute the laws, as they do both in the U.S. and the former U.S.S.R., there is no true freedom, only token freedom. So bureaucracies do comprehensive damage to both *"land"* and *"labor."* Today, in the U.S., we have the right to swim around in a very limited manner. Relative freedom is truly no freedom at all. True freedom comes from self-governing men and women who adhere to a higher law, God's law. This results in covenanting and contracting, and taking the long-term view. Then bureaucracies and civil government become minimized and effectively neutralized. Power returns to the local decentralized level, where it can be kept in check.

It adds insult to the injury of our tradition of Western freedom, republican democracy, honest money, and Hebrew/Christian ethics for communism and socialism to exist (or have existed) at all. The former U.S.S.R. was first financed and built by multinational Western debt capitalism. As French writer Anatole France (1844-1924) wrote, *"You believe you are dying for the fatherland - you die for some industrialist."*

Third World Myths

It is equally naive to believe that undeveloped Third World countries live in harmony with their environment. *"The Noble Savage"* is an environmental exploiter. Both World Bank and United Nations studies have consistently shown this to be the case. The U.N. Conference on Trade and Development recently called displaced persons in poor Third World countries *"environmental refugees."* Environmentalism is, like art, a luxury which comes with the excess (savings) of free market capitalism. Where people live off the land, as natural men and women do, much like animals, they increasingly degrade the environment. So the direction this *"Earth Day"* deception is taking us is toward a greater delusion and abuse of the environment, toward less freedom and economic prosperity. The masses are being told to grab a *"tiger by the tail."* They think the tiger is a pussy cat. They are deceived.

More Reflections and Models

As longtime REAPER readers know, the concept that *"government is always religion applied to economics"* has proven out time and time again in our market turning points, in our economic analyses, and in our political discernment over the years. Those of you who have been willing to take the risks have made fortunes based on this word. The basic theoretical model I work with now is this: A personal God through law, love, sound and light works holographically in a clockwise spinning matrix/spiral of electromagnetic energy (only 5% of which we see), primarily in the infrared and ultraviolet ranges, in setting up standing electromagnetic waves, slowed down below the speed of light, existing in what we call matter. In terms of science, we move from the realm of quantum physics, through Einsteinian physics, to the Newtonian realm. Our challenge as humans is not to get too wound up, or rather, wound down into matter and the darkness of the bowels of the earth, where the *"Dark/Black Arts"* (witchcraft) reign as the governor of religion, government and economics. Our challenge instead is to unwind counterclockwise (while remaining grounded in the earth through law and work - salt), and to move from darkness to light, to allow the biological resistors of error in our spiritual/mental/emotional/physical beings to be dissipated so we become truth and light, balanced with salt.

While I have learned a great deal from all religions, what I like basically, practically, about the Christian model is its unique Creator/creature separation, which requires Law, Spirit and salvation to come from outside of man, demanding true humility; and its holographic abstract model, which answers the basic philosophical, political and economic question which has always plagued mankind, to wit: *"How does one balance off the rights of the individual with the collective rights of the majority?"* Not through civil government, which has historically been the oppressor of the people through its bureaucracies and military, but rather through covenant and contract, which is freedom based. Such at one time was basic to the Christian West. The God of the Bible is both the *"One and the Many,"* Father, Son and Holy Spirit, separate and yet united. This provided the holographic model, the dialectic tension, for resolving the dilemma of how to balance off the rights of the individual versus those of the collective majority. Further, this God works through the means of covenant and contract - Old Testament (Old Covenant) and New Testament (New Covenant). So the holographic model from this *"Father of lights"* thus wound down clockwise through quantum, Einsteinian and Newtonian physics to the created realm; and man, made in the image of God, emulated God by the use of covenant/contract and Law-abiding behavior.

Of course, covenant and contract requires human freedom, and maximizes individual responsibility while balancing off collective rights, also maximizing individual power and economic prosperity. Further, covenants and contracts are the essence of how *"government is always religion applied to economics"* on an individual and social level. Both bring true power to the people.

When men operate according to covenant and contract, they take a long-term view, aligning themselves with God in the hologram, who is eternal; they serve their fellow man before they serve themselves, which balances off the rights of individuals with the rights of the collective majority. The covenant/contract provides mankind with the only way to achieve both love and money, thus meeting both of the created needs of *"made in the image of God"* (love) and *"formed from the dust of the earth"* (money). A covenant/contract is also a religious document because it's no better than the morality of both parties to the contract. It is a legal document with recourse, and is an economic instrument because it provides economic benefits and sanctions for both parties to the contract. Using the covenant/contract, men emulate their *"Father of lights."* There is then peace and harmony in the hologram, between the super-natural and the natural. When men covenant and contract horizontally, they balance with the vertical. On the other hand, the predators and parasites in bureaucracies have no moral accountability, no legal exposure, no incentive to serve. They effectively play god-making, administering and judging their own laws. They are the epitome of evil.

At this other end of the spectrum we also find the earth-based *"Dark/Black Arts"* of witchcraft. Such literally derives its power from the dark bowels of the earth, from hell itself, where the burning of sulfur reigns supreme and dark-room light exists. (Yes, Martha, this is just like the smell of sulfur which emits from the bowels of the earth at the geysers of Yellowstone, and also like the colors of Halloween - orange and black.)

What is the favorite type of wood used in making the wands and other instruments of witchcraft? The wood of the holly tree. In other words, *"Holly-wood."* As the February 5, 1990 *USA Today* reported, *"Hollywood is casting the spotlight on environmental issues."* Now let's link up these models with present reality.

From the Earth

Names and symbols are important. In the infrared range, form, frequency and substance all are interrelated. A form, matter, will emit or attract a certain frequency, depending upon its shape and substance. In other words, everything is an antenna. We live in part of the infrared range, literally where we do not see. *"We walk by faith, not by sight."* So while all actors and actresses are by no means witches or warlocks - far from it - a significant number are. It could not be otherwise, given the infrared reality of *"Hollywood."* And many actors and actresses have been innocently caught up in the deception of this *"Earth Day"* environmental movement. They have literally caught the *"tiger by the tail."* How could it be otherwise? The concept of *"Mother Earth"* is basic to witchcraft, too. Witchcraft - Mother Earth - Hollywood - Earth Day. *USA Today* provided a list of the celebrities who have followed Robert Redford's lead in the environmental movement.

Celebrities Lend a Hand

A sampling of stars and organizations or causes they support.

Greenpeace

Brigitte Bardot	Christie Brinkley	Belinda Carisle
Pee-Wee Herman	John Hurt	Jeremy Irons

Earth Communications Office

Roseanne Cash	Mel Gibson	Ron Howard
Quincy Jones	Dudley Moore	Oliva Newton John
Ron Reagan	Meg Ryan	Dennis Weaver

Enviromental Media Associates

Kevin Costner	Melanie Griffth	Don Johnson
Norman & Lyn Lear	Edward James	Bette Midler
Olmos	Robert Redford	Robin Williams

Rainforest Foundation

Sandra Bernhard	Sting	Gelnda Jackson

Brazilian Rain Forest

Tom Cruise	Harrison Ford	Peter Gabriel
Richard Gere	Grateful Dead	Jennifer Grey
Daryl Hall	Harry Hamlin	Gelnda Jackson
Madonna	John Mellencamp	John Oates
John Ritter	Mimi Rogers	Sade
William Shatner	Carly Simon	Oliver Stone

Heal the (San Francisco) Bay

Justine Bateman	Kim Carnes	Morgan Fairchild
Goldie Hawn	Ken Olin	Patricia Wettig
Dweezil Zappa	Moon Unit Zappa	

American Oceans Campaign

Lloyd Bridges	Carol Burnett	Ted Danson
Danny DeVito	Sally Field	Kris Kristofferson
Chris Lemmon	Marlee Matlin	Rhea Perlman
Ally Sheedy		

Others

Linda Evans - Take Pride in America

Michael Landon - Kids for a Clean Environment

Paul McCartney - Friends of the Earth

Meryl Streep - Mothers and Others for Persticide Limits

Barbara Streisand - Environmental Defense Fund

Source: USA Today

Now, don't get me wrong or take this out of perspective. *"Earth Day"* would not have the massive following it enjoys if it were not doing a lot of good things. But then again, the greatest deceptions normally are at least 90% true. (Last chapter we discussed how communism conceptually seemed like a good idea. It captured and deceived millions.) It's just that all the good people caught up with *"Earth Day"* have missed that 10% hook (root) which spins off into darkness.

This writer and few others would have any issue with the goals, the agenda, set for *"Earth Day"* and the *"Green Decade."* (Basic to Christianity doctrinally and historically is environmental stewardship.) It's the means to achieving this end which is at issue - that of global bureaucratic slavery versus freedom, of further environmental degradation versus environmental integrity.

Black Time

So why does this *"Earth Day"* cauldron brew during the month of April each year? Astrologically, this time was predestined, as discussed in the last chapter. The concept of *"Mother Earth"* is basic to witchcraft. The earth is coming alive at that time; it's spring. It's a time of earthly power. May 1 is the highest day of the year of the ancient religions of witchcraft, and is known as Beltaine - *"May Day."* It is geometrically 180 days/180 degrees/6 months, the equal opposite, of Halloween.

Isn't it interesting that the word *"Mayday"* is also the word of distress broadcast by ships and aircraft in trouble. Further, it was no accident that communism was unleashed on the world on May 1.

Because government is religion applied to economics, this spiritual clash of the titans should have a dramatic influence on government, economics and markets as it filters down, if past history holds true. Earth Day on April 22 is a mere prelude to the May 1 confrontation. And Hollywood (the wood of witches) is in the thick of it. The April 12, 1990 *USA Today* declared, *"A two-hour 'Earth Day' special will be among the most star-studded events on April 22. Participating will be Bette Midler, Robin Williams, Barbara Streisand, Kevin Costner, Goldie Hawn, Jane Fonda, Dan Akroyd, Meryl*

Streep, Kurt Russell, Jessica Lange, Sam Shepard, Dustin Hoffman, Danny De-Vito and Rodney Dangerfield. USA Today further declared in its April 12, 1990 cover story: *"Environment is right for chic cause....Environment is a 'risk-free' cause."* This is the same issue of *USA Today* which warned us about *"The Debt Bomb."*

The April 9, 1990 *WSJ* headlined, *"Countdown to Earth Day: Ecology Goes from Hippies to Recycling."* The *Journal* declared, *"No one is sure how the change occurred, but environmentalists agree something remarkable is sweeping the nation. People in all walks of life are worrying about the health of the planet. Fear of the Earth's future has taken a grip on the mainstream."*

Easter/Earth Day

In the last chapter, I didn't want to muddy the waters by trying to make too many points at once. Therefore, I focused on how this grand Earth Day deception, formulated over 20 years ago by multinational debt capitalists, is back-door socialism/communism. The same folks who financed and gave us atheistic, satanic communism over 70 years ago with the upbeat idea of collective rulership by the people and abolition of the state, are now bringing us environmentalism as a means of also enslaving the masses. Communism/socialism was the front door, direct, *"people"* approach to the one world order. Environmentalism is the *"land"*/indirect/back door attempt to achieve the same thing. Now, here's what I edited out last time and saved for this chapter because I did not want to confuse the primary issue. It is this: Easter in its historical sense is directly linked to Earth Day and antagonistic to Christianity. Allow me to explain.

The crucifixion, death and resurrection of Jesus is an extension of the Jewish Passover. Easter is something entirely different. Easter has been as much as three weeks removed from the Passover, as was the case in 1989. As religious historian David J. Meyer wrote, *"The epitome of age-old pagan religions of Lucifer, as practiced in Egypt and Babylon, was the worship of Mother Earth, also known as Gaia or Gaea. Gaea or Mother Earth was considered the oldest of the deities and all gods were subject to the laws of this goddess. The religion of the Gaea was the worship of nature and environment, also called mother nature or nature..."*

Meyer stated that the rainbow symbolically was/is seen as the *"necklace of the Great Mother."* The pot at the end of the rainbow stems from the pot as the womb symbol of *"Mother Moon"* or *"Mana"* in which she kept the souls of the dead. This in turn is directly linked to the witches cauldron. *"The rainbow was also referred to as the seven veils or stoles of Isis, the Egyptian goddess that the Babylonians called Ishtar (pronounced Easter)."* The ancient religious teaching *"...is that the goddess Easter (Ishtar) used the rainbow to block the sacrifices and prayers to the Heavenly Father in order to punish him for sending a flood upon the Mother Goddess's earth people..."*

Note that originally the rainbow was a symbol of a covenant between God and man not to again destroy the earth with water. Is it any wonder Greenpeace named one of its ships the *"Rainbow Warrior?"* Ever listen to the Muppet, Kermit the Frog, sing *"The Rainbow Connection?"* It's about magic.

Meyer continued, *"...We know that Easter has its origin in Egypt and Babylon, which accounts for the adoration of Easter's Egg. The ancient people believed that the moon goddess ovulated on her 28 day cycle at the time of the first Vernal or Spring Equinox. The egg fell to earth and landed in the Euphrates river, where it hatched and Mother Ishtar (pronounced Easter) was born. The ancient people colored and venerated the egg as a symbol of the mother goddess. Since the moon had to be impregnated by the sun in ancient Babylonian religion, Easter day always had to be on a Sunday or day of the sun. Thus, we have Easter Sunday which is followed by Easter Monday or (Moonday, day of the moon)...Easter is always the first Sunday after the first full moon after the Spring Equinox. This is pure witchcraft as witches always reckon time by the full moon. God told His people Israel to mark time by the new moon...The festival of Easter is mentioned only once in the Bible (Acts 12:4), as a day that the heathen king Herod kept."*

And who was crowned Miss Universe on Easter, April 15, 1990? A girl from *"Hell"* - Hell, Norway - named Mona Grudt. Coincidence, of course. Mona Grudt was even nicknamed the *"beauty queen from hell"* (AP).

Past and Present

In the book of Revelation, specifically Revelation 13:14-17, the evil model for how *"government is always religion applied to economics"* is presented. (What goes around comes around in the hologram.) Economics is the new means to be used to the end of global slavery for the purpose of achieving a one world political order and a universal religion. Bureaucratic control of the environment through the deception of environmentalism is control of economics. When people lose control of their means of production, of material things, of their ability to buy and sell without governmental approval, they are totally enslaved. So the decade of the '90s as the *"Decade of the Environment"* is going hand-in-hand with increasing one world governmental control over economics. Ken Gerbino wrote in his *Investment Letter*: *"The United States' military muscle is now of less importance with the fall of communism, and the U.S. does not have as much power as it had in the past when we were the 'protectors of the free world.' Economic muscle is what will count in the future. This will put Germany and Japan in a stronger position than we've seen since World War II, and it's going to make the U.S. monetary policies more dependent upon them."*

With the reunification of Germany and the establishment of the EEC in 1992, the reestablishment of the old Roman Empire in Europe will be intact to establish global economic slavery. Margaret Thatcher saw the EEC as a means of establishing social and political control and eliminating national sovereignty. This is why she was under so much pressure. She was resisting the beast.

Some establishment writers have even recognized this. Alexander Cockburn, writing in the April 12, 1990 *Wall Street Journal*, declared, *"So the newly emerging world model is not the notion of 'free market' but authoritarian capitalism...In Latin America, moving from military fascism to market fascism..."* The same folks who raped the environment in the first place are now bringing us the economic solution? Market fascism is Hegel's dialectic in practice.

Finally, Ron Paul, in his *Investment Letter* reported on a *"Wish List"* produced by Wall Street insider David Lipschitz, written for Shearson. This wish list included all national currencies being converted to a new world currency effective December 31, 1996. This new currency would be backed by the debt of the World Bank, which has the power to tax Americans, the Swiss, Europeans and others. A checkless and cashless society would exist by 1998, eliminating all black market activities (free market activities) and tax fraud. A computer system would exist to control and drive the world's financial system, and would be housed in Basle, Switzerland, in the former Bank for International Settlements, which was renamed the Bank for Global Settlements. Everyone would have an International Debit Card by which they would transact business. Use of this card would be the only way in which people could *"buy and sell."*

Interesting. Trilateralist professor Richard Cooper, writing in *Foreign Affairs* magazine, the insider Council on Foreign Affairs magazine, announced that a global one-world currency could be achieved by the year 2000. *The Economist* forecast a one-world currency, the Phoenix, would be possible by 2020. Australia just announced a New Money: plastic notes with holograms, new colors and raised printing on both sides. In a very real sense, the world is coming down to God or money.

Let's face it. There are very few of us left, less than 4% of Americans, who have any capital in the historical free enterprise sense of the word. As investors, we are a fleeting remnant. Therefore, we have to husband our *"nest egg,"* so to speak (pardon the pun). At minimum, we want to be out of debt (death). We, the middle class, are the target of a plot to reestablish an ancient global system comprised of only rulers and slaves. This decade is the set time for its implementation. The environmental pussy cat the people of the earth think they are grabbing hold of is really a tiger intent on consuming the unwary and deceived. We want to make sure we don't grab a *"tiger by the tail."*

* * * * *

When it comes to conservation and environmental integrity, on a scale of one to ten, I rate myself a solid eight. We live in the country. Our family activities focus heavily on staying close to the earth - gardening and animal husbandry. I would dare say there is not another family out there which has won as many prize ribbons as our family has at the annual county fair for our plants, produce, flowers and animals. Further, I risked my life working in Guatemala in 1983, in an attempt to turn that country into a natural foods growing center. These earth-based activities keep us grounded, settled down, with a root in ourselves. We are *"formed from the dust of the earth"* and basically created to be *"gardeners."*

The essence of good physical health lies in the biofeedback mechanism of staying close to the earth and its Schumann resonant frequency of 7.83 Hertz, the frequency, incidentally, at which all healers heal. In fact, healers of all religions who get too far away from the earth and are still attempting to heal become weakened. It follows therefore that cities are basically unhealthy for man. Today, we live in a sick city-based world, literally and otherwise. (The city is a jungle.) So I tend to not trust intellectuals from all camps who are not grounded. This deep abiding suspicion carries through to an Earth Day celebration which has its origin in the pagan world cities.

The very name and nature of THE REAPER is earth-oriented. I have written in THE REAPER from time to time throughout the years about my love for animals, wildlife and God's creation. Further, having a child whose pancreas is locked up with pesticides has heightened my environmental concerns (no thanks to corporate agriculture, herbicides, pesticides, and absentee ownership of the land).

I guess when I boil it all down, I believe God basically created us to be stewards of the earth and to live peacefully with everyone. Before the good Lord used any of His great saints He had them spend time out and away (Moses and David for example). This means each of us need to be gardeners, and to sit literally under our own vine and fig tree. This is the only way we can ultimately stay healthy and balanced. After all, the color green, the green of life and of the creation, is the middle color, the balance color, in the visible electromagnetic spectrum.

From both my study and work around the world, in both developed and undeveloped countries, I have concluded that the only procedures that work long term to bring about environmental integrity are: (1) Strict limitation on absentee ownership of land - people must own the land where they live and work and be accountable for it; (2) no man should own more land than violates (a) the spirit of community, and (b) environmental integrity; (3) honest money, created in the country, out of commodities or representatives of commodities; and (4) men who take a long-term view, operating in a free-enterprise, primarily local economy, who covenant and contract with one another. This way power is localized and the nuclear and extended family are the bloodline natural safety net, while the local church and community are the non-bloodline spiritual safety net. In the fall of 1987, Dr. Lester Thurow (MIT) and I discussed how modern technology, distribution systems, transportation and communications make this possible today.

Needless to say, we have just the exact opposite of this today. Absentee ownership of land is rampant. City magnates centralize governments and through their bureaucratic minions and debt capitalistic corporations maximize the absentee ownership of land. These folks are not accountable for the land they use in absentia. We have lost our sense of local community and with it environmental integrity.

We are equally far removed from honest money, gold, silver and monetized commodities or the receipts for those monetized commodities, including computer entries. Today instead we have fiat money and fractional reserve banking where money is created (counterfeited) out of thin air through the multiplier effect. Caribbean pirates never had it so good.

Further, power is centralized rather than decentralized. The masses of individuals have very little power today. There are no local, caring safety nets. Nearly everyone is short-term oriented, in an evolutionary, dog-eat-dog, every-man-for-himself world. As a result, the land has been mined, drugged and poisoned, and depleted of its inorganic and organic nutritional value. So how are the sickest people, who manifest characteristics the exact opposite of those necessary to bring about environmental integrity, going to pull this rabbit out of a hat and save the environment? Answer: They're not. A tiger does not change its stripes. We are going to be pulled down as these predators attempt to make us slaves and further destroy the environment. The coming earth changes - earthquakes and volcanic eruptions - will cleanse the earth where man fails.

SECTION III

Science and Technology

THE END OF THE AGE OF OIL
April 4, 1985

(The Cornucopia of Energy)

If you were fascinated by Bruce Cathie's comments in his book *The Bridge to Infinity*, then the interviews in the August and September 1984 issues of *The Moneychanger* with Colonel Thomas E. Bearden of Huntsville, Alabama and Mr. Joe Newman of Lucedale, Mississippi are worth their reading weight in gold, or at least in energy.

To titillate your interest, here are some of the quotes extracted from those interviews with Colonel Bearden and Joe Newman.

Colonel Thomas E. Bearden: *"...What upsets me about our Western science is the prevailing attitude of trying to suppress anyone who wishes to study anomalies. They attempt to impress upon a graduate student that there are no anomalies, that everything is already completely explained...all the electromagnetic textbooks are totally wrong at base level."*

Regarding Tesla, *"There are subtle energies that can be set up in the electromagnetic realm and you can tap them from now to infinity.*

"I tell you this: their basic control mechanism on which control of everything else is founded, control of finance, energy, etc., is the control of science.

"And I believe Morgan did that, and the reason was because Tesla, in trying to get more money to finish that tower at Wardencliff had finally revealed to him that he was going to give the world free energy. Morgan knew, if all you could do was sell them an antenna, you couldn't sell them the energy, that would end his lock on energy and end his empire. I believe there have been hundreds of other scientists similarly crushed in pure Mafia style. Tesla wasn't one of them. They made him a non-person by pulling the financial rug out from under him. Their fundamental keystone support is the control of science. It's not accidental that we get the hounds of hell on us when we come up with an heretical idea in science. It's not accidental that you can't get a dollar from the vast sums of money spent on the energy problem. Look at where the money goes. Nobody is doing research on what we're talking about. Physics verifies that a vacuum has plenty of energy. Just ordinary physics."

Bearden goes on to talk about the Philadelphia Experiment, and why we support Israel. The reason the United States continues to support Israel economically is not only because of the Jewish financial and political clout in this country, but also because Israel is the only other country that can militarily offset Russia in the use of Tesla weapons of war, such as the Tesla Howitzer.

Bearden commented, *"If I reach out and put energy in (instead of taking it out) you get what's called a high pressure cell. If I can reach out and cause lows and highs, I can control the weather all over the continental U.S. They [the Russians] have been doing it since early 1983."*

Bearden commented further concerning the Russians, *"They are not going to do it with nuclear weapons, because they don't care about New York City or you and me, but they do care about that farm land and they don't want polluted, radioactive farm land. If I put a cold explosion on New York City, everybody freezes within seconds, regardless of their arctic clothing. Layers of clothing or walls or electric blankets do no good because it sucks the heat out of every part of your body on the inside. There is no barrier to it. You can't get in a foxhole or a pillbox; it does no good because I can just place a cold explosion inside there and it sucks all the heat out and you freeze to death."*

Tom Bearden is no slouch. He has just signed a multimillion-dollar contract with Energy Resources Unlimited, a Sacramento-based corporation. He holds a Masters degree in nuclear engineering from Georgia Institute of Technology. He has also confirmed that globally at least four energy-motors are working or are in advance development. One exists in Switzerland. The Japanese (Hitachi) have one based upon Sieki's work. But the most publicized is in Germany.

The German equivalent of our Department of Transportation had its engineers take a normal motor scooter, power it by an electric motor, put a battery on it and run the machine until it stopped. It ran eight kilometers before it drained the battery. Next, they took the same scooter, put on a fresh identical battery, but then clamped on the energizer. The scooter ran for forty kilometers before the German engineers shut it off. The battery was fully charged and was overheating. Free energy!

The Soviet Union was conducting tests and experiments with free energy on Bennett Island in the Bering Sea. The Russians were very near to a commercial breakthrough.

Comments by Mr. Joe Newman: *"I'm 48 years old, I invent for a living, and have since 1961. I've always been curious all my life. I didn't get along well in school; I always asked the teachers questions they couldn't answer...I will not be intimidated by people."*

Newman had done some startling work with some revisions of the scientific work of Michael Faraday and James Clarke Maxwell. Regarding this he comments, *"I'm sure there are a few people motivated by money and power, but I think the major resistance that one runs into is the general scientific community. You see the same thing in science throughout history. Those who made the great contributions are always persecuted by their colleagues. If a person just looks at the facts and asks himself why is it that way, he makes discoveries, if he isn't chained to the ideas of his time."*

Regarding the U.S. Patent Office, Newman commented, *"The guy was so biased and prejudiced he told me at a meeting, 'I don't think I'll ever be able to give you a patent no matter what evidence you present to me'...The patent examiner did not even read my information, and readily admitted that he had not read it, which is totally against the law. "* In the U.S. Court for the District of Columbia, on October 31, 1984, the former commissioner of the Patent and Trademark Office, Special Master William E. Schuyler, Jr., commented on Joseph Newman's work: *"Evidence before the Patent and Trademark Office and this court is overwhelming that Newman had built and tested a prototype of his invention in which the output of energy exceeds the internal input of energy; there is no contradictory factual evidence."*

Newman has done some interesting work in explaining the commonality between magnetic fields and gyroscopic action. This, according to the reading that I've done over the years, also ties in to the UFO phenomenon, which I am increasingly understanding in a mechanical sense, not a mystical one. Once the scientific basis is discovered, the so-called magic disappears. The problem historically has been that much avant-garde technology was and still is controlled by occultists or suppressed. It needs to be recaptured.

Newman also has done some excellent work regarding energy and matter conversion in an electromagnet, linking it with gyroscopic action and Einstein's $E=MC^2$. It's not that difficult to understand either.

What is becoming increasingly clear to this writer is that the work of Nikola Tesla, Bruce Cathie, Michael Faraday, James Clarke Maxwell, Joe Newman and Colonel Thomas E. Bearden and others in energy is similar to what the Wright brothers accomplished in aviation. We are on the verge of a scientific revolutionary explosion in our new understanding of physics, mechanics, energy and chemistry which will make our present technological age look like a dark age. Perhaps most chilling of all is the probability that this scientific information has been available for decades and is being exploited secretly by the government. We already know it has been suppressed. What has become obvious is that these marvelous scientific breakthroughs are purposely not being taught in our public schools or universities.

There are a number of other creative, competent scientists and inventors who have been literally run out of this country because their entire approach to physics has been nonestablishment. And all of these men are operating under the same principles in open energy physics as I have found operable and fundamental biblically in open-system economics. You see, as long as we are fed the lie that we live in a closed system of limited resources and limited energy, man remains in conflict with every other man. This justifies the rise of an empirical, tyrannical government as the great mediator, the Great Mother, who equalizes, redistributes wealth, and resolves conflict, while really feeding its own bureaucratic parasite. But oppressive government today, planned by the coercive utopians (as an economic parasite), also yields to the dictates of high-placed money interests. So, ultimately, money is the god of this world.

Rather than have a bottom-up decentralized system where freedom, responsibility, accountability and prosperity are evident, we have flipped it upside down. We now operate like all the pyramid-type, pagan, slave-state empires that went before us. The order, from top to bottom, should be God, government, economics. With this order comes decentralization, freedom, responsibility and prosperity. Today, it is flipped over - economics, government, and then God is effectively dismissed.

Benjamin Franklin saw this empire problem clearly. He opposed salaries for those who worked in the executive branch of government. Benjamin Franklin recognized that men have two passions, both of which have a powerful negative influence on the affairs of men when combined. These are ambition and avarice, the love of power and the love of money. United they are poison. Today, with government and money united, (a fact since the late 1800s, the age of the Robber Barons) men have blocked out, for their own selfish short-term interests, through manipulation of education, the glorious information and explosive technology possible through wealth for all economics and wealth for all energy.

Special interests do not want all men becoming prosperous in time. Men who are prosperous are free on earth. They can't be controlled. So, those in power limit the access to wealth for all economic activity and energy.

Back to energy. Dr. Carey Reams, in one controlled experiment after another, measured the amount of soil, water, and nutrients fed to food-producing plants. And yet, consistently, the total weight of produce yielded by the plants (not to mention the weight of the plants themselves) was far in excess of the weight of the materials that went into them. Where did the extra weight come from?

I have noticed this phenomenon in my own greenhouse. Energy and matter being interchangeable ($E=MC^2$), from where does the extra energy/matter come that produces an abundance of tomatoes whose weight far exceeds the amount of soil, water and nutrients utilized by the tomato plant? It comes from the sun (photosynthesis), from the air. Energy from the air is transformed into matter. It's free. Matter is commodity. Commodities are wealth. Unlimited energy means unlimited wealth; wealth for all!

The concept of economic wealth for all and the perspective of the earth as an open system are what I am finding possible in energy - open energy systems. Hilscher, in his book, *Energy In Abundance*, listed generators that interact with surrounding energy fields, designed as open systems. This is in stark contrast to our present closed systems of energy technology, such as gasoline and diesel engines, steam turbines, and nuclear power generators.

There is simply no such thing as empty space. There is even energy in a so-called vacuum. Space is filled with an extremely energy-rich subatomic, prephysical state of matter which can be utilized as an energy source or converted into matter. This is what Tesla accomplished and kept trying to tell us. This is what this new physics' technology is all about. Tesla planted an antenna in the ground and presto, instant energy. Bruce Cathie has recently confirmed that antennas are planted on the ocean floor and on land at the exact locations where the earth's energy acupuncture meridians pass. Instant, free energy! The earth is alive, much like the human body.

A REAPER subscriber, who is also an M.D., wrote to shed some more light on Cathie's and Tesla's work:

"...The system of grid-like energy projections which Cathie discovered and wrote about in his book have been written about for the last century by the British Ley hunters. Alfred Watkins was the one who originally described ley lines in England and essentially all he did was rediscover the old ley system which was in use from prehistoric times. There is now a ley hunters guide, ley hunters journal, etc., in England and this is a fascinating topic. When Cathie describes the location of the British Observatory where Greenwich mean time was originated he was probably unaware of the original siting of English cathedrals along ley lines. Alfred Watkins and others in their original descriptions told how the Greenwich Observatory was sited along the previous energy grid. The people who did this were not ignorant of what they were doing. At any rate, the ley lines which cover the earth connect points of energy. These points of energy are essentially areas where non-physical matter is condensed into physical matter. You might look at them as tiny white holes. Aborigines to this day use these spots as communication devices. If one were to sit, for instance, on a confluence of ley lines one can communicate with someone sitting on a similar spot around the world simply by thought. In prehistoric times this was a major means of communication."

The March 1985 *W.D. Gann Technical Review* noted that Gann believed that our solar system acts like a large transformer. The sun is the primary coil and the planets are the secondary coils. The size of the planets and the speed at which they circle the sun determine the current, according to Gann's theory. The moon acts as a magnet as it circles the earth. The earth, in turn, acts as a conductor of the electrical currents.

Dr. Chalfin of Cal Tech discussed the pulsed capacitator discharge electric engine, Patent Number 3,890,548, produced by American inventor Edwin W. Gray: *"There does not exist an even distantly similar engine to this one in the world. Conventional engines use up power. In this system, energy is used up for only a minute part of a millisecond. It operates without heat loss and there is no energy loss whatsoever with this system."*

The work of John R.R. Searl with the levity disc in England is under investigation. It is a gyro-flywheel high energy density mechanical magnetic device that shows antigravitational and inertia-free properties. It's a lot like what we call UFOs. It is similar to the mag-lev technology (magnetic-levitation) being utilized now experimentally in Germany and Japan for passenger trains.

Dr. R. Schaffranke frankly stated, *"We are not running out of natural resources or intellectual talent; we are running out of the freedom of innovation that made the countries on the North American continent the most advanced nations on earth."*

The energy that exists free in space can be collected, focused, magnified and compacted by magnets or magnetic materials used as new core materials for converters of all kinds, utilizing available cosmic energy for new technological applications.

If I were a young man (or woman), seeking an exciting, prosperous field, in which to make a contribution to society, this is the direction and the field of study I would pursue.

More information on this subject is available from Energy Unlimited (P.O. Box 493, Magdalena, NM 87825-0493). Also write the Tesla Book Company (1580 Magnolia Ave., Millbrae, CA 94030) and ask for their catalogue of books for sale. Engineers particularly, take a look at the work *Bedini's Free Energy Generator* by John C. Bedini.

Dr. R. Schaffranke has additionally declared, *"As in the past, a formidable inertia of the establishment is not only based on inaccurate, incomplete and outdated information, but also on its reluctance to accept new ideas. The honest search for the truth requires that we first demythologize generally-accepted claims of so-called experts of the past."*

Science, like theology, is layered. The deeper we get, the closer we come to the truth, the more powerful and positive and simple is the answer.

We are very, very close to developing and applying the unified field theory. U.S. astronaut Edgar Mitchell, in a paper delivered in Amsterdam in 1972 declared, *"History has shown time and time again that important scientific discoveries generally happen only when someone steps outside the limits of his traditional discipline and looks at something from a fresh point of view. Then what should have been obvious all along comes into focus. I think we are very close to a breakthrough, very close. In the next few years I predict the development of a Unified Theory of Universal Functioning."* Mitchell made this remark more than two decades ago. We're there now.

In all honesty, it's very possible we've had this unified field theory operative all along, since the late 1940s, only the government has kept it under wraps. In this country, we are continuously sheltered from the truth in so many areas.

Prototypes of the French Kromrey converter have been tested in Strasbourg, France and in Switzerland with efficiency ratings of 140% to 180%. This converter operates on the principle that a very powerful energy field fills all of space, and that this special energy can be tapped and utilized.

The N machine of American physicist Bruce de Palma (whom I have written about before) has an efficiency of 330%. It has been duplicated in both Sweden and Germany. The work of de Palma is based upon Faraday's scientific work. How many American scientists have ever studied in detail or have even seen the work of Faraday? Next to none. It's been blocked out by the establishment.

American inventor T.T. Brown has been able to pull electricity from the crystalline structures of certain rocks, as has the late Marcel Vogel in California. American engineer Edwin V. Gray moved to Holland when his capacitator discharge engine achieved an efficiency of 200% or more, because he was persecuted in this country. It's Semmelweis all over again, who was run out of town (Vienna - 19th century) for suggesting that doctors who had been handling corpses wash up before delivering babies.

The establishment always persecutes the creative avant-garde in every civilization where the pagan/religious, humanistic, socialistic collective dominates and suppresses the individual. As scientist T. H. Huxley wrote, *"'Authorities,' 'Disciples,' and 'Schools' are the curse of science, and do more to interfere with the work of the scientific spirit than all its enemies."* True science was built upon the assumption that the natural order could be understood and put to good use because it was created by a God of order (see *Wealth For All: Religion, Politics and War* pp 79-81).

Just think: the silent air around us is full of words, music and pictures which we can pick up if we have a radio or TV set. The same is true with other energies, if we have the right technology. It's just that simple. Plants have been using free energy all along. And now man has captured free energy from the air and earth, and can put it to good use.

Tesla physics employs opposing forces - not Hegelian thesis, antithesis, synthesis - but opposing forces, truth in tension. Tesla's work in physics is exactly the same in principle as the conversion of matter to energy in an electromagnetic field, which in turn is exactly the work of a gyroscope. All this avant-garde energy technology operates on the principle of opposing forces - truth in tension, the simultaneous coexistence of apparent opposites. This is also the nature of the creative thought of all geniuses - truth in tension, the ability to hold two seemingly contradictory ideas simultaneously separate, yet without conflict - in fact, resolving conflict. It is the principle of the double helix, for example. It is the essence of the dual nature of Christ.

It is also the fundamental modus operandi of biblical law - truth in tension. For example, the ultimate political question is *"whose rights are superior, those of the individual or those of the group?"* These are two opposing forces. The answer is neither. Nor is the answer some conflict-ridden, Hegelian downward spiral of thesis, antithesis, synthesis. Rather, the answer is that both opposing forces, both the individual and the group, have rights, duties and responsibilities. They both simultaneously coexist, in harmony, by the rules of God's moral law. This is truth in tension - TNT! So, what biblical law does is stand between the two, and by so doing, transform the conflict between the individual and the group into harmony by defining the rights, duties and responsibilities of both the individual and the group. It stabilizes Yin and Yang. This is what is also happening as the particles of matter go to the smallest particles of matter in a magnetic field. The particle moves forward at the speed of light and simultaneously spins at the speed of light. This is the speed of light squared, $E=MC^2$. And mechanically it follows the laws of the gyroscope which operate on the principle of opposing forces.

The point here is that the same principle which provides for an open system in harmonious human action (self-interest is best served by service, balancing off the rights of the individual as a byproduct of meeting the rights of the group) is also operative in an open system of wealth for all economic activity and in free energy (Tesla/magnetic, field/gyroscopic) physics! And these free-energy devices can be built with off-the-shelf technology in a machine shop! TNT produces harmony and wealth for all!

We are blind to the potential all around us. We are living in a technological dark age. Science is only a few hundred years old. It's still in its infancy. It's in its prenatal stage, which is the way Dr. Norman Cousins described our civilization in a recent interview in *The Mother Earth News* - *"prenatal."* We are still barbarians who can't handle the technology we've developed.

Let's try another example. Tests have been done where a photograph has been taken of fields infested with insects. Insecticides have been put on the photograph with a resonant pattern of that insecticide then projected onto the field. The result in these tests, where the field was sectioned off into grids for careful scientific control, is that the bugs in those grids treated on the photograph with insecticides have been killed. So we don't need all those chemicals that poison our food and water. We can use sound to kill the insects, as well as let the land lie fallow every seventh year to break up the insect breeding cycle and also let the ground replenish itself.

Colonel Bearden stated bluntly, *"In one cubic centimeter, there is a normal energy, enough to build this whole universe."* Energy and matter are interchangeable. The space between the molecules is so extensive that Bearden's statement has credibility. To bring this down to something we can relate to, how else can a straw be driven into and through a telephone pole during a tornado? There has to be lots of space in molecules, in matter, to allow it. We are the only ones who are dense (pun intended).

We don't need genetic engineering. We don't need to split the atom. (By the way, a scientist in L.A. has discovered that radioactivity is an atomic abnormality, much like fever is to the human body. Radioactivity can be corrected and has been neutralized experimentally, bringing the *"split"* atoms back into the Creator's natural alignment. That's right, radioactivity can be neutralized and corrected. It is an abnormality, and the technology to neutralize radioactivity is available now.)

Cathie has found the key to utilizing the energy locked in the energy meridians of the living earth, just as the Chinese utilize the acupuncture meridians which run the length of the human body. Gravity, electricity, magnetism, and inertia planetary motion, along with new sources of energy, can be explained in terms of opposing forces, the simultaneous coexistence of apparent opposites, existing in gyroscopic action, the TNT (truth in tension) principle.

Again, to restate, because this is so important: what we are discussing here is the fundamental operating principle that God gave man in the abstract moral realm, duplicated in the scientific laws in the physical realm of His creation, which transform conflict into harmony and release an explosive unimaginable cornucopia of plenty in wealth for all economics and energy.

It is mind boggling. It is glorious. It is heaven come to earth, again. It is a unifying principle between the abstract and the concrete, between God's moral law and the long-hidden principles necessary to recapture His creation from disorder, conflict and poverty - indeed from Satan himself.

The oil industry is obsolete. Opposition physics is to the oil industry what the automobile was to the horse and buggy. Utilities as we now know them are horse and buggy vintage. The entire multinational oil, multinational banking, communistic/debt capitalistic empires, with all their support institutions, are potentially finished, done for. Our options will be either a "Brave New World," or freedom and wealth for all.

We are so close, oh so close, to being able to use this technology for the good of man, that twenty years from now it will make our lifestyle of today look like that of the cavemen. And yet, we are also oh, so close to blowing ourselves to hell.

Technology is neutral. It can be used for either good or evil. We are moving fast down the spiral road toward a culmination of an unimaginable evil in the 1987-2012 time period, the end of which will be the logical cause and effect result, the most bloody, brutal, pagan and warlike century in human history. We had better get our act together and get it together fast.

What is also troublesome is that if all this technology is already in existence, waiting on the government's shelf so to speak, to bail us out in the next few years as we face perhaps a trumped-up nuclear confrontation, then, the price of our temporal salvation will cost humanity the exchange of its freedom for the security and peace found in a one-world empire, which is united politically, religiously and economically. C.S. Lewis's *That Hideous Strength* comes to mind. The word that comes to my mind to describe the next ten to twenty years is simply *"awesome." We are living in the twilight of the end of the age of oil, and the dawning of the age of free energy.*

BRUCE CATHIE REVISITED
May 15, 1986

Without question, one of the most controversial REAPERs I have ever published was the October 4, 1984 REAPER, which featured Bruce Cathie's book, *The Bridge to Infinity*. Anytime, it seems, when we are not dealing with something readily accepted by the Establishment, the quick label of *"kook," "nut,"* and *"occultist,"* are just a few of the labels thrown out by those who fear the unknown and dislike having the comfort of the status quo disrupted. All this just goes to show that we are no different from our ancestors, who did exactly the same thing when anything new and different was introduced.

Everything new is first laughed at, then attacked by the Establishment. Finally, people wonder why this wonderful *"new thing"* wasn't with us all along. Ignaz Semmelweiss, who in Vienna in the 19th century had the audacity to suggest that physicians should wash up after handling cadavers before delivering babies, was labeled a *"kook"* and an *"occultist"* and driven out of Austria. Columbus was called *"demon possessed"* and told he would sail off the edge of the earth. Pasteur's concept of germs was initially labeled *"satanic."* The controversy between Ptolemy and Copernicus was first a question of theological heresy. The telephone, airplane and computer were all labeled to be *"of the devil"* by various churchmen of their day. Two years after the first motorized flight of the Wright brothers in December 1903, *Scientific American* reported (1905) that the flight was a hoax and a prank contrary to the on-site observation of approximately 500 witnesses. Meanwhile, the less religious and more secular members of the general public just dismissed the geniuses of their times as *"kooks"* and *"nuts."* Never mind that it is such *"kooks"* and *"nuts"* who bring us the quantum advances and scientific leaps forward that make a better world for the average man. It just never pays to be too far out in front.

(A quick word to my theologically inclined readers: The word *"occult"* means *"secret, hidden knowledge."* Power, mysteries and magic which cannot be repeated by anyone or explained openly may indeed be occult, *of demonic origin*, as a theologian would put it. However, all things were originally created good. And so it seems that both men and material are supposed to be recaptured theologically and scientifically from the cursed natural order of conflict, chance and cycles to harmony, linear times and dominion. This includes the *"occult."* How often have pagans labeled technology and science that we easily understand as *"magic"*? The American Indians once thought that what made corn pop were the little demons inside. Could it be that *"magic"* may in some cases be technology and science which we do not yet understand, that needs to be recaptured? Chemistry came out of alchemy. Albert Einstein wrote, *"Science without religion is lame, religion without science is blind."* Certainly, the history of new science and the human response to it would suggest that Einstein was correct.

For Christian working purposes, I describe the occult as: (1) anything that God specifically defines as occult; (2) anything that is elevated from the created natural realm to God's eternal realm, which is not directly linked to the sacrificial provision of His son Jesus Christ; and (3) anything from the natural order, man or creation, which is not recaptured from the curse of the earth to the peace of the kingdom.

As many of you know, in late 1985 I was in New Zealand on business. I therefore took the opportunity to look the tiger in the eye and arranged an interview with Bruce Cathie. (Rumor had it that Cathie was dead, an old Establishment trick, designed to kill interest in someone.) What was expected to be a casual two-hour chat turned into an intense eleven-hour discussion of point and counterpoint, followed by illustration, demonstration and documentation. Here is the bottom line: I am not a qualified scientist. Therefore, what I am presenting here hopefully will lead to further study, research and careful investigation and scrutiny. But my pressing question is: Is Bruce Cathie to *"insider"* Establishment modern science and technology what Dr. Antony Sutton is to *"insider"* Establishment history and geo-political affairs?

Dr. Antony Sutton, of course, formerly a researcher at the Hoover War Institute of Stanford University, has carefully documented the occult nature of The Order, a one world political socialistic conspiracy, into which George Bush was initiated at Yale. Dr. Sutton has also documented the fact that the former Soviet Union and the United States are effectively working together. An alarming 95% of the technology the former Soviet Union had procured was given to it, sold to it, or financed by Western civilization. Bruce Cathie, in like manner, discovered a possible occult, geometric, scientific link between the United States and the former Soviet Union. This confirms the observations of authors and philosophers, Gore Vidal and Norman Mailer, who declared that in an overall historical context, the U.S. and the former U.S.S.R. are natural allies. This strongly suggests a one world socialistic scientific conspiracy. Furthermore, this is in keeping with the Hegelian dialectic of thesis versus antithesis equals synthesis. The thesis, the individualistic extreme of monopolistic evolutionary debt capitalism, versus the collectivist extreme of communism, forms a synthesis between the one and the many in a one world socialist state.

Communism is obviously failing. Communists, both in the former Soviet Union and Red China, are loosening up and allowing some state controlled *"capitalism"* in order to survive. Debt capitalism is also failing in the West. How could it do otherwise? The words *"debt"* and *"capitalism"* are incompatible long term. Putting the two words together, is in fact, Orwellian. *"Debt"* is borrowing from the future by mortgaging the past to consume in the present. *"Capitalism"* requires savings from the past through the present for investment in the future. So the *"debt capitalism"* of today is present oriented, while *"capitalism"* itself is future oriented. Thus, debt capitalism collapses into bureaucratic socialism. The synthesis came easily with the bureaucratic Soviet Union, which after all was the Union of Soviet *"Socialist"* Republics. (The

U.S.S.R. collapsed as the West fell, too, since it was dependent upon Western loans, technology and foodstuffs, not to mention the population and pollution problems there.)

Bruce Cathie pretty much fits the stereotype of a research scientist, mentally sharp as a tack. A voracious reader, surrounded by his computers and calculators, Bruce Cathie is a meticulous perfectionist when it comes to his calculations, a man who refuses to compromise the integrity of what he is doing for money or publicity. In short, while I don't agree with him in some matters, I found him to be dedicated to a search for truth. His family exhibits the hallmarks of a tightly knit, mutually supportive group, which has been harassed, questioned and haunted by global intelligence agents. I noted the continuous, careful, guarded evaluation of me, stemming from years of having visitors drop in and out, some scientists, some legitimate inquirers and fascinated readers, some government undercover agents.

Bruce's wife, Wendy, who has read my *Wealth For All* books, is a strikingly beautiful woman, who is deeply loved by the Cathie family. I watched one son, Stephen, read *The Bible For Children* and relate to me the story of Abraham, Moses and David, and how they were all God's *"good men."* Cathie's other son, Mark, a bright entrepreneur in his early 20s, is rightfully protective of his father.

Bruce Cathie is no lightweight when it comes to science and technology. He was educated at Otahuhu Technical College. He was an engineering apprentice prior to joining the Royal New Zealand Air Force, where he became a pilot. In March of 1977 he became a qualified Boeing 737 pilot for Air New Zealand.

Cathie commented that present day airliners have been obsolete for at least 20 years. It was back in 1952, when Captain Bruce Cathie was a pilot with National Airways Corporation, that he and a group of friends made a prolonged evening sighting of a UFO at Mangere, Auckland. Cathie's first book, *Harmonic 33*, presented the theory that the whole world is crisscrossed by an electromagnetic grid system. His second book, *Harmonic 695* contained evidence that this grid system is known to our scientists and being used for secret experimentation, particularly by the nations involved in atomic bomb tests. Cathie's third book, *The Pulse of the Universe, Harmonic 288*, provided formulations of a series of unified field equations. In his last book, *The Bridge to Infinity, Harmonic 371244*, Cathie demonstrated the harmonic nature of physical reality, and today's scientists have at their command a fantastic store of knowledge with which they could dramatically advance the welfare of the human race. This knowledge, however, is being carefully guarded.

One cannot help but wonder, if at some time in the future, during a created and controlled crisis, in order to centralize government totalitarian power, the Establishment globally might drop on us an exchange of food for our firearms, the reappearance of flying saucers and advanced technology with *"wealth for all"* type solutions to our problems - free energy like that discovered by Nikola Tesla, Joseph Newman and Bruce Cathie, and consistent medical healing, such as those which existed before 1930 in hospitals in this country using the multiwave oscillator invented by George Lakhovsky. (The multiwave oscillator healed at the frequency [energy] level rather than the matter level, by electrically energizing the body's cells.) 2010?

Most of us deal with three dimensions - length, breadth and time. However, Cathie related that ten to fifteen years ago New Zealand scientists commented that they were working in fifteen dimensions. A dimension can be jumped, according to Cathie. It has something to do with the idea that each of the eight spaces for electrons in the shell of an atom is first *"filled."*

I watched with a critical and somewhat skeptical eye as Bruce pulled out three full three-ring binders of letters documenting the military and intelligence officials he had worked with in the United States and New Zealand. There was the September 18, 1968 letter in which New Zealand Prime Minister Mr. Holyoake referred to the *"facets"* that scientists in New Zealand used in two-way communication with UFOs. There were also the letters from Colonel Burnett and Col. Lewis H. Walker of Wright-Patterson Air Force Base in the United States, our UFO center. There was the correspondence with leading U.S. scientists, and the documentation of how Bruce Cathie was taken to Seattle to interview for a job with Boeing. But when Bruce refused to sign away his New Zealand citizenship, and a form pledging total secrecy, he had the job offer withdrawn.

There were letters from New Zealand intelligence officials who provide Bruce Cathie with protection now, as has been the case for several years, as he provides the New Zealand government with the results of his latest work. There were also the copious files obtained through the Freedom of Information Act that the U.S. intelligence community had accumulated on Bruce Cathie. And on and on it went.

Question: Why would the clandestine upper level *"insider"* Establishment military, intelligence and scientific community be interested in Bruce Cathie's work (going back for years) if it wasn't valid? Cathie's work is very similar in theory to that of Joseph Newman in Lucedale, Mississippi, inventor of the free energy machine featured in the chapter *"The End of the Age of Oil."* Joseph Newman discussed principles of physics and his invention on nationwide TV on NBC's Johnny Carson's *"The Tonight Show"* (February 27, 1986). Newman has received patents in Spain and South Africa.

Cathie had never heard of Newman. The history of science is the history of the simultaneous discovery of like principles at various places around the world. One may be overcome with the sneaky suspicion that the *"insider"* Establishment is lying to us in physics and basic science, just as it has lied to us in political theory, economics and theology.

For his free energy machine, Joseph Newman's theory proposes gyroscopic motion at the speed of light, spinning at the speed of light and moving forward at the speed of light. Centrifugal force is manifest. Bruce Cathie demonstrated that the harmonic wave-form which creates an atom of matter and antimatter in alternate pulses also has three simultaneous movements - directional, spinning and rotation. But again, Bruce Cathie has never heard of the work of Joseph Newman, and I suspect that Newman has never heard of Cathie.

This Cathie theory harmonizes with part of quantum theory, that life (matter) exists in pulses. We view matter/life as we view a motion picture. There are separate frames of still photographs sped up to make motion appear evident. Cathie postulates this is the matter/antimatter sequence. This in turn links to jumping into a new dimension. To quote Cathie, *"Matter and antimatter are formed by the same wave motions in space. The waves travel through space in a spiraling motion, and alternately pass through positive and negative stages. Matter is formed through the positive stage, or pulse, and antimatter through the negative pulse.*

"Every spiral of 360 degrees forms a single pulse. The circular motion of an electron about the nucleus of an atom is therefore an illusion. The relative motion of the nucleus and electrons through space gives the illusion of circular motion. The period during the formation of antimatter is completely undetectable, since obviously all physical matter is manifesting at the same pulse rate, including any instruments or detectors used to probe atomic structures.

"The period or frequency rate between each pulse of physical matter creates the measurement which we call time, as well as the speed of light, at the particular position in space of which we are aware, at any given moment.

"If the frequency rate of positive and negative pulses is either increased or decreased, then time and the speed of light vary in direct proportion.

"This concept would explain time as a geometric, as Einstein theorized it to be.

"A rough analogy of physical existence can be made by reference to a strip of motion picture film. Each frame or static picture on the film strip may be likened to a single pulse of physical existence. The division between one frame and the next represents a frame of antimatter. When viewed as a complete strip, each frame would be seen as a static picture - say one at either end of the strip - then the past and the future could be viewed simultaneously. However, when the film is fed through a projector, we obtain the illusion of motion and the passage of time. The divisions between the static pictures are not detected by our senses because of the frequency or speed of each projection on the movie screen. But by speeding up or slowing down the projector, we can alter the apparent time rate of the action shown by the film...

"The theory outlined above explains why life has been described as being caused by both a wave motion and a pulse. Both explanations are correct."

The harmonic of the circle is determined by multiplying the radius of the circle times two to get the diameter. The diameter is multiplied times pi to obtain the circumference, which is then divided by eight and then divided by six. Increasing divisions, or multiples of six, provide new harmonics according to Cathie (666). It is Cathie's firm conviction that the unified field equation expressed in terms of light is pure electromagnetic wave form, the key to the universe, and that the whole of existence has been known for some time. As Cathie states it, *"All of creation is light."* Interesting. God is light, but He is also personal.

Joseph Newman stated on February 27, 1986, on *"The Tonight Show"* with Johnny Carson, *"I just set out to figure out the how, why and what of things. To prove to myself that this energy was the real energy, I had to come up with the unified field theory mechanically explaining gravity, electricity, magnetism, inertia, planetary motion and a new source of energy. It took me over fifteen years to do that."*

When a couple of U.S. intelligence agents visited Cathie, he opened up to them and explained how his unified field theory applied to the gravitational fields, making possible the antigravity flotation of discs, as well as the geometrics of the atomic bomb. He said one of the agents became drunk during their discussions and kept saying over and over again, *"How could a common man like you uncover this? How could a man like you find out about this?"* Cathie related that the gentleman was quite frustrated that this *"secret"* had gotten out.

Once Cathie presented it, the concepts of antigravity and antigravitational discs in motion became quite simple. *"The earth is simply a huge magnet, a dynamo, wound with magnetic lines of force as it coils, telescopically counted to be 1257 to the square centimeter in one direction and 1850 to the square centimeter in the other direction (eddy currents), indicates that natural law (sic) has placed these lines as close together as the hairs on one's head."* Interestingly, the Bible speaks of how the very hairs on our head are numbered.

"A spectroscope shows that there is an enormous magnetic field around the sun. And it is the present conclusion of the best minds that magnetic lines of force from the sun envelop this earth and extend to the moon, and that everything, no matter what its form on this planet, exists by reason, by magnetic lines of force." Again, interesting. The Old Testament particularly refers to the sun, moon and earth in what could be regarded as in harmony with Cathie's statement.

Cathie believes that the magnetic lines of force enter the earth at the poles and then carry out a loop path through the body of the earth before passing out of the opposite poles.

"The flow is not in one pole and out the other, but in both poles and out both poles, although the field intensity both ways is unbalanced. It is imbalance that creates gravity. The lines of force of the magnetic field form a lat-

tice, or a grid pattern due to the spin of the earth. This is just like a machine-wound ball of string. The length of string has taken on the form of a ball, and at the same time has formed a crisscross pattern. A small vortex is created at the trillions of points where the lines of force cross each other in the lattice pattern. Each vortex manifests as an atomic structure and creates within itself what we term a gravitational field. The gravitational field is nothing more than the effect of relative motion in space. Matter is drawn toward a gravitational field just as a piece of wood floating on water is drawn toward a whirlpool. So matter is effectively the slowing down of light at the intersections of these lines of force."

Cathie states, *"...my belief that as a harmonic of light is fractionally decreased, the energy which is released is converted to form physical matter."* This is what Joseph Newman has said about his free energy machine, which he has demonstrated and had verified by scientists all across the country. Both Cathie's and Newman's work confirm Einstein's declaration that physical matter is nothing more than a concentrated field of force.

Now let's carry this discussion over into antigravitational discs. The difference in the force fields going into the earth as opposed to those coming out of the earth is equal to 3928.371. This excess of energy flowing into the earth as opposed to energy coming out of the earth (through vortices) is what creates gravity. Stated differently, there are more lines of force (vortices) penetrating the earth than there are coming out of the earth. The resultant difference between the two creates gravity. Or, the lines of force weaken after having worked their way through the earth's resistance, thereby permitting gravity. All an antigravity disc has to do then is to be tuned to a frequency to balance out the difference of 3928.371 to get it to float or become antigravitational. Then, only the pulse rate has to be increased or decreased, which decreases or increases time, to cause movement. It is all so incredibly simple. There is really nothing much to what we mistakenly call a UFO.

Cathie further provided me with a December 1956 Establishment paper entitled, *"The Gravitics Situation."* This work was produced by Gravity Rand Ltd., of 66 Sloane Street, London, S.W.1. Now, as you read direct quotes from this paper, remember it was written nearly forty years ago. How far have we come since then?

"Electrostatic disks can provide lift without speed over a flat surface. This can be an important advance over all forms of airfoil which require induced flow; and lift without airflow is the development that deserves to be followed up in its own right and one that for military purposes is already envisioned by the users as applicable to all three services. This point has been appreciated in the United States and a program in hand may now ensure that development of large-size disks will be continued."

The word *"continued"* tells us that we had these floating antigravity disks over forty years ago. In fact, there was/is a Dr. Townsend Brown who had/has a patent on them. A Project Winterhaven recommended major efforts be concentrated on electrogravitics, based upon the principle of Brown's disks.

We are a movie projector in a sense. We can expand or contract the "T" (time) factor. Angular velocity is the same while linear motion changes. With the speed of light, angular velocity is constant while linear velocity is variable. This gives us our spiral, or our combination of linear and cyclical time.

Imagine if you will a spinning bicycle wheel with a bug crawling up a spoke at the same speed. The bug is moving at the same speed angularly, but at a faster speed linearly the farther out he gets from the hub. (All this links to temperature as well, because at absolute zero we hit antimatter. So to change matter, we use both frequency and temperature.)

In Einstein's equation, $E=MC^2$, E is energy, M is mass, and C is the speed of light.

"Einstein declared that physical matter was nothing more than a concentrated field of force. What we term a physical substance is in reality an intangible concentration of wave-forms. Different combinations of structural patterns of waves unite to form the myriad chemicals and elements, which in turn react to one another to form physical substances. Different wave-forms of matter appear to us to be solid because we are constituted of similar wave-forms, which resonate within a clearly defined range of frequencies - and which control the physical processes of our limited world.

"Einstein believed that M, the value for mass in the equation, could eventually be removed and a value substituted that would express the physical in the form of pure energy. In other words, by substituting for M a unified field equation should result, which would express in mathematical terms the whole of existence - including this universe and everything in it." What Cathie explores in *The Bridge to Infinity* are harmonic unified equations 1, 2 and 3.

I asked Cathie about Tesla's work. He said it was incredibly simple. The earth is covered with static electricity. All you have to do is oscillate this electricity and you can use it. For example, every time a raindrop hits the earth, a static charge is set up. This provides us with an unlimited amount of potential electricity if we can just find a way to oscillate it, which is what Tesla did. Interesting. This is exactly what John Bedini's Free Energy Generator does. It captures and utilizes a static charge.

Regular waves that we use every day flow from the atmosphere to an antenna, to a radio (or TV) and then to earth (ground) in terms of the signals we receive. Tesla discovered how to reverse the process - from the earth (ground), to the radio, to the antenna and into the atmosphere. Thus, we literally have the potential to electrify the entire earth (or the atmosphere as Tom Bearden claims the Soviets were doing with scalar waves). All some poor peasant would have to do in Brazil, for example, is to put a probe in the ground and presto - instant power, once we resonate the whole earth. At the crossover points of the ley lines, the intersection of the earth's energy acupuncture meridians (much like the nerve intersections of the chakras of the human body), are points where energy can be generated or used as well (matter created?). Through the earth's own network this energy could be transferred all over the globe and put to good use. Remember, the earth is simply a huge magnet, a dynamo, with magnetic lines of force. A recent underground nuclear test was conducted at one of these earth energy intersections, and the result was a huge crater and radiation readings popping up out of the earth, all over the earth.

Now, here comes a blockbuster. There are four significant U.S. military installations in New Zealand: Kauri Point, where there are transmitters and electronic research is carried on; Blenheim Station, where the USAF operates an electronic high altitude research station; Tangimoana where a high-frequency receiver is located that falls perfectly on one of Cathie's harmonics; and the Bakernun Space Camera Center located at Mt. John. It was the link up between Mt. John and the New Zealand Russian embassy where Cathie smelled a rat.

Using his harmonic research, Bruce Cathie found in the results of a mathematic survey of the two positions (the Russian embassy in New Zealand and the American scientific observatory at Mt. John), a significant geometric harmonic relationship. The relationship was/is a communication harmonic. The latitude of the Russian embassy location also created a mathematical harmonic relationship to the unified equation. The actual latitude of the observatory also showed a mathematical connection with geometric light harmonics. Therefore, to quote Cathie, *"It would appear that any electronic activity carried out at Mt. John could be monitored with extreme efficiency by the Russians."*

On the surface, this appears to be incredibly stupid on our part, to have a Russian embassy set up on the same harmonic where the Soviets could monitor highly sensitive U.S. scientific/military activity. Being the careful researcher that he is, Bruce Cathie began to dig deeper. Pouring over courthouse records, Cathie found an October 3, 1946 *"Memorandum of Transfer"* which confirmed his suspicion that the Soviets and the Americans were working together, even after World War II was over. (The Soviets were our ally in World War II.) The United States gave the land in New Zealand to the Soviet Union so that it could locate its embassy at the perfect harmonic location. This October 3, 1946 document was signed on behalf of the United States by its senior representative in New Zealand, Avra M. Warren. This *"Memorandum of Transfer"* was also signed on behalf of the Soviet Union in New Zealand by its senior representative, Ivan K. Ziabkin.

We now come to perhaps the most controversial aspect of Cathie's work. Bruce Cathie is protected by the SIS in New Zealand (the Security Intelligence Service) because he has for years been providing his government with data on his work, including predicting exactly the dates, times, and position of nuclear tests. (I inspected the confirming letters.) According to Cathie, a nuclear device itself is geometric, and so falls within the confines of the frequency (harmonic) physics with which he is working. Cathie declares that it takes three things for a nuclear device to explode: The correct sun/earth position and relative motion; a precise geometric point on the earth's surface; and the geometric make-up of the bomb itself. This is why, he declares, the ABM systems, when they were first proposed, were at such weird locations. An antiballistic missile system, for example, might have been located 50 miles outside of a city in a remote rural location, rather than around a major city. People asked why. Cathie asserts that one reason the ABM system was junked was that, although fighting a nuclear war is not impossible, it is impractical, because the opposing parties can predict all of the locations, times and dates when such a surprise attack could be launched. So, from Cathie's perspective, the threat of a nuclear war is a gigantic hoax.

Is this why the New Zealand government has established its extreme and lonely antinuclear position, its *"nuclear free"* zone?

Now, honestly, I don't know what to make of this. What about backpack nuclear weapons and nuclear tipped military shells in antitank weapons? What about the conflicting testimony of Jacob Beser, who dropped both atomic bombs on Japan?

Cathie says a nuclear explosion simply drives the electrons out of their shell into the next orbit. And the reason we can never have a clean nuclear bomb is because we can never perfectly displace all of the atoms angularly. Thus, all such bombs will remain dirty. In any case, it goes without saying that this aspect of Cathie's work deserves some close scientific attention.

Finally, Cathie has confirmed fascinating harmonic relationships in Washington, D.C. involving the geometric placement of the Pentagon and the CIA. The bottom line of this work is that he believes there is some type of unseen, below the surface, controlling, all-powerful government which has knowledge and use of this secret harmonic geometric power to manipulate the apparent economic and political powers of today's world. This brings us full circle back to Dr. Antony Sutton and his work in a different field (using different evidence), which has strongly documented that the same thing is true. It further lines up with the possibility that the world's central banks are in cahoots also. Money runs the world. And it confirms the Hegelian dialectic as it operates today.

I asked Bruce Cathie if he would go to Washington, D.C. to testify, or travel to the United States to speak and lecture. He said he would only consider doing so if he had *"protection."* He said that any time he leaves New Zealand now he is followed, tailed by New Zealand and U.S. intelligence agents. The man is literally awestruck by the worldly power that is behind the geometric harmonic work which he has discovered.

Bruce Cathie is not a confrontational tiger like Joseph Newman. He is (again) a quiet, somewhat frail, humble, rather shy man, but courageous in his own right. I was not able to find in all his years of documented records a willingness to compromise his integrity or his search for truth in exchange for money, position or power. Based upon the evidence I have seen, Bruce Cathie's more than two decades of research deserve careful and open scientific attention, particularly since it is also his allegation that the unified field theory has been operative in high scientific technological levels for years. If this is indeed true, then we have to ask why such tremendous advances are being withheld from the open arena of public information. The answer to that question may be clearly sinister.

* * * * *

Antigravity is evident throughout nature. Water rises through evaporation (antigravity). Trees grow (antigravity). Hurricanes and tornadoes through vortex mechanics lift objects (antigravity). We need to recognize that the other side of heat/death physics is growth/life physics. Newton should have focused on how the apple got up there in the first place, before it fell due to gravity.

* * * * *

One type of UFO, an antigravity disk, probably operates like a gyroscope. If the antigravity disk, the UFO, is gyroscopic in nature, when pressure is exerted on it from the top down, it rises. If pressure is applied from the bottom up, it falls. A gyroscopic antigravity disk (UFO) moves opposite to the direction in which force is applied. So, once the gravitational lines of force are offset, allowing the antigravitational gyroscopic disk to float, then the appropriately applied pressure determines the direction of movement.

* * * * *

The Searl effect was discovered by an English electronic technician named John Searl in 1949. He noticed a small EMF or voltage was induced in rotating metal objects. The negative charge was on the outside, and the positive charge was around the center of rotation. He reasoned that free electrons were thrown outward by centrifugal force, leaving a positive charge in the central portion. It followed that an electrical generator might be built utilizing this principle.

He constructed his first generator in 1952, and tested it outdoors. Its performance and behavior far exceeded his expectations. The armature was rotated by a small engine. It produced a powerful electrostatic effect on nearby objects, accompanied by crackling sounds and the smell of ozone. Beyond a critical rotational speed, the armature continued to accelerate without the aid of the engine. The generator finally lifted off the ground, while still accelerating, and rose about 50 feet, breaking the connection between it and the engine. It remained at this height for a brief period, while still increasing its rotational velocity, at which stage it rapidly gained altitude and disappeared.

Since 1952, Searl and others have constructed numerous generators of varying sizes from three to thirty feet in diameter. Some of them have been lost in a similar manner. They claim to have developed a means of controlling them in the process. — Source: *The Awesome Life Force*

* * * * *

The following is quoted from a late 1985 West German publication, *"Vertrauliche Mitteilungen"*:

"On the 14th of November the Vertrauliche reported (No. 2590, Para. 11), in connection with the theme 'Free Energy', about the CASIMIR-EFFECT, with the help of which zero-point-radiation in space may be changed into usable energy. On the same day, on which you received that issue (namely 15th Nov.) there was entered in the Berlin office of the German Patent Office the patent report of the 'Inventors Association For Energy'. Categorization:

"'Directions or procedure to produce a varying Casimir-analog force and release of usable energy.'

"Now we will see if the Patent Office can free itself from a dogmatic defense of the current theories. Physicists hold their breath! More: Casimir is a Dutch physicist, who worked in the Phillips research labs and in 1948 demonstrated that there are electromagnetic fields in a vacuum.

"The motor of the Berliner 'Inventors Association For Energy' is a young physicist, Sven Mielordt, whose introductory book, 'Tachyonenergy/Hyperenergy/Antigravitation,' you will find on our book list enclosed today. 'Vertraulichen' has, with Herr Mielordt, promised that everyone who orders the book will receive gratis a copy of the patent report.

"To fill things out further: In the October 1985 issue of 'Spectrum of Science,' the American physicist/professor Timothy H. Boyer of the City University of New York published the noteworthy article entitled, 'The Vacuum in Modern View.' Quintessence: In spite of its characterization, the vacuum is no way 'empty.' Each space-area which is free from matter and heat radiation remains filled with a fluctuating electromagnetic field."

* * * *

"I do believe that at least one nation other than the Soviet Union has weapons and devices based on scalar electromagnetics. I have very good data to lead me to make that statement. I do believe that a very, very small part of the UFO phenomena is indeed ships made right here on this world by that nation and by the Soviet Union...The work that was being done in electrogravitics simply went under classification...." - Physicist Tom Bearden in *The Moneychanger*, August 1985

THE RAINMAKERS
June 30, 1988

In 1956 Burt Lancaster and Katharine Hepburn starred in a black-and-white movie which has become an American classic entitled *The Rainmaker*. Predictably, given the fact that Burt Lancaster was cast in the role, *The Rainmaker* was about a man who conned a community, which was caught in the throes of a drought, into believing that he could make it rain. Of course, everyone knows that no one can control the weather. Oh, really?

If we stop and think of weather as nothing more than the result of energy changes in the atmosphere, then we can rationally begin to consider that there is a cause-and-effect logic to the process, the physics of which can be discovered and harnessed. We know, for example, that the heat energy (radiation) from the sun draws moisture from the earth into the atmosphere. Clouds are formed as this moisture condenses on atmospheric particles. When there is enough atmospheric buildup, and the condensation becomes too dense and heavy, it rains.

Man is already duplicating some of the atmospheric weather processes. The equivalent of snowstorms are manmade at ski areas all over North America. Snow machines create the white fluff so necessary for this industry during times when Mother Nature is stingy with her crystallized manna from heaven. Also, *National Geographic Explorer*, in its special, *"The Restless Sky,"* showed how laboratories today duplicate the natural production of a hailstone.

Our atmosphere is literally alive with energy. If we can just discover the physics of how to tap it, there is free energy available for all. If we can also discover how this energy creates weather, then we can move toward controlling the weather.

The March 23, 1987 issue of *Insight Magazine* reviewed the work of German zoologist Urich Warnke, of the University of Saarbrucken. Dr. Warnke, using an oscillograph, was able to measure the electromagnetic fluctuation in flocks of birds as they flew in formation. Warnke discovered that electromagnetism (in the atmosphere) is the probable means birds use to communicate with each other while in flight. There is energy in the atmosphere.

The *National Geographic Explorer* TV feature, *"The Restless Sky,"* also indicated that when a supercooled water drop freezes into hail it releases heat. When atmospheric water condenses into a raindrop, heat is released, too. Heat is energy. So the physics of a heat-release/energy exchange process is clearly involved in weather.

When we stop and think about it, who among us has not seen the awesome power of a lightning bolt streaking across the sky - millions of volts! That's real energy, free energy, in the atmosphere. What if a lightning bolt could be tapped and utilized constructively? Better yet, what if the energy already inherent in the atmosphere, which gave rise to the lightning bolt in the first place, could be tapped? A good thunderstorm shows us the casual relationship between thunder and lightning, and the rain which falls from those energy-excited cumulonimbus clouds. Germany and Russia have both done significant studies on the relationship between electromagnetism and weather, and have reportedly made significant progress in the area.

THE REAPER has reported on Goesta Wollin's observations, confirmed by the Fredericksburg Magnetic Observatory. When there is a radical change in the solar magnetic field, this change is consistently registered in the magnetic records of the earth two to five days before a snowstorm hits. It is as though the sun's magnetic field transfers electromagnetic energy to the oceans. The oceans, which are electrically conductive, then transfer this energy to the atmosphere. This then triggers the snowstorm. It's cause and effect.

We need to realize that whenever light (energy) of any sort radiates a substance, that substance becomes energized due to the photon energy exchange of light. The sun does this naturally. It has been known since 1934, for instance, that excited molecules will emit energy which can be picked up. In 1954, it was discovered that electrons were released by plant photosynthesis.

The purpose of the foregoing mental exercise is to loosen you up intellectually so you may at least consider the possibility that science may well have advanced to the point that it can understand the physics of weather, and possibly engineer weather as well. In fact, such is precisely the case. This writer knows of three gentlemen who have been consistently successful in engineering the weather. They are literally *"the rainmakers."*

Now, please ponder this a moment. We are already living at *"The End of the Age of Oil."* There are at least half a dozen proven free energy devices operating on the North American continent alone at this time. You further know from my *Wealth For All* books and *No Time For Slaves* that there is no excuse for economic scarcity. And now the physics, engineering and technology is available to control the weather. This means there need be no deserts or droughts. The deserts in the southwest United States, Mexico, Africa and Australia, for example, could literally bloom. With *"the rainmakers,"* we can literally have rain on demand. We can unhook ourselves from the public utilities too.

Since control of energy is control of people, with these avant garde systems, the ball game is over for the manipulators of mankind, once these systems become widespread. Since money and power control every society, it is no small wonder that news items concerning these *"rainmakers"* have been spiked, just as the controversial free energy and anti-gravitational demonstration of Mississippi's Joseph Newman have been ignored. What will it take to shake the common man out of his Establishment-induced trance?

The first of the three *"rainmakers"* we will discuss is Jack Toyer, who resides in Australia. Jack lives on Palmers Island, a few kilometers from

Yamba, on the northern coast of New South Wales (NSW). Toyer's home sits on the Clarence River. He is a naval architect and a renown inventor, who has invented such things as a surf ski, an underwater sled, and a therapeutic bed which is used in the Casino hospital there.

Jack Toyer's rainmaking machine has become so consistent that it is now considered a nuisance by the local community. Toyer's *"rainmaker"* is basically a mirror disc, which is three meters across, with small mirrors around its edges. Attached are three infrared lamps. Located in the center is a generator which emits static electricity.

This mirror disc catches the solar rays and reflects them back up. The small mirrors start the solar rays rotating clockwise. The infrared rays given off by the lamps provide extra heat to make the solar rays travel upward at a faster speed. The vortex this *"rainmaker"* creates rises until it literally bores a hole in the stratosphere. When this hole is bored, a vacuum is created which pulls together all the electrically charged particles which are floating about in the atmosphere. These particles then literally short circuit. This in turn causes an electrical storm. The storm pushes down to the earth and causes low barometric pressure. Then the rain comes tumbling down. Quick, neat, simple.

A seven kilovolt ampere generator operates Toyer's rainmaking machine, turning the mirror disc at half the speed of the earth's revolution.

The principle of putting a vortex up into the atmosphere is a very powerful concept. Think about a whirlpool, a hurricane, or a tornado which occurs naturally in nature. There is no more powerful natural source known than these vortexes. Toyer has, in a sense, recreated the vortex process which occurs naturally in nature, and put it to work for the good. ...Wonder if a large enough vortex could be engineered in reverse to stop a tornado or a cyclone?

Our second *"rainmaker"* is Trevor James Constable. He demonstrated time and time again, between February and August 1985, that he could generate rainstorms at will on the high seas of the northern Pacific. Constable videotaped his weather experiments aboard the U.S. Merchant Marine ship *"Maui,"* which belongs to the Matson Navigation Company of San Francisco, California. En route to and from Hawaii, using no chemicals or electricity, Constable repeatedly created rainstorms from high barometric pressure, nearly clear skies (fair weather conditions), using his geometric weather guns. These experiments were witnessed by Captain Ted Dobbs, Commodore K.R. Orcutt and other crewmen.

Trevor James Constable is no novice when it comes to engineering weather changes. He has spent 17 years involved in the research and study of weather modification. His three assumptions, upon which his work is based, are quite straightforward: (1) There is free energy in the atmosphere; (2) this atmospheric energy is technically accessible with some simple, carefully positioned, geometric forms (primarily cylinders and cones - coils and vortexes); (3) this energy inherent in the atmosphere operates like an ocean. It has a tide that flows, which is specific to latitude, season and other factors.

Weather modification, according to Constable, is obtained by simply opposing these various geometric forms (called translators) to the tide of these atmospheric energy flows.

The cones and cylinders used by Constable (vortex/electrical coil geometric forms) are all constructed to *"golden section"* ratios. When Constable's ship moved at right angles to the atmospheric energy flow (for best results), these geometric forms literally begin to stack up the atmospheric energy in a line perpendicular to the heading of the ship. This atmospheric energy buildup effectively caused moisture to accumulate in clouds. The clouds stacked up like cars on a freeway in rush hour traffic until the atmosphere became so overloaded it could no longer sustain the weight of the water. Then it rained.

Each of Constable's experiments had to be conceived and engineered in conjunction with the prevailing specific conditions of both the atmosphere and the ocean. Latitude and the season of the year were also taken into consideration in this weather engineering process for the purpose of achieving weather modification. Simply put, the compression - the buildup of atmospheric potential - caused atmospheric water to accrete. As this wall of energy grew, the moisture in the atmosphere became denser and heavier until it literally rained.

Contrary to Establishment-taught physics, Constable's experiments show that primary force flows from low potential to high potential. This is the reverse of mechanical and electrical potentials as we presently know them.

I reviewed Constable's work in a one-hour videotape produced by TCJ/Atmos Productions. The tape was graciously provided by the late Johnny Johnson of Research Publications. Dr. Anthony Sutton has also reported on Constable's research and experiments in *The Phoenix Letter.* Constable's weather guns were built by Dr. Walter O. Stark of the Technical University of Zurich, Switzerland. Dr. Stark is a top Swiss expert in the field of ionization. Dr. W. Gordon Allen has also been technically involved. Dr. Allen has worked in weather control at Georgia Tech and at Boeing. So we are not talking about con men or oddballs here. We are talking about men of science, engineering and academics, with distinguished track records in the field. Will these men be to the National Weather Service what Apple Computer was to IBM?

(For more information on Constable's weather engineering techniques contact Irv Trent, 1586 Mitchell, Tustin, California 92680, 714/544-7612. Also, contact Borderland Sciences Research Foundation, P.O. Box 429, Garberville, California 95440.)

Before we proceed to a discussion of our third *"rainmaker,"* Dr. James De-Meo, a little more background work in science is appropriate. This digression will help us to understand and accept what is going on here scientifically, rather than viewing *"rainmaking"* as some mystical, occult activity, or a con job.

Of all the frequencies which God has created, the human eye/camera only picks up about 5% of them. In other words, we are just babes on the threshold of science. We've only cracked the surface. We are barely competent scientifically with the 5% we can see. What about the other 95%?

The rods and cones in our eye's camera only *see* and pick up from 0.4 to 0.7 microns/micro-meters in the infrared range. We can only see what the sun makes visible in this 0.4 to 0.7 range. But there is a lot more to the infrared range which is invisible to the naked eye. Interesting is the reality that we live at 10 microns, 10 micro-meters, literally in a frequency range which we cannot see. Given this reality, it is not surprising that 10 microns is where the spy satellites operate. The insects also live and operate primarily in this infrared range. The spy antenna on a spy satellite is nearly an exact duplication of one of the many hundred insect antennae which already exist in God's created realm. Also, the sensilla (spine) structure, which exists on insect antennae, resembles to a startling degree what man has designed to catch frequencies in the microwave region of the spectrum.

What is very important to realize, in this unsensed environment, is that in the infrared range, *form* and *frequency* are inescapably intertwined and interrelated. You can't separate the two. The infrared range therefore is the important scientific link between energy and matter. The form or shape of an object determines the frequency it attracts and emits in the infrared range. Furthermore, the *substance*, the material which an object is made of, determines whether it will give off less or more energy than it absorbs, and how that energy will be dispersed. (All substances are either paramagnetic or diamagnetic in varying degrees.)

This writer spent a day two years ago with Dr. Philip S. Callahan in Wichita, Kansas at the Olive W. Garvey Research Center. We did experiments from the laser computer which demonstrated this *form, frequency, paramagnetic/diamagnetic* reality in the infrared. (Dr. Callahan has spent a lifetime in the study of insects in the infrared range. He retired from a long-time research position with the USDA. He was also professor of entomology at the University of Florida.)

I know all of this is strange and new to most of you. Think of it this way. You know there is energy in the air. Your transistor radios and TV satellite dishes pick up energy from the atmosphere all the time. The sound and sight of these energy waves become heard and visible in your reception units, which we call radio and television respectively. Also, remember back when you used to have a TV antenna on your house. The direction that TV antenna was pointed was important in picking up the correct frequency, the correct channel. But also, the design of the antenna, the shape, the *form*, determined the *frequency* which was received. The *material* the antenna was made of was also important. This is roughly similar to what we're talking about.

You might also think of the work of Trevor James Constable as the man-made equivalent of when a cold front and a warm front collide naturally. An atmospheric line builds up and it rains.

Quoting from Dr. Philip S. Callahan's 1975 book, *Tuning in to Nature* (The Devin-Adair Company, 143 South Beach Avenue, Old Greenwich, CT. 06870), *"The radio band includes the long wavelengths of broadcast radio and the very short wavelengths of TV and the EHF (extremely high frequency) wavelengths of radar. All frequencies shorter than 1 meter long (100 centimeters) down to 1 millimeter long are called microwave frequencies. High-resolution radar and guidance systems operate in this region. From 1 millimeter down to 0.7 micrometers (red), where human eyes see, is the infrared portion of the spectrum. This almost unexplored region of the spectrum contains 17 octaves of radiation and is the largest region. It is also in the natural 'sea' of radiation where we dwell day and night on this spaceship Earth. Human beings cannot see beyond 0.4 micrometers (violet), but insects see into the ultraviolet to slightly below 0.36 micrometers. Insect spines represent the transition between the long metal bars and horn antennas that collect and guide radio and microwave frequencies, and the short insulative (substances like glass) lenses that collect and guide visible and UV wavelengths. A lens may be thought of as a foreshortened and rounded antenna. In the infrared portion of the spectrum, the study of antenna engineering and the physics of optics overlap, and the techniques and mathematics of both must be utilized."*

Water vapor emits energy in a laser-like fashion. I watched Dr. Callahan prove this with his laser computer at Wichita. Further, it is the understanding of the relationship between *form* and *frequency*, and whether the *cones* and *cylinders* in the case of Constable's work were *diamagnetic* or *paramagnetic*, that explains how a *"rainmaker"* functions. Working with paramagnetic and diamagnetic materials in the form of cones and cylinders (vortexes and coils), Constable was effectively engineering antennae in the infrared range, relative to the specific latitude, season, primary atmospheric energy flow, and the prevailing oceanic and atmospheric conditions (barometric pressure) of a particular location. This created, in cause and effect fashion, a buildup of energy, followed by a buildup of clouds to the atmospheric water saturation point, followed by rain.

What we are not talking about here is cloud seeding or chemically changing the atmosphere to cause it to rain. Cloud seeding has been around for years, with questionable success.

Dr. James DeMeo is our third *"rainmaker."* He consented to a stimulating interview with Charlie Walters, editor of *Acres USA*, in the October 1986 issue of that publication (1008 East 60th Terrace, Kansas City, MO 64133). Jim and I have visited about his rainmaking work several times since that interview.

Dr. James DeMeo, formerly a professor at Illinois State University, spent nine years doing field research in the American Southwest with what he calls his *"cloudbuster."*

Dr. DeMeo discovered that the same type of health or sickness exists in the atmosphere as is found in the human body. When the energy in the human body is moving around actively, people are healthy. When it slows down, people get sick. So, too, when there is activity in the atmosphere, the atmosphere is clean, healthy and nontoxic. The weather cycles can flow, which result over time in rain.

When there is a pulsing energy field which is moving and sparkling in the atmosphere, clouds form, rains come, and the weather phenomenon undergoes its natural cycle between rain and dry, back and forth. But the atmosphere can go dead. Energy can cease to flow. In a sense, the atmosphere can become toxic, constipated. When the atmosphere reaches this stale and toxic state, there is no movement of energy. There is no rain. So what Dr. DeMeo's *"cloudbuster"* effectively does is insert fresh, alive energy into the atmosphere, while drawing out the toxic material, and - by an analogy - gives the atmosphere an enema. This way the atmospheric energy can be made to flow again so the rain-to-dry and dry-to-rain cycle can be reactivated.

When the atmosphere goes stale, clouds simply cannot build up. When clouds can't build up to the point that it subsequently rains, we experience what we call a drought. Life forms, whether animal, human or plant, show the sluggishness which results from stale, toxic, and dead energy in the atmosphere. In other words, the atmosphere's toxicity negatively affects the life quality of plants, animals and humans.

Obviously, under drought conditions, in a toxic, stale-energy atmospheric environment, there is little water movement. So what Jim DeMeo's *"cloudbuster"* does is simply revitalize and restore normal conditions to the atmosphere, beginning with having the *"cloudbuster"* grounded into live running water. This grounding into live water allows the atmospheric/surface energy exchange necessary to provide literally a spark of life for the atmosphere. It takes life to create life. (Remember that water vapor emits energy in a laser-like fashion.)

Somewhat like Constable's devices, DeMeo's *"cloudbuster"* apparatus consists of a series of hollow tubes/cylinders (coils).

While DeMeo's *"cloudbuster"* will work in quiet water, like a lake, the *"cloudbuster"* works best in an active, energetic flowing river or stream. This way, as the toxicity is drawn out of the atmosphere into the water, the surface water does not become saturated. There is an intensive and active energy exchange between the active, alive water and the stale water-hungry atmosphere. The cleansing of the atmosphere can continue until a normal healthy state is established.

When done correctly, after the atmosphere is given its *"cloudbuster"* enema, rain will usually follow in 24 to 48 hours, even under persistent drought conditions. DeMeo has consistently demonstrated this in experiments in Kansas, Florida and Illinois. The *"cloudbuster"* even works under cloud-free conditions. Rainworks, the firm with which DeMeo is associated, has experienced an 80% success rate. This has followed over 29 *"cloudbusting"* experiments accomplished with students of Dr. DeMeo at the University of Kansas.

The range of influence of these *"cloudbusting"* experiments is very extensive indeed. Experiments in Kansas had an affect on the weather all the way from the Gulf of Mexico to Canada.

Just how does our atmosphere become so toxic and create drought conditions in the first place? Excessive chemical pollution from industrial processes, agricultural spraying, nuclear power plant operations, nuclear bomb testing, deforestation, and overall general abuse of the earth's living plant cover are primarily to blame.

Everything in the infrared range is an antenna. This includes particularly trees. Trees are the antennae which activate and regulate the water flow exchange between atmospheric, surface and subsurface water. This is why, where deforestation occurs, where the trees are removed, drought conditions follow. Without trees to activate and regulate the environmental movement of moisture, water cannot move. Next, the atmosphere becomes toxic, the land dries out, drought conditions occur, and both the air and land become stale. Depression usually follows.

Rainworks, in its experiments in the American Southwest, Israel and Australia, has found that regions suffering from drought are almost identical to those in the desert. This is consistent with our explanations given above. What does this also say for the toxic, polluted, stale nature of the atmosphere (and the unfortunate people) in the world's cities which control the earth at this time? Their destructive aggressiveness is aggravated by the paramagnetic structures which surround them (asphalt, concrete and steel). World cities are accelerating our civilization's death cycle. How much better, by contrast, is it to decentralize the population by allowing no absentee ownership of land and by permitting only honest commodity money, produced in the hinterlands?

When men live close to nature, they are continually refreshed by the supportive, calming, diamagnetic nature of plants and trees, as well as by the Schuman frequency. Perhaps this is why city people rush off to the parks and the countryside on the weekends - to literally escape, to get recharged, to detoxify, to re-discover life. This is why it is declared, *"...everyone shall sit under his vine and under his fig tree,..."* (Micah 4:4).

The life of the good earth and the life of man are inescapably intertwined. Trees provide us with vital oxygen. We provide trees with vital CO_2. We need each other. But, as one becomes toxic, so does the other. As one is death oriented, so is the other. And man is the determining factor. Man determines the use or abuse of the earth.

With *"Wealth For All"* economics, plus the technology of free energy and *"the rainmakers,"* we can decentralize like never before, even to the point of making the deserts bloom. For, with the engineering of weather by *"the rainmakers,"* we have opened up vast lands (deserts) which were heretofore uninhabitable. Under these circumstances, there will be no such thing as the myth of overpopulation. In fact, we would not even have enough people on the earth to fill the deserts which presently exist. And who knows, with a little advancement in the technology of *"the rainmakers,"* we could probably restore the transparent water canopy which used to hover protectively over the earth prior to the time of Noah's flood. This transparent water vapor canopy not only descended and watered the earth at night, it also rose with the radiation heating of the earth by the sun during the daytime. But most importantly, this water vapor canopy shielded out the harmful radiation which now strikes the earth and reduces the age of mankind. With the restoration of this water vapor canopy, men could again live to be 800 to 1000 years old.

In a sense, life is water. Our bodies are 80% water. There are no prosperous economies where there is a lack of water or rainfall. These three *"rainmakers,"* Toyer, Constable and DeMeo (and perhaps others yet unknown by this writer), have made it possible for us to choose life. We must so choose.

* * * * *

"21 May 1987

"Dear Mr. McMaster,

"...the Southeastern drought of 1986 is a case in point. In that case, the drought was anticipated to last until October, but rains actually began falling on the day after we arrived in the Southeast with the cloudbusters, on August 6. Within a week, heavy rains were falling all across the Southeast, and the drought was broken. The tragedy was that we could not find the $8,000 funds to pay for our expenses until August. If we had such funds earlier, much of the $1.5 billion crop losses could have been avoided.

"I am presently convinced that this technique, in trained hands, has the capability of ending any drought anywhere. Furthermore, it has the capacity to also bring rains in desert lands, which one may consider to be suffering from semi-permanent drought conditions..."

James DeMeo, Ph.D.
Robert D. Morris, M.P.H.

FREE ENERGY BREAKOUT
February 9, 1989

Just about the time man's plight will appear hopeless with regard to climatic deterioration, we will see this new free energy trend explode to the surface. Because we both serve mankind and profit financially from correctly anticipating the needs of man in the earth in the future, I am taking the wraps off some of this energy technology now.

For those of you new to the concept of *"free energy"* and *"free energy devices,"* free energy devices have the ability to use a small amount of power as a catalytic action to allow a large amount of molecular action to become available. These devices then feed back a small portion of the output power to continue the reaction, thereby becoming self-sustaining. An initial power source is required to start the reaction, whether it be a battery or a hand crank. Then the device runs on its own.

The Planetary Association for Clean Energy on July 4, 1988 (Independence Day) released its Communique specifying how new energy technologies could offset the greenhouse effect. This is a dramatic statement of hope, backed by solid research. We do have a bright future in free and clean energy, and in maintaining the integrity of the climate.

COMMUNIQUE

The Planetary Association for Clean Energy, Inc.
La société planetaire pour l'assainissement de l'énergie, inc.

191 promenade du Portage / 600

HULL, Québec J8X 2K6 CANADA (819) 777-9696,

HULL, QUEBEC
July 4, 1988

NEW ENERGY TECHNOLOGIES COULD OFFSET "GREENHOUSE" EFFECT

Clean energy systems that may shape our future as well as clean up our past were discussed and demonstrated at the Third International New Energy Technology Symposium/Exhibition held at the Maison du Citoyen (City Hall) of Hull, Québec, Canada, June 25-28th, 1988.

This symposium was opened by the **Hon. Michel Légère**, Mayor of Hull and closing remarks were delivered by the **Hon. Eugene Whelan**, former Canadian Minister of Agriculture and recently Chairman of the **World Food Council**. The event was sponsored by the **Planetary Association for Clean Energy, Inc.**, an international Learned Society, which has its headquarters in Hull and whose president is **Dr. Andrew Michrowski**, and by the **Advanced Energy Research Institute** (AERI), which has its headquarters in London, England. AERI, whose chairman is **Sir Ian MacGregor** (former chairman of **British Steel Corporation** and the **National Coal Board**) was represented by its executive director, **Mr. Leonard Holihan**.

The 150 conferees from three continents adopted the following conclusions and recommendations:

THE PROSPECT FOR NEW CLEAN ENERGY SOURCES IS EX-TREMELY PROMISING AND WHAT IS NOW NEEDED IS OPEN-MINDED ASSESSMENT BY THE SCIENTIFIC AND INDUSTRIAL COM-MUNITIES AND A WILLINGNESS TO FUND PRACTICAL R & D AND APPLICATIONS BASED ON THE EVIDENCE PRESENTED AT THIS SYMPOSIUM.

WE NOTE THAT SIMULTANEOUSLY WITH The Third International New Energy Technology SYMPOSIUM/EXHIBITION, THE World Conference on the Changing Atmosphere WAS BEING HELD IN TORONTO, OR-GANIZED BY **Environment Canada,** WITH SUPPORT FROM THE **United Nations Committee on the Greenhouse Effect,** CHAIRED BY **DR**. **Kenneth Hare,** WHO IS CHAIRMAN OF CANADA'S **Climate Program Planning Board....**

The Third International New Energy Technology Symposium/Exhibition declares that, we believe that revolutionary technologies which permit a gradual transition from current polluting energy sources can be developed in time, based on what was presented and demonstrated at our conference.

Specifically the Canadian Planetary Association for Clean Energy and the U.K. Advanced Energy Research Institute recommend the international promotion and funding of the crucial developments of the following Symposium highlights:

1) REVOLUTIONARY SOLAR CELL TECHNOLOGY WHICH, BASED ON INEXPENSIVE PLASTIC FILM (BY DR. ALVIN MARKS, INVENTOR OF POLAROID FILM), COULD BRING SOLAR CELL PRICES DOWN TO 5% OF THE CURRENT LEVEL, MAKING THEM COMMERCIALLY FEA-SIBLE AND WIDELY AVAILABLE AT LAST - AND THE U.K. DEVEL-OPMENT OF ACCURATE, FLEXIBLE MIRRORS FOR SOLAR RAY CON-CENTRATION - AND ALSO THE MARKS CHARGED AEROSOL DEVICE TO BE RETROFITTED INEXPENSIVELY TO INDUSTRIAL SMOKE-STACKS AND CHIMNEYS...;

2) U.K. BREAKTHROUGHS IN LOW-COST NEW METHODS FOR MANUFACTURING HIGH-OUTPUT, EFFICIENT THERMOCOUPLES TO

TURN WASTE HEAT INTO ELECTRICITY, THUS ENABLING WASTE HEAT FROM UTILITY AND INDUSTRIAL PLANTS INTO A NEW, RENEWABLE ENERGY SOURCE;

3) THE "MIGMACELL", WHICH MAY MAKE FEASIBLE SMALL-SCALE, NON-RADIOACTIVE FUSION, NOW 4/5 COMPLETE (BY **DR. BOGDAN MAGLICH** OF PRINCETON);

4) RECENT DEVELOPMENTS IN NEW ENERGIES FROM MAGNETIC FIELDS, THE VACUUM OF SPACE-TIME, AND THE EMERGING ETHER PHYSICS (FOCUSED BY **DR. HAROLD ASPDEN**, FORMER HEAD OF I.B.M.: EUROPEAN PATENTING);

5) DEMONSTRATED NEW USES OF ENERGY FOR NOVEL MODE OF PROPULSION USING INTERNAL INERTIAL THRUST WITH POTENTIAL FOR LAND, SEA, AIR, SPACE UTILIZATION;

6) THE POTENTIAL FOR TRANSMITTING ELECTRICITY TO ANY PART OF THE EARTH WITHOUT WIRES, WITH NEGLIGIBLE LOSSES AND CAPITAL COSTS (WITH CONSTRUCTION OF A PILOT PLANT UNDERWAY)....

The directors of the Planetary Association for Clean Energy and the Advanced Energy Research institute have long been aware of a large group of scientists, discoverers and inventors operating at and beyond the frontiers of recognized science. Because these organizations are also aware that these people as a group have largely been talking among themselves, we have assumed the challenge of establishing links and discourse between these pioneers on one hand and established scientists and leaders of government and industry on the other. Both sides were well represented at the conference, and a respectful dialogue occurred.

The Planetary Association for Clean Energy and Advanced Energy Research Institute foresee the need for future such conferences and invite interest and support.

Entrepreneurs who want to establish themselves on the inside track of what may be the next IBM or Exxon should order the transcripts of the First, Second and Third International Symposiums of Non-conventional Energy Technology. These three sets of papers may also be ordered from The Planetary Association For Clean Energy.

Also, for original research, investors should delve into the presentations of the work which has been presented at the Tesla symposiums. Nikola Tesla was the pioneer genius of much of this new free and clean energy technology.

Two other free energy/renewable energy conferences are held in the U.S. each year. They are the Alternate Energy Resources Organization (AERO) Conference, 44 North, Last Chance Gulch, Helena, MT 59601, phone (406) 443-7272, and the International Renewable Energy Conference (IREC) of Mary

Charles and Associates, 2334 S. King Street, S-205, Honolulu, Hawaii 98226, phone (808) 942-9655.

A REAPER subscriber has founded Virtual State Productions, Inc. in Long Island City, New York. Grants have been made by Virtual State Productions for the purpose of establishing a semi-private forum for various technologies. One individual, who has worked with Virtual State Productions, has invented an extraordinary generator with upwards of 150% crossover efficiency, without violating any of the laws of thermodynamics. For information write Virtual State Productions, Inc., 29-14 40th Avenue, Long Island City, New York 11101.

In Seattle, All Source Systems (6018 24th N.W., Seattle, WA 98107 206/782-664) sells an important book, *Superefficiency: Beyond 100%* ($288.00). This book contains important discussions on the Berg motor, Nikola Tesla, The Faraday disc dynamo, the Kromrey patent, Ed Gray's patent, super-conductivity, heat pump technology, the Joseph Newman motor, the self-re-charging battery circuit, Alexander's patent, Howard Johnson's permanent mag-net motor, the Bedini motor, and the SUPEREFFICIENCY rotary power device which has an operational efficiency exceeding 200% after the external power is disconnected. The SUPEREFFICIENCY rotary power device is self-sustaining while driving an output load of 120/240 VAC, 60 Hz, etc.

Old friend Dr. Antony Sutton reported in his December 1988 *Phoenix Letter* on free energy development. The Swiss M-L Converter is an electrostatic device which draws energy from space and converts it into electrical energy. The Swiss system uses the Wimhurst generator and Tesla magnifying coils. In the U.S., Don-ald Kelly, an electrical engineer from Florida, is building similar devices. Dr. Sut-ton also reported on the German Schumacher device with ratings from 4 KW to 27 KW. Also, the WIN (World Into Neutrinos) device, constructed by Dr. Wingate Lamberston of 216 83rd St., Holmes Beach, Florida 34217, phone (813) 778-1274, is based upon the neutron sea of conventional physics. Additionally, the Sunburst machine, which produces electricity from ambient space, was first developed by Bruce DePalma of 1060 Channel Drive, Santa Barbara, California 93108, and du-plicated by Indian electrical engineers. The DePalma "N" machine, rated at 3:2:1 (320% efficiency) is being produced in Germany by Rhewum, Tommernstrasse-12 D-7562 Gernsbach, Mr. Chrystowski, Manager, phone 07224-50550.

Solar Tracking of South Texas, Inc. (1319 N. Mesquite, Corpus Christi, TX 78401, phone 512/882-9722) is working with Bill Muller of Penticton, B.C., Canada in producing a 300% efficiency device. Ulrich Schumacher, 4800 Bielefeld, Germany, is working on permanent magnet motors, as is Shigeru Minato, Permanent Magnet Motors Gijutsu-Shuppan Co., 2-24-6 Tamagawa, Setagaya-ku, Tokyo, Japan 158. Dr. Sutton has a new book on the press, *Handbook of Future Technology.* Contact Donn Peden, (406) 245-6841.

Stan Meyer of Grove City, Ohio, holder of 42 patents, has developed a water fuel cell to produce hydrogen on demand. This water fuel cell can be retrofitted to conventional gas and diesel engines, burns nothing but water and causes no pollution. He has further compounded the technology into producing electricity by using magnetized gas in a cyclotron. The military has picked up on this technology. Contact Water Fuel Cell, 3792 Broadway, Grove City, Ohio 43123, phone (614) 871-4173. Incidentally, the atomic energy yield of a gallon of water exceeds 44,000 barrels of oil.

The technology is now available across the spectrum to solve all of the problems which are facing humanity these days. It just takes collective will and leadership to provide us with a promising future.

* * * * *

Important speakers and papers by speakers delivered at the Symposium on Energy Technology in Hannover, held November 27-28, 1980 were:

Diploma Engineer Hachim Kirchhoff of Herten, Germany. Kirchhoff is a specialist in technical and historical material about the conversion of gravity field energy.

Prof. Dr. Walther Peschka of the Division for Electrical Propulsion Systems and Energy Conversion, German Aerospace Research Institute, Stuttgart, Germany. Prof. Dr. Peschka is a specialist on the research of the propulsion system phenomenon which is based on the conversion of gravity field energy.

Diploma Engineer Rolf Schaffranke of the United States is one of the best students of the history of gravity field energy conversion. He worked with Wernher von Braun at NASA in Huntsville and was employed by Boeing. Mr. Schaffranke is credited with recognizing the original important work of Prof. Townsend Brown. Schaffranke wrote a book entitled *Ether Technology*.

Professor Shinichi Seike, Director of the Gravity Research Laboratory in Ehime, Japan is a worldwide leader in the area of experimental research on gravity field energy. His work in the experimental production of very energetic bundled tachyon radiation is highly respected. The output energy obtained is many times higher than the prime induction energy. Professor Seike is involved in the construction of conversion systems and gravity conversion devices. His book, *The Principles of Ultra-Relativity*, is standard reading in modern experimental gravity field energy conversion.

Bruce DePalma is an American physicist involved with the construction of gravity field energy convertors. DePalma constructs N-machines. DePalma studied at MIT and was a physicist with Polaroid Corporation.

Prof. W.A. Tiller of Stanford University, Menlo Park, California, has worked on the interaction between the space field and biological effects. He is called the successor to the Austrian physician and physicist Wilhelm Reich.

Dr. Hans A. Nieper of Hannover, Germany has spent over thirty years in the area of gravity field research. In 1972, Dr. Nieper's paper, *"Shielding Theory of Gravity,"* related to the tachyon theory of the American physicist Gerald

Feinberg of New York. In May of 1983, Dr. Nieper spoke to the Space Commission of the U.S. Senate and strongly recommended rapid development of practical applications of gravity field energy.

* * * * *

In Australia, Yull Brown of Sydney (Auburn) has made water a major source of fuel. Jules Verne would have loved it - water into fire. A hydrogen economy, based on the electrolysis of water, could be in our future. Brown has demonstrated how an electric current may be used to separate water into its two constituent elements - hydrogen and oxygen. Brown has apparently been able to solve the explosion problem and make a safe gas. Brown has over 100 patents in 31 countries. Effectively a controlled thermonuclear device, Brown's fire is expected to be able to destroy plutonium and other toxic waste.

* * * * *

An organization doing important work on superconductivity and other energy related matters in England is the Watt Committee on Energy, Savoy House, Savoy Hill, London WC2R OBU, Telephone 01-379-6875. This is the organization of Sir Ian MacGregor.

* * * * *

In the United States, Energy Unlimited Publications (P.O. Box 493, Magdalena, NM 87825-0493) is doing important work on *"vortexian mechanics."* Contact Rhetta Jacobson, editor of *"Causes"* newsletter there. Also, excellent free energy research is being done at Borderland Sciences Research Foundation (P.O. Box 429, Garberville, CA 95440).

Additionally, Peripheral Industries, an OTC company, has turned nuclear waste into a safe battery which has a useful life of 40,000 years. Phone Phil Talbert at (503) 257-0912. It won't be long before folks will unplug from the public utilities forever. Henry Worden of MIT has built six solar cars, one of which recently won a 160-mile race at an average speed of 52 miles an hour. Worden plans to manufacture the cars for $3,000 apiece. Sandia National Laboratories of Albuquerque, New Mexico has developed a photovoltaic cell which can transform 31% solar energy into electricity, compared to 10% for silicon cells and 34% for traditional thermoelectric coal and petroleum systems. Even bacterial fuel cells are being developed by scientists at King's College in London. These cells produce up to two amps using sugar as fuel. *"Free Energy Breakout"* is almost here!

* * * * *

India is planning on harnessing the ocean's waves to generate five megawatts of electricity. India will use technology conceived by Britain's National Engineering Laboratory in Glasgow. The wave motion of the ocean will drive the horizontal windmills. Norway and Indonesia are already utilizing this technology.

* * * * *

Dr. Lonnie O. Ingram at the University of Florida has developed a microbe which readily converts inedible and cheap vegetable wastes, such as stalks, stems and leaves, into ethanol at 95% efficiency. Ethanol is the key ingredient in alcohol-added fuels.

* * * * *

For the short-to-intermediate term, from now possibly until the year 2012, I am overall pessimistic regarding the plight of mankind and Planet Earth. However, I am long-term optimistic.

There are only two parts of the economic equation: people and things. If one studies the history of either, one comes to the conclusion that, over time, things are getting better. For example, on the *"people"* side, the history of child-rearing is one of improvement, as is the history of medical care. On the *"things"* side of the equation, technological advances are exploding exponentially. Therefore, the long-term trend for people and things (economics) is bullish.

This hopeful human and technological evidence is in keeping with the two great positive philosophical perspectives which are battling for supremacy in this world: post-millenialism versus evolution.

EXTRAORDINARY SCIENCE
September 24, 1991

Please read this chapter when you're sitting down, it's quiet, and you have time to reflect. Otherwise, it is likely to distract you the rest of the day.

What We Know

It was over 45 years ago that we split the atom and unleashed on the world the *"big bang,"* the atomic bomb. The hydrogen bomb and nuclear power followed. It was also in the 1940s that the Nazis began developing the technology of flying saucers, antigravity devices, and cruise missiles. ICBMs followed. Biological and chemical warfare techniques of hideous magnitude were also created in World War II. Genetic engineering has now come of age. In the Korean War, the reprogramming of man took a giant step forward. The Soviets moved forward with the development of the perfect *"Manchurian Candidate."* We continue to see bits and pieces of how we can program the subconscious and change man. We have sent men to the moon, probes to Mars and Venus. The space shuttle is now an everyday event. Recallable memory can be stored in the electromagnetic field off the edge of a chip. Superconductivity has become reality. Solar power is coming of age. Cold fusion is with us.

What Don't We Know

The foregoing is just a partial list of what we have been told exists today in the realm of science and technology. And even though this is what we have been told, the man on the street, the average American, knows, understands, or cares little about it. But how much really exists out there that we don't know? How much of *"that hideous strength"* is the offshoot of the spiritual realization of Einstein's relativity and quantum physics, which has been developed into verifiable, repeatable and usable science and technology? What truly exists with regard to our ability to reprogram the mind of man down in the theta region of the subconscious? How far have we really come in genetic engineering, anti-gravity devices, free energy devices, and scalar, non-Hertzian technology? Just what really does go on, what has already been established, at those super-secret government scientific labs at Los Alamos, New Mexico? What is truly the state of the art at Pine Gap, located in the middle of Australia? What is the Navy experimenting with and already using in its top-secret research facility in Norfolk, Virginia? After all, the first time/space experiment, which displaced matter in space instantaneously, occurred in the Philadelphia Experiment in 1942. That was over 50 years ago! And we know that science and technology has taken a quantum exponential leap since then. So exactly where are we today? ELF, where are you? Hidden radionically?

We know that press releases on anti-gravity devices went underground in 1956, and have remained classified, out of the public view, since that time. Is it possible that if true science and modern technology were exposed to the general public today, people would react to it in the same manner as aboriginal tribes in Africa react to helicopters? Would they see *"that hideous strength"* as an act of God? Is the spread between what the common man knows about science and technology and the reality which exists today wider than it's ever been in history, even wider than it was in the so-called *"Dark Ages?"* I no longer think so, I know so.

Suffering Scientists

Thank God that government and government-subsidized scientists at their well-financed labs, universities and research centers are not the only ones who receive illumination through the *"skylights,"* or from below, as it were. The history of science and technology, the history of significant breakthroughs for mankind, which has launched him into new eras, is the history of *"tinkerers,"* of private individuals who have been given and are obsessed with the creative urge, who have sacrificed their lives, time, money, reputations and families to research and experiment in their garages and basements in search of truths, the applications of which in their hearts they know exist. These are the *"off-the-shelf men,"* who use *"off-the-shelf technology,"* or who develop their own. They are the counterparts of the *"Death Star,"* *"Star Wars"* oriented government-sponsored research facilities. These are the men of passion, of character and professionalism; great minds, holistic and synergistic minds, blessed with hands-on mechanical skills, working to bring scientific theory and concept into practical, working, useful, productive technology.

These are the men whom a life, love, liberty, law, light-oriented, long-term biased society would lift up. Unfortunately, the character of the modern world is just the opposite of these six *"Ls."* And so such men suffer, are persecuted by the government and the culture-at-large. They scramble for funds, are abandoned by their families, suffer the ridicule of their colleagues, are forced to suppress their thoughts and keep their mouths shut. They are lonely. And yet, they drive on in their relentless pursuit of truth to make this a scientifically and technologically better world.

There is something about the non-stop pain of long-term suffering which humbly grounds a man in reality. Under such continuous pressure, men break and either become bitter or better. They neither have the time nor the interest in the airheads who are wrapped up in the materialism, conflict and leisure orientation of today's world. Nor do they belong to the group of intellectual acid-heads who read books, gather facts, and are ever learning and talking, but do not have the hands-on skills or the hearts to help their friends and fellow man when the need arises. Rather, such men are the point men, on the dangerous edge of life. They are self-assured and have few good, reliable friends. And when these point men get together, it's like the reunion of a platoon of Vietnam War vets. The camaraderie, the rapport, the love is there, perhaps unstated, but never more real. For once, there, they belong and fall under the bell-shaped curve.

Extraordinary Conference

This writer has attended conferences of such men, the Nikola Teslas, the Dr. Iben Brownings, of today. I have attended and spoken at a wide variety of conferences, conventions and seminars. So I speak with authority when I tell you, these are the most unique conferences and groups of men with whom I've ever had the privilege of being associated. I was the invited guest of the 1991 Extraordinary Science conference. I was allowed to be truly on the inside.

Mind Warp

The first day I scrambled to find my footing. Then I got my feet on the ground and made contact. By the end of the intense, four-day conference, my mind had soared to dizzying heights never before dreamed of. I was exhausted. Bombarded by 16 hours of presentations, discussions and interactions during two full days and two half days, mentally filled to the brim and overflowing, I was wrung out. But I had taken another quantum leap in my level of understanding. It was worth it.

I had danced with the men on the cutting edge, the men of courage who dare to dream and break with the chains of culture and conventional scientific thought. These are the men who challenge the new frontiers and the old order to make a better tomorrow. These are the loners who have been persecuted by both industry and government, who have endured grave injustices in search of scientific truth. And not surprisingly, they have been as severely persecuted by their own government than the right-wing tax protestor-types, if not more so.

To Know the Truth

It was alarming to learn that there is just as much disinformation in the public schools and universities today in the areas of science and technology as there is in economics, politics, history, theology and every other subject. This was a conference of mavericks; not bitter men, but caring, concerned men. And believe you me, the earth is in far worse shape than I ever imagined in my wildest nightmare. At the same time, all the answers necessary to solve every social, economic, technological and environmental problem we face out there exists today. And when one speaker talked about how he was consistently able to regenerate life at the microscopic level from death (a dormant state), confirmed by other scientists and videotaped, I asked him how that affected him metaphysically. His eyes began to water, his voice trembled, and he talked about the three lights that leave when life passes from the Newtonian life state as we know it, into the dormant state, the state of sleep, which we call death. (The Bible talks about death and sleep interchangeably.) He spoke with proven conviction as he discussed how there was no way that we could have evolved from monkeys, that the intelligence necessary to create what he had seen and documented through many tedious years of research at the microscopic level demanded the acknowledgment of the existence of a Higher Power, a Creator whose intelligence was beyond any of our abilities to grasp. At that point, the 400-or-so attendees erupted into applause, one of the very few times that occurred during the four-day conference.

Unlike many conferences and conventions, the attendees at this conference were often as bright and as highly respected as the speakers. It was a reunion of great minds, gifted with great hands-on abilities. It was a cross-fertilization process, a reunion, to prepare for the next great leap forward.

The Men and Their Machines

Who were some of the men who attended and spoke at the 1991 Extraordinary Science conference? Dr. Yoshiro NakaMats, the prolific Japanese inventor, holder of over 2,200 patents worldwide, one of the most highly respected and richest men in Japan, inventor of the ENEREX engine, which extracts energy from water, was there. Dr. George Merkl, one of the world's leading biochemists, and holder of over 400 patents globally, spoke, too. Dr. Glen Rein, formerly of Harvard and Stanford, made an impressive presentation. Dr. Roger Billings, whose research and funding by the federal government in hydrogen power spans three decades, talked also. Two of the world's leading experts on the energy, scientific nature, and therapeutic quality of water, Rhetta Jacobson and Walter Baumgartner, made a thought-provoking presentation. Warren York expounded on the unified field theory, bringing Tesla's original work in this area up to date with modern research and documentation. The unified field, as Bruce Cathie has long declared, is not still some unknown. It has been with us for some time.

The ever-stimulating and informative Larry Spring made an excellent presentation on how electromagnetics are neither wave nor particle, expounding on energy and antennas. Mr. Spring is an inspiration and challenge to all men in their 70s to have active minds and make productive contributions. For those who are interested in the Tesla concepts of the steam turbine, turbine pump, and gas turbine, Chuck Parker, Frank Macon, and Sev Bonnie were on hand back-to-back. Dan Davidson spoke about the gravity field sensor, and R. Andrew Michrowski talked on *"Y-Field Scalar Aerial Units."*

Stan Meyer made a powerful presentation on his new hydrogen fuel technique, perfecting the splitting of the water molecule so our internal combustion engines no longer have to run on fossil fuel, but instead on water. Bill Wysock spoke on advance spark gap technology; James Hardesy on vacuum tube technology; Ron Kovac on the working model of Tesla's 1899 power wave. I found the documented slide presentations of the history of this technology to be absolutely fascinating. Why wasn't I taught this in school? Mark Benza talked about the development of the biochip.

Global Attention

The director of The Advanced Energy Research Institute of London, England, Leonard Holihan, was on hand to introduce Stan Meyer and verify his hydrogen fuel technology. A record was made for the BBC. Videotapes of Dr. NakaMats were also recorded for Japanese television. NASA and World Health Organization officials were on hand, perhaps Soviet agents, too. And where was the American media? The conference only made the local news. Sad, but typical. No wonder the U.S. is eating scientific dust globally. (Now, we're even driving our electronic and chip industries overseas with stupid bureaucratic regulations.)

The Highlights

Given all this mind power, it should come as no surprise that the 1991 Extraordinary Science conference was like a good book or a superb motion picture. You have to work through it three or four times to get it all. That's at least the way I felt. Information overload shut me down from time to time. The highlights of this conference would take a 20-page REAPER just to catalogue. The off-the-podium, after-the-speech discussions with the speakers, remarks made by other key avant garde scientists, mavericks in their own right who still work in leading industries or for the government, provided much food for thought. Just one example: I went to dinner with a leading biochemist from Merck, who works in their drug quality control section before drugs are released. Was he ever a fountain of insight. So with the qualification that what follows are just a few of the many high points of this conference, here are some of the peaks which I gleaned from the 1991 Extraordinary Science conference. I think they will titillate your thinking.

Fuel From Water

Remember the chapter entitled, *"The End of the Age of Oil?"* Well, it's here. The age of fossil fuels is for all practical purposes over, done with, finished, dead. Texas Instruments has developed a solar cell which makes solar power competitive with conventional sources of power. Eighty-year-old scientist Alvin M. Marks of Athol, Massachusetts has patented a process he claims is 80% efficient in converting sunlight into electricity. He works with Lumeloid, a thin polarizing film covered with tiny molecular antennas that absorb sunlight and produce an electrical current. Marks claims that production cost comes to only one cent per kilowatt hour. That's a fifth of the typical cost of fossil fuels.

But more importantly, we are about to enter the age of safe hydrogen fuel. The technology exists now - proven, workable, consistent, verifiable, ready for mass production. And this hydrogen fuel technology is popping up from a number of sources. Dr. Yoshiro NakaMats' ENEREX engine derives energy from hydrogen in water. Dr. Roger Billings' hydrogen Lasercel is now safely on line. Can you imagine driving your car on 25-cent-a-gallon fuel? But the most impressive source of hydrogen fuel from water comes from Stan Meyer. Stan pointed out that there is 2.4 times more energy in a glass of water than there is in a glass of gasoline. For about $1,500, you can buy a set of these water fuel cells and install them in your car. It's simple, quick, easy. Simply take the present spark plugs out of your 4- or 8-cylinder car and plug in these water fuel cell *"spark plugs."* Then turn on your garden hose and fill up your fuel tank with water. Off you go. There's no air pollution. Water vapor is the only exhaust. And it doesn't matter if you use distilled water, rain water, salt water, or mineral water. Stan Meyer of Grove City, Ohio is taking us into a glorious non-polluting, fossil fuel-free future.

The End of the Age of Food

The evidence presented at this conference has now convinced me that we must now phase out, as quickly as possible, fossil fuels and nuclear power. Not only is our sun losing its energy, but the conductivity of the atmosphere has been massively diminished due to an increased build-up of carbon dioxide and pollution. This is not only negatively affecting mankind, but it's now approaching the point where it is a direct threat to agriculture. At the present rate of atmospheric deterioration, it won't be many years before plants are unable to grow, before we're unable to raise food. Dr. George Merkl confirmed this in chilling fashion. Also Rhetta Jacobson and Walter Baumgartner, from a totally different perspective, discussed how the energy in Americans' drinking water today is substantially reduced. The best water comes from pure bubbling mountain streams where the water turns and churns in vortexes over rocks which are energized by sunlight. Such water has energy, power. Rhetta and Walter demonstrated the energetic reality of water for the audience by showing how water, properly directed, can light up a disconnected neon light tube, held a few feet away from the H_2O. Water minus energy cannot do the job it's intended to do in the human body. Our water today is woefully lacking in energy. The worst water Rhetta and Walter have tested in their experiments all around the country was in San Francisco. ...Figures. We are mere shadows of what we (mankind) were originally created to be.

Biotech

What is the state of the art in biotechnology? Would you believe regenerating life from death (sleep) and cloning? It's already with us. Frankenstein is antiquated. We're far beyond that. Cloning via scalar technology is alive and well. Try this on: Cellular material, literally a biochip the size of an off-the-shelf cold capsule, can be programmed using fiber optics and laser technology, and implanted in the head. Want to be able to fully reference the *Encyclopedia Britannica*? No problem. Desire to have the biochip programmed with a foreign language? You have it. Want to know everything you need to know about the state-of-the-art vocabulary and research in chemical engineering, effectively a Ph.D. in the subject? Program it into the biochip and then implant it. *"Total Recall"* is here.

How about programming the biochip to attack and destroy cancer cells in the liver? Program and swallow. How about programming the biochip to totally change the personality, thinking and emotional pattern of a person? It's here, too. Arnold Schwarzenegger's *"Total Recall"* is not futuristic, it's today. If the government decided to paternally make us all alike and perfectly fulfill George Orwell's *"1984,"* it could do so. We'd never know we'd been altered.

How about taking a piece of steak off a supermarket shelf, removing a few cells, inserting a few life crystals, and regenerating the whole original cow from that steak? No problem. We're on the road there already. For that matter, you could take some cells off the leather of your shoe and do the same thing.

Why not clone yourself? Take a few drops of your own blood, add a few life crystals, and watch yourself regenerate. If you want to absolutely ensure your own continuation, you could also freeze, freeze-dry, or dehydrate some of your blood now, wait for cloning to become commonplace, and then effectively regenerate a whole new you in, let's say, the 22nd century.

The technology for cloning exists. The technology for such complete reprogramming exists. What do we do if someone wants to clone Saddam Hussein, Michael Dukakis or Dan Quayle? A better idea is to pull out of the freezer some of those old mastodons and regenerate them. Or, some mummy from an Egyptian tomb.

Longtime REAPER readers will recall that I wrote years ago that Dr. Stephen Smith at the University of Kentucky was successfully working with chemicals and the electromagnetic field in the regeneration of truncated limbs in living organisms, rodents, etc. But in the area of cloning and biochip technology, we're talking about technology far beyond that. The *"Brave New World"* is with us today. C.S. Lewis's *"That Hideous Strength"* is alive and well.

Spiritual Creativity

Dr. Yoshiro NakaMats made an inspiring and thought-provoking presentation on what it takes to become an inventor. On camera, I later pointed out to him that his 21 samurai points of spiritual creativity were almost identical to the Puritan Calvinistic work ethic which built early America. The only difference was that the samurai philosophy was minus any mercy, compassion or charity. (That's a big difference!) Dr. NakaMats was gracious. He revealed publicly for the first time ever at the 1991 Extraordinary Science conference his new, effective perpetual motion machine. This machine's one moving part (flywheel) touched nothing, absolutely nothing. That was, as Dr. NakaMats called it, the *"invention."* Further, this machine ran on any kind of energy - heat, light, beamed microwaves, etc. Installed on the roof of a house, it would be able to heat, light and power the entire home perpetually. Homeowners would be able to literally unhook permanently from the utility company. (A battery using nuclear waste already exists to accomplish the same thing.) Installed in an unmanned aircraft, this engine would keep it aloft indefinitely, with all the benefits of that reality.

* * * * *

I have written many times in THE REAPER that I thought the best way to bring in the New World Order would be to spring the UFO (perhaps alien) issue on the American people and the world in a dramatically staged event. In such an event, all the superior technology that's been quietly developed over the past fifty years or so would be brought to the surface immediately, perhaps in a staged global crisis as a means of uniting the world and forcing all mankind into the New World Order, perhaps against a common enemy. Such would also allow the destruction of the belief systems of the world.

The only group which would stand today against a New World Order is the Moslem community. Islam is the only religious group which is willing to fight and die for what it believes in. Also Islam has an honest banking system, is experiencing exploding population growth, and is evangelical. We must remember that 90% of Africa is Islamic, as is 90% of the Middle East and 50% of East Asia. There are 100 million Chinese Moslems. The Moslem population is expanding rapidly in Southern Russia and also in Europe.

THE SPACE-TIME QUESTION
August 5, 1987

As I have pondered the *"Bruce Cathie Revisited"* chapters over the years, I find most troublesome the space-time question. If it's true that we now have knowledge and utilization of the unified field theory, and UFOs are able to manipulate space-time, then history is threatened. Time is history, as the superior linear aspect of time and the subordinate cyclical aspect of time move forward in a progressive spiral. Thus, if time can be altered, history can be changed.

The time manipulation of history has long been a goal of man. Who of us is not at least vaguely familiar with H.G. Wells', *The Time Machine*. And recently, three box office hit movies have dealt with the manipulation of time/history. Arnold Schwarzenegger's movie, *The Terminator*, dealt with a successful attempt to go back in time, but an unsuccessful attempt to manipulate history. Steven Spielberg's smash hit, *Back to the Future*, focused on going back in time for the achieved purpose of successfully manipulating the future. So, too, was the focus of the flick, *Peggy Sue Got Married*, the space-time question.

If this was all sci-fi (science fiction), I wouldn't give it a second thought. But remember, science fiction all too often precedes scientific reality. Literature and art (movies) project the future accurately often enough to chill this writer in this particular space-time case. If, just what if, men with a lust for power, inclined toward evil, were truly able to get a handle on this space-time thing. What if men could literally go back in time and, assuming they were strong supporters of the British Empire, were able to eliminate Paul Revere, Benjamin Franklin, John Adams, James Madison, Thomas Jefferson, Patrick Henry, and George Washington? What if these Founding Fathers were eliminated (terminated) when they were children? Where would we be today? What if some satanist and occultist with the money, power and inclination went back in time and eliminated King David, or Solomon, or Mary or Joseph? Then Jesus would never have come on the scene and the lineages of Matthew 1 and Luke 3 would not be history.

Sounds crazy, doesn't it? And yet, we're actually dealing in the space-time question with the application of the scientific thinking of two of the greatest scientists of all time - Albert Einstein and Nikola Tesla.

Einstein's search for the unified field theory as well as his *"theory of relativity"* are well known. Less known, but probably just as important, if not more important, was the work of Nikola Tesla (1857-1943). Nikola Tesla invented the first electric clock, the first computer circuit designs, the first x-rays, the first fluorescent light, the first system to harness alternating current (AC), the first radio (two years before Marconi), conceived the first VTOL aircraft (Vertical Takeoff and Landing Aircraft), the automobile speedometer, the bladeless turbine, and on and on. In fact, Thomas Edison received credit for most of the inventions which really belonged to Nikola Tesla. J.P. Morgan, George Westinghouse and Thomas Edison fought over Tesla for his time and the rights to his inventions (*Freedom Magazine*, March 1986). Tesla, with the financing of J.P. Morgan, built a tower in New York that would have provided the world with free energy. It was only under the persuasion of oil baron John D. Rockefeller that J.P. Morgan jerked the financial rug out from under Tesla and left him adrift, unable to complete the project.

The *"Bruce Cathie Revisited"* chapter documented beyond question the existence and involvement of at least the U.S. and the former U.S.S.R. in UFO activity, going back, at minimum, 35 years. Quoting again from Bruce Cathie's *The Bridge to Infinity*, *"The period or frequency rate between each pulse of physical matter creates the measurement which we call time, as well as the speed of light, at the particular position in space of which we are aware, at any given moment.*

"If the frequency rate of positive and negative pulses is either increased or decreased, then time and the speed of light vary in direct proportion. This concept would explain time as a geometric, as Einstein theorized it to be."

In other words, the essence of Bruce Cathie's title to his book, *The Bridge to Infinity*, is that by manipulating time, man can literally bridge the limits and boundaries of time and become infinite. Let's get down to brass tacks: What we're talking about here is man playing and/or becoming God. Furthermore, one does not have to be too well read to be troubled by the fact that all this *"time jumping"* involves the 666 harmonic.

As I wrote in the *"Bruce Cathie Revisited"* chapter, *"All an anti-gravity disc has to do then is to be tuned to a frequency to balance out the difference of 3928.371 to get it to float or become antigravitational. Then, only the pulse rate has to be increased or decreased which decreases or increases time, to cause movement."* The fact that sighted UFOs behave exactly in accordance with this theory is indeed troubling. (See the May 29th, 1986 REAPER, Page 7, the reprint from *U.S.A. Today*, 5/24/86 on *"Brazilians Investigate UFO Reports."*) Numerous June 1987 UFO sightings in Florida made this relevant.

The Soviets have been involved with the physics of Einstein and Tesla since the advent of the atomic bomb. American physicist Tom Bearden in a speech delivered in 1984 declared, *"We've gone through...a one-way door. This is the final technology. You can engineer physical reality itself, with the full implications eventually as the technology develops...of that thing, that statement. So we have two burning problems. No. 1 - We must quickly develop counters to the Soviet weapons so that they might not decide to move when they could use them. I should point out one other disadvantage of these weapons. They have a limit of how much you can use because they shake space/time. Can you imagine what happens if you cause time to oscillate, and time in half cycles is running backwards?*

"Suppose you were shot in the breast and blown apart in such an oscillation in positive time. And then time backs up in the negative half cycle and you sit there and blow apart, come back together and restore your life, blow apart and die, come back together and restore your life. That's possible. That's real.

"Do you know what gravity is in negative space/time? It's a repulsion, not an attraction, so all the...buildings sit there and jump up and down and so do you. You go flying up and crashing down. You see what I mean? You can only use these things on a limited scale or you'll blow your own leg off. But the ability to engineer things like that is now in our hands as ill-prepared as we are. So the first thing is, we must buy some time, counter the Russian weapons that are already sitting there in the Soviet Union and have been. They've been developing them for 30 something years."

Downright mind blowing, isn't it? Unbelievable? And yet, I haven't met many fools in my life. Every man who knows something and puts it to good use has a handle on some truth, in some form or fashion. On the other hand, I've met deceivers, liars, and men who have been deceived or lied to, but where there's smoke there's usually fire. And there's been entirely too much smoke over the past 35 years in this UFO space-time area, and too much money, too many high powered Establishment brains and insider Establishment support to cause this analyst to just dismiss it all as science fiction. Beyond question, when we're dealing with manipulating space/time/history, we're dealing with the supernatural as well as the normal science of the created realm. The two are integrated like no place else when it comes to space/time/history. Religion and science are becoming one.

Now, we all have presuppositions (assumptions) about the ultimate nature of reality. This is inescapable because all of us have limited time, limited knowledge and limited minds. My ultimate presupposition is that there is a sovereign God. This being the case, it logically follows that there are limits to man's capability of manipulating time if in fact this purported space-time manipulation is not an illusion (or man is being deluded). Jesus said to His disciples in Acts Chapter 1, verse 7, *"It is not for you to know times or seasons which the Father has put in His own authority."* This to me means, just like matter and energy, the buck stops in the manipulation of time with a sovereign God. But there is no question in my mind that we (mankind) are fooling around with it. And if I had to put my money on the line, my best guess is that there will be some hair-raising events in this area openly manifest before the year 2012 rolls around. (Remember the movies *2001* and *2012?*)

What we can't do is shrink from our responsibility to investigate and exercise dominion over this area - time. Because we have not been judicious and responsible in exercising our dominion in the area of economics and finance, we now again have the Babylonian occult, freedom-stealing money system running this world. As we have shrunk from our governmental responsibilities (primarily self-government and local government, the government of the local school, job, family, and church), we are now back to the establishment of vertical pyramids, structured bureaucratic pagan empires. It's the tower of Babel all over again. And these government/gods, like all gods, demand tributes and sacrifices, human sacrifices. So we are becoming poor through debt, inflation and/or high taxation, while becoming more enslaved by administrative, bureaucratic law by edict. This means we can't leave the scientific arena unchallenged either, particularly given what is going on with space-time. To do so is to further guarantee the loss of our freedom, peace and prosperity.

* * * * *

"Relativity is presently regarded as a theory or a statement about fundamental physical reality. In fact, it is only a statement about FIRST ORDER reality - the reality that emerges from the vector interaction of electromagnetic energy with matter. When we break down the vectors into scalars, shadow vectors or hypervectors, we immediately enter a vastly different, far more fundamental reality. In this reality, superluminal velocity, multiple universes travel back and forth in time, higher dimensions, variation of all 'fundamental constants' of nature, materialization and dematerialization and the violation of the 'conservation of energy' are all involved." — T.E. Bearden

"Comments on the New Tesla Electromagnetics," 1982

* * * * *

"Presently, gravitational field and electrical field are considered mutually exclusive. Actually, this is also untrue. In 1974, for example, Santilly proved that electrical field and gravitational field indeed are not mutually exclusive. In that case, one is left with two possibilities: (a) They are totally the same thing; or (b) they are partially the same thing...With the new Tesla electromagnetics, pure scalar waves in time itself can be produced electrically, and electrostatics (when the charge has been separated from the mass) becomes a 'magic tool' capable of directly affecting and altering anything that exists in time - including gravitational field. Anti-gravity and the inertial drive are immediate and direct consequences of the new electromagnetics." — Ibid

* * * * *

"Then Joshua spoke to the Lord in the day when the Lord delivered up the Amorites before the children of Israel, and he said in the sight of Israel:

'Sun, stand still over Gibeon;

and Moon, in the Valley of Ajalon.'

So the sun stood still,

And the moon stopped,

till the people had revenge

upon their enemies.

"Is this not written in the Book of Joshua? So the sun stood still in the midst of heaven, and did not hasten to go down for about a whole day." (Time-space was altered, in this case stopped.) Joshua 10:12-13

* * * * *

"'Behold, I will bring the shadow on the sundial, which has gone down with the sun on the sundial of Ahaz, ten degrees backward.' So the sun returned ten degrees on the dial by which it had gone down." (Time-space was reversed.) — Isaiah 38:8

Some controversial computer retracements of time-history have confirmed both Joshua 10:12-13 and Isaiah 38:8.

* * * * *

The following is taken from C.S. Lewis' 1971 book, *The Screwtape Letters*. A letter is written from a senior demon (Screwtape) to a junior temptor (Wormwood).

"Our policy, for the moment, is to conceal ourselves. Of course this has not always been so. We are really faced with a cruel dilemma. When the humans disbelieve in our existence we lose all the pleasing results of direct terrorism, and we make no magicians. On the other hand, when they believe in us, we cannot make them materialists and skeptics. At least, not yet. I have great hopes that we shall learn in due time how to emotionalize and mythologize their science to such an extent that what is, in effect, a belief in us (though not under that name) will creep in while the human mind remains closed to belief in the Enemy. The 'Life Force,' the worship of sex, and some aspects of Psychoanalysis may here prove useful. If once we can produce our perfect work - the Materialistic Magician, the man, not using, but veritably worshipping, what he vaguely calls 'Forces' while denying the existence of 'spirits' - then the end of the war will be in sight. But in the meantime we must obey our orders. I do not think you will have much difficulty in keeping the patient in the dark. The fact that 'devils' are predominantly comic figures in the modern imagination will help you. If any faint suspicion of your existence begins to arise in his mind, suggest to him a picture of something in red tights, and persuade him that since he cannot believe in that (it is an old textbook method of confusing them) he therefore cannot believe in you."

* * * * *

"Witchcraft is flourishing because of its positive benefits to participants and the entire planet. Most rituals have some focus or concern for healing our ravaged Mother Earth. Women are especially drawn to it because of the emphasis on a female divinity which has been denied us in all formal Western religions.

"...Satan has nothing to do with witchcraft, Wicca, or paganism. None of these groups even believe in the devil's existence. Most feel Satan is a figment of the medieval church's collective imagination used to coerce people into becoming tithe-giving churchgoers." — Brigid Beth Kelly - Tempe, Arizona - Source: *Insight* Magazine - Letters to the Editor, 7/13/87

* * * * *

Emerging science today belongs to the New Agers. They have in their grasp the proven beneficial technology to: (1) clean up the environment; (2) heal the sick (including cancer and AIDS); (3) recapture the earth from a wasteland to a garden; (4) make it rain and stabilize the weather at will any place on the earth; (5) provide free energy; and (6) neutralize radioactivity. And that's just for starters!

This marvelous science and technology is repeatable, verifiable, and can be done by almost anyone. The New Agers literally have the technical tools to create widespread peace and prosperity on earth. And this technological explosion is about to surface. (In other words, the New Agers have achieved what was the church's dominion responsibility.) ...So much for the good news.

The bad news is that many New Agers are the evolutionary result of the revolutionary 1960s *"me generation."* Into their spiritual void has come Eastern mystical humanism, every man as his own reincarnated god, every man with his own *"spirit guide"* or *"entity."* (What nice names for demons. Too bad this bloody occultism is not in the open as it is in the Philippines and Haiti.)

Since the New Age technology is operative in the frequency range where demons comfortably operate (outside of normal human sight), and because these New Agers have no frame of reference for demons, they are right at home in linking their science and technology with natural occult religion and these alien and possibly, demonic *"spirit guides"* and *"entities."* Here then is the danger of a successful coup, about which C.S. Lewis warned us in *The Screwtape Letters.*

* * * * *

"...it is appointed for men to die once, but after this the judgment." — Hebrews 9:27 NKJV

TIME TO REWRITE THE TEXTS
August 18, 1993

For a full eight days I slept in a spartan, unairconditioned room, all night hearing nothing but Russian spoken around me. Where was I? On the ninth floor of Sandberg Hall on the campus of the University of Wisconsin at Milwaukee. The occasion? The Joint 1993 Conference of the International Association for Psychotronic Research, and the United States Psychotronics Association. This Joint 1993 Conference of the I.A.P.R. and the U.S.P.A., held from July 9-18, focused on the theme, *"Science and Spirit - A Merging of the Technology of Man With the Spirit of Man."* I was one of only two journalists invited to report on this special event. (The other was *Discover* magazine.)

What was my impression? In a word - mind-expanding!

Scientists from over 14 countries attended, including some of the avant-garde scientific thinkers from the former Soviet Union, Eastern Europe, Japan, South America, Canada, France, and England. The names with which I became familiar after a week, primarily through the efforts of a translator, were Zdenek Rejdak, Yvonne Duplessis, Andre Sandor, Toshiya Nakaoka, Valentina Ponomaryova, Ivan Ploc, and on and on. Papers which were given through translators (or in broken English), and were published in the proceedings of the I.A.P.R. included the following topics: *"Psychotronics and the Spiritual Sphere," "The Consequences of No-Material Environmental Pollution," "The Biological Object - Unity of Matter and Spirit," "The Existence of the Soul - A Bridge Between Religion and Science," "The Immaculate Conception, Antioedipus and the New Culture," "The Parapsychological Significance of Certain Gestures in the Christian Religion," "Exploratory Precognitive Dream Studies," "Determining the Age of Objects by Bioindication," "Psychotronics and the Spiritual Sphere," "Screening of the Geoactive Zones," "The Science of Yoga and Psychotronics," "Man and Hu-Man," "Meditation and the Laying On of Hands," "Choice of Transducers for Bio-Energetic Transfer," "The Quantum Theory and the Reality of the Internal Experience," "Bioenergy - A New Diagnostic and Healing Frontier," "Psychotronics in the Orient," "Psychotronics and the Sects," "Technical Channeling for Remote Healing," "Warning Messages in Dreams and Psychograms," "Subconscious, Music, and Biotherapy,"* and so forth.

The scientists from the former Soviet Union paid their own way to Milwaukee, the equivalent of a month's pay! Originally, the proceedings' papers were to be given in Bulgaria in 1991. That I.A.P.R. Conference was canceled due to upheavals in the Balkans. The complete proceedings from this Milwaukee I.A.P.R. conference are available from the International Association for Psychotronic Research, P. O. Box 8276, Silverspring, MD 20910, phone (301) 587-8686. The price is $45.00. Some of the papers are in Russian.

By July 13, it was nice to get back to English at the 19th annual U.S.P.A. Conference on *"Science and Spirit."* The 1993 U.S.P.A. proceedings are also available for $45.00 from the U.S.P.A., P. O. Box 354, Wilmette, IL 60091. If I had to opt for buying one of the two proceedings, I would spring for $45.00 and buy the 1993 U.S.P.A. proceedings from the Wilmette, Illinois address. For hard core investigators, after you have read these proceedings, if you like, audio and video tapes are also available. I found particularly enlightening the presentations of Bob Beutlich, Moray King, Eldon Byrd, Jim Windsor, Dr. Roger Taylor, Henry Monteith, Glen Rein, Murray Bast, and Marcos Rodin. Personal presentations and/or the proceedings included Murray Bast's *"Nature's Most Nearly Unperfect Food,"* Bob Beutlich's *"Parallel Worlds of Time"* and *"Expanded Three Dimensional 8x8 Matrix,"* Steven Halpern's *"Relaxation, Recovery and the Healing Powers of Music,"* Moray King's *"Fundamentals of Zero-Point Energy Technology,"* Eugenia Macer-Story's *"Naturally-Occurring Time Chambers,"* Dr. Henry Monteith's *"The Dual Nature of Free Energy Systems,"* Glen Rein's *"Local and Non-local Effects of Coherent Heart Frequencies on Conformational Changes of DNA,"* Marcos Rodin's *"The Dandelion Puff Principle,"* Dr. Roger Taylor's *"The Crop Circle Phenomenon,"* and James Windsor's *"The Body/Mind/Spirit Connection."*

Life is never stagnant. If we are coasting, we're heading downhill. We either constantly grow or we die. To me, growth is an integration now of the spiritual, scientific, political and economic. So, to spark your interest, I'll titillate you with just some of the many gems of information I picked up from this fascinating joint conference.

Consciousness, the limbic system, the immune system and neuropeptides are all interrelated. Where there is conflict between action and conscience, there is dis-ease.

Bob Beutlich gave several fascinating talks. He observed that 80% of the world's population is the equivalent of only eight years old emotionally, and that 19.9% of the world's population are only 14-15 years old emotionally. (All politicians are at best 14 years old according to Beutlich.) Then, only one-tenth of one percent of the people reach maturity, which is the equivalent of 21 years of age. Beutlich pointed out that two dimensions below the proton is what we call the psychic world. We live primarily in the Newtonian world of three-dimensional space and one-dimensional time. The world of two dimensions below the proton is three dimensions time and one dimension space. The physical body effectively lives in a different dimension than the mind which interfaces with the physical body through the astral or emotional body. (See the June 30, 1993 REAPER, *"The Great E-Motion."*) Furthermore, according to Beutlich, the four primary worlds of earth, air, water, fire, the molecular, atomic, ether and primal-will worlds respectively are accessed via the speed of light at 1C, 3C, 9C, and 27C respectively. This is done via scalar FM modulation. The scalar precedes the electromagnetic field according to Beutlich. Time and gravity are a scalar. There are seven fields in a magnet, relating to seven of the ten strings in the ten-string theory, but we only know of one field presently in physics.

An important book is Paul Davies' and John Gribbin's *The Matter Myth*. Science has come full circle to the deeply theological concept that creation was as the Bible said it was. *"Zero-Point Energy"* is significant in this regard. Eldon Byrd discussed how man has progressed from Newton's view of a materialistic universe where people were no more than cogs in a machine, to a theory of relativity which demolished Newton's concept of space and time. Then came the quantum theory which destroyed Newton's theory of matter, followed by quantum field, which said that solid matter doesn't exist at all, but that the field is everything. Next came chaos, specifically deterministic chaos, with its non-linear effects where matter behaves miraculously and changes in random and unpredictable ways. The shift has been from reductionism, to holism, to mysticism.

I have never heard the Bible quoted so many times at a scientific conference. But, at the same time, one speaker said, *"The ultimate scientist today is a shaman."* Spirit and science are uniting. It is interesting to contemplate that all the matter in the universe can be put in a box three foot square, and that one cubic centimeter of energy equals all the entire universe. The concept of scalar energy is key to understanding the universe. At issue is the fact that reality is not based on measurement. Reality is subjective. Science is based on measurement. Therefore, inescapably, science is incomplete. We cannot ever know perfectly.

Bob Beutlich did a fascinating job of linking DNA, the I Ching, and correlating YHWH, the Hebrew letters for Jehovah, into an 8x8 matrix. There are 64 energy fields generated and we only have knowledge of eight or nine of them. Thus, we are only 12.5% of the way there. Fascinating. My work indicates by 2008-2012, and by no later than 2030, we will know all of these. This means we are due many quantum leaps in the next few years.

Bob Beutlich stated, *"The Bible is a physics book."* I have started to understand that. In checking a concordance, where Scripture refers to the *"kingdom of heaven"* and/or the *"kingdom of God,"* it is speaking of the existence above the Newtonian realm, the quantum, chaotic scalar realities which exist beyond three parts space/one part time, beyond the second law of thermodynamics, entropy and death. This existence has been open and available to us since the temple veil was torn at the time of the crucifixion of Jesus Christ. This moved us potentially from a Newtonian world across the Einsteinian relativity bridge to a quantum world. Until Jesus' crucifixion in linear, progressive history, the temple was an external physical structure available only to the priests, gemstone breastplate and all. But after the temple veil was rent, the kingdom of God went within, and the body became potentially the temple of the Holy Spirit. The kingdom of God within made possible the kingdom of God without, for which the creation groans. *"Born again"* means living beyond the Newtonian world of conflict, chance, cycles, poverty and death, in a quantum, integrated, holographic world by being obedient first, and living a Second Great Commandment lifestyle in the Newtonian kingdom of conflict, the natural world. This means that for nearly 2,000 years the *"church"* has not grasped what the New Testament had to say regarding being *"born again"* or the *"kingdom of God."* But it's not entirely the church's fault. Most often, the church learns from science and reorders its theology based upon the work of science. It has only been within the last two decades that we have come to an increased awareness and understanding of what the world beyond Newton really is about.

Dr. Henry Monteith discussed how the word *"human"* means *"hu-man,"* or animal-man. That's our natural state in the Newtonian world. He stated that women, *"female bodies,"* particularly are being indwelt increasingly by *"animal spirits."* This is what the Bible refers to as demons. This is consistent with the theology of the Chinese, Muslims, Hindus, and Christians regarding an uncovered (ungrounded) woman. Women are naturally always in the natural spiritual realm (unless they are grounded and covered), because of their negative polarity and dominant scalar, holographic, chaotic right brain. This makes them vulnerable.

Moray King discussed how the Zero-Point Energy flux is from hyperspace. Zero-Point energy is a turbulent virtual plasma. Self organization occurs under three conditions: 1) non-linear; 2) far from equilibrium; and 3) an energy flux. Self-organizing chemical reactions involve self-forming vortices. Coherence equals zero-point energy plus self-organization.

Free energy is with us. Cold fusion is being repeated successfully all over the world. Paul Brown has a U.S. patent on a resonant nuclear battery, U. S. Patent No. 4,835,433. Stan Meyer, through water disassociation, is tapping into unlimited energy, too.

Jim Windsor discussed how in L.A., when people prayed for peace in a specific area, crime went down, fears were reduced, and love became more apparent. Windsor traced the history of the mind-matter interface. He discussed the work of Herbert Bensen, and that when the parasympathetic has been trained to relax, the fight or flight impulse disappears from consciousness. It is the sympathetic division of the autonomic nervous system which triggers the fight or flight response. Helplessness and hopelessness are two keys to death that the mind uses to kill the body. Windsor next discussed Norman Cousins' *Anatomy of an Illness*, and how the mind can be used to overcome the body's illnesses as with funny movies. Mood swings produce biochemical changes in the body which affect the immune system. Brain cells and immune cells are in direct communication with each other. Faith, hope, love, and joy are key to good health. The front of the hypothalamus controls emotions while the back of the hypothalamus inhibits stress. Chopra, in *Quantum Healing*, notes that the mental is more important than the physical. This is discussed in my recent REAPER on *"The Great E - Motion."* When the mind changes it goes deep enough to erase the physical pattern that exists in the body. A shift of awareness usually occurs before a physical cure. What we see is what we become. Personal reality is subjective. This is what Michael Ryce developed in his tapes, *"Why is This Happening to Me...Again?"* (800-755-6360). When the mind shifts, the body cannot help but follow. The immune system can be classically conditioned. Men have been found to have a greater will to live when they feel their wives love them, and have no will to live when they feel their wives don't love them. Do wives have power or what?

Dr. Roger Taylor gave a fascinating talk on crop circles. Laura Faith talked about psychokinesis and its relationship to animate and inanimate objects in the former Soviet Union. Dr. Peter Moscow, who works regularly with animals, talked about the state of consciousness of the animal's owner being critically important to the state of consciousness of the animal. Taking a very strong stand against vaccines, Dr. Peter Moscow stated, *"Vaccines of all types have the ability to weaken the immune system and do tremendous biological damage."* Steve Halpern pointed out that refrigerators resonate in the stomach area, that under fluorescent lights people crave sweets, and that the old European Christian gothic cathedrals had a great deal in common with New Age art. Sound creates images. The body heals when it's relaxed, and music can help the body heal. He described music as a carrier wave for consciousness. Halpern took a very strong stand against heavy metal music and rock and roll because of the damage it does to the physical system. Mark Benza discussed how we were all at risk of becoming cyborgs like *"The Borg "* on *"Star Trek."* Benza expressed his concern that *"Data"* on *"Star Trek"* may be about to become a reality, and that people could be programmed to be Ph.D.s in the likes of nuclear physics through simply a chip implant in the human body. It was Benza who stated, *"...Physicists are learning the basics from shamen."* Vladimir Terziski is a treasure trove of information on UFOs (10970 Ashton Ave., #310, Los Angeles, CA 90024, phone 310/473-9717). Vladimir thought all UFOs had a Luciferian connection, with important links to secret societies. Dr. Henry C. Monteith was very excited about the Japanese cars that are running on water, Ken McNeil's atom machine, cold fusion which has now been proven globally, and the free energy motor of Mr. Troy Reed of Tulsa, Oklahoma. Dan Davidson gave a fascinating talk on Gravity Field Sensor experiments, including UFO detectors.

* * * * *

This writer was also a featured speaker at the 1993 Extraordinary Science Conference held July 22-25, 1993 in Colorado Springs, Colorado, sponsored by the International Tesla Society, Inc. (1-800-397-0137). My subject was the unification of science, Christianity, politics and economics.

What the IAPR and USPA were to the interface between mind and matter, science and spirit, the Extraordinary Science Conference was to the hands-on application of mind and spirit to technology. Hands-on technology, working devices, were clearly the highlight of this Tesla conference. Packing the auditorium was Gaston Naessens with his fascinating work on somatids. A full house was also present when Dr. Yull Brown's people talked about Brown's Gas. Joseph Newman and his energy machine literally almost brought the house down. Fascinating presentations were additionally given by physicist Larry Spring, Al Bielek on the Philadelphia Experiment and time travel, Scott McKee on the Phoenix Project, Bert Werjefelt on the magnetic battery, George Wiseman on the advanced energy conserver, John Crane on *"The Cancer Cure That Worked"* (north pole-green side of a magnet), Klark Kent on the Lakhovsky oscillator, Dr. Thomas Peterson on absolute electrostatics, and many more. For the cutting-edge, hands-on electrically, mechanically, and magnetically oriented, the 1993 Extraordinary Science Conference was the place to be. The technology was there on display. (I was like a kid in a toy store.)

Tesla torrid coils which sent lightning bolts six to eight feet into the air above the stage were demonstrated by William Wysock. Larry Spring's physics experiments, batteries and solar machines which worked with incredible efficiency, were featured. Electromagnetic devices were on display by Klark Kent of Super Science. Super Science's multi-wave oscillator was an attendee stopper throughout the conference. I broke down and bought one - $1,889 each. Now that I've worked with it, I have concerns that someone who is not knowledgeable about the mind could get in real trouble with it. Extreme caution is advised. You might, though, write Super Science for a free copy of their catalog (Super Science, P.O. Box 392M, Dayton, OH 45409, phone 513-298-7116). As Super Science says, *"The Multi-Wave Oscillator is your personal invitation to experiment with a high voltage Tesla Coil. Experience every cell in your body resonating to its own natural frequency. It is quite stimulating!"* ...Approximately ten years ago, my science and medical reading exposed me to the history of Lakhovsky's multi-wave oscillator as it was used in hospitals in this country up until about 1930. Then last year, Dr. Fuller Royal, M.D., at his Clinic for Preventive Medicine in Las Vegas, Nevada, as part of my treatment had me sit in front of his multi-wave oscillator for 15 minutes. But, again, the MWO is no toy or gadget. It is electricity-based, and could shock, harm or potentially kill someone. I'm the only member of our family who goes near it.

Back to the Extraordinary Science Conference. Dr. Thomas Peterson, Jr. confirmed that dia-electrics at the earth's surface are negative. Thus, Mother Earth is feminine. Gaston Naessens, whose *"somatids"* have been made famous in a book by Christopher Bird, talked about how somatids are present in all forms of living matter. Somatids are tiny particles observed in the plasma of human blood. They are nearly impossible to kill. By tracking the 16 stages of the somatid cycle, a Naessens practitioner can predict the diseases that will hit an individual up to two years in advance, and head them off at the pass. Naessens' associated 714X treatment has been widely used in the treatment of cancer. ...The product 714X liquifies the lymph. It is made with camphor molecules. The purpose of 714X is to liberate the immune system, so that the body can get organized and bring forth its own defenses. For more information contact C.O.S.E., Inc., 5270 Fontaine, Rock Forest, Quebec J1N 3B6, Canada, telephone (819) 564-7883, fax (819) 564-4668. Books, cassettes, the condenser, and the 714X product are all available from the C.O.S.E., Inc. address, with an attending physician.

Cell division is accompanied by somatids. Growth hormone release is controlled by somatids. If there are no somatids, there is uninhibited growth hormone release. All degenerative diseases are a result of this uninhibited release of growth hormones, according to Gaston Naessens. Somatids are a precursor of DNA. They cause genetic information. Somatids are present at birth and also at death. At death, the somatids remain alive and go back into the earth.

Dr. Yull Brown's associate's presentation on the technological breakthrough of Brown's Gas was very encouraging. Brown's Gas is an implosive, not explosive, gas. Brown's Gas can totally deactivate nuclear waste. This means that presently 96%-99% of both toxic and nuclear waste can be neutralized using Brown's Gas. The California Department of Energy knows it. The U.S. Department of Energy knows it, too. Transmutation of radioactive material is now an accomplished fact. This means the world has a viable way to eliminate radioactive waste. It is no longer an unsolved problem. And there's the added benefit to the internal combustion engine using Brown's Gas, which has been viable since 1972. The only exhaust of this engine is water vapor. Bye-bye to pollution. Moreover, using Brown's Gas with a solar panel has proven to be 95% efficient. It's time to unhook from the utilities. Say goodbye to the diamond cartel as well. Brown's Gas used on certain bricks turns them into diamonds. Brown's Gas also can be used to weld unusual materials together, to glass for example. Christopher Bird is going to write a book on Yull Brown. For more information on Brown's Gas, contact MAXA, 1420 NW Gilman Blvd., S-2266, Issaquah, WA 98027, phone (206) 868-9875, fax (206) 391-2384.

Finally, we come to Joseph Newman, who is as volatile as his invention is controversial. Joseph Newman may still be contacted at Route 1, Box 52, Lucedale, MS 39452, phone (601) 947-7147. Newman pointed out that the obvious is something that is never seen until it is explained simply. By contrast, from the perspective of bureaucrats, *"Everything that is not forbidden is compulsory."* Newman's energy machine is able to convert salt water to fresh water. This means fresh water is no longer a problem for the world. We have a potentially endless supply of fresh water. Newman's device has also been able to explain as well as demonstrate levitation. His work is consistent with the work of Maxwell and Faraday, whose original work has been altered and distorted by modern scientific textbooks.

From these two conferences, back to back, I have learned it is clearly time to rewrite the scientific textbooks. Here is just a minute sampling of what else I picked up. Electromagnetic phenomena is mechanical energy. Magnetic energy is a wind in the ether. Two vectors multiplied together yields a scalar. If you multiply two scalars together, it equals an electromagnetic wave. All psychic transmissions are pulsed FM. The 64 hexagrams of the I Ching can be explained in terms of electricity, magnetism, gravity and time, as well as YHWH and 1C, 3C, 9C, 27C. This links further to the ten string theory of 3-7, the three being electrical (a trinity) and the seven magnetic fields in a magnet.

Time is scalar. T.E. Bearden's work on *"Free Energy: The Final Secret,"* is must reading (Explorer magazine, vol. 4, nos. 3 and 4, 1993, Phone: 1-800-845-7866). The energy from the vacuum is unlimited. The materials a magnet is made of are key. The action of the gyroscope is basic to the laws of the magnetic field. Moreover, gyroscopic action is fundamental to UFO technology. The magnetic field of a UFO device as it interfaces with the earth's magnetic field is basic to levitation. Gyroscopic action exists throughout the universe, and explains how the heavenly bodies are positioned. *"Spikes"* in electrical systems can be harnessed and provide excess energy (overunity). This is just like when the same input at a rock concert is applied to an amplifying speaker, it will explode, giving off more energy than was put in with the sound. This "spike" energy has now been captured.

We are on the verge of a scientific and technological explosion in the next 20 years that will surpass everything that has existed from the dawn of man to the present. Get ready. We are moving into the age of Extraordinary Science.

SECTION IV

Economics

THE <u>REAL</u> STATE OF THE NATION AT THE START OF 1989

January 18, 1989

The Consumer

Consumer spending comprises 70% of U.S. economic activity. Because the consumer is so deeply in debt, and since assumption of more debt is a function of confidence, consumer confidence must be sustained so that borrowing will continue, so the economy can roll on. The problem is, the consumer is up to his neck in debt with a pitifully low savings rate, the lowest of all industrialized nations! Both mortgage debt and consumer debt, as percentages of personal income, are at record highs. Meanwhile, the savings rate has dropped to record lows, having fallen irregularly since 1975. The level of savings in any society determines the degree of investment in any country and, in turn, its living standard. In other words, a low savings rate equals low investment which equals a low living standard.

The American consumer has become poor, but is attempting to maintain his high-flying lifestyle by such activities as borrowing and mortgaging his wife to the work force. The number of two-income couples as a percentage of all married couples in the United States rose from 28.5% in 1960 to 49% in 1985. Additionally, both husbands and wives have taken moonlighting jobs or joined the underground economy, which has rocketed to $400 billion a year.

In the first half of 1988, the median family income was $31,341. Of course, the bureaucrats in Washington, D.C. topped the income list with the nation's highest median family income of $44,859. Only 8% of the U.S. population earned more than $50,000 a year, and to make the top 15%, an income above $40,000 a year was necessary. To be in the top 15% of net worth, which is rich by the U.S. government's measures, a person's income equivalent had to be just under $50,000 a year.

The inflation-adjusted incomes of the nation's poorest families had fallen more than 10%. The number of people below the poverty line grew from 23 million in 1973 to more than 35 million in 1988. The poverty rate for blacks in 1987 hit 33.1%. This is a seething social cauldron.

The middle class in the United States fell from 54% of the population to 49% in 1985. Effectively, the middle class has been stagnant for the past 20 years, during rampant, then creeping inflation. It has been a growing middle class which historically has been the backbone of the stable U.S. political and economic system. It is the U.S. middle class which is threatened.

U.S. consumers could not be in worse shape financially at a worse time in American history, at the end of a 510-year civilization cycle. Most of Americans' net worth is in their single-family homes, which many analysts view as an

investment bubble. Single-family homes are not investments, they are consumer items. The baby-boomers, have saturated their demand for single-family
homes while loading up on debt. This leaves a glut of real estate on the market
as we enter the *"baby bust"* era, and as the *"gray panthers"* pass on. With the
fastest growing sector of the U.S. population now over 85 and passing on, what
will happen to all the extra houses coming on the market? Who will buy them?
The Japanese? Mexican immigrants?

Rental houses today earn less than 5% per year of market value. It's
cheaper to rent than it is to buy a home today. This type of flip-flop in real
estate has been an inevitable forerunner of lower real estate prices. With single-family housing unrentable for a positive cash flow, the housing market cannot long sustain steady, much less higher, prices.

Economic stress is reflected in stress elsewhere. Immune systems are compromised and the Epstein Barr Virus is epidemic. America's youths are in turmoil. American teenagers also have the highest rate of abortion in the developed world, almost double that of teenagers in Europe. Drug use is epidemic.
First amendment rights are being violated right and left in the war on illegal
drugs and U.S. citizens protesting abortions are being jailed without being
charged. A blue ribbon panel of the American Bar Association declared regarding crime, *"The criminal-justice system cannot provide the quality of justice the
public legitimately expects."* In Los Angeles, for example, convicts found
guilty of drug violations and sentenced to five-year terms are out of jail in only
six weeks.

Americans have lost their sense of personal responsibility and duty as basic
to freedom. The public schools and the media do not explain that real freedom
walks on the legs of a religious system which emphasizes self-government,
debt-free honest money, and economic self-sufficiency. Only 5% of the people
in the U.S. are self-employed, according to the Small Business Administration.

AIDS is creeping into American homes. The Children's Defense Fund reported that U.S. teenagers are <u>not</u> changing their sexual behavior to avoid
AIDS. The virus is latent in many of our youth, ready to spring forth in a
stressful crisis.

Finally, there is little understanding of climatic and weather changes as
they have historically affected the country's religious, economic and political
systems. The overall global cooling trend and earthquakes all threaten between
now and the year 2000.

The Financial and Business Sector

In 1950, the U.S. accounted for approximately 45% of the free world's GNP.
Today, the U.S. is lucky to muster 20%. The rest of the world has caught up and
surpassed us. Manufacturing, like agriculture, the two critical pillars of the economy, has fallen. *Business Week* reported in its December 12, 1988 issue, *'The*

factory rebound may be more fantasy than fact." As it turns out, manufacturing's much-vaunted productivity gains have not been all that impressive. The U.S. is falling behind in the global industrial race. This *Business Week* article was confirmed by the Commerce Department and the Brookings Institution, which reported that manufacturing, as a share of U.S. GNP, has fallen over two percentage points from 1978 to 1988. Further, the U.S. has fallen behind most of its major industrial rivals in productivity growth. This means the U.S. has to rely on a weak dollar, wage restraints and steady erosion in U.S. living standards in an attempt to reduce the troublesome U.S. trade deficit.

Back in 1960, the U.S. accounted for 34% of all manufacturing jobs; today, only 24%. Meanwhile, service sector jobs have jumped from 56% to 73% of the economy. Nearly nineteen out of twenty new jobs are low-paying service sector jobs.

The United States used to produce and sell 50% of the world's automobiles. That percentage has dropped to less than 20%. The United States used to lead the world in fifteen major industries. It now leads in only two: aircraft and computers. In 1980, the United States accounted for nearly half of all computer exports. It saw its computer lead dissipate to only 31% by 1986. The United States has lost 600,000 highly skilled jobs to foreign competition from 1980 to 1988. Foreigners captured 46.6% of U.S. patents in 1987. The U.S. share of consumer electronics dropped from 100% to 35%, and in VCRs from 10% to 1%.

The United States will have a shortage of 500,000 scientists by the year 2010. Presently, between 1,300-1,800 faculty positions at U.S. colleges and universities are vacant. Fully 60,000 high school math and science teachers in the United States are not qualified. By 1995, the U.S. will need an estimated 300,000 more secondary school math and science teachers. Meanwhile, U.S. students spend only 180 days in school, while Japanese children spend 240 days a year under instruction, and European children 220 days. Poorly qualified workers mean American business is far less competitive now and in the future.

U.S. corporations have dangerously low liquidity and alarmingly high debt levels. U.S. corporations doubled their debt from 1982 to 1988 to nearly $2 trillion. Debt service jumped to 40% of cash flow, with new corporate debt amounting to 90% of the total value of all corporations combined. There is now more than a dollar of debt for every dollar in equity, a most dangerous situation.

The leveraged buyout mania of 1987 and 1988 was scandalous and nonproductive. With the LBOs, financial sharks were allowed to pay nothing for assets they acquired with effectively no personal risk. High risk loans were arranged for these scoundrels by high rolling lending institutions, which were gambling with the faith and deposits of their customers. These lending sharks would do anything for high interest rates, betting on the gamble they could liquidate (or fire sale) the targeted company for a profit.

Of the junk bond total, 30% were purchased by insurance companies, 30% by mutual funds, 15% by pension funds, 8% by thrift institutions (S&Ls), with the Japanese buying the balance. (No wonder insurance companies are in trouble.) These financial shenanigans did nothing to enhance Wall Street's reputation. But then again, Drexel's concession to plead guilty to six felony counts and pay a $650 million fine caused the public to view Wall Street as primarily a den of pocket-picking thieves.

But this is not the end of the problems in corporate America. Foreign producers are increasingly winning a bigger chunk of American capital spending business. This even further endangers the slim hope of reducing the trade deficit. Sales by small businesses, which create 80% of all new jobs, began to slow in September 1988. There is a glut of commercial real estate all over the country. When the last recession hit, this glut of commercial real estate led to a crisis in the lending institutions - mortgage companies, investment banks, insurance companies, S&Ls and the like.

Finally, American business is faced with an accelerating health crisis. Over 75% of U.S. companies with more than 5,000 employees have reported AIDS among their employees and dependents according to the consulting firm of Foster Higgins. The AIDS epidemic in business is a volcano waiting to erupt during a stressful economic recession, political or climatic crisis. Of course, U.S. businesses are increasingly being looked to by the federal government to foot the bill for all these medical costs. In 1988, U.S. profits after taxes and dividends were $59.6 billion. A federal medical insurance bill of $25 billion would wipe out 42% of these profits. Imagine what this would do to the U.S. stock market.

The time to borrow is when interest rates are below the rate of inflation. This was the case up to 1980. Then for the remainder of the 1980s, we had high real interest rates, interest rates above the rate of inflation. This was the time to save and pay off debt. So overall, U.S. consumers, businesses and the federal government did precisely the wrong thing at the wrong time in the business cycle - borrow when real interest rates were high.

Remember that only a few things can happen when it comes to debt. Debt can either be paid off, refinanced, defaulted on, or inflated into oblivion. We have reached the point where U.S. debt will likely be defaulted on and/or inflated away.

Debt is like a drug. In fact, it could be said we have a drug epidemic because we have a debt epidemic. Both lead to death, one physical, the other financial. It takes more and more drugs for an addict to get high. It takes more and more debt to sustain a debt-based economy. We're in a Catch-22 situation. Businesses in a recession will borrow to avoid bankruptcy. But if the economic recovery continues, because of maximized industrial capacity, other corporations will need to borrow for expansion.

Even the religious ministries have gotten high on debt. But with the Jim Bakker and other scandals, religious organizations are facing sharp revenue fall-offs, creating more financial crises.

The nationwide *"devil-may-care"* attitude toward debt has led to a gambler's perspective. Volume in U.S. futures trading has quadrupled to more than 200 million contracts in the past decade alone. This means that Chicago is now the world's leading financial center, when the volume of all futures contracts are totaled.

Third World Debt

As with the little boy who cried wolf too often, investors have dismissed the problem of Third World debt, assuming the problem is either resolved or will simply go away. And yet, the Third World debt situation has reached another crisis point. Poor Third World countries are transferring their wealth to the richer developed countries of the world at a rate that is alarming. The year 1988 saw record wealth transfers from these destitute Third World countries to the world's richer nations. The World Bank warned that the drain of funds from these impoverished countries *"of the speed and magnitude recorded in recent years represents a new and significant constraint on their expansion."*

In 1988, the 17 most highly indebted countries of the Third World provided the rich countries and multinational lending institutions with $31.1 billion more than they received in return. This is triple the amount of wealth transferred in 1983. Key countries in Latin America involved in this wealth transfer via debt repayment are Brazil, Mexico, Argentina and Venezuela.

In 1987, the total debt of the Third World developing countries increased 10.4% to $1.2 trillion. It is now even higher.

Mexico, located at the U.S. soft underbelly (border) is the most dangerous basket case. Mexico's population of 80 million includes 30 million under 17 years of age. Mexico's unemployment rate is higher than it was during the depression of the 1930s. Plus, over the next decade, Mexico's work force will double. Mexico's external debt is now above $100 billion, with almost a $10 billion a year annual debt service. A striking 60% of the Mexican federal budget goes to pay interest alone on its foreign debt.

Mexican workers go underground and cannot afford to pay taxes since the real wages of Mexican workers have effectively fallen 66% since 1982. Former president of Mexico, Miguel de la Madrid declared, *"We repudiate the vision of a world integrated economy which relegates us to the margin. The effort and sacrifice of Latin America's people have not met with fair reward."*

The president of Mexico, Carlos Salinas de Gortari, called for a renegotiation of Mexico's $104 billion foreign debt when he was sworn into office in early December 1988, amid street protests and job walkouts. He warned, *"I declare emphatically and with conviction: above the interests of the creditors are the interests of Mexicans. It is unacceptable and unsustainable for Mexico to continue to transfer its resources to other countries."* Sadly, when President Bush and President Salinas discussed Mexico's horrendous debt problems, they ate chocolate truffles, dusted with 24-karat gold. So much for the words versus the actions of politicians.

The situation is not better in the rest of Latin America. Few Americans have any knowledge of how dangerous this Third World debt crisis has become. For example, Peru's president, Alann Garcia, stated in late November 1988, *"Norms and theories of the International Monetary Fund have exhausted themselves, blocking the possibility of a reconstruction of the international economic system."* Peru, like Mexico, is effectively in revolution. The former president of Argentina, Raul Alfonsin, declared that Latin America is in the midst of *"the most serious economic crisis in all its history."* Of course, Argentina had just dealt with a major military revolt, an event forecast in an early 1988 REAPER.

A December 1988 issue of *The Wall Street Journal* headlined, *"Unfunny UN Money: Brazil's Price Spiral Nears Hyper-Inflation, Could Ruin Economy."* The government of Brazil, saddled with extreme double-digit inflation, has been facing wave after wave of angry protest, which culminated with army units firing on striking steel workers. Anarchy is almost the situation in major urban centers in Brazil, such as Rio. Soaring inflation, political impotence, labor unrest and falling living standards all plague Brazil.

The Third World generally is facing an aging population crisis too. Developing countries account for 58% of all people age 55 and older. These Third World countries also account for 80% of the 1.2 million people who pass their fifty-fifth birthday every month. So there is little hope of these Third World nations ever paying off their debt. Old people don't work. They have to be cared for. This costs money. These Third World debts, therefore, will either be inflated away or defaulted upon, probably a combination of both. It was deceptive for the Bush administration to come up with a scheme whereby the U.S. and Japanese taxpayers buy Third World debt at a discount, in order to bail out the big international banks and support the corrupt and bankrupt governments of Latin America. Such a program was only a band-aid on a major financial wound. And it will only intensify the crisis longer term.

U.S. Government Debt

Far from reducing the federal debt, the Reagan administration dramatically increased it. The welfare state under President Reagan also expanded substantially. The Reagan revolution of welfare reduction was a myth.

The federal government under Jimmy Carter took 19.4% of GNP in taxes. In 1988, under President Reagan, it also took 19.4% of GNP. In 1980, U.S. government spending, according to the Congressional Budget Office, was $591 billion. In fiscal 1988 it reached $1 trillion, an increase of 80% in eight years. Interest on the national debt rose from $53 billion in 1980 to $151 billion in

1988, a rise of 185%. Defense spending grew from $134 billion in 1980 to $293 billion in 1988, a rise of 118%. Social Security rose from $278 billion in 1980 to $498 billion in 1988, up 79%. Every 1% increase in unemployment increases the federal deficit approximately $40 billion. Plus, the federal government has $745 billion outstanding in subsidized loans and loan guarantees, made by the likes of the VA, SBA and Export-Import Bank. A former Reagan administration budget official, M. Kathryn Eickhoff declared, *"It's a system waiting for an accident to happen."*

Then President-elect George Bush's ideas on eliminating the federal deficit through an Orwellian *"flexible freeze"* was a pipe dream. The General Accounting Office warned it would be impossible to *"freeze our way out of the deficit problem."* The nation's budget deficit has over $500 billion in hidden costs and so is much worse than reported. According to the GAO, higher taxes were *"probably unavoidable."* (The GAO is the congressional watchdog agency.) The GAO further reported that the $150 billion deficit reported for the fiscal year ending September 30, 1988 was a sham, masked by growth of surpluses in committed reserve accounts such as the Social Security trust fund. The Social Security surplus was estimated to be $52 billion, which means the true budget deficit was over $200 billion, not counting all the *"off-the-budget"* items, just taking into consideration Social Security factors alone. The real federal deficit was not $155 billion, but actually $252 billion, camouflaged by $97 billion in excess taxes collected by Social Security and other trust funds.

The October 20, 1988 *Wall Street Journal* reported, *"To truly narrow a budget deficit, most analysts agree that the nation must raise taxes and curb the exploding cost of such programs as Medicare and Social Security."* The chairman of the Federal Reserve, Alan Greenspan, declared, *"I want to stress that the long run is rapidly becoming the short run. If we do not act promptly, the imbalances in the economy are such that the effect of the deficit will be increasingly felt with some immediacy."* In other words, we're in a monetary crisis. Former Fed chairman Paul Volcker chimed in, *"We are hostage to the psychology of markets in moving money to the United States from abroad."*

On and on it goes. There is no apparent end to it. Do our politicians and federal bureaucrats really think the world will continue to finance us and support the U.S. dollar as the world's reserve currency when our twin deficits (trade and federal) continue to mushroom?

From 1979 to 1988, private foreign holding of U.S. Treasury and corporate securities increased 600%. The annual need for financial capital from abroad leaped from $1 billion to $154 billion over those ten years. The U.S. degenerated from being the world's largest creditor, with net foreign assets of $95 billion, to becoming the world's largest net debtor, with net foreign liabilities of more than $400 billion.

Japan then bought 30% of our debt. But as Hiroaki Mohri, a pension fund manager for Yasuda Trust and Banking Company warned, *"Many Japanese investors just don't feel safe in the U.S. After the crash, survival called for a new strategy. Part of that is to reduce our U.S. exposure."* There is simply no way, given the present spendthrift trends which the U.S. is pursuing, that the U.S. will be able to maintain its present level of foreign borrowing at these interest rates. We are well on our way to becoming a *"banana republic."*

The American public is far more astute than its politicians or financially secure civil service bureaucrats. The 1988 voter turnout was the lowest for a presidential election since 1924 - a 64-year low. Only 50.1% of those eligible to vote did so. So half of the U.S. population eligible to vote did not vote, while nearly half of those who did note, voted for the loser. The U.S. obviously is a fractured nation. This was further aggravated by the divided rule between the Bush administration and the Democratic congress.

Most blacks and Hispanics did not vote, but those who did vote voted 90% Democratic, for Dukakis & Co. Clearly we had a fragile political and civil state of affairs held together by a very thin economic thread.

Not that voting really makes any difference when it comes to the U.S. Congress. In 1988, 99% of the 408 members of the U.S. House of Representatives seeking reelection were successful. And these congressmen had the audacity to ask the American public for a pay raise to $135,000 a year, when by a 40-to-1 margin the public told *USA Today* they opposed the pay hike.

During the primaries in 1988, the Republican and Democratic regulars voted for candidates who gutlessly did not face the issues. As Anthony Lewis declared, *"The notion that the public controls governments has all the elements of myth. In 1988, it became a groaning fiction."*

The problems facing the state and local governments were equally severe. Sarah Johnson of Data Resources reported that neither state nor local governments any longer had the financial cushion necessary to weather a downturn. Over 80% of Americans live in a major city. Therefore U.S. cities, with the growing AIDS and drug epidemics, disgruntled minority populations, and financial bankruptcies, are a time bomb.

The U.S. Dollar and The Trade Balance

In 1981, the U.S. was the world's largest creditor nation with a net investment income of $34 billion. This resulted in a current accounts surplus. By 1988 the United States was the world's largest debtor nation with net liabilities approaching $550 billion. The annual net interest on debt owed to overseas investors doubled. U.S. investment income slipped into the red in 1988 for the first time in more than sixty years. It became worse in subsequent years. The U.S. trade deficit and current accounts are in dismal shape.

Bridgewater Associates provided some insightful perspectives on the U.S. economic situation as it impacted world commerce in 1988. The U.S. current accounts deficit was approximately 3% of GNP and 30% of a year's exports.

U.S. foreign debts of $550 billion were 11% of GNP and 150% of exports. Therefore, if the U.S. reduced its trade deficit by 20% a year, it would not be able to stop borrowing until sometime between 1995 and 2000. At that time, the U.S. would have a foreign debt of approximately $1 trillion. If the U.S. then ran a trade surplus so that its exports exceeded its imports by 20%, it would not pay off its debt until between the years 2025 and 2050. For foreign investors to have a positive real rate of return on their investment in the United States, they must assume the U.S. is willing to allow an enormous transfer of wealth, and be willing to wait a long time for the payback.

Further, in order to make the U.S. dollar attractive, U.S. interest rates had to move up. The U.S. dollar was increasingly competing with other nations which ran large current accounts deficits, such as Great Britain, Canada and Australia. When the U.S. eases and Great Britain, Canada and Australia tighten, the U.S. dollar falls. U.S. real interest rates had been too low, which is why the yield curve had to become inverted.

Competition for necessary global funds is the name of the game. If the U.S. continues to maintain its tremendous appetite for borrowing, it faces a financial crisis. Inverted yield curves exist in Australia and England. But neither Australia nor England run federal budget deficits, unlike the U.S. So the U.S. has to offer an even more attractive situation to retain international investors' confidence. Thus, the U.S. is indeed hostage to the international financial markets.

As Ray Dalio of Bridgewater explained, the U.S. was running a huge current accounts deficit because investment assets in the United States were cheap. In order for there to be a net inflow of capital into the United States, and therefore a surplus in the capital account, the U.S. has to run a current accounts deficit. Current means short-lived and capital means investment. When a country is running a current accounts deficit and a capital accounts surplus, it is effectively selling off its investment assets in order to pay for its immediate consumption. This is unhealthy. Put differently, the United States was squandering its birthright.

The Japanese were key in this scenario, purchasing nearly 30% of U.S. debt. When the Japanese saw that they could not receive a positive real rate of return, they no longer invested in the United States. Also, with recession approaching, the risk of investing in U.S. plants and manufacturing facilities for the Japanese was rising. The Japanese already owned over 600 U.S. manufacturing plants, not counting those located in Mexico, just south of the U.S. border. The Japanese investments in U.S. real estate and manufacturing plants were based upon the premise that the U.S. would remain the world's most important consumer. Most of the assets purchased by the Japanese are primarily valuable because they serve the U.S. market, even though increasingly the Japanese were using U.S. manufacturing facilities as a cover for export to Europe. But by and large, in order for U.S. capital assets to be profitable to the

Japanese, both U.S. consumption and the U.S. dollar had to stay strong. This was difficult to achieve. This meant the United States would have to dramatically cut consumption and/or lower prices in world terms, the latter through further depreciation of the U.S. dollar long term. This in turn caused foreign investors to shift out of U.S. dollar denominated debt. As U.S. creditors moved their assets out of U.S. financial assets, and even away from U.S. tangible assets, interest rates rise and hasten the decline in the U.S. standard of living, the trade picture, and U.S. consumption. Why? Because they withdraw the credit and financing which the United States today finds vital to sustain itself.

There were other growing problems in global trade. For example, the international financial press reported that a scandal was brewing in one of Switzerland's big three banks and protectionism was on the rise. The U.S. slapped protectionist measures on European imports when the Europeans refused to accept U.S. beef. Such led to a slowdown in global trade. The breakdown in Montreal of the 96-nation GATT talks was another example of this increasing economic friction. Clyde Prestowitz of the Carnegie Endowment for International Peace reported, *"Day by day the world is slipping into protectionist, regional bloc trading."* Protectionism is historically a forerunner of war. The U.S. War Clock projected the U.S. facing a high risk of war between 1988 and 1992.

All of the world's developed countries were heavily in debt and competing for funds. This means local, domestic economies were being sacrificed to the high interest rates necessary to hold hot international investment money. The growth rate in national debt among G-7 countries from 1980 to 1987 was as follows: Italy up 23%; France up 17.3%; Canada up 16.8%; U.S. up 15%; Japan up 11.4%; Great Britain up 10.6%; and Germany up 9.6%.

Globally we saw an inverted yield curve in Great Britain, Australia and the United States; subsequently we saw the entire world slip into a recession. The harsh fundamental factors affecting exchange rates and the U.S. dollar particularly truly came into play: the supply and demand for the U.S. dollar; the supply and demand for each particular foreign currency; the level of interest rates of each currency; purchasing power parity; and finally, public confidence. Against this criteria, the U.S. dollar was unimpressive. With the financial situation of nearly all the world's governments (perhaps with the exception of Switzerland) being so dismal, why would investors opt for any currency at all? Will they not instead choose gold?

In summary, *"The Real State of the Nation"* can be summed up in one word - *"CHAOTIC!"* The United States is a poor country that is still behaving like it is rich. The U.S. is still living in an economic illusion, oblivious to ever-approaching and encroaching reality. It is the dawning of this reality, the busting of this bubble, which will lead to all the shocks, fallouts and major readjustments in the upcoming years. So, being out of debt, being liquid, cash rich, and owning gold, gems, agricultural real estate, one's own home and international currencies is prudent. International diversification should also be pursued. Being a citizen of one country (United States), with a corporation established in another country (Great Britain), banking in a third country (Switzerland), operating out of a fourth country (Bermuda), while marketing and investing worldwide make an awful lot of sense. Bureaucrats treat foreigners better than their own citizens because government bureaucracies own their own citizens. The common people today are seen as *"pawns in the game,"* to be sacrificed. Federal bureaucrats today are anything but *"public servants."* And they're not even civil, so they can hardly be called *"civil servants."*

This may not be the last train out, but it could be the last chance to comprehensively get one's affairs in order. A word to the wise is sufficient, once *"the real state of the nation"* is comprehended.

ECONOMIC PERSPECTIVES
May 24, 1990

King Pin

Since World War II, the United States has had pretty much its own way with the rest of the world. Despite the fact that this situation changed dramatically in the 1980s, particularly in the financial and economic arenas, the nation still gives lip service to the decline of its supremacy. The United States intellectually acknowledges that the economic playing field is broader, with many more substantial players. However, the U.S. still acts as if it rules the roost. It is this wide gap between perception and reality which now is in the process of being closed, probably painfully, during the next few years. My War Clock projects the risk of civil unrest and war to be very high during this time frame, too. *"Peace, peace, when there is no peace?"*

If a worker in a business acts as though he is sovereign, that he can do his own thing, he doesn't last long. Of course, given legal precedent these days, the boss may tolerate this aberrant and rebellious behavior for a while. But over time, a nonconforming worker who refuses to be productive will lose his job.

Boss

In like manner, U.S. creditors are the *"boss"* of the United States. Japan, for instance, finances 30% of U.S. debt. European investors also contribute significantly. But the U.S. is not getting its economic and financial house in order, in either the public or private sectors. And so foreign creditors are uneasy, insecure, and slowly but surely looking for investment havens outside of the United States for additional capital placement. Outright withdrawal of capital from the U.S. is on the rise as well.

Concerns

Just what is the foreign perspective? Basically, the United States is viewed as being a debt junky, a spendthrift, with little consideration, appreciation or understanding of its subordinate financial status or foreign financiers. Financier Carl Icahn was quoted in Dan Dorfman's *USA Today* column: *"I'm worried. There's too much debt. The savings rate is too low; too many people are living way beyond their means, and the day of reckoning is coming. The stock market is overvalued and I think it's headed lower."*

Foreigners are alarmed that the people of the United States think economic progress can be achieved through the ballot box and the courtroom. The surging number of elected minority officials to head U.S. major cities emphasizes this point. Economic progress via political power makes foreign investors shudder. The classic *"American way"* of boot-strapping one's way up economically is dead. And if the ballot box is unavailable, there is always an all-too-eager attorney, ready to sue someone to obtain riches for his client. The U.S. has the highest per capita of attorneys of any country in the world, and 96% of the world's civil lawsuits.

The S&L bailout, and particularly the high level political corruption associated with Lincoln Savings, raised international eyebrows. All-in-all, the clear message the United States is sending foreign investors is that the United States will not discipline itself fiscally, and that the country will continue to spend as if it has a bottomless money well. This results in foreigners tactfully withdrawing their investments from U.S. Treasury debt securities, a reluctance to establish factories in major U.S. cities, and effectively a willingness to sell the U.S. short. This is a precarious position for the United States. The U.S. is not owning up to the ever-true reality that *"the debtor is servant to the lender."* The Japanese, for example, now control almost 900 U.S. manufacturers, and employ over 300,000 Americans. Five of the top ten California banks are Japanese.

To echo Oswald Spengler from the 1920s, we are living in a time of world cities, when our civilization is *"frozen"*. The climatic, economic and political changes we are experiencing should lead to massive decentralization between now and 2012. This will in turn create racial unrest within the United States as the minority groups come to realize that their major political victories in U.S. cities are hollow and of short-term benefit. Therefore, diversification of business and investment interests outside of major U.S. cities, into small towns and rural areas is recommended. Further diversification into gold and hard currencies held outside the United States in major conservative banks is prudent.

The Economic Cycle and Capital

Back to basics. The business cycle is a function ultimately of the expansion and contraction in the use of credit. Normally, such an expansion takes 50 to 60 years to work its way from one extreme to the other and back again. Generally speaking, the economy moves from depression to thrift and savings, and from there to a sense of confidence. Confidence leads to investment. Investment leads to increased confidence and expanding economic activity. Economic activity rolls on to good times, and people forget the lessons of the previous debt-contracting depression. The use of credit springs up. Prosperity soars. The use of credit eventually results in the abuse of credit, and inflation. Inflation leads to economic corruption, unwise use of human and natural resources, overbuilding, excess capacity, and dog-eat-dog speculation. Interest rates rise and eventually move from below the rate of inflation to above the rate of inflation. (The currency of the realm falls until this occurs.) But when interest rates become real, providing a real rate of return after inflation and taxes, the economy effectively shifts from favoring the borrower to the lender. This occurred in the early 1980s in the U.S. economy. The continuation of the debt binge for all sectors of the U.S. economy during the 1980s was only made possible by the willingness of foreign creditors - primarily European and Japa-

nese - to continue to finance the U.S. economic party. With Europe now focusing on reorganizing itself with the EEC, Germany reuniting, and Eastern
Europe (the new Third World) opening up and requiring huge capital infusions,
competition is stiff for global funds. Capital routinely placed in the United
States by Europe during the 1980s is being withdrawn in the 1990s. On the
other side of the world, the Japanese are facing their own economic problems,
political unrest and earthquake threats. Meanwhile the other Asian tigers nip
away at the Japanese economic empire as the Japanese trade surplus shrinks.
Japanese capital is no longer available to the degree it was in the 1980s to
finance U.S. debt. This means it's time to pay for the economic party of the
1980s.

THE BEST LONG-TERM INVESTMENTS
September 1, 1988

The Best Investment

Investing is ultimately personalized if it is to be comprehensively successful long term. Why? Because investing is the personal expression of an individual's wants, needs, desires and hopes in the financial arena.

I consider the best investment any one of us ever makes is in our spiritual, mental and psychological welfare, our physical health, our knowledge, and in our skills, and in that of our families, friends and church. Next to this, I think owning and operating our own business, even if it's only a part-time occupation, is an unequaled investment.

Real Estate

In real estate I like irrigated, organic, rural farmland best of all, preferably located in the South, Southeast or Southwest, and not much farther north than Iowa in the Midwest. The abrupt changes in climate, the probability of a colder climate, more drought and a shorter growing season as the crop growing regions shift further south, are limiting parameters on agricultural investments.

With some shopping around, a careful investor should be able to pick up properties at excellent if not bargain basement prices. In the South, particularly in Louisiana, Texas and Oklahoma, there are great values to be gleaned with cash from banks, S&Ls and from federal agencies such as the FDIC and the Farmers Home Loan Administration. Not only should the value of irrigated, organic farmland increase on a per acre basis, but the prices of crops grown on these properties should also increase over the next 20 years.

Also, in real estate, we are on the cutting edge of the *"baby boomers"* now beginning to think about retirement. With the climate in the northern states overall becoming colder, the shift to the Sun Belt will accelerate as the *"baby boomers"* become *"gray panthers"* in the next 20 years. California prices are sky high, and in Florida real estate retirement communities are not cheap either. On the other hand, Texas and Louisiana, having gone through an economic bust due to the collapse of the oil industry, have numerous desirable retirement home properties for sale. All along the Gulf Coast, from Texas to Florida (including Louisiana and Mississippi), a wise investor will look for bargains to buy and hold long term, with rental potential in the meantime.

In terms of multi-unit structures, the banks are still under tremendous pressure in Texas, Oklahoma and Louisiana, particularly. For example, apartment units have been purchased for as little as $800 per unit, with cost of construction of $15,000 per unit. Such properties are available under the most favorable of financial terms where bargains still abound in Houston, Austin, Dallas, Corpus Christi, Denver, Tulsa and Oklahoma City.

Oil and Gas

Employing the principle that we like to buy investments when they are out of favor, I think we will see a revived bull market in the petroleum oil complex, most probably in the early to mid-1990s. A bull market in natural gas has already begun. We should look to invest in petroleum oil complex stocks once the stock market has bottomed out.

With avant garde money, we should consider placing some venture capital into the new free energy areas, the soft energy fields. The best investment areas with this new free energy technology should be in the medical field, as well as in firms which replace public utilities and big oil companies.

Currencies

With Japan facing increasing intense competition from the other Asian *"Tiger"* countries, coupled with the likely risk of extensive earthquake and volcanic damage to the Japanese islands, I think the currencies of choice will again become the European currencies. With Eastern Europe and Russian opening up, the next century's focus could be on Europe, outside of China and the Far East.

Stocks and Bonds

With the threat of military conflict increasing, investment in key military sensitive stocks and military commodities should do well, beginning in the early to mid-1990s. Also food stocks which benefit from the harsh and variable climate should move up in price.

An International Perspective

Finally, I still think it is best to be a citizen of one country (the United States, for example), live in a second country (let's say, England), bank in a third country (like Switzerland), have your business operate out of a fourth country (perhaps Bermuda), and market a product out of a fifth country (like Canada). This type of widespread distribution of persons, assets, power base, political moorings, business base and tax liability maximizes freedom. Remember, under the religion of humanism, the state (civil government) really believes it owns its citizens. Thus, to keep from being a slave or being harassed, this global perspective is the best strategy.

For example, an English taxpaying productive citizen living in the United States is treated with more respect and a more *"hands-off"* approach by American bureaucrats than is a U.S. citizen. That's the way it works pretty much in every developed country of the world. Governments treat foreigners better than they treat their own citizens. Perhaps needless to say, this international approach also better enables us to avoid devastating legal entanglements.

Commodities

Because today nearly every investment is a commodity, because nearly every liquid investment is traded on the futures market, to not know how to deal with futures now is to miss the boat. Furthermore, due to dramatic upcoming changes all around, the opportunities to make fortunes in futures will be unequaled in the '90s. Whether for direct investment or to hedge, expect futures to be hot!

Conclusion

Overall, I look for volatile and abrupt changes in the world during the next 20 years. These recommended diversified investments should better enable us to survive and prosper during these times of change.

THE WINDOW OF CHANGE
January 28, 1988

Beginning in 1980, extending through the year 2012, I think this 32-year time period should be one of the most tumultuous and exciting in the history of mankind. We are in the middle of a massive *"window of change."* The metamorphosis began its acceleration in 1987.

Cities

Nothing should go untouched. The decrepit trend of centralization has now topped out and should decline precipitously. The fresh, new emerging trend of decentralization is picking up speed. The vertical bureaucratic institutions and the cities which birthed them are in rapid decay.

Cities were never meant for man anyway. As Oswald Spengler pointed out in his massive tome, *The Decline of the West* (written in the early years of the 20th century), cities consume both people and resources. World cities are the capstone of a civilization. Cities are effectively lifeless and death oriented. The concrete, asphalt, glass and steel of cities sucks in the natural and human resources from the country and draws the very life out of them. Life begets life. Man and nature thus can only flourish in a decentralized rural, village oriented economy.

China

Western civilization as we know it is in critical condition, a terminal case. As the University of Pittsburgh pointed out in a major study produced back in 1944, the baton of civilization has been passed to the Far East. China over the next 500 years will be what the United States and Western Europe were in the 19th and 20th centuries.

Singapore

Forward-thinking people, both young and old, will learn Chinese and relocate to the Far East Pacific Basin now. The cities of choice there include Singapore, an English-speaking former British colony, which has the best port in the region. With oil again rising to pre-eminence in the early 1990s, Singapore should again boom.

Australia

Western civilization's outpost in the Far East Pacific Basin is Australia and New Zealand. New Zealand has already radically moved to free up its economy. Australia is beginning to take note of the success enjoyed by its *"little brother"* nation to the east. Moreover, it is not by accident that 26 of the wealthiest families in the world built massive mansions in Australia's capital city of Canberra. These generation-to-generation extended families know very well where the future lies. It is no coincidence either that as far back as 1973, at *"war game"* exercises held at NORAD Headquarters in Colorado Springs, Australia was painted red and labeled *"New China."*

Already the Japanese/Australian connection is well established. The more time that passes, the more the World War II wounds between the Japanese and the Chinese will heal. The Japanese need new markets. China is a natural. China, surrounded by the new Industrial Tigers—Singapore, Hong Kong, Taiwan and South Korea—will look to these countries and their mentor, Japan, for the future. Hopefully, the Australians will sober up as they watch our demise from a distance. Such an empathetic lesson, coupled with the emerging technology which controls the weather, will allow the Australians to develop their vast desert areas which to this point have limited Australian growth to primarily the coastal regions.

Perth

Another choice city is the freewheeling entrepreneurial city of Perth, located in progressive Western Australia. Perth could very well end up with America's heritage. Already the freedom-oriented government officials there in that resourceful continent are moving back to sound money.

"The Western Australian Government has announced plans to launch what is believed to be the first international gold bank in the world.

"The bank, which will have its headquarters in Perth, is to be developed as a result of the success of GoldCorp Australia and the launch of the Australian Nugget gold coin programme during the past year.

"It is to be known as the Gold Banking Corporation and will trade internationally as the Gold Bank of Australia.

"The decision to establish the new corporation was announced by the Premier and Treasurer of Western Australia, the Hon. Brian Burke, when he introduced the necessary legislation in the Western Australian Legislative Assembly...

"The bank will:

— Provide international banking and investment services in gold and foreign currencies to gold producers, private investors, international banks and government authorities;

— Issue coinage and securities denominated in gold and other precious metals and generally utilize gold as an international currency;

— Operate the internationally accredited Western Australian Mint and gold refinery and carry on the crushing, milling and gold recovery operations previously undertaken by the Western Australian State Batteries;

— Develop and market internationally, products made of gold and other precious metals. " Source: *The Australian Nugget Journal*

Vancouver

If the decision is made to remain in North America, then the city of choice is Vancouver in British Columbia, Canada. Resource rich Canada, with this fabulous port city and the Vancouver/Hong Kong connection, all make bustling Vancouver the North American, West Coast city of the future. Once the Red Chinese take over the free market in Hong Kong, and the inevitable synthesis there occurs, the natural link between Chinese Hong Kong and the wealthy Hong Kong businessmen who have already relocated to Vancouver will provide a rich pipeline of commercial opportunity.

Chinese Reciprocity

Less than 200 years from now, I would not be at all surprised if communism is seen as an aberration in the long, proud history of the industrious Chinese. The Chinese should return to their roots in Confucius, and from that base build a major civilization. Confucius' basic operating principle of *"reciprocity"* is the Eastern version of what we call in the West *"covenant"* or *"contract."* Early American Christianity was based upon *"covenant"* or *"contract."* From that religious decentralized base of personal responsibility and freedom, Americans built a society based upon self-government which economically rewarded individual initiative through service and cooperation.

The religious, governmental and economic decentralized nature of the *"covenant"* or *"contract"* is the only method of resolving the age-old governmental, religious and economic question of how to balance off the rights of the individual with those of collective society. Given this covenantal and contractual base in Confucius' concept of *"reciprocity,"* the Chinese are thus grounded philosophically. (Government is always religion applied to economics.)

It would not be surprising either to see the Chinese exchange a language which is graphic and perceptual, for one which is more linear and conceptual.

Cut free from bureaucratic restrictions, the dynamism and creativity of the Chinese is unequaled. Hong Kong shows us this clearly. And despite the fact that throughout the rest of Southeast Asia, the Chinese are the most persecuted of minorities, they still prosper economically wherever they are. The Chinese are hardworking, have strong family ties, study and learn skills, save and are creatively industrious. Unlike the Australians, who see recreation (play) as the *"end all"* in life, the Chinese by contrast regard recreation in its proper meaning of the word, as *"re-creation,"* creative, fun work, in other words.

The Chinese could organize the first society ever to resolve the problem between the individualism of capitalism and the collectivism of communism. How? By requiring individual initiative and productivity as basic for earned local communal ownership of businesses in a debt-free environment. Thus, the Chinese could resolve the dialectic tension between man's need for community (love), and man's need for individual self-worth (personal incentive). In such a manner, the Chinese workers could earn the ownership of the means of production from the bottom up, rather than through the failing bureaucratic communistic top-down methodology in operation today.

The United States

Being honest intellectually, I do not believe the United States of America will be a good place to live between now and 2012. We have too much painful error to be cleansed. Too many of our leaders are spoiled, self-centered, materialistic and violent. The common people are captured by illusion and strong delusion. If Moses with all God's miracles could not change the Hebrew slaves coming out of Egypt with 40 years of basic training in the desert, what makes us think any man or any group of men are going to change the violent, dependent hedonists of the United States over the next 20 years?

As existentialists who live for today, Americans have no vision of the future. The time horizon of a people has always determined their level of wealth. The longer the time view of a society, the greater its savings for the future and thus the greater its wealth long-term. (Savings produces capital which provides the necessary base for the creation of wealth.) The shorter the time perspective of people, the poorer they are. When a people live for today, as is the present situation in the United States, they are one breath away from poverty. This is our present status. The debt-laden middle class is only one paycheck away from bankruptcy and skid row.

We are also an aging population. By the year 2020, a third of the U.S. population will be at least 55 years old. But the sham known as the Social Security System is already bankrupt. Due to selfishness, there will be few youngsters to take care of the post-World War II baby-boom generation when they are old.

We shy away from creativity and development of new products because of the fear of lawsuits. Indeed, 96 percent of the civil lawsuits in the world are filed in the United States. This legal civilized conflict can (will) quickly degenerate to physical conflict during a time of economic and political breakdown, particularly in our world cities.

Moreover, as Peikoff pointed out in his important book, *The Ominous Parallels*, we are moving rapidly toward the tyranny of fascist socialism, not unlike that which dominated Nazi Germany. And the rise of occultism in this country, which is filling the present religious void, is almost an exact repeat of what happened in Nazi Germany. The backlash against Hispanics, blacks, Jews, Asians, homosexuals and fundamental Bible-believing Christians is coming. Just give it time. The WASPs are historically the most violent people who have ever walked the face of the earth. (Just ask the American Indian.) Between 60 and 80 percent of the U.S. population still has its roots in the WASP tradition.

Communist-trained terrorist camps are located just across the U.S. southern border in Mexico. Our vital imported strategic industrial mineral and metal resources from Africa and South America are being cut off by the Soviet Union, Cuba and Nicaragua. We are being cleverly alienated from our Western European allies.

Only hapless Haiti has a worse AIDS epidemic per capita than the United States. And yet we treat what is clearly a public health concern as a political issue.

Our children, educated in the statist schools, are illiterate, emotional, demineralized and know little about history, science math or geography. They are puppets, waiting to be manipulated.

South Africa

One final thought. During this window of change, what is the ultimate contrary opinion country? South Africa! South Africa, like Australia, could be a pivotal country in the 21st century, provided Russian and U.S. State Department plans to destroy that nation are short circuited by economic, political and social collapse at home in the former U.S.S.R. and the U.S.

* * * * *

The next 510-year civilization cycle, as I have long pointed out, belongs to the Chinese. There are 50 million Chinese in Hong Kong, Taipei (Taiwan), and Singapore. The Chinese now dominate the economies of most of Southeast Asia. In Thailand, 20% of the population is Chinese, and that one-fifth controls the majority of the corporate assets. In Indonesia, the 5% of the population which is Chinese controls 75% of the corporate assets. In Malaysia, where the Islamic culture discriminates against the Chinese, the Chinese still dominate the economy anyway. Singapore is 75% Chinese.

* * * * *

The average wage in China is 27 cents an hour. This means Chinese in an 8-hour day make basically $2.00 a day, or $10.00 a week, or $40.00 a month. The U.S. standard of living is dying because wages are so cheap everywhere else around the world, and because U.S. capital is being shipped abroad to build high-tech plants in these low wage-earning countries.

GM is opening a plant in northeastern Red China, thanks to an October 10, 1992 trade agreement in which China exempted U.S. automakers from rigid government limits on the number and types of cars which foreign companies may produce in China. There go more American jobs in the auto industry, courtesy of *"The Heartbreak of America."*

Where are American jobs in other industries going? To China, financed with American workers' money deposited in multinational banks. Wing-Merrill is building $2 billion worth of power plants in China, Arco a $1.2 billion natural gas project, AT&T $1 billion plus telecommunications, semiconductor, mobile phone and R&D facilities. Boeing is receiving $800 million for filling China's order for six Boeing 777 jets; Coca-Cola $150 million for ten additional bottling plants; General Electric $150 million for aircraft engines; and Motorola $120 million for pagers, cellular telephones and semiconductors.

* * * * *

"The Far East is going to overtake the West economically sometime during the next four decades. We can see this coming. The Far East's culture combines respect for family, enormous thrift, a willingness to work hard and long, and a desire to escape poverty. There is no way the West can keep pace with Asians without matching them. They are leaving the welfare State;... Apart from...bankruptcy...we have no chance of matching Asia...

"The welfare State mentality is never voluntarily abandoned by the older generation that is totally dependent on it. The welfare State mentality is still alive and well in Western Europe, just as it is in East Germany. People do not abandon the welfare State mentality; the welfare State just dies, the way a parasite dies when its host expires." — Dr. Gary North - *Remnant Review*, February 19, 1993

...This is the end of the 510-year cycle I began writing about in 1977, when power shifts from the West to the East, which will probably occur by 2012. ...No wonder the gold is flowing to Asia.

* * * * *

China's population of 1.1 billion means that one out of every four human beings on earth is Chinese. China has moved into the 21st century. Marxism is no longer taught at the University of China, replaced now by business courses. China is a major buyer of gold. The Chinese work hard, and are smart in producing quality goods. They have business know-how, and they save and invest. The U.S. trade deficit in 1992 with China is estimated to have exceeded $18 billion. By 2020 China could have the world's largest economy. The savings rate in China is 35% — Richard Russell's - *Dow Theory Letters*, March 3, 1993

* * * * *

"If the Asian Pacific region continues to grow at a 6% rate, by the year 2009, Asia's share of world GNP will rise to 41% compared with 27% in 1989. North America's contribution will fall to 31% from 38% in 1989. That's a big decline. Western Europe will make up 28% of global GNP compared with 35% in 1989." — Bert Dohmen - *The Wellington Letter*, March 1993

SUN, EARTH, AND ECONOMY
September 18, 1993

Those of you who have followed my work over the years, particularly my turning point analysis, know that often when I have an *"enhanced cluster"* of turning points it is joined by extreme solar activity and/or significant disruptions in the earth's geomagnetic field. For years I have been using the data published weekly by the National Oceanic and Atmospheric Administration (NOAA) for all types of analyses, as these *"electrical"* natural forces affect the *"body electric"* and *"E-motions"* (energy-in-motion) of man in his many natural behavioral manifestations. Thus, you can imagine my delight when the May 1993 issue of Cycles published the correlations between: 1) the annual rate of change in the Dow Jones Industrial Average and the geomagnetic model projections; 2) the annual rate of change in 30-year bond yields and Ap projections; 3) the annual rate of change in spot gold changes and Ap geomagnetic change projections; 4) the annual rate of change in the U.S. CPI and Ap geomagnetic field changes; 5) U.S. manufacturing production percentage change and sunspot areas; and 6) annual rate of change in real U.S. GNP and Ap change.

What these charts clearly show is that the solar and geomagnetic field alterations have a direct effect (and correlation with) stocks, bonds, gold prices, the CPI, U.S. manufacturing and GDP.

Question: If there is obviously a close correlation between the sunspot areas, geomagnetic field changes and model projections with what takes place in U.S. stocks, bonds, gold, the CPI, U.S. manufacturing, and GNP, why isn't this taught widely in universities, discussed in the mass media, and generally well known? Could it be because it might awaken the *"natural man"* to his real state of affairs and open him up to a higher awareness, an *"open system"* reality which would be detrimental to the powers-that-be which control economic, political, scientific and religious life in the dark, closed Newtonian system in which we operate today?

In this regard, recall that in the chapter, *"Our Coming War With Iran,"* I stated, *"Radical Islam would like to attack Israel within three years. The director of the U.S. CIA recently stated that Iran and its allies pose a military threat to the United States within three to five years. Lawrence H. Berg of Omaha, Nebraska, writing in the July/August 1992 issue of Cycles, stated, 'The Astral Indicator bottoms in 1992 and peaks in 1995, making for an increased probability for war, peaking stock markets, and low temperatures in 1995.' Solar Cycle 22 (sunspots) bottom in 1995-1996, the same time the 18-1/3-year real estate cycle in the United States bottoms. So, my war cycle work, which projects our next significant U.S. war for 1995-1996, is right on the button. The year 1995 is when Harry E. Figgie predicts the U.S. will default on its debt (BANKRUPTCY 1995)...."*

We are also in the time frame between 1994 and 1997 when we remain affected by the 178-179-year sun retrograde cycle, a planetary alignment cycle, which dovetails with the 60-year cycle and the 100-year cycle, the 180-year volcano cycle, the next El Nino cycle for 1994-1995, the 170-year political trauma cycle which peaks in 1996, and the 510-year civilization supercycle which peaks in 1996-1997. Thus, this 1994-1997 time frame could be horrific.

What do the SESC Regression Models Prediction of Smoothed Sunspot Number and 10.7 cm Radio Flux project for this time frame? These are expressions of the factors that correlate so closely with what's happening with U.S. stocks, bonds, gold, the CPI, U.S. manufacturing and GNP. The SESC Regression Model Prediction of Smoothed Sunspot Number and 10.7 cm Radio Flux project turning point lows between mid-1994 and the end of 1997. In short, we are entering the worst of the maelstrom. The decline in sunspot numbers suggests significant economic contraction now.

TURNABOUT

September 9, 1992

When we say that someone is out of touch with reality, it is another way of expressing that they are ungrounded, and out of touch with the reality of Newtonian physics. If they are too far out of touch with reality, we say that they are touched in the head, or even crazy, perhaps insane. At the very least, we state that they do not have their feet on the ground.

The markets made a turnabout in 1980 when short-term interest rates soared to 22%-plus and went above the rate of inflation. At that point we experienced a key financial shift. Unlike the 1970s, it no longer paid an investor to borrow in the '80s, because interest rates were well above the rate of inflation. Rather, it paid an investor (and consumer and businessman) to lend, thus the turnabout, the shift to financial assets (stocks and bonds) as opposed to commodities, collectibles, gold, silver and the like in the 1980s.

That segment of society closest to the earth, to being grounded, to being in touch with Newtonian reality - commodity producers - learned the lesson of this great financial turnabout first. Oilmen, miners, ranchers, growers of crops - all went through a rolling depression in the 1980s. Business, which must also respond to the reality of the marketplace, learned as well, particularly manufacturing. Slower on the uptake were real estate, the service industry, and consumers. This should come as no surprise. These segments are further removed from grounded reality. Unfortunately, the segment which did not learn the economic and financial lesson or adjust was the great fiction we call civil (sic) government, the parasitic entity that lives at the expense of everyone else who is productive. Cites, states, and the federal government accelerated their flight from reality. Total U.S. debt is now at $14.3 trillion. In 1980, it was only $4.6 trillion. Federal debt today increases at a staggering rate of $18.14 billion a week. The U.S. government took nearly 200 years to accumulate its first $1 trillion in debt, and since then has increased it another $3 trillion to over $4 trillion. Federal spending in the first nine months of FY 1992 rose 10.8%, four times faster than the economy.

One thing the now immensely unpopular Ronald Reagan did get right was his statement, *"The closest thing to eternal life on earth is a government program."* But an actor in the White House, who made everyone feel good, was the perfect pied piper to lead the country on its flight from reality. Now, the spread between *"we the people"* and our federal government becomes even wider as we have two elitists, who have never had to be in touch with reality in their entire lives, leading this country. The Clintons are so far to the left, that after them there will be nothing left. No wonder discerning historians say that we are dangerously close to a period in U.S. history similar to the French Revolution.

Climatically, this is a revolutionary era. We are being hammered by extremes - the riots in L.A., Hurricane Andrew and the 7.4 California quake, extreme lows in the U.S. dollar, commodity prices and gold, and extreme highs in stocks and bonds.

Isn't this what we would expect at a turnabout? Everybody knows there are hard times now, and are starting to get back to reality, except for those farthest removed from reality - those who invest in paper in the cities and who sit in the seats of government.

Let's look at some of the extremes which suggest the turnabout is imminent. Climatically, the sunspot cycles headed down hard in 1992. The climate is becoming accordingly colder and more harsh, with more weather extremes. Historically, such has accompanied economic depressions, people getting back to basics - in other words, getting grounded. A bounce is not due until the trough of both the sunspot cycle and the 18-1/3-year real estate cycle in 1995-96. This is also when we're due to have another war. So the government disarming is doing precisely the wrong thing at the wrong time. I would suspect, accordingly, that both defense stocks and raw material stocks, particularly water stocks, should do well in this great turnabout.

It's significant that the Fed's lowering of the discount rate in 1929-1931 and 1990-1992 parallels the decline in sunspot cycle numbers. As I've written for years, the two run together, economic activity and solar activity.

Producer prices of all commodities are back lower than they were in nominal terms in the early 1950s. In real terms, they are off the bottom of the chart. Do not wise investors buy markets at extremes of price and time, particularly when investor sentiment toward the investment is deep, dark and dismal? Such is the attitude toward commodities now. Inflation has not yet kicked off. If it does, it's likely to be a flash fire.

Because the U.S. is the farthest removed from reality of all the countries in the world, accounting for 40% of all manmade heat, and the world's leading debtor, it is the least accustomed to the grounded reality of suffering. Thus, it is most prone to the extremes of social, economic and political instability. It has taken quite an effort for the U.S., which at the end of World War II had the world's greatest gold reserves, was supreme technologically and militarily, the only major industrial power which was still intact after the war - in other words, the world's preeminent power - to squander in less than 50 years its political preeminence, its gold reserves, become the world's greatest debtor nation, and have its currency become the laughing stock of the globe. Even though people do get the government they deserve, the alienation of *"we the people"* from Weak Willie's Washington could not be higher.

Ironically, in terms of the emerging fundamentals, of the Trilateral blocs of German-led Europe, Japanese-led Asia, and the U.S.-led North American common market, the U.S. is emerging in the best condition industrially. The U.S. dollar is now way undervalued in terms of purchasing power parity. Its exports are more competitive. Europe is in an economic crisis because of high interest rates and fragmentation of the EEC, civil unrest in Germany, climatic instability, and an Islamic assault.

Great Britain is in a depression. European labor costs are 50 times greater than that of China and India, and almost that much higher than Eastern Europe. Because reunited Germany accounts for 27% of European GDP, Germany would like its currency to become the universal European currency. But splintered Europe, which has had to unite to defeat Germany in two world wars during this century, is unlikely now to submit to Germany economically. This European reluctance is reinforced by the Neo-Nazi violence against foreigners (non-whites) in Germany. The break-up is spreading. As *The Economist* stated, *"The new Europe forms a whole still found only on maps, in conferences on the continent's future or in selected memories of Europe's warlike past. The new Europeans are divided, as were the old, by wealth, work habits and ambitions; by language, by culture and by that potent mystery, national sentiment."* German extremists tossing fire bombs in refugee shelters in Bonn rekindles old fears among Europeans.

And Japan? The Japanese yen I view as a high-risk currency due to its increasing severe geophysical risk, which could devastate that country economically. Also, Japan is going through its own version of 1929 and learning the hard way. Japanese real estate, the backbone of that economy, is broken.

Could we see investors opt for undervalued raw material currencies, like the Australian dollar and New Zealand dollar? These resource-based currencies in the still economically viable western Pacific Basin, are also the most undervalued of the world's major global currencies on a purchasing power parity basis. We want to monitor them closely.

Last, but not least, there is gold. Gold is definitely shaping up as a superb contrary opinion play. FWN reported that if the central banks eliminate 25-30% of their gold inventories, the *"bottom end is $250."*

"After the Second World War, most of Europe was a pile of rubble and it was unbelievable to get a hold of an ounce of gold. The generational central bankers, thought it was wonderful to build up their gold reserves. Now, you're looking at a new generation and these guys have MBAs from Harvard and they're looking at gold reserves and they're not worth anything."

Are these Harvard guys, Ted Kennedy types, grounded? How's that for an ungrounded extreme in the time frame of a turnabout? Gold, the only historic money which is not simultaneously someone else's liability (or debt), is now worth nothing to these Harvard-educated central bankers.

* * * * *

"If the precious metals bottom in 1993-94, then they are likely to experience at least a five-year bull market, into 1998, and as much as an eight-year bull market, into 2001." — The Elliott Wave Theorist, December 31, 1992

* * * * *

"There's certainly no guarantee that dropping interest rates will lead to economic recovery. During the Depression, lest we forget, interest rates dropped to zero." — Former Federal Reserve Chairman Paul Volcker

OUT OF DENIAL
November 11, 1992

The people of the United States are slowly coming out of denial. (This means they next will become very angry.) They are awakening to the reality that the federal government, rather than being a benefactor, is a parasite; rather than being a servant, it is an oppressor.

Civil government takes its concepts for legislation from the abstract realm of religion, and at the same time, draws its means of sustenance to maintain its concrete existence from the taxes paid by the people. Thus, civil government is literally a paper shuffler that can only redistribute wealth on the natural grounded side of the equation, and enact laws drawn from the supernatural, ungrounded realm.

Despite this initial awakening, Americans are a long way from regaining control over their own lives, where primary governmental, religious and economic power are again posited in the individual. The classic American concept of every man as a king, priest and steward is almost extinct today. But this should not be surprising since we stand in time at the end of a 510-year civilization cycle, a time of world cities, and particularly coastal world cities. World cities are historically the hallmark of a slave state, just the opposite of the decentralized state of free men.

A primary reason the American people are starting to emerge out of denial is that they are realizing that the parasite, the federal government, is now consuming the host, *"we the people."* (Thank you, Ross Perot.) But thus it has always been. Just as the concept of being self-governing is foreign today, so too is the concept of stewardship and honest money. (The United States was historically a country of self-governing men where *"ignorance of the law was no excuse"* because everyone knew the law of the land - the English common law and the Ten Commandments. Also, two primary reasons for the American Revolution were that the King of England was going to impose Bank of England money and Church of England bishops on the Colonies.)

As I have written in my earlier books, *Wealth For All* (both volumes) and *No Time For Slaves*, the boom/bust economic cycle is an aberration, an anomaly that would not occur in an honest money system. The result of an honest money system should be increasing wealth for each generation so that economics effectively becomes a non-issue, as it was in the Middle Ages and in early American history. The business cycle is primarily a function of the expansion and contraction of credit, giving rise to inflation and deflation. The problem presently is that despite the soaring growth in M1 (money made available by the privately owned Federal Reserve monopoly), there's little borrowing by the private sector, and so M2 and M3 are in decline. Only the federal government continues to borrow, and now the Federal Reserve is monetizing the federal debt (inflationary). Recognizing this upcoming explosive problem, large U.S.

corporations are switching rapidly to foreign banks for safety, exiting U.S. banks. The prospect of exchange controls is looming even larger.

That M1 has moved inexorably higher due to the Federal Reserve's making ample reserves available to the banking system - and yet borrowing has not occurred by the private sector - is evidenced by declining M2 and M3, and the flat velocity of money. Both money supply and velocity have to increase for M2 and M3 to kick in to the upside and the economy recover.

What continues to amaze me is how much pain and suffering it takes for mass consciousness to reach the point where it is willing to even consider coming out of denial. It is to the nefarious credit of the federal government, the Federal Reserve, the banking cartel, the public schools and the mass media that the American public is so brainwashed and uninformed with regard to a matter which is vital to them - their grounded economic existence! In money and economics, *"we the people"* consistently act contrary to our own best interest long term and rabidly defend a system that leads to our own destruction. That the American people are still taxed at a rate greater than ancient Egypt taxed its slaves, than slave-owning plantation owners taxed the *"Negroes"* of the Old South, than the Vietcong extracted from its peasants, goes right by the board. The fact that in the Middle Ages, during the first Industrial Revolution, as well as in early American history, a man only had to work a third of a year to meet all his annual economic needs and live debt-free is incomprehensible to the working slaves today trapped in the win-lose, closed system of fractional reserve debt banking. That there are honest, successful banks which work for the people, which grow by leaps and bounds, which have never had a loan failure, such as The Bank of the People's Labor in Mondragon in the Basque region of Spain, is a reality unknown to the American people. There is also the Islamic banking system, where the bank effectively acts as an investment agent for its depositors (the community) who earn profits from businesses the bank invests in, rather than interest, thus enriching the community overall. These alternatives are not discussed at the educational or professional level in the United States, or by the mass media, much less the politicians. The U.S. fractional reserve debt (death) system is anything but people and profit-sharing oriented. There is no equitable balance between the *"one and the many"* in the U.S. fractional reserve debt system. It can only be a win-lose system short term, a lose-lose system long term.

Look at it this way. If five people each borrow $200 (for a total of $1,000) at 10% simple interest for a year, at the end of that year, unless more money is created by the fractional reserve bank (inflation), the result is that one of these five borrowers (maybe several) will lose, because each owes $20 interest ($100 total). They have no means (money) to repay. Thus, they will have to liquidate their assets at a loss and/or go bankrupt, in order to satisfy their debt. On the larger scale, the fractional reserve debt banking system is accordingly inflationary and deflationary long term, with few winners, many losers, and eventually, all losers when the civilization collapses under the weight of debt, which is close to being the case today. It's simply a closed system, locked into the death spiral of the second law of thermodynamics and Newtonian physics, not recognizing the reality of Einsteinian, quantum and chaos physics, which open up the probability of endless *"wealth for all"* in an open system. Yet, this open system is what has occurred during brief moments of human history (the Middle Ages and early American history), which gave rise to tremendous peace and prosperity.

We use money to buy goods and services - commodities. Since money is only the representative of a commodity, then any commodity can serve as money and have a receipt or a computer entry issued for it, representing it. This means free market money, just like the free market in automobiles, where the consumer is sovereign and his needs are met. Moreover, since energy is neither created nor destroyed as Einstein taught us in his classic equation $E=mc^2$, energy is interchangeable with matter. This is something that quantum physics has expanded on, that matter is nothing more than energy slowed down below the speed of light and held together by a standing electromagnetic field. Economically this means the creation of unlimited money with free energy coming in from the sun in an open system, allowing potentially the endless production of the likes of food commodities and timber, with in turn, a potential for monetizing the unlimited commodities. There is accordingly unlimited wealth available. When we add to this open system equation the geometrically expanding scientific explosion (with its subsequent leaps in technology which make more efficient and effective use of both human and natural resources), and the wealth that is passed on generationally through inheritance, it becomes quickly obvious that in an honest, open economic and financial system economics should be a non-issue for mankind (personal and natural catastrophe to the contrary). All it takes is for man to have a long-term view, and act in his own self-interest long term by developing his talents, and meeting simultaneously his two basic needs for both love and money by serving his fellow man, and thus himself. This is the win-win covenant between God, man and his fellow man.

By applying chaos, quantum, and Einsteinian physics to economics, the nature of an open, expanding system in the realm of energy means that economics can also be quickly translated into an open, expanded, unlimited system in matter (commodities), which can in turn be monetized, fulfilling the needs of all. Mankind has had to work hard at the present economic and financial lie to get himself in the position of trillions of dollars of debt and unbelievable shortages and deprivations which exist today for so many millions.

The reality is that the closed, win-lose, lose-lose, debt-based slave system of today persecutes the free and open system of prosperity. Specifically, as agricultural income declines (representing the free and open system linking grounded Newtonian physics economically to energetic Einsteinian, quantum and chaos physics), the debt (death) based system expands. Put differently, as agricultural income declines, bank loans increase. This is inflationary, and results in shortages and widespread poverty.

As the real prices received by farmers - the connecting link between energy and matter - decline, both debt and inflation increase, particularly for necessities, even in an asset and credit deflation such as exists presently.

In summary, if *"we the people"* are really ever going to come out of denial, if we're going to truly get grounded economically as a people, we must scrap the existing fiat currency, fractional reserve debt banking system. It is a death-oriented system, a closed system, which is win-lose short term and lose-lose long term. We must instead - which is possible as never before in this computer age - transition to a free market in money, where any commodity can be monetized, thus allowing a win-win system both short term and long term, providing the unity between energy and matter, and the harmonious connection between Newtonian, Einsteinian, quantum and chaos physics in an open system. It further means our financial system must be reorganized on the order of the Islamic banking system and the bank in Mondragon, Spain. The former allows profit sharing by the community with individuals with whom the bank invests, thus eliminating interest (usury), and putting an effective cap on how long *"interest"* can run, essentially no longer than the life of the project. There is no such thing as the crushing geometric compounding of interest under Islamic banking. There are only higher profits and losses for the community at large, as well as the businessman, thus maintaining the balance between the individual and the community, not allowing, as does Western debt capitalism, an individual to become excessively rich at the expense of everyone else, a la Donald Trump, David Rockefeller, Ross Perot, and Michael Milken. It is this balance between the one and the many, between the individual and the community, that provides peace, harmony and stability long term, the bell-shaped curve, the Gaussian distribution in society so to speak, economically. The lesson of the super successful bank in Mondragon in the Basque region of Spain is that the key investment a bank makes is in its people, not in projects or in things. Why? Because people are more important than things; because people make, use and consume things. So a sensitive, people-oriented banking system to replace the insensitive, non-people oriented financial institutions which exist today is vital. Under such a comprehensive open system, there is inevitably always a shortage of labor. Unemployment ceases to exist.

Finally, what is even more incredible is that even under today's twisted, warped, python-like, debt-based dishonest money system, a backwater Third World country like Singapore was in the 1960s can, in less than three decades, produce a first class civilization that is debt-free, with huge gold reserves, possessing the third largest foreign currency reserves in the world, by simply ordering its governmental structure according to principles of spiritual and economic reality. In short, it has taken a concentrated, deliberate effort to get the United States and the American people in the impoverished state in which they find themselves today financially and economically.

A U.S. Treasury agent who has studied a true U.S. $100 bill can easily recognize a counterfeit. Why? Because he knows what the real thing looks like. So, too, it is relatively easy to see the bankruptcy of the present economic/financial system once the reality of the historically valid, scientifically unified, open system is presented. To my mind, the reality of the overwhelming economic debt (death) cloud which has blackened this country is a primary testimony to the existence of evil. After all, because the love of money (greed) is the root of all evil spiritually, the grounded reality becomes for the masses that the lack of money is practically the root of all evil. The Establishment will work its way out of this debt mess the way it always does - debt (death) default and war (death).

Men (and women) are inescapably consistent with their presuppositions about the nature of reality. If today's natural man continues to be earthly-oriented and lives exclusively according to Newtonian physics and the second law of thermodynamics, in the downward death spiral, he will accordingly be debt (death) oriented in every area of life. This includes the orientation of the lose-lose, fractional reserve debt money system, which will find its death-based harmonics in abortion, divorce, high crime, violent entertainment, arms exports, dead food, death of the political order (riots and revolution), and in war. This means that as the debt-based money system dies, and the associated parasitic political system with it, we die in riots, revolution and war. (We are already dying in debt, dead food, divorce, high crime, and abortion.)

The return to pagan, natural religions and feministic cults is an attempt to escape this death spiral's reality. But such too falls short as history has consistently documented. Nature-based religions are by character still trapped in the death spiral of the second law of thermodynamics. Feministic cults and goddesses have historically given rise to bloody bureaucratic empires, symbolized by the pyramid (such as appears on the U.S. currency), with a few elite living well while many suffer in the masses. In both old world Egypt and new world Aztec and Mayan civilizations, the bloody elite ruled and the masses suffered. Death and human sacrifice were common. The individual human life had no worth. And while nature-based religions and feministic cults had access to a plane of the supernatural, it was still the plane of the fallen, created (natural) spirits, thus condemning their efforts long term inescapably and irretrievably to death. (It was/is the natural, automatic, ungrounded access to this natural/supernatural plane that is the reason why biblically women always had to be *"covered,"* for their protection.)

Modern man has flipped reality around. It's not that mankind is evolving and nature is constant. Rather it's that nature, linked between Newtonian, Einsteinian, quantum and chaos physics is changing, while human nature is the constant. The hearts of the men and women of the Roman Empire were no different than the hearts of the men and women of the New World Order of today. But when man, individually and collectively, is not grounded in eternal, enduring principles of character, he falls victim to becoming a slave of nature (and the Newtonian second law of thermodynamics), with all the conflict, chance, cycles, poverty and death that brings. Such a natural man is tossed to and fro like a reed upon the water with every wind of natural change and darkened doctrine.

As geometric planetary alignments set up gravitational stresses on the sun, which in turn emits specific electromagnetically charged solar particles in solar flares and sunspots (which bombard the earth's magnetosphere, ionosphere, and collect at the earth's poles to then run the gamut of the ley lines over the earth's geomagnetic field), natural man is victimized and acts according to this electromagnetic stimulus. Only character, grounded in enduring eternal principles, is the restraining factor by which man can resist and overcome such cosmic electromagnetic influences. It is this spiritual anchor which grounds out and neutralizes such electromagnetic stimuli. Such is rare today in modern man, particularly the modern natural man who lives in the cities, where the health-bringing free electrons and negative ions are all but nonexistent.

The reason that astrology, Elliott Wave, and Gann analysis work increasingly well in modern markets is because these methodologies are based in the electromagnetic nature of the natural man, which determines his emotional and mental activity and his subsequent physical actions in markets. When it comes to money, men in masses (mobs) are emotional in markets. Money is a matter of the heart today, because it is so closely tied to survival. The greater the number of natural men (slaves to Newtonian nature), the greater the predictive accuracy of astrology, Gann and Elliott Wave, because these systems come from the natural electromagnetic plane which determines physical reality as we know it. Incidentally, the primary operating realm of the fallen spirit world is the supernatural, the infrared range, which rules (deceives) the earth. Put differently, in an honest, open, free market money society, where the mass of humanity is grounded and lives by enduring principles of character, there would be life orientation marked by sustained, consistent, predictable growth. Love, life, light, liberty, law and the long-term view would be the norm. Cycles in human action (such as in markets) would become effectively insignificant. Cycles in human action are evidence of natural, unstable man, a term which the Bible calls "fallen."

In Section 6, "Where We Stand", Chapter 1, "Where Our Culture Stands in Time: Back to the Future - Through 2012," I write regarding the years 1995-96, "The sunspot cycle low is made and begins to move up in 1997-98. Solar activity accordingly is at a minimum. Volcanic activity peaks; earthquake activity peaks after a large quake. Commodities make a low, particularly 'protein gold.' Gold makes a low (the low in gold possibly coming in 1994). There are high international tensions which could result in a war, perhaps between the U.S. and Japan, but probably in the Middle East. The stock market recovery rally ends in 1995-96. There are high interest rates and low bond prices (this may occur in late 1994). There is a severe recession/inflationary depression Latin American-style in the U.S. The recession ends in 1996, but the final depression low is not yet in. The year 1996 marks the trough of the 18-1/3-year real estate cycle. In 1996 there is a secondary drought in the United

States.'' ...I wrote this in 1991. Now the evidence is increasing that there is a high probability of war in 1995-96, consistent with the death harmonic of our debt (death) based system.

It is now widely recognized that the U.S. will have probably defaulted on its debt by 1995. When a country's currency becomes worthless, the fallout is riots and revolution. Riots and revolution are usually diverted into war by the civil government as a convenient distraction for the people, preventing them from focusing on the real issue. The vacuum of anarchy (from riots and revolution) in government is usually filled by a man on a white horse. The political human action cycle of fallen natural man is from rule by one (such as a king), to rule by a few (as in a republic), to rule by many (a democracy - short-term mob rule), to anarchy, and back to the rule by one in a New World Order of global fascism/socialism. Under such conditions, it would not be at all surprising to find real estate totally washed out and on bottom in 1996, commensurate with the bottom in the 18-1/3-year real estate cycle.

According to the July/August 1992 issue of *Cycles* Magazine, comparing planetary cycles, temperature and war, nearly every major peak in the war index coincides with bottoms in temperature (cold) and tops in the Astral Indicator. On the other hand, when the Astral Indicator is low and temperatures are high, the war index is low. Again, when the Astral Indicator is high and temperatures are low, countries move against countries in war.

The Elliott Wave Theorist, 10/30/92, put it another way: *"Inclusionism peaked on the world's stage three years ago with the ideas of (1) a new world order, (2) European unity and (3) the North American Free Trade Agreement. Exclusionism is manifested in the break up of unions. The last Grand Supercycle bottomed in the late 1700s, and saw the American colonies break from Britain. The Supercycle wave II low of 1859 saw the south split from the north in the U.S. Peace and alliances were certainly broken in World War II during Supercycle wave IV. The large degree bear market that started in 1989 globally is producing the same style of events.*

"R.I.P.

"U.S.S.R. (1991)

"Yugoslavia (1992)

"European Community (1992-?)

"Canada (?)

"In the past, the ultimate result of exclusionism and disunion has always been war."

Lawrence H. Berg of Omaha, Nebraska, writing in the July/August 1992 issue of *Cycles* Magazine, stated, *"The Astral Indicator bottoms in 1992 and peaks in 1995, making for an increased probability for war, peaking stock markets, and low temperatures in 1995."* ...How's that for a lineup of natural harmonics? A peak in the Astral Indicator in 1995, a bottom in the sunspot cycle in 1995-96, a peak in the stock market, a high probability of war, a high probability of higher prices for gold and oil at a time when the U.S. defaults on its debt and war breaks out, accompanied by the trough in the 18-1/3-year real estate cycle.

Elsewhere in *Cycles*, it was written, *"The public cry for 1996 will be for a 'man on horseback,' like Jackson. Economic distress will bring demand for a 'strong leader.'"* This is inconsistent with the work at MIT presented in *The Bank Credit Analyst* which shows the Long Wave In Political Values moving from conservative to parochial in 1998. (We don't become progressive again until 2011, which is very close to my 2012 date when we complete this social transition.)

There are other natural factors which will stir up the pot considerably in 1996. The next El Nino is expected in 1996. In fact, 1993 through 1998, that five year period, could see global shortages of food due to unfavorable weather. The worst could occur toward the end of this time period as it becomes colder. According to John C. Cochener, writing in *Cycles* of July/August 1992, it should be coldest in 1997-98. (Solar Cycle 22 bottoms in 1995-96.) Cochener thinks the earth will be approaching another abnormally cold period following 1996: *"Based on the 178-year retrograde sun cycle and the last recorded bitter cold period in 1816, a renewed cycle of cold temperature is likely to begin after 1994."*

All this puts us in the time frame of 1995-96 when the fat hits the fire, leading to the possibility that the 1992 election may very well have been the last peaceful election for a president of the U.S. It's likely the vicious portion of this leg of the bear market of our thoroughly *"natural"* Western civilization begins now and does not conclude its dark, dismal death assault until 1995-96. We are under siege.

* * * * *

"The Maya, far from being the flower children of 19th century archaeological fantasists, were blood-drenched, cruel and autocratic. They not only conducted massive human sacrifices, but practiced a form of warfare that included the slow, excruciating torture of captives. Even their games were bloodthirsty; they considered their gods to be insatiable in their hunger for human blood, and they rivaled the Aztecs in their diligence in providing it.

"The Aztecs had, of course, an equally hideous religion: their practice of tearing the hearts out of living virgins, war captives and young men is too well-known to require description.

"Since history is now being used as a weapon against the white race by racists, it is impossible not to point out that only the white race ended slavery - enforced emancipation upon all others, but also that only Christianity ended human sacrifice in all other religions..." - Otto Scott's *Compass*, 11/1/92

BEHIND THE FIRE

January 6, 1993

Burn Out

Our concerns have been confirmed. From a classic, conservative, Hebrew-Christian, traditional American investor perspective, President Clinton's cabinet selections are far afield. Lloyd Bentsen is okay as Secretary of the Treasury, but from there it's downhill. Clearly, the Clintonistas are in power. That's bad news for us. Bill Clinton, like Ronald Reagan and George Bush before him, is a figurehead for the CFR and the New World Order, and will follow the CFR agenda. That agenda is radically leftist - fascist in fact, socialistic and communistic in theory. The loss of personal and financial freedom, increasing regulations, controls, and accelerating taxes are upon us. The Clintonistas now look at it as *"their time"* to *"get even"* for the last 12 years. Not that most of the American public cares, mind you. The majority of the American public is broke. But for those who are not, and for the few who still have a long-term view, the full court press is on by the Washington, D.C. bullets (pun intended). They are the shooters, we are the shootees. Even the December 28, 1992 issue of *U.S. News & World Report*, in its *"1993 Predictions"* section, declared, *"Hillary Clinton, directing a sweeping 'children's crusade,' ...Regulation Returns ...Gore Shapes Green Policy ...Planets Align for Health Reform...*

With an initial approval rating of 67%, what was to stop Bill Clinton? Not much right away. It all began with his inauguration, which included, of all things, an Animal's Ball. Hosted by the People for Ethical Treatment of Animals, fur and leather were banned at this official inaugural event. Bartenders and hostesses wore nothing but aprons with the slogan, *"I'd Rather Go Naked Than Wear Fur."* Welcome to the Clinton administration.

Make no mistake about it. We have had a political revolution. In fact, we've been had. The 85% of Americans who say it's very important to have a good home life, and the 69% who believe it's important to have a good life at work - all are in deep doo-doo with the Clintonistas, following being in deep voodoo with King George the Bushwhacker. The two presidential scorpions in a bottle, both CFR, both from Yale, get you with their stingers going and coming. And now Hillary throws her stinger into the battle as well.

Clintonomics plans to gore us (pun intended) with 300 more agencies and programs, including a national police force of up to 100,000 new officers, and boot camps for non-violent first-time offenders. Also on the agenda is a requirement for all Americans to carry a smart card, effectively a national I.D. card, a la George Orwell's *1984*. Coming on stream, too, is a national information network linking every house, business and classroom with a government agency. Who today is willing to echo the words of Patrick Henry, *"Give me liberty or give me death"*? Or for that matter, who is willing to quote the

Bible, *"Where the Spirit of the Lord is, there is liberty"*? With government employees now comprising more than one-third of the civil work force, which when added to unemployment and welfare rolls, totals more than 40% of the population, we must recognize that slavery to the state already exists. When more than 40% of the population depends on tax revenues extracted from the gainfully employed, that voting bloc cannot be overthrown short of a catastrophic upheaval. But we are at the point in time in the business cycle, confirmed by climatological events, when such a big economic and political bear market for this country should accelerate down, from 1993 through 1996.

Blinded by the Light

It remains incredible how easily Americans can be manipulated and deceived by the media. Fully three out of four Americans initially backed the use of troops in Somalia. Then why weren't we in Ethiopia when thousands more died there during the famine a few years back? Why in Somalia? So American troops, if necessary, could be airlifted to South Africa to establish a U.N. provisional government there prior to the ANC effectively taking power? It's a short five-hour flight from Somalia to Botswana, where American taxpayers' money has already built an airfield, the staging area necessary to transport U.S. troops into South Africa. Watch platinum.

The leftist mass media tells us that the Clintonistas are the return of Camelot, reminiscent of JFK, to the White House. Sober reflection reveals it's more akin to the return of stray pit bulls to your backyard. Actors, bureaucrats and the CFR rule the White House and dupe the American people. No wonder we're held in so much scorn and disdain internationally, in Europe particularly. It's all-out warfare against traditional beliefs and policies that Americans have long held sacred. And the generals are in the Clintonistas' camp, all the way from the surgeon general to the attorney general, ready for the assault.

Ultimately, a country is held together by either faith or force/fascism. Americans have long since lost their faith in freedom. Now they're in for a good taste of harsh force/fascism. Faith, after all, is the willingness to look to the future and brave the unknown. It involves the willingness and the ability to incur risk and develop an intangible concept into a viable, tangible one. This is anything but the *"stop time,"* end of history, security-oriented, feministic perspective of American serfs today. As Ian McAvity put it in his December 15, 1992 issue of *Deliberations*, *"The Yuppies of yesteryear have progressed from DINK's (Double Income, No Kids) to SINC's (Single Income, No Cash); and many are now NEBBies (Negative Equity Baby-Boomers)."* If we're going to go to hell, I'd much rather do it in the Cayman Islands.

Here comes the Clinton-istas. In your face! Camelot? Not on your life! Renowned black economist Thomas Sowell of the prestigious Hoover Institute stated, *"The next four years should be good for lawyers, parasites and criminals."* My old acquaintance, John Rutledge, declared regarding his encounter with Bill Clinton and his economic advisors: *"By the end of the meeting my skepticism was gone. I was terrified."* Listen for the buzz word *"economic democracy."* It is the same thing for the Clintonistas as communism and socialism.

Clintonomics Revealed

The normally staid and conservative *Bank Credit Analyst* had some harsh words in its *"Outlook 1993"* released at year end 1992. Says the BCA, *"George Bush lost the election because he failed to goose the economy enough in 1991. Bill Clinton was elected by promising to correct that error. The accepted wisdom is that the people voted for change. The reality is that they voted for the status quo - more short-term palliatives to create the aura of prosperity and postpone the correction."* Continuing, *'There is a growing awareness that the U.S. is suffering from a structural malaise (much of it government-induced) and that, if it continues, the nation will be placed in great jeopardy.*

"The U.S. political system works very well to deal with a clear and imminent danger. It does not work when slow and persistent rot gradually destroys the supporting beams of the entire country."

Analyzing the American public deep down, the BCA comments, *"People feel that their standard of living is dropping and that the trend will continue. They are terrified that the build up in government debt will eventually cause national bankruptcy, that their pensions might not be available when they retire, that they won't be able to afford medical care and that their children will face an even bleaker economic future."*

Let the point sink in. Nothing has fundamentally changed financially or economically. It's only gotten worse. What has changed and is presently occurring is nothing short of a revolution politically and socially. The country is polarized and has lived for years on the veneer of economic good times. Now that this veneer is being stripped away, the harsh realities of a country at war with itself, bound together effectively by nothing, is bringing forth the heavy hand of tyranny.

Opportunity Locks

Don't get me wrong. There will be tremendous opportunities to make big money in the United States during *"the next four years."* It will be a volatile time. The trick will be to stay out of jail for some error in business judgment or for missing some obscure regulation that some bureaucrat sees as a ripe opportunity to hang your scalp on his tepee as a way of climbing up the Clintonista bureaucratic ladder. And don't forget envy. Good, old-fashioned envy from these Clintonistas will be enough on its own to land you in the slammer. With raw power now ruling supreme at the federal executive and bureaucratic levels, the Clintonistas won't need an excuse to throw you in jail. They'll just make it up as they go.

* * * * *

It is argued that the male is "individually" oriented while the female is "community" oriented. That's the one and the many in conflict. The New World Order is feminine. It is collective, and harkens back to Mother Earth and witchcraft as its religion. By contrast, the Hebrew-Christian heritage of Western civilization is masculine and individual. Strong individuals, it is thought, build a strong community. A chain is no stronger than its weakest link, so to speak. History is, at the end of a civilization cycle, when the security-oriented, collectivist, naturally ungrounded (polarity) feminine spirit is strongest, men become irresponsible and women become dominant, e.g. Weak Willie and Hillary Clinton. The following crisis brings on a male dictator to re-establish grounding. Perot is the perfect person for the part. H. Ross Perot will cause the federal bureaucracy to be efficient and effective. Perot's entire being is wrapped up in the centralization of power.

THE SPIRITUALITY OF MONEY: INVESTING IMPLICATIONS
April 14, 1993

In Season

Springtime is the time of year when both religion and money are prominent in men's consciousness as the earth springs literally to life. Islam completes its holy month of Ramadan. Jews begin the Passover. Christians and pagans celebrate Easter, and the pagans observe Earth Day (April 22) and then May Day, the high day of the year for witchcraft, May 1. Cashing in on this phenomenon, Time magazine in its March 15, 1993 cover story headlined, *"In the Name of God."* Then the April 5, 1993 issue of Time again headlined (with a cross on the cover), *"The Generation That Forgot God."* For once I agree with Time. If God is love, we sure must have forgotten Him, given all the seething violence in the world today.

Go For the Gold

If we stop and think about it, there are two Golden Rules, one having to do with a godly attitude toward man, the other having to do with money, reflecting the spiritual and physical natures of man respectively. The biblical Golden Rule is: *"Do unto others as you would have them do unto you."* It is also restated as Christ's Second Great Commandment, *"Love thy neighbor as thyself."* Then there is the Golden Rule of Money: *"Whoever has the gold makes the rules."* It's not that one or the other is true; it's that both Golden Rules are true, simultaneously. Moreover, regarding our biblical heritage, if we really want to be in good health and prosper in a way that we can enjoy our money, we have to seek God first, or as Jesus put it, *"Seek ye first the kingdom of God and His righteousness and all these things will be added unto you."*

Interesting. We seldom think about making it a priority to line up with God's laws to achieve financial success in this day and age. But I have found it instructive that in the 46-64 age group, Time magazine says 54% read the Bible at least weekly, and 80% agree that the Bible is the *"totally accurate"* word of God. In the 24-45 age bracket, Time stated that 43% read the Bible in the past week, and that 73% agree the Bible is the *"totally accurate"* word of God. That's certainly significantly different from what the mass media and Hollywood tell us is the case in Amerika. But then again, holly-wood is the wood used by witches for all their incantations and spells.

As a Man Thinks

If we stop and think about it, we know that the religious values which give rise to our correct thinking and disciplined emotion are vital to our trading and investing success. Investment psychologist Van K. Tharp and author Jack D. Schwager in *The New Market Wizards* make clear that a major key to successful investing is the psychological make-up of the individual, particularly hard work and emotional discipline.

Greed and Shortages

One more spiritual perspective on money before we get to the meat/money of this article: We were taught growing up that the love of money (greed) is the root of all evil. Given this truth therefore practically speaking, because greed results in scarcity, the lack of money ends up in reality being the root of all evil for most folks. Greed dominates socialism, communism and debt capitalism. This is of course unnecessary, as I have demonstrated in my books and THE REAPER time and time again. It is our closed system of debt money which results in inescapable conflict, shortages, scarcity, cycles, poverty and death. As I wrote in the chapter "Out of Denial," *"In summary, if 'we the people' are really ever going to come out of denial, if we're going to truly get grounded economically as a people, we must scrap the existing fiat currency, fractional reserve debt banking system. It is a death-oriented system, a closed system, which is win-lose short term and lose-lose long term. We must instead - which is possible as never before in this computer age - transition to a free market in money, where any commodity can be monetized, thus allowing a win-win open system both short term and long term, providing the unity between energy and matter, and the harmonious connection between Newtonian, Einsteinian, quantum and chaos physics in an open system. It further means our financial system must be reorganized along the order of the Islamic banking system and the bank in Mondragon, Spain. The former allows profit-sharing by the community with individuals with whom the bank invests, thus eliminating interest (usury), and putting an effective cap on how long 'interest' can run, essentially no longer than the life of the project. There is no such thing as the crushing exponential compounding of interest under Islamic banking. There are only higher profits and losses for the community at large, as well as the businessman, thus maintaining the balance between the individual and the community, not allowing, as does Western debt capitalism, an individual to become excessively rich at the expense of everyone else [OPM], a la Donald Trump, David Rockefeller, Ross Perot, Michael Milken. It is this balance between the one and the many, between the individual and the community, that provides peace, harmony, prosperity and stability long term, the bell-shaped curve, the Gaussian distribution in society so to speak, economically. The lesson of the super successful bank in Mondragon in the Basque region of Spain is that the key investment a bank makes is in people, not in projects or in things. Why? Because people are more important than things, because people make, use and consume things. So a sensitive, people-oriented banking system to replace the insensitive, non-people oriented financial institutions which exist today is vital. Under such a comprehensive open system, there is inevitably always a shortage of labor. Unemployment ceases to exist."*

The answers are here, folks. The question is just whether we have the will to implement them. Isn't this what the spirituality of money is all about?

Three Flips

Given that such a life-giving money and banking system doesn't exist today, investors have at least three significant problems facing them, one short-term, one intermediate-term, and one long-term in nature (1995-96 and years following).

One

Short-term, we have a situation in the interest rate market where either interest rates have to rise as borrowing picks up to sustain the economic recovery, or if interest rates fall due to lack of borrowing, the economy slumps. (Of course, the Fed could/would monetize the debt, holding interest rates lower for a short period of time, but that's an inflationary stop-gap solution.) All this is negative for stocks, higher interest rates short term, a slumping economy long term.

We're in the time frame now when stocks are topping out and investors are becoming quite nervous. Investors are disenchanted with the Clintonistas, and are wary of the economy and the stock market. Consumer confidence is on the wane as hiring is also sluggish. The freefall in stocks like Philip Morris and U.S. Surgical has left investors gun shy.

Those who live at the margin, the violent, the ungrounded, naturally see a manifestation of their personalities in the harmonic of the unstable geophysical realm. In summary, we're forming a top in intangible assets - paper (stocks and bonds), and a base for more upside in tangible assets - precious metal and mining stocks, commodities, energy, etc.

Two

Over the intermediate term, we have to be troubled with the out-of-touch shenanigans of the Clintonistas. This ungrounded, radical fringe, which represents perhaps 3-10% of the American general public, doesn't have a clue about how to deal positively with the real world problems facing the common man. How could it? Most of the Clintonistas are elitists who have never held a real job, who have been educated at the best socialist schools, and who have worked for elitist, bureaucratic organizations (primarily government), poisoned with elitist ideas. They have no constructive political answer to the U.S. losing 2.5 million jobs a year to overseas competition, U.S. industry relocating overseas, technology replacing labor, downsizing, and a global recession. There is no easy solution to a federal deficit that is growing at a $1.3 billion-a-day rate. There is no easy answer for a consumer whose savings rate is hovering just above record lows, and who has tapped out his borrowing capability at a time when he is scared of losing his job. Consumer borrowing (spending) is 70% of GNP. So far, not even negative real interest rates in the U.S. or Federal Reserve monetization of the debt, which should be inflationary, have been able to soundly kickstart the deflationary nature of the economy. This is evident from unemployment, sluggish and/or contracting consumer borrowing, slow retail sales, and minimal wage increases. There is no easy way out for California, effectively the world's seventh largest economy. California is plagued with a 40% increase in business failures, an $8 billion budget deficit, with real estate off 25-30%. Moreover, we ought to sell the Clintonistas short anyway, just on the basis of contrary opinion, what with Bill Clinton on the cover of Time magazine as *"Man of the Year"* and all, not to mention Hillary on the cover of the April 11, 1993 issue of Parade magazine.

The Clintonistas will be an absolute disaster for the U.S. economy. There are several major reasons for this: 1) The Clintonistas are ungrounded elitists, totally out of touch with reality. They don't have a clue as to how the real world works for the average American. 2) The Clintonistas are exactly the wrong thing at the wrong time for what this country needs in its economic and national progression cycle, not to mention absolute poison for where we stand in terms of climatological history. 3) The Clintonistas are treating the economy as a closed system, subsidizing non-productive, death-oriented behavior and penalizing life-bringing, open-system, productive behavior. If this is not a suicidal equation, I don't know what is.

People everywhere respond to incentives. Even in the old Soviet Union, workers responded to the lack of positive incentive to work by getting drunk, missing work, and/or taking their time in leisure. The Clintonistas are not providing positive incentives for the economy to expand. Moreover, what the Clintonistas are subsidizing, the poor and the less prosperous, we'll get more of, more poor and more less prosperous people. This inescapably breeds conflict within their closed system, promoting the false idea of a limited economic pie. The Clintonistas are penalizing and providing disincentives for the creation of wealth, and shunning subsidies that would make people more productive so we'll have less of that, less wealth and less productivity, and less of an open system, less freedom.

Finally, 4) the Clintonistas' personal histories are marked by emotional chaos, conflict, and turmoil. Their bodies personally emit chaotic radiation in massive doses. Like homeopathically attracts like. It was no accident that a natural harmonic of Clintonista reality, the largest nuclear accident since Chernobyl at Tomsk-7, occurred commensurate with Bill Clinton's meeting with Boris Yeltsin in 1993. ...An organization or nation reflects its leadership. Both the U.S. and Russia are headed for chaotic times, literally radioactive times, reflective of their emotionally ungrounded, radioactive leadership.

Three

This brings us to our long-term concern: We are headed for a major war, most probably involving nuclear weapons and rampant terrorism, in 1995-96.

It will be precipitated by Iran. This war will be religious, economic and political in nature, and will involve water and oil, not to mention territory. I tell you clearly, this nation cannot stand a war with Iran, even if we win it. The cost is too high. It could bring down this government and the U.S. dollar.

To Arms

So, on that cheery note, just how do we invest and make lemonade out of lemons? The general principle is that we want to move from intangibles (paper - stocks and bonds) back into tangibles (commodities, precious metals, agricultural land, energy, etc.). We want to get grounded in our investments.

In tangibles, as a general rule, we like gold - real gold, the metal, along with silver and platinum; we also favor paper gold in the form of gold and precious metal mining shares; liquid gold in the form of water stocks; black gold in the form of energy and energy stocks; and we literally want to go to where the gold is to invest, the golden Far East.

Stocking Up

First off, the Far East has its emphasis on the work ethic, productivity, family and savings, even under low wage conditions. The Far East, specifically China, is in the emerging phase of the new 510-year civilization cycle, the super-growth phase. The Far East is the part of the world that is buying up all the gold that the Europeans are selling. Red China, for example, bought 800 tonnes of gold in 1992. Singapore, Taiwan, Malaysia and Hong Kong are not far behind in gold purchases. In fact, more gold is traded in Hong Kong than in Zurich, London and New York combined. Additionally, the savings rate of Singapore is 43%, Malaysia 33%, Hong Kong 31% and Thailand 21%. That's capital power!

Accordingly, the stock funds I like in China are Wardley China Fund Ltd., China Fund, Greater China Opportunities Fund, China Region Fund, and China Opportunities Fund.

In the Far East generally, I like Scudder New Asia Fund, T. Rowe Price New Asia Fund, Fidelity Pacific Basin, R.O.C. Taiwan Fund, Thai Capital Fund, Korea Fund, Malaysia Fund, and Singapore Fund. Specific stocks I favor are Bangkok Bank, Singapore Telecommunications Pte Ltd. (when it comes out this year); in New Zealand, Telecom of New Zealand and also Fletcher Challenge; and in Hong Kong, Jardine Strategic Holdings, Sun Hung Kai Properties, Hong Kong and Shanghai Bank, Hutchinson and Whampoa, and Swire Pacific. Of course, some of these stocks which are situated on islands could be subject to a real shakeout, literally, geophysically, over the next few years. The geophysical risk is greater in Taiwan and New Zealand. Hong Kong has a China wildcard risk. Korea faces a military risk.

Regarding Japan, trading opportunities in the Nikkei Dow appear in the Japan Fund. Japanese stocks which have excellent cash-rich positions long term, and which should do well short of an absolute geophysical disaster, are Hitachi, Toyota, Sony and Matsushita.

Stateside, the energy stocks I like are numerous and include: Baroid Corp., Unocal, Barrett Resources, Phillips Petroleum, Marathon Oil, Plains Petroleum, Parker Drilling, Galveston-Houston, Smith International, Oryx Energy, Tidewater Marine, Comstock Resources, Columbia Gas, British Petroleum, Petro-Canada, Talisman Energy, New Jordan Petroleum, Global Marine, Thermo Electron Corp., Louisiana Land and Exploration Royalty Trust, Arch Petroleum, Ashland Oil, Burlington Resources, Amoco, and Consolidated Natural Gas. These energy stocks are best purchased on pullbacks.

In the precious metal and mining stock arena, here too are my favorites, also best purchased on corrections: Benham Gold Equities Index Fund (1-800-472-3389), American Barrick, Pegasus Gold, Amex Gold, Placer Dome, Glamis Gold, Asarco, Inc., ASA, Vaal Reefs, Minorco, Freeport McMoRan Copper and Gold, Battle Mountain Gold, Echo Bay Mines, Homestake Mining, Newmont Mining, Royal Oak Mine, Chase Resources, Golden Star, and Tiomin Resources. This covers the major U.S. gold stocks, some Canadian speculative plays, and some South African gold stocks, the Canadian and South African stocks being really risky.

Water stocks I like include American Water Works, Ionics, Pall Corp., and Millipore (Ehrenkrantz picks).

Funeral home stocks which unfortunately should do well in the mid-'90s are Service Corp. International, Loewen Group, Stewart Enterprises, and Hillenbrand.

Defense stocks which I favor include Martin Marietta, E-Systems, Bowmar Instruments, and International Airline Support Group.

There you have it. If I had to put my money on the line, walk away and come back in 1997, these are the intangible investments (stocks) which I would want to hold. Why? Because they invest in tangible assets in line with what I perceive to be the primary trend between now and 1997. But, as always, timing can increase total return substantially. Next up, we are due a good overall shakeout in stocks. Then your stock broker should be able to assist you in monitoring some of the above stocks, picking an entry point on oversold conditions into support, from which you can make scale-down purchases.

SECTION V

Where We Stand

WHERE OUR CULTURE STANDS IN TIME: BACK TO THE FUTURE - THROUGH 2012

November 6, 1991

Where We Stand In Time

It is crucial to our personal and financial decision-making that we know where we stand in time. Knowledge of where we stand in time is almost unconscious during our daily, weekly and yearly routines. For example, our activities during the morning versus the afternoon are normally substantially different. What we eat at breakfast usually varies greatly from what we consume at dinner. During the week, the activities which we schedule and engage in on Monday are not at all like those we enjoy on Saturday and Sunday. During our lifetime, over the span of 80 years, our interests and activities at age 18 do not approximate those which occur at age 45, and even less so at age 65. But what about where we collectively stand, where our culture stands, in time; in its linear and cyclical spiral, in its historical progression?

To 1980

In 1943, an obscure chartist at the University of Pittsburgh put away his graph for the last time. This graph projected a 1980 top in U.S. wholesale prices commensurate with a 1980 peak in sunspot activity. This unfinished graph, as it turns out, accurately predicted reality which occurred 37 years later. For 1980 was indeed the peak of the 11-year sunspot cycle. It was the time when Mount St. Helens blew. U.S. wholesale prices accordingly peaked, as did U.S. commodities. Gold and silver topped. Many areas of U.S. real estate peaked, particularly farmland. (The federal debt then was only $1 trillion.) Most importantly, interest rates peaked. Short-term interest rates exceeded 22%. But most significantly, 1980 changed the rules of the investing and financial game from what they had been during the entire post-World War II era since that obscure University of Pittsburgh chartist put away his graph.

In 1980, when interest rates soared, all of a sudden it no longer paid to be a borrower, but rather a lender. Why? Because, unlike the 1970s, interest rates went from being below the rate of inflation to above it. Financial reality flipped. It paid to borrow in the 1970s when interest rates were below the rate of inflation. It paid to lend in the 1980s, when interest rates were above the rate of inflation. However, the general public, including the financial sector, was slow to catch on. It took the better part of the 1980s, the Kontratieff plateau period, for this financial and investing rule change to sink in. If it had sunk in quickly, in 1980-82, the early 1980s would have experienced a depression. The 1981-82 recession would have been a harder but shorter depression than the adjustment we face now with many trillions more in debt ($20 trillion). Nevertheless, the most sensitive sector of the economy, the grounded sector, the raw material and commodity industry, learned the new financial rule first. This basic industry went through its own depression in the early 1980s. The general business sector, manufacturing, real estate, the service sector and consumers, followed as the 1980s progressed with consumers and the service sector learning the lesson last of all. In fact, they are still learning the lesson today, in the 1990s. Government never did acknowledge or react to the financial rule change.

Opportunity Squandered

I can remember in March 1981 speaking to Dave Stockman, Alexander Haig and Cap Weinberger about the fact that the newly elected Reagan administration had incredible momentum while the Democrats were in disarray. I told these three cabinet members in no uncertain terms that if they would seize the initiative, cut federal taxes and cut the federal budget then, in 1981, they would go down in U.S. history as financial heroes. But, if they delayed, the 1982 recession would sweep away the opportunity and lock us into a spiral of everexploding federal debt and taxes which now burden us today. I will never forget the looks of shock, disbelief and scorn on the faces of those three gentlemen when I related this reality to them.

Climate, Culture and 1980

The year 1980 was also the peak of Dr. Raymond H. Wheeler's Drought Clock, which was completed in 1945, 35 years before this top. The Drought Clock marked the completion of the 510-year civilization cycle which included three 170-year cycles and five 100-year cycles. Dr. Raymond H. Wheeler was a man far ahead of his time. Under his instruction, more than 200 researchers worked for over 20 years, studying the influences of weather on mankind. Wheeler was not searching for facts that would prove a previously accepted theory. Rather, he was a researcher yearning for truth. Over 3,000 years of weather were evaluated, along with nearly two million pieces of weather information. Over 20,000 pieces of art were studied, as was literature throughout history. In excess of 18,000 battles were examined. All parts of the world were investigated. No stone was left unturned. Wheeler's efforts were comprehensive and exhaustive.

Now, exactly what did Dr. Raymond H. Wheeler conclude? Here are his comments: *"It seems highly certain that the initiative is again passing from the West to the East for a 500-year period. The present 500-year cycle is due to end around 1980.*

"The changes that are now taking place will, of necessity, alter many of our patterns of behavior. Our economic system and the world of business are not exempt."

Dr. Wheeler saw that the time at the end of the 510-year cycle, our time, would be a time evidenced by mass migrations, devastating revolutions, and literally the death of the old world and the birth of a new world. He was *"right on."* Dr. Wheeler expected the death of our world to last until the end of this century, the year 2000. It is his conclusion that the end of the 510-year cycle is a time when governments break down and nations collapse, and that there is a wave of international wars which will bring down nations. These wars trigger civil strife and revolution.

Let's look at some more of Dr. Raymond H. Wheeler's conclusions: *"The fifth 500-year cycle since the sixth century B.C. is just now terminating. The end of the cycle is due around 1980 at the center of an expected cold-dry period corresponding to the one in the first century A.D. and the one in the tenth century.*

"Profound revolutions over the whole known world of humanity, regardless of race or culture, have occurred during each of these centuries, often amounting to cultural convulsions."

Dr. Wheeler went on to state: *"Current events show that another world convulsion is occurring second only to: (1) the emergence of rational thought in the sixth century B.C., (2) the fall of Rome and other ancient civilizations in the fifth century and the beginning of a medieval world based on feudalism, and (3) the final collapse of the Middle Ages in the fifteenth century. The current convulsion is comparable to the birth of Christianity in the first century and to the growth of the modern nation as a feudal principality in the ninth and tenth centuries."*

To the Heart of the Matter

Dr. Raymond H. Wheeler's work has been confirmed by Peter Kelly of Interdimensional Sciences, who has noted that the earth is losing its magnetic field charge at a rate and to a degree that is comparable to the time of Jesus Christ. If we stop and think about it, man's mind, systems and society are like a computer. They are information held together by magnetic charge. Energy is information held together in a magnetic field. As the field breaks down, so does the information, systems, and everything else.

Mankind himself is electromagnetic, as the work of the Center for Frontier Sciences at Temple University, the Tesla Society and Extraordinary Science in Colorado Springs have demonstrated. Dr. Robert O. Becker in his books *The Body Electric* and *Cross Currents* has conclusively demonstrated this reality. These electromagnetic and geomagnetic field activity changes go directly to the heart of man. Dr. E.G. Stoupel at the Toor Heart Institute in Israel writes, *"The earth's natural magnetic field is variable. With suitable sensitive equipment, called magnetometers, it is possible to detect the very small variations in the intensity of the earth's magnetic field. The intensity variations occur both over time, i.e. temporal fluctuations, and over space, that is spatial gradients. The amplitude of these variations is about 0.35-10 trillionths of a Tesla.*

"The temporal intensity variations, or pulsations, occur over a wide frequency range from DC level changes; to frequencies much below one cycle per

second (micropulsations); to brainwave frequencies (1-30 cycles per second); and higher frequencies. These temporal variations in the earth's magnetic field strength are called geomagnetic activity or GMA. As a result of energetic changes from events on the sun (and other objects in space), the geomagnetic activity of the earth is substantially influenced.

"Recent studies indicate that changes in geomagnetic activity, can affect one's cardiovascular health...

"The following links can be found between the level of the GMA and some physiological parameters and the natural history of diseases. In the course of my studies, I have identified:

"1. Higher hospital cardiovascular and cerebrovascular accident mortality on active and stormy days of high GMA...

"2. Higher number of deaths of outpatients from acute myocardial infarction (heart attack) on days with higher GMA;...

"5. Greater human blood plasma viscosity on unsettled and active GMA compared to quiet days;...

"8. More severe migraine headaches on days with high levels of GMA...

"9. Significantly more frequent heart rhythm disturbances...

"10. A high number of sudden cardiovascular deaths on these low GMA days compared with three higher GMA levels..."

So why aren't we sensitive and responsive to all this important information? Simply because we live in a time of world cities, when our civilization is frozen. Recall that there are only two parts of the economic equation: land and labor, things and people. Everything in our society focuses on people, labor. There is a lack of balance. When was the last time the Nobel Prize in economics was given to an agricultural economist or a climatologist?

Now, let's run down the significant correlation between astrophysical/energetic events and economic, climatological and financial realities as they have occurred in the late 1980s, projecting them forward through the year 2012.

1986

The sunspot cycle trough was in June/July 1986, a time when commodities bottomed in the CRB Index and wholesale prices also made their trough. The Comet Halley reappeared in the sky. (The federal debt hit $2 trillion.)

1987 - Year of the Breakout

The year 1987 was the real peak in the U.S. economy, according to most graphs, and the real peak in the Dow Jones Industrials on an inflation-adjusted basis. The first stock market crash occurred in 1987. From 1987 through 1989, what remained of the Kondratieff plateau period in real estate peaked. This peak was delayed due to unwise use of debt in the 1980s. The year 1987 was also the important year of the planetary Harmonic Convergence, setting off a sequence of events carrying into the year 2012. At about the time of the August anniversary of the Harmonic Convergence each year since 1987 we have seen a nominal stock market peak, Iraq's invasion of Kuwait, and the Soviet hardliner coup attempt in the former Soviet Union. Perhaps we should beware of the Ides of August.

Pieces of Eight

Let's now focus on the acceleration of events carrying up to the year 2012.

Robert Anton Wilson, in his 250-page book, *Cosmic Trigger*, made important observations regarding the historical progression which is presently carrying us through to the year 2012: *"The Law of Octaves was first suggested by Pythagoras in ancient Greece. Having observed that the eight notes of the conventional Occidental musical scale were governed by definite mathematical relationships, Pythagoras proceeded to create a whole cosmology based on 8s...*

"In China, roughly contemporary with Pythagoras, the Taoists built up a cosmology based on the interplay of yang (positive) and yin (negative), which produced the eight trigrams of the I Ching, out of which are generated the 64 hexagrams.

"In India, Buddha announced, after his illumination under the Bodhi tree, the Noble Eightfold Path. Patanjali subsequently reduced the science of yoga to eight 'limbs' or, as we might say, eight 'steps.'

"The game of chess appeared, somewhere in the East, with a grid based on 8 x 8 (64) squares.

"In the 1860s, English chemist John Newland showed that all the chemical elements fall into eight families...

"In the 1870s, with much more detail than Newland, the Russian chemist Mendeleyev proved once and for all that the elements do, indeed, fall into eight families. His Periodic Table of the Elements, an octave of hauntingly Pythagorean harmony, hangs in every high-school chemistry class today...

"...Nikola [Tesla],...also intuited a basic Law of Octaves governing universal energy.

"Modern geneticists have found that the DNA-RNA 'dialogue' - the molecular information system governing life...is transmitted by 64 (8 x 8) condons.

"R. Buckminster Fuller, in his Synergetic-Energetic Geometry, which he claims is the 'co-ordinate system of the Universe,' reduces all phenomena to geometric-energetic constructs based on the tetrahedron (4-sided), the octet

truss (8-sided) and the coupler (8-faceted with 24 phases). Fuller argues specifically that the 8-face, 24-phase coupler underlies the 8-fold division of the chemical elements on the Mendeleyev Periodic Table.

"The eight families of elements are: (1) alkalis, (2) alkalines, (3) borons, (4) carbons, (5) nitrogens, (6) oxygens, (7) halogens, (8) noble gases.

"Working independently..., Prof. Peter Flessel of the University of San Francisco has begun developing correlations between the 8 x 8 condons of the genetic code and the 8 x 8 hexagrams of the I Ching...

"In the 1890s, Henry Adams became convinced that technology was following a geometric or exponential law...

"Korzybski, Buckminster Fuller, Alvin Toffler and others have shown, with countless examples, that many things in technology are advancing exponentially, and the one general tendency is clearly that there will be more basic breakthroughs (both in scientific theory and in technological applications) in each generation than in any previous generation.

"As Toffler in particular emphasizes, there are more scientists alive in the 1970s than in all previous history added together. Thus, this generation should witness more breakthroughs than all previous history added together.

"This, indeed, is the thesis of a remarkable book offering the final set of models and metaphors... 'The Invisible Landscape,' by Terrence L. McKenna and Dennis J. McKenna.

"There are 64 time-scales in the hologram of our universe, they say, and each one is related to one of the 64 (8 x 8) hexagrams of the I Chings.

"The McKennas have programmed a computer with their 64 I Ching time systems and the answer is that everything goes jackpot around A.D. 2012.

"The McKenna scenario is somewhat more dramatic than the exponential accelerations suggested by Henry Adams, Korzybski, Fuller, Toffler and even Leary, because, within the McKenna theory, all of the 64 time-scales peak together. That is, they assert: a 4,300-year cycle from urbanization to the dawn of modern science; a 384-year cycle in which science has caused more upsurge of novelty than in that 4,300-year cycle; a 67-year cycle (from the technological breakthroughs of the 1940s, including nuclear energy and DNA, to peak in 2012) in which there will be more acceleration than there was between Galileo and Hiroshima; an 834-day cycle in 2011-2012 when there will be more transformations than in all the previous cycles; a 6-day cycle at the end of that in which things will move even faster; and so on, down to a grand climax in which, as they say, 'in the last 135 minutes, 18 such barriers (i.e., barriers comparable to the appearance of life, the invention of language)...will be crossed, 13 of them in the last 75 x 104 seconds.'"

Art often predicts reality. Remember the movie, *2010: The Year We Made Contact?* With the earth's magnetic field breaking down, and the Newtonian reality as we know it being subject to fluctuations, the crossover between quantum and Newtonian reality through the Einsteinian relativity bridge will increase. This means that supernatural/spiritual manifestations should increase substantially between now and 2012. We are in the time frame when quantum, Einsteinian and Newtonian reality should again be moved toward reunification as we move from the dark, acid, degenerate, deoxygenated end of the scale toward the light-oriented, alkaline, regenerated, oxygenated end of reality.

Recall, too, that the years 2008-2012 are when Dr. Iben Browning's work on climate also focuses on a final climatic upset. Additionally, the Mayan calendar, which began in 1313, ends in 2012, in what historically has been a universal disaster, according to the four previous time eras for the Mayan calendar. Around the year 2012 we could see a maximum acceleration in the rate of change, ending what the establishment now sees as the *"hell period"* of our civilization.

According to Herb Frizzell, Bible prophecy also zeros in on the year 2012. In Daniel Chapter 8, from the time Alexander invaded Asia in 334 B.C., it is 2,300 days (years) until the 1967 Six-Day War in Israel (Jerusalem). (In the Bible, one day is a year - Ezekiel 4, Numbers 13 and 14.) The difference between 1,335 days and 1,290 days (Daniel, Chapter 12) is 45 days (years). The year 1967 plus 45 days (years) brings us to the pivotal year 2012.

What was the purpose of the foregoing exercise? To demonstrate that some of the best climatological, scientific, philosophical and mathematical minds, artists and, even Bible prophets, think the *"hell period"* of our civilization extends until the year 2012. But during that time frame, at least some members of mankind will become progressively smarter and wiser, until we get it all together in 2012. So, there is hope, there is light at the end of the tunnel. We only need to endure for 20 years.

So much for the historical squaring of history in time. An upcoming master turning point for the human race is the year 2012.

Progress Into 2012

Stop and think a minute of what progress will be achieved by then. Look how much would be available to us now if it weren't for the frozen nature of our civilization and politically protected institutions which refuse to allow quantum progress to surface. As you know, for some time now I've worked with a substantial number of highly respected global scientists. At the rate things are going, it is doubtful that their breakthroughs, which are available now, will begin to be manifest until around the year 2003. For example, when will we see a free market in education, which has been demonstrated to be the most effective educational approach in England and Singapore? This concept of *"P.C."* (political correctness) which has gripped our schools, universities and political arena is straight out of George Orwell's *1984*. It's a throwback to the Hitlerian Nazi era, which persecuted nonconforming thought as Adolf Hitler rose to power. *"P.C."* is uniformity at any price, suppressing and oppressing the smorgasbord of ideas which fertilize the human mind. *"P.C."* is effectively mental sterilization.

In medicine, leading research MDs are focusing on the medicine of the future, captured by the word *"psychoneuroimmunology."* Psychoneuroimmunology sees man's spirit, mind, energy systems and physical systems as an integrated whole. This is as it should be, consistent with the *"light man"* perspective. How long, for example, do we let the politically oriented actuarial liabilities of the Social Security Administration, and the $5 billion legalized drug industry, suppress the research being done in curing cancer? It is now well documented that cancer cannot live in an alkaline environment of oxygenated cells. Cancer, to live and thrive, must exist in a dark, toxic, acidic cellular environment which is deoxygenated. What about the treatment of cancer using north pole magnetic energy established by Davis (and Rawls) at the Columbia School of Medicine? North pole magnetism has shown approximately 90% effectiveness in curing cancer. How about the work of Ed Sopcak and his Cancell therapy, which literally starves the cells of energy so that the weaker cells, the cancer cells, die? What about the work of Dr. Evans Rapsomanikis with his electromagnetic free electron chair, which as a byproduct of treating pain has cured some cancers? What about the work of Dr. George Merkl used at the Century Clinic in Reno, Nevada and elsewhere, where Life Crystals and Chondriana, precursors of the mitochondria, literally become Pac Mans in the body's immune system and chew up the cancer cells and turn them into usable energy? What about the work of Dr. "Washington" Ayuko in Birmingham, England and his homeopathic remedy for cancer? How about the labors of Doug Leber and Ralph Cryzak in Miami and the Bahamas? Why aren't these men, who have experienced some spectacular successes in treating the likes of cancer - some as a byproduct of other alternative health methods - being brought into the public eye, and financed by taxpayer grants? Why hasn't the federal government funded the above projects with the necessary grants so that the consistency and proof of the alleged ability of these methods to cure disease, including cancer, can be confirmed or denied?

In the area of technology, how about all the new-generation Tesla free energy devices which Extraordinary Science has brought to the public's attention? How about harnessing the earth's natural energies in the geomagnetic field and ley lines, which Bruce Cathie has discussed in his books, and the federal government presently uses in energy transport in California? What happened to Bernelli's free energy generator? How about Dr. NakaMat's water engine, and more importantly, his perpetual motion engine, in which the one moving part touches nothing? The end of the age of oil is already with us. The ability to unhook from the public utility companies exists now. Additionally, Stan Meyers has the technology to provide safe hydrogen fuel for our cars, literally using the backyard water hose, antiquating Exxon's gas stations.

What about the rainmakers, the men who have the ability, using Reich technology, to cause it to rain on command? The work of Trevor Constable and James DeMeo, and their success in Malaysia, Israel and Singapore, has not been put to use in this country. How come? Why hasn't the Rife microscope and its innovative ability to recognize cellular dysfunction and treat such with light been exploited? What about the anti-gravity devices which the U.S. government has been working with since the early 1950s?

How about the flying wing concept for airliners, rather than the *"flying sausages"* which exist today, as Dr. Antony Sutton so disdainfully calls them.

In the area of law, why are we using antiquated systems to try to discern if an individual is lying? The Judge Thomas versus Anita Hill Supreme Joke affair would have been totally unnecessary if the French system of Kirlian photography had been admitted. The French have demonstrated that Kirlian photography can be used to determine precisely whether an individual is lying or telling the truth. This can be reconfirmed by the back tracking work done by David Oats, which correctly analyzes the subconscious thoughts behind the actual words and determines the voracity of an individual's statement. This technique has been so successful that the Dallas police have used it in cracking tough crime cases.

What about the age-old freedom-oriented concept of self-government, rather than external government by the city, state, or federal government? Why is it today that only 14% of Americans say they believe in all the Ten Commandments, which are basic to self-government, when in multi-racial, multi-religious, and economically variant group sessions, conducted by a prestigious foundation in Illinois, it has been established that there is nearly always an 84% consensus that the correct collective human values approximate the Ten Commandments? What ever happened to the common law which is basic to our heritage?

Finally, when will we see a free market in money, money based upon commodities, money that is spent into existence, rather than borrowed into existence? In other words, when will we have an open system in money rather than the closed, debt, death-oriented cyclical system which exists today? We now have the technology and the communication methodology for a free market in money. The boom-bust debt cycle is no longer necessary. We live in a day and age when the standard of living for each generation should be higher than the one that preceded it, except for natural and personal disasters, so much so that economics should not even be a major consideration for the average individual. John F. Kennedy caught a glimpse of this reality, as is apparent from his speech made at Columbia University ten days before he was assassinated. JFK was about to radically change the money system of the United States, having the U.S. Treasury spend into existence its own money, probably eliminating the Federal Reserve system. For this he was assassinated, just like Abraham Lincoln before him. How about back to the future with President Andrew Jackson, who also fought the central bankers? The tax system needs to be changed, of course, from an income tax to a national sales tax. This will encourage savings and capital formation, rather than consumption, and provide the base for sustained long-term growth.

1988

This was the year U.S. *"protein gold"* supplies (corn, soybeans, wheat, other feed grains) went into dangerously short supply, less than 60 days in some cases, as a U.S. drought ravaged the country.

1989

In the year 1989 the sun went retrograde. Historically, when the sun goes retrograde, droughts, earthquakes, volcanic eruptions and tornadoes begin to appear. This has certainly been the case this time around. The effects of the sun going retrograde could last into 2009-2011. (There are those key dates again). The retrograde activity of the sun should keep the earth very active geophysically at least until 1995 and possibly into 1999.

Retrograde activity of the sun occurs every 178.7 years, coinciding with the 180-year vector sum high tidal cycle. The last time the sun went retrograde, in 1810-1816, the U.S. experienced the year without a summer after a major volcanic eruption (Mount Tambora) flooded the stratosphere with volcanic ash. The retrograde motion of the sun, of critical mass around the barycenter (center of mass of the solar system) is caused by the tidal forces at the major outer planets, especially Jupiter and Saturn. It is no accident that as light peaked and the sun went retrograde in 1989, that the world economy also peaked. (In 1989, the federal debt also exceeded $3 trillion for the first time.)

1990

It will be the *"Nasty Nineties"* for the establishment, and the *"Nifty Nineties"* as freedom-loving entrepreneurs go through the time of trend transition from darkness to light. The New Age-oriented New World Order is out of sync with approaching astrophysical/geophysical reality. But there's always turmoil when an old trend tops out and a new trend begins. The year 1990 was when the U.S. standard of living declined and did not recover. It was the time when the Kondratieff Wave plateau period terminated after a ten-year run, following the previous three decades' (1950s through 1970s) up-leg. The 54-year Kondratieff Wave cycle clearly turned down beginning in 1987-89. According to the late climatologist Dr. Iben Browning, the Kondratieff Wave corresponds with climatological cycles. The Kondratieff Wave correlated with the 30 degrees north latitude vector sum high tidal forces multiplied by inverse sunspots. Dr. Browning also noted that the University of Copenhagen has shown that the isotope analysis of oxygen contained two main oscillations, a strong one for 180 years, and a weak one of 78 years. These two oscillations (180 years and 78 years) correlated with the 180-year vector sum high tidal cycle in the Northern Hemisphere and with the 73-year cycle of these tidal forces at the equator. It was thus demonstrated that the summative beat is 54.5 years. The Kondratieff Wave business cycle is, of course, 54 years. Thus, the two are almost identical: the Kondratieff Wave business cycle and the 54.5-year tidal beat are at about the same amplitude in their effect on business. Dr. Browning projected these two would fall together in the 1990s, just as they did in 1776, and that the 1990 depression would be more severe than any depression since the time of the American Revolution.

1991

The secondary sunspot cycle peak occurred along with the 18.6-year lunar cycle which peaked October 24, 1991. An El Nino manifested, probably the strongest El Nino in the past 125 years. This El Nino (which is Spanish for child, specifically Baby Jesus at Christmas) was probably the result of the Mount Pinatubo eruption, according to Dr. Paul Handler. Warmer Pacific currents of +4-5 degrees Fahrenheit were recorded. In 1991, the earthquake and volcanic activity increased and should do so through 1994 minimum, possibly 1995, and maybe until 1999. Earthquake and volcanic activity should at least carry through 1994 due to high tidal forces and solar retrograde activity. Unknown to most Americans, Mount Hudson in southern Chile erupted, sending debris 20 miles up, effectively 100,000 feet into the stratosphere. The ozone layer accordingly thinned. War broke out in 1991 within one month of the December 1990 high tidal force. The Persian Gulf war was then accurately projected by the dovetailing of Dr. Iben Browning's high tidal force projection and my 1992 U.S. War Clock. Silver bottomed out in the first quarter of 1991. And there is one other very significant event which occurred in 1991.

Recall the chapter entitled "Light Man." This chapter was preceded by the June 10, 1991 cover story of *Time* Magazine, *"Evil"*, and followed by a *U.S. News & World Report* special report, *"What Did Jesus Really Say?"* This *U.S. News* report basically attacked the U.S. Hebrew/Christian heritage. In this time frame the City of Angels, Los Angeles, experienced a severe 6.0-Richter quake. Also Michael Landon, the angel on *"Highway to Heaven,"* died suddenly. Following this time of the summer solstice and in the time frame of the celebration of U.S. independence at the Fourth of July, the Arnold Schwarzenegger movie *Terminator 2: Judgement Day* was also released. I projected *Terminator 2* would be the hit movie of the year, a forecast which proved to be accurate. All this occurred in the late June/early July 1991 time frame. In fact on June 27, 1991, astronomers found a bright light in space which measured 30,000 times brighter than all the known stars in the universe. This light was moving rapidly toward earth, even though it was at that time a vast distance away. ...Is the earth being prepared for a reset function? A scientist at the Extraordinary Science conference in 1990 said so, that a cosmic pulse is headed this way which will literally reset the earth. Could this light be the actuator of such a reset? After all, we live in a holographic universe. Just like a computer can be reset, so can the human body and the earth be reset. I've had this technique, a result of years of research by a world-renowned Dallas chiropractor, done on me. It is a jolting experience, similar to what the earth will experience between now and 2012.

1992

This is the year that extended sunspot and solar activity ceased. The year 1992 was the worst year of high tidal forces, focusing initially on January 18-19, 1992.

1993

Sunspot activity is off substantially, down hard. The effect of the sun's going retrograde on weather may ease or cease in its dramatic severity in 1993, but possibly not until 1995.

1994

Prices in *"protein gold"* fall off, possibly sharply so. The stock market makes an intermediate low in its decade lasting ongoing bear market. The U.S. recession/depression continues, but ends this leg by late 1996 at the latest. There begins to be key rumblings in the financial system and key shifts in exchange rates. The U.S. dollar will be called into serious question. Significantly, socially and politically, the neo-pagan, barbaric and violent nature of the American people becomes manifest in 1994. The elitist Skull & Bones fascist, occult, feministic, environmental New World Order becomes obvious where non-*"P.C.s"* are persecuted.

1995-1996

The sunspot cycle low is made and begins to move up in 1997-98. Solar activity accordingly is at a minimum. Volcanic activity peaks; earthquake activity peaks after a large quake. Commodities make a low, particularly *"protein gold."* Gold makes a low (the low in gold possibly coming in 1994.) There are high international tensions which could result in a war, perhaps between the U.S. and Japan, but probably in the Middle East. The stock market recovery rally ends in 1995-96. There are high interest rates and low bond prices (this may occur in late 1994). There is a severe recession/inflationary depression Latin American-style in the U.S. This recession ends in 1996, but the final depression low is not yet in. The year 1996 marks the trough of the 18-1/3-year real estate cycle. In 1996 there's a secondary drought in the United States.

1997

Solar activity begins to pick up from the solar/sunspot cycle trough. The *"protein gold"* complex is marked by high yields and falling prices. Another top in bonds occurs.

1998

The sunspot cycle begins to clearly move higher. The *"protein gold"* complex is still marked by high yields and falling/low prices, although a maverick drought could occur. There is a stock market low. Gold makes a major high in accordance with the 64-year cycle. The federal debt exceeds $10 trillion and monetary reform becomes the frantic, violent call of the day. There's a key shift in exchange rates with the attempt to establish a New World monetary system, possibly using the *"phoenix."*

1998-2000

There is an economic panic in 1998-1999, resulting in severe economic conditions. A war threat of considerable significance follows between 2000-2003. Monitor August 10, 2000 for another possible crash in stocks.

2001-2004

In 2002, the sunspot cycle peaks. The *"protein gold"* complex makes a high (9-year and 12-1/2-year cycles), with low yields and high prices in 2001-2004. In 2003, El Nino returns. Also in 2003, the economy bottoms out. This is the latest date for the economy to ultimately bottom out. The year before, 2002, should mark either the secondary stock market low or the major low in stocks. In 2003, there will be a key shift in exchange rates, when we may establish an equitable New World monetary system. The economic washout will be completed, and the new up-wave in the Kondratieff economic cycle will begin, although it will remain cold. Traditional values and conservative, decentralized politics will be the new major trends. The equivalent of the *"Death Star"* in Star Wars, the New World Order, will be seen for what it truly is, an elitist attempt at a global power and money grab, a throwback to the oppressive empires of ancient history.

2005-2012

The year 2008 is the sunspot cycle minimum. The year 2008 is also the time of high tidal force when there's an increase in earthquakes and volcanic activity. The years 2007 and 2011 are years of El Nino, when there should be a significant *"protein gold"* bull market, offset by the sunspot minimum. In 2010, according to Dr. Iben Browning, northern Mississippi's climate will be like Toronto's in the 1940s. Crops will move about 700 miles south. In 2012, the Mayan calendar, which began in 1313, ends. It is marked by universal disaster and change. By 2012, world population could be reduced one-third to one-half due to war, pestilence, famine and disease, not to mention cataclysmic earth changes. We will have again learned the lessons of the Aztecs, the need to be *"earth sheltered"* during such times.

There you have it, the rocky road map of the future. Crises and opportunity both exist. We will, of course, fine tune and make adjustments in our road map as time goes on. At least we have an overview from which to plan. Those who plan long term win. It's time now to become really grounded, established and rooted - spiritually, mentally, emotionally, and physically.

FIVE FATAL FLAWS
April 10, 1986

There are five fatal flaws which have gripped Western civilization, five egregious errors which are leading to the compounding of the problems we face today. These five fatal flaws fall in the areas of religion, political philosophy, economic philosophy, financial systems, and the mistaken idea that climate is not important.

The primary religious flaw is a widely held belief that government can play the role of God, that government can solve all of our problems legally through legislation, and economically through the redistribution of wealth. It is generally held today by the majority of Americans that government is the great insurer of all of our welfare in both the guns and butter areas. The federal government provides for its people from womb to tomb. However, reality is that the federal government is in fact an emperor who has no clothes. The federal government playing the role of God is the maximum distortion of reality, because the federal government is in reality an economic parasite. The federal government cannot create wealth. It can only redistribute wealth obtained by taxation (conflict), from the economic production of hard working men and women, at a tremendous bureaucratic cost. Furthermore, the myth that government can legislate peace and justice on earth is quickly wilting as we become strangled by bureaucratic rules and regulations; all the while social unrest builds. We have lost the abstract truth that government is always religion applied to economics.

The political philosophical flaw which grips Western civilization is that debt capitalism and the evolutionary market produce the greatest good for the greatest number long term. Clearly however, as historically documented, it was the evolutionary debt capitalists who financed communism originally, and continue to finance communism today. Communism is supposedly the arch enemy of debt capitalism. In truth, the two work together.

Evolutionary debt capitalism focuses upon the radical rights of the individual. Communism focuses radically upon the rights of the masses, the group. Because both are radical in the extreme and do not focus on a harmonious balance between the individual and the group, both are radically flawed. Both generate conflict long term. Conflict long term never produces economic prosperity. It is only a peaceful environment that produces wealth long term through the specialization and division of labor leading to trade. This is why flight capital flows to havens of safety. So, neither debt capitalism or communism today balances the rights of the individual with the rights of society. Therefore, conflict is not resolved by either system today.

Both debt capitalism and communism hold in their political philosophy that the big bureaucratic state, the federal government, is evil. Debt capitalism holds to the theory that the dog-eat-dog market best allocates resources, and best produces and distributes wealth. Debt capitalism holds in theory that the government which governs best, governs least. Debt capitalism holds that the only purpose of the civil government is to protect the marketplace by enforcing contracts, ensuring domestic tranquillity, and protecting its participants against all enemies, both foreign and domestic. But this is simply not the case today, regardless of how good the theory sounds. The evidence that debt capitalism is bankrupt today is best seen by the never-ending growth of the federal budget and the explosion of the alphabet agency bureaucracies which rule over our economic processes, stifling the marketplace. The worst have gotten to the top and have become an undesirable elite under evolutionary debt capitalism. Thus, the political philosophy of debt capitalism is, in practice, bankrupt.

The political philosophy of communism is also bankrupt. If communism worked, it would not have had to depend upon the loans, grants, technology and foodstuffs provided by the West in order to survive. If the political philosophy of communism were not bankrupt, it would not have had to be imperialistic and sub-due people and nations by military means. It would instead be able to convert people peacefully to communism, which it was clearly unable to do. Communism is more hypocritical than debt capitalism. The stated end goal of communism is the withering away of the state, according to the author of communism, Karl Marx. Not only is the communist state not withering away, it is growing larger, more elitist, and more bureaucratic, a clear sign of its theoretical bankruptcy. (Bureaucracy is the greatest institutional manifestation of human evil).

A megabureaucracy is planned for humanity as the bankruptcy of debt capitalism and the bankruptcy of communism merge in a Hegelian dialectic thesis (debt capitalism) versus the antithesis (communism) into the synthesis (bureaucratic socialism - a one world government). This is the direction we are moving presently. What we need is good old-fashioned, moral free market equity capitalism and honest money.

The third fatal flaw which has gripped Western civilization is found in its economic philosophy. Economics today is considered the dismal science, because both of the operating assumptions about the land and labor sides of the economic equation are indeed dismal. Today, we incorrectly hold that we live in a world of limited resources and too many people. Both of these false assumptions about the nature of reality are indeed dismal. The concept that we live in a closed system, one of limited resources, ignores the reality that we live in an open system where unlimited amounts of energy from the sun potentially can produce unlimited amounts of renewable commodities which, when monetized, produce a potentially unlimited amount of wealth. Furthermore, we can always make better and higher use of present resources, and find new and different ways of doing things than we have in the past. To the Indians, oil was only good for making paint and for medicinal purposes.

What resources are available in the desert and on the ocean floors? What about in space? What about recapturing through desalinization plants the unlimited supply of water in the oceans? What about the fact that hard research has indicated that we now have more natural resources than we have ever had before at any time in human history? The concept of limited resources is a myth.

We do not have too many people on the face of the earth, either. Present agricultural technology, although radically flawed, utilized on today's arable land, could produce enough food to feed 31 billion people, six times the earth's present population. We could take all the people in the world today, put them in a single family home, give them a typical front and back yard, and they would all fit in the State of Texas. And we could recapture land from the sea, just like the folks in Holland do.

Man does not have to be the ultimate predator. He does not have to prey on his fellow man. Neither does he have to be the ultimate parasite, as he leeches from his fellow man. Both are forms of slavery. Man can instead be the ultimate resource, when he disciplines himself, limits his wants, and practices deferred gratification. He can save for the future and build capital for investment. As he serves others in the marketplace he serves himself long term. The myth, the fatal flaw in our economic philosophy that we live in a world of limited resources and too many people (seen as either predators or parasites) gives rise to the federal government bureaucracy as a necessary evil to redistribute wealth.

The fourth fatal flaw is financial. The myth here is that there is such an animal as *"debt capitalism."* The term *"debt capitalism"* is much like the expression *"mercy killing." "Mercy"* has to do with caring, nurturing, and saving precious human life, *"killing"* with the ruthless, brutal destruction of human life. Putting the two words together is therefore an oxymoron. So it is with *"debt capitalism." "Capitalism"* requires saving, from the past and in the present, for investment and production in the future, looking for long-term rewards. *"Capitalism"* therefore requires a long-term view. *"Debt,"* however, is short term in nature. *"Debt"* consumes savings and thus is the long-term enemy of *"capitalism." "Debt"* is borrowing from the future by mortgaging the past to consume in the present. Thus the words *"debt capitalism"* are a contradiction in terms.

"Debt" destroys *"capitalism,"* particularly where you have a fractional reserve banking system and the compounding effect of interest as we have today. That debt will eventually either be repudiated through a default or inflation. If at the time of Jesus, one of the Wise Men, instead of giving Jesus gold, had given him one cent to put out on interest at 6%, and if Jesus had cashed in that one penny compounding at 6% for 1,977 years, the amount of gold Jesus could have bought when gold was selling for $150 an ounce would have made a ball so big, that, when placed in the center of the sun, it would have displaced all the planets in the solar system. That's the power of compound interest. Therefore, when people don't save, capitalism effectively dies, particularly when the

financial system gets behind the power curve of compound interest as it has today.

A fatal flaw in the religious, political and financial arenas today is the myth of *"natural law."* Politicians wave their hands in the air and appeal to *"natural law"* as justification for their actions. Market analysts hold sacred the works of W.D. Gann and R.N. Elliott, the two foremost proponents of *"natural law"* as the key to understanding the markets. But the concept of *"natural law"* is also a contradiction in terms. *"Nature,"* from an evolutionary humanistic perspective, operates on the basis of chance. *"Law,"* by definition, is enduring, absolute, eternal and certain. Therefore chance and law are antagonistic. Therefore *"nature"* and *"law"* are incongruous when joined together. The concept of *"natural law"* is Orwellian. Sure, there are high probability rules of behavior in nature and in the markets which exist given specific sets of circumstances. But when we really boil it all down, there is no such thing as scientific law. As physicist Tom Bearden declared, *"There is no such thing as a 'Law of Nature.' No such thing ever existed. What exists is a general rule of behavior of physical systems under very general conditions. But it is just a rule. There is nothing sacred about it at all. If you change those conditions, you blow that rule right out of the window. But when you elevate it to the phrase, 'Law of Nature,' you are substituting for the phrase, 'Law of God,' and you are now practicing religion, not science. And that is what Western science is doing today."*

In other words, while the *"law"* of gravity is operational for us as we walk around here on earth, it is inoperative in space where different conditions exist. When the environment changes, variables act differently. In an enduring, eternal sense then, there are only scientific rules of behavior which hold true under specific, given conditions. The same thing holds true in the market. The more men become slaves to the cycles, chance and conflict of nature, the more they will fall under the influence of astrology and become predictable by *"natural"* probabilistic systems used to analyze the markets. But none of these systems are perfect. They all only work some of the time, when conditions are just right. They are probabilistic, not certain. Therefore they are not laws. The concept of *"Law of Nature"* is a myth, a religious, political, and financial fatal flaw.

The fifth and final fatal flaw which grips Western civilization is the myth that climate is not important. We live during a time of world cities, where 80% of the people of the United States live in the top 100 urban centers. Because of this, our economic theories are all man-centered. The economics of Keynes (big bureaucratic government), Austrian economics (human action), monetarist theory (the theory of money), supply side economics (incentives for men), and labor theory (communism/socialism) are all man-centered. We have forgotten about the other half of the economic equation - land.

It takes both land and labor to make up the two parts of the economic equation. Because we are blind to the importance of climate as it affects the affairs of men, we have ignored the works of Dr. Raymond H. Wheeler, the agricultural economists, and Dr. Iben Browning. Thus we do not know that we are in the midst of a time of major climatic disruption and change. Such times lead to upheavals in civilizations that are dominated by world cities and their bureaucratic governments. Indeed, we are doing exactly the wrong thing at the wrong time. We are destroying the small family farms. Our correct response to these climatic changes should be to decentralize, to provide incentives for our civilization to develop horizontally, through networks in the country and small towns, and move toward self-sufficiency and a sense of community if we are to respond successfully to the climatic changes that are upon us.

In summary, the five fatal flaws - religious, political, economical, financial, and climatic - are setting the stage for the Four Horses of the Apocalypse to ride in Western civilization. These five fatal flaws have left the door to the barn wide open. It will soon be too late to close it because all the horses will already be out. To complicate matters, the laborers who are responsible for keeping that barn door shut are bickering among themselves and ignoring their work. The unholy trinity of politicians, government bureaucrats and special interest groups are frozen into inaction. We are no longer responding to the challenges we face as a civilization. The failure to respond to reality is inescapable bankruptcy. Reaping what we have sown, it will soon be every man for himself. Will a misguided, confused, miseducated, slave state population look for a man on a white horse to lead them out of the valley of the shadow of death? The federal bureaucracy is in place to handle emergencies, awaiting the ruling tyrant. Is the created crisis about to be unleashed/orchestrated? Between now and the year 2012 we should see the most radical changes ever experienced in the history of mankind. It is therefore time to live in small towns or in the rural country with strong family, church and community ties, in an environment of self-sufficiency, if we are to avoid the claws of the five fatal flaws.

* * * * *

"In the twentieth century, Christians have remained servants in the judicial and cultural households of their enemies. This century has been a century of bondage for God's people. I am aware of no other century since the fall of Rome in which God's people have been more universally in bondage." — Dr. Gary North, *Biblical Economics*, January 1993

* * * * *

There will be one million lawyers in the United States by the year 2000, according to the American Bar Association, a 34% increase in attorneys in the decade of the 1990s. ...And we seriously expect things to get better?

SOCIAL BREAKDOWN

July 24, 1986

The end product of the evolutionary doctrines of *"survival of the fittest"* and *"do your own thing"* is inescapably social breakdown.

Society is ultimately dependent on a religious and moral base which provides the practical working answers on how to resolve the conflict between individual rights and those of collective society. When those answers are not forthcoming from the religious, philosophical and political sectors of society, then society degenerates into *"man the animal,"* with *"every man for himself."*

The *"yellow light"* indicating that this breakdown is quickly approaching is the explosion in the number of lawsuits being filed in this country. Criminal and civil lawsuits involving alleged violations of personal and property rights are a result of the lack of respect for the rights of others, the disintegration of the ability of men to honorably contract and covenant with one another, and the loss of character, which in earlier times resolved differences quietly.

A contract is a religious/moral, legal and economic document. (Government is religion applied to economics.) When men are no longer self-governing in a moral/religious way, they inevitably breach their contracts, with lawsuits the result.

The world looks at America cynically. One international economist recently quipped that it seems that Americans believe the only way to be economically productive today is to sue one another. A publication which is immensely helpful in monitoring what all is going on in today's courts is *Lawyers Alert* (30 Court Square, Boston, MA 02108, $99 yr.) Insanity seems to be the norm.

Lawsuits are civilized, respectable conflict. They are only a breath away, however, from outright social breakdown and violence. Such is what our movies are telling us is up next on the horizon.

The glorified explosion of violence in American cinemas today consistently repeats the message that the inescapable answer to our problems is violence. Again, violence is without a doubt the sign of the bankruptcy of a culture - religiously, morally, philosophically, and politically. Why? Because violence only erupts when there are no other peaceful ways to justly resolve differences.

Movies, a form of art, project where society is headed, reflecting the thoughts and emotions which are welling up from the subconscious of the general public. The Clint Eastwood *Dirty Harry* series; the Sylvester Stallone *Rocky*, *Rambo*, and *Cobra* series; Charles Bronson's *Death Wish - I, II, III*; the Arnold Schwarzenegger movies, such as *The Terminator 1 and 2*, and *Raw Deal*; and the Chuck Norris movies *Missing in Action I and II*, along with *Invasion, U.S.A.* - all are warning us loud and clear that big time social violence is just over the horizon.

The city is truly about to become a *jungle*, as these *urban western* movies are telling us. When 80% of the people live in the cities, as is presently the case, while the rural country is going bankrupt, now is the time to relocate to a small town or the rural country.

Immorality never begins in the country. Neither does social breakdown. It begins in the city. If you want to destroy civilization, you must destroy its countryside, its moral and resource base. If you just destroy its cities, the civilization will rebuild. But if you destroy the countryside, the cities will die and civilization will not return.

We are well on our way to destroying the rural countryside. The bankruptcy of the agricultural community is testimony to it. The cinemas are telling us that the cities are not far behind. If city violence doesn't get you, the bureaucrats or AIDS will, so to speak.

FIT FOR A KING
(TO LIVE AND DIE IN L.A.)
May 12, 1992

Most of the facts and insight into incidents in this chapter were gathered from eyewitnesses who were there, in L.A., at the time of the Rodney King trial and riots. Their names are being withheld for their own safety, and for the protection of their families.

The Media Line

I think it's fair to say that this writer followed the Rodney King trial, verdict, and subsequent L.A. riots as closely as any white middle class American who didn't live in L.A. Here is a brief summary of the sequence of events as the mass media portrayed it, the party line so to speak:

Rodney King was pulled over in his car by the L.A. Police. In the process of his arrest, he was savagely beaten by the LAPD. The white LAPD officers went on trial for police brutality. An all-white jury in this case of egregious racial injustice acquitted the white officers. The L.A. black community then exploded in rage, and rioted and looted as an expression of their protest of this unjust verdict. The mayor of L.A., the governor of California, and the President of the United States joined with the black leaders nationwide in calling for new programs for the black community - more welfare, better housing, Head Start, etc. - as a solution to the problem. ...This is the essence of what the American people were told occurred in L.A.

Legal Aliens

Now, let's face it. Americans generally, not just blacks, are alienated from the legal system today. Federal judges particularly are notoriously unresponsive to the wishes of the people. Justice has become largely a money game, where winning in court depends upon the best lawyer money can buy. The laws themselves are so numerous and complex, and often contradictory, that the average man feels powerless when he becomes ensnared in this legal monopoly controlled by the American Bar Association. The laws today are also relative, no longer having any moral foundation where truly *"ignorance of the law is no excuse,"* because everyone knows the Ten Commandments upon which our law was based (*Texas Tech Law Review*). So, under the decaying evolutionary legal system under which we live today, might makes right, rather than right making might. This means power rules. The police represent power and the establishment. Again, Americans generally, not just blacks, are in awe of the establishment which exercises power. Americans are today the most obedient people on the face of the earth. A police uniform mesmerizes a jury.

Black Plight

The rich got richer in the '80s, while the blacks fell further behind (as did the middle class). The average family income of blacks is 60% that of whites, compared to 62.5% in 1967. The black unemployment rate is double that of whites. Forty-five percent of black children live in poverty. Over 64% of black children are illegitimate, compared to 15% of whites. Black women have 635 abortions for every 1,000 babies, compared with 274 per thousand for white women. Twenty percent of black males spend at least some of their lives behind bars. Blacks are responsible for nearly 90% of violent crime in the U.S.A. Black and Hispanic women comprise nearly 75% of the reported AIDS cases in the United States.

The Way Out

Why haven't blacks broken out of poverty in the ghetto the way the Irish, Koreans, Chinese and Vietnamese have done? Insightful black economists Dr. Walter Williams and Dr. Thomas Sowell have asked, researched and answered this important question. They put the blame firmly on the back of the federal government, which has enslaved through welfare, housing programs and the like, the black community, just as it did the native American Indians. Both Dr. Williams and Dr. Sowell point out that the way out of the ghetto and poverty is the same for all minority groups: A strong nuclear family headed up by a father, emphasis on work, education, learning skills, and saving. It's no more complicated than that, according to Williams and Sowell.

Back in the 1930s, before the federal government was so involved in the welfare system, subsidizing illegitimate black babies, black men still had their dignity, and were responsible heads of black households. The literacy rate was far higher, and the illegitimacy rate far lower, in the black community then than it is today.

If the federal government were really serious about helping the black ghetto it would eliminate the minimum wage to allow more blacks access to employment. The federal government would reduce taxes, reactivate the investment tax credit and discard the capital gains tax, sharply reduce regulation, restrict absentee ownership of land, and allow free market honest money. It would imitate Singapore's example of housing policy and a business/labor savings plan. Singapore has eliminated its racial strife. It would institute Germany's education system. It would implement France's job training techniques.

My friend at MIT, Dr. Lester Thurow, in his book *Head to Head*, comes up with many good solutions to this nation's problems, based practically on what has worked around the world. The trick is getting the viable solutions implemented in a frozen culture.

Staying Hooked

There is just something about people, all people, when they are given something they haven't earned, particularly over a long period of time, and can't either repay it or pass it on, that the end result is their enslavement and embitterment. They ultimately return evil for good. And the more people take, regardless of race or creed, the more they want and expect, once they get hooked on the treadmill of dependency. Then they start viewing the property of others as an entitlement, rather than as a short-term charitable response. But property rights are human rights, because property only comes into existence as a result of the sweat, time, money, and energy expended by individuals. So when property rights are violated, human rights are violated. So the burning and looting in L.A. was a violation of human rights. But, why would not the ghetto-based black community feel justified in stealing, when the federal government steals through taxation, inflation, and other means of illegitimate property (wealth) transfers? But again, as I have looked into it, it was not the black community itself which was primarily responsible for the rioting and looting which took place in L.A. It was the gangs of lawless black youths, hundreds of which exist in L.A., along with young and old minority criminals, who committed the crimes. The riots in most cases had nothing to do with Rodney King. He was just a convenient excuse that allowed these thugs to loot, plunder, burn, beat and kill, knowing full well because of the Rodney King verdict, they would not be shot on sight, which has been the traditional response when it comes to riots, and globally, the one surefire solution to ending riots immediately - shoot on sight! The lower class simply saw a free ride, an opportunity to loot the middle class with impunity.

Black Shame

In a fit of black racism and externalized envy, the black gangs took their toll on the Koreans, Vietnamese and Hispanics who had bettered themselves by providing goods and services to the black community. White America has little or no understanding of the rampant racism which exists between blacks, Hispanics, Vietnamese, Chinese and Koreans in south central L.A.

I can still talk about this subject with some authority. Just out of the University of Houston in 1969, when the memory of the '60s race riots was still fresh on the minds of most citizens, I can remember day after day being the only white teacher willing to teach in the Houston black ghettos' junior high schools and high schools. So I can say with conviction, *"I've been there. I know of what I speak."*

The Response to the Verdict

Now let's look at the Rodney King incident and the trial which purportedly led up to this civil upheaval. What we're going to find is that the reality of what occurred in this trial and subsequent events are far different than the liberal, hysterical media's inaccurate portrayal. Now, I viewed the edited film clips which Ted Turner's network kept hammering into our consciousness over and over again. And so I, too, was initially shocked when the jury acquitted the four white L.A. police officers. But I also know the mass media has a value structure which has nothing in common with the broad-based ethics of hardworking Americans. And this is the media that lied to us about KAL 007 and the Persian Gulf war. So my reasoned response to the King verdict went something like this: *"Look, I wasn't there. And I know the media can make things look however they want to make them look. There were 12 impartial jurors, acceptable to both the defense and the prosecution, who examined all the evidence over a three-month period. And these 12 jurors aren't immune from the culture. They certainly felt the social pressure to bring back a guilty verdict, despite the intimidation of police authority on the witness stand. The fact that the jurors unanimously brought back a not guilty verdict means that the evidence must have been overwhelming to not convict these white police officers. I have to, in humility, go with their judgement. They saw the evidence. They were there. I was not."*

What is stunning is that only 11% of the American people agreed with this reasoned response. Fully 89% bought the media line that injustice occurred in the Rodney King trial. On what basis? Edited film clips shown by CNN? What else? Is this what our country has come to? Have we become this programmed and emotionally conditioned, that 90% buy a mass media position against hard evidence looked at by 12 impartial jurors? Couldn't the general public at least withhold judgment pending appeal? Is there so little understanding in the land about the rules of evidence and the way our jury system operates? The jury system is one of the last, best hopes this country has for returning true power to the people. But a jury is no better than its members.

Suppressed Trial Evidence

Here is the essence of the key evidence which did <u>not</u> come out in the mass media but was evident to the jurors in the trial, and to attendees who were in the courtroom with Rodney King. First of all, L.A. is a high crime area, particularly central L.A. When the police pull people over in L.A., they do what is called a *"felony stop."* The reason for this is obvious: So many L.A. policemen have been shot, or shot at so many times, that the *"felony stop"* had to be implemented to protect the lives of these law enforcement officers. A *"felony stop"* means that when the L.A. police pull an individual over, they have their guns drawn in most cases, and they will tell the person to get out of the car and lie in the street face down. This is very humiliating to anyone who is stopped, and particularly to blacks. But because policemen's lives have been endangered by doing anything else so many times, and because central L.A. is such a high crime area, probably the highest in the United States, this *"felony stop"* technique had to be implemented. It was the only thing that worked. Also, the media did not bring out the fact that there were two other people in the car that Rodney was driving, and that no harm came to them.

Why was only Rodney King allegedly beaten with police batons? It is standard procedure by convicted felons on parole to try to incite the police to acts of brutality so that all charges against the felons will be dropped and they won't be returned to prison. This could have been a reason for Rodney King's resistance. He was a convicted felon, for robbery. He was also involved in soliciting for prostitution. In any case, if you were a policeman chasing a 6'4", 240-pound felon, who was speeding away from you for 6-7 miles at speeds up to 100-110 miles an hour, who, when he got out of his car, came at you, and you shocked him with 50,000 volts of electricity, and then he still got up and came at you yet again, you certainly would have reason to be in fear for your life and think that Rodney King was on PCP. In such a split-second decision, how would most trained police officers respond, black or white?

The mere 87 seconds of the Rodney King tape which was shown over and over again by the media was just a small edited fragment of the entire video, which was taken, by the way, at a considerable distance from the scene. The media did not explain that it is a taught, long-implemented police technique to surround a resisting subject and flail away at him with batons which do not touch him, but merely graze him and/or hit the ground close to him in order to intimidate him into submission without injury. Nor did it come to public light that many of the injuries Rodney King sustained were a result of his running away from the police and falling headlong onto the pavement, a part of the film clip not shown. Indeed, Rodney King's skull would have been fractured if he had been hit with the night sticks as brutally as the film clip showed, not that possibly excessive police force wasn't used. Attendees in the courtroom re-ported that the evidence was overwhelming that it was when King tried to es-cape that he stumbled and fell and hurt his head. When Rodney King fled, and tried to escape the L.A. police officers, in any other state the cops would have had every right to shoot him. Only in California and Washington, D.C. can police not shoot a *"fleeing felon."*

One individual called the media's portrayal of events a cruel hoax, and blamed the media and the L.A. black politicians/leaders for inciting the riots which followed. Another man stated that the whole event turned into a political ploy to destroy the white element of the Los Angeles police force, which is rated as one of the best in the country. Perhaps the one good thing which will come out of this tragic affair is that police, many of whom are really toxic, will act with restraint in the future.

Juror Media Intimidation

As it turns out, the jurors, feeling the social pressure to convict the white law officers, took longer than they needed to reach their decision. They didn't want to return a not guilty verdict on the four white police officers, because they knew such would be unpopular. They just had no choice, based on the evidence. And another thing has come up from the world of attendees at the trial. It was not an all-white jury. There were several Orientals and several

Latinos on the jury, along with the white jury members. (There were no blacks on the jury.) But the mass media, in what I consider to be an egregious breach of ethical conduct, printed the names and work addresses of the jurors who brought in the not guilty verdict. Two other newspapers then followed suit. These jurors received numerous death threats. This means in the future jurors will be intimidated into conforming to the *"politically correct"* perspective. This means justice will not be served, but that the liberal, lawless, reprobate, unethical media will further suppress the truth in unrighteousness to the detriment of this country.

Media Generated Violence

The mass media considers violence entertainment. That's what much of Hollywood-produced movies and television are all about. And when it becomes the real thing, like the L.A. riots, they have much greater viewing audiences, and the potential for garnering increased advertising revenue. It becomes a media event. They are center stage. Moreover, with the graphic violence depicted by the media today in what is sickly called *"entertainment,"* once these evil holographic thought forms and values are established in an impressionable teenager's (or younger) subconscious, it is just a small step to bring these thought forms to fruition in the actual acts of violence committed.

The Big Lie?

Ronald Walters, chairman of Howard University's political science department, who was deputy campaign manager for Jesse Jackson in his bid for the presidency, wrote in the May 7, 1992 *Wall Street Journal, "The perversion of justice in the Rodney King verdict was possible because a group of jurors dehumanized a black person and sided with the police officers who unjustifiably beat him. As such, this case raised to a very visible level the treatment many blacks experience in the criminal justice system daily. But the institutional racism in this verdict was undoubtedly stimulated by the same set of factors that produces the wider violent reaction in Los Angeles.*

"The human explosion occurred under the cloud of an ideology of denial and cynicism,..." The evidence of the trial, the evidence of economic history, the careful and accurate research by black economists Dr. Walter Williams and Dr. Tom Sowell paint Ronald Walters, to put it mildly, as an opportunist.

What A Riot

The riots, lootings, burnings, beatings and killings in L.A., which allegedly resulted from the Rodney King verdict, were only minimally the result of that decision. The riots probably would not have occurred at all if it had not been for the slanted portrayal by the mass media, and if some black leaders had not fanned the fires of hatred, specifically L.A. Mayor Bradley and state assembly-woman Maxine Waters. Also, a black minister stated, *"I have one thing to say on television. The Crips and the Bloods in central L.A. must quit fighting each other. We have to band together. We will have a war in the streets. We need to go after these people and fight."* ...Isn't it a crime to incite a riot?

Eyewitness testimony at the scene, contacts within the Long Beach, L.A. and Inglewood police departments, men who were there, declare the vast majority of the destruction which occurred in L.A. had absolutely nothing to do with Rodney King. It had to do with opportunistic young and old criminals, and the gangs, going on a shopping spree with no threat of reprisal. It had to do with black racism against whites, Hispanics, Vietnamese, Koreans and Chinese. It had to do with black gangs and their penchant for wanton violence. The alleged Rodney King beating looked like a Valentine's Day party compared to the abuse inflicted by the black gang members on their helpless victims. And ironically, there also ended up being far worse police beatings of some blacks than the alleged Rodney King beating, but these went unreported by the press because of fear of even worse violence than what they'd already stirred up.

The looting fed on itself. It became Christmas Day, so to speak. A few blacks looted, and then, typical of the mob, others joined in. It was just that everyone else was looting and shooting, so the mob mentality became, *"Everybody else is doing it. Why can't I?"* Police officers stated that on the way to answer one call, they got as many as 15-20 more calls and couldn't be every place at once, so they'd end up just shooting into a building where the looters were, to try to drive them out. As one former police officer put it, *"Hasn't anyone ever taught these people that stealing is wrong?"* (*"Thou shalt not steal."*)

Many of the fires were started after the looting of a store had been completed so that the looters' tracks were covered. A store would be looted, a gallon or two of gasoline would then be poured inside, and next the place set on fire. Many of the looters were smiling and laughing with glee. After all, it was Christmas! Anything they wanted was free, and they had an excuse (the Rodney King verdict) to steal. Many postal substations were burned down, and the media showed a crowd of black women and children massed before a postal substation expressing their outrage that their welfare checks were late.

As it turns out, only a few of the black businesses were looted and burned after the signs went up on the buildings saying, *"Black Owned."* But nearly all of the Korean buildings were burned. This had to do with the Latasha Harlen victim, the black girl who was shot in an L.A. Korean-owned liquor store.

One arrested individual stated he was being paid to set fires. This suggests there was some method to the apparent madness which occurred, some nefarious planning. There was a pattern to the fires, and most were set by pros. But what the riots may have really boiled down to, is the black gangs got together and started war in the streets. The rumor is they had this planned well beforehand, and that it didn't make any difference what the Rodney King verdict was, guilty or innocent. (More on this later.)

The riots weren't over, and the violence wasn't over, nearly as quickly as the media portrayed it, either. A SWAT team member from the Long Beach Police Department reported that he took over 50 rounds in his car two days after the looting, when supposedly the streets were quiet. The media reported only *"light shooting"* at the time. Light shooting is not the attempted assassination of a police officer with 50 rounds of ammo fired into his car.

Police Story

The belated response by the police made the riots worse. This was a political decision. Law-abiding blacks called for the police, but the police were told to retreat after the riots began. The police were so intimidated by the abuse they'd received from the media and from the political authorities over them, they became afraid to act. And then the police in the Korean neighborhoods took the shopkeepers' guns away from them, and when the mobs attacked the Korean stores, looted them and set them on fire, the police stood by and did nothing.

Reinforcements for the police were slow in coming also. Mayor Bradley and California Governor Pete Wilson showed their ineptitude (and some say cowardice) in taking so long to respond and in the way they responded. A police officer on the Long Beach force stated that they began putting SWAT team members in stores they felt were going to be looted. One officer sat behind boxes in a building waiting for the windows to be broken. After the windows were smashed, he said specifically he watched a 300-pound black woman start to come through and then stop, pick up her 10-year-old daughter, and say, *"Here honey, let me lift you through the window. You go in and get us whatever we need, because if I go in, I'll probably get arrested, but they won't arrest a child like you."* ...Is this any way to train a child?

On Guard

About 80% of the destruction in L.A. happened on Thursday between noon and 10:00 p.m. But it wasn't until late afternoon on Thursday that the National Guard actually got armed and out on the streets. The National Guard's ammunition was supposed to be shipped to the Long Beach Police Department, but it didn't go there. It went to the Highway Patrol's office. For 12 hours the National Guard did not have ammunition. Finally, the Long Beach Police Department supplied the National Guard with ammunition. The same thing happened in Inglewood. The Inglewood P.D. finally had to provide the National Guard with ammo because no one remembered to send it to them. So there were four or five hours where the National Guard could have made a difference when they were literally and effectively disarmed. Adding insult to injury, the National Guard members were told not to load bullets in their guns as long as they were in *"safe"* neighborhoods, unless they were attacked. This meant that these National Guardsmen would have to reach down into their pouches, draw out their bullets, load their guns, and then prepare them for firing before they could defend themselves. That's like fighting with one arm tied behind your back. This was not a Clint Eastwood movie.

The Toll

The outcome of all this official bungling is that as of the Monday night following the Rodney King verdict, there had been 58 deaths in L.A. County alone and 2,383 injuries, 226 of which were critical. There were 12,111 arrests in Los Angeles County, and 5,273 buildings on fire and either heavily damaged or completely destroyed. It's hard to grasp that there were 2,383 people who didn't just fall off of their skateboards, who instead were savagely beaten, kicked, hit with sticks, rocks and fire extinguishers, innocent bystanders! All this in L.A. County over a 3-4 day period. By 7:00 a.m. Sunday morning, in some cases, it was business as usual back on the streets. One man told me that he was driving down Long Beach Boulevard at 7:00 a.m. Sunday morning and two hookers tried to wave him over for sex. A couple of other guys were standing on the corner selling cocaine, at 7:00 a.m. To live and die in L.A.

As it turns out, hundreds of shootings went unreported, including those at the L.A., Long Beach, and Inglewood police officers. A prominent L.A. official stated on TV that all individuals arrested would be sure to receive their *"constitutional rights."* What if the police had been told to *"shoot to kill"* rioters and looters, as was the case in the 1906 San Francisco earthquake and fire? How many innocent lives would have been spared? How many businesses and jobs would have been preserved?

The Aftermath - A Shot in the Dark

The potentially most dangerous violence yet to come is from the black L.A. gangs.

The black gangs broke into a store named Western Surplus. There they stole over 1,100 guns. They also broke into a dry cleaners and stole over 200 police uniforms belonging to the L.A.P.D. and Inglewood P.D. None of the weapons or uniforms have been recovered. The black gangs have already purchased 7,000 rounds of ammo for automatic weapons and have attempted three police assassinations.

The New York Times News Service reported on May 8, 1992, *"L.A. gang truce raises fears of united attack on police."* *"Instead of shooting each other, we decided to fight together for black power, a Crip nicknamed 'Oz Dog' said at a news conference."* ...Another black gang member interviewed stated, *"Tear it down, break it up, and rebuild it."* Also, in his opinion, the government had to go. This is revolution. This is *"order out of chaos,"* the basis of the plan for the New World Order.

One of my well-placed L.A. sources told me a *"Council of 12,"* the leaders of the L.A. gangs, came together and declared that as soon as the National Guard left they were going to get even with the businesses, police, and firemen with whom they had a vendetta. The fires in L.A. are a long way from being extinguished. Remember Billington's book, *Fire in the Minds of Men: Origins of the Revolutionary Faith*? And just think, none of this would have happened if Rodney King had simply pulled over and stopped like any other normal person.

Deliberations/Questions

What happens if there is another major earthquake in L.A.? As one REAPER subscriber wrote, often after riots, earthquakes and major earth changes occur, all over the world. This is electromagnetically consistent, once we understand the electromagnetic nature of both man and the earth, and the relationship between the two. (This is why in the Old Testament of the Bible, there had to be a blood sacrifice on the site where a murder was committed, when the guilty party could not be found.)

What happens when there are food shortages in L.A.? Can we really afford to have the Eastern Establishment allow California to be destroyed when the L.A. region is one of the key manufacturing centers of the U.S.?

Why is black racism allowed in this country, while white racism is the ultimate offense? The politics of guilt and pity? Why is it open season on WASPs, the Silent White Majority, but if a WASP speaks out, he is destroyed by the media, by the bureaucrats, by the legal system? Of the 1992 presidential political candidates, only Pat Buchanan faced the L.A. riots issue squarely.

How can the U.S. condemn South Africa, given what has occurred here? What kind of example is the U.S. democracy to the world today? Isn't democracy eventually always mob rule, which leads to an autocratic form of government? If riots break out again, couldn't the current administration declare martial law, a national emergency, and confiscate firearms?

We are at the end of a 510-civilization cycle. It is the time when world cities die. It is the time, during such times of major climatic changes, when racial strife always occurs. It is time to have a place to live outside of the dying cities. The L.A. riots prove that neither the state nor the federal government can or will effectively rule. Anarchy and lawlessness can occur on a whim, and be emotionally triggered with no basis in fact.

This brings up the question whether the U.S. government can survive. Lawlessness and the federal debt are two sure signs of collapse. Is it possible that the U.S. empire could collapse just like that of the U.S.S.R.? The hard truth is that many of the people are so alienated from the federal government that they hate the federal government. Politicians are resigning in droves because they know the system is gridlocked. French government officials have already written off the United States as a viable power in the 21st century. The always pragmatic French observe the U.S. is not recognizing or dealing with its problems.

What about the law-abiding, hard-working, tax-paying, God-fearing U.S. middle class which is already stretched to the limit financially and stressed out?

Will it stand for an increase in the $230 billion annual cost of poverty programs? Why have foreign welfare when we can't take care of our own at home? What about all the small farmers who went bankrupt in the 1980s? Conflict always results from legalized theft.

People sat glued to their TV sets in disbelief as the Rodney King-inspired (sic) L.A. riots were an apparent repeat of the '60s cry, *"Burn baby, burn!"* Welcome to the *"Nasty Nineties."* The '90s will make the '80s make the '60s look like the '50s. As I wrote in the March 11, 1992 REAPER, quoting my old Cherokee friend, *"People will be so afraid of what is happening they will be afraid to leave their TV sets."* His words were remarkably restated by Dr. Gary North, quoted in the same REAPER, *"In one day, everything that the typical urban dweller regards as familiar will disappear forever. He will sit transfixed in front of a TV screen, watching through telephoto lenses a CNN broadcast about the city..."* A forecast of our future?

* * * * *

"Under natural conditions, the earth's surface is negatively charged; the positive charge of living things are grounded, producing positive currents. And in contrast, urban and industrial areas do not allow the grounding of positive ions, which are at a higher level than in the natural setting. The negative surface retains its charge and continually attracts positive ions, which typically accompany storm fronts. Thus, more and more people are being affected by natural disasters, such as violent storms and floods. Urban and industrial areas show an accumulation of ions in the atmosphere. Insulating materials prevent grounding of the predominantly positive ions found in urban and industrial areas. This also contributes to the higher rate of crime, accidents, and civil unrest in urban and industrial areas." — Richard Pasichnyk— "The Solar-Terrestrial Linkage in Climate and War," *Cycles* Magazine

THE IDES OF AUGUST
July 30,1987

Historical Evidence and Celebrations

So potentially potent is this *"Ides of August"* time frame, that I decided to do some historical research on it. I thought such might give us a clue to see if history will repeat itself.

We don't have to go back very far to find financial significance for August 15th. It was on August 15, 1971 when Richard Nixon closed the gold window and permanently took the United States off the gold standard. But beyond this, our research turned up a fascinating sequence of historical events which tie into this three day time frame.

Napoleon Bonaparte was born on August 15th, as was Edward Lawrence, popularly known as *"Lawrence of Arabia."* So, two *"liberators"* lead the list in this time frame. And amazingly, there are a whole host of *"liberation"* festivals celebrated at this time as well.

August 15th is Congo Independence Day. August 15th is Independence Day in India, as well as Korean Liberation Day. On August 15th Laos celebrates Laotian Memorial Day while Liechtenstein celebrates Liechtenstein National Day.

August 16th is Cyprus Independence Day. In the Dominican Republic, August 16th is Political Restitution Day. August 17th is Gabon Independence Day and Indonesia Independence Day.

During this three-day time frame there are also a significant number of religious festivals underway. The Buddhists celebrate the *"Feast of the Dead"* in mid-August, after the harvest in the rural areas throughout Asia. In India, a holiday is celebrated in honor of the birth date of the baby Krishna. This involves the prayer and anointment of the infant god and recountings of his life. In Malaysia and Singapore, the *"Feast of the Hungry Ghosts"* or *"All Soul's Day"* are celebrated. In Belgium in August there is a *"David and Goliath Day"* festival where Goliath is vanquished but declares, *"I'm not dead yet."* In China on August 15th, the Chinese make offerings to the *"Hungry Ghosts."* These are spirits who either have no descendants to look after them or who had no proper funeral.

Prayer Power

We should never discount the effect of human prayer and meditation on either other people or the cosmos. For example, in the spring of 1985 when over 40,000 witches and warlocks in this country prayed and fasted for 30 days for the destruction of Christian families, it happened. Ministers with whom I visited all across the country in months subsequent to then repeatedly commented about the breakdown of Christian homes. Christians by and large had no knowledge of this occult event.

There is also an impressive statistical correlation between times of mass prayer and meditation coinciding with reduced solar flare and solar storm activity. This computerized statistical correlation of these two simultaneous events has all but ruled out that this was a chance occurrence. Probabilities instead favor cause and effect, that prayer and meditation by masses of people globally do in fact reduce solar storm, flare and sunspot activity.

This type of religious activity is emerging in the public's consciousness. Dr. Paul Pearsall's 1987 book, *Super Immunity*, disclosed evidence that people who are prayed for, even if they don't know that they are being prayed for, heal faster. For an excellent discussion on the importance of the power of prayer in healing, see John Wimber and Kevin Springer's 1987 book, *Power Healing*. As Wimber and Springer point out, if you're going to use *"spirits"* for healing purposes, you might as well use the King of Spirits, the *"Holy Spirit."*

The New Age Link Up

On the other side of the fence from the *"Holy Spirit,"* the New Agers link up with their *"spirit guides"* globally on August 16th and 17th. The New Agers gather at the locations of ancient astronomical alignments such as Stonehenge, the Ruins in Zimbabwe, the Temple of the Sun in Cuzco, Peru, and at Uxmal in the Yucatan, among others. According to the New Agers, the Ancients believed that these man-made astronomical alignments allowed the power of the reflected light of the sun, moon and stars to energize these power centers. The Ancients made pilgrimages to gather for ceremonies at these locations during special times of the year such as the full moon, at solstice and at equinox. Their purpose was to anchor *"light"* and receive *"healings."*

The New Agers have learned that during times of prayer and meditation, the brain oscillates at approximately 8 hertz, in harmony with the sun and the earth. They hope to link up and achieve this *"harmony,"* anchor *"light,"* and receive *"healings"* during the *"Ides of August."* One time the New Agers linked up like this was on December 31st, 1986, the time of highest tidal force in 168 years! On this exact December 31st date, both the stock and bond markets bottomed and gold broke out upside.

Global Acupuncture

Quoting from the *Sacred Sites International Festival* release (sent to me out of the blue by a REAPER subscriber), *"By gathering together at each Sacred Site around the world we are unified in thought and energy, linking the earth ley lines as an accupressure treatment of the world. This is much like Chinese acupuncture, where needles are placed in the Ch'i or energy points of the human body to redirect the positive and negative currents of energy."*

French scientists have confirmed the existence of acupuncture points and meridians. Small microscopic particles of radioactivity were placed under the skin of tested individuals at the acupuncture points and found to flow around the human body precisely on the acupuncture meridians. As a crosscheck, radioactivity was placed at other points under the skin where there were no known acupuncture points or meridians. The radioactivity remained stationary at those locations.

Acupuncture meridians which make up the human body's energy field can only be seen with Kirlian photography. This electromagnetic human energy field is commonly called the *"aura"* or biblically, the *"countenance."*

Continuing to quote from the *Sacred Sites International Festival* release, *"Today there is a need to explore the global power centers, ley lines and the importance of the individual working in harmony with life forces. It seems wise to let yourself expand your awareness to give love and service to this magnificent planet. Let your connection with the Sacred Sites elicit within your inner knowledge the rediscovery that we are not separate from our world."*

Arguelles' Harmonic Convergence

"According to Dr. Jose Arguelles of the Planet Art Network, August 16th and 17th of 1987 mark the 'precise calibration point in the galactic and planetary harmonic scales.' He calls this point 'Harmonic Convergence.' Jose has referred to his work as a new-Mayan science and a basis for a post-industrial scientific pattern he calls a 'resonant field paradigm.'"

Wild stuff, right? Then why did the *Wall Street Journal* during late June 1987 run a center column, front page feature article on Jose Arguelles entitled, *"New Age Will Dawn in August, Seers Say, and Malibu is Ready."* Regarding the *"Ides of August,"* the *Journal* commented: *"...That's when a bright new era for mankind will be ushered in. Either that or nuclear annihilation.*

"At that time, when the Earth starts to slip out of its time beam, ordinary mortals are going to feel a bit disoriented. The metaphysically inclined will experience recurring deja vu. Coincidences will proliferate. So will UFOs."

Continuing with the *Wall Street Journal* commentary: *"Mr. Arguelles says the choice between a 'new age' and all-out destruction is ours, and we had better decide within the next eight weeks. A new beginning can be assured only if enough people gather at sacred spots around the globe like Machu Picchu, Peru - on Aug. 16 and 17.*

"If the attendance is sparse, he warns, we lose our chance at joining a federation of extraterrestrials. It is Mr. Arguelles' hope that the United Nations will arouse and support his drive."

The Journal quoted Dr. Carl Raschke, a humanities professor at the University of Denver: *"You have these periods of religious upheaval whenever a society is making a transformation from one underlying social and economic structure to another."*

The 144,000

You can bet your boots Shirley MacLaine was linked up on August 16, 1987. The *Journal* cited the popularity of her seminars, book, and television movie, *"Out on a Limb."* Curiously, the *Journal* also contained the following: *"...Mr. Arguelles, the guru who is counting the days until the new age dawns on Aug. 16...wants people - 144,000 of them - to go to places like the pyramids, Machu Picchu and even Idaho. Once there they should 'resonate.' This will usher in the new age and prevent catastrophe, which explains why the new age press is hailing his plan as 'Armageddon Averted.'"*

This *WSJ* commentary coincided almost exactly with the commentary taken from the *Sacred Sites International Festival* release. Quoting the *SSIF*, *"According to the Rainbow People prophecy of the Intertribal Medicine Societies, a great psychic shift will occur at this time, 1987 is the year of Initiation. 144,000 Sun Dance enlightened teachers will totally awaken in their dream mindbodies. They will become a major force of the light to help the rest of Humanity to dance their dream awake. A Sun Dance teacher is any human being who has balanced their shields, who has gained the dream mindbody and who honors all paths, all teachers, and all ways. A true Sun Dancer will not say they have the only true way, for all ways are true. In 1987, 144,000 enlightened will sit down in Gathering Together Circles saying, 'Here it is brothers and sisters, openly, totally - come and receive it.'"*

There is quite a contrast between the New Age *"Sun Dancers"* who say that *"all ways are true"* and who honor *"all paths, all teachers, and all ways"* and what Jesus Christ said in John 14:6: *"I am the way, the truth and the life. No one comes to the Father except through Me"* (NKJV).

We are coming to a clear division among mankind spiritually. It is no accident that the ultimate in curse words today has become, *"Jesus Christ!"*

There is quite a difference between the persons, purposes and peaceful events of the 144,000 *"Sun Dancers"* and the 144,000 spoken of in Revelation 7:4, *"One hundred and forty-four thousand of all the tribes of the children of Israel were sealed..."* (NKJV).

Biblically, these 144,000 who are sealed in Revelation chapter 7 are called *"the servants of our God."* These elite 144,000 are sealed *"on their foreheads"* before the angels harmed the earth, the sea, or the trees, before a *"Hell Period"* began. In other words, these 144,000 biblically are the protected ones. (I don't think the 144,000 Sun Dancers are what the Jehovah's Witnesses have in mind, either).

The Big Island Connection

It is perhaps not surprising, given that the United States is the present Babylon of the world with its Babylonian debt monetary system (which is why Iran's Ayatollah Khomeini referred to the United States as *"The Great Satan"*), that the geographical focal point of the *Sacred Sites International Festival* was also located in the United States. In which of the United States is there maximum earth energy by way of volcanic activity? Which state in the United States has the most fertile soil, made possible by the paramagnetic charge of volcanic ash? Hawaii, of course. The *Sacred Sites International Festival* handout stated, *"The Big Island-Harmonic Energy Convergence...Pila of Crystal Visions, says, 'There are special places on your planet called power vortices where certain laws of physics do not prevail. These are places out of the norm, exceptions to the rule. Legend and myth portend them to be gateways to different worlds. The strongest of these vortices is the Big Island of Hawaii, directly opposite the Great Pyramids of Egypt. Hawaii is the birthing energy of this planet, the only 'living' vortex and the pulse of all energy on this planet. The Big Island is nicknamed the living 'Fantasy Island.' It is steeped in folklore and legend from Madame Pele, our Goddess of the Volcano Abode, to the Night Marchers, Fire Balls of the Kahunas and, of course, the little people, the Menehunes. Saddle Road between the majesty of Hawaii's two great mountains, Mauna Kea and Mauna Loa, is one of the world's most active hotbeds of UFO activity.*

"Reports of spiritual and physical healings are ever-increasing on the Big Island. It is said that anything you ask for in earnest here will manifest for you in the following few months, from forgiveness to successes, to physical healings. It is suggested that you meditate over your wish at one of the sacred power centers, such as the Place of Refuge (at sunset), Waipio Valley, the Volcano, etc....

"In this year of Harmonic Convergence for Planet Earth, more and more eyes will shift toward the Big Island. The guidance and enlightenment of her vortex of scientists and philosophers are sure to become a major seat of learning in the New Forming Order of Energy."

Undoubtedly, the Big Island of Hawaii is located on a key energy ley line, since it is 180 degrees opposite the Great Pyramids of Egypt. The ley lines of the earth are effectively the earth's acupuncture lines or meridians. These are a primary source of free energy. It is on these ley lines that old churches are located all over Ireland, England and Europe, and even in this country, such as in the Midwest states of Wisconsin, Indiana, Ohio and Illinois. Older Mormon temples are also located on key ley lines in this nation.

The church used to struggle with the pagans for location of their sanctuaries on these key ley lines. But the church gave up dominion in this area centuries ago. As Bruce Cathie has pointed out, the ley lines are now the primary energy tracks used by UFOs. This brings us back to *"Close Encounters."*

A Parting of Company

Now, let's close in on the core of all of this. So far we have just *"danced"* (excuse the word choice) around the issue. The *Sacred Sites International Festival* release quoted Dr. Jose Arguelles, *"...Harmonic Convergence signals a phase shift which marks the passage from a collective determination to view things from a perspective of conflict, to a collective determination to view things from a perspective of cooperation. It will be universally experienced as a vibrational ripple momentarily dissolving the current mental frame and evoking a release of archetypal memories...."*

In other words, Arguelles expected a *"Hundredth Monkey Syndrome,"* a time when all of a sudden everyone becomes aware of *"what's happening."* It's all supposed to happen like magic. Presto! Instant awareness! This is a far cry from the biblical requirements of character, righteousness, faith and work to achieve such.

The *SSIF* release also quoted Jim Berenholtz, *"...And it is being seen that the Sacred Sites of Planet Earth, be they natural shrines or timeless temples, are calling us back to reactivate their energies and link them in the ways that are appropriate to now. These sites are here to help us do what must be done. Like acupuncture needles, they channel the healing energies and link them in ways that are appropriate to now. When used properly we all benefit.*

"...People can answer the calling for two days of prayer and ceremony from wherever they are,...

"...Our ancestors have left us a great gift knowing the Time of Remembrance would come. Never before have human beings simultaneously coordinated their prayer, meditations and ceremonies at Sacred Sites throughout the world. What a remarkable opportunity we have. If we can focus our energies as clearly as our ancestors have focused the creation of the Sites we will be using, imagine the potential for healing and positive changes."

I don't quarrel with the importance, power and potentially beneficial effects to be derived ecologically, technologically and humanly from the understanding and proper use of *"earth energies."* After all, *"all things are created good.."* For too long our rationalistic, materialistic society has had the order of reality reversed. We put matter ahead of spirit, mammon over God, and things before people. The correct order is spirit - energy - matter, God over mammon, and people as more important than things. This perspective the New Agers have is therefore partially correct. However, where I radically part company is with the *"gods"* and *"spirits of this world"* the New Agers have chosen to serve, or the *"extraterrestrials."* It smacks of the revival and calling forth of Satan and his demons, just as C.S. Lewis warned us in *That Hideous Strength* and *The Screwtape Letters*.

For most people, this is spiritually often a very subtle and difficult distinction. But it is a basic one. After all, Satan comes disguised as *"an angel of light."* II Corinthians chapter 11, verses 13-15, declare *"For such are false apostles, deceitful workers, transforming themselves into apostles of Christ.*

"And no wonder! For Satan himself transforms himself into an angel of light.

"Therefore it is no great thing if his ministers also transform themselves into ministers of righteousness, whose end will be according to their works" (NKJV).

Hell To Pay

Central to this whole August 16th-17th human, planetary, extraterrestrial demonic, sacred site link-up is the Aztec prophecy concerning the Mayans. According to this prophecy, there are thirteen heavens and nine hells, each of which lasted 52 years. For the Aztecs, the end of the thirteenth heaven came on April 23, 1519, when Cortez and his Spanish conquistadors landed on the Yucatan coast. That signaled the end of the Aztec empire. Each of the succeeding nine hells was expected to be worse than the former one for the entire world. Quoting from the *Sacred Sites International Festival* release, *"Finally, on the termination day of the Ninth and Last Hell, Texcalipoca, the God of Darkness, will rise to the fullness of his power and might, at the end will suddenly remove his Jade Mask, to reveal his true nature beneath, Quetzalcoatl, Bringer of Peace. The Hells will come to an end, and a New Heaven day will come in our calendar on August 17, 1987.*

"The ancient prophesies of the Mesoamerica pinpoint the return of Quetzalcoatl, Lord of the Dawn, to the time that correlates with the time of August 16/17, 1987 in the Gregorian Calendar. Quetzalcoatl represents the force of the cosmic intelligence, the spiraling pattern that governs the movement of all things in this Universe.

"Quetzalcoatl is the enlightened state, the Kundalini energy soaring to the Crown Chakra. Quetzalcoatl lives as a potentiality, a seed within each of us. It is written that 144,000 Human Beings will emerge to be the sprouting of that seed on the day of Harmonic Convergence, and will grow to flower and seed again toward the awakening of all humanity in the years that follow."

In other words, Satan, the god of this world, the god of evolutionary humanism, is about to become *"a good guy"* and install *"heaven on earth."* Satan's original name was Lucifer, meaning *"Light-bearer."* Therefore, it would appear that Satan is looking to re-establish himself again as the *"Light-bearer,"* Lucifer - *"Lord of the Dawn."*

One of the most sophisticated of the satanic religions is Luciferianism. It holds that Lucifer is the elder *"son of God,"* and that the younger son, Jesus Christ, wrongfully replaced Lucifer in his position of glory by deceiving God the Father. Therefore Luciferians look to re-establish Lucifer as the rightful son to sit at the right hand of God the Father, equal to God.

Notice another hook. When we're dealing with the Kundalini energy of the human body and the crown chakra, we're dealing with the strongest energies in the human body. The satanic appeal is to *"the autonomous god within us,"* a twisted distortion of man as *"made in the image of God,"* a denial of man's *"creaturehood"* and need for God. Thus, we're back again to basic humanism, *"man as his own sovereign god,"* matching Lucifer's first lust to be his own god, to *"be like the Most High"* (NKJV).

There is a sharp distinction between man naturally in his present state already being an autonomous god, and the opposite basic Christian perspective. The basic Christian perspective is that man is lost, helpless, hopeless, and in need of salvation from the slave market of sin (error), this salvation coming from outside of nature. From the basic Christian perspective, man must have the supernatural saving grace and work of Jesus Christ to restore man's legal and personal fellowship with God the Father. This saving work alone allows God to implant the Holy Spirit (God) within each believer upon the point of realization (faith) of his eternal salvation. This also establishes each redeemed man as a *"son of God,"* operating not independently, but instead under the authority of God and His Law. This in turn progressively eliminates the inherent natural conflict between men so nature can be recaptured to harmony.

False Harmony

This idea of living in harmony with Planet Earth is a basic tenet of witchcraft. There is no natural harmony or primary goodness in Mother Nature or Mother Earth. Mother Earth/Mother Nature is no *"mother."* Mother Earth/Nature is naturally known for her conflict, chance, cycles, confusion, disintegration and death. For this reason, man biblically is called to *"occupy"* and exercise *"dominion"* over nature in order to peacefully recapture Mother Earth/Nature to harmony.

The Possession

As the state (civil government), *"god walking on earth"* as Hegel put it, breaks down, humanistic collectivist man is being replaced by humanistic, individualistic man who is supernaturally empowered by *"spirit guides"* (demons). This in turn will cycle back to a one world, bureaucratic, *"spirit infested"* super state. Again quoting from the *Sacred Sites International Festival* release: *"There is an obscure Zapotec Indian prophecy which also predicts that at sunrise on The Morning, something special will occur near Oxacian in southern Mexico, at the El Tule Tree. The El Tule Tree is a magnificent towering being, cousin to the Sequoia, and one of the oldest living things on the planet. According to Zapotec tradition, one of the incarnations of Quetzalcoatl is buried beneath the roots of the tree, and as the first rays of the dawning new heaven cycle sink into the depths of the Earth, billions of tiny spirits will burst from the heart of Quetzalcoatl. They will slowly rise through the trunk, through the limbs and branches, appearing as sparkles of light, finally erupting from every leaf and seedling, to circle the globe, each spirit to implant itself within the heart of a human being and plant a crystal of peace and hope."*

What a beautiful way to describe massive demon possession, white magic at its finest. Biblically speaking, it would appear as though Satan and 144,000 of his most powerful demons were about to be loosed on the earth for 25 years, until 2012.

Finally, to tie things down, both the Ute Indian tribe of North America and the Mayans of Central American held the belief that our world and its civilizations move in cycles of 22,880 years, known to them as a Universe of time. Within each Universe are four ages. The fourth Universe is one of education and spiritual awakening. Quoting from *SSIF*:

"...According to both civilizations, the final day of the fourth age in the current Universe is August 16, 1987. The first day of the first age in the New Universe, the age of wisdom, will be August 17, 1987...."

* * * * *

Farmers who are REAPER subscribers in the Tri-Cities, Washington area regularly see UFOs. These sightings are quickly followed up by visits from government officials informing these farmers that *"Last night you saw nothing. This is a secret government project."*

* * * * *

On August 14, 1935, the Social Security (SS) swindle system became law. This evil system undermined self-reliance and broke down the traditional family and church *"safety net."* It replaced them with the federal government as Big Brother at a budget-busting cost.

RELIGION IN AMERICA:
THE OUTER LIMITS

March 11, 1992

Rocky Mountain High

Promptly at 7:00 a.m. every morning, seven mystics sit on mats in a circle around a fire built in a pit. Accompanying them from a ground-level shelf is a collection of seven deities which also face the flames. The fire ceremony begins when a woman begins to sing in Sanskrit. Thus begins the pre-Vedic ritual which dates back thousands of years, rooted in the Hindu faith.

A clear crystal is anointed with various substances. Grain is tossed into the fire along with fruits and flowers as an offering to the god. There is the passing of a candle flame which serves the purpose of *"singing the praises of the Universal Mother."* The candle ritual is followed by these fruit lovers throwing a coconut, some apples and bananas into the fire. Charred fruit salad anyone?

What is all of this, anyway? Where is it? Some mystical Hindu religious service being held in the high Himalayas? Perhaps instead it is what remains of a cult of 1960 hippies who have been strung out and wasted on drugs. But neither is the case. Every morning, promptly at 7:00 a.m., this ceremony takes place in the woods behind the Aspen Institute for Humanistic Studies in the Colorado Mountains! (Source: *The High Valley Independent*, Crestone, Colorado)

You're correct. The Aspen Institute has gone bananas, so to speak. But we've known that for a long, long time. The problem is, we just weren't told that the Aspen Institute was all that religious.

What happens at the Aspen Institute for Humanistic Studies affects us all. The Aspen Institute is one of the leading intellectual think tanks for the Eastern Establishment which runs this country, politically and economically. It often links up with the left-leaning, legislation drafting Brookings Institution. So once again we confirm that government is religion applied to economics. It is the Hindu religion which is primarily influential on the U.S. establishment's governmental and economic policy. Just how far has Hinduism taken India economically?

This is just like God, mother, country and apple pie, right? The good old-fashioned all-American way, correct? Car 54, driven by Bill Moyers and Mortimer Adler, where are you? Going/throwing bananas, too, up at the Aspen Institute? Has the thin air of 7,900-foot-high Crestone, Colorado gone to your heads?

Located high in the central Colorado Rocky Mountains lies the once sleepy mountain town of Crestone, Colorado. Nestled in the shadow of the three

14,000-foot-plus Crestone peaks, what was at one time a nice little all-American mountain town has now become what some local residents call *"just a cover for an elite group to control things throughout the world."* Obviously, some of the locals aren't all too hip or *"Rocky Mountain High"* about it all. Nancy Hood called Crestone *"cult city."* She talked of human sacrifices and dueling curses.

Interesting that this would occur at Crestone. The Crestone peaks are part of the Sangre de Cristo mountains, which translated from Spanish means *"the blood of Christ."* There is anything but *"the blood of Christ"* at Crestone these days. Perhaps this is why some of the locals would like to change the name of Crestone to Prestone and send it into a deep freeze. Can hell freeze over?

Let's gather around the fire and have a roll call of these all-American types (sic) who have now squatted at The Baca in Crestone. This formerly was the domain of all-American mountain men, of whom John Denver is definitely not one. We have the Lindisfarne Mountain Retreat and Chapel, the San Luis Valley Tibetan Project and Monastery, the Taoist Retreat, the Muslim/Sufi Learning Center, Dingo Khentse Rinpoche, the Tibetan Buddhist Monastery, the Zen Institute of Japanese Culture, Eiheja, Zen Buddhist Temple, the Carmelite Chapel and Retreat, the Carmelite Hermitage, the Lam Gampo, Tibetan Buddhist Retreat, the Babaji Ashram, Mother's Temple Shrine of Shiva, Sri Aurobindo and Savitri House Learning Center, the College of the Adepts along with the Library and Archives of Ancient Knowledge, the Suncircle Archaeological Site, the Center for Development Alternatives, the World Garden, Flowers and Herbs of World Religions, the Bistro Restaurant, the Native American Elders Council, the Shontu Arabian Farms, the Experimental Gardens, the Wisdom Education Center, the School of Hebraic Studies, the Sierra Blanca High Altitude School and Experimentation Farm, the Agricultural Center and Seed Bank, the Baca Wildlife Sanctuary for Indigenous and Endangered Species, the Rediscovery Four Corners Wilderness Camp, the Native American Center of Traditional Medicine, the Spiritual Life Institute, the Liberty Hermitage, the Essene School of Life, the Karma Triyana Dharmachakra, the Colorado State University Experimental Farm, and oh yes, a Baptist church.

What? A Baptist church? What's a Baptist church doing here? *"In over their heads?"* Actually, the Baptist church was here first. Oh well, maybe they're meditating on James Jordan's book, *The Failure of the American Baptist Culture.*

Strange. I don't see any Puritan Development Center, NFL Showcase or John Wayne Center for Western Art named among this august list at Crestone. But this is not America today - or is it?

I talked to a young man at Christ for the Nations in Dallas, Texas about the summer he spent at Crestone on a religious retreat. He said strange people would regularly gather around their dormitory in Crestone at night and chant and cast spells.

John Wayne would never have let the Indians get this far. But then again, John Wayne was a straight arrow. The living waters which flow from the Sangre de Cristo mountains are apparently taking on a whole new meaning at Crestone these days.

Mental giants such as Farrah Fawcett have visited the area. Shirley MacLaine spent her birthday here. (You could say that Crestone and the Baca Corporation, which runs this whole religious thing, are *"out on a limb."* Should someone hand a conjured up John Wayne a chain saw?)

Just what are all these alien religious groups up to here in the heartland of America's mountains? Not contemplating *"In God We Trust,"* I assure you. On July 5, 1987, ground-breaking ceremonies were held for the Temple to the Divine Universal Mother at the Haidakhandi Universal Harham. One could say it was kind of a late 4th of July celebration, Divine Universal Mother style. Of course the Universal Mother's handmaidens, *"the sun and moon were in very auspicious positions according to the Indian astrological calendar."*

"The significance of the ground-breaking ceremony is to worship Mother Earth. Worship is also offered to the mineral kingdom, the animal kingdom and the plant kingdom. The beings that live in the underworld are offered prayers. Prayers are also offered to the protectors of the eight directions and all the planets of the zodiac."

An invocation was given to the Universal Mother, *"the Creatrix and Protectress of all Creation...*

"Ceremonies were made to Ananta, the king of snakes, who is considered master of the underworld, for protection of all beings on the site. A gold replica of a snake representing Ananta was made..."

All-American to the core (COR) (sic)... I guess you would be run out of Dodge by a Chrysler if you brought to these folks' attention (assuming they can understand English) that slavery, snakes, serpents, witchcraft and occultism have all been linked together from the time of the empires of ancient Babylon and Egypt forward. And undoubtedly, they would throw you out on your ear if you pointed out that *"Mother Earth,"* when left to her whims without the reconciliating and subduing efforts of dominion man, is nothing more than a cruel, parsimonious witch. Somebody needs to tell these yahoos that the natural characteristics of *"Mother Earth"* include conflict, chance, cycles, poverty and death. Some mother! (Men of the cloth would say these negative attributes of *"Mother Earth"* are pretty close to those of the Prince of Darkness, too.) Oh well, some cynic will just whisper the chorus from the Doobie Brother's hit, *"But what a fool believes he sees no wise man has the power to reason away..."*

It seems that anybody who is somebody in this world today knows about this little hot spot of international global religion in Colorado, with the exception, of course, of typical red-blooded Americans. But then again, how long has it been since typical red-blooded Americans knew what was really going on in their country? They've been duped and seduced since at least 1913.

A prince from Thailand, Suchart Kosolkitiwong, who calls himself the *"World Peace Envoy,"* and who is president of the International Federation of Religions in association with the United Nations, made a trek to The Baca at Crestone. He was there July 1 and 2, 1987. (So, American Independence Day was surrounded by two non-American ceremonies.) Prince Suchart Kosolkitiwong, who is also with the World Constitution and Parliament Association, and who is prime director of the Religious Land Hooppa Sawan, is considering building a religious center at The Baca.

Let's see. The United States is the origin of the debt-based world reserve currency, the U.S. dollar. (Did I ever tell you that the crescent, the circle and the truncated pyramid on the back of the U.S. one dollar bill is identical to that of the sign of *"Tanit?"* *"Tanit,"* of course, was a consort of Ba'al Hammon to whom the Carthaginians offered child sacrifices for over 200 years. And, of course, in the infra-red range of light spectrum, where frequency, form and substance are all interrelated, the symbol of *"Tanit"* and that which appears on the back of the U.S. one dollar bill attract and emit the same frequency. A continuity of evil? Abortion today is the equivalent of child sacrifice by the Carthaginians.) Continuing, the U.S., is, of course, the headquarters for the United Nations, the symbol of the global political movement toward a New world Order. The Council on Foreign Relations and The Trilateral Commission, both located here, could vie for this One World honor (sic), too. So, it should come as no surprise, given this internationalist economic and political reality, that the center for One World religion should be established here in the United States as well. Government is always religion applied to economics.

Now, as you might suspect, this *"Rocky Mountain High"* area was not chosen whimsically. The Sangre de Cristos have long been a site of major religious significance for American Indians. Blanca Peak, located 40 miles south of Crestone, is one of the Hopi Indians' four sacred mountains. Considerable archaeological religious evidence has been unearthed there, too, including the discovery of ancient shrines, underground kivas, and burial grounds. Shamans used to make annual pilgrimages to *"power points"* located on these mountains, in a quest for knowledge. For thousands of years this area was considered to be one of the holiest of holy places on earth. These transplanted people here now believe that Crestone is where *"the preparation for the new world will take place."*

Government and economics spring from religion. Should we feel safe and secure as investors about now? Think these folks harbor warm thoughts and feelings toward materialistic American capitalists and investors, debt-infested or otherwise? Hardly. Does it sound like these mystics are interested in preserving our traditional American way of life? Not by a long shot. Want to invest in prosperous (sic) India? The Indians have invaded America! Is turnabout fair play? Dr. Barry Fell, where are you?

Forget grabbing your musket or six-shooter. Grab your mantra and chant or hum. Maybe then these body and soul snatchers will pass you by. Psst, Rambo, or is it Ramtha, where are you?

By now, it has probably occurred to many of you that this type of thing did not *"evolve"* naturally. It took someone besides *"Hannah and Her Sisters"* to pull it off. But that's not far off the mark. Actually Hannae and her *"Strongman,"* literally her husband, Maurice Strong, wove this web of religious internationalists together.

Maurice Strong, who heads up The Baca project, is no 90-pound weakling. He has been called *"Custodian of the Planet," "Anti-poverty Warrior," "Salesman for Relief,"* and *"Mystic Millionaire."* His entry in *Who's Who* is three inches long. He holds 26 honorary degrees from universities in the United States, Canada and Europe. He has linked together the twin carnal gods of money and power with his internationalism, couched in religion, humanitarianism and environmentalism.

Canadian by birth (Oak Lake, Manitoba), Maurice Frederick Strong has served as Undersecretary General of the United Nations. As Undersecretary General of the UN he was responsible for the World Conference on Environment held in Stockholm in 1972. Out of that arose the United Nations Environment Program. Strong sat with Michael Sweatman and Edmund de Rothschild at the World Conservation Bank Caucus, where the plans were laid to capture one third of the earth into a one world land trust, under the guise of environmentalism. He was also responsible for the infamous Earth Summit held in Rio in 1992.

Strong is the Director of Finance of the Lindisfarne Association, which relocated its headquarters from New York to The Baca in 1979. Its relocation was followed soon thereafter by the Aspen Institute. (Strong donated 300 acres to the Aspen Institute.) One of Strong's partners is William Ruckelshaus, a prominent Republican and former head of the EPA.

Under internationalist Canadian Prime Minister Pierre Trudeau, Strong organized the Canadian national energy agency - Petro-Canada. Petro-Canada is the most controversial socialistic Crown corporation ever created in Canada.

Strong has made his mark (and his fortune) in private industry as well. He developed a graphite mine in Africa, along with a string of gas stations in Eastern Africa. (He learned to speak Swahili.) He made a fortune in Canadian mining stocks. He was active in the early stages of the oil and gas development boom, headquartered in Calgary, Alberta, Canada. A millionaire at age 30, his corporation was appropriately named *"Power Corporation."* (Who financed all this?)

Strong is or has been a director of over 40 other corporations, too. He has served as the Canadian Deputy Minister for External Affairs, where he assumed responsibility for foreign aid as these issues came before the United Nations and the World Bank. He bought Prochemo, a Texas-based company, through which he was able to buy control of the Arizona Colorado Land and Cattle Company. He later merged AZL with TOSCO, the second largest independent oil refining company in the United States at that time. He now heads Hydro-Quebec, which has been getting flak over its treatment of Canada's native peoples who are affected by the utility company's development projects.

Strong also headed up the Canada Development Investment Corporation, which was the overall umbrella for many corporations owned by the government of Canada. CFR member and former U.S. Secretary of State George Schultz awarded Maurice Strong a humanitarian award as a result of his work with the UN Office for Emergency Operations in Africa. Says Strong, *"I'm hoping to connect what I'm doing at Baca on a grass-roots level with the global level."*

Should someone bind this *"Strong man?"* Then again, perhaps *"Mother Earth"* will do it on her own. If then the late climatologist Dr. Iben Browning is correct, we are headed for a time of tremendous earthquake and volcanic activity. Now, mountains weren't formed by a nice, neat, peaceful, evolutionary process. Mountains were formed violently and sit, by their nature, along earthquake faults. If, just what if, the Sangre de Cristo mountains came tumbling down on top of Crestone, the Baca and Strong during a violent earthquake? Well then, the *"Strong man"* would be bound and his internationalist project would have more *"Mother Earth"* than a mouthful with which to deal. Ironically, if such an earthquake occurred, the *"Strong man"* would literally be covered by *"the blood of Christ."*

This is, of course, an unlikely possibility. Earthquakes and landslides which cover up entire towns are few and far between. So if the *"Strong man"* has his way, the trend toward One World religion, government and economics will continue, based in the United States, backed unknowingly by the American people and their tax dollars.

Perhaps tomorrow morning when they again hold that fire ceremony behind the Aspen Institute, someone will toss in that *"golden snake."* Where's the beef? If it worked for a *"golden calf"* long ago, it might work for a *"golden snake"* today.

(Credit for much of the research for this chapter goes to REAPER reader Mr. Donald R. Hood, the staff writers of *The Valley Courier* of Alamoso, Colorado and the staff writer of *The High Valley Independent* of Crestone, Colorado.)

* * * * *

The March 1, 1992 issue of *Parade* Magazine had a full-color, 3-page article by left-wing environmentalist and atheist Carl Sagan, entitled, *"To Avert a Common Danger."* Sagan talked about how religion and science, old antagonists, are now forging a new alliance. Sagan stated that we are at risk everywhere on earth, that there are 5.4 billion people on the earth, and the earth's population is growing at the equivalent of the population of China every decade.

He stated, *"And at each step, we have emphasized the local over the global, the short-term over the long. We have destroyed the forests, eroded the topsoil, changed the composition of the atmosphere, depleted the protective ozone layer, tampered with the climate, poisoned the air and the waters, and made the poorest people suffer most from the deteriorating environment. We have become predators on the biosphere - full of arrogant entitlement, always taking and never giving back. And so, we are now a danger to ourselves and the other beings with whom we share the planet.*

"The wholesale attack on the global environment is not the fault only of profit-hungry industrialists or visionless and corrupt politicians. There is plenty of blame to share.

"The tribe of scientists has played a central role. Many of us didn't even bother to think about the long-term consequences of our inventions. We have been too ready to put devastating powers into the hands of the highest bidder and the officials of whichever nation we happen to be living in. In too many cases, we have lacked a moral compass. Science from its very beginnings has been eager, in the words of Rene Descartes, 'to make us masters and possessors of nature,' and to use science, as Francis Bacon said, to bend all of nature into 'the service of man.'...

"The religious tribe also has played a central role...The notion of 'us against Nature' is a legacy of our religious traditions. In the book of Genesis, God gives humans 'dominion...over every living thing,' and the 'fear' and 'dread' of us is to be upon 'every beast.' Man is urged to 'subdue' nature, and the word 'subdue' was translated from a Hebrew word with strong military connotations. There is much else in the Bible - and in the medieval Christian tradition out of which modern science emerged - along similar lines...

"True, there is nothing in the Judaeo-Christian-Muslim tradition that approaches the cherishing of nature in the Hindu-Buddhist-Jain tradition or among Native Americans. Indeed, both Western religion and Western science have gone out of their way to assert that nature is just the setting and not the story, that nature should not be viewed as sacred...

"It has been my good fortune to participate in an extraordinary sequence of recent gatherings that have helped wet the stage for the May meeting in Washington and other, similar meetings throughout the world: The leaders of our planet's religions have met with legislators from many nations, and with scientists, to try to deal with the rapidly worsening world environmental crisis...

"The interconnectedness of all human beings was a theme constantly stressed...

"Since the Oxford and Moscow meetings, many parliamentarians and environmentalists have worked to prepare for this June's 'Earth Summit' of na-

tional leaders in Brazil, which may lead to true international commitments to fix the global environment - or at least to slow the rate of its degradation...

"Religious leaders in many nations, including the United States, have moved into action...U.S. Sen. Al Gore is playing a central role...

"Cleaning up the environment and changing industrial practices that threaten it take money, of course..."

Next, Sagan, also in *Parade*, reprinted a text sent by scientists to religious leaders. Part of this text includes the following statements: *"...We are close to committing - many would argue we are already committing - what in religious language is sometimes called Crimes against Creation...*

"The environmental crisis requires radical changes not only in public policy, but also in individual behavior. The historical record makes clear that religious teaching, example and leadership are powerfully able to influence personal conduct and commitment.

"As scientists, many of us have had profound experiences of awe and reverence before the universe. We understand that what is regarded as sacred is more likely to be treated with care and respect. Our planetary home should be so regarded. Efforts to safeguard and cherish the environment need to be infused with a vision of the sacred...

"We believe the environmental crisis is intrinsically religious."

Isn't it interesting that the only attack Carl Sagan made against any religion was against the uniquely monotheistic Judaeo-Christian-Muslim tradition. Said Sagan, *"True, there is nothing in the Judaeo-Christian-Muslim tradition that approaches the cherishing of nature in the Hindu-Buddhist-Jain tradition or among Native Americans."*

Sagan's remarks are revolutionary. The Hebrew-Christian heritage is the backbone of our political and economic structure. Besides, the environmental scare tactics spewed out by these high priests of the earth are pure garbage, lies, intellectual pollution! Moreover, real environmental distress occurs in non-Christian, non-free market cultures, in the undeveloped Third World, and in statist countries like the old U.S.S.R.

Christians in the fifth century in Syria referred to God as Allah. Interesting. In the Judaeo-Christian-Muslim tradition, man is created by God to be a steward over the garden (nature), which is in sharp contrast to all these other religions in which man is seen as an evolutionary part of nature who can become his own autonomous god.

* * * * *

The Earth Summit was held in Rio de Janeiro, Brazil on June 1-12, 1992. This was the coming-out event for the New World Order, which was kicked off with the World Wilderness Congress held in Denver, Colorado in 1987. The

Earth Summit was officially called the United Nations Conference on Environment and Development. Representatives from 140 countries attended. All total, 6,000 government officials gathered in Rio.

This Earth Summit was the official global launching of the New World Order under the guise of environmentalism. It was an exercise by *"watermelons,"* green on the outside but red on the inside. It was the fulfillment of the synthesis of the Hegelian dialectic of the evolutionary, collective thesis of communism versus the evolutionary radical individualism of debt capitalism into the synthesis of the New World Order as fascist mercantilism - one world socialism. The Tower of Babel, Old Babylon, is rising.

Now the U.S. government has a series of global treaties set to be signed that will gut U.S. sovereignty and merge the U.S. into the New World Order. A treaty is the only document that supersedes the U.S. Constitution. All this, of course, will be accomplished in the name of *"saving the planet."* Look for a series of orchestrated articles and catastrophes to be used as catalysts to bring about this New World Order. (You have to break an egg to make an omelet.)

Beware the Ides of March, particularly the time of the full moon of March 18 and up until spring equinox March 20. It is a time when the snakes come out of hibernation and thus is a good time to get *"snakebit,"* literally, figuratively, and spiritually.

In 1991, the creature of the year was the *"wolf,"* and *"Dances With Wolves."* Of course *"Dances With Wolves"* was opposed to the Western tradition, grounded in the biblical record of *"ravenous wolves,"* werewolves, Wolfen, wolf it down, cry wolf, and a wolf in sheep's clothing. In 1992, in our devolution into darkness, where the worship of the creature/creation takes precedent over that of the Creator, the creature of the year was the *"snake."* Here again, Hebrew-Christian Western civilization has a negative perspective when it comes to the snake/serpent. A real scoundrel is said to be *"lower than a snake's belly."* I have occasionally heard someone called a *"viper."* A lying and conniving man has been referred to by women as *"a real snake."* Of course, going back to the religious roots of the Western political and economic system, the biblical record refers to a cunning serpent, the poison of the serpent, trampling the serpent underfoot, wounding the serpent, giving your son a serpent when he asks for a fish, etc. And with finality, in Revelation 12:7-9, as a result of the war in heaven, *"that serpent of old, called the Devil and Satan, who deceives the whole world; he was cast to the earth, and his angels were cast out with him."* No accident that the serpent/snake is held in such low esteem in Western civilization.

What emanates out of Crestone, Colorado, the Baca and the Aspen Institute are amply found in Colorado State University at Fort Collins, in Boulder, Colorado, and in Austin, Texas. I carefully monitor daily what happens in Austin, Texas in this regard, as well as the mass media as they orchestrate nationally the *"creature of the year."* In 1992, as the foregoing makes clear, I knew something big was up, given the *"Earth Summit"* which occurred that year. It is no surprise that we're going back to the roots of the pagan religious systems, the old empire of Egypt, king cobra and all, run by the greatest bureaucracy in the world, the epitome of what the *"New Age"* represents in the *"New World Order,"* with its emphasis on serpents/snakes. Remember Cecil B. de Mille's movie, *"The Ten Commandments,"* where God turned Aaron's rod into a serpent which swallowed up all the serpents of the magicians in Pharaoh's court? What goes around comes around.

The weekend of March 7-8, 1992, Austin, Texas held its *"Psychic"* Fair. On March 15, 1992, ten Tibetan lamas put on a sacred dance at the Paramount Theater in Austin, Texas for world purification and planetary healing. Ted Turner's network featured all the old occult movies, including Conan the Barbarian, with his war against the snake cults. The first week in March 1992 the Discovery Channel featured nationwide a major presentation on the pyramids of the Mayan and Aztec cultures and the snake, Quetzalcoatl, whose slithering figure runs from the top to the bottom of the pyramid. Quetzalcoatl, as many of you will recall, is the *"feathered serpent,"* who was the central focus at one of the Central American power points during the harmonic convergence of August 1987. (I first came across the importance of Quetzalcoatl when I worked for the president of Guatemala in 1983.) So it was no surprise that the Discovery Channel, among others, aired major features on the Central American Indian empires. The University of Texas at Austin held an introductory lecture on the Mayan culture Friday, March 13, 1992, including workshops on hieroglyphic writing at the UT Art Building.

The *Austin American-Statesman* on March 7, 1992 featured as a major story a Knight-Ridder News Service piece on the Sunday night, March 8 ABC *"World of Discovery"* presentation entitled, *"Realm of the Serpent."* Of course, the program was blatantly pro-serpent. Harry Greene, renowned herpetologist at Berkeley (where else) *"is an unabashed snake booster."* *"The shy and incredibly patient snake is no man-killer, says Greene. It's more like a Zen master."* The narrator, E.G. Marshall, states, *"Most snakes in most circumstances are totally harmless to man."* So much for *"Realm of the Serpent."*

The *"green"* picture is coming together at Austin. The Sunday, March 8, 1992 *Austin American-Statesman* quoted Austin City Council member Max Nofziger: *"I predict this teaming up will become an important new force in determining this city's path into the next century. For once, the entire city appears to be coming together on the environment."* In Austin, one of the most popular radio stations, whose call letters are KKMJ, calls itself *"Majic."*

There is, as also would be expected, an offset. Some good old boys - old-fashioned, grounded Americans/Texans in Taylor, Texas - hold their annual *"Rattlesnake Roundup,"* sponsored by the Taylor Jaycees. The March 7, 1992 *Austin American-Statesman* reported on that event: *"There is a Texas saying that the only good rattlesnake is a dead rattlesnake. But at least 100 Texans are expected at Taylor's annual rattlesnake roundup today to defend the state's rattlers.*

"Herpetologists, biologists and snake lovers will be at Murphy park in Taylor to protest 'the cruel and inhumane' treatment of Texas wildlife, said Duz Crawford, director of the Reptile Defense Fund."

And former California Governor *"Moonbeam"* Jerry Brown, won Colorado's Democratic primary March 3, 1992 on a pro-environment platform. Colorado is home of *"Devil's Head," "Garden of the Gods,"* Manitou Springs, and the huge Albertson, Ward, Freeman volume entitled *Paranormal Research*, published by Rocky Mountain Research Institute, Colorado State University. Both Boulder and Austin house the states' universities, and are high tech and New Age centers. Colorado Springs has all of that paramagnetic red rock (Garden of the Gods), while pink granite is prominent in the Hill Country outside of Austin. There is even an *"Enchanted Rock,"* composed of paramagnetic pink granite, the same stone which lines the king's chamber in the Great Pyramid of Egypt. On the Pharaoh's head-piece was a cobra. And then there was that ceremony up at Crestone to Ananta, the king of snakes, who is considered the master of the underworld.

The Arts & Entertainment channel in 1992 featured, *"David L. Wolper Presents,"* a special on the Great Pyramid. John Denver's album, *"Earth Songs,"* was being advertised all over TV.

As many of you know, I have worked with the global scientists on a regular basis since the mid-1980s. I have come to learn that in the world of quantum physics and living energy, there is an indistinguishable crossover, an integration of science with the supernatural. Religion and science are becoming bonded as one. For example, it can easily be explained today scientifically why voodoo works in some cases and doesn't in others. There is also something very important and significant about bringing the essence of the *"dark arts"* to light; it destroys their power. (Chemistry came out of alchemy; astronomy out of astrology. So, too, did the new physics out of the *"dark arts."*)

In Numbers 21 of the Bible, the people spoke against God and against Moses. As a result, the Lord sent fiery serpents among the people. Many of the people died from serpent bites. The people then repented for their sins (errors) and asked Moses to pray to the Lord to take the serpents away. Moses did pray for the people. The Lord told Moses to make an image of the fiery serpent and set it on a pole, *"and it shall be that everyone who is bitten, when he looks at it, shall live."* Moses obeyed, made the bronze serpent, and put it on a pole. After that, if a serpent had bitten anyone, when that individual looked at the bronze serpent, he lived instead of dying. Religion, Newtonian reality and the new physics were all linked together.

Several years ago I contacted a research group that the Japanese government used exclusively to *"clear"* an old samurai site in Japan. I wanted to find out if they could discover the nature of what was coming down. They uncovered that there were blood sacrifices being performed on the 666 negative ley lines (energy grid lines) of the earth, and that *"satanic groups were readying to usher in the Beast in 1992 who would be in control by 1993."* Their words, not mine, on June 13, 1990. Then in 1992 came the assault of the serpents prior to the Earth Summit at the time when all the planning for the Earth Summit was taking place, just before spring equinox.

Before I wrote this chapter, I sat down on Saturday, March 7, 1992, picked up the phone and called my old friend in Missouri who is one-quarter Cherokee (considered to be a full-blooded Cherokee), a naturally earthy and grounded man, who was struck by lightning and ever since has been blessed with uncannily accurate visions, dreams, prophecies, healing abilities, and the like. Time and time again over the past few years, when the two of us have been given the same perception separately, and then talked to each other on the phone, we independently confirmed what the other was seeing.

When I called Bob on Saturday, March 7, before I said anything at all, he told me that on Monday, March 2, 1992, he had a vision that, *"The rattlesnake is coming again, and I must reach past him. The rattlesnake had bit me last year,...that the snakes meant emergencies that eroded the foundation stones of this country like grains, the auto industry, strategic metals."* He stated he must *"wait upon the Lord to make a way through...People will be so afraid of what is happening they will be afraid to leave their TV sets."* He further stated that the little snakes that he'd seen before (last year) had grown up in 1992. So again, independently, using totally different methodologies, we came to the same conclusion.

There you have it, the revision of a REAPER I first wrote in 1987, published the week of March 16, 1992, the week of the full moon and spring equinox, the week when the religious sector of the new World Order attempted to bring to full power the *"year of the serpent"* - 1992.

Now this is amazing. In the March 6, 1992 issue of Dr. Gary North's *Remnant Review, "Scary Gary,"* as he is occasionally affectionately called, talked about how the United States had let dangerous Saddam Hussein off the hook, and how Saddam Hussein's only successful weapons against the West were used against civilian targets, terrorism, whether nuclear or, dread of dread, biological - anthrax. Gary stated, *"In one day, everything that the typical urban dweller regards as familiar will disappear forever. He will sit transfixed in front of a TV screen, watching through telephoto lenses a CNN broadcast about the city. If the city in question is New York City, there will be no CBS, ABC, or NBC national evening news."* This is almost word-for-word what my old Cherokee Indian friend/prophet said on March 7: *"People will be so afraid of what is happening they will be afraid to leave their TV sets."* Coincidence? Neither man knows the other. The March 16, 1992 cover story of *US News & World Report* headlined, *"The Nuclear Epidemic: The West's attempt to prevent the spread of nuclear weapons has failed, and a dangerous new era of nuclear proliferation has begun."* There goes the neighborhood and the environment.

IN TOUCH

May 15, 1991

World Cities

Oswald Spengler, in his classic work written in the 1920s, *Decline of the West*, noted that Western civilization entered the wintertime of its civilization when it became frozen. This is a time of world cities, when a civilization no longer responds to the challenges it faces. This is what seemed to be the case in April and May, 1991, during the secondary peak of the 18 1/3-year sunspot cycle (Solar Cycle 22), with the subsequent severe climatic and weather fallout. The ramifications of these geophysical upsets became magnified and more intense over the next two to three years. And yet, the thoroughly modern media paid little heed to these disasters, at least when it comes to their implications for civilization generally. Such was to be expected. At the end of a 510-year civilization cycle, during civilization's wintertime dominated by world cities, the land (climate) side of the economic equation of land and labor is all but ignored. It is not considered to be an influence, much less a determinant, of human action. Yet over 2,500 years of documented climatic history argues to the contrary.

Out of Touch

It was amazing to observe, during all this solar and geomagnetic field upset, that the TED spread went to new lows, representing high levels of financial confidence; and that fund managers poured their money into stocks, reducing their cash reserves to record low levels and sending the stock market to new highs where yield was all but nonexistent. Similarly, small investors were flooding into stocks and bonds. From the world city perspective, good times were here again, not to be confused with the reality of a world literally coming apart at the seams, climatically and geophysically. But during the time of world cities, during the wintertime of a civilization, is when illusion and delusion capture the minds and hearts of men. This is a reason why the heroes of the city populations today are actors, actresses and sports stars. These idols' lifestyles have little to do with reality. It's illusion that counts. But climate has the last word, and forces itself to be heard and reckoned with eventually. This is the *"truth shock"* facing a frozen civilization which is out of touch with reality.

Recovery?

It was sobering to discover that so few Americans have even a marginal awareness of these climatic events, much less their significance. Are we too toxic to sense reality? There is a sense within the intelligence of the energy behind matter, in the realm of quantum physics, that we all are interconnected, that we all are one. There is a common grace, so to speak, that links us all together. The ripple effects of what occurred in the Persian Gulf and in Bangladesh in 1991, for example, both directly and indirectly affect us all. But this did not stop seven out of ten economists from saying that the U.S. recession would be over in May or June. Nor did it stop the consumer confidence index from reaching a higher-than-expected 80%. FWN reported in April 1991: *"People are pretty convinced the economy is going to recover in a couple of months..."* A survey by Consensus Economics in London of 170 international analysts projected that all four leading English-speaking countries - the United States, the United Kingdom, Canada and Australia - would recover strongly in 1992 following the deep recession of 1991, and that the recovery would bring sustainable non-inflationary growth. *Business Week* boldly reported on April 29, 1991: *"You Heard It Here: Recession Won't Last the Summer."* Whoa! Hold it. Climatic history argues to the contrary. The type of climatic upset we saw in April and May 1991, if history repeats over the next 21 years, should put an anchor on economic activity. After all, the cost of these climatic rampages is exorbitant, not to mention their draw-down on human energy and the time required to return things to the status quo. Climatic upheaval also undercuts confidence.

Shake, Rattle & Blow

These significant earth changes began in our projected mid-to-late April to early May 1991 time frame. On April 18, 1991, an earthquake struck Soviet Central Asia in the republic of Tadzhikistan. It destroyed more than a hundred homes, resulted in human casualties, and registered 6 or 7 on the Soviet 12-point scale. A 7.5-Richter scale earthquake slammed Costa Rica and northern Panama on Monday, April 22, 1991, killing 74, injuring 800, and leaving 9,000 homeless. Over 80,000 were left homeless and 100 people died, while 500 were injured, when an earthquake struck Georgia in the former Soviet Union on April 29, 1991. This quake measured 7.1 on the Richter scale. A 6.0 quake on the Richter scale triggered rock slides and caused damage to buildings 110 miles northwest of Anchorage, Alaska on May 1, 1991.

The Volcano of Fire erupted on April 18, 1991, spewing lava rock and smoke, forcing the evacuation of nearby villages. This volcano is 300 miles west of Mexico City, and has not had such a violent eruption since 1913. (This is the time frame when the stock market topped.)

Of course, the tragedy in Bangladesh received widespread publicity. There, as many as 200,000 died in the most powerful cyclone in Bangladesh's 20-year history. Thunderstorms and tornadoes then whipped that battered nation mercilessly, increasing the death toll and the number of homeless. Some sources put the final death toll at approximately 500,000, which would equal Bangladesh's worst natural disaster to date, a 1970 cyclone. This latest cyclone packed 235-kilometer-an-hour winds and created 6-meter high waves. Bangladesh residents said the waves were *"as high as mountains."*

That's not the end of it. Snow fell in the Mideast country of Oman for the first time ever in April 1991. Africa faces its worst famine ever. More than 20 million Africans faced starvation in six countries. The Ethiopian famine was rated worse than it was in 1984. Also in April 1991, northern France recorded record cold temperatures. Billions of dollars of vineyards there, which produce the famous Bordeaux wine, were destroyed. As of May 13, 1991, a typhoon with peak winds of 150 miles an hour was racing toward the Philippines, threatening coconut and rice farmlands there on the main northern island of Luzon.

Back Home

Stateside, the weather was just as ugly in late April/early May 1991. Iowa recorded the wettest April on record. Heavy rains in Iowa continued into May and delayed corn planting. President Bush declared Louisiana a major disaster area due to the severe storms, tornadoes, torrential rains and flooding that began in April 1991, particularly in the Ouachita and Union Parishes. In Louisiana, 8,000 were left homeless by heavy rains in late April, and 17 of 64 parishes were declared federal disaster areas. At least 34 Louisiana parishes experienced some damage. Damage topped $50 million. State health officials offered cholera and typhoid shots. (Cholera, as you will recall, was a problem in Peru. It had also become a health issue among the Kurds.) Mississippi was likewise hard hit, sitting next door as it does to Louisiana. April 1991 was the wettest month on record in the Delta region.

Touch Down

A record number of tornadoes were recorded in the Midwest and Southeast. Between April 27 and April 29, 1991, over 100 tornadoes touched down in the continental United States. Pity the poor folks in Andover, Kansas, where a mobile home park housing 700 people was almost totally destroyed. Mobile home residents account for more than one-third of all tornado-related fatalities. Of course, mobile homes, just like warehouse districts, are energy magnets, both being made of metal. The *"freight train"* sound produced by a tornado, the sound of energy crunching, is attracted to such sites. Disaster agencies were beside themselves, having dissipated their financial and other reserves, as they were swamped with all these natural catastrophes at once.

Crop Talk

In Australia, parts of Queensland and New South Wales were very dry. Dry conditions in Australia delayed planting of winter wheat. Argentina's soybean harvest crop has been an off-and-on affair due to drought also. Excessive rains, in turn, negatively effected Brazil's soybean harvest. Drought in South Africa in fourth quarter 1990 delayed planting of the South African corn crop. In the U.S., Delta flooding drowned out potential cotton, corn and soybean fields. Louisiana and Mississippi were a disaster in this regard.

Disconnect

No connection was made publicly between solar storms and geomagnetic field upset and severe weather and climatic disturbances, with disruptions in the human realm, most typically, human violence. Let's just laundry list what had been going on around the world. Following the Persian Gulf war, a record number of rapes occurred in Kuwait. Saddam Hussein's methodically attempted genocide of the Kurds is now history. A black racial civil war rages in South Africa. Twelve people were injured or killed in violent clashes in Tunis. Yugoslavia finds itself in a state of civil war. Solidarity called a day of protest on May 9, 1991. The Soviet army intervened in the revolutions in Armenia and Azerbaijan. Riots broke out in Washington, D.C. Killing continued in India's Jammu and Kashmir states. Bombs exploded in Pakistan as the Hindus and Muslims in India and Pakistan continued to fight it out. The civil war raged in Afghanistan. Violence between Israel's security forces and the Palestinians continued. Rebels attacked a major hydroelectric dam in El Salvador, leaving six dead. Demonstrations by South Korean dissidents, numbering at least 200,000, almost paralyzed Seoul, in the worst anti-government violence in three years. (It's difficult for Americans to imagine 30,000 protesters in Yugoslavia and 200,000 protesters in South Korea. But such are literally signs of the times.) Labor strife in the largest workers' union in Uruguay broke out May 10, 1991. We are living in a time of global climatic and human upset, well into a 25-year transition period which began in 1987, which should carry at least to the year 2012.

Gunslingers

The riots which occurred in Washington, D.C. were dismissed as a fluke. And yet, the United States is the second to third most vulnerable geophysical country on the face of the earth. And we are a lawless country. Law is evolutionary and relative here, home of the best justice money can buy. Even the Christian religious population is lawless, some 86% claiming to be Christian, but only 13% believing in or abiding by the Ten Commandments. (The old adage in this country, *"Ignorance of the law is no excuse,"* had its origin in the fact that everyone knew the Ten Commandments, the basis for the law of the land.)

Violent crime in the United States jumped 10% in 1990, continuing a six-year uptrend. Only 17 perpetrators of each 1,000 major felonies are put behind bars in the United States today. The world cities, headed by New York, Los Angeles, Chicago, Houston, Detroit, Philadelphia and Washington, D.C., lead in violent crime statistics. And if history repeats, it's going to get worse.

Security should remain a major growth industry in the 1990s. Being *"in touch"* means recognizing the solar, geomagnetic, and ensuing climatic and weather effects on men individually, society collectively, the economy generally, and food production particularly.

We all know the old saying, *"Save the best for last."* Will this apply (from a global perspective) when it comes to violence in the United States? Bruce Landry provided some haunting insight in a Letter to the Editor in the April 22, 1991 issue of *U.S. News & World Report.*

Imagine a society where violence is glorified as a massive entertainment machine spews forth film after film loaded with blood-spilling, brain-exploding violence. Imagine a society where every 12 or so minutes of TV are spiced with flashy ads reminding people of the things they can never be or have unless they take them with force, if need be. Imagine a society where compassion is considered a weakness and greed a strength, where *"getting away with it"* makes one some sort of folk hero and where the premise of law applies only to those unfortunate enough to lack the funds, prestige or gumption to lie their way around guilt. Now, imagine this society reacting with shock to the actions of its youth, stating that guns, drugs and greed are the problem. Our children, so ready to kill, are merely the reflection of what we have taught them and tolerated. — *Bruce Landry, Hollis, N.H.*

INTEGRATION OF PERSPECTIVES
October 18, 1990

Craziness

Markets have a way of getting carried away and moving into the outer fringes of insanity. Who would have believed that the hardheaded and stubborn Dutch would have ever gone crazy over tulips? And yet for years, during the ill-fated Tulip Mania, tulips were the equivalent of gold to the Dutch. How about the masses of investors involved in the show animal market? In order to increase the hair length on Maltese show dogs, arsenic was fed to these cute little Maltese. Sure enough, their hair length increased, but they were short lived.

Then there is the llama market, in which I have been involved for over a decade. I thought, logically, that investors would have opted for good conformation, solid muscle and bone, gentle disposition, medium wool and good color in llamas as a prerequisite for determining value, and therefore price. I was wrong. The llama market, where one sire sold in 1990 for $175,000, instead went for the nonfunctional variety of llama, probably inbred with alpacas, lacking athletic ability (packing), the standard being *"cute and cuddly,"* like a teen-aged girl's stuffed animal. In other words, the best-selling llamas today are the equivalent of shaggy dogs. It's Maltese, part 2.

The main point of this exercise is that markets are usually not rational. We should expect them to become more irrational during this decade, too, as mankind collectively becomes more unstable. We are, as the late Vern Myers wrote, in a time of global *"rollover."* Myers was speaking economically. This is the human side of the equation equivalent to the 500-year civilization cycle on the climatic side of the equation. It is the latter - climate - about which the late Dr. Iben Browning has written so much.

Energy Input

Taking this a step further, this time of global upheaval and change is marked by accelerated deterioration of the earth's magnetic field charge, last seen to this degree at the time of Jesus Christ. Since man is an electromagnetic being, and since the breakdown in the magnetic field means that the electrically charged information held together by the magnetic field is deteriorating rapidly, only individuals who are well grounded spiritually (electrically) and physically (magnetically) are likely to stay rational and survive this rollover between now and the year 2012. The electromagnetically ungrounded masses we should expect to go berserk, and the mob in the markets literally crazy.

Recall the intricate designs which mysteriously appeared in the fields of England. Scientists are extremely puzzled over what has been forming these strange circles and intricate geometric designs on earth. There is no question that this is not random, natural (Newtonian) activity. This is the work of an intelligence. And this design is also an antenna in the infrared range. So it means something.

Now these mysterious circles have come to the United States. Farmers in Bates City, Missouri have noticed circles up to forty feet wide, similar to the ones seen in England. These circles have popped up on other farms in Kansas and Missouri, too. These energy balls, I think, were linked with the rapid decay of the earth's magnetic field charge, the peak of the sunspot cycle, and the high tidal force leading to significant earthquake and volcanic activity in December 1990 and January and February 1991.

Incidentally, eyewitnesses who have seen these energy balls describe them as amber in color. Interesting. Some leading charismatic Christians say the color of the Holy Spirit is amber. Doesn't God use earth changes to wake his people up? On the other hand, the color of hell and of the demonic realm is *"dark light,"* the red infrared light such as in a film processing darkroom. That's right, Martha, the colors of Halloween, orange and black, also echo the colors of hell.

This breakdown of electrically based information, due to magnetic field deterioration, could result in an alteration of the normal light spectrum visible to the human eye. We normally see between 0.4-0.7 micrometers, only 5% of all light frequencies. Mystics and heavy drug users have long broken through this limited visual spectrum of the human eye camera and have seen the spirit world. In fact, the earliest, and many recent reports of UFO sightings, have come from just such sources.

Is the breakdown of the magnetic field charge why reported sightings of UFOs now are increasing so dramatically? Are *"ordinary"* men and women now able to see things which earlier were visually obscured, but now are visible due to changes in the electromagnetic environment? Some scientists have stated that the 666 major energy ley lines which circle the earth and keep the earth's magnetic field intact are deteriorating and allowing this phenomenon to be manifest. These ley lines - energy lines - are electromagnetic lines of force which Bruce Cathie long ago proved are the highways of the UFOs.

Holographic Life

The expansion of the world of quantum physics has taught us that life is indeed holographic. It is spiritual, energetic, and material in nature - three in one. This, not surprisingly, reflects the three functions of the Christian Godhead: God the Father (spiritual), God the Holy Spirit (energetic and delicate), and God the Son - Jesus Christ (material). It is also an expression of what we are now learning in terms of the holographic nature of physics: quantum (all in all), Einsteinian (relative and energetic), and Newtonian (physical reality). The three all work together. Religion and science are becoming integrated.

Ideally, one begins the spiritual thought and meditation process with prayer. This is the quantum realm. This in turn activates the electromagnetic energy level of reality, which ultimately must be grounded by action (human works) in the physical, Newtonian, material realm. In other words, religion comes down to economics. Faith without works is dead.

The electromagnetic realm is the transition plane between electromagnetic and magneto-electric; from the spiritual to the material and from the material to the spiritual. This is why potentially in prayer, one can put a thousand to flight; two, ten thousand.

None other than *The Wall Street Journal* has really been getting into this realm, with articles in the October 10 and 11, 1990 issues, respectively, on transcendental meditation (TM-Sidhi) and Belgian scientists' pursuit of a triangular UFO. The yogis in TM have worked out the math and science in the area and say that the square root of one percent of any population is critical to bring about change. From what I know about work in another related field, homeopathic medicine, this is true. A very small amount of a substance, or even its energy pattern, energetically can induce massive changes in a physical property.

We are living in a time when the transmutation of our reality is accelerating. Only absolute truth - spiritual, energetic and physical - will survive this shift. Everything else could very well be destroyed. Today, both an anchor and a plumb line are vital.

Years ago, we moved out of the simplicity of Newtonian physics into the relativity of the physics of Albert Einstein when we split the atom. We changed matter into energy. $E=mc^2$ was confirmed. (Actually earlier, in 1942, the Philadelphia Experiment demonstrated this reality from another perspective, the alteration of Newtonian time-space.) Since scientists were able to split the atom, and turn matter into energy, for the last 48 years they have been working feverishly to reverse the process, to move from energy back to matter, or to have energy influence or alter matter. This is what the field of radionics and psychotronics is all about.

Can viruses and bacteria be transmuted, changed from one to the other and back again, and/or destroyed electromagnetically? Beyond question, research in Russia, Germany and England confirms this. It has long been established that animals and humans transmute elements, too. Studies of the calcium content in chicken eggs, where chickens have been deprived of calcium, as well as among calcium-deprived prisoners of war, have confirmed that both chickens and the human body have the ability to transmute one element into another. Scientists have also been able to do this with inorganic matter, either by changing the electron structure of the atom of a substance or, by going one step back, altering the energetic frequency pattern of which the substance is composed. Either approach can and has turned lead into gold, theoretically and actually.

One thing for sure, the further one moves from the physical Newtonian realm, through the Einsteinian electromagnetic and energetic realm, into the quantum realm, the closer one moves to total integration and cooperation with the spiritual realm. (In the quantum realm, subatomic particles communicate in matched pairs, just like the electromagnetic positive/negative duality of sunspots as they rotate through the 11- and 22-year sunspot cycles.)

The quantum basis, commonly referred to as the etheric realm, where literally all is one and interconnected, gives rise to the energy patterns which make up the distinctive aspects of the created Newtonian world. This inter-relationship is the basis of intuition and the 100th monkey syndrome. Mankind, with the computerized information explosion accompanying massive earth changes, is approaching this point. When we throw in scalar reality and phase conjugation with their inescapable alterations not only of matter but also of space-time, we can see that the present spiritual, political, educational, cultural, military, financial and economic reality are in for a drastic restructuring. The works of physicist Tom Bearden, Warren York, Matt Campbell, Henry C. Monteith, Moray B. King, Oliver Nichelson and G. Harry Stine are key in this regard.

By the way, what do you think the feds have been doing with all of our tax dollars in those top secret research laboratories in New Mexico all these years? If the American general public had any idea what was occurring at the Sandia National Laboratory at Albuquerque, New Mexico, for example, it would blow their minds. The NFL-minded American general public is farther removed from the scientific reality of today than the peasants were in the so-called *"Dark Ages."*

In this reality shift, particularly as the information-holding magnetic environment breaks down at an accelerated pace, thought forms (as a man thinketh, so he is) are going to become increasingly important. There is a physical basis for man literally creating his own reality, which gives rise to the phrase, *"ye are as gods."* As Jesus Christ stated, *"Greater things than I have done you shall do."* Scientists are just now discovering, that with laser-like faith and the integration of the human mind, (left-brain/right-brain, literally Newtonian and quantum, respectively) with an energetic crossover through the corpus callosum, coupled with the phase conjugate integration electromagnetically and magneto-electrically through the body's energy centers, it is possible to tap into the whole realm of transmutation, space-time, and alter the spiritual, energetic and physical reality. Want to move mountains? No problem. Want to send spirits scurrying? No problem.

The political superstate has always found it in its best interest to have man operate only at the lowest levels of his potential, at the physical/Newtonian/economic level. Men are better slaves this way. But we are approaching the crossover point, when there will be no time for slaves. The lid is about to come off. Mankind is on the verge of discovering what it truly means to be *"fearfully and wonderfully made."*

The subtle and delicate world of the piezoelectric charge of the human body, the subtle nature of piezoelectric charges in gemstones, which appeared both on the breastplate of the high priest of ancient Israel as well as in the new heavenly city, is beginning to be understood. The intricate anti-gravitational nature of the cerebral spinal fluid (called by the ancients the *"tears of Jesus"*), is part of the equation. So in view of all this, our present market systems do indeed appear antiquated.

Nature's Law

We are still working from a frame of reference which states that markets operate according to *"Nature's law."* *"Nature's law"* is simply Newtonian physics. But Newtonian physics (*"Nature's law"*) is incomplete and inadequate. What scientists have been teaching us is that there is no longer any such thing as *"Nature's law."* *"Nature's law"* is nothing more than a rule that repeats itself under the replication of a precise set of conditions. But with the tremendous changes taking place in the quantum and electromagnetic realms, this stream's end of reality, nature and Nature's rules (laws), are subject to tremendous change, variation and volatility, due to higher laws and functions. This is another reason why being diversified in markets, never having all of one's eggs in one basket by way of either investment or location, makes a tremendous amount of sense today. It is also why more catastrophes, abrupt lurches and changes, and literally *"acts of God"* should increasingly be expected to shake the marketplace.

Investing Shift

If I'm correct in this, the days of good old-fashioned trend-following moving averages and classic investing are over. Such systems and methodologies are likely to be whipsawed unmercifully. So, too, are all the *"Nature's law"* systems, whether they be Elliott Wave, Gann, astrology or other philosophical systems which were more valid probabilistically when the earth was stable electromagnetically. This may also mean that the technical indicators which were so valuable in the '60s and '70s, and developed such a massive following in the 1980s, will become less useful. Accordingly, I am attempting to break out into some new and creative approaches to trading the markets. Obviously, I don't intend to totally depart from what I've done best for years. I tend to stay grounded until I have proven that these new approaches are consistently effective.

The next few years should be quite interesting. For practical purposes, I think investors will be best served by taking an unleveraged or low-leveraged approach to the marketplace, buying extremely undervalued investments and selling extremely overvalued ones, and then holding and waiting for time and abrupt jumps and lurches to make them money. Buying put and call options in futures, rather than taking outright positions, may be the way to go also.

Silver, platinum and *"protein gold"* would qualify for this investing perspective when purchased in cash accounts on a scale-down basis. Other grounded investments on a local level are well-advised, too. Hardware stores, appliance and car repair, and spare part operations should all do well, as should organic agriculture. I do expect that by the year 2012 our entire present political and financial system will be totally overturned and reformed.

Rational Investing?

Does it make any sense today, with record global debt, that investors would flock to debt-based currencies which offer the highest interest rates? High interest rates have historically always meant greater risk and less security. Investors traditionally are more security oriented than profit oriented. In other words, fear overrides greed in the mindset of investors. This is why bear markets (fear) occur three times faster than bull markets (greed). So why are security-minded investors opting for high interest rate, debt-laden currencies? Haven't they learned from the junk bond game?

Are markets rational? Is mankind rational? Is the mob, which is exactly what the herd of investors is, rational? No. Markets are psychological. Value, which sets price, is a subjective concept.

Is the mob/market ever correct? Yes, sometimes. If we accept the model that there are three stages up in a bull market, investors are usually right, the mob is usually correct, on the second leg up. The first leg up is usually short covering, and the third leg up is the overvalued leg. The masses/mob/market are correct in the middle, in the *"fairly valued"* range. So, if an investor can be savvy enough to take the middle third out of a move, he has done quite well. Otherwise, he has to buy an oversold market and wait for the trickle-up effect (first leg), the return toward fair value. Or, he can make money with high risk in the fastest bull leg of all, the third up-leg, where greed and panic take over as a market moves to overvalued levels.

Suggested Reading

For those of you whose eyes have glazed over, whose minds have shut down, or who are totally confused or blown out by what you have just read, hang tight. Occasionally I have to stretch you and prepare you for what is coming. Over time, what I've just written will make sense to you. For additional reading in the area I recommend the following books: *Subtle Energy*, by John Davidson, ISBN 0-85207-1841; *Vibrational Medicine*, by Richard Gerber, M.D., ISBN 0-939680-46-7; *Blueprint For Immortality: The Electrical Patterns of Life*, by Harold Saxton Burr, ISBN 0-85435-281-3; *The Secret Life of Plants*, by Peter Tompkins, ISBN 0-06-091112-3; *Secrets of the Soil*, by Peter Tompkins, ISBN 0-06-015817-4; *The Dark Side of the Brain*, by Harry Oldfield and Roger Coghill, ISBN 1-85230-025-6; *The Body Magnetic*, by Buryl Payne (848 Walnut Avenue, Santa Cruz, CA 95060); *The Body Electric* and *Cross Currents*, ISBN 0-87477-536-1, by Robert O. Becker, M.D.; John Gribbin's *In Search of Schrodinger's Cat*, ISBN 0-553-341000 and *In Search of the Double Helix*, ISBN 0-553-34434-3; and *Recovering the Soul*, by Larry Dossey, M.D., ISBN 0-553-34790-X.

* * * * *

"The swift succession of catastrophic events on a steeply mounting gradient inevitably inspires a dark doubt about our future, and this doubt threatens to undermine our faith and hope at a critical eleventh hour which calls for the utmost exertion of these saving spiritual faculties. Here is a challenge which we cannot evade, and our destiny depends upon our responses.

"'I dreamed, and behold I saw a man clothed with rags, standing in a certain place, with his face from his own house, a book in his hand and a great burden upon his back. I looked and saw him open the book and read therein; and as he read he wept and trembled; and, not being able longer to contain, he broke out with a lamentable cry saying "What shall I do?"'

"It was not without cause that Bunyan's 'Christian' was so greatly distressed.

"'I am for certain informed (said he) that this our city will be burned with fire from heaven - in which fearful overthrow both myself with thee my wife and you my sweet babes shall miserably come to ruin, except (the which yet I see not) some way of escape can be found, whereby we may be delivered.'

"What response to this challenge is Christian going to make? Is he going to look this way and that as if he would run, yet stand still because he cannot tell which way to go? Or will he begin to run - and run on crying 'Life! Life! Eternal Life!' - with his eye set on a shining light and his feet bound for a distant wicket gate? If the answer to this question depended on nobody but Christian himself, our knowledge of the uniformity of human nature might incline us to predict that Christian's imminent destiny was Death in his City of Destruction. But in the classic version of the myth we are told that the human protagonist was not left entirely to his own resources in the decisive hour. According to John Bunyan, Christian was saved by his encounter with Evangelist. And, inasmuch as it cannot be supposed that God's nature is less constant than Man's, we may and must pray that a reprieve which God has granted to our society once will not be refused if we ask for it again in a humble spirit and with a contrite heart." —
Arnold J. Toynbee - *A Study of History*

THE CORE VERSUS THE MARGIN
March 2, 1993

Every nation has at its center a core, the establishment, the politically correct, as it were. Every nation also has those mavericks who operate at the margin, on the periphery, on the cutting edge, the outer edge of the envelope, the avant garde, as it were. The dialectic tension between the core and the margin is, in essence, stability versus change, continuity versus discontinuity, stagnation versus growth.

The tug-of-war between the two is incessant. However, the intensity of the conflict's pull and push is often dictated by where a nation or civilization stands in its progressive spiral, its age. For example, in a young nation or civilization, the conflict between the core and the margin is less intense. By contrast, in a 200-year-old nation, such as the United States, or at the end of a 510-year civilization cycle, such as in Western civilization today, the conflict is more severe.

The younger and more vital the nation's civilization, the larger, more flexible, more adaptable, more vital and permeable is the core. It encompasses a larger percentage of the people of a nation or civilization. And such a core is fed by the nourishment of the creativity of change coming from the margin. As Thomas Jefferson would put it, the core is fed by the *"natural aristocracy."* The best gravitate to the center. In such an era, those who operate at the margin are more comfortable with those at the core and do not feel threatened. Indeed, those at the margin often find support for their activities at the core. By contrast, in an old and frozen nation or civilization, the core is small, compact, cold, dense, hard, harsh and dark. It is all but impermeable. It is made up of an elite few who enjoy their position by way of birth, privilege, established status or adoption by the core. It is at such a time that the vast majority in the social system are alienated from the core. Those who operate at the margin are seen as the core's arch enemy. The core, to those at the margin, is the equivalent of the Death Star of the *"Star Wars"* movies. The core operates exclusively and comprehensively in its own brutal self-interest in a win-lose fashion, to the direct detriment of those at the margin, whom it actively persecutes. Those at the margin flee the core. Injustice reigns supreme.

Intent on maintaining the status quo, having accrued to itself maximum power (as opposed to the decentralization and dispersion of power when it was young), the core takes on a life all its own, unresponsive to the challenges fed it from the real world and the cries of those outside of it. The core becomes sterile, insulated, arrogant, brutal and degenerate. It is in such a frozen and unresponsive state that the core inevitably brings a revolution against itself.

This is where we are today at the end of a 200-year nation cycle and a 510-year civilization cycle. At the frozen core of Western civilization today, we find the New World Order, despite the revolt against it in Europe, the

United States and Canada. In the United States, we find the lightless core dominated by Golden Dawn magic, Luciferianism, other forms of neopagan occultism, astrology, witchcraft, membership in the CFR, elitist establishment universities who promulgate the politically correct myth, special interest groups who via government-installed monopolies - such as the Federal Reserve, the American Bankers Association, the American Bar Association, the American Medical Association, the FDA, the NEA, and the mass media - strangle the society. Avant garde technology and free energy devices are suppressed. The core exists of itself, by itself, and for itself to the exclusion and harm of the interests of the masses-at-large. It is polarized. Having lost the power to engender peaceful support for its causes, it then operates the only way a bankrupt philosophy can operate, through force. Through unjust economic, civil and criminal sanctions, the likes of the IRS, OSHA, the DEA, the FDA, BATF, the EPA, the Department of Energy, the Department of Health and Human Services, the Justice Department, ad nauseam, the core sucks the life and sustenance out of all from the margin inward to the core. It was no wonder that Roman citizens welcomed the infestation of the barbarians who sacked the empire. It was a relief from the oppressive taxation and regulation of the decadent core. So, too, do many Americans today wish the former Soviet Union had nuked the Washington, D.C.-New York City corridor. Such Americans were simply expressing their frustration and need for relief from the life-depriving core. Life inside the Beltway is an illusion to most Americans; it is only reality to politicians and bureaucrats, the faceless, nameless soldiers of Darth Vader.

The core faces a problem today. Having sucked the essence of grounding life from those who surround it, it has rendered the social order unstable. This is particularly dangerous during our era of accelerated and severe earth changes. Historically, where we stand in time in climatological history is a time of the breakdown of the core, the repudiation of the establishment, and the setting up of a new core, possessed of life. But never before has the core had so much technological power, information as power, and mass media power where it can manipulate the masses to operate consistently contrary to their own best interests long term. Never before have those outside the core been so weak and out-gunned - spiritually, emotionally, mentally and physically. The masses have been co-opted. They are vulnerable.

One would almost think that a racial war was being fomented in this country to further increase the concentration of power at the core. Then dictatorial executive orders would be used to eliminate the few remaining freedoms, to confiscate firearms, to bring the United States into the New World Order. Of course, a concomitant financial crisis would serve to bankrupt the country so that the United States would be poor enough to be merged into the New World Order. Moreover, with the Clintonistas ruling at the core, whose psychological make-ups thrive on collision, whose values are alien and hostile to over 80% of the people over whom they reign, we should expect the use of dictatorial, "divine right of kings"-type executive orders.

Four years of the volatile reign of the Clintonistas in our time of climatological, social, and economic turmoil will leave the nation in an exhausted, chaotic state. A Machiavellian stroke of genius then would bring a supposed *"man of the people,"* a Ross Perot-type, to the core as a solution. This would apparently give the people what they desire, while actually locking down tight and guaranteeing a New World Order. A Ross Perot-type, after all, would make the core's Death Star efficient and effective, abolish the U.S. Constitution, centralize all power, make everything uniform, and enforce it all with high tech. Those at the margin would thus cease to exist as the core became the great all-in-all. It would be, effectively, the end of history.

Do I think this will occur? Unlikely. Both the sovereignty of God and the nature of the geophysical changes we are undergoing argue against it. And then there is the compounding factor of $17 trillion in debt. This argues for decentralization and the return of spiritual, political, and economic power to individuals. It's just like in markets when a trend goes exponential and seems to never end (in this case the trend toward centralization of power); it turns in a twinkling of an eye. Put differently, the long, old bull market in centralization is topping out, and the new emerging bull market in decentralization is beginning. Thus, we live at a time of tremendous change in human history, spiritually, politically, economically, geophysically, technologically, medically, educationally, and just about every way imaginable. The challenge will be to live through the blowoff in the centralization trend, which is occurring between now and 2000-2004. We must ever keep in mind that in order to withstand the buffeting forthcoming, and acceleration under the Clintonistas, we must continue to build up our reserves and invest in ourselves and our families - spiritually, physically, economically, emotionally, educationally. Our psychological preparation should give us a tremendous advantage over those who believe the propaganda pumped out by the core. Information is power. The age of computers is the age of information, and with accurate information, the age of the individual and small organizations, literally cottage industries - decentralization.

TWO SHIFTS IN CONSCIOUSNESS
July 6, 1994

Both the individual and collective levels of awareness are dependent upon how people subjectively interpret objective phenomena. Put differently, all of us interpret the objective world subjectively based upon our vocabulary, categories of understanding, frames of references and experience. One of the overwhelming influences of technology is that technology establishes, indeed dictates, the way in which people generally interpret their world. For example, we are living at the end of the Mechanistic Age, brought on by the advent of the automobile. Industrial nomenclature, the verbiage of the factory, is still the primary mindset the majority uses to describe its political and economic processes. It permeates our contemporary news. Even our schools still maintain the design and methodology of the industrial factory. But a shift is most definitely and definitively taking place. The shift is from a mechanistic (mechanical) world view to that of a computerized world view, and more specifically, a bio-computerized, virtual reality world view.

The explosive growth and widespread use of computer technology, filtering into the mindset of the general public over the past two decades, has led to this change in our perception of the world in which we live and the way it works. Couple that with the fax machine, fiber optics, and holographic reality, and the result is we are now beginning to "see" the world differently. But these shifts take place slowly, and normally take at least a generation (40 years) to become primary. When the shift reaches the explosive exponential point of mass human consciousness, a significant alteration will take place in all our institutions. We are approaching such a threshold, as the Information Age expands.

One of the painful fallouts of this massive adjustment/readjustment is that the synergy between computers and mechanization is eliminating jobs, permanently. People, workers, are becoming increasingly unnecessary. Until the *"Nasty Nineties,"* it was widely held to be true that the level of a person's income and status in life was dependent upon his level of education. Education was the economic god, so to speak. This god has now been slain. The plague of the *"Nasty Nineties"* is chronic unemployment. We are learning what the Argentineans learned by economic fire in the 1980s, that it is the demand of the marketplace in a chaotic (feminine) economy that determines economic wherewithal, not formal, factorylike, status-based education. (Here, by the way, is where the Clintonistas miss the boat. They are still living in the old paradigm - status-based, fascist/socialistic, educationally expert and immoral. It is bringing on chaotic disaster.)

Who makes it economically in today's world? Those who have demand-side, hands-on education, avant-garde education, and experience in providing the goods and services demanded by the marketplace. Today's world of speed-of-light communication (fiber optics/satellites) goes to those who are visionaries, entrepreneurs, risk-takers, those on the cutting edge who deliver the demanded goods and services, as well as those who are long-term and service oriented, who supply the basics of life in a state-of-the-art way. This "new world disorder" in which we live, requires - nay, even demands - a yin and yang, positive/negative, acid/alkaline, clockwise/counterclockwise, masculine/feminine balance. It requires an integrated linear vector and a cycle, vortices - spirals if you will - to achieve in a balanced way the demands of the age. The pre-creation void, the black hole of space, the energy-rich charged potential of the womb, so to speak, needs the directional, life-bringing masculine linear vector to frame it with laws, give it direction, and anchor its creativity so it can be productive and progressive. In a world struggling to find the balance between the one and the many, between the collective and the individual, between the feminine and the masculine, recognition of this truism is vital. Without the horizontal balance and the simultaneous vertical hierarchy of authority, chaos and anarchy reign. Why? Because we are already too close to the edge of the dark abyss of total chaos (feminine). It takes a real juggling act today to maintain balance, direction, and creativity in life.

Few can conceive of the importance of the Eastern yin/yang balance and of the simultaneous Western directional/hierarchal/masculine lead vector. It is the emphasis on diversity, individuality, a masculine impulse, which leads to risk-taking, progress, the multiplicity of richness of the marketplace, and eventually unity in society. Yes, diversity produces unity because the diversity of specialization in the division of labor yields to cooperation in the exchange of goods and services and thereby harmony. The many voluntarily become the one. At the same time, without the gentle, kind and collective chaotic feminine impulse to balance, the marketplace becomes cutthroat and warlike, legalistic, harsh, destroying itself. Thus the acid legalism of the masculine impulse, by itself, kills. It needs the alkaline feminine offset.

While this overemphasis on masculinity has been a primary issue in earlier Western civilization, it is not the primary issue today. Today the pendulum has swung too far the other way, toward the collective, the democratic, the feminine, where the focus is on security, acceptance/approval and control. These natural basic biological instincts, when not held in check, destroy the very essence of themselves, resulting in chaos and anarchy, a dark empty economic womb, if you will. This tragically is where we are rapidly moving today, at a time when the effort to stop time, call an end to history, kill progress, establish total control, security, and politically correct approval, is at its height. We would expect as much, with lesbian-based witchcraft, the extreme of the feminine democratic collective principle, running the country today.

The ruling natural occult sequence is to cycle from order to chaos in the fulfillment of the Hegelian dialectic of thesis, antithesis, synthesis. But cycles are, by definition, non-progressive. Thus, out of the emerging chaos and anarchy we should expect to arise, in the natural order of things, a compensating hyper-masculine figure, our version of a pharaoh if you will. It will be an ugly synthesis for the freedom-loving, but then again, freedom is an open system, and the primary paradigms in operation today remain Newtonian, closed system.

This brings us to the second major shift of consciousness which is just emerging among those who think, live and work at the cutting edge. This perspective has not even yet begun to dawn on the mass consciousness. It is this: It is the now-proven spiritual, scientific, economic reality that the "*field*," electromagnetic phenomenon, not only influences but determines - is prior to - physical Newtonian reality. Living energy, energy as information, determines matter. I am convinced that the reason the likes of honest money, true free markets, free energy machines, energy and alternative medicine and the like are brutally persecuted and shut down by the closed system-loving establishment is because they bring about a radical transformation in the conceptual thinking of the mass mind, literally a paradigm shift. If open-system thinking became widespread and generally accepted in mass human consciousness, it would shortly render the establishment powerless. The establishment, after all, depends on a comprehensive campaign of ongoing deception through public education and the mass media to maintain power. The New World Order establishment can maintain its control, its elitism, and get filthy rich as long as the public is trapped in the lie of an exclusive Newtonian closed system with its second law of thermodynamics, entropy, and its modus operandi of conflict, chance, cycles, poverty, and death. After all, if the masses can remain convinced that we live in a world of scarcity, of conflict, of chance, etc., then the ruling elite can justify its existence by protecting life (in a token way), and doling out in some inequitable fashion, so-called scarce resources. There is never enough to go around in a closed system. Therefore, someone has to referee the conflict. That's the establishment, the New World Order government, the global parasite.

On the other hand, with a massive shift in consciousness from a closed to an open system, from death to life if you will, from a dark spiral down to a plentiful open-ended light spiral up, the Newtonian closed system philosophy of conflict, chance, cycles, poverty, and death wilts. Time and time again, in brief flashes of history, where the open-system of freedom, free markets, free energy machines, of energetic health, and honest, open, free market money in an open system of self-governing (supernatural) law is allowed to manifest, mankind flourishes, with the parasitic bureaucratic government and ruling elite diminishing accordingly. This is what is emerging. It is all the insider establishment can do to keep the lid on it. There either has to be total control now under a comprehensive suffocating New World Order or, the international banking system which has plagued us for nearly 500 years with its ruling elite, are dead in the water. Thus, the urgency of the New World Order. It is a race against time, against the computerization and dissemination of knowledge and information, bringing about knowledge and understanding of the many ways in which man can better himself through the open system's abstract and concrete reality.

The primary contradiction (so designed) of the New Age, with its emphasis on the natural earth-based religion of environmentalism, is that it focuses in large part on open system technology, while maintaining a closed system (natural) philosophy of government, religion and economics. Again, this is not accidental. It is deliberate, purposeful. For example, *"Hillary the Hippie,"* as she was known in the '60s, established her values in the radically chaotic 1960s when God was officially pronounced dead. This spiritual void was attempted to be filled in the '70s, and in the '80s particularly, by materialism, of which Ronald Reagan was the foremost proponent. Thus, the egregious expansion of debt (death) in the 1980s, the Reagan era. This orgy of materialism (debt-based death) proved to be unsatisfying, empty, to the human spirit and so the pendulum has now swung back toward spiritualism. But this time, since God is officially dead, it is a neo-pagan spiritualism, a return to the "natural" Newtonian earth-based religions with their fallen spirits of antiquity. It is the religion of empire, of Babylon, of ancient Egypt.

In this neo-pagan framework, one is either in the elite, or the ruling bureaucracy, or one loses. It is as simple as that. Power accrues at the top. Thus, the strategy of the New World Order banksters is to bring about global crises, resulting in chaos, from which the New World Order can emerge, with a world central bank, a world court, effectively a world parliament, a global religion, and all the rest of it. Then, once in total control, probably aided and abetted by a high-tech sound and light show of UFOs (which have been around since at least the early 1950s), the ruling elite of the New World Order can take the lid off all of this quantum, open system-based reality and give the masses free energy, open-system energetic medicine, gold-based money, and on and on, which paradoxically, they would seek to totally control, and then only after the global population has first been dramatically reduced to approximately 2-3 billion. After all, in a world of computerized technology, what in the world are we going to do with all these useless people? "Mother Earth" must be cleansed.

In this New Age of Dark Enlightenment, since *"God is dead,"* who gets to rule religiously? The biblical concept that *"God is light"* has been replaced by the New World Order elitists. It is about to be resurrected in a new form, by a new god. Who indeed but a substitute *"light bearer"* will fill the bill? A natural, created angel of light? The logical candidate to fill this "light" void is Lucifer. It is thus no accident that for the past several centuries, Luciferianism has been the guiding religion of what has now evolved (sic) into fascist New World Order elitism. With the breakdown of the earth's magnetic field, and the resultant boundary between open and closed systems becoming increasingly indistinct, expect New Age magicians to shortly begin *"wowing"* the masses in preparation for the neo-pagan spiritualistic New World Order. The old paradigm, which is dead at the cutting edge, is the old theory of evolution, as we were taught it, the concept that we all evolved meaninglessly by chance out of the primordial mud and slime. The new reality is that the *"field,"* energy as living information, light, created the physical Newtonian world in which we live. We're back to spirit preceding matter, sans Creator.

* * * * *

The summer of 1993, as Providence would have it, I was in Aspen on the 6th anniversary of the Harmonic Convergence. This was when the Pope met Clinton in Colorado. I walked, appropriately enough, over the grounds of the Aspen Institute for Humanistic Studies, the think tank which is responsible for much of the legislation which ends up governing this country. Aspen dictates your future, your life, in many ways. I found it instructive that the grounds of the Aspen Institute feature pagan religious symbolism.

UNRESTRAINED
Spring, 1993

My sense of things was that effective May 1, 1993, the unseen restraining hand in this country was removed. The country became theologically, politically, economically, socially and geophysically ungrounded, unrestrained. The rush toward madness accelerated.

For all practical purposes, we have seen clear evidence that this trend is already in motion. We began documenting this sad state of affairs in the chapter *"Behind the Fire."* Next, there was the important discussion in the chapter *"The Core Versus the Margin."*

What this means socially is that we should see an increasing number of no-win situations like the tragedy in Waco. To my mind, the worst circumstances in life are the lose-lose situations. But that's what normally occurs during the accelerating down phase of a bear market in a closed system. And this is where we are theologically, politically, economically, socially, and geophysically into at least 1995-96, and probably into 2000-2004, maybe 2008-2012. Comprehensively, we don't have any ground to stand on. That means upheaval, personal and physical.

The culturally dominant ungrounded feminine E-motion (energy in motion) force, effective May 1, 1993, became unrestrained. This meant the Clintonistas' radioactive drive for approval, for control, and for security tightened in its death spiral. All three drives are earth-based, falling victim to Newtonian physics and the second law of thermodynamics, none of them faith-centered. Thus, the dominance of the conflict-based, chancy, chaotic, cyclical, limited resource, poverty-ridden, uncreative, joyless, death-oriented, closed system over an open system. For example, in the BATF/FBI versus David Koresh's Branch Davidians in Waco, there were no win-win options. W.A.C.O. - We Ain't Coming Out - was an initial acronym replaced by B.A.T.F./F.B.I. - Batter, Assault, Torch, Fumigate/Firestorm, Browbeat, Intimidate. The BATF planned this operation for eight months. It was a media event - machine guns, battle gear and all. It backfired. Whatever happened to the process of quietly, properly serving a warrant? And this wasn't the first time this bullying by the feds has happened.

In 1992 in northern Idaho, several hundred of these Nazi-like BATF storm troopers invaded Vietnam veteran Randy Weaver's land on a specious firearms charge, shot his dog, shot Weaver's young teenage son in the back (killing him), and shot Weaver's wife dead between the eyes while she stood in her front door holding their baby. BATF then burned their bodies to conceal the evidence. Randy Weaver went on trial, even though he never fired a shot. Did the mass media report any of this? Come on, Dan Rather, what went on in the Randy Weaver trial? Moreover, the man who wrote a book on the Randy Weaver tragedy had his home in Portland, Oregon surrounded by 200 of the same BATF ninja crowd. The charge? Allegedly cutting timber on government land without a permit. That calls for a BATF strike force? Only if you want to condition the American people to a police state in the New World Order. Did all this make you want to give up your guns, or buy more?

No one ranks higher on psychological tests regarding the craving for security, approval, and control than bureaucrats. Bureaucrats look out for themselves first. It now turns out there were only two suicide/murders in Waco within the compound. Moreover, the FBI, once it learned from an escaped cult member that the Branch Davidians had no armor-piercing bullets inside the compound which could pose a threat to the FBI, decided to attack. And where did the FBI attack first? Precisely where they were told the children were. That's where the federal bureaucrats first dumped the gas before everything caught fire. Incredible. Arson experts state the FBI *"tear"* gas was inadvertently perfectly placed to torch the Waco compound. ...And we allow these tax-guzzling Rambos to run roughshod and to vote?

David Koresh was no better. People today are desperately looking for something to believe in, to belong to, that adds real meaning to life. David Koresh preyed on this basic human need. His adulterous actions, taking of multiple wives, was blatant evidence of his unquenchable craving for approval. His absolute dominating, elitist control over the compound crowd is unquestioned. And the very nature of the compound itself spoke of unrestrained insecurity. Thus, the lose-lose. But there can be only one god in a closed, earth-based system, the BATF/FBI or David Koresh. And now we have gays, liberal politicians and black leaders threatening violence unless their legislative agenda is enacted. This is blackmail, backed by the threat of street violence. There is no restraint.

At the extreme, at the margin, in a revolutionary society when human behavior becomes unrestrained, there is literally an electromagnetic polarity flip (not counting the angry homosexuals). Primarily, men become irresponsible and women become dominant. Their Creator-given estate is abandoned. Eventually it becomes too much to stomach, particularly the short period of anarchy that inevitably follows the inescapable death of chaotic democracy. It results in tyranny, a police state, ruled by a Caesar-like individual. We could be there by 1995-96. This is another good reason why, as investors, we are making the increasingly grounded shift from intangibles (paper - stocks and bonds) into tangibles (precious metals, resource stocks, agricultural land, Earth Manna, etc.).

By analogy, in the present stage of things, the fear- and flight-based feminine pancreatic power center goes alternately hyper- and hypoglycemic, which throws the naturally spiritual, chaotic, ungrounded, non-Hertzian female-dominant right brain into a tizzy. At the same time, the anger/fight, masculine, law-based gall bladder/liver grounding meridian has blown out, giving rise to the likes of the World Trade Center bombing, Waco, Lucasville, Ohio, Srebrenica, the murders and violence in South Africa, Somalia, and on and on. Anger and fight - violence - is unrestrained. And yet the majority of Americans, literally following *"the 80-20 rule,"* acknowledge the importance of the calm, grounded, masculine, law-based Hertzian carrier wave, the intact gall bladder/liver complex and meridian, and its associated law-based left brain/right foot masculine grounding anchor, although not a power center, as the necessary foundation for the yin, feminine, pancreatic, E-motion (energy in motion) complex, in order to avoid a totally chaotic state. How do we know this? Because according to the March 7, 1993 Washington Times, 79% of Americans say the most important thing in their families while growing up was *"discipline when you did something wrong."* There it is, the ground, the anchor, the law-based masculine discipline of the established nuclear family. Such a *"ground"* is all but smashed today. And so we move quickly toward chaos, which is consistent with the theology of the ruling humanistic Clintonistas' occult closed system, the death-based religion which dominates the country today. Government is always religion applied to economics. It is self-conscious, though. This Clintonista death wish, which has enslaved us, is looking with faith for a phoenix to rise out of the ashes of the chaos it is fomenting. In that sense, Waco was an accurate and instructive holographic model of what is set to befall the nation as a whole, particularly those who do not conform to the New World Order. No wonder psychiatric hospitals are now overflowing as never before (at least in Austin, Tex.). People are blowing out right and left.

Remember, we live in an integrated vortex of reality. Truth is truth at all levels. When we are in touch with truth on multiple levels simultaneously, we are in touch with the plumbline of reality, the center line of progressive history, if you will. Put differently, there is physics and metaphysics. There is science and religion. There is natural (closed system) and supernatural (potentially open system). There are men and women. These coexist at different ends of the same spectrum in the vortex of reality. It's not either/or, it's both, simultaneously. But since we're so worldly and natural today (not to mention miseducated), caught in both a materialistic and an earth-based spirit of a closed Newtonian system, reacting as it inescapably does to the second law of thermodynamics, the fruit of such faith and focus are poverty, cycles, chance, confusion, shortages, anger, fear, insecurity, chaos, conflict and death. We should accordingly expect more Wacos or worse.

A society either consciously, or by way of cultural assimilation, establishes its theology (the nature and character of God); its ontology (what actually is - the nature of being and what actually exists); its axiology (the study of values - ethics and aesthetics); its teleology (the purpose and meaning of life and where it came from); its cosmology (the origin and structure of the universe); its anthropology (the origin and nature of man, the good and evil complex); its psychology (the nature of the mind and thought, the spirit/brain cell considerations); and its sociology (the appropriate institutions of society, such as family, state, etc.). We are working these out presently, with the power elite being consistent, although mad (ungrounded). Talk about a flip. We're now getting $4.80 of taxes for every $1.00

of spending cuts under the Clintonistas, an administration at war with every solid, grounded principle that built this country, an administration intent on establishing an occult Nazi-like New World Order, ruled by an elite and their bureaucrats, exercising total economic and financial control over people and property. ...Have these people ever experienced true love?

Recall that the hideous global environmental movement began as an elitist CFR plot at the World Wilderness Congress in Denver, Colorado in 1987 as a way to inflict socialism on the world in a New World Order. The earth-based religion of witchcraft attempts to ground out economically in environmentalism via the political action of the Clintonistas, hippies turned Baby Boomers. Again, government is always religion applied to economics. Never mind that their system leaves in its ashes an elite few, many poor and enslaved, and awful bloodshed. There is always a grounding blood sacrifice. Every religion, and therefore government, demands it. But consistent with the Clintonistas' New World Order, Mikhail Gorbachev moved into his U.S.-based think tank in the Presidio at San Francisco. The commanding general of the 6th U.S. Army handed Gorby the keys to a prime building at the Presidio in April 1993. And Bank of America during that same time opened an office in Hanoi. Also, former Federal Reserve chairman, Paul Volcker, became chairman of the Trilateral Commission-North America. There goes your money again.

In chaotic times, the old reliable market-analysis systems cease to function reliably. Discontinuous events occur. The very nature of discontinuous events is that they are unexpected and unpredictable. This is why now more than ever staying grounded long-term in tangible investments is important, leaning toward a cash basis. The time of having sufficient knowledge to accurately forecast the future, as well as the ability to time entries and exits in and out of markets, is coming to a chaotic close. (Just look at the stocks that are falling out of the sky unexpectedly.) Such approaches could suffer devastating losses due to the onset of an accelerating series of discontinuous events. Funds could be devastated. Earth changes are just one of these discontinuous manifestations. Terrorism is another.

In a sense, as goes the earth, so goes man. Or, as goes man, so goes the earth. It's a chicken and egg thing. The magma which runs along the fault lines where the tectonic plates join carries a piezoelectric charge. This manifests on the earth's surface by way of an electromagnetic spike prior to a significant earth change (earthquake). Animals, such as cats and dogs, sense this, which is why so many of these domestic critters leave home just prior to a significant earthquake. They want to literally get the heck out of Dodge. It is why tracking geologist Jim Berkland's Lost Dog and Cat Index from The L.A. Times is consistently useful. When the number of lost dogs and cats increases significantly, the probability is very high that an earthquake there is right around the corner. People also react. They get equally as crazy, but in different ways. You see, a piezoelectric charge is also the charge carried by the human cranial and skeletal system, and on the human skin. The piezoelectric charge is intrinsic to gemstones, too, when put under pressure. In their natural state, it is also the charge of the major organ systems of the human body. Thus, when mankind becomes unrestrained, the earth becomes likewise unrestrained, and vice versa. Unrestrained, and Clint Eastwood-style, unforgiven.

Does the connection now become more obvious between unrestrained human activity and increasing forecasts for unrestrained earth changes, not to mention market chaos? Each is a piezoelectric reflection of the other. The late, great climatologist, Dr. Iben Browning, wrote that the severity of the earth changes we would experience between now and 2008-2012 would result in every major government that existed in the 1980s going through radical alteration so that 25 years later, at the end of this time period (which began in 1987), governments would no longer be recognizable in the form in which they existed 25 years earlier. Today's prevailing political, bureaucratic and dominant radical feminist spirit, craving security, approval and control, is in for a real shaking. This is a time of risk, standing alone, and re-emerging freedom. After all, when you boil it all down, economics comes down to its two most primitive parts, to people and their relationship with the earth. As the earth changes, people change. As people change, the earth changes. The piezoelectric charge is the common ground to both the earth and man. And so, too, are the earth's electromagnetic fields and ley lines interfaced with man's fourteen meridians and his lymphatic system, both of which are electrical and effectively identical. It's time to ground out!

(By the way, it is not physically possible for women to ground out without a male covering. Women are negatively charged [feminine (-)], as is the earth's surface negatively charged [-], and thus *"Mother"* Earth. A negative [-] repels a negative [-]. Both the Hebrew-Christian West and the Eastern Hindus understand this religiously.)

What we need now, at the end of this 510-year civilization cycle, when the earth is again losing its magnetic charge, becoming unstable and too acidic, when the masculine gall bladder/liver meridian complex is blowing out, and anger and violence are becoming unrestrained, is courageous, secure, coolheaded, calm, grounded, law-abiding, moral, risk-taking, freedom-loving, and yet kind and gentle men, husbands who are responsible, whose faith and practice is sufficient to rise above the craving for control, approval and security, who share an equality with their wives, and yet, in authority over their wives as the grounding element, provide, defend and instruct in a loving way, and serve their wives, while providing a protective covering under which the wife can flourish. That way she can in turn nurture and provide the constructive subconscious programming vital to the psychological health of the children up to age 12, while children are still in the formative delta, theta and alpha regions of the brain, so that the children's basic control, approval and security (love) needs are met and constructively channeled. Then she can also harness her incredible power center of E-motion constructively in the world of business, church, the arts, and charity. Women and wives can exercise indirect control over almost everything through business/money. Given this as the balanced theological/scientific dialectic polarity model, it is obvious we don't even come close today in the United States. Real meaning in life comes from work, family, church and community - from love, from people.

Natural curiosity has led investigators to research why, for nearly 2000 years, the church has excluded women from eldership and the priesthood, a law-based function, and why for 400 years the U.S.' Founding Fathers saw women as too powerful to be involved with the law on almost any level, in any capacity. Late 20th century research has suggested that men better understand justice tempered with mercy, because men naturally tend to be weak and irresponsible. Women, by contrast, tend to be strong, to lack mercy, as evidence reveals from the study of both female gangs and women jurors. Moreover, overwhelmingly, women like working for men rather than other women, because men are typically not as tough or cruel. Women have a natural dominant characteristic, just as men have a tendency to be irresponsible, and thus merciful. The holistic feminine need for security, control and approval, found in both genders, also centralizes power in a statist bureaucracy which attempts to solve all problems, stop time, eliminate risk and individuality, and legislate all of life, going bankrupt in the process. A religious and economic parasite, civil government has no ground. But civil government attempts to fill the groundless vacuum left by irresponsible, wimpy, effeminate and macho men. ...What does this tell us about Yale-educated Hillary Clinton, one of the top 100 lawyers in the country? Has she ever been truly loved?

In a 1957 book, THE COMING CAESARS, French historian Amaury de Reincourt wrote, *"Toward the end of the Hellenistic Age, there was no greater revolution in Rome than that of women's rights. In the Second Century B.C., they became emancipated in every way, including economically. The United States' declaration that all men are created equal in terms of practical ability excluded women. Apparently, the difference in essence was enough. The growing role of women in the United States has led to many changes in public opinion, including the following: the desire for freedom to be replaced by security, the tendency to focus on the child and the youth worship syndrome, the suspicion of individualism, the desire to avoid risk, and the emotional personalization of issues. In Rome, the increasing voice of women in formulating public opinion resulted in the establishment of a virile Caesar. Masses of people, such as are found in the cities of the United States today, display the emotionalism collectively that is common to women. They must instinctively look for compensating masculine leadership, which cannot be found in a congress, but in a Caesar."*

What did Hillary say before the election? *"I want to be the voice of America's children."* Hillary advocates *"the immediate abolition of the legal status of minority...the extension to children of all procedural rights guaranteed to adults; the rejection of the legal prescription of the identity of interest between parents and their children...."* ...There go our children and grandchildren, wards of the state under Hillary. In other words, as the prophet Isaiah warned, *"...children are their oppressors and women rule over them...Those who lead you cause you to err and destroy the way of your paths."* ...In addition to the Billary-backed return of abortion, with the Clintonista vaccination program and all, child sacrifice is taking on new meaning. ...It will not be Hillary-ous when the effeminate Clintonistas get their heads handed to them by the compensating masculine warrior demons and terrorists emerging from Iran. Watch out come 1995-96!

This brings us to focus on Hilly and Billy Clinton, the Hill-Bill-ies of Arkansas, come to Washington, D.C., in reality silver spoon-fed Yale and Fabian New World Order demagogues. Just as a family reflects its head, or a business reflects its executives, so too does a nation reflect its political leadership. As I've pointed out over and over again, the Clintonistas are out of touch with reality. They live in their heads on images, on illusions, in ivory towers; they are ungrounded. Their ill-placed reliance on so-called experts was demonstrated to be bankrupt in the Waco tragedy. (Is Janet Reno ever a piece of work.) They are literally radioactive because they are so toxic, in thought, action, word, and deed, as well as body chemistry. They live by theories that have never ground out in the real world of having a job or running a business. Their values are alien to over 80% of Americans. This is a revolutionary situation.

Bill has an insatiable desire for approval, as demonstrated by his constant need to talk, his wish to appease and please everyone, and his tireless escapades with women, both during and following the campaign. He is most vulnerable. But Bill Clinton never had a male influence or role model in his family that he could rely on. His mother was married five times to four men. Small wonder he's indecisive. He has no ground, no sense of security. I grieve for the country because of it.

Hillary, the lawyer (her profession alone speaks volumes), literally wears the pants in the family. Talk about craving control and anger! Here we have it in spades! So here we have a polarity shift, a sex role reversal. When Chelsea Clinton was sick in school and wanted to take an aspirin, the school nurse required Chelsea to call her parents to get permission. Chelsea called her father, not her mother.

The stories filtering out of the Secret Service and the Fraternal Order of Police (FOP) in Washington, D.C. regarding the private exploits of the Clintons are mind-boggling. Newsweek reported that a Treasury Department official told the Secret Service to put a lid on its agents' spreading the word regarding the Clintons, or the responsibility for protecting the Clintons would be assigned to another agency. That's how bad it's gotten. A marriage of convenience is putting it mildly. That's how black things have become in the White House.

The jokes filtering through the grassroots speak to the reality of Hillary's dominance. Let's just run down a few of them: *"I don't trust the president, nor her husband."* ..."*Why does Hillary Clinton have so many Secret Service agents assigned to her? Because if anything happened to her, Bill would be-come president." ...."When Bill Clinton expresses his opinions, he qualifies them by saying that they are those of his wife." ... "Reporters are having a field day in Washington these days. It's fun to cover the new leader of the Western world, and her husband."*

When Hillary Clinton was in Austin, Texas to speak on the full moon of April 6, 1993, she and Gov. Ann Richards both wore the upper chakra emotional color of lavender/violet, a sign of unrestrained emotion. Fourteen thousand women turned out at the Erwin Center on the University of Texas campus to hear Hillary Rodham Clinton speak at this time of the full moon, which was the last major preparation for the witch covens around the country prior to May 1, 1993, the high day of witchcraft. Moderator Bill Moyers asked both women what it was like to govern. Gov. Ann Richards commented, *"I think that Hillary's not in any position to be as frank as I am."* Hillary then responded, *"I am also - just to set the record straight - not really governing, either."* Gov. Ann Richards then responded, *"If you believe that, I've got a bridge I want to sell you."*

When Hugh Rodham, Hillary's father, died the week of April 10, 1993, Hillary lost her last male covering, leaving her totally ungrounded. In 1993, the Year of the Woman, which was really the Year of the Goddess, or the Year of the High Priestess, Hillary became unrestrained. She has no covering, no grounding, by a male pastor, her father, or her husband. It was thus well timed that the cover of Parade magazine of Sunday, April 11, 1993 featured Hillary Rodham Clinton with the headline, *"Hillary Rodham Clinton is one of the most influential Americans of our time."* Well said. Absolutely true. As goes Hillary, so goes the nation.

It is no accident that an ultra pro-lesbian and pro-abortion magazine, Ms., allowed one of its top writers, Judith Warner, to publish a very flattering book on Hillary entitled, HILLARY CLINTON: THE INSIDE STORY. It praises Ms. Rodham and takes great delight with her agenda as first lady. The book noted that many regarded her as the governor of Arkansas in practice over the past ten years, and that President Clinton is already being called Hillary's husband in many prominent circles. Too true.

The February 8, 1993 issue of U.S. News & World Report, as a cover story, stated boldly, *"Hillary Clinton: The Co-President?"* Perhaps preparing for her May 1, 1993 enthronement, the media reported on February 23, 1993 that Hillary Clinton had consulted with the spirit of Eleanor Roosevelt. This is a kind of witchcraft known as necromancy. A recent letter that appeared in the Southwest Times-Record of Fort Smith, Arkansas, talked openly about Hillary Clinton's shamanism: *"...[O]ur very powerful first lady's practice of it."* ...Oh, the seductiveness of those earth-bound spirits.

An expert in the field, David J. Meyer, wrote, *"In the occult, the female force is dominant."* And Bill Clinton is supportive. David J. Meyer penned in February 1993: *"Here let it be known that those who have been involved in the occult know that witches have a very definite jargon or descriptive way of speaking. Years ago, I was very much part of that world, and I know that jargon fluently. When William Jefferson Blythe Clinton gave his inaugural address, I listened with amazement as I heard the familiar words and phrases on the radio. I was listening to the words of high level witchcraft as the jargon poured forth from the lips of this New Age Illuminist."*

Candidly, dear readers, given what exists in many researchers' files these days, what I'm telling you is going relatively easy on the Clintons. By contrast, for example, you ought to see the file that Floyd G. Brown, author of SLICK WILLIE: WHY AMERICA CANNOT TRUST BILL CLINTON, is building (Floyd Brown, Citizens United, Washington, D.C., 703-352-4788).

We Texans had the first real opportunity to send a resounding judgment to Washington on the Clintonistas when we voted in the special election for U.S. senator in 1993. The Democratic nominee, Bob Krueger, heavily backed by Billary, was nonetheless defeated by his Republican opponent, Kay Bailey Hutchison.

You know, when I was younger and read the book of Revelation, I used to wonder about the tie between the seven last plagues, ushering forth from the seven bowls, and their relationship with the great harlot spoken of in Revelation. I don't wonder anymore. I know both are symbolic of an ungrounded humanity and an earth in upheaval, both unrestrained. The media is foretelling what is coming. Here's what the Austin American-Statesman had to say on April 23, 1993 regarding TV in May of that year: *"The season of murder and mayhem continues in force during the May sweeps, with the heavily hyped rating period producing a higher-than-usual body count.*

"Ripped-from-the-headlines movies and miniseries start with the 1958 case of a Nebraska serial killer and end with the painfully recent story of the Branch Davidian standoff in Waco. If you're looking for lighthearted springtime fare, you won't find it on the networks in May.

"Although studies consistently show that an overwhelming majority of people believe there is too much violence on television, Nielsen surveys show that bloody TV movies do boffo business. If the audience truly has reached the saturation point, it's not reflected in the ratings." ...Yes, on May 1, 1993, we became ungrounded and unrestrained, also unforgiven.

SECTION VI

Solutions

AN ANSWER TO THE UNANSWERED ECONOMIC QUESTION

Sept. 11, 1986

Dr. Lester C. Thurow is a Rhodes scholar and Oxford educated. He was formerly a professor at Harvard before he moved on to Massachusetts Institute of Technology, and is clearly identified with the Eastern Establishment. He authored the best seller, *The Zero Sum Society*, which sold over a million copies globally. Thurow has been a member of the President's Council of Economic Advisors. I was honored when he took a couple of hours out of his busy schedule to visit with me at my Montana llama ranch. We have both been successful enough, have read enough, have a basic love for truth, and have been frustrated enough by the traditions of men (politicians) that we quite naturally put our pretenses aside and got down to basics. (Llama discussions came first, of course.)

As Lester put it, he is as far out on the radical fringe as he can be without being kicked out of the Establishment. Yours truly, on the other hand, is clearly anti-establishment in his thinking, having been tagged at a national conference as the *"Indiana Jones of Christian Economics."*

The bottom line of what Lester and I both have in common is an intense desire to see what he calls *"social justice"* instituted in the corporate and governmental affairs of men. *"Social justice"* is nothing more than *"government as religion applied to economics."* Sound familiar? This should not be surprising, given that Lester is Montana born and raised and the son of a Methodist minister. He has some of the same zeal as I found in David Stockman, who was a Harvard-trained divinity student.

I did not find it at all surprising that Lester's basic analysis of global economic problems and his subsequent pessimistic outlook is almost identical to my own. He thought President Reagan would be remembered historically for the federal and trade deficit. He said he looked forward to reading my book, *No Time For Slaves*, on his flight home. His observations are included in the following article:

By DAN BLACK
The Daily Inter Lake

WHITEFISH - A nationally known economist has mostly discouraging words for delegates to a two-nation conference on regional development.

Dr. Lester C. Thurow of the Massachusetts Institute of Technology said *"there is no such thing as regional economic development"* until the nations of the world abandon protectionist policies.

Thurow was the keynote speaker Thursday at the opening session for 20 delegates from Japan and 20 from Montana.

Pointing to record high unemployment rates, Thurow said the system of economic regulators that served the world well following World War II is no longer appropriate in a world changed by high-tech communications and economic development. He said using that system in today's economy is like driving today's automobiles with roads and regulations designed for the horse and buggy. He said the federal reserve board only thinks it controls the money supply. It is possible to bypass the Fed's control, he said, by doing business in German marks or Japanese yen, neither of which is controlled by the Fed.

"We have a world money supply with no one controlling it," he said, "or worse, with three or four governments thinking they control it."

That lack of a world money policy means that nations acting independently could have a catastrophic effect on the world economy. For example, he said, if the United states were to cut spending enough to balance its budget it would mean the loss of 5.5 million jobs, 3 million in the U.S. and 2.5 million elsewhere, and that would produce a recession.

Another problem, he said, is trade imbalances that have produced a huge trade surplus for Japan and an even huger trade deficit for the United States. The world economy cannot run for long with those deficits. Eventually the U.S. will cure its deficit, he said, and when that happens the rest of the world will lose 7 million jobs.

"We don't call that a recession, we call that the Great Depression."

Yet he said, neither the United States nor any other nation is instituting the necessary reforms in money policies.

Governments are pressured politically to adhere to protectionist policies. Third-world nations have borrowed more than they can repay, and the amounts they are required to pay are blocking economic growth. For example, he said, Mexico would have to cut its standard of living by 25 percent for at least 50 years to repay its debts.

"No democratic leader in the world can do what we are asking those leaders to do," Thurow said. But unless these problems are solved, there is no such thing as regional economic development.Lester Thurow, however, being an integral part of the Eastern Establishment now, has opted for statist answers. (He could hardly do otherwise and be influential in today's Democratic Party.) By comparison, he is more academic, corporate and pragmatic than your editor, who is more market oriented, individualistic and philosophical.

Given the dependent, slave-like nature of the American public today, it might well take central government implementation of biblical law in order to provide the incentives necessary to reestablish the decentralization which brings freedom, peace and prosperity to all of society. It took God forty years to let the Hebrew slaves of Egypt die out before their descendants were tough and courageous enough to conquer the Promised Land.

Dangers For Thinkers

Change comes slowly to most people, and this is a constant source of frustration to both Lester and myself. The August 15th issue of *Vital Speeches* featured a key address by Stephen Joel Trachtenberg, president of the University of Hartford, entitled, *"Five Ways In Which Thinking Is Dangerous."* Lester and I both suffer in all five of these areas:

1) Thinking becomes depressing at times, because there are so many people who don't make use of the brain power they have available, who have lost their inquisitiveness, who could improve things for the benefit of themselves and their fellow man, but do not do so.

2) Those who think become disliked. Today, most people, rather than recognizing and rewarding excellence, become resentful, envious and feel inferior to thinkers and risk takers.

3) Those who are older begin to feel *"obsolete"* when someone younger knows more than they do. This contributes to the isolation of a thinker. (This is also one reason why your editor grew a beard and mustache. I got tired of people telling me I was too young to know what I knew.)

4) Often, despair comes with the fast pace required to keep up with the information explosion in our society today. (The high standard that both Lester and I have set for ourselves is a very demanding pace, sometimes overwhelming to others with whom we work.)

5) Perhaps most frustrating is the desire, which accompanies the impact thinkers have on the world around them, to bring about more changes. They also have to live with the changes they have made, right or wrong.

The Loss of Creativity

Lester and I discussed how the short-term orientation of the U.S. economic and political order today has led to a loss of creative thinking, initiative, and cutbacks in research and development. As a result, we are falling behind as we are now forced to compete in a global economy. We arrogantly still refuse to acknowledge in our national consciousness that we are part of that arena. For example, why haven't the wood products, copper and aluminum industries of Montana thought of ways to make better use of those raw materials by vertically integrating their raw material activities into end use products? How many Montana lumber and wood products operations have traveled to the Scandinavian countries to investigate the technology used there in the wood products industry? When a country is short-term oriented, as ours is, it has no vision. Without a vision, without a long-term view, the people perish.

How many economic regions have gone to the trouble to list the ten best things about their area, as well as the ten worst things, and done so honestly? Few, according to Thurow. People tend to deceive themselves, particularly about the bad things. Until we recognize both our strengths and our weaknesses, we cannot win. We have to be both wise as serpents and harmless as doves. We have to know both the bulls' and the bears' case. We have to know both our enemy and ourselves, just like in warfare, if we are to be successful long-term.

The Unanswered Economic Question

Lester noted that the advances in both communication and transportation today should effectively lead to decentralization and widespread GNP over large geographic areas. However, such is not the case. He commented, *"No economist has a good reason for the observed phenomenon...For some strange reason millions of people like to live on top of each other."*

Here is a case in point where Eastern Establishment thinking, with its pre-supposition that the federal government has all the answers, coupled with its focus almost exclusively on the *"labor"* side of the economic equation, breaks down. People simply cannot think outside of their given mind set. They cannot reason beyond their assumptions about the nature of reality, or beyond the facts/information which they have available to them. Put simply, you can't know *"there is more than one way to skin a cat,"* if you've only been taught *"there is only one way to skin a cat."* In other words, we all tend to *"rut"* think.

When Lester observes (rightfully) that the decentralization revolution should occur because of the advances in transportation and communication, but such has not been the case; and that, *"No economist has a good reason for the observed phenomenon,"* he is recognizing the bankruptcy of present day human action-centered, central government-dominated, economic thought. I told Lester, as we strolled in the pasture among the llamas, that I had answered his question in my *Wealth for All* books. Here again is the essence of it.

An Answer

An answer to Lester's dilemma lies in the age-old urban versus rural conflict. This can also be characterized as a vertical (urban) versus horizontal (rural) phenomenon; a collectivist (urban) versus individualistic (rural) conflict. Such a confrontation, a slave (urban) versus free (rural) situation, has to do with a lack of balance between the *"labor"* (urban) and *"land"* (rural) parts of the economic equation.

The challenge for any civilization is to maintain its balance between city and countryside, its balance between its vertical and horizontal institutions, between the tendency toward collectivism versus the rights of individuals, in order to minimize slavery and encourage freedom, and to balance off labor and land in economics. The two parts of the basic economic equation, *"labor"* and *"land"*, are the essence of man as God created him - *"made in the image of God"* and *"formed from the dust of the earth."* Maintaining the balance between urban and rural should rightfully come through decentralization because the advances in the technologies of communication and transportation are in essence decentralizing. Things really must be out of kilter for a phenomenon which should occur naturally - decentralization - to be short-circuited.

The *"specialization and division of labor"* occurs most naturally and conveniently in the city, while the intellectual aspect of cities gives rise to the development of *"technology."* Both of these create and increase wealth long-term and should naturally harmonize with the *"raw materials and resources"* of the *"land"* found in the rural countryside.

The problem comes when the decentralizing, peace-bringing, prosperity-producing work ethic of the Golden Rule, *"Self interest is best served first by service,"* is replaced by the evolutionary *"survival of the fittest"* norm.

There are in this life two *"jungles."* There is the jungle found in the natural environment, such as in parts of Africa and regions of Latin America. This is the *"land"* jungle. But there is also the *"labor"* jungle, the evolutionary city. The city becomes a jungle when man is no longer a God-ruled, self-governing *"ultimate resource"* but instead, becomes in an evolutionary way, *"the ultimate predator"* or *"the ultimate parasite."*

When the city becomes a jungle, as it becomes increasingly evolutionary, it uses its *"labor"* power in the *"survival of the fittest"* mode and tends, both politically and economically, to oppress, exploit and eventually bankrupt the rural countryside. (Man ultimately rules over and determines the use of nature.) This short-term perspective is not to the city's benefit long-term, because the rural countryside is the natural resource lifeline, the umbilical cord, which brings life to the city. The rural countryside can survive on its own because it is self-sufficient with regard to the necessities of life - food, water, clothing, shelter and fuel. The city, on the other hand, is dependent on the rural countryside for these basic subsistence needs. Therefore, when the rural countryside dies, the city cannot be far from extinction.

Military strategists have long known this truth. If you want to totally destroy a civilization, if you destroy only its cities, but leave its rural countryside intact, the civilization will come back. Why? Because its roots, both resource-wise and value-wise, are grounded in the rural countryside. However, if you destroy a nation's countryside, its cities will wither and die. The subsistence base which supports the cities' fragile life support systems is cut off.

(This is why it took General Sherman four years to destroy the Old South during the Civil War. He had to destroy the countryside - its plantations and farms, its churches, its work ethic. He could have marched directly to Atlanta in 90-120 days.)

The checks and balances between the city and the rural country are achieved by implementing two key biblical economic principles in the social order:

1) Strictly limiting absentee ownership of land; and

2) Allowing the rural countryside to be the primary, if not the exclusive, creator of money through the monetization of commodities, the issuing of receipts for commodities, or computer entries representing actual commodities. In other words, free market money, honest money, is produced in the rural country.

People flow to where the money is. Where the money is, there the jobs are. If the money is created in the countryside, people will migrate to rural areas. Decentralization occurs. However, if the money is created by a fiat currency, fractional reserve debt banking system in the city, with its unlimited compounding of interest as it is today, then people are sucked through the resource pipeline from the rural areas to the city where they are digested, used up, and spit out. No rural decentralization or dominion of the earth can occur. There is no subduing of the conflict, chance and cycles of the natural earth. The technological advances in communication and transportation are not allowed to work in harmony with decentralized, rurally created honest, free market money. As a result, few prosper.

With rurally produced, honest, free market money, 80% of our people who now live on approximately 1% of the land in the cities, would be geographically dispersed throughout the countryside.

The federal government today owns 42% of the land in this country, contrary to the Constitution. And, according to *Town and Country* magazine, less than 5% of the people in this country own approximately 95% of the land held by the private sector. The rest of us are dispossessed.

By strictly limiting absentee ownership of land to small plots primarily owned by seasonal residents, by restricting absentee ownership to less than 50% in any major land or capital venture, by requiring at least six months annual residence in an area, and by encouraging instead long-term land and/or capital leases of less than 50 years in the rural countryside, decentralization is further encouraged. Land generally becomes less expensive and more affordable the further removed it is from the city. This makes migration to the country more attractive. The absentee ownership of land, which is also so evident today in economically stagnant Europe, Scotland, Great Britain, Guatemala and other Latin American countries, is minimized. The status of folks in the rural country would amount to something more than feudal serfs. The lower cost basis in land would enable them to earn a better living. Government-owned rural lands, with the possible unconstitutional exception of a few parks and wilderness areas, would disappear, too. The federal government would no longer be able to bankrupt the farmers as they are doing today in this country, or starve ten million to death as the Soviet communists did in the Ukraine in the early 1930s. (Government involvement in the economy long-term is always a curse. It follows that all land taxes would be abolished as well.)

When I worked in Guatemala City in 1983, I found that the large land owners lived not on their income land in the countryside, among their laborers, but rather in the city. The people who worked the farms, ranches and plantations in Guatemala were dispossessed. They stayed perpetually poor, with no incentives, inclined toward communism. In Ireland, during the famine of 1847-1849, thousands of Irish literally starved to death along the sides of the road, begging for the food which they had produced, as it was being shipped off in carts to be sold by the absentee landlords who owned the property and resided in London.

The only workable solution to Third World economic development problems comes in the working ownership of small family farms.

Absentee ownership of land destroys the spirit of community (harmony), which is necessary for widespread prosperity long-term. It inhibits decentralization. Furthermore, it limits personal accountability, which is vital in human affairs. Absentee ownership of land not only prevents men from being held personally accountable for environmental damage and abusive actions to those who live and work the properties, it also alienates the city from the country, weakening the nation.

Tenants who work the land have no real stake personally in nurturing and improving the land long-term for some absentee owner. They can't get rich either. The Westlands, California experiment demonstrates this, aggravated by federal government subsidies. This, in turn, leads to such evils as migration to the already choked and polluted cities, rural land and water pollution, demineralization of the soil, substandard food, and increased toxicity of the environment. This long-term turns the rural country into a wasteland, and wrecks the general vitality of the people. The city then dies, too. This is why deserts reign supreme today and the land is depopulated where formerly civilizations existed. The vertical bureaucratic city/state empires of long gone civilizations were noted for their absentee ownership of land. Northern Africa, for example, today a desert, used to be a swamp area.

No man should own more land than that amount which he can turn into a garden. Absentee ownership of land is a no-no!

Countries which have strong laws requiring local ownership of land, and healthy restrictions on absentee land ownership, include Switzerland and Bermuda. We do not have to reinvent the wheel in this matter. We can and should study the solutions of other countries.

When the city controls through political edict, the monopolistic issue of non commodity money by special interest groups (banks), which allows all wealth to be concentrated increasingly in the city, into fewer and fewer hands, it encourages (and results in) the buying up of the rural countryside, dispossessing the country folk. The rural folk migrate to the city. Then the city has effectively signed its own death warrant long-term. When "land" and "labor" die, the economy dies. When the economy dies, the city, the rural country and the entire civilization die.

We now know why the natural advances in communication and transportation today have not led to the decentralization of GNP over a widespread geographic area in this nation. The imbalance of power, brought about by city-created dishonest money and the promotion of absentee ownership of land, has led to this massive distortion.

I told Lester there is an explanation for the observed phenomenon. We no longer need to live in THE ZERO SUM SOCIETY. When the rural country monetizes commodities, we have unlimited wealth, because earth is an open system, thanks to unlimited sunlight, which is transformed into commodities, which can be monetized. We have the resources available to us for both unlimited wealth and unlimited money. So, there was a good reason, after all, that the Pilgrims celebrated Thanksgiving and the blessings of an abundant harvest. It was a blessing in that day, rather than the curse which the abundant harvest brings today, thanks to a dishonest monetary system and widespread absentee ownership of land.

One day soon, I hope every man will live under his own vine and fig tree.

* * * * *

"I personally think the notion of the 'city' is becoming obsolete. Cities grew up originally because you had great access to natural transportation. We have a terrific harbor here [N.Y.] - which is also the case in Boston, Washington and other cities that have been around for a long time. Transportation and distribution were a definite need. So you built up a tremendous infrastructure, railroads, ports and terminals, everything else. But now communications, technology and the movement of goods have advanced so far that the whole idea of the city - having this tremendous infrastructure to support the economic activity that is at the center of the nation's prosperity - doesn't make sense anymore."
— Michael Aronstein - *Barrons,* October 23, 1992 September *11, 1986*

* * * * *

"Workers are not well trained, American products rarely meet the standards of international markets. Brand name goods and quality are secondary in importance - managers are looking for quick profits and high quarterly dividends. University graduates prefer careers in marketing and finances than a career in production. And what is worst: The average American is completely disinterested in the rest of the world. The world is changing rapidly - the United States is not... In the 21st century, the winning edge will lie in production technology and no longer in new product development. Americans still invest two-thirds of research funds into R&D or new products and only one-third into the development of new methods of production. In Japan for instance, it's the exact opposite." — Lester Thurow

PONDERINGS ON THE CRISIS OF DEBT CAPITALISM

January 15, 1987

The Middle Ages

Contrast the sad state of affairs which exists today in Western civilization with conditions in the Middle Ages, when men had full use of their productivity and taxes were 33% or less, and in many cases, only 12%. In the Middle Ages, according to Thorold Roger's studies at Oxford, a laborer could provide all his yearly necessities for his family by working only 14 weeks - 3½ months. European historian Sombart revealed that in Middle Age Europe hundreds of communities averaged half a year in holidays, from 160 to 180 holidays a year. This meant the common working man only labored three to four days a week. People had all they could eat by way of protein and plant variety. They were abundantly clothed, had households full of furniture and bedding, and possessed all the implements they needed for the tools of their trade.

There was a church every four square miles throughout England, and 35 magnificent Gothic cathedrals. Externally imposed laws were minimal. The church, the king, the municipalities and the guilds had limited power. The church interpreted the laws and the laymen wrote pamphlets with regard to commerce. The main issues were those of economic justice, with strong prohibitions against usury.

The prosperity, harmony and debt-free lifestyle of the Middle Ages was overturned near the end of the 17th century with the Industrial Revolution. But it wasn't the Industrial Revolution in and of itself which destroyed the lifestyle of the rural farmer, the village dweller, the lower class and ultimately the middle class. It was instead the modern, fractional reserve, debt capitalistic banking techniques that came with the Industrial Revolution that compromised and limited the vast majority.

Today, the evolutionary, humanistic, socialistic, statist liberals call the *"Middle Ages"* the *"Dark Ages."* The pot is calling the kettle black. The Middle Age lifestyle was far better and a far cry from the escapism of today's world, where men run to drugs, alcohol, professional sports, television and movies. People are into rampant escapism.

Producer Sovereignty

The concentration of power today, primarily in the hands of about a dozen big Eastern Establishment multinational banks and other Dow Jones-type corporations, guarantees no-risk business situations. Their multi-million dollar sales abroad are guaranteed by U.S. taxpayers via the Export-Import Bank, the International Monetary Fund, the World Bank, etc. The end result is that basically only these behemoths of business can afford to borrow from the big banks, because they have risk-free, taxpayer-guaranteed sales at the other end. Therefore, these producers determine in many cases the rate and degree of new investment, based upon expectations of profits, not based upon changes in consumer demand. In other words, too often today the producer is sovereign, not the consumer.

Furthermore, because American consumers have never been taught in the public government schools to husband their money, they have made their deposits in many of these multinational banks. These deposits have in turn been borrowed by the multinational corporations to finance manufacturing investments in Third World countries, where labor and raw material prices are much lower than those stateside. These multinational banks and businesses, using their political leverage in Washington against tariffs and other forms of trade protectionism, then import these cheaply produced finished goods from the Third World back to the United States where they are sold to American consumers, thereby undercutting American manufacturing (steel, TVs, leather and plastic goods, textiles). American workers are thrown out of their jobs. Coming full circle, the American worker, by first depositing his money in multinational banks, has financed his own unemployment.

The high financial cost of entry into various highly developed fields today limits competition, as does the high cost of government red tape. And then there is the squeeze play. The airline industry is a case in point. After deregulation, air fares were driven sharply lower. Weak airline companies who did not have the staying power (by way of financial backing) were forced to sell out, go belly up, or merge. Now that the dust has settled, the result today is that we are stuck with five big major airlines which control 73% of all air traffic. And predictably, now air fares are being raised with all carriers pretty much in agreement. It's the same old evolutionary debt capitalist technique made famous by Rockefeller, Morgan and the other robber barons of the 1890s: (1) Garner a huge financial pool of financial staying power, courtesy of your friendly big banker; (2) drive prices through the floor (below cost) thereby eliminating the weak, the small, the *"uncompetitive,"* and those with little financial staying power; (3) buy up the busted competition's businesses and their assets for a song, or merge with them on favorable terms; (4) once the consolidation is complete and only a handful of the big boys control the vast majority of the market, then set prices and raise them consistently. The consumer is forced to pay up. In this way producer greed, not consumer desire, becomes the dynamic force under debt capitalism.

Mature Debt Capitalism

Debt capitalism faces another problem. We are in the mature phase of industrialization. The productive plant of the nation in terms of manufacturing finished goods, as well as the production of raw commodities, is in excess of that required for subsistence living. It is only through the emotional appeal of clever psychological advertising to an undisciplined consumer, who is willing (and has been taught) to take on unwieldy amounts of consumer debt, that this game can be continued. Everything is in surplus worldwide - commodities and manufactured goods. This is why the exploitation of the Third World and now Red China is so popular. It is also why wars are necessary from time to time, so the excess that would naturally produce global prosperity can be destroyed, and the debt game can be played all over again. Think of wars as *"urban renewal,"* or as ways to bring Middle Age countries quickly into the 20th century, or as ways to aid and abet the spread of communism and socialism.

Certainly, if the debt capitalists raise the working man's living standards by reducing profits, the game could peacefully continue longer as well. But such is not the nature of greed inherent in human nature. And, of course, reduced profits reduce the incentive for new investment and enterprise. Checkmate. Unless living standards are raised by increases in real wages (after inflation and taxes), or at the expense of profits, the necessary market cannot be maintained for full production and employment. And how can interest be paid on the debt? Through an escape valve, such as overseas investment, particularly in the Third World.

This is all part and parcel of the problem brought about by bankers not allowing a global free market in money, where commodities are monetized, and by not having strict limitations on the absentee ownership of land around the world. Both of these economic standards, when implemented, allow for an ever higher standard of living, lower prices, decentralization, and incentives for endless growth, which literally returns the earth to a garden.

What we have now is excess without beneficial, meaningful growth. It is mind blowing to realize that the United States has stored in limestone caves around Kansas City literally over 181,000 tons of butter, 363,000 tons of cheese, and 1.5 million tons of dried milk powder. The cost of refrigerating this commodity excess is $60 million a year. Excess is also the case in Australia, New Zealand and the European Economic Community.

Technology and Unemployment

Increasingly efficient technology under the present debt capitalistic system, instead of becoming a blessing, has become a curse for the vast majority. As we move increasingly toward the era of total automation, with *"smart"* computer-controlled robotic factories, the blue collar worker, the non-thinking laborer, the middle manager, and many white collar workers become totally expendable and unnecessary. With these ultimate labor-saving techniques, all that is left by way of necessary human labor are high-tech repairmen, the technocrats, and those who control them - the political, military, banking, business and other bureaucratic elite.

Who will buy all these robot-produced goods, perfected by the smart computers? Who will buy all the fish sandwiches poured out by unmanned fast food outlets? (Who needs the bank tellers in a cashless society?) The consumer market will inevitably diminish as unemployment increases due to these ultimate labor saving devices. It's Catch 22. The greater the efficiency of labor saving technology, the greater the unemployment in the developed world (the U.S.), means a smaller consumer market for finished goods and services. As a society, we are not even addressing the problems, much less coming up with answers today.

The Technological/Unemployment Dilemma

The technological/unemployment problem, of course, stems from the fact that these efficiencies in technology are financed with debt capital, rather than with equity. There is no way to spread the technological labor-saving wealth around under debt capitalism. There is no way under debt capitalism to widely distribute the benefits of such labor saving techniques and ultimately lower prices to the society-at-large. The economic benefits today are increasingly realized by the elitist debt capitalists, who can afford to borrow. So, here again, it is the working man, who has made his deposits in the big banks (who have in turn loaned his money to the debt capitalists) who has financed his own unemployment.

Today, labor union men sit idly beside high-tech machines, doing nothing. Talk to railroad men. It's a joke. More and more men and women are being laid off and unemployed, as their jobs are shipped overseas, or as they are being replaced by high tech and a contracting economy, forcing men and women into menial tasks, scrambling for whatever scraps are left in the shrinking job market. Perhaps even worse is the disguised unemployment of make-work bureaucrats. Small wonder then, given this sad state of affairs, that the three largest items in the federal budget today are the military budget, entitlement programs, and debt service. We reap what we sow. All three of these big budget items are the direct result of the foundational errors of debt capitalism.

Equity Capitalism, the Solution

By contrast, the answer comes readily under equity capitalism, whereby the worker, by being unwilling to loan (deposit) his money to a bank, instead requires an equity interest in all investments. The bank serves as his investment broker/agent. The worker becomes a participating owner of the means of production, and benefits from the profits generated by labor-saving technology, such as computer robotics. This in turn completes the circle, allowing the worker to enjoy a share of the income from high technology, and thereby remain a part of the consumer market for the goods and services produced by these technological advances.

In other words, the worker, by working, saving, and investing through equity ownership, rather than being paid next to nothing in interest by a bank, is able to thrive long-term. If he finances his own unemployment through high-tech advancements, so what? He is compensated as a capitalist because he has invested his hard-earned dollars in the high-tech devices which have replaced him. Small wonder then that the Hebrew, Greek, Christian, Muslim and Middle Age economies all condemned usury.

Today, with honest free market money, under equity capitalism, we should have a far higher standard of living than did the debt-free Middle Age man and woman. Work today should be creative - the development of one's talents - rather than drudgery.

Communism

In contrast, Communism has no answer at all. Communism depends upon debt capitalism to survive. Communism was given life by debt capitalism, both in the Soviet Union and in Eastern Europe. There is no incentive to produce under communism, and so there is little quality production and without ownership, no worker equity. The only way the bureaucracy of communism can be supported is by the excess production thrown off the debt capitalism.

The misery of the human spirit under communism is evident from rampant absenteeism from the workplace, epidemic alcoholism, and a lifestyle which is much akin to bugs crawling around in the sludge of a stagnant barrel of water. Thus, the bureaucracies of both communism and debt capitalism today are simply layered personal pigeonholes, where people waste their time until they die. Bureaucracies are escapist institutions, where people hide from the real world, become dehumanized, and disguise the unemployment of their creative talents in submission to a job.

The worker should be the owner of the means of production, but not as Karl Marx declared, not by politically enforced communal ownership, brought about by a violent political bureaucracy working from the top down. Rather, ownership of the means of production by workers should be earned - with incentive, initiative and rewards provided for workers who save and invest as equity capitalists, from the bottom up. A legitimate, debt-free market in stocks would be a good place to start.

The Devastation of Free Trade

As historian Otto Scott wrote in the Chalcedon Report, given the present inequities and failures of the debt capitalistic system, global free trade is suicidal for this country at this time. We are letting the world defeat us economically, just as surely as if it had defeated us militarily. Economic slavery is as real as military/political slavery. Otto makes the point that in the 1870s the abolition of agricultural tariffs in Great Britain led to a flood of imported cheap American wheat and beef produced in Argentina. As a result, British agriculture predictably collapsed. Four million people left the rural English countryside and crowded into the cities. By the turn of the century, for the first time in its history, Great Britain could no longer feed itself. Sound familiar? Isn't this exactly the road the U.S. is traveling today?

Great Britain, practicing free trade in this manner, while the U.S. and Germany erected high tariff barriers and upgraded their technology, allowed both Germany and the United States to become rich, much of it at the expense of Great Britain.

The problem with free trade is that the world has an endless supply of cheap labor. And, thanks to debt capitalism, we have the means to finance the exploitation of this cheap labor and raw materials in the Third World while cutting out the American worker. This, when fused together with exported debt-financed high technology from the developed world, results in the production of both basic and sophisticated goods in the Third World. These goods are then exported back into the developed world, thereby bankrupting U.S. industries and throwing the American middle class and working class into the unemployment and welfare lines.

The remaining high-tech jobs and low level service occupations cannot make up for the massive unemployment which occurs as a result of this economic dislocation. As things are going now, the economies of the high wage developed world are being destroyed, the people who work there being progressively unemployed. Furthermore, we are being set up, with our basic industries destroyed, to be defeated in a war. Our industry has been decimated by multinational monopolistic debt capitalism. It can no longer produce the war material required to sustain us in a major conflict. This, in turn, increases the likelihood of high-tech nuclear war.

Free Markets Are Ideal

Ideally, free markets globally are the only way to go. When goods and services do not cross borders, armies eventually pave the way for them. Protectionism is a forerunner of war, because protectionism brings on economic, social, political and finally military tensions. But free trade only works where there are open markets, no political involvement in the economic sphere, relatively equal standards of law among nations, and preferably free market money and strict limitations on the absentee ownership of land. In other words, when nations are relatively similar, as is the case between the various states in the United States (California and Oregon, for example), free trade works. Otherwise, a defense has to be raised against economic warfare for the protection of the working people. This is why trade barriers, although undesirable, are necessary when men institute political economies and grant debt monopolies over money. The curse causeless shall not come, as the Bible says.

Trade Barriers

While trade barriers protect against massive domestic unemployment and the breakdown of the domestic industrial economy, at the same time they also promote domestic inefficiency, poor allocation of labor and resources, and support subsidized special interests. Perhaps as a short-term compromise, the foreign company which has to pay the U.S. government-imposed tariffs placed on their exports to the United States will have to take American produced goods and services as repayment. In other words, the payment of the tariff would not go to the federal government. It would instead be established as a credit for the foreign company to be collected by way of American produced goods and services. This establishes effectively a balanced barter system and therefore free market money, which effectively renders the trade barrier less onerous.

In a sense, trade barriers are to economic prosperity what government bureaucracies are to freedom. They are both detrimental long-term. But both may be necessary short term if the philosophical and operational base of the system is in error, as it is today. Politically, freedom is ideal, but people must be responsible (and therefore moral) to be free. (The act of being responsible is the act of being moral.) Unless men are moral, responsible and self-governing, decentralization results in anarchy. So, where men are not moral, responsible and self-governing, the freedom-killing bureaucracy arises to prevent anarchy. So in like manner are trade barriers a necessary evil. Where there is not an open and free market of equity capitalism, with free market money, with mutually agreed upon common laws of trade, then trade barriers and protectionism (like bureaucracies) arise to keep the country which is attempting to implement free trade from collapsing internally. This is the case with the United States today, both with human freedom and free trade. Government bureaucracies and trade barriers are signs of our failure.

This is the price we pay for being irresponsible, for not having a free market in money, for not husbanding our economic production and installing equity capitalism, and for not being self-governing in controlling the laws and lawyers/legislators/bureaucrats which rule over us. It is a sign of the loss of freedom.

It's time therefore to opt for liquidity - cash/T-bills and gold, held both domestically and out of the country. It is time to own fully paid for assets, preferably income producing. It is a time to be out of debt. It is a time to only speculate with risk capital. It is a time to be cautious.

Economics

Economist Joseph Schumpeter saw capitalism as characterized by creative destruction, where entrepreneurs seeking profits introduced innovations that attracted competition because of the high returns available. As innovation moved to the status of commodity, profits were drastically reduced, destroying the value of past investment. This was economic progress as a result of a perennial gale of creative destruction.

In his later writings at Harvard after World War II, Schumpeter explored the ominous implications for democracy implicit in the near universal acceptance of Keynesianism as espoused by economists who took control of most Western economies. He saw the dangers as twofold. First, democratic economies would have a bias toward inflation because governments courting popularity would redistribute income from the areas of savings and investment toward consumption. This has indeed been the case. The second danger was that the redistributions of the welfare state will result in a *"new class,"* such as the nonproductive or parasitical elements of an economy - bureaucrats, lawyers, professors, journalists, intellectuals.

* * * * *

"The beginning of the end of capitalism in America, which was also the beginning of the rise of totalitarian communism, came in 1913...

"Some students would place the beginning of the end of American capitalism earlier. They would date if from 1862, when the first federal income tax was imposed...

"This is why the decline of capitalism should be dated from 1913, when the 16th Amendment authorizing the federal government to impose an income tax was adopted...

"The capitalist forces seemed to have won a great, and possibly decisive victory when Ronald Reagan came into the presidency in 1981. He had campaigned on the promise of a big tax cut and delivered one almost immediately. Conservatives were jubilant. But 10 years later that victory seemed pyrrhic and even Ronald Reagan became suspect. He had once been a Democrat and head of a labor union. Intimates later said he had never really believed that cutting tax rates would raise the revenue. He had gone along with tax increases in every year of his administration except the first. Worst of all, he had laid his hands upon George Bush and pronounced him his heir.

"Conservatives had always had their suspicions of Bush. He was a graduate of Yale, the institution whose radicalism had been exposed by William Buckley in his famous book, 'God And Man At Yale.' Bush had never been able to explain what he did during his time in Communist China. And he revealed a side of himself in 1980 by describing Reagan economics as 'voodoo economics.'

"But still, Bush's apostasy came as a shock to conservatives. In October 1990, encouraged by his Rasputin, the long-haired budget director Darman, he had conspired with Congressional Democrats to raise taxes..." — Dr. Herbert Stein - *WSJ*, January 9, 19

LET FREEDOM RING

July 1, 1987

Presidential Warnings

Much has been said and written about liberty. The president of Princeton, in fact, the 28th president of the United States, Woodrow Wilson, on May 9, 1912 in an address to the New York Press Club declared, *"Liberty has never come from government. Liberty has always come from the subjects of government. The history of liberty is the history of resistance."*

In 1913, in his speech entitled "The New Freedom," Woodrow Wilson thundered, *"The government which was designed for the people, has got into the hands of their bosses and their employers, the special interests. An invisible empire has been set up above the forms of democracy."*

President Wilson also stated, *"The great monopoly in this country is the money monopoly. So long as it exists, our old variety of freedom and individual energy of development are out of the question"* (Brandeis' "Other People's Money").

These quotes from President Woodrow Wilson are nearly 75 years old. Question: If this was indeed the case 75 years ago, and I tend to believe that President Wilson told us the truth, then how much more liberty have we lost since then?

What happened in 1913? (1) The 16th Amendment, the income tax amendment, was passed despite the fact that the Supreme Court had held the income tax to be unconstitutional in 1895. (2) The Federal Reserve System was established. The Federal Reserve System is a *private* corporation that works for the interests of the big international banks. (3) The 17th Amendment to the U.S. Constitution was adopted. This provided for the direct election of U.S. senators. This amendment stripped the states of their checks and balances, centralizing control in the hands of the federal government.

Let's look briefly at some of the key phrases of President Wilson's quotes: From the first quote it becomes obvious that liberty never comes from the top down, but always from the bottom up, from the grass roots, from people like you and me. And liberty has to be wrested from those above. This means that freedom/liberty is never free. Liberty has to be earned, worked for, and fought for when necessary. A man is not free unless there is something he is willing to die for. (Domestic resistance should be nonviolent.)

The second quote from Woodrow Wilson demonstrates that by 1913 the federal government was no longer *"of the people."* The government works for someone else, specifically *"bosses," "employers." "We the people"* don't know who these *"bosses"* are, because they are *"invisible."* An *"empire"* exists, not a republic nor a democracy. By 1913, the federal government was in the hands of the money-oriented *"bosses"* and *"employers."* At that time, the federal government became *"empirical"* in nature.

From the third Woodrow Wilson quote we can make the following observations: The biggest monopoly which exists in this country is the money monopoly. Again, recall that in 1913 the federal income tax and the Federal Reserve System were established. These both had to do with money. The Federal Reserve specifically is the establishment of a *money monopoly.* Thomas Jefferson warned us: *"I sincerely believe that banking establishments are more dangerous than standing armies..."*

Just what about government-granted monopolies? Any economist worth his salt will tell you that a government-granted monopoly always results long-term in the least consumer satisfaction. Monopolies are the most inefficient and ineffective of all organizations in the production, distribution and use of resources. Monopolies are also abusive and corrupt. They have no incentive to serve, cut costs, or produce quality products. Monopolies have no competition to spur excellence. The 7th president of the United States, Andrew Jackson, declared, *"Every monopoly and all exclusive privileges are granted at the expense of the public..."*

In his Farewell Address of March 4, 1837, President Andrew Jackson emphasized, *"The mischief springs from the power which the moneyed interest derives from a paper currency which they are able to control, from the multitude of corporations with exclusive privileges which they have succeeded in obtaining...and unless you become more watchful in your States and check this spirit of monopoly and thirst for exclusive privileges you will in the end find that the most important powers of government have been given or bartered away, and the control of your dearest interests has been passed into the hands of these corporations."*

Recall that President Andrew Jackson's words were delivered 150 years ago. How much worse have things gotten since then? You see, the Bible declares in I Timothy 6:10, *"For the love of money is the root of all evil."* Because the <u>love</u> of money (greed) is the root of all evil <u>spiritually</u>; therefore <u>economically</u>, in our practical world, the <u>lack</u> of money ends up being the root of all evil.

How many of us could use more money? As I have shown practically, logically and historically in my book *No Time for Slaves,* under an honest money, Christian economic system, the potential supply of money is endless. The average working man and woman in this country today should have an annual income of $60,000 a year, earn it in 14 weeks to six months, and be debt free. We should also have falling prices. Instead, if we leave out real estate, today the top 10% of all families own 86% of all net financial assets, the bottom 55% of all families hold zero or negative financial assets in this country.

Back to President Woodrow Wilson's third quote. It becomes obvious when the money monopoly is established we lose our freedom and individuality. This occurred, according to President Wilson, nearly 75 years ago.

The Legs of Liberty

What should become inescapably clear from all of this is that the body of freedom, the body of liberty, stands on the legs of both law/government and economics.

With regard to laws, remember that liberty and freedom are the absence of externally-imposed law. What do most people think of today first when they think of government? The federal government! And yet classic American Christian government, the government of free men, has always been primarily that of self-government. Can you imagine, for example, departing from Kansas City, headed west in a covered wagon, and hearing a highway patrol's siren screaming up behind you? Can you imagine our ancestors, the pioneers, being issued a ticket for passing in the wrong lane, exceeding the speed limit for covered wagons, for not having a current license, or for having a broken tail light?

Under self-government right makes might, rather than might making right. The number of laws spewed out today by the local, state and federal governments tie us down. Our representatives and senators don't even read the proposed laws they vote on. There are too many laws and they are too lengthy. Plus, approximately 50,000 pages of laws a year go into the Federal Register. These laws next to no one reads. The Federal Register laws are put there by the federal alphabet agencies, like the SEC, the Securities Exchange Commission. The federal government's alphabet agency bureaucrats today have less accountability than the tyrannical feudal lords during the Dark Ages, according to historian Otto Scott. Our alphabet agencies today, such as the IRS, make the law, administer the law, and then judge the law. Our Boston Tea Party forefathers would have called this a sham of justice at minimum, and certainly not liberty.

What about economics? Let's take money. Today we use debt money. That's what a Federal Reserve *"note"* is, a debt. Being in debt has always been a form of slavery. The ancient Assyrian empire first sent its merchants in to enslave a people with debt in order to soften them up, before their armies marched in to enslave them militarily and politically. The word *"debt"* means *"death."* The French word *"mort," from which we derive our word "mortgage,"* means death. You know - *"mort,"* as in *"mortuary." "The wages of sin is death."*

If someone controls us economically, through debt or otherwise, then that person determines how we spend our time, with whom we spend our time, where we spend our time. This is not freedom. This is not liberty.

Because money represents a person's life, time and energy, control of a person's money economically is control of his life. This is why we dare not lend our money out to others for a meager rate of interest, particularly for economic development outside of the local area. OPM, *"other people's money,"* makes *"other people rich"* at our expense. This is one reason why Americans are unemployed. Their hard-earned money deposited in U.S. banks has been used to build factories in the former Soviet Union, Red China and Taiwan, for example. These overseas, American worker-financed factories produce cheap competitive goods which are shipped back to this country, throwing Americans out of work. Americans end up financing their own unemployment. If Christian banking existed in this country, as it exists in most Islamic/Moslem countries, the average American working man or woman could make 35% a year on his money. At this rate, our $100 deposit would be worth $200 in slightly over two years. You see, Mohammed took his economics from Moses, from the Old Testament of the Bible.

Excessive taxation ends up being a form of both economic and political slavery. Today we have an income tax. The graduated income tax was the second plank of Karl Marx's Communist Manifesto. As President Reagan remarked, *"The income tax is the brainchild of Karl Marx."*

The greatest tyrannical government bureaucracy of the ancient world was entrenched in Egypt. The Egyptian pharaohs enslaved the Hebrews of the Old Testament of the Bible. And yet, the maximum tax imposed by the Egyptian bureaucracy on its subjects was 20%. How many of us pay only 20% in taxes?

In the Middle Ages, the average serf worked only two or three days a week for his lord. The average serf only paid a tax of about 1/12 of his income. In the Old South, the average black slave forked over only 10% to 12% of his production to the slave owner. And the Viet Cong in Vietnam took only 30% from the peasants.

The higher the level of taxation, the greater the level of economic slavery in any society. It is obvious that we in the United States today are taxed at a higher rate than the slaves of both modern and ancient history. Beardsley Ruml, former chairman of the New York Federal Reserve, said that the real reasons for income taxes today are not to raise revenue. The central bank can do that. The real reasons for income taxes are to inhibit the inflation caused by government spending, to finance pork barrel projects, and to redistribute wealth.

Sure, it's true, we today do live in the most free country on the face of the earth. But freedom is relative. The problem is today the whole world is enslaved with both debt money and civil government law.

In 1800, less than 2% of free Americans worked for someone else. To work for someone else then was viewed as one tiny step above slavery. Today, however, 95% of Americans work for someone else. We need to dramatically encourage independent contractor status, and the establishment of Employee Stock Ownership Plans (ESOPs). Today too many American workers are pawns in the game of big finance, mergers, buyouts and takeovers.

Government is Religion Applied to Economics

Again, the body of freedom stands on the legs of both government/law and economics. And yet, government is always religion applied to economics. Every government legislates laws which are religious ideas about right and wrong, ethics, morality, and good and evil. Every government takes religious principles about right and wrong, good and evil, and then enacts these religious principles into laws that seem to fit the ever-changing facts of day-to-day society. These laws frame the arena of *"human action."* *"Human action"* is a working definition of economics. Therefore, government is always religion applied to economics.

The question is, *"Who is the final authority in the society?"* The buck does have to stop somewhere. *"Who is the lawmaker?"* Because all laws are religious ideas about right and wrong and good and evil, the lawmaker of any society (where the buck finally stops) is effectively the god of that society. And the lawmaker/god of a society determines the economic well-being of that society since laws determine and define economic activity. Just look at the differences between the economies of Mexico and the United States. The average American earns seven times that of the average Mexican. Latin America never had a decentralizing Protestant Reformation, which triggered a Protestant (religious) work (economics) ethic (government).

If we want true equality in our society, then *"all men must be equal under the law."* This legal concept is derived from the principle that *"all men are created equal"* under the law. What this means is that we can't have men make ultimate laws, or all men aren't truly equal under the law. Men cannot play god without going insane and becoming tyrants. Men cannot establish the ultimate laws, the ultimate principles of right and wrong, and good and evil. Men can only implement God-given laws and apply them economically to the society-at-large. This means our laws, if we're going to have true equality and justice in our society, must come from above both man and nature. This means our laws have to come from God. They have to be given to us supernaturally. Where both the *"spirit"* and the *"letter"* of the law of God exist - from whence we derive our concept of *"justice tempered with mercy"* - there all men are equal under the law. There freedom can exist.

Remember that we are told by our legal authorities that *"ignorance of the law is no excuse."* This phrase comes from our history when everyone knew the law of the land because everyone knew the law of God, based in the Ten Commandments. The Ten Commandments were taught in the homes, the churches and the schools. Who today, by contrast, can know or keep the approximate 3,500,000 civil laws?

Where there is legal equality, there is the basis for liberty. This is why the Bible in II Corinthians 3:17 declares, *"...where the Spirit of the Lord is there is liberty."*

Who do any of us trust to play God? What man do we trust to be our god and lawmaker? If we all hopped into our automobiles and drove down to the

Flathead County, Montana courthouse, there we would discover, etched in granite out beside the front steps of the county courthouse, two tablets containing
the Bible's Ten Commandments. Why does a granite monument containing the
Ten Commandments sit on the lawn outside the Flathead County courthouse?
To remind us that the purpose of our judicial civil servants is to implement the
laws of God according to the facts of the case, to remind us that government is
religion applied to economics.

The Flathead County Courthouse is not unique in this respect. Copies of
the Ten Commandments sit outside of courthouses all over this country. And
yet today, the Ten Commandments are ripped off the walls of the federally
funded public schools. Why? Because the federal government plays god today. The federal government is the final authority, the lawmaker, the god of
our society and that's what our children are taught. All education is inherently
religious because it involves a search for truth.

Government playing the role of god is the maximum distortion of reality,
because civil government is really an economic parasite, dependent upon taxes
paid by people like you and me.

The purpose and duty of politicians and judges is to apply the never-chang-
ing laws of God to the ever-changing facts of His creation. We still have *"In
God We Trust"* engraved on our coins. The President still puts his hand on the
Bible, historically on Deuteronomy, when he is sworn into office. We pledge
allegiance to *"one nation under God."*

Church and State

This does not mean there is not a separation of church and state. There
certainly is a separation of church and state. As John Calvin wrote, there must
clearly be a separation of church and state. Separation of church and state
means that the men who run the church are different from those men who run
the government, the state. The churchmen have the responsibility of communi-
cating the principles and meaning of God's laws to the politicians and judges.
But the politicians and judges bear the responsibility for the application of
God's laws to economic society.

The American Indians

An early American patriot, William Penn, declared, *"Men must be governed by God or they will be ruled by tyrants."* Men are ultimately either
freemen under God's governance or they are slaves to other men. We either
assume the risks of freedom under God or the risks of tyranny under men.
There is no such thing as a risk-free life. When men play god, or in other
words, when men are the ultimate lawmakers in a society, as is the case today,
they become tyrants, passing endless laws. Tyrannical government inescapably
leads to a loss of liberty and resultant economic poverty for *"we the people."*
For instance, just look at the plight of the American Indians under the Bureau

of Indian Affairs. According to noted black economist Dr. Walter Williams of George Mason University, if we took the Bureau of Indian Affair's entire budget in 1976, and divided it up equally among American Indian families of four members each, each American Indian family would receive an annual income in excess of $30,000 a year. Only slightly more than 11% of white American men make more than $30,000 a year. What does this tell us? It tells us that the federal government bureaucracies eat up our wealth while they regulate our freedom out of existence. Federal bureaucracies cost us four times the cost of meeting people's needs at the local level. Freedom stands on the legs of government/law and economics.

Just how well off today are the American Indians who live on the government's reservations? (The Indians have been the recipients of government welfare longer than anyone else.) According to the Department of the Interior, of American Indians who live on reservations, 58% are unemployed versus only 8% of Americans nationally. Forty-one percent of American Indians who live on the reservation live below the poverty line versus a 12% poverty rate for the nation-at-large. A startling 27% of these American Indians have less than an elementary education compared to only 10% in the rest of the country. Finally, 22% of American Indians are on welfare versus only about 8% of the rest of the country.

The point is simply this: We are not well-served, in fact, we are enslaved by government bureaucracies which also keep us poor. The Nobel Prize in economics went to James Buchanan for telling us, in public choice theory economics, that government bureaucrats and politicians make decisions to advance their own self-interest and not that of *"we the people."* Ironically, even government workers would enjoy greater peace and prosperity under a Christian government and economic system. Today there are 5100 bureaucrats for every elected official.

On the other hand, self-government, freedom and prosperity run hand-in-hand. Liberty means subordination only to God, not slavery to man, not slavery to anything manmade, not slavery to anything natural. Liberty means humility and obedience to God and His laws. Liberty means self-government. Liberty means being out of debt and having savings and honest money.

Liberty: Our Founding Fathers' Perspective

Government is always religion applied to economics. When a God and His law come supernaturally from above and outside of nature, men have established where the buck ultimately stops. Final authority and responsibility for justice are established. It is no accident, but rather cause and effect, that this country has enjoyed the greatest liberty and prosperity in the history of the world. Why? Because this Christian civilization is based on a God and His absolute laws which come from above and outside of nature, leaving Americans self-governing. Founding Father James Madison declared, *"We have stacked the whole of all our political institutions upon the capacity of mankind for self-government, upon the capacity of each and all of us to govern ourselves, to control ourselves, to sustain ourselves according to the Ten Commandments of God."*

Dr. M.E. Bradford of the University of Dallas discovered that of the 55 men who drew up the U.S. Constitution, 30 were orthodox Christians. These 30 men understood in their own way that Jesus Christ is the personal embodiment of how government is religion applied to economics. Jesus Christ is both our Savior <u>and</u> our example. Jesus Christ, in his humanity, was perfectly self-governing. He perfectly kept the Law. Jesus Christ, as King of Kings, is the Lawgiver and Judge. That's government. Jesus Christ is the personal incarnation of God Himself. He is Lord of Lords. That's religion. Jesus Christ is Creator and Sustainer of the universe. That's economics. Government is religion applied to economics. John tells us in his gospel, chapter 8 verse 36: *"...if the Son sets you free, you shall be free indeed."* That's liberty!

Rome

In the latter days of the Roman Empire, when Constantine was emperor in the 4th century, the Roman courts were so corrupt that even Roman citizens went to the Christian church courts of law to be judged under biblical law in order to receive true justice. Constantine, recognizing the popularity of the church courts of law, brought them under the umbrella of the Roman Empire. He made the Christian courts of law and their judges the legal courts of Rome. We still see evidence of this today in the purple robes worn by some members of our clergy.

The Middle Ages

In Western civilization, beginning in the Middle Ages, historian Richard Maybury discovered that our common law had its roots in biblical law, specifically the Ten Commandments, and the first five books of the Old Testament of the Bible. During the Middle Ages, many of the courts of justice were run by the clergy. The two basic root principles of our common law are: (1) *"Do all you have agreed to do;"* and (2) *"Do not encroach on other people and their property."* In other words, men are required to keep their word and to honor their covenants and contracts. Men are held responsible and accountable for their representations and commitments. Additionally, a person's life and property are sacred. Notice how perfectly this extends from the Ten Commandments, The Golden Rule, and Christ's Second Great Commandment.

William Blackstone was an 18th century English jurist whose *Commentaries on the Laws of England* deeply influenced the development of common law. The following quotation is inscribed on the wall of the Supreme Court of Pennsylvania in the state capital at Harrisburg: *"The Law of Nature dictated by God himself is Superior to any other. It is binding over all the Globe, in all countries and at all times. No human laws are of any validity if contrary to this, and such of them as are valid derive all of their force and all their authority mediately and immediately from this Original. Upon these two foundations, the Law of Nature and the Law of Revelation depend all human laws. Human laws are only declaratory of and act in subordination to Divine Law."*

See how closely religion is related to laws and economics? G.N. Clark, in his history, *The Wealth of England From 1496 to 1760*, pointed this out very clearly, as did Fortescue, Lord High Chancellor under Henry VI in his book, *Praise the Laws of England*. Quoting Sir John Fortescue concerning English life in the 15th century: *"...The King can not alter the laws, or make new ones without the express consent of the whole people in Parliament assembled. Every inhabitant is at his liberty fully to use and enjoy whatever his farm produceth, the fruits of the earth, the increase of his flocks and the like. All the improvements he makes, whether by his own proper industry, or of those he retains in his service, are his own, to use and enjoy without the interruption or denial of any. If he be in anywise injured, or oppressed, he shall have his demands and satisfaction against the party offending. Hence it is, the inhabitants are rich in gold, unless at certain times upon a religious score, and by way of doing penance. They are fed in great abundance with all sorts of flesh and fish, of which they have plenty everywhere; they are clothed throughout with good woolens; their bedding and other furniture in their houses are of wool, and that in great score. They are also well-provided with all sorts of household goods and necessary implements for husbandry...and all have all things which conduce to make life easy and happy..."*

How many of us are this well off today?

Four Modern Monopolies

Since we have lost our biblically based common law, how much governmental, legal and economic freedom do we have remaining today? Remember our earlier discussion of monopolies. Both Presidents Woodrow Wilson and Andrew Jackson told us that monopolies are contrary to our governmental and economic self-interest. Then why today have we granted an effective legal monopoly to the American Bar Association? An outrageous 96% of the civil lawsuits globally are filed in this country. Two-thirds of all the lawyers in the world practice in this country. According to a Harris poll, only 15% of Americans have *"a great deal of confidence"* in lawyers, and yet 60% of U.S. senators are lawyers. Today, we have one lawyer for every 354 Americans. Are our lawyer gods going to bring about peace and prosperity by having us sue each other and by passing endless laws? Jeffrey Nugent's University of Southern California study found that in 52 nations, economic growth slowed in direct proportion to the number of lawyers.

And why have we granted an economic money monopoly to the Federal Reserve? American individuals, families and businesses are saddled today with an overwhelming debt. The federal government owes over $4 trillion. Americans' real income has fallen since 1973, and the median income of Americans is only slightly over $12,000 a year. The United States is the most indebted country in the world today.

Furthermore, how can we think and feel we are free when our thinking is monopolized by our educational system, and our health, physical, mental and emotional feelings are subjected to a medical monopoly granted to the American Medical Association? Out of 165 nations rated, the United States ranks between 40th and 50th in both education and health care. We have upwards of 60 million Americans today who are functionally illiterate.

The Geometry of Freedom

The geometry of liberty, the geometry of freedom, is always horizontal, side-to-side. The geometry of slavery is always vertical, up and down. Freedom is man with man, operating according to the law of the contract, based in Christian common law. Slavery is man over man, which is vertical in nature. Free men work and contract for a living. Slaves live off others.

The Contract

Let's focus on the covenant and contract. The covenant and contract is horizontal, side-to-side. A contract is a peaceful means by which man interacts with man. Contract law is therefore the operational basis of liberty in common law and biblical law, whether the contract is a handshake, a verbal agreement, or a written instrument. The contract is the instrument of freedom.

Every contract is governmental, religious and economic in nature. A contract is governmental because it is a legal document which describes the rights, duties, benefits and punitive damages of both the party of the first part and the party of the second part. A contract is religious because it is a moral document, no better than the character and ethics of the two parties to the contract. A contract is finally an economic document because it defines the exchange of economic goods and services to be given and received by the parties to the contract for their mutual benefit. The contract establishes voluntary equality between free men.

Even God operates by way of a contract. The Old Testament and the New Testament mean the Old Contract and the New Contract. Further, the contract resolves the basic religious, political and economic question which today is both the unasked and unanswered question. This question dominates every society. The question is, *"How do you balance off the rights of the individual with those of the collective masses?"* *"How do you establish unity amid diversity?"* *"How does an individual get along peacefully with everyone else?"* The answer is only by the use of the contract, based in common law, which stems from biblical law. Thus, it was no accident that in Old Testament times, contracts were established between individuals outside the gates of the city in open public forum. An open contract meets both the needs of the individual and society. A contract resolves conflict. Both parties win. A contract, after all, is a barter arrangement. This is why barter money, honest money, is contract money - commodity money, not debt money. We had private money mints in this country in places like California and Colorado up until about the time of the Civil War. This free market money was preferred to government money.

The U.S. Constitution

The U.S. Constitution is a contract between *"we the people"* and the federal government. The ultimate purpose of the U.S. Constitution is to maximize and protect the freedom of individuals. The Constitution was intended to provide the framework to protect the self-government of individuals and their families, with primarily local government established in the nuclear family, then the extended family, then the government for the local church, the local school, the local workplace, and the local community. All of these separate local governments, each under God, set up a system of checks and balances, a balance of power which allowed liberty to flourish.

The U.S. Constitution grants appropriate limiting powers to the states. And finally, the U.S. Constitution established a federal government, and at the same time, according to Jefferson, chained the federal government by both limiting its powers and establishing a division and separation of powers. The primary purpose of any federal government should be limited to the enforcement of contracts, the prevention and punishment of fraud, and to provide for protection of its citizens against revolt, insurrection, revolution and invasion by all enemies, both foreign and domestic. The federal government has no business having any involvement in the production, distribution or use of economic resources. The purpose of the federal government is not to keep us as children and slaves, or to protect us against our own foolishness and mistakes. The purpose of the federal government is not to provide for us economically. As responsible, free men, we are to do that ourselves by way of the contract.

The first ten Amendments to the U.S. Constitution comprise the Bill of Rights. The purpose of this Bill of Rights is to protect the liberty of the individual. Thomas Jefferson wrote to James Madison, *"...a bill of rights is what the people are entitled to against every government on earth."* Dr. Erwin N. Griswold, Dean of Harvard Law School declared, *"The right to be left alone is the underlying principle of the Constitution's Bill of Rights."*

North Carolina did not ratify the U.S. Constitution until the Bill of Rights was added. And incidentally, Rhode Island was the last of the original 13 states to ratify the Constitution. Rhode Island wanted cheap, counterfeit, paper money. But Rhode Island lost out. The other states would have no part of such monetary fraud.

In a 1987 poll by the Hearst Corporation regarding the U.S. Constitution, it was learned that almost 50% of Americans wrongly thought the U.S. Constitution contained the Marxist communist phrase, *"From each according to his ability, to each according to his need."* Forty-two percent of Americans wrongly believed the U.S. Constitution guaranteed the right to free health care; 75% incorrectly believed the U.S. Constitution guaranteed the right to a free public education through high school; and 54% of Americans mistakenly thought the federal government could restrict the right to publish and distribute printed matter.

Free Men and Slaves

There is no left wing or right wing. There are no conservatives or liberals. There are only two kinds of people, free men and slaves. Slaves take the easy way out short-term and reap hell long-term. Free men understand the importance of short-term pain for long-term gain. Slaves are takers. Free men are givers. Free men give when they contract for goods and services before they receive back the benefits of the contractual exchange. Free men thus resolve the governmental, religious and economic conflict between individual rights and group rights. This is why it is always more blessed to give than to receive. These free men are thus the ultimate resources of any society.

There are two types of takers, two kinds of slaves. One type of slave is a parasite who depends upon others to take care of him. Such a slave is effectively a child, whether he is four years old or forty. Today 81 million Americans live off the government while 71 million pay taxes. Presently 80% of all Americans have their lives directly or indirectly affected by government programs. How free are *"we the people?"* At age 65, only 2% of Americans are financially self-sufficient.

The second type of slave is a predator who preys on other people. A predator takes advantage of those under him. Predators include bureaucrats and those who operate with OPM, other people's money. Both types of slaves, parasites and predators, prey on other people. Parasites take from the people.

Requirements of Freedom

It should be obvious that in order for us to be free, we must contract for what we need, for the goods and services we require. Any time we let someone *"take care of us,"* like the government, we lose our freedom. We must husband our resources and our money. We must not depend upon others, or prey upon others, even if it is by government-granted license, monopoly, extortion, privilege, or special favor. Remember that government involvement in economics is both immoral and criminal. It is both theft and a curse long-term. Because an individual has no right to steal the property of another individual, it therefore follows that government collectively has no right on behalf of individuals to steal property from other productive individuals. *"Thou shalt not steal."*

Without exception, as black economist Dr. Walter Williams has demonstrated, any benefit that government involvement in economics brings short-term always creates a worse problem long-term. A quick example: Federal government involvement in public education has led to far greater rate of black illiteracy now than in the 1930s. Federal welfare has resulted in the emasculation of the black American male and the subsequent destruction of the black family. Today nearly one out of two black babies born in this country are illegitimate due primarily to welfare incentives.

When we contract for what we need, we are effectively self-governing. After all, self-government is the only thing that works long-term. Civil government law does not work. When men are evil, legislated laws are broken. When men can be entrusted to become self-governing, legislated laws are unnecessary.

Four Virtues Necessary to Contract

To be able to contract successfully requires four virtues. These four virtues are the four basic virtues in the Bible. They are humility, empathy, responsibility and duty. To be able to contract successfully we have to have the humility to listen, to learn, to ask, to grow, to change, to admit we're wrong, to ask for forgiveness, to serve, and to give before receiving. We have to have the empathy to understand and meet our fellow man's needs through our contracts. We have to take responsibility for ourselves, our families, and our property. We have to perform our duties to our fellow man, to allow him his liberty as he allows us ours, to keep our word and honor our commitments and contracts at all times.

When we exercise humility, empathy, responsibility and duty as we contract with our fellow man, we are inevitably required to take the long-term view. The long-term road is always the road traveled by free and successful men. Every biblical principle for self-government is long-term in nature. Civil government, by contrast, always fills the vacuum of unbelief and irresponsibility with slavery.

Guns and Butter

What about society? What about *"guns and butter?"* Primarily the nuclear family, the extended family and the local church (by way of the congregation's offerings) should be responsible for the health, education and welfare needs of the people - the *"butter"* needs. Today in America, if each church took responsibility for just one family on welfare, there would be no welfare in America. Women and children account for 77% of those in poverty today. The local church is God's voluntary collective. The local church is God's answer to socialism and communism. Communism and socialism always fill the vacuum of unbelief and social irresponsibility. See Acts chapter 2 and II Corinthians 8 and 9.

And *"guns?"* A local militia and civil defense should be our primary line of defense. This is what our Founding Fathers intended. This is what functions so effectively today in both Switzerland and Israel. We cannot afford either the expense or devastation of a military/industrial complex, built to protect us against our World War II ally, the former Soviet Union, particularly since the former U.S.S.R. was and is today still financed by U.S. banks and U.S. tax-payer-subsidized world banks. Responsible businessmen and local government can fill in the gaps in the *"guns and butter"* equation.

Changes Necessary for Freedom

By now, it should be clear that we have a lot of work to do, not if we are to remain free, but if we are to regain our lost freedoms. If Presidents Woo-drow Wilson and Andrew Jackson are correct, we are now third generation slaves. We need to do something besides watch seven hours worth of mindless TV a day.

Our state governments need to force the federal government to balance the budget. We need to establish a high-tech, local, Swiss-type militia and civil de-fense system. We need to return to having the state houses elect U.S. senators. We need to provide tax breaks and incentives for those individuals who give their tithes and offerings to local churches that specifically meet the health, education and welfare needs of the people at the local level. We need tax breaks for men and women who opt out of the Social Security contract to take care of their elderly parents. We need to establish tax incentives for employee-owned businesses, fam-ily-owned businesses and small, locally-owned businesses. We need to abolish both the income tax and the property tax. All we require long-term are a head tax for men and perhaps a state and national sales tax.

We need the elimination of debt money and the Federal Reserve, and in-stead establish free market, honest commodity money as recommended by Jef-ferson, Jackson and Lincoln. We need to outlaw inflationary fractional reserve banking. We need to limit debt to less than seven years. We need to privatize all state and federal government involvement in economics. We need to estab-lish Spanish Mondragon-type economic cooperatives and Lebanese-type family associations. These are workable, proven, successful, social *"safety nets."* For over 40 years the Christian bank and economic cooperatives at Mondragon, Spain have not had a bad loan or a single business failure. Not one! And these people are among the most progressive, successful, productive, secure and happy people on earth, according to the Anglo-German Foundation for the Study of Industrial Society.

We need to put our best legal minds and scientists to work to rediscover how God's law works for our own benefit and blessing long-term. We need legally to return to biblical law, our common law heritage and contract law. We need a Switzerland-type citizen-initiated referendum. The primary basis of criminal and civil justice should be the biblical principle of restitution, to make things right. With 69% repeat criminal offenders, we can't do any worse, par-ticularly at a cost of $20,000 per inmate per year. The basis for both making and judging the law, in terms of the facts of the case, should lie ultimately with the jury. Judges should be elected. All government granted monopolies, li-censes and privileges should be abolished. Change should be implemented gradually, over seven years, by way of sunset laws. Tax incentives meanwhile should be provided for progressive decentralization, for returning responsibility for self-government to the local level.

We need to establish strict limitations on the absentee ownership of land by individuals, large corporations and governments, such as is the case today in Switzerland and Bermuda. This should be done at the county level. No man should own more land than he can turn into a garden, or that destroys the spirit of community. This is the economic lesson of Leviticus 25.

These are the lessons of liberty. Etched on our Liberty Bell in Philadelphia are the words *"Proclaim Liberty throughout all the Land unto the Inhabitants thereof."* This phrase was taken from Leviticus 25:10. We need to ring out that biblical phrase throughout all the land today. We need to let freedom ring!

A BANK MEN CAN BANK ON:
THE MONDRAGON EXPERIMENT

March 31, 1988

Tucked away in the Pyrenees mountains of northeastern Spain, nestled in a long-persecuted area known as the Basque, lies the all but unknown village of Mondragon. Establishment forces have many times attempted to oppress the people there. For example, in this century during the 1920s, many Basque towns and villages were active in the Spanish anarchist movement. The people even went so far as to eliminate government money from their villages and replace it with a simple barter system. Not only does this financial action show the fierce independence and rugged individuality of the area, but it also demonstrates that these people have some idea about what real money and honest economics are all about.

The Basque stood and fought against Franco. When Franco achieved victory, he outlawed their language and required them to speak Spanish. All this did was reinforce the solidarity and community spirit of these rugged people.

In 1941, a Catholic priest who had fought in the Spanish Civil War, Father Jose Maria Arizmendi, was assigned to Mondragon. Father Arizmendi, understanding that faith without works is dead (James 2), began implementing social and economic systems at Mondragon which prove indeed that religion does come down to economics (human action). Since the Catholic Church had never officially supported either capitalism or socialism, Father Arizmendi sought to pull the best from both systems for use in his development plans at Mondragon.

It is not surprising that this priest was successful. For, since debt capitalism emphasized radical individualism and socialism stresses radical collectivism, if the strong points of both systems can be harmonized, then the basic problem of humanity is resolved, to wit: *How do you balance off the rights of individuals with those of collective society?*

Despite nearly a half century of success, Father Arizmendi's work at Mondragon is just now coming to light. The BBC produced a film entitled, *"Mondragon: An Experiment."* Perhaps the most knowledgeable individual on Mondragon in the United States is Dr. Terry Mollner, who authored *The Mondragon Cooperatives and Trusteeship* (Trusteeship Institute, Inc., Shutesbury, MA). Dr. Mollner also wrote a short summary of the history and results of the Mondragon economic experiment for the April 1986 issue of *Green Revolution* (R.D. 1, Spring Grove, PA 17362). The facts concerning Mondragon are drawn largely from Dr. Mollner's work.

The linear sequence from the abstract to the concrete runs as follows: religion - philosophy - creative ideas unifying thoughts with matter - work - material achievement (economics). Father Arizmendi struck the right sequence and chords in human nature in structuring both his worker cooperatives and the bank at Mondragon. Small wonder then that his economic experiment is successful. Thoughts precede action. Ideas have consequences. When the rights of the individual (capitalism) are balanced off with the rights of collective society (socialism/communism), harmony results.

The strengths of pure capitalism are its emphasis on individual character development, professional performance of a task, freedom, incentive to work, the primary use of the contract which permits horizontal relationships (equality), and finally when correctly formulated, that self-interest is only served as a byproduct of first serving one's fellow man. The worst of capitalism - dog-eat-dog evolutionary conflict for the survival of the fittest, OPM, debt money which is not a commodity, and competition for the purpose of win/lose - is discarded.

The worst aspects of communism/socialism are also discarded - forced cooperation and communal activity (slavery) enforced by a militaristic, oppressive bureaucracy, no individual incentive to be productive or to work, no individuality which allows the development, expression and free use of one's unique God-given talents. The best of communism/socialism is retained - the idea that *workers should be the owners of the means of production* (if they earn it), the emphasis on cooperation, harmony and community spirit, *the greatest good for the greatest number,* but not at the expense of killing individualism. (Balance must be maintained.)

While no student of economic theory, Father Arizmendi stumbled upon the reality that economic prosperity only flourishes long-term in an environment of cooperation rather than conflict. (Competition rightfully implemented short-term is only for the purpose of serving, not win/lose. If conflict produced economic prosperity, there would be no such thing as *flight capital.* Instead, people would invest in Lebanon, Nicaragua, Iran, etc.) Father Arizmendi, because he was a priest, captured this cooperative idea in terms of a primary characteristic of God - *love. God is love.* Because of God's love, he effectively reasoned, *people* are more important than *things.* Furthermore, when and where there is *love* between *people,* they treat *things* differently than where conflict exists. Where there is *love,* there is more voluntary sharing, justice, and give and take - more cooperation concerning *things.* Where there is not *love,* however, where conflict reigns between men, *things* become a catalyst for even greater conflict. Instead of sharing, there exists hoarding, envy, theft, suspicion, injustice and greed. *Things* become more important than *people* in a conflict-ridden society which lacks *love.*

Matter exists in time and space. On the other hand, people and their relationships can become timeless and spaceless. Therefore, *people* are more important than *things.* With this handle on economic reality, Father Arizmendi set to work.

Permit me to digress for a moment and put into American economic terms the similarity between this writer's work and that of this Spanish Catholic philosopher. The work of Father Arizmendi is akin in both philosophy and in implementation to what I came up with for Guatemala when I worked there in 1983.

There are only two parts of the economic equation: land and labor, or in other words, *people* and *things*. *People* are more important than *things* because *people* determine the production, distribution and use of *things*. *People* make and destroy *things,* including money. Stated differently, all problems are human problems.

Man faces four basic conflicts on this earth: conflict with God, conflict within himself, conflict with his fellow man, and conflict with nature. When these four conflicts are resolved, peace and prosperity exist on earth. God is served, our fellow man is served, and we ourselves are served, in a healthy environment. This is much of what my last book, *No Time For Slaves*, is all about. This is a win-win-win covenant.

The final point of progression of Father Arizmendi's work, the crowning glory of his economic experiment, is the Caja Laboral Popular *("The Bank of the People's Labor")*. This bank, headquartered in Mondragon, is active in nearly every village throughout the Basque region of Spain. This cooperative bank has 120 branches, and is both a custodian and investor of the deposits of nearly 400,000 families. Not bad expansion for a bank founded in a church basement 30 years ago (1958).

This bank has a clearly defined objective: to create worker-owned jobs for the community. So in its purpose, The Bank of the People's Labor has given incentive to individuals to work and also become owners of the means of production for the purpose of serving their fellow man, and as a byproduct, serving themselves. And it all began with a man who was seeking first to serve God. As a result, the Mondragon bank has a 100 percent success rate at forming industrial cooperatives and making loans. It has experienced no failures. By contrast, in the United States, only one out of ten new businesses will survive the first five years. But then again, the investment philosophy and approach of the Mondragon bank is to invest in *people*, not *things*. As we have already seen, *people* are more important than *things*, for good or for evil. Therefore, the best investment is always in *people*, if *people* can become the ultimate resource, rather than a predator or a parasite in society.

The investment priorities of the Mondragon bank are: (1) workers; (2) managers; (3) the goods or service to be produced; and (4) capital/money. This is just the opposite of what exists under the Western debt capitalistic system today. Here the emphasis is on: (1) capital; (2) the goods or service; (3) management; and (4) workers.

Western debt capitalism and communism both stress the development of capital/*things*. (Dialectic *materialism* is basic to communism.) But because capital/money is effectively stored energy or stored labor, we inevitably get back to the character, professionalism, incentive and work habits of *people* as primary for producing *things*, or for making money. So we are reaping what we have sown today in the West. Because we put *things* first - *things* before *people* - we are under economic, political, social and spiritual distress. Only 2% of Americans are financially and economically self-sufficient at the age 65, while 96 percent are flat broke, or dependent upon shaky pensions, bankrupt Social Security, etc. to stay alive economically. Then we have the bankrupt federal government and the pitiful U.S. dollar. We are effectively bankrupt economically as a society.

Debt capitalism does not produce *the greatest good for the greatest number*, either. Far from it. Only two-tenths of 1% of all Americans are millionaires. Only 15% of Americans are capitalists these days. The bureaucrats who produce nothing constructive consume our wealth, if the international banks don't give it or loan it away first. And 3% of the U.S. population owns 85% of the private land in the United States. This is worse than in El Salvador. In California, only 1% of the population owns two-thirds of the private land.

Spiritually, we are also dead ducks. Our sad spiritual state of affairs is readily seen by the fact that the largest sales in U.S. drug stores are for: (1) Mylanta; (2) Anacin; and (3) Bayer aspirin. In dollar amount of sales in U.S. drug stores, No. 2 is Anacin, No. 3 is Tylenol, and No. 4 is Advil. The bankruptcy of our governmental, religious and economic systems is literally giving all of us a collective headache and worse. The cancer death rate is up 8.7%. We are in a death spiral downward. Further reflecting this death spiral, the United States ranks first globally in military expenditures, and leads the world in military technology, military bases globally, and nuclear warheads and bombs.

Of course, it's worse under communism. There the bureaucracy is far more extensively developed. (Bureaucracy is the greatest institutional manifestation of human evil.) The greatest class distinctions economically in the world existed in the former Soviet Union. The high ranking members of the Communist Party and their obedient bureaucrats lived like kings, like gods, while the masses of people stood in line to buy toilet paper. Furthermore, every Russian woman on average has six abortions, while Russian men drink themselves to death. The eyes of the people of the former U.S.S.R. show no sparkle of life. Reflecting this, the former U.S.S.R. ranked 44th globally in life expectancy and second in weapons' expenditures. The U.S. and the former U.S.S.R. together, with less than 11% of the world's population, account for 60% of global military expenditures, 80% of the weapons research, and 97% of all nuclear weapons. It's a miserable life at either extreme of individualism (debt capitalism) or collectivism (communism).

Because Mondragon has discovered rightfully that *people* are more important than *things*, the Mondragon bank invests first and foremost in *people*. The Mondragon bankers figure the goods or service produced will be self-perpetuating in time. If the investment is made in the right people, and people can work cooperatively, professionally, effectively and efficiently, then the bank and business can always change the goods or service produced to meet the needs of the marketplace.

Based in this philosophy of a primary investment in people, because the bank is a cooperative bank where the people themselves have a stake, the result is that the entire community backs the bank and the businesses it creates. The entire community is business-oriented. The workers, managers, owners, consumers and bankers as owners of the means of production are all one and the same, or at least closely tied to one another. People in Mondragon are literally investing in themselves. Business is a blessing at Mondragon in the Basque region, rather than the curse it has become here in the West.

Furthermore, the bank backs the people and their businesses when they get into trouble. Why shouldn't it be that way? The people are simply backing themselves. In fact, the bank makes a commitment to both the people involved and the business to back them until they succeed. If the goods or service produced has to be changed, so what? It's changed. *People* are more important than *things*. *People* produce *things*. Therefore, the primary investment is in *people*! You can desert the *thing*, but not the *people*.

If a business falls on hard times or is struggling, the bank's entrepreneurial division has a policy of lowering the interest rate on loans to these worker-owned cooperatives as business gets riskier. This is a long-term view. *Short-term pain for long-term gain* has always been necessary for success in any human endeavor. At Mondragon, *all for one and one for all* voluntarily, with incentives, maintains balance because workers, managers, owners, the bank depositors, the bank and consumers are all one and the same and all tied together. Everyone has a vested interest in seeing that every worker-owned business is ultimately successful. This further provides lifetime job security, even though the business itself may change by way of new or different goods or service, depending on what the market demands. Crisis management is thereby also avoided. Stress is minimized if not mostly eliminated.

If these people had honest free market money, based in some ultimate physical reality, such as they effectively did during the Spanish Civil War, the sky would be the limit economically.

Can we as Americans imagine an economic and financial system where our investments are secure, our savings are indeed safe and growing in real terms, without inflation or deflation, where workers do not have to worry about absentee ownership, new management, being fired, transferred, or losing their jobs due to a plant or business closing?

Just how does a business get started at Mondragon? First of all, a group of men (friends) voluntarily get together and decide they want to start a new business. So people who already have a covenantal and contractual relationship with one another (love), get together and decide to work together (things/money). Thus, spiritual and economic realities are in basic harmony to begin with. Each member of this business starter group has to *put his money where his mouth is*. He is required to have a financial stake in the venture. He is required to be a true capitalist. Each member loans the business some of his own capital. Therefore, the individual group members are literally at risk. Then they go to the bank.

At the Mondragon bank, the bank's entrepreneurial division interviews the business starter group regarding their request for the bank's assistance. The bank's first priority is to determine if there is truly a loving bond and solid relationship between the various people in the proposed business start-up group. This is the basis, the foundation, for the new business - people and love. If the bank is happy with both the character and covenantal relationships of the group members seeking to start a new business, the bank then joins into a partnership with the business on behalf of its depositors, for the purpose of creating this new worker-owned cooperative.

Both the bank and the group desiring to form the new business are committed to work and provide capital until the business is running profitably, effectively and efficiently. Everyone has a stake in the venture, both short-term and long-term. The investment is by way of both *people* and *capital*, with the priorities being in that correct order, followed by *things* or *service*.

Next, democracy comes into play. The business start-up group meets by itself and chooses one of its members to be the manager of the new business. Next, important long-term strategic planning commences. This elected manager is required to spend two years working with an expert of the bank for the purpose of developing both a plan for the business and a community development plan. Thus, the goals of the individuals of the business group are required to be in harmony with those of the community generally. Community considerations such as housing, parks, commercial development and other community services are considered.

Now, when all this is eventually accomplished, the goods or service to be produced is finalized. This product or service must be determined to be in the best interest of the people of the community long-term before the bank will finance it in partnership with the business group. In other words, the people are deciding with their own money what they really want in the marketplace and their community. Consumer sovereignty is effectively king by determining producer investment.

Now, practically speaking, the process is not all this cut and dried. The group of friends who decided they wanted to work together and form a business to serve the community (and as a byproduct meet their personal needs), had a good idea going in about what goods or service they wanted to produce, before they got into partnership with the bank and established their worker-owned jobs. The members of the group came together, bringing their strengths of character, commitment and specialized professional skills, such as in electronics. It's how they will use these skills, let's say in electronic technology, to produce a specific electronic product which is decided last of all.

An extensive market study is conducted to determine the true needs of the community. In fact, everything that makes for a successful business is carefully covered at Mondragon. Most businesses fail due to insufficient capital, poor accounting, inadequate and inept management, labor problems, no strategic or tactical business plan, no marketing plan, and goods or a service produced which is not desired by the marketplace. All of these problems are solved front end, going in, to the maximum extent possible, before the business ever gets off the ground at Mondragon. No wonder Mondragon has a 100% success rate. They are doing everything right. Success - making honest money - is a byproduct of doing things correctly.

The bank's entrepreneurial division has two bank worker-owners who are involved full time in identifying new products needed by the community, which require new businesses to produce them. So the emphasis is clearly on research and development, and production over and against consumption. Smart! This is true, progressive capitalism. Furthermore, down the line if the manager is found to be incompetent, he is demoted back to the group and a new manager is chosen. He is not fired, just demoted. If the product or service is found to be inviable, a new product or service is developed, even if it means new, expensive capital equipment has to be purchased. So, excellence in both people and product are demanded at Mondragon. Incompetence and failure are rectified in a caring, loving way. These Mondragon cooperative businesses stress both responsiveness to the marketplace by way of consumer demanded goods or services, as well as excellence in individual productivity and management. Small wonder the bank has never suffered a loan default.

Mondragon, with its primary and correct emphasis on people, finds group strength is a function of individual strength coming together voluntarily in a loving and supportive atmosphere. Individuals find themselves and meet both their love and money needs by voluntary, contractual exchange (with incentives for hard work), by giving themselves in their service to their community. Thus, the balance between their individual self-identity and the community's collective identity are in balance. Harmony, peace and prosperity inescapably have resulted.

Since 1958, the Mondragon Bank of the People's Labor has produced 20,000 worker-owned jobs and over 100 cooperative businesses. Eighty-six of these cooperatives are industrial enterprises. These industrial enterprises produce everything from home appliances, such as toasters and refrigerators, to tools, such as sophisticated die presses, down to plastic rulers.

These eighty-six cooperative industrial enterprises are the top producers in all of Spain. Their productivity per worker is also the highest in that country. Their profitability is nearly double that of their competitors. An independent study by the Anglo-German Foundation for the Study of Industrial Society found the management of these cooperatives (which was chosen by the group of owner-workers and approved by the bank) to be some of the most aggressive and innovative ever witnessed by the Foundation's staff. Needless to say, these worker-owners were also found by the Foundation to be highly motivated and fulfilled by their jobs. If we do things right, things usually turn out right, given justice and honest money.

Projects other than industrial ventures have proven to be successful as well. There are pre-order and storefront-type food cooperatives which have been successfully established. A consumer cooperative, Eroski, has 120,000 members and 72 stores throughout the Basque region. Some are small mom and pop-type operations. Others are more like K-Mart. Additionally, there are six agricultural cooperatives, fourteen housing cooperatives, forty-three cooperative schools, and four separate cooperatives which provide services to the other cooperatives. These four service cooperatives are the bank itself, a technical research institute, a League of Education and Culture (which has a technological division, a business and professional school), and a social security and medical cooperative. In other words, the people through their work and productivity in their own businesses, and through their own bank, have financed their own health, education and welfare needs. Government involvement is not only unnecessary, it is totally unwanted!

Can we imagine the results of totally eliminating the civil government's involvement in economics and in the health, education and welfare segments of the federal budget? HHS is the largest item in the federal budget. The simple people of Mondragon are telling us that such civil government involvement is totally unnecessary, not to mention the fact that HHS primarily serves the bureaucrats and doesn't really meet the needs of the people whom it purports to serve.

Give these tough-minded people at Mondragon their own high-tech self-defense militia, which they would naturally gravitate toward anyway, along with a good civil defense, and no power on earth could challenge them. (This is why the world leaves Israel and Switzerland alone. The people in Israel and Switzerland are responsible for their own defense, beginning on the local level.)

Local civil government is more responsive, frugal and responsible. Civil government literally becomes what it should be, a service for which the people contract (a constitution), for the limited purpose of providing for defense against all enemies foreign and domestic, for putting down insurrections, revolutions and riots, and for enforcing contracts. That's it, the total purpose of civil government. Civil government has no legitimate function in economics, in the areas of the production, distribution, or use of resources.

There is an aspect of the Mondragon worker-owner program with which I take issue (in addition to their lack of free market, honest, commodity money). The salary scale among the worker-owner group business cooperatives is restricted. No worker-owner can receive a salary greater than four and one-half times that of the lowest paid worker in the worker-owned business. While this keeps economic equity (and therefore real power) balanced in the community, it would seem to come at the expense of maximizing incentive long-term. (By the way, the salary ratio from the highest to the lowest paid worker in the United States today exceeds 100 to 1.) Furthermore, because the lowest salary paid is only slightly above minimum wage, the highest salary paid at Mondragon is significantly lower than the salaries paid to men who work in the more conventional business sector. However, because these Mondragon workers are owners of the means of production, the worker-owners' share of profits usually makes up for the lower salary.

It would seem that the percentage of the profits and dividends paid by the business each year should be in proportion to the contribution made, and therefore include, the salary earned by each individual worker-owner. In other words, in this manner, a natural aristocracy would arise. Those who earn more will be those who produced and therefore served the most. Who could argue with this? An individual who has worked and produced to provide *the greatest good for the greatest number* is entitled to the greatest reward. Additionally, a buyout arrangement between worker-owners and/or the bank would quickly resolve any irreconcilable personal differences between men in the business, or facilitate a job change if desired.

As I reflect on all I've written above, it becomes clear how we in America have lost our way. The destructive and death-rendering consequences of our era are all around us - in our families, our health, our communities, our economic and financial systems, our jobs, our governments, our legal system, our medical bureaucracies, our educational institutions, our military-industrial complex, our labor unions, our courts and in our religious institutions. We are individually and collectively bankrupt, literally caught in an accelerating death spiral. But there is hope. We are not dead yet. Our heritage is that of the greatest spiritual and economic freedom the world has ever seen, given to us by God-fearing, self-governing men. And we now have with Mondragon the abstract and concrete solutions. We have the spiritual and economic answers necessary to put our national house back in order. Furthermore, we have the technology necessary to achieve these desirable ends. The only question is whether we have the faith, the individual and national character, and the will to go to work to change things. If we do, then a glorious future awaits us long-term. If we do not, then we will effectively, by our sins (errors) of omission and commission, commit suicide. We shall die.

The choice is ours. The two paths available are clearly before us. One is easy short-term, but brings death long-term. This is the path we are on presently. The other path is painful short-term, but brings the abundant life long-term. We will reap what we sow. The people at Mondragon were worse off than we are now when they got started. They turned things around. Can we do any less?

MONDRAGON: FINAL REFLECTIONS
April 27, 1988

The Nature of Society

Human action is never static. Anytime we're coasting, we're headed downhill. We are either building up or we are tearing down. We are either acting constructively or destructively. Destruction comes naturally.

There is nothing quite like a crisis to bring out the true character and mettle of a people. When the pressure is on, people either pull together or they tear each other apart. A people's spiritual values, the laws which stem from these religious roots, and the individual and collective behavior patterns taught and applied, determine largely whether a people will pull through together during tough times, or self-destruct.

In this sense, people reap what they sow. People cannot for long act contrary to their religious beliefs, mental perspectives, internalized laws, cultural indoctrination and habits, for when the pressure is on, most people react. They do not think.

Of course, people need to have the basic physical stamina, the calcium, enzyme, potassium, vitamin and mineral base of live, nontoxic foods and pure water in their diet if they are to have the energy to persevere. The quality of the food not only determines whether the advanced (cerebrum) or primitive (limbic) brain centers are used, but also how the immune system and the brain interact. Stress is simultaneously mental and physical. Our bodies are byproducts of the earth.

Crisis is an inevitable challenge in life for individuals and their collective institutions. This is why a society must be rooted religiously, governmentally, and economically in correct perspectives if it is to survive. A crisis brings out the errors of men's ways. A society collapses when the last of its illusions are shattered.

If an individual is taught the principles of humility, empathy, responsibility and duty, a long-term view, the necessity of short-term pain for long-term gain, the importance of service before reward, and these values are worked out in time in bio-regional societies, then you have an individual who can bring strength to collective society. Such an individual is in harmony with himself, God, his fellow man, and the creation. He understands the balance between love and economic self-interest, and his need to be a good steward of the earth. He is a resource, an asset to society, rather than a predator or a parasite.

A healthy society collectively will be decentralized, architecturally and structurally, applying in the agriculturally-based social order the contract - the covenant. The religious, governmental and economic nature of the contract established true equality amid desired inequality throughout society, based upon service first, followed by self-interest. It established the worth of the individual and establishes unity amid diversity. Self-interest, incentive, and risk-assumption are balanced off as byproducts of duty and service, human need and security. People are seen as more important than things, as ultimate resources, because people determine the use of things. Thus, people are like-minded, and this unity of love is established socially.

The constitutional covenant with government works its way back to its roots in an individual, through the church (God's non-bloodline voluntary communal body), and the extended and nuclear family. With every man living effectively under his own vine and fig tree, eating primarily fresh foods which have the same magnetic charge as where he resides, blessed with pure air, soil, and water, a man has the necessary calcium, enzymes, vitamins and mineralization in his body to live in peace physically, too.

None of these things characterize our society today. Therefore, reaping what we have sown, in cause-and-effect fashion, our society, particularly our cities, will probably not meet the challenge of the next comprehensive crisis. We shall fall. Aside from a supernatural miracle, I see no hope for the revival or reformation of our cities. We are completely out of touch with religious, political, economic, social and ecological reality.

Early America

In early America, 90% of Americans owned and worked the land in a horizontal, decentralized, covenantal fashion. Today, farmers make up less than 3% of our population. In 1800, less than 2% of free Americans worked for someone else. Today, 95% of Americans work for someone else in a vertical hierarchy. Some 80% of our people live in the cities, too, and are dependent upon government in some form, shape, or fashion. Our society is built vertically. Vertical is bureaucratic and marks a dying slave state.

Debt Capitalism and Communism

Debt capitalism is Orwellian. Capitalism (savings applied) requires short-term pain for long-term gain. Savings (capital) must be accumulated from the past and in the present for investment in the future. Debt, on the other hand, involves short-term gain with no consideration for the long-term pain it brings through compound interest and slavery. Debt is a form of slavery. Debt is borrowing from the future by mortgaging the past to consume in the present. It is the antithesis of equity capitalism/free enterprise. How can our people not be in conflict personally when our basic system of economic debt capitalism is intrinsically a contradiction? They cannot.

Debt capitalism, which focuses on the radical rights of the individual, puts man in conflict with his fellow man, elevates the destructive principle of the survival of the fittest, and has led in its true evolutionary perspective to the emphasis on things rather than people. Communism, on the other hand, with its radical focus on the collective masses, with its power-endorsed, top-down bureaucracy, not only destroys the individual building blocks of society in terms of character, initiative and the family, but also puts its emphasis on things rather than people (dialectic materialism). And yet, where we see people who are truly the earned owners of the means of production, where individual incentive is made possible through equity non-debt capitalism and service, the balance between unity amid diversity is achieved. The conflict between capitalism and communism is neutralized.

Worker-Owned Businesses

Worker-owned businesses in this country do far better, especially during crisis, than other types of debt capitalistic ventures. The work of Dr. Tom Peters has confirmed this anew. Where ESOPs exist (employee stock ownership plans) for example, businesses are more productive, more competitive, marked by higher profits, better employee morale, and less absenteeism. The business is seen as a family. The family is the basic social unit of society, one place removed from the individual, whether it is the nuclear family, the extended family, the spiritual family in the local church, the economic family in the local business, or the political family in the local community. Man's need for love, his spiritual need for family, is as high a need as his need for economic sustenance.

Why Mondragon Is A Winner

The reason the experiment at Mondragon, Spain has been successful for over four decades is because people found the correct balance between individual rights and collective society. The conflict between individualistic capitalism and collective communism was resolved at Mondragon. Individual needs were first balanced off with those of the community. Leadership was local, earned and accountable.

The crisis of persecution brought out the best in the people at Mondragon, too. They did not self-destruct. They created a system that's a shining example for us all. America particularly needs to study and learn from Mondragon.

Where else are there societies in crisis? In the Soviet Union, Sri Lanka, in parts of Asia, Africa and South America. And guess what? In these areas, too, facsimiles of Mondragon have sprung up independently. Poland, for example, in 1940 began an investment trust which operates effectively just like the bank at Mondragon. Over 175,000 people work in Polish cooperatives. The Poles and the people in the Basque region both, without knowledge of each other, set up almost identical systems. This gives us a sense of hope. Are we about to see the hundredth monkey syndrome manifest itself as we purge the errors of this age and the foundations of our culture are shaken? The radical individualism of debt capitalism and the radical collectivism of socialism and communism are both dying. Furthermore, their focus on things as more important than people will accelerate their death in a world caught in comprehensive crisis.

When things are more important than people, inevitably conflict is manifest. How do we divide the economic apple? Who decides? Conflict! But when people are more important than things, where spirit is more important than matter, there can be like-mindedness and love. Common ground is sought. This then established the basis for cooperation and the just and merciful division of things in collective society without destroying the initiative of the individual. The contract (law) becomes the primary instrument of love. (Such is next to impossible where the time value of money rules [compound interest]).

Mondragon has proven that it can outperform both socialism/communism and debt capitalism. We know a people and a society by its fruits, by its works. The fruits and works of Mondragon, in terms of the spiritual, mental, physical, emotional, governmental and economic health of its people, slam dunk both fault-ridden debt capitalism and communism/socialism. Furthermore, the consistency in Mondragon between means and ends, between process and goals, is a shining light of truth which illuminates the inconsistencies and contradictions of both debt capitalism and communism/socialism. The United States is now a class structured society as the middle class has been progressively destroyed under debt capitalism. The former Soviet Union, far from bringing about the classless society promised by Marxism, was the most class-structured society in the world. Position there was not based upon merit or service. It was based upon status in the party, in the bureaucracy. The fruits of communism therefore confirm the error of Karl Marx. The end cannot be different from the process, from the means, and maintain its integrity and validity long-term.

Mondragon's Organization Structure

What are some of the specifics, the technicalities incorporated at Mondragon, which have made it successful? Each division of 20 to 50 worker-owners conducts at least a monthly work Group meeting to discuss any and all issues. Management and their Social Council representative are part of the Group. This numerical division of 20 to 50 is important. Studies in large churches in the United States have indicated that most people never get to know more than 20 to 50 members of any congregation. The more successful churches have thus divided up their larger churches into these smaller numerical units.

At Mondragon, each worker-owner Group of 20 to 50 members elects a representative. This representative then meets with all the other representatives of the worker-owner businesses in the Social Council. The ruling Board has delegated to the Social Council all the worker issues with which unions are normally concerned - salaries, safety, fringe benefits, job descriptions, etc. Furthermore, the Social Council is responsible for deciding to which charities 10% of the annual company profits will go (a tithe).

Every worker-owner can be involved in managing every aspect of the business. All worker-owners have one share of voting stock. Therefore, they all have equal power. Management and labor are distinctive, but both of them fall under the umbrella of the cooperative, and both are subservient to the Board. This assures total integration and coordination. If the Board, for some reason, should fail in its task, then the General Assembly of all worker-owners, which wields the ultimate power within the cooperative, can overrule the Board. This results in total accountability at all levels. A member of the Group who has also been elected to the Board may also participate when it comes to the more mundane worker-owner matters.

Each cooperative (worker-owned business) elects representatives to the Association of Cooperatives. This Association elects the Board of the secondary cooperatives which include the Bank at Mondragon, the Research Institute, and the Insurance and Social Security institutions. However, the main focus of the Association of Mondragon Cooperatives is to create worker-owned jobs.

The Positive Results

This primary business/serve thrust of the Association of Cooperatives enhances current worker-owner job security and gives the current worker-owners an incentive to be enthusiastic about automation. The worker-owners are equity capitalists. For this reason then, the cooperatives at Mondragon have moved aggressively forward in robot development. The worker-owners realize that their jobs are not threatened by automation and progress, and that new jobs are being created in which they have a stake. And so, the worker-owners enthusiastically embrace computerized automation which eliminates repetitive jobs, dirty jobs, and increases the productivity and the viability of a product produced for the international marketplace.

The worker-owners at Mondragon can be progressive and embrace change, even if it eliminates their own particular job, because they own the business themselves. They are not threatened. New jobs are being created for them, and as a member of the Mondragon cooperative, having a job is guaranteed for life.

The civil government has no involvement in this process. No worker-owner in the Mondragon cooperative is ever dependent upon public assistance. The purpose of the cooperatives is to contribute to the needs and development of society, which means the health and welfare of the individuals within the cooperative society. Beautifully then, each worker-owner in the Mondragon cooperative has the incentive to provide for himself and simultaneously serve society. It is unity amid diversity personified. It is social harmony. It is the balance between the one and the many. It is the balance trade-off between individual and collective rights.

Individual Benefits

What do the Mondragon cooperatives do with their profits from their businesses? Presently, 70% of the profits are distributed among the worker-owners. This distribution is based upon an earned salary scale, as well as the number of years an individual has been involved with the cooperative. Thus, individual productivity is balanced off with time commitment to economic society in the profit distributions.

Moreover, the profits are not cash distributions. They are instead allocated to the worker-owner's internal capital account, where they are regarded as a loan by the worker to the cooperative. Therefore, the worker-owner becomes an investor, an equity capitalist, by way of investment in both his own business and the community-at-large.

The worker receives dividends each year in cash just before Christmas. An interest rate of 6% is paid annually on his internal account. As the worker-owner's investment in a cooperative increases, the cooperative re-invests his profits to create more worker-owned jobs, more profits, more dividends, and more job and financial security for the worker-owner. This methodology is very important. It allows newly-formed cooperatives to receive uncollateralized capital at low interest rates. In the West, this start-up capital is normally the most difficult and expensive capital to borrow, and primarily the cause of failure for most new businesses - lack of sufficient capital! Mondragon has solved this basic problem!

What happens if the cooperative for one reason or another ceases to exist? The remaining amount of funds, which is collectively owned, is given to charity and managed for the general welfare. There is therefore no owner or banking incentive at Mondragon to arbitrarily bankrupt businesses, to go out of business, or to cash out of a business which is profitably providing a needed social good or service. Only those businesses which really have no hope and should be liquidated are in fact liquidated.

The worker-owner does have use of his portion of his 70% of the profits if he needs it. This 70% capital account can be used as collateral at the bank for a personal loan. On this personal loan, the interest rate which is charged the worker-owner is only 1% or 2% above the 6% which he is earning via the cooperatives' use of this capital in the new job creation process.

The Full Life At Mondragon

Compare and contrast what the Mondragon worker has going for him - a rich life individually and socially; and a productive, profitable, economic life - to that of his American counterpart. The Mondragon worker-owner has job security, tenure, financial security, a say in all aspects of his business where he is a worker-owner, a voice financially and personally in community affairs, a sense of belonging, and the incentive to be progressive, creative, and productive. He experiences the excitement of personal involvement with his own (and the community's) bank, research institute, insurance program and social security system. He is an investor, a consumer, an important individual with dignity, and yet at the same time, he is encompassed by a strong sense of belonging as a significant, loving member of the community. He has it all - love and money, heaven on earth - *"thy Kingdom come, thy will be done, on earth as it is in heaven."*

When we see what has been accomplished and proven at Mondragon, Spain for over 40 years by way of the answers necessary to meet both the love and money needs of man; the answers which already exist with regard to meeting individually and collectively man's biological, safety, social, egotistical and self-fulfillment needs, and then compare it to what exists in this country today, it's enough to bring tears to our eyes.

People Power

There are effectively two aspects of real power: (1) being able to act effectively to accomplish what you want; and (2) not being under the control of other people, but instead cooperating with other people. Both of these are achieved at Mondragon.

People's Express almost got it right in this country, too, with the company organized as worker-manager teams without supervisors. Low salaries but generous profit-sharing plans and stock dividends provided for both individual incentive and group cooperation.

When a corporation decides to enter a new product market, it is coming close to duplicating Mondragon. The corporation already has established its primary investment in people, in its management, staff and workers. Capital, accounting, marketing and feedback systems already exist. So, *"pick a product."* People are more important than things.

The May 1987 issue of *Inc.* magazine, in an article entitled, *"Every Worker An Owner?"*, pointed out the advantages of ESOPs (employee stock ownership plans). This is as close as we've come in the United States to the successful experience achieved at Mondragon. This *Inc.* magazine article documented that companies with high degrees of employee-ownership outperform similar-size competitors. They also grow faster than they were growing previously.

Knowledge of how to run ESOPs and other worker-owned collectives in this country is widespread, but it is so contrary to cultural norms that those ESOPs established are few and far between. It will take a crisis to establish them.

The Trammell Crow Company, for which I worked over a decade ago, caught a glimpse of this *business people principle* in its early years. It became the largest real estate development company in the country partly because it provided its bottom line leasing agents and staff personnel with the individual incentive of *owning a piece of the action* of the projects developed. Local partner power established a check and balance with the central Dallas office. Entrepreneurs primarily were hired. Real estate development, after all, is an entrepreneurial business.

Lessons for America

We Americans are a proud, stubborn people. We are devoid of love, as we war with one another over everything, filing 96% of the civil lawsuits in the world. *"Who do you know in Idaho? Does anyone there know you? Who do you know who lives next door, or is he a stranger too?"* (Killough & Eckley)

We are dead spiritually. We declared some twenty years ago that *"God is dead."* We are impoverished economically. Everything we own today is in hock, in debt.

We are dead physically as we eat lifeless stale foods produced from poisoned air, soil and water. We live in dead cities of glass, concrete, asphalt and steel, and thereby miss the life-giving diamagnetic charge so necessary for our peace and tranquillity, which is provided only by the trees and plants of God's Good Earth.

The colors blue and green, which are so vibrant in a decentralized *"vine and fig tree"* agricultural economy, are vital to our spiritual and physical health as their wavelengths impact and nourish our pineal and pituitary glands respectively. All this is missed in the cities, the heart of our civilization.

Spengler was correct. Our civilization peaked 90 years ago with the rise of world cities. City-produced chemicals have brought rampant toxicity to the countryside and our farmers are now poisoned, too. Undertakers tell us it takes a third less embalming fluid to preserve us. We are therefore already one-third dead. We only await our final burial.

Seen in this light, the American fitness craze, the emphasis on *looking good,* is a sad, cruel joke. What we need is radical surgery on our hearts (figuratively speaking) to begin with. We need a spiritual, mental, physical, emotional, individual and collective renewal. But such seems not about to come until we suffer much pain, until the system comes crashing down on our heads, until our cities die. And the sun of that sad date is about to dawn. For the sun of love, joy, peace, patience, kindness, goodness, faithfulness, gentleness, and self-control has long ago set and departed from the American urban spirit.

(Again, thanks to Dr. Terry Mollner for the facts on the Mondragon Cooperatives and Trusteeship.)

SECTION VII

Love and Money

KEYS TO SUCCESS

September 28, 1988

Success/Wisdom

How do we become successful? By making good decisions. How do we come to make good decisions? By experience. How do we acquire experience? By trial and error, by making bad decisions or by learning from the wisdom of others.

Success means different things to different people - freedom, money, power and recognition, just for starters. Similarly, the most startling conference experience I have ever had came at a speaking engagement in front of more than 300 self-made millionaires held at The Anatole in Dallas, Texas. To my surprise, I learned these self-made men were only successful because they happened to be at the right place at the right time. They had successfully met the collective human need for goods or service in the marketplace, and had worked hard to *"deliver the goods."* By and large, however, they were no smarter, wiser or knowledgeable than the average American. They were, in short, *"lucky."* They too were lost at the 1980 turning point in the economy.

In 1980, when inflation shifted to disinflation, these successful men had no idea what it all meant or how to adjust for it. This experience then, first and foremost, caused me to make a serious inspection of what success is really all about.

Our Only Resource

The only resource that all of us truly have is our time. Therefore, the wise use of our time determines whether or not we are successful. Time needs to be our servant rather than our master. If time is our master, Parkinson's law kicks in, and the task at hand will expand to fill the amount of time allotted for it. Thus, a person who has fallen victim to Parkinson's law has squandered his true wealth and unsuccessfully managed his most important resource, his time. A person who wastes his time is by default unsuccessful, a loser. On the other hand, a winner will value his time so greatly that he will always have to select against important alternatives in the use of his time. In other words, a successful person will be forced to constantly make painful choices among equally good choices.

Balance

To me personally, being successful means freedom - the ability to spend my time doing what I choose. It also entails balancing the use of precious time among work, rest, exercise, family, church, civic duties, friends and recreation. This need for balance comes from the observation that we all have multi-level needs.

All of us have varying degrees of basic biological/economic needs, safety and security needs, social and self-esteem needs, and self-fulfillment drives. Walking through a cemetery one Memorial Day, reading and studying the headstones, I discovered that the overwhelming theme of the cemetery is two-fold - *"God"* and *"love."* The problem is, while we are here on earth, we have to make do economically. We need basic economic provisions to survive.

The only way I have found to harmoniously and simultaneously meet my need to serve God and my fellow man, and to in return receive love and approval, and to also meet my basic biological/economic needs, is to first serve my fellow man and then as a by-product receive compensation (psychological and material) for that service. This then is the harmony between the *"Two Golden Rules"* of life: *"Do unto others as you would have them do unto you;"* and, *"Whoever has the gold makes the rules."*

Adopting a *"win-win-win"* lifestyle brings spiritual, interpersonal and personal harmony. It requires a long-term view. Thus, the essence of success (in the sense that peace and prosperity are the hallmark of success) is the diligent use of time within a long-term perspective. Additionally, if one can also assume the risks in providing goods and services for others, and thus meet their security needs and make all offers effectively *"risk free,"* then one has it made. The public will flock to your door. A *"win-win-win"* philosophy, coupled with providing desired goods or a service risk free inevitably leads to success in the marketplace of life. The world will give us anything we want if we will first give it what it wants.

Success/Freedom

Being successful when it comes to freedom means assuming responsibility personally for oneself, and simultaneously performing one's duties toward one's fellow man. Only in both personal responsibility and duty toward others does one find the balance necessary to achieve both individual and collective freedom. The risk and pain of responsibility in turn brings the real security of freedom and following prosperity.

It is risky to take the long-term view to become successful. It's easier to *"live for today."* The *"time"* motto for the successful life therefore becomes, *"Short-term pain for long-term gain in all things."* We dare not let the *"urgent"* things of life overwhelm the *"important"* things either. *"Urgent"* things are always short-term in nature, the *"important"* things long-term.

Information and Success

With regard to information, *"ignorance is bliss"* is a short-term perspective. In the long-term, *"truth kills those who hide from it."* Long-term vision requires us to *"look before we leap."* But when the time comes to act in any circumstance it takes courage. *"He who hesitates is lost."* Patience and courage are also aspects of success.

Character, Professionalism and Health

Being successful requires both character and professional attention to detail, both abstract concepts and concrete facts blended together. Additionally, one must maintain one's health, since we are a psychosomatic biological/spiritual computer. Ultimately, we are not *"wealthy unless we are healthy." "We are not successful unless we are healthful."*

The Formula For Success

The formula for success is well established in every culture: (1) work hard; (2) save and accumulate capital; (3) learn skills which can be used to meet the needs for goods or a service in the marketplace. Then investment follows. Ideally, a solid family will instill children with character, the work ethic, and professionalism in their calling.

We should all develop our personal talents, and strengths. We can then hire or contract with others for their strengths and pay them to compensate for our weaknesses. It's a myth that we should work to compensate for our weaknesses. The *"wealth of nations"* comes from the specialization and division of labor, leading to trade. Trade is the result of men maximizing their strengths and relying upon others to provide for their weaknesses. *"One man's strength is another man's weakness." "One man's meat is another man's poison."*

Service, The Future, and Success

We must anticipate what the needs for goods and services will be in the future if we are to be ultimately successful. So we have to *"Think and Grow Rich,"* as Napoleon Hill declared. In giving the world what it wants, we have to: (1) provide better goods or service at less cost; (2) provide new goods or service which will result in the stimulation of demand by the consuming public; or (3) solve problems with which other people do not want to deal. To accomplish any or all of these three goals requires personal *"humility"* so that we are able to listen to what the market environment is telling us. It also requires *"empathy"* so that we can discern the consumer's true needs. *"Humility"* and *"empathy"* are the essence of the *"Golden Rule"* and the *"Second Great Commandment,"* applied to the marketplace: *"Do unto others as you would have them do unto you." "Love thy neighbor as thyself."* The *"Second Great Commandment"* and the *"Golden Rule"* are therefore effectively a covenant, a contract. A covenant/contract is governmental, religious and economic in nature. It is the essence of *"reciprocity,"* the word Confucius pointed out as the key to all of life.

Future Perception and Success

To be able to accurately perceive the future, we have to escape our culture. Ve must rise above the traditions of men, the old staid ways of looking at ʾlity. Culture is present and past oriented. Success and profit come from ᴈing future oriented.

Recall that wealth is first a concept, an idea, which eventually takes form in physical reality. For example, the idea of a real estate developer is communicated to an architect, who then draws up the plans, which are engineered for the construction crew, to build a shopping center, to serve the consuming public. The public purchases goods and services at the shopping center so that the tenants can pay rent to the real estate developer. Ideas produce action and physical substance.

Along this same line, we must never forget that the purpose of competition is to disseminate information about the best goods and services. The greater the competition, the greater the service to the consuming public in a market free from government regulation. Thus, in perfect competition, there exists a harmony of interests.

OPE and OPM

Beyond our own energy and our own money, we can make use of OPE (other people's energy) and OPM (other people's money). Life is time. Time is work. Work is energy, and energy is money. Therefore, life, time, work, energy and money are all (in a sense) one and the same. Accordingly, if we are able to contractually capture other people's energy and/or money, we have a greater chance long-term of more successfully meeting our own objectives. The problem comes when one man takes unfair advantage of another. The equity of horizontal covenant and contract is set aside. The rise of labor unions and today's menace of monopolistic debt capitalism (which produced and supports communism) are examples of the abuse of OPE and OPM. Ideally, however, under equity capitalism, OPE and OPM are synergistic. The whole is greater than the sum of its parts.

The Family Aspect of Success

Every business takes on the characteristics of a family. It has its own norms and standards. Ultimately, the first and second rules of business apply: Rule No. 1, *"The boss is always right."* Rule No. 2, *"If in doubt see Rule No. 1."* There has to be a final authority. The buck stops at the boss's desk.

In a small business, with less than seven workers, the operation is essentially the same as that of a homogeneous nuclear family. Therefore, it is critical for the success of a small business long-term that all members be like-minded, at least in a working sense. For the small business owner, it is very significant that his wife be supportive, because of the tremendous sacrifices he is required to make in order to be successful.

We should not deceive ourselves into believing that we can accomplish everything on our own, and at the same time maximize our opportunities for success. We cannot do everything well. We have limited time, resources, skills and energy. Therefore, we must either hire employees, which sets up a vertical relationship, or delegate our responsibilities horizontally through independent contractual relationships.

In the case of employees, the boss is always in the middle, attempting to serve his customers, and to keep his employees happy. Thus, it is only when a working society sees the importance of a harmony of interests all around that it can succeed and prosper long-term. Then ownership, management and labor have a commonality of interests.

Economics is a peaceful activity, which only thrives in an environment of freedom, responsibility, duty, and peaceful, contractual exchange. When the laws which govern a society are conflicting and bring on class warfare, reflecting a lack of religious and moral unity in that society, inescapably long-term poverty will result.

Employees and Contractors

When evaluating potential employees or independent contractors, it's important to be able to discern in the prospective individual(s) both the *"will to win"* and a *"heart given to service."* Learning how a person spends his time, particularly his spare time, his discretionary income, what he reads, and who his children, friends and family say he is, will tell us a great deal about that person. Testing both aptitude and motivation are critical today. It is an extremely dissipating failure-oriented mistake to attempt to build long-term with inferior workers. Build with quality. This means building with men who are like-minded, have character and are competent. As the old saying goes, *"You can't fly like an eagle when you're surrounded by turkeys."*

Employees should be: (1) Held accountable for their representations. They should be able to do what they say they can do, and what they agree to do. (2) Employees should contribute to profits; or (3) employees should contribute to cost savings. These are the only reasons to have employees, because the employees' primary contractual purpose is to serve the business (customers and boss), for which he in turn is rewarded. (This also applies to independent contractors.)

Employees derive meaning in the work place from: (1) recognition; (2) rewards, financial and otherwise; (3) a stable routine or regimentation; and/or (4) responsibility/freedom. Nearly every individual who is an employee will derive motivation from at least one of these four factors as an incentive to be productive.

With regard to our *"time"* motto that success is always built on, *"short-time pain for long-time gain"*, we must provide our employees/contractors with *"enough rope to either build a bridge or to hang themselves."* This is also the human application of the principle found in the marketplace of *"cutting your losses short and letting your profits ride."*

In order to build any relationship we have to assume risk. We have to open ourselves up short-term to be hurt in order to build a meaningful relationship long-term. We treat all people on the basis of our character, not theirs. But long-term, we always do the right thing - justice tempered with mercy. The standard is nothing less than perfection, but error is forgivable.

Musts in Every Business

Regardless of what business one is in, there are six areas that are a must if the business is to be successful long-term. Every business must: 1) provide desired goods or service; 2) have a marketing/sales plan; 3) accumulate adequate capital/financing; 4) have good accounting for both planning purposes and financial feedback; 5) be run by effective and efficient management with feedback loops for better decision making; and 6) have the right people to do the right job at the right time - good, competent personnel.

Planning

A successful business must have both a long-term strategic plan and a short-term tactical plan. A combination of principles and facts must be mixed with both the strategic and tactical plans for success to be manifested long-term. Good businessmen will *"never guess if the information is available." "If in doubt, they will check it out."* And *"if still in doubt, they will stay out."* It's always easy to get into something, but usually difficult (and painful) to get out. It is all too easy to over-schedule our time and commitments. Therefore, we should be slow to invest our time, money, energy, thoughts and emotion in any particular venture or activity.

Equity

When investing in a business, or in the trading marketplace, the most successful people either do it themselves, or they give it to someone with the character and skills to do it, and then give that individual a piece of the action. People just won't perform unless there is an incentive to do so. This also promotes a harmony of interests. Here, too, as in any other venture or market investment, the principle is to *"cut the losses short and let profits ride."*

Timing

Understanding business cycles, particularly since they are created by our fractional reserve debt banking system, helps us better discern the potential risks and rewards in any business or investment in the future. Knowing where we are in the business cycle can be the ultimate determining factor of success today. Today, the expansion and contraction in the use of credit determines the ups and downs of the business cycles and, therefore, is very influential in determining success or failure.

CEOs

Gathering all the facts concerning the business or investment via the left brain, and then letting them filter through the right brain functions, where the subconscious can reflect upon these facts and return an intuitive feel for the matter, is the key to success for nearly all CEOs. Of course, first it takes hard work to gather and sort all the facts, and then organize them before ultimately reflecting on them. And even after such hard work is done, success requires courage to act, to put our decision, time and money on the line in the assumption of risk. An individual who is successful must have a plan, implement it, and follow up. This requires courage, discipline and a long-term view. A successful businessman or investor who is really doing his job right is much like an artist, at least in the sense that he must be creative and intuitive.

Where to Put the Eggs

When we are young and have few eggs, we can better assume both the responsibility and stress of risk. We can go for the big one. We can put all our eggs in one basket and then watch that basket carefully. When we become older and more successful, we have other interests. Then we should diversify our investment eggs into a number of baskets in order to reduce risk, accepting in exchange a more modest return.

Buying and Selling

Since personal humility is the ultimate virtue, followed next by empathy toward our fellow man, it should come as no surprise, given the lack of both humility and empathy today, that *"the greatest bargain available to man is the low cost of good advice."* Men consistently underprice the value of good information. Too often the operating rule is, *"When all else fails, read the directions."* (I wonder if God feels this way about us.)

To be successful in the investment markets, we must follow the tried and true adage, *"Buy low and sell high."* Of course, we can *"buy high and sell higher"* if we can find a *"greater fool"* who will pay more than we did. Also, it's important to remember we can *"sell high and buy low,"* or *"sell low and buy back lower,"* and profit. Markets fall at a rate three times faster than they rise. So, profits can be accrued three times faster on the short side of an investment than on the long side.

It is difficult in the American culture to understand how one can be successful by selling something one does not yet own. But if I sell you a Cadillac for $30,000 for delivery at Christmas, and between now and then I am able to purchase that Cadillac for $27,000, then I have sold you something I did not have at that time. But by buying it later cheaper than when I sold it to you, I thereby profit.

Except for new goods and services, high technology, venture capital and the like, traditional investments over time move from being undervalued to overvalued and then back again. Usually, an investment which is undervalued is accompanied by fear and a paucity of information, or negative data. An investment which is overvalued is usually accompanied by greed and a plethora of information distributed about the glories of that particular investment.

When an investment is undervalued, the risk, which seems at that time to be the greatest, is in fact at a minimum. There is no profit if there is not risk.

When an investment is overvalued, this is the time when risk seems to be minimized, but is actually when risk is maximized. Profit (success) is only realized when there is risk present. And risk is present when there is little information (or negative information) available about an undervalued investment.

Basic Market Movements

This *"undervalued-risky-limited information"* analysis helps us understand why markets tend to move up in three stages: From (1) being undervalued (short covering); to (2) becoming fully valued (true value recognized by the marketplace), to (3) being overvalued.

Because by nature men are both gregarious and like to feel secure, and because the crowd is usually wrong, it is important to recognize that to be successful long-term we must be both loners and risk takers. We have to become comfortable with being unpopular. We have to be entrepreneurs in the business world or in the investment markets. We have to be mavericks. This demands character, competence and confidence.

In this world, we all have limited time and imperfect information. This means that life is indeed *"risky."* A wise man accordingly will build himself a buffer zone to allow for his own limitations. That buffer zone will include not scheduling all of his time, intellect, emotion, energy or money. Remember the *"Peter Principle,"* that it is very easy for all of us to *"promote ourselves to our level of incompetence."* Stated differently, *"The greatest tendency of mankind is the tendency to self-destruct."* Avoid like the plague people who walk around nurturing their own destructive tornado.

Reserves

There is wisdom in storing up material reserves, time, money, emotion, intellect and energy for a rainy day. This is not hoarding. This is providing an effective insurance policy against inescapable human and/or natural error. Having available food, clothing and shelter totally paid for, along with two years' disposable income, is a form of insurance. Beyond this, however, money is like manure. The more it's spread around, the greater its velocity, the greater its potential return. Remember the biblical parable on the use of talents? Talents (money) are not to be buried. They are to be invested. Particularly in today's world, the power of compound interest cannot be discounted or underestimated in its ability to multiply talents.

Two Types of Capital

In our quest for success, it is indeed critical that we recognize that all of us possess only two types of capital - psychological/physical capital and financial capital. If either is in short supply, we will short-circuit on our road to success. When the opportunities become obvious in the investment or business arena, we have to be ready to take advantage of them. We need the courage to commit both our psychological/physical and financial capital reserves. This requires patience to wait for the opportunities to arise. We have to have a plan. We have to be prepared. We have to recognize and act on opportunity.

Harmony

It is never wise to force a business deal, an investment or a relationship. Things forced usually don't work out well. They break. Good deals, profitable investments and good relationships tend to come together naturally with a following harmonious flow. In a sense, thinking about the integration of the fundamental, technical, psychological and timing aspects of any deal, investment or relationship is key to success long-term.

Ideal Freedom

If success means maximization of freedom, then the ideal set-up today is to be a U.S. citizen, living in a foreign country, banking in a third country, with a business operating in a fourth country, held by a corporation in a fifth country, with marketing headquartered in yet a sixth country, selling worldwide.

Trap Doors to Success

There are trap doors on the staircase to success. For men in the business world, the most common ones are money, sex and power. These are identical to the same three which snare the clergy - gold, gals and glory. We have to know what these look, smell and act like (along with drugs and alcohol), when they come ambling our way. We have to recognize our enemies in order to side step them. When we make a mistake, we learn from it. We forgive, forget, move on, and never look back.

Our life is our own in a sense. It is personal and unique in every sense of the word. (Therefore, one's investment portfolio should be personal, like a trading system that is tailored to the psychological makeup of the user.) But in the same vein, it is important to always keep in mind, *"Real meaning in life comes from relationships with people."* We are born into this world as parasites. We initially depend upon others to meet our needs. Hopefully, we do not stay parasites or grow up to be predators, preying on others. Rather, we want to be a resource (hopefully, the ultimate resource), as men possessed of character and professional skills who take a long-term view and covenant and contract successfully.

Old J.R. on the TV series *"Dallas,"* who has all the money in the world, frustrates his own love, approval and self-esteem needs by operating in a predatory win-lose manner. J.R., like most of us, is his own worst enemy. We should never underestimate our ability to fool ourselves, to falsely rationalize our errors, bad judgments, or our incompetence. And when we're under pressure, we should recognize we are then most vulnerable to aggravating our own worst self-destruct tendencies. Thus, we must always blame ourselves first for anything that goes wrong. At the same time, we must not quit until we are sure we have given our chosen project, activity or relationship our best effort, our best shot.

Being successful is a by-product of doing things right, of first serving our fellow man in our God-given calling. Any other approach leads to the misery which goes with the adage, *"Friends come and go, but enemies accumulate."* A truly successful man, therefore, will even live at peace with his *"enemies,"* as well as prosper.

THE ONLY WAY TO
BOTH LOVE AND MONEY
April 15, 1987

From conversations with typical Americans in airports and planes when I travel, it has become alarmingly clear to me that, as a people, we have lost our basic concepts of what freedom, love, and money are all about. To many Americans today, life itself is wrapped up by the subjective emotionalism of *"do your own thing."* Indeed, our philosophical concepts of freedom, love, and money are superficial at best. This sad fact is a far cry from our historical roots.

Classically, freedom was basic to Americans because we saw ourselves as created by God to be free, so that we could pursue the calling and purposes on earth for which we were created. Because we were created (in this religious sense) to be free, we had to be free governmentally and economically if we were to be truly free to do *"God's will for our life"* on this earth.

The body of freedom stands firmly on the legs of law and economics. External regulation and control (laws and statutes) are by definition limitations on freedom. So, too, is economic enslavement (debt, and a monopoly on the issuance of money via the Federal Reserve) a limitation on freedom. Therefore, in any society, the working out of freedom comes down to individual control over law and economics. The legal and economic/monetary institutions of a society are ultimately determined by the philosophical/religious presuppositions concerning freedom which precede them. In other words, government is always religion applied to economics.

It all boils down ultimately to one of two systems: (1) a centralized society, ruled by a natural or man-made religion, where the buck stops with some man-made institutional laws, formulated and implemented by and through a bureaucracy, which in turn limits personal freedom, increases slavery and produces poverty long term; or (2) a decentralized society of self-governing men who are ruled by God and His laws, which come from above and outside of nature (supernatural), the result of which is a leveling of human institutions (non-bureaucratic), all of which compete to serve man. This self-government in turn results in minimal external regulation, maximum freedom, and therefore maximum prosperity. Freedom, the responsibility for self-government, and prosperity always run hand-in-hand. On the other hand, slavery, externally imposed government, and poverty also run together in the same harness. It's ultimately an either/or thing. Men must be governed by God or they will be ruled by tyrants.

Long-term, we can't legislate morality. And yet, all of law is by definition the legislation of morality - ideas about right or wrong, and good and evil. Therefore, the only thing which works long term is self-government, brought about by preceding religious conviction.

Where men are good and self-governing, external laws are unnecessary. Where men are evil and lawless, externally imposed laws do not work, because evil/lawless men will break them anyway. This is why the growth of big, bureaucratic government is inescapably eventually an exercise in futility. This is why empires inevitably fall. Externally imposed law does not work. Evil/lawless men disobey such laws, and long-term the society cannot economically support the bureaucrats who create and enforce these laws.

Looking at freedom geometrically, freedom is always structured horizontally, not vertically. This pertains whether we are looking at the architecture of the horizontal country versus that of the vertical city, or at human relations. Slaves are like children in a sense. They are dependent. The relationships of both slaves and children are vertical. They look up to others for their support. The key to growing up, to becoming free, is to grow from being dependent (vertical) on someone, to being independent (horizontal). Horizontal interaction is contractual.

When men contract horizontally for the goods and services they need, they become a resource to society rather than a parasite who is dependent upon other people. Of course, some folks remain dependent upon other people, like children, not by taking from others from below (slavery), but rather by taking from other people from above, by preying on others. Thus, the natural instinct of man is to remain a parasite, or become a predator. Both are takers. Both are conflict oriented. Neither contribute to the peace, harmony, and productivity of society long-term.

This natural instinct of man to take rather than to give, to remain as a child, a parasite, or to become a predator, is why communism and socialism do not work. Under communism or socialism, individual self-interest can best be served and realized only by being non-productive, by maximizing one's *"wealth"* by way of leisure time. Sounds much like the United States today, doesn't it? What incentive exists to become a human resource, a giver?

This is the same reason the Pilgrims at Plymouth almost didn't make it in the first couple of years, and why the initial experiment at Jamestown was a failure, and why the English *"commons"* was also a failure. In all three of these community experiments, the basic religious assumption was that man was naturally good and giving, rather than naturally inclined to maximize his own self-interest first. It was only when the English *"commons"* was broken down into private ownership, and only when Jamestown and Plymouth abolished communism and allowed private property rights, concomitant with incentive and merit, that Jamestown and Plymouth boot-strapped their way up from poverty and starvation to prosperity and ultimately *"Thanksgiving."*

The contract is the working instrument of the free man. A contract is by definition governmental, religious, and economic. A contract is governmental because it defines the legal rights, duties, and expectations of both parties to the contract. A contract is religious because it is a moral document. It is no better than the ethical covenant and morality of both parties to do what they say they will do. A contract is finally an economic arrangement by which the needs for goods or services by the two contracting parties are met.

God operates by means of a covenant/contract with His people - Old Testament/Old Contract, New Testament/New Contract. The Founding Fathers operated by means of a contract when it came to the federal government. That document was called *"the Constitution."* The Constitution was a contract by which free men reserved the greatest amount of authority and power for themselves and their local communities, then the states, and finally gave very little power to the federal government. In fact, the purpose of the *"Bill of Rights"* was to put chains on the federal government so it would not become a vertical, centralized, bureaucratic monster, which enacted endless legislation, taxed excessively, and played the role of God like the pagan empires of old. The Founding Fathers wanted to avoid a replay of the *"divine right of kings,"* where the federal government played the role of God and became the maker of laws rather than the implementor of God's law, while requiring tribute and sacrifice like a god. The Founding Fathers did not want the buck to stop at the federal government (or the Supreme Court) as the final authority of what was right or wrong, good or evil. The Founding Fathers knew if this became the case (as it is today), that the federal government would play the role of God, and then all men would not be equal, but instead privileged classes would arise.

All men are only equal when they are equal under law. Therefore law needs to come from a God above and outside of nature (supernatural), from a place higher than man, or all men are not equal under the law. If men both make the law and enforce the law, these men have power over other men and true equality ceases to exist. Freedom begins to die. Furthermore, when you combine legal and economic/financial special interests with God-like authority, the result is the centralizing of man as the epitome of government as religion applied to economics. This is when self-governing freedom and economic prosperity cease to exist for the masses, and only continue for the elite few at the top of the bureaucratic order.

The most class distinctive society in recent times existed in the former Soviet Union. There, the central government played the role of God, made and implemented all laws, and totally controlled the society economically. The result is that the Soviet bureaucratic party elite lived like gods, eating in their own elite restaurants and shopping in their own elite stores. Meanwhile, the masses wallowed in poverty amid shortages of such basic items as toilet paper. Washington, D.C. is becoming like this today. Washington is the only U.S. city where home prices have not fallen since 1933.

Again, the contract is the basic operating instrument of the free man. It is the way by which our God-given inequality makes us equal. When we are all educated alike, act alike, and think alike (thanks to the federally funded public schools and TV), none of us are important as individuals. We can be easily replaced. In other words, we are expendable. However, when we are all unequal, and have developed our unequal skills and talents according to our God-given calling, then we all need each other. This is the specialization and division of labor that leads to harmonious trade/exchange in the free market. In this process, our inequality results in us needing our fellow man and in his needing us. It is our inequality, our differences, that make us unique and important. It is, therefore, the contract, this governmental, religious and economic instrument, which is basic to solving the ultimate political, religious and economic question, *"How do we best balance off the rights of individuals with those of collective society?"*

The contract is the instrument of reciprocity, the instrument of balance between the one and the many, the instrument of freedom, peace and prosperity. Perhaps this is why the majority of Jesus' disciples were businessmen. They knew how to contract!

There are four basic ethical religious characteristics which each man must possess if he is to contract successfully. Two are personal, and two apply toward his fellow man; two of these are abstract ideas, and two are concrete and operational. These four foundational principles are humility, empathy, responsibility, and duty.

The two abstract principles are humility and empathy. The two operational principles are responsibility and duty. Personally, an individual must have humility followed by personal responsibility. Toward one's fellow man an individual must possess empathy, followed by duty. None of these four virtues come naturally. All must be taught. All four are foreign to the *"do your own thing"* philosophy.

All four principles must become basic to individuals for the contract to be the primary modus operandi in a society. An individual must develop the humility to first perceive that he must meet someone else's needs before his own needs can be subsequently met. He must have the empathy to understand what the other person's needs really are to be able to covenant and contract successfully. He must have the personal responsibility (character, discipline) to be able to fulfill his half of the contractual bargain. And this personal responsibility must be activated by a sense of duty toward the contractual obligations owed his fellow man if the contract is to be completed. In other words, self-interest is best served by service. Making money is a byproduct of doing things correctly. Service precedes and results in the fulfillment of self-interest. Incentive leads to service, which in turn results in the fulfillment of personal needs. Fulfillment of needs is not a right. Fulfillment of needs is a byproduct of humility, responsibility, empathy, and duty.

If a person is to be free, he must have the humility to be personally responsible rather than remain dependent as a parasite or a predator. In other words, he cannot economically live on the dole or be a bureaucrat. Freedom and personal responsibility always run hand-in-hand. At the same time, if a person is to be free, he must have the empathy to recognize the rights and freedom of his fellow man. In other words, he has a duty to allow his fellow man to also be free. Men must work out their differences and fulfillment of needs by way of the horizontal contract, thereby maintaining equality. The contract both permits freedom and defines the limits of freedom through voluntary commitment and consent.

This principle of the reciprocity of the contract as a basic governmental, religious and economic document, and as foundational to freedom, peace and prosperity, is summed up by The Golden Rule and Christ's Second Great Commandment. The Golden Rule states, *"Do unto others as you would have them do unto you."* Christ's Second Great Commandment declares, *"Love thy neighbor as thyself."* They are both effectively the same thing. They balance out the inherent conflict between individuals by way of the contract. The Golden Rule and the Second Great Commandment equalize self-interest and service, giving and receiving, the rights of the individual with the rights of collective society. The rights of others are seen and defined first (humility, empathy), but in terms of one's own individually understood rights and needs (incentive). It is simply a matter of giving/serving (responsibility/duty) and, as a by-product of giving/serving (through the contract), taking or receiving what is earned. This sets up a win-win situation. Actually, it's a win-win-win situation. God wins because man is obeying His basic dictates. Our fellow man wins. And we win. This is far better than the lose-lose evolutionary humanistic philosophy which dominates our society today, which has resulted in emotional emptiness, a frantic search for happiness, rampant subjectivity, the breakdown of the family, a loss of freedom, pervasive debt, increasing poverty, and the growth of big, bureaucratic regulation-spewing institutions which increasingly make us miserable. Ideas have consequences. Thoughts precede action. We reap what we sow.

When, according to The Golden Rule, we *"do unto others as we would have them do unto us,"* and when we, according to the Second Great Commandment, *"Love our neighbors as ourselves,"* we are inescapably forced to implement the virtues of humility, responsibility, empathy, and duty. We are further forced to covenant and contract with our fellow man. We are additionally required to utilize the long-term view as superior over and against the short-term perspective. All biblical principles are long-term in nature. It is the closest we can come to imitating God, who is eternal. And, furthermore, because God is the epitome of success, the application of these principles are basic to success in all areas of life.

"Short-term pain for long-term gain," the long-term view, is necessary for success in all areas of life. In athletics, where rigorous training precedes excellence in performance, in academics, at work, in the family - everywhere we find success we discover that men have paid the price short-term, even to the point of holding their tongue short-term. (He who laughs last laughs best, even if by so doing he shows little compassion.)

Men who have humility have the ability to listen, learn, change, grow, adapt, and respond to their environment - in other words, to be successful. Responsibility following personal humility leads to leadership, power, freedom, and prosperity. Power, and therefore money, inescapably flows to those who accept responsibility. Empathy toward the needs of others enables one to eventually anticipate what those needs will be, which direction the market will go, which way the running back will cut, etc. In other words, empathy leads to success because empathy, which is based in humility, fueled by personal responsibility, leads to the effort necessary to produce the goods and services demanded by one's fellow man. Duty is the follow-through. This results in success. By performing one's duties in line with one's contractual responsibilities, one earns freedom, dignity, respect, appreciation, approval, power, security, and prosperity.

When you boil it all down, man has two basic needs - for love and for money. Man has a spiritual need for love, for appreciation, acceptance, belonging, and approval because man has a spiritual nature, *"made in the image of God." "God is love."* Nearly all of our music today cries out man's need for love. Man also has a need for money, an economic need for food, clothing, shelter, fuel and safety because God made man, *"formed from the dust of the earth."* Even if we take psychologist Abraham Maslow's hierarchy of human needs, it becomes obvious that his biological and safety needs are economic/money needs, while the social, ego and self-actualization needs are love needs - spiritual needs. THE ONLY WAY HUMANLY POSSIBLE FOR MAN TO MEET BOTH HIS LOVE AND MONEY NEEDS, BOTH OF WHICH ARE VITAL TO HIS TOTAL SELF-FULFILLMENT, IS TO LIVE ACCORDING TO THE GOLDEN RULE AND THE SECOND GREAT COMMANDMENT!

Only when man operates according to the basic biblical virtues of humility, responsibility, empathy, and duty can he successfully operate according to the basic biblical instrument of the covenant/contract. The covenant/contract is the only way a man can operate with regard to his fellow man and receive in return both love and money, meeting both his spiritual and economic needs. This is why it is better to give than to receive. Because only when we give and then, as a by-product receive, does both love and money come flowing back to us. Sure, we can win economically in this life, much like J.R. Ewing on *"Dallas,"* through conflict-ridden, self-centered, humanistic, evolutionary *"survival of the fittest"* techniques. But the people that we defeat in this short-term win-lose battle for the almighty buck certainly aren't going to love us, approve of us, support us, or meet our love needs as a result of being defeated. In fact, just the opposite occurs. And this is just what happens to J.R. Ewing on *"Dallas."* J.R. gets rich, but his underlying spiritual need for love, approval, recognition, and status is always frustrated. On the other hand, when we covenant and contract according to these four basic biblical principles and utilize the instrument of the contract, as a result of first serving our fellow man with regard to his needs (whether spiritual or economic), our fellow man then in return, according to the terms of the contract, meets our economic and spiritual needs. In other words, when we contract in the marketplace of life, and first subordinate our interests and tie our personal incentives to meeting the spiritual and economic needs of our fellow man for love and/or money, the inevitable feedback and by-product of this action of giving and service is that we are repaid accordingly. (If not, then we cut our losses short.) Then, word spreads about us because people talk. And our love and money needs begin to be met geometrically and exponentially when we first meet the love and money needs of others. Everyone wins. No one loses. And because we have inexhaustible energy coming from the sun and therefore inexhaustible commodities which can be monetized, we have endless resources. And so no one has to lose - ever!

The Golden Rule is indeed golden. It is enduring. It is valued above all else by wise men because it is the only route to serving God, serving our fellow man, and to meeting both our needs for love and money. On earth, there are two Golden Rules. The first is spiritually (love) based: *"Do unto others as you would have them do unto you."* The second Golden Rule is economic (money) based: *"Whoever has the gold makes the rules."* Both are true in the real world. Because spirit rules over matter, those who live according to the first Golden Rule long-term end up owning the gold and making the rules according to the second Golden Rule. It takes first humility - meekness - to live this way, according to the first Golden Rule. Humility is the basic biblical virtue. It is what Jesus referred to when He said, *"The meek shall inherit the earth."* The earth is not conquered by conflict and money. The earth is subdued by love and then money.

The only thing that works in life, that brings success in the two basic areas of love and money, is to live according to The Golden Rule and The Second Great Commandment. It is the basic law given to us by God to be obeyed. Didn't He give it to us because He loved us? Didn't He give it to us because He knew our nature? Didn't He give it to us because He knew it was the only way that our own personal needs for both love and money would be met? Isn't this why it is no accident that where men live according to The Golden Rule and The Second Great Commandment, and covenant and contract in line with the basic biblical principles of humility, responsibility, empathy and duty, captured by the long-term view, they in turn worship God, are self-governing, and are free, happy and prosperous? Their realm of dominion subsequently grows.

Sadly, the reciprocal is all too true today. When in the '60s the university campuses declared, *"God is dead,"* they announced effectively the death of man, the end of the vestiges of personal humility, responsibility, empathy and duty, the demise of the covenant and contract, the disintegration of personal dignity, self-esteem, love, cooperation, peace, happiness, freedom and prosperity. It was the announcement of the will to death. It was the fulfillment of Proverbs 8:36: *"But he who sins against Me injures himself; All those who hate Me love death."*

* * * * *

Not only does living according to The Golden Rule and The Second Great Commandment provide the only way to both love and money, such living is also the only way to resolve man's four basic conflicts in life on earth.

Man's four basic conflicts here on earth are: (1) conflict with God; (2) conflict with his fellow man; (3) conflict within himself; and (4) conflict with God's creation, nature.

By living according to The Golden Rule (TGR) and The Second Great Commandment (TSGC), man resolves his conflict with God. Man cannot give God anything since God is the source of everything. (Man can only worship God.) Therefore, the only way man can serve God is by doing what God tells him to do, which is, generally to serve his fellow man. This way man resolves his conflict with God. In the process, he also resolves his conflict with his fellow man, because he gives/serves (contracts) before he receives. This way balance is established and conflict eliminated between the individual and collective mankind. Furthermore, as a byproduct of serving God and his fellow man, man serves himself. So, his internal conflict is also resolved. A man who serves both God and his fellow man as a result ends up meeting his own love and money needs. His biological, safety, social, self-esteem and self-actualization needs are all met long-term.

Man's fourth basic conflict on earth, his conflict with nature/God's creation, can be resolved once the first three conflicts are eliminated. In the economic equation of land and labor, man is more important than land as man determines the use of the land and its resources, for better or for worse. When man has resolved his three preceding conflicts, he can then obey God and cooperate with his fellow man for the purpose of eliminating conflict in nature. He can then overcome the conflict, chance and cycles of nature, and exercise dominion over the earth to the benefit of all concerned. Conflict-free men, who take a long-term view and covenant and contract with one another with humility, empathy, responsibility, and duty, decentralize over the earth and recapture it from a wilderness to a garden. Peace and prosperity result. This is dominion. God wins. Mankind generally wins. The individual man wins. Nature wins.

THE TIME VALUE OF MONEY
April 27, 1988

As we have seen, people are more important than things because people create, use and destroy things. Furthermore, when people are treated as more important than things, there is harmony and cooperation in a society. What follows is more voluntary sharing, justice, and give and take concerning things. This cooperation, covenanting and contracting in turn creates more prosperity, more things. So, prosperity long-term for any society rests upon having its priorities straight, placing its primary emphasis on people rather than things (and money).

This emphasis on people rather than things (and money) is the essence of why the Bank of the People's Labor at Mondragon, Spain has been so successful long-term. No business failures. No loan failures. Highest productivity in all of Spain, highest profitability (nearly double that of its competitors), highest morale and innovation ratings possible - all characterize Mondragon. Success there has been achieved in all areas. Success is a byproduct of doing things correctly. Ideas have consequences.

Critical to the success at Mondragon, although unstated and possibly unrecognized even by these people, is that they have established their priorities on people systems and effectively checkmated the natural inclination to focus on the time value of money with its compounding effect. The compounding of money in a fractional reserve, debt-based, interest sensitive society inevitably leads to a focus on things (and money) rather than people. The reason for this is because the challenge of compounding is a challenge which no individual or society can meet or beat long-term. The compounding of interest, money earning money on money, is relentless, ruthless, eternal, mistake-free and eventually exponential. By contrast, men make mistakes, need rest, do not forecast the future perfectly, make poor use of human and natural resources, and are fortunate if they can simply achieve arithmetic economic growth. Therefore, it is no surprise that the slave-like god of debt money and compound interest eventually forces all to bow at its altar. Forced to serve this god of money (mammon), inescapably then, money and things become more important than people.

The key chapter of my book, *No Time For Slaves*, Chapter 3, is also entitled *No Time For Slaves*. Therein I discuss the dangers and pitfalls of debt slavery. Human nature has not changed. We should hail back to the sound advice given us by the Hebrews of the Old Testament, the Greeks, the great Christian teachers of the Middle Ages, and the Founding Fathers who built this country. These wise men outlawed fractional reserve debt money, compound interest, usury and paper money. They spurned debt generally. They found reprehensible the concept of money earning money on money - compound interest. And they were prosperous.

The bottom line is this: If a people in a society are to be prosperous, peaceful and happy long-term, the economic structure of society must establish people as superior to things and money. This is the lesson of Mondragon. But in order for this to occur, a society must establish the rules (boundaries) of monetary law. Such monetary law must first and foremost include prohibition of fractional reserve debt money, paper money, and the compound interest factor, whereby money earns money by simply being money. Strict limitations on the nature and length of debt itself are also important. Such prohibitions forbid non-productive financial activities, such as we have seen run rampant in recent years by way of junk bonds used for leveraged buyouts, mergers, greenmail, and the weakening, dismantling and selloff of productive business corporations. Such prohibitions are the only way to establish the correct priority of people over things.

If people are indeed primarily spiritual beings, made in the image of God, then they are eternal, and more important than things (and money), which are temporal. Therefore, the very concept of the time value of money as eternal is a myth, as debt-based society after debt-based society has demonstrated time and time again down through history. These societies have crumbled and disappeared. When a society focuses on the time value of money and such things as discounted present value, as does our social order today, it has bought the lie of money as a god. It has elevated money and things to a more important position than people. It has relinquished its freedom and prosperity in exchange for a walk up the ever increasing angle of inclination, on the treadmill of compound interest, to exhaustion. To hold as absolute the concept that life is time and time is money, is to equate life with money. Then money and things become more important than people and the society begins to die as conflict over money and things accelerates. Conflict brings about poverty, not prosperity. The result long-term is less things for people. So, unless there are laws which establish money as a commodity, or as the representative thereof, unless there are laws which tie money to man's real, finite world, there's no hope for establishing cooperation over conflict, for establishing people as more important than things, or for escaping the long-term exhaustion and bankruptcy resulting from the tyranny of the time value of money.

I would be remiss if I did not mention that as a byproduct of establishing the time value of money (and things) as superior to people, that people, particularly children, become a curse rather than a blessing. Children are expensive. They are sacrificed to the god of debt service. So, it is no accident that with the increasing debt load in a society that there is a concomitant increase in abortion.

A people who do not reproduce themselves and murder their young by definition commit suicide long-term. Thus, the time value of money which establishes the priority of money (and things) over people inescapably destroys mankind. It is no accident that one of the root meanings of the word *debt* is *death*, just as the root meaning of the word *mort*, as in *mortgage*, is also *death*.

SECTION VIII

Health

THE TWO WORST MISTAKES YOU'LL EVER MAKE
(AND HOW TO PREVENT OR CORRECT THEM)

July 31, 1991

The two worst mistakes you'll ever make are: (1) choosing the wrong vocation; (2) choosing the wrong marriage partner.

If we stop and think about it, a meaningful life really comes down to love and work. Therefore, if we choose the wrong vocation and the wrong marriage partner, we strike out in life. Even if we're wrong in only one out of two, we have squandered 50% of our life.

We all grow up in a family which programs our subconscious regarding both marriage and vocation. Plus, we each come into this world wired in a unique way regarding our deep personal needs, desires and calling. If we do not line up our vocation and our marriage partner with our basic work and love needs, we frustrate ourselves in life. We also do ourselves considerable emotional damage, with the inevitable fallout being physical disease. Leading doctors today say that 80% of all disease is emotionally based. So choosing the right vocation and the right marriage partner is literally a life and death matter.

Punching the Clock

Look at how we spend our time in a 24-hour day: When we're young, we spend it with family and in school. This programs us for the type of marriage partner we will choose and our life's work (vocation). When we're older, having left our nuclear formative family, and having completed our education, we still spend at least 50% of our waking hours and one-third of our 24-hour day working at our chosen vocation, with nearly all the rest of our time spent with our marriage partner or in that family environment.

So again, what I am saying is this: The two most important choices and decisions you will make in life are: (1) the education, training and subsequent work in your chosen vocation; (2) the choice of your marriage partner.

Financial Fallout

In a materialistic culture such as ours, inevitably both of these choices carry tremendous financial consequences. A person who has both the motivation and aptitude, along with the opportunity, to do his life's work/calling/vocation has the greatest probability of succeeding. Such an individual literally loves his work. Work for him is fun. This stimulates all the intuitive and creative juices necessary to succeed and prosper. The financial payoff is a big one.

Unfortunately, the opposite is equally true. If an individual is in a job/calling/vocation where he has little aptitude for the job and no motivation, his conscious and/or his subconscious will self-destruct at the task. The payoff here is poverty, financial mediocrity, depression, perhaps even physical and financial ruin.

Marriage has an important financial payoff, too. The most successful and happy people in the world are couples where the man and the wife work together as a team with shared values, shared goals, like-minded interests, protecting each other's backside, with each partner's weaknesses being offset by the other's strengths. Three examples in this country come quickly to mind (regardless of what you think about their politics): Lyndon and Lady Bird Johnson, Jimmy and Rosalyn Carter, and Ronald and Nancy Reagan. The payoff for all three of these couples was a big one, not only financially, but in terms of power, self-esteem, and self-actualization.

We should also realize that there is a huge downside loss financially, emotionally, psychologically and physically associated with choosing the wrong marriage partner. Divorce is devastating comprehensively. In financial consulting sessions, I tell my clients that the worst financial loss they'll ever suffer will be in a divorce. And make no mistake about it, the subsequent mental, emotional, depressive psychological and physical drawdown resulting from a divorce takes its toll on an individual's future earning capacity as well, often for an extended period of time.

Cultural Counterpunch

The healthiest, happiest and most productive people on earth are those who live in harmony with their vocation and their marriage partner. Tragically, our culture today does everything possible to ensure that neither of these occur. In short, the institutions in this society work at making us miserable, and deceive us into making the two worst mistakes possible in life, in our choice of a vocation and a marriage partner. Here's how:

9 to 5

First of all, we are programmed by the mass media and 12 years in the State Indoctrination Network (public schools) to be Manchurian candidates, serfs and bondslaves of the state (civil government), or of some big corporation. We are told that there is nothing unique or special about us, but that we are to fit into some 9-to-5 corporate or government peg hole. We are taught that we are statistically insignificant, just a 9-digit social security number, a chance product of some slime that has evolved, and lives and dies without meaning. The last thing in the world we are taught is the reality that we are made in the image of God, the Father of Lights, literally *"Light Men,"* who are unique, special, and have been programmed by God for a special purpose/calling/work/vocation here on earth. We have destinies to be fulfilled!

With rare exceptions, the public schools, the big corporations, and the federal government don't have a clue to understanding the subconscious of the individual, identifying his motivation and aptitude, and thus predicting his behavior and ideal vocation from that information. But, for nine years the Los Alamos National Laboratories have used the PDI system. Why not the rest of us? Why not? Aren't we entitled to become *"the best and the brightest?"*

Merry Marry

Then there is the way Hollywood and the mass media program us to select a marriage partner. It's totally emotional. When have you ever seen anyone succeed long term who makes their decisions based primarily on emotion? Never! Not that emotions aren't important. Emotions are the appreciator of the soul. But emotions, just like a small child, have to be disciplined, trained, harnessed and directed. The natural tendency of unbridled emotions is to self-destruct. So, it is no coincidence that over 50% of American marriages today are on the rocks. They have no solid, long-term foundation on which to build.

A good marriage is built upon covenant, shared values, mutual interests, complementary strengths, and shared vocational interests. Real emotional satisfaction and sexual compatibility follow long term. This is just the opposite of the way our culture has programmed us. But then again, in almost every way possible today, from the environment to federal debt, the federal government and culture are death oriented. Small wonder it would be so, too, in the key areas of vocation and marriage, the two most critical decisions any of us will make.

The Brass Ring

Okay, so what's the way out? From my training in college in behavioral management to today, I have spent over 25 years pursuing the answer to these two vital questions. I am comfortable that I now have the unique tools available to answer both of them successfully, with about a 90% probability of accuracy! Most testing services (of which there are many), look at behavior in an attempt to identify motivation and aptitude, leading to vocation. That's backwards. It is why people continue to flounder in choosing both their vocation and marriage partner despite the proliferation of testing and counseling services across this country. The correct approach is to begin with consciousness, insight into the motivation and aptitude of the individual emerging from his subconscious, and from that base predict behavior and select a vocation and marriage partner. It is thus not surprising that a number of competing firms have attempted to steal PDI's software program. This is not at all your typical *"behavioristic psychology,"* no way.

Let's face it, it is next to impossible to reprogram an individual's subconscious. We are what we are. For all practical purposes, you can't change people. The Catholic church has known this for years. It's why the Catholic church has always said if you give it the first six years of a child's life, and then add to it the first six years of schooling (the first 12 years total), the Catholic church will own that child for life. Why? This is the time frame when the subconscious of an individual is programmed, from age 2 to 12. The odds that an individual will break out of this mold in any meaningful sense is less than one in a thousand. Further, an individual will never change the natural wiring he brought with him into this world regarding his vocation.

Atlas Shrugged

Here's another way to look at it: If a person has the motivation to do a particular work but doesn't have the aptitude for it, he will work hard at the task but probably fail long term. He just doesn't have the natural gear for the job. On the other hand, if the individual has an aptitude to do a job, but has no motivation (or drive) to accomplish it, he will likely fail also. He'll squander his time, be distracted by other interests, produce a run-of-the-mill performance, etc. But if an individual has both the motivation and the aptitude to do a particular job, and knows this early in life, and then can obtain the education and training necessary to fulfill his natural calling, and further chooses a marriage partner who is like-minded and synergistically complements his efforts, well, that person is destined for greatness! Blessed is such an individual indeed. Today, this can be all of us!

Tried and True

I now consider one of the most important things I can do for my children and grandchildren is provide them with the information which gives them the unique understanding of themselves, their basic makeup, their motivation and aptitude, so they can choose both the right vocation and marriage partner. To me it is an expression, perhaps the best expression, of my love.

Potentials Development, Inc. (P.O. Box 55339, Seattle, WA 98155-0339, Tel: 206-364-0737, Fax: 206-364-3303) can provide you with what I call the *"Vocation Report,"* the basic personal appraisal which tells you your subconsciously based motivation and aptitudes and following logical vocational choices. This is great for children and grandchildren, too. We, too, deserve the opportunity to become the *"best and the brightest."* Plus, a really neat aspect of the PDI instrument is that it works for everyone in a kind and gentle way, regardless of age, education, culture, race, creed or religion.

What I call the *"Marriage Report"* includes the analysis of both people in the marriage partnership, each of their basic makeups (aptitudes/motivations/logical vocational choices) and then the critically important interpersonal crossover report which shows how they will fit (or not fit) together. This interpersonal crossover report reveals with a high degree of accuracy whether a partnership in marriage (or business) will make it or fail, whether the two individuals seeking a union will meet each other's needs, compliment each other, and pull together as a team, or tear each other apart.

* * * * *

UP THE DOWN ESCALATOR

The mask of the theater, a smile, a frown, positive or negative, which will it be?

I've never considered myself to be either an optimist or a pessimist, but rather a realist. I adopted the Lebanese proverb, *"Truth kills those who hide from it."* If you live in Lebanon, in order to survive, you pretty much have to adopt this proverb. You have to stay in touch with what is.

Is the glass half empty or half full? It doesn't matter, the real issue is, *"What is the trend?"* Is the glass being filled, or being emptied? Once we discern true status, reality, and then know trend (direction), we can next determine what the worst case scenario might be. What is our maximum downside risk? If we manage the downside, eventually the upside will take care of itself.

It is no different in life than in the markets. If we are in a leveraged market investment position, we'll put in a stop loss to prevent a multiplication of our error/pain on the downside. In non-leveraged investments, we can either run quickly (use a protective stop loss), or not run at all. In a non-leveraged situation, time is on our side. Not so when leverage is involved. Good things and bad things in life happen to us all. The most healthy outlook with regard to the bad things is: (1) We view them as temporary, that they will pass; (2) we see them as isolated and not affecting everything else; and (3) while we discern our culpability, naivete and mistakes in the matters, we also determine that they are not totally our fault, and that there are other people and circumstances who are involved who also shared responsibility.

With regard to the good things that happen to us in life, the most healthy attitude we can take is to: (1) Believe that we caused them to happen or influenced them, in other words, take some credit for them; (2) think that our good fortune positively affects and permeates everything else in our lives; and (3) that good things have a beneficial long-term effect.

Some medical doctors today think that 80% of all diseases are emotionally based. From a 50-year study of the health of 200 Harvard men, George Vaillant and psychologist Martin Seligman found that optimism at age 25 strongly predicts an individual's health at age 60. Around age 45, the pessimists begin to develop more of the diseases which are common to middle age. They also suffer more severe symptoms as well. Psychosomatically, as a man thinketh, so he is.

Who is the primary influential person in determining whether we are naturally optimistic or pessimistic? Our mothers! But this instilled attitude can be changed. Martin Seligman's book, *Learned Optimism*, presents a persuasive case that we can change our inherited outlook on life.

In tune with reality and the trend, I think we are on the pessimistic downside of the cycle near term (between now and 2012). But I am very enthusiastic and optimistic long term, particularly after 2025. Also, my trading history reveals my market bias is clearly bullish. I prefer to go long rather than sell short, by a ratio of 2:1.

Finally, there is a six-part test that I took which determined my degree of optimism and pessimism. I ended up *"average"* in four of the six categories, extremely optimistic in one case, and only extremely pessimistic in one of the six categories. Where was I overly pessimistic? In thinking I could not personally make a difference and change things. You see, I've been beaten up a lot during the last ten years trying to change things in the world, in this country, for the American people, in the church, and in my family. I guess I had resigned myself that the only thing I could really change was myself. I'm having to rethink this position now.

Incidentally, Marian Sandmaier, in the March/April 1991 issue of *New Age Journal*, authored a piece entitled, *"Living on the Bright Side."* Inside that article, on pages 41 and 98, is a 48-question optimism/pessimism test and 6-part scoring mechanism. I recommend it to you. (So, you see, Martha, there are some nice things I can say about Kevin Costner's New Age. The most dangerous errors, however, are those which are 95% true. So, we have to be good sifters.)

We're entering an era when we, the people, individuals, are again going to be able to make a difference. At a time when we have no heroes, and the individual man is all but bludgeoned into insignificance in accordance with the *"Death Star,"* the New World Order, we are about to see a major contrary opinion rally of individualism. So there is an optimistic silver lining to today's pessimistic black cloud.

HUMAN POTENTIAL
November 10, 1988

Garden or Wasteland

Beyond question, the most squandered resource on the face of the earth is human potential. We have over five billion people on this globe who have the *"potential"* to turn the earth into a garden rather than a wasteland. Since we are moving toward the latter, it follows we are doing something wrong, squandering *"human potential."*

There are only two parts of the economic equation - people and things. People are more important than things because people create, use and destroy things. So if we are to function successfully, we must focus first and foremost on the development of people.

I have written a great deal about *"people systems"* over the years. Section 7, *"Love and Money"* and the conclusion of this book really lay out the individual and social systems necessary to recapture the earth from a wilderness to a garden. For good measure, we could also throw in the Lebanese family associations and the requirement that the church not abdicate its health, education and welfare responsibilities. With just these four elements properly operative in any society, the curse of cold bureaucratic civil government, whose existence is nothing more than the resulting curse of local irresponsibility, will wither away.

Human Capital - U.S. and Japan

The cover story of the September 19, 1988 *Business Week* was *"Human Capital: The Decline of America's Work Force."* Leading off in this article *Business Week* stated: *"The U.S. has lost much ground to competitors, and investing in people looks like the way to retake it. After years of neglect, the problem of human capital has become a crisis."*

Amen! America's literacy rate has dropped dramatically from 90% in 1851. Today in Japan, blue-collar workers interpret advanced mathematics, read complex engineering blueprints and perform sophisticated tasks on the factory floor. By contrast, in New York, Chemical Bank interviews forty applicants to find one qualified to be trained as a teller.

Adam Smith wrote in *The Wealth of Nations, "A man educated at the expense of much labor and time to any one of those employments which require extraordinary dexterity and skill may be compared to one of those expensive machines."* So public education just isn't cutting it these days. American high school students are consistently beaten by their foreign counterparts in math and science. America's youth test two to three years behind the Japanese.

In the U.S.A., we have given status to the working mother. In Japan, by contrast, the mother plays such a strong role in teaching her children that she is known as *"education mamma."* My friend, Lester C. Thurow, Dean of the Sloan School of management at MIT says, *"The big reason for Asian-American success in public schools is family; family means some parent telling you that some education is important."*

Unprepared Minorities

Between now and the year 2000, more than half of all new workers hired will be from minorities, nearly three times the current figure. A fourth of all children born in the U.S. will be on welfare some time in their lives, while 25% will be born out of wedlock, and 42% will live in single-parent families before they reach age eighteen. Most of these will be members of minority groups. Blacks and Hispanics have the highest school dropout rate in the country and consistently score the lowest on tests. As a result, the productivity of the unskilled, emotionally scarred American worker is plummeting, while worker productivity abroad is soaring, with foreign workers often being paid lower wages as well. Over the intermediate term, this almost ensures an increasing U.S. trade and current accounts deficit. More dangerously, this increasing spread between the top and bottom half of society makes for social tension, with ambitious men using the politics of envy to fan the fires of economic strife.

Three Economic Forces

Business Week points out that three forces active in the economy now are requiring more skilled and educated workers. These forces are: (1) more sophisticated technology; (2) high-skilled occupations in the service sector; and (3) Japanese-style work organizations.

Against these requirements, the Hudson Institute found that three-quarters of the nation's new workers will have limited verbal and writing skills while competing for 40% of the new jobs. The math and science skills the workers are bringing to the jobs are abysmal. Only 22% of the workers will be able to function at the level required of them. Most of the jobs will require above a high school education. And alarmingly, only 5% of the employees will be able to actually meet the demand levels required by the job.

This means 50 million workers will have to be trained or retrained in the next twelve years, 20 million new workers and 30 million current workers. Over 30 million employees will need new math and science skills to operate in our computerized and robotic service and industrial sectors. Reading and writing skills will have to be upscaled dramatically also.

Science & Engineering

U.S. companies are presently spending $30 billion on worker training, much of which is used to upgrade present employees. Some 2.3 million workers were displaced in the 1980s due to the changing nature of the economy. Scientists and engineers are in short supply. According to the National Science

Foundation, over the past thirty years, only 3.7% to 4.3% of college degrees have been awarded in science and engineering, while the demand for scientists and engineers has mushroomed. By the year 2000, the U.S. will be short over 400,000 science and engineering college graduates. Plus, fully 50% of the engineering graduate students in the U.S. today are foreigners. It is projected that the U.S. will be short 27,000 Ph.D.s in these two critical fields by the year 2000.

Youth Dearth

Some futurists are saying that a decline in the birthrate after 1960, primarily due to economic pressure, abortion and self-orientation, has slashed the number of young people available to fill jobs until after the year 2010. This labor shortage is complicated by the fact that 73% of all working women are of childbearing age, and 60% of all school-aged kids have mothers in the work force. This means time away from the job for women. Further, women with children under age six are the fastest growing segment of the work force. This not only makes child care an expensive issue, but by the year 2000, more and more workers will have to take responsibility for their parents as well. Needless to say, there is no way the federal budget can support the welfare which will be demanded at both ends of the spectrum, by the very young and the elderly.

Presently, the federal government provides a $3.9 billion dependent-care tax credit, $660 million for day care, and $1.5 billion for the Head Start early childhood program. Businesses are starting to pick up the slack in these areas. Such is becoming a particularly significant expense for businesses where minorities are involved. Not only are businesses being increasingly asked to pick up the day care expense, but the retraining cost for minority members is substantial. In New York and Washington, D.C. for example, the high school dropout rate among minorities, mainly blacks, is 35% and 50% respectively. Nationwide, the dropout rate for blacks is 17.5%, and 29.3% for Hispanics. Furthermore, Harvard sociologist David Ellwood predicts that two-thirds of children who grow up in a single-parent household will spend at least some of their childhood in poverty. These children are also three times more likely to drop out of school. The situation at present is so dismal that a National Assessment of Education Progress study discovered that only 60% of white young adults could locate information in a news article or an almanac, while only 25% of blacks and 40% of Hispanics could locate such information.

Old Age Recall

More and more men who have retired are being called back into the work force by attractive salaries, and out of sheer economic necessity. Presently, only 15% of those over age 65 are in the work force today. Only 68% of men aged 55 to 64 work presently. This is liable to change dramatically, not only due to demand and incentives provided by the work place, but also due to strains put on the economy by monetary inflation, higher costs of goods and services, higher taxes, more expensive health care, and greater expense in educating and caring for children. Retirement at middle age will become less and less the norm over the next twenty-five years (middle age being 58-year old retirement). Retirement at age 65 is likely to go by the boards as well.

Inner Cities and Immigrants

The federal government is compounding the problem by providing welfare incentives in the inner city ghettos for black teenagers to become single mothers. As black economists Tom Sowell and Walter Williams have long pointed out, federal welfare programs have emasculated the black American male, who previously took charge and responsibility for maintaining the integrity of the black nuclear family unit. Additionally, four out of five foreigners the INS is allowing to enter the United States have not been screened for job skills. Family ties and refugee status have priority. When the two to four million illegal immigrants are added to this number, the work force/welfare dilemma is aggravated even more.

Today, too many black families with children are headed by women. An overwhelming majority of these children end up in crime and/or on welfare. Charles Murray's alarming book, *Losing Ground*, is proving to be true. Federal welfare policy has discouraged marriage and work while rewarding out-of-wedlock childbearing and unemployment. Only half of adult black men who live in the cities work, compared to 80% back in 1969. The federal government's welfare programs do little to encourage work.

How badly are the public schools failing? In the inner cities, 50% of high school students drop out. Of the 2.4 million who graduate, 25% cannot read or write at the eighth-grade level, a functionally literate level. Most seventeen year olds in school cannot summarize a newspaper article, write a good letter requesting a job, or solve real-life math problems. Sadly, they can't even follow a bus schedule. When a man can't read, write, do arithmetic or think, he cannot be rational. He then is left to what comes naturally: being reactive, animalistic, emotional and violent. We desperately need a free market in education in this country.

This human capital crisis the United States faces will affect us all. The September 19, 1988 *Business Week* is must reading for investors, for employers, for parents with children, and for students who will be entering the work force shortly.

Government Regulations

The holistic profitable use of human potential has suffered badly in the American work place over the past few decades. Productivity, effectiveness, efficiency, profitability, creativity and safety have all seriously declined in American industry. This trend must be reversed if U.S. business, its management and workers, are to successfully compete in the global marketplace. The challenge to business today is even greater with the increasing *"social responsibility"* placed on both manufacturing and the service sector by the federal government. The EEO regulations and their interpretations, plus the July 1988 decision of the U.S. Supreme Court in *"Watson vs. Ft. Worth Bank and Trust"* make attention to this area a must.

Contrary to popular opinion, the EEO regulations and the court decisions are not anti-business. Nor do they mandate or favor quota hiring on the basis of race or sex. To the contrary, both EEO regulations and recent court decisions are strongly pro-business if business management can fulfill three basic hiring procedures: (1) identify essential functions of the jobs which must be profitably performed by the persons in the jobs; (2) identify the vocational potential of job candidates; and (3) have a valid way to match the potential of job candidates with requirements of the job.

If business management can adequately fulfill these three mandated employment functions, then the EEO regulations, their interpretations, and court decisions encourage and even support the selection of qualified candidates for jobs, even if sexual and/or racial representation in the workplace is not quickly achieved. It is only if management cannot perform these required functions that the EEO regulations, interpretations and court decisions have mandated quota hiring on the assumption that vocational skills are equally distributed among all races and sexes. Of course, corporate attorneys have argued that such capability, with the known techniques available today for evaluating human potential, make the fulfillment of these three requirements virtually *"impossible."* So the challenge to business is for individuals to have equal opportunity, to have their vocational potential identified and measured, relative to identified job requirements. This puts the onus on the back of employers. If the employer has such capability, then he has the right to select the best candidate as a *"business associate."*

Perhaps needless to say, American business, reflecting the culture, finds these requirements a curve ball it has been unable to hit. Then again, American culture, and the business which seeks to serve that culture, has for the better part of this century focused on things rather than people. So this quandary in the workplace is no surprise.

Handwriting Analysis

As a result of groping in the dark for answers on how to match the right person to the right job, within the guidelines of federal regulations and court decisions, a number of exotic evaluation techniques have appeared. For example, the August 25, 1988 *Wall Street Journal*, on the front page of the second section, featured an extensive article entitled, *"Handwriting Analysis as Personnel Tool."* *The Journal* discussed how major firms are beginning to use handwriting analysis as a way of determining if a particular individual is suited for a specific job. The WSJ mentioned the following professional handwriting analysts: Shirley Hawe of Portland, Oregon; Handwriting Resource Corp. of Phoenix, Arizona; and Jay Larsen with Professional Management Consultants of Richardson, Texas. The burgeoning number of reputable firms which are using *"graphology"* to match people with jobs listed in the WSJ is quite impressive.

Color Analysis

Then there is the use of color in analyzing an individual's personality, motivation and potential with regard to his likely performance in the workplace. Color Information Systems, Inc. of Las Vegas, Nevada specializes in this area. Dr. Richard Wedaa, a brilliant color analyst, has dedicated over twenty years of his life to understanding the effects of color on people, as well as how the color of an individual's name gives important clues to the personality makeup of that individual.

Dr. Wedaa keeps his analytical techniques proprietary. Color analysis must work because Dr. Wedaa charges a healthy fee to major corporations for his evaluation of the color of a candidate's name who is applying for a top managerial position. Dr. Wedaa claims 90% accuracy.

Let's see if I can explain Dr. Wedaa's color analysis. In the visible light spectrum in which we live, 0.4-0.7 micrometers, we all have a handle, a name. Now, in the infrared range, form, frequency and substance are all interrelated. This means each letter and each combination of letters in a name emits its own frequency. So a name is frequency, and of course, color is also a wave length or a frequency. So through the use of sophisticated computer software, a name can be changed into a color combination, which in turn can be broken down into the color elements of the periodic table, where resonant frequency can be determined, providing important clues concerning the chemical makeup of that individual on the electromagnetic level. This in turn is psychologically critical in determining the basic psychological makeup of that individual. (It has long been established that chemicals, like drugs, alter human behavior, just as human behavior may be altered by such things as diet.)

Color and Biblical Names

This link between a name - color, basic elements, resonant frequency - and psychological makeup is not all that farfetched. (Besides, who can argue with accuracy?) The Bible says, *"The word of God is alive and powerful."* In this perspective, that biblical sentence should be taken literally! Also in the Bible, in Genesis, God changed Jacob's name to *"Israel."* With that name change came a personality change. Jacob meant *"supplanter"* or *"chisler."* Israel meant *"God strives."* Throughout the Bible, names meant something. Biblical names describe behavior and personality types. For example, Christ means *"The Anointed One."* In Revelation 4:3, Jesus Christ is described in terms of color, particularly gemstones - a jasper, a sardius, and an emerald. Fascinating!

I went back as far as the Middle Ages in my study of gemstones, color and their effect regarding people's health, behavior and spiritual state. What I learned regarding the description of Jesus Christ as a gemstone in Revelation 4 was absolutely mind blowing. But that's another long and involved discussion, more appropriate for another time and another forum. Suffice it to say, I now also understand the meaning of the color patterns of countenances, which are emitted by each of us, but visible only to a few.

Conventional Business Management and Investment Consultants

Dropping back down in the realm of the conventional, I have been blessed with the opportunity to work with a number of excellent management consultants. In my early twenties, I worked with business psychoanalyst Dr. Bob Schaffer, recently retired from Rohrer, Hibler and Replogoe, Inc. (55 West Monroe, Chicago, Illinois 60603). Dr. Schaffer's former company works with major corporate clients and is expensive, but well worth it according to their reputation.

Bob Eskridge, president of Growth Management Center (796 Via Del Monte, Palos Verdes Estates, CA 90274) has worked with a large number of corporations, including Jack Daniels and Holiday Inn. Bob's Growth Management Center is highly respected. I found the time I spent with Bob Eskridge to be extremely valuable and constructive for my personal and business planning in sorting out my work situation.

When it comes to helping investors understand their personalities and internal conflicts as they relate to markets and investment success, the work of Van K. Tharp, Ph.D. is unequalled. Dr. Tharp helped me recognize and deal with unconscious internal conflict which inhibited my trading success. Dr. Tharp may be reached at Investment Psychology Consulting (1410 East Glen Oaks Blvd., Glendale, CA 91206). He offers a superb set of cassettes and books in the area of investment psychology.

For building communication and relationship skills, I found the *"Effective Communication and Relationship Building Seminars"* of Selwa Said useful (25 Quendale Avenue, Monterey, CA 93940).

Testing Services

When it comes to testing, one of the most reasonably priced and comprehensive battery of tests available is put out by Palmer Testing Service (93 Main Street, Andover, MA 01810). Palmer Testing Service's reports include Aptitudes Summary, Personality Summary, Career Interests Summary, Job Function Interest Summary, Industry Interest Summary, and an IQ Test. Palmer Testing also includes an Indepth Personality Profile for Executives. This profile includes Personal Orientation, Job Preference, Satisfaction Values, Self-management Style, Relations with Others, Conflict Resolution, Leadership Style, Information Processing, and Interpersonal Style. Palmer Testing Service also provides a *"Stress Map Report,"* which is an evaluation of stress in a person's life. This test identifies stress symptoms, sources of stress, satisfaction levels, and coping mechanisms. These reasonably priced Palmer Testing Service reports provide a Thinking Style Profile as well.

Aptitude and Motivation

Many tests on the market today test just aptitude. So what? Aptitude alone does not determine behavior. The world is literally crawling with people possessed of tremendous aptitude who have squandered it because they had no motivation to use it. It is the link up between aptitude and motivation which leads to the true development of *"human potential."* Mark Cramer (working with Ken Neils) goes a long way toward resolving this age old problem. And I may be understating the case a bit. The men I have talked to who have worked with Cramer and Neils say their system is so refined that pegging people is no longer an art, but a science. (Refer to the previous chapter, *"The Two Worst Mistakes You'll Ever Make"*)

Conclusion

We have the tools available to us today to identify precisely the aptitude and motivation of an individual, and match it almost perfectly to a calling. So as I see it, the nature, degree and orientation of education and job training can now be clearly targeted. The type of job to be chosen subsequently can be clearly identified. The ultimate result is both the person (work) and the firm are synergistically fulfilled in a win-win transaction. The resulting fallout is that society-at-large is both well-served and more competitive globally.

I am convinced the utilization of the systems and techniques formulated by the above-discussed people and firms will dramatically help you personally, your family, and your business in helping America regain its cutting edge in the global marketplace.

People make, use and destroy things. People are more important than things. When we use these above-stated systems professionally, rather than *"winging it,"* we will move a long way toward maximizing *"human potential."*

GREEN GARDEN GOLD
October 7, 1987

Slowly, but surely, as the research has emerged, I have come to the conclusion that one of the best investments I can make is in my own garden.

What the Federal Reserve and the fractional reserve banking system have done to our money, the food processing industry has done to our food. Both have *"gutted"* the value of their product.

We are what we believe; we are what we think and feel; we are also what we eat. And what we believe, think, feel and eat are all interrelated. Each area affects the other. The body is an extension of the mind, a reflection of the mind and a part of the mind. To put it more crassly, when we are junk food junkies, we become junk. The average American puts 26 types of poisons into his system daily. This scrambles the digestive and endocrine systems, and overtaxes the immune system. Chronic metabolic disease is at an all-time high presently in the United States as a result.

Since the mid-1920s, when the food processing industry began stripping our flour of all its nutrients (promoting white flour products), the average American male's sperm count has dropped over 75%! Sperm count is a sign of physical vitality. One out of five American men will have a heart attack before age 55. No wonder American men are becoming increasingly irresponsible. They have lost their physical vitality, and with it their will and their discipline.

Ever wonder why our children crave sweets? It is because they have a legitimate need for sugar. The food they're eating is not giving them the high levels of natural sugars which their growing bodies require. So, they ingest the *"quick fixes"* - the colas, candy bars, sugared cereals and the like.

Life comes from life. How can we eat dead, stale food and expect to live well and long? Food needs to be as fresh, nutritious and wholesome as possible. Otherwise, particularly in the case of much of the junk food, we literally draw down our bodies' reservoir of stored energy reserves - minerals, vitamins, calcium, enzymes and the like - in order to digest the junk food we are eating. It's much like eating snow when we're thirsty. Our bodies burn up more energy and utilize more water in melting the snow in our mouths, than the moisture content derived from the melted snow itself. It's a losing situation.

This depletion of our bodies' calcium, enzyme, vitamin and mineral reserves is another reason why the exercise fad which has captured much of yuppie America is potentially deleterious. Without the underlying proper nutrition, exercise fanatics are drawing down their bodies' basic calcium, enzyme, vitamin and mineral reserves. They are doing themselves more harm than good long term.

Ever have jet lag? We read regularly that a good diet, abstinence from alcohol and tobacco, and being in good physical shape reduces the effect of jet lag. So be it. Also, eating food which is grown at the same longitude and latitude where we reside is best for us. This means that the magnetic charge of our homegrown food is in harmony with that of our physical bodies. So, there is a good reason why every man ought to live *"under his own vine and fig tree."* (Jet lag actually is nothing more than the amount of time it takes our electronic bodies [countenances] to adjust to the new longitude and latitude. And this is a function of the overall health of our physical bodies.)

Good nutrition is vital for the health of the *"aura,"* the *"electromagnetic - chemical field,"* the *"countenance"* which radiates from the human body. The *"countenance"* is also our body's first line of defense against disease. This is what medical research in both France and West Germany has confirmed in thousands of cases. We can ill afford a hole in our countenance. With the plagues that inevitably come at the end of a civilization, we can ill afford today to have weak *"countenances"* and weak immune systems, particularly given the likes of AIDS.

There is well documented agricultural research that if the land is not given a sabbatical (rest) every seven years, if there is not good crop rotation, if the soil is not nurtured, protected, built up and balanced, that effectively the soil is mined out and depleted of its calcium, humus, minerals and magnetic charge after only three generations. The soil, in other words, is exhausted. This is what has happened with the land on which our food is grown today. It has been depleted and exhausted, literally mined out. But to make matters worse, to further stimulate the exhausted soil to produce, toxic fertilizers, herbicides and pesticides are dumped onto the land. This subsequently weakens the soil long term as well as makes it more toxic. Small wonder that the sickest people in America today are the farmers.

The quality of our food can be no better than the soil on which it is produced. Because the food we eat today comes from weak, poisoned, toxic plants, even this non-junk food is substandard in calcium, minerals, vitamins, enzymes and percentage of sucrose/brix. We receive inadequate nutrition from this toxic, substandard food, leaving us with poor physical constitutions and easily blown countenances, even if we eat a so-called healthy, well-rounded, relatively fresh diet of fruits, vegetables, nuts, seeds and whole grains. We are what we eat. We get out of our food what was put into it.

How can we possibly receive adequate nutrition from the food we eat today when it is harvested from weakened and toxic plants, which were grown in toxic, depleted soils? Plus, our food has been sprayed with who knows what while in the field, picked green, sprayed again before being shipped to us, and sprayed and reprocessed yet another time to *"look good"* before it is merchandised on the supermarket shelves.

Heavens, as a result of what we eat, we are hardly even human today. We are mere skeletons of what God originally created. Morticians tell us that we are already so well preserved that by the time we're cold and reach the undertaker, it now takes one-third less formaldehyde to preserve us. The forensic divisions of major police departments inform us that 50 years ago when they dug up a grave, the skeletal system was still intact. Now if a body is dumped or buried in a shallow grave for only two or three years, when it is dug up, the bones have already dissolved. Only a trace of them remains. We have effectively no calcium left in our systems. We are *"holy"* all right! How can we as a nation have any character when we have no backbone?

We may have *"heavenly"* (good looking) bodies on the outside, but on the inside our bodies are like dead men's bones, like termite infested supports. The whole system collapses from the inside out, regardless of what it looks like.

The older generation today is plagued by broken hips. (It will be a worse plague too for the malnourished, now aging, *"hippie"* generation.) Broken hips occur because the body has used up all its fluid calcium and is forced to steal calcium from the larger bones, like the shoulder bones and hips.

Unless the calcium is adequate in our bodies, the pH cannot be maintained between 6.2 and 6.6. The body's pH needs to be between 6.2 and 6.6 in order for vitamin C to be assimilated and utilized by the physical system. Thus, the assimilation of vitamin C is dependent upon calcium. Calcium is in turn dependent upon adequate vitamin D. Vitamin D in turn is dependent upon vitamin A, which is available in all healthy fresh fruits and vegetables.

Nutrition turns into a chemical-electrical charge. As Dr. Robert D. Becker wrote in his fascinating book, *The Body Electric*, we are effectively an electrical system. The chemicals we use and the electromagnetic charge derived from them, come from the minerals in the body's system. Calcium is the primary, basic mineral needed for good health. (Excessive protein intake restricts calcium assimilation.)

Another reason I need a garden is because socialism ultimately creates such an imbalance between the number of people living in the cities versus the food supply, that famine inevitably results. (When we analyze the nutritional value of our food today, we are already being starved to death.) Food shortages and socialism/communism go hand-in-hand. Those who did best economically under the rule of atheistic, occult, socialistic, fascist Nazi Germany were small, rural farmers. This is the political direction we are headed today. So, it's again time to become a small, rural farmer.

All around us people are breaking down physically (and as a result mentally and psychologically). Chronic metabolic disease has reached an all-time high. The ever-increasing lifespan in this country is peaking out. Long life has been primarily due to dramatic, high-tech medical advancements, coupled with the fact that people who are old today were born and raised before both this rape of the land and our food occurred. The older generation had good physical constitutions which they could mine and abuse. But we don't have the constitutions of our fathers, grandfathers and great-grandfathers. And our children are really in sick shape.

In today's high-stress environment, can we risk being nutritionally deficient? All the food we eat ought to add up to about 12 brix of sugar to support our health. The conventional corn crop in America only comes up to about 3 to 4 brix, whether it's used for animal feed or human consumption. If our food does not measure up, we get excess nitrogen in our systems which puts stress on the liver and kidneys, not to mention the heart. Mankind develops kidney, liver and heart problems from insufficient energy in a crop or food in relation to nitrogen.

An added complication is sugar imbalance and stressing of the pancreas and the adrenals. The adrenals attempt to compensate for a stressed pancreas. This results in an ever-increasing number of Americans becoming either hypo- or hyperglycemic.

Faulty nutrition is a contributory reason why we have become a society consumed by sex and violence. Our movies are obsessed with sex and violence. The brutality of professional football is an addiction. A bumper sticker recently read, *"Be a Road Warrior - Drive California Freeways."*

When food is of poor quality and low nutritional value, the primitive (violence-prone) brain center of mankind takes over. On average, America has the worst staple diet of any civilized nation in the world. Americans consume the stalest food in history. Dr. Steven Schentahler discovered in his research regarding the metabolism of the brain, that deep within the primitive brain is the limbic system. The limbic system requires only one-fifth of the energy required by the higher frontal brain centers. If there is inadequate nutrition, the forebrain is less efficient than the deeper, more primitive brain centers. Thus, man literally degenerates to behaving like an animal when he eats the typical American diet. He is prone to the animalistic activities of violence, immorality and immoderate sexual activity. On the other hand, research done with teenagers in prison and in teenage reform schools indicates that a wholesome nutritious diet has become fundamental for character and behavior reformation. This is what the Roloff schools in Corpus Christi, Texas proved.

Today, the average American has a dangerously wide spread between the alkalinity of his saliva and the acidity of his urine. His sugar levels are generally below normal and fluctuate wildly. His body is full of cell debris and excessive salts, and his kidneys and liver are loaded with nitrates. His lower intestine (the colon), which requires the same three basic elements as the heart - sodium, potassium, and calcium - is disfigured and loaded with putrefied debris. The physical system is literally clogged up, shut down in part, and compensating like mad while it depletes its vital reserves. Small wonder then that we are in a national health crisis.

Of course, health is different from the practice of medicine. If we were all healthy, then there would be less need for the practice of medicine, surgery, hospitals, etc. There is a negative financial incentive for Americans to get or stay healthy, as far as the medical establishment is concerned. Why are many veterinarians required to have over 1000 academic hours of nutrition, while some medical schools offer only a token course or two in the area? Why did President Harry Truman refer to the American Medical Association as *"just another damned trust?"*

For further readings see the books of Robert S. Mendelsohn, M.D., *Confessions of a Medical Heretic* and *How to Raise a Healthy Child...In Spite of Your Doctor.* Mendelsohn has served as Chairman of the Medical Licensing Committee for the state of Illinois.

Americans are spending a record low amount of their disposable income on food - 14.4%. Are we getting what we pay for?

Each generation, generation after generation, is inheriting a weaker constitution than the one which preceded it. How can we continue in this vein without a massive, collective physical breakdown? Presently, 97% of Americans are deficient in minerals.

And our water? Just forget for a moment about the fluoridation (banned by most European nations), the chemicals, the herbicides, the pesticides and all the other toxins which have polluted our water. All tap water, unless it is passed through brass pipe, has cadmium leeched into it. In a decade, we end up with enough cadmium in our systems to give us high blood pressure. Cadmium replaces zinc in the body's system. Zinc is vital for enzyme transport. Zinc is also necessary for the reproductive organs and the pancreas. Some 14% of insulin is zinc. We're not unlike the Romans who were poisoned by the lead in their water pipes. This leaves us with the necessity of drinking distilled water, natural spring water, or using reverse osmosis. The other option is a water purifier.

Hopefully, this brief overview is enough to at least grab your attention. It was enough to motivate me to consider the benefits of a garden. But just any old garden will not do. Remember, the soil has already been depleted. So throwing out a handful of seeds on just any old ground won't cut it anymore. The soil has to be built up and balanced. This means the soil requires adequate lime (calcium), usually additional soft rock phosphate, and adequate mineral content from powdered rock (electrical charge). (The addition of gravel which has been crushed to powder - 12 to 14 mesh - will perform the mineralization task.)

We must remember that the soil is alive. It is made up of microbes, earthworms, humus, etc. It must be fed and nourished if it is to provide us with good food to produce healthy men. This means our gardens should have a soil test and a sort of *"annual checkup."*

For an avant garde publication which covers agriculture in detail, consider an annual subscription to *Acres U.S.A.* (10008 East 60th Terrace, Kansas City, Missouri 64133, $19 per year, phone 816/737-0064.)

Also recommended is a book by Ronald F. Schmid, N.D., *Traditional Foods Are Your Best Medicine* (Ocean View Publications, 2420 Main St., Stratford, CT 06497). This book demonstrates that the industrialization of our food supply is at the root of our modern ills. (Another useful book is *Diet and Nutrition* by Rudolph Ballentine, M.D.)

A helpful newsletter is the *Tufts University Diet & Nutrition Letter* (P.O. Box 10948, Des Moines, Iowa 50940).

For academic sources, contact the American College of Nutripathy (6821 East Thomas Rd., Scottsdale, AZ 85251) and the American Quack Association (P.O. Box 550, Oviedo, Florida 32765).

I rigorously test the food I grow and buy. A Japanese firm (wouldn't you know it) named Extech makes a nifty little device called a *"hand refractometer"* for just such a purpose. This helpful little instrument can be used to check the nutritional value of both food and crops. Calibrated from 0 to 32, the fruit, vegetable or grain with the higher refractive index will have a higher sugar content, a higher mineral content, higher protein content, and a greater specific gravity or density. This means that the fruit or vegetable is sweeter tasting, more minerally nutritious, and has a lower nitrate and water content, as well as better storage characteristics. (The *"hand refractometer,"* Model #2132, can be purchased for $145 from Trans National Agronomy, Ltd., 470 Market Street S.W., Suite 101, Grand Rapids, Michigan 49503, 616/456-6878.)

The only other instrument I require to check the nutritional value of my food is a hand-held *"garlic press."* (A *"garlic press"* can be purchased for about $4 from any kitchen supply firm or from a five-and-dime store.)

Armed with my *"hand refractometer"* and *"garlic press,"* I made my pilgrimage to the local supermarket to purchase a strawberry, broccoli, zucchini, summer squash, beet, turnip, carrot, red onion, green bean and red potato. With the *"hand refractometer,"* I then checked the nutritional value of each fruit and vegetable, calibrated in percentage sucrose or brix. The ratings were as follows: Strawberry 6, Turnip 5.2, Broccoli 8, Carrot 3, Summer Squash 4, Zucchini 0.7, Red Onion 6.5, Green Bean 3, Beet 4.6, Red Potato 0.7

Now note from the following the *"poor"* and *"excellent"* ratings of the fruits and vegetables listed. The supermarket strawberry with a 6 reading barely passed the test with a *"poor."* The broccoli at 1.8 might as well have been dumped and not eaten. The zucchini at 0.7, along with the summer squash at 4, couldn't even make it up to the *"poor"* category. We had good news, however, on the supermarket beet. At 4.6, the beet was 2.6 points above the *"poor"* category.

The turnip at 5.2 also passed inspection, slightly better than *"poor."* The carrot at 3 did not make the grade. The red onion at 6.5 was barely acceptable. The green bean at 3 was worse than *"poor."* And the red potato at 0.7 was disaster, not worthy of consumption.

So much for the nutritional value of the fresh fruits and vegetables at my local supermarket (a well-known national chain). This evidence presented quite a compelling argument for me to have my own balanced soil and to grow my own food if I wanted to have true freshness and nutritional value.

Next, I went out and checked the produce raised in my garden. For purposes of establishing percentage sucrose or brix ratings, I rose early and picked the following fruits and vegetables just before sunrise. This is when they (the root crops) are at their highest nutritional value. (It is always coldest before daybreak and so the plants store their energy [% sucrose/brix] in their *"future,"* in their seeds, in their roots. Once the first light of the sun hits the leaves of the plants, then the energy [% sucrose/brix] leaves the seed, particularly the root crops - beets, turnips, onions, carrots, potatoes - and travels back up to the leaves to begin the whole photosynthesis process all over again. This is why garden produce [particularly root crops] should be picked before first light and consumed preferably within 3 to 4 hours.)

The percentage sucrose/brix nutritional value of the fruits and vegetables from my garden were as follows: Strawberry 9.5, Turnip 5, Broccoli 3.6, Carrot 7.5, Zucchini 5, Red Onion 11, Summer Squash 4, Green Bean 4.5, Beet 14, Red Potato 6.5.

It is immediately obvious that my garden's percentage sucrose/brix numbers handily beat the supermarket readings.

My strawberry was a solid *"good."* The broccoli was unfortunately unacceptable, but twice as good as the supermarket's. The zucchini did not make the *"poor"* category, nor did the summer squash, even though they too were better than the supermarket's. (In the future, I'll pick these *"above ground"* crops in the heat of the day.) My beet was better than *"excellent,"* tipping the scales at 14. My turnip was slightly better than *"poor."* My carrot was *"fair."* My red onion was better than *"excellent."* My green bean was slightly better than *"poor."* But my red potato was almost *"excellent."* Overall, three cheers for the excellence of my root crops. They slam dunked the supermarket's produce.

The bottom line of food is, *"if you want something done right, grow it yourself."* There are few things more important than the food we put into this physical body, which hangs on this God-given, spiritual, electronic structure (countenance),

Later, I checked the root crops from my garden in the heat of the day for the percentage sucrose/brix level. The sugar levels had dropped substantially. The beet, for example, fell from a 14 to a 6.2; the carrot from a 7.5 to a 3.7; the red onion from an 11 to a 4; and the red potato from a 6.5 to a 3.2. In other words, nutritional value increased in excess of 100% when the root crops were picked just before first light. That says it all. *"Early to bed, early to rise, makes a man healthy, wealthy and wise."*

Although my garden originally came from virgin soil, it has been in use for eight years now without a sabbatical, a real no-no. The land must have one year of rest every seven years in order to kill off the harmful insect breeding cycle and to allow the soil microbes to replenish themselves.

Despite the addition of llama manure every fall to the garden, I have not yet balanced the soil by way of adding lime, soft rock phosphate or powdered mineralized rock. So, in some ways, my garden is *"typical."*

But we have by some standards a better than average garden. It was developed out of glacial fill soil, which has relatively good mineralization and calcium. It is all organic. Natural fertilizer (llama manure) has been added every fall along with other humus matter.

There is another factor to consider: I know that the fruits and vegetables which I eat, homegrown in my garden, have not been sprayed or contaminated with any toxic fertilizers, herbicides or pesticides. Nor are there any toxins in my soil. I don't know if this is the case with regard to the produce I purchased from the local supermarket, which has been subjected to the food industrialization process of toxic fertilizers, herbicides, pesticides and sprays before it reaches the attractive display counters. Anyway, increasing food irradiation is on the way.

Americans are obsessed today with appearance rather than substance, with *"looking good,"* rather than with quality built from the inside out. The inescapable conclusion I draw from all of this is that we are on the verge of a disastrous national health crisis, not even considering the horrors of the encroaching AIDS plague. As the offspring of third generation junk food junkies, we are *"wasted."* We have squandered our national constitutional heritage in a physical sense, just as we have squandered it in a legal sense.

We are vulnerable. We must get back to basics. Our children must have the support systems by way of good nutrition because they don't have the physical constitutions which our parents, grandparents and great-grandparents had to carry them through stressful times. (And stressful times are here and ever-increasing.) We no longer have the physical constitutions to compensate for the junk food which draws down our calcium, mineral, vitamin and enzyme reserves. These reserves simply don't exist in our physical constitutions or those of our children, for the most part.

If we do get back to basics, then we can provide both ourselves and our children with the support systems so that the DNA/RNA structures which they pass on to our grandchildren will be better than our own. This then is another challenge before us. This is an unrecognized and unaddressed major problem facing Americans, which is sneaking in the back door. *"The curse causeless shall not come."* Nearly any family, church or community group can get back to the basics of a garden. And we need to do so now. All too soon we may have to re-learn the reality, *"We're not wealthy unless we're healthy."*

* * * * *

Trading market psychologist Dr. Van K. Tharp's research has revealed that our physical health is very important to the success of our investing. Dr. Tharp has written that only a 10% drop in an investor's overall health is enough to turn his market trading from being a winner to a loser. Here then is another reason to value *"Green Garden Gold."*

*   *   *   *   *

I would also be irresponsible and less than comprehensively truthful if I did not include some comments regarding the spiritual aspect of a garden.

My underlying assumption is that everything God has given us is for our own good, long term. Certainly, the foregoing empirical evidence is convincing enough regarding our need for a garden and the produce derived therefrom. We just have not recognized how basic the garden is, not only for our personal health, but also for the health and well-being of our beloved children and society-at-large.

God created man for the explicit purpose of tending and keeping a garden (Eden) (Genesis 2:15). The Hebrews were given the Promised Land for the purpose of restoring it to a garden. The disciplining of nations is for the specific eventual purpose of returning the earth to a garden. Isaiah 2:2-4 and Micah 4:1-4 make it very clear that the responsibility of nations is to: (1) learn the law of God; (2) teach the law of God to the people so the people will be self-governing; (3) for the purpose of beating political *"swords"* and political *"spears"* into the economic gardening instruments of *"plowshares"* and *"pruning hooks"* respectively. In fact, the end goal for every individual is to *"sit under his vine and under his fig tree."* In other words, after all is said and done, the self-governing, spiritually edified man is to be returned to his original and ideal status as a gardener. We are returning to Eden.

What a condemnation this is of our moribund cities, built of lifeless concrete, asphalt, glass and steel. No wonder men are aggressive, conflict-ridden, and yearn to make war. They are supercharged by the paramagnetic nature of these lifeless materials day in and day out. Isn't this why historian Oswald Spengler referred to the *"wintertime"* of our civilization, when we are *"frozen"* in our *"world cities?"* Spengler also observed that cities consume people and resources.

Men are also enslaved today by the vertical institutions which operate by *"man over man."* This is reflected in the very architecture of today's *"world cities"* - the skyscrapers and high rises.

By contrast, when a man lives, works, and sits *"under his own vine and fig tree,"* he can be at peace. The diamagnetic charge of the live, green plants and trees soothes and calms a man's spirit. (Is this why all the city folk rush to the parks and the country-side on the weekends, in order to get in touch with themselves, to restore themselves spiritually, to renew their strength?) The covenantal and contractual nature of gardeners, whose institutions and physical structures are spread out horizontally, reflects self-governing free men.

God wants the best for us. He loves us. He tells us in Proverbs 8:36, *"But he who sins against me wrongs his own soul; All those who hate me love death."* King David wrote in Psalm 119:127-128, *"Therefore all Your precepts concerning all things I consider to be right; I hate every false way."* In this regard then, the importance of every man living *"under his own vine and fig tree"* cannot be minimized.

The color of a *"vine"* and *"fig tree"* is obviously green. When a man sits under his own *"vine"* and *"fig tree,"* he is sitting under the live color green. This is just like with God. Surrounding the throne of God is the color emerald green (Revelation 4:3). God has given man a throne room to match His own.

What's so important about the color green? Many, many things! First of all, green is the balancing point, the centering frequency, the color of perfect peace and harmony, balancing out the seven colors of the rainbow. Red, orange, yellow - GREEN - blue, indigo, violet. Green corresponds to the location of the corpus callosum located between left-brain oriented man (law) and right-brain oriented woman (love). Green is the color therefore which is the balance point between the aggressive red, orange and yellow colors of left-brain oriented man, and the blue, indigo, and violet peacemaking colors of right-brain oriented woman. Green is the color of the frequency which balances out the paramagnetic and diamagnetic charges which are the two basic ends of the magnetic spectrum in all of God's natural creation. Green is the color which resolves conflict!

Color psychologists and industrial psychologists who do interior design in office buildings, airliners and the like know this color green well. The primary psychological character trait of the color green is HUMILITY! The basic virtue which God requires of us is humility! But that's not the end of it.

The master gland which regulates the body is the pituitary gland. Which color is associated with the pituitary gland? You guessed it - the color green! A great deal of the calcium our bodies assimilate is derived from green leafy vegetables from the garden.

Did you ever wonder why so many of the city-based leaders - the politicians, the bureaucrats, the judges, the hot-shot lawyers, the big business and labor leaders, the intellectuals, the theologians, and the scholars - who know so much but never work with their hands outside, tend to be proud, arrogant, sickly, harsh, unloving, angry, lack common sense, and are generally out of touch with day-to-day reality? They are literally not grounded under a green *"vine"* or *"fig tree."* They are out of touch with the reality of God's creation, His green garden. (Wisdom in the Old Testament meant to work with one's hands.)

They are out of touch with themselves, too. Their bodies are out of whack - thanks in part to a malfunctioning pituitary gland, which is identified with the color green. They are toxic. They neither sweat, get enough sunlight, or eat correctly. How can they think correctly when their toxic bodies are part of their minds? They are literally full of _____. They lack humility, the character trait of the color green and the basic requirement of God, and so they are ultimately out of touch with God. Not receiving adequate sunlight, their key spiritual gland, the pineal, is calcified, too.

Any love they claim to have for mankind is couched in terms of mankind generally, because they lack the ability to love mankind personally and individually. They are effectively frozen when it comes to their fellow man's personal needs and burdens, living often so far above *"with their heads in the clouds"* that *"they are no earthly good."*

As religion always comes down to economics, so is the lifelessness and godlessness of our religious leaders reflected in the lifelessness and godlessness of our people who live in this country, particularly in our cities. As a society, we are out of touch with physical life - human, animal, soil, insect and plant life. So as we are out of touch with our gardens, we are therefore out of touch with our living God. It follows, for collective man, that an economy which is not built upon an ecologically sound agricultural base, a garden, is theologically and historically death oriented. Historians have documented that when the rural country dies, the city is not far behind. God destroys those who destroy the earth (Revelation 11:18).

"Green Garden Gold" is God's emerald green! It logically follows that a theological, political or economic reconstruction of our city-based society is very unlikely.

* * * * *

Personally, I have taken the responsibility of sitting under my green *"vine"* and *"fig tree"* and *"tending my green garden"* very, very seriously. It has literally changed my life - physically, mentally, emotionally and most importantly, spiritually. I find now that I am much better equipped to serve my fellow man, bear his burdens, and to obey God as a result (Christ's Second and First Great Commandments respectively). Working in the green of my garden has worked wonders on both my pituitary gland and my sense of humility, according to my doctors and my wife. Being a gardener has also reaped fruit in a number of other ways as well.

In the summers of 1986 and 1987, as a family we entered our garden grown vegetables, flowers, llamas and horses in the regional fair. In 1986, as a family we won 15 ribbons at the fair - 6 first place blue ribbons, 3 second place red ribbons, and 6 third place white ribbons. In 1987, we achieved even better results. Our family won 20 ribbons at the regional fair - 7 first place blue ribbons, 10 second place red ribbons, and 3 third place white ribbons.

I don't think I've ever done anything more enriching and satisfying than harvesting these *"marks of excellence."* These ribbons are the hallmarks of our *"Green Garden Gold."* Perhaps a garden is an investment you, too, should consider.

* * * * *

"Pleasant words are as a honeycomb, sweet to the soul and health to the bones." — Proverbs 16:24

* * * * *

"For we have great joy and consolation in your love, because the hearts [bowels] of the saints have been refreshed by you, brother." — Philemon verse 7

* * * * *

"For as a man thinks in his heart, so is he." — Proverbs 23:7

* * * * *

"Science without religion is lame, religion without science is blind." — Albert Einstein

PUT ON A HAPPY FACE AND
A TRUSTING HEART

July 26, 1990

"I have spent over eight years and thousands of dollars researching the material included in this series on health. This quest was launched out of a family health crisis. Because health is foundational to the creation of wealth, it is my deep pleasure to now share with you and your loved ones what I have learned at considerable personal cost."

Emotions and Health

Modern medical science is finally wising up and confirming ancient wisdom. When it comes to health, there is no separation of mind, spirit, soul and body. It has even been demonstrated that an actor who smiles playing a role boosts his own immune system. Also, in a controlled experiment reported by *Psychology Today*, a group of viewers watched a one-hour film of the work of Mother Teresa. Half of the viewers liked Mother Teresa, half of them did not. But that didn't make any difference. The before-and-after blood tests revealed that *all* the viewers enjoyed an enhanced immune response after viewing Mother Teresa. Why? Because Mother Teresa does good and we benefit physically from even watching her.

Has this study influenced the movies and TV programs I watch? You bet. I seldom watch anything negative, violent, lawless or bloody which weakens my countenance and immune system. So, needless to say, the TV stays off 90% of the time at my house. Hollywood, the *"wood"* of witches, can keep its *"wands,"* thank you. Dr. Branden Canterwall, in a study published in the *American Journal of Epidemiology*, found TV a factor in 10,000 U.S. homicides, rapes and other violent crimes each year.

Dr. David Spiegel, at the 1989 meeting of the American Psychiatric Association, reported on the results of a 10-year study at Stanford and U.C. Berkeley which demonstrated that cancer patients who receive emotional and social support through group therapy tend to live twice as long as patients on medical treatment alone.

Dr. Mary Ann Fletcher, director of the clinical immunology laboratory at the University of Miami, has found that cells in the immune system have receptors for brain chemicals, and that there are links between the nervous system and the lymph nodes and spleen, where some immune cells are stored and manufactured.

We process and store our emotions in the red energy (magnetic) area of the bowels, just as the Old Testament of the Bible says. When a negative thought comes out of our mind as a particle/wave, it has an unhealthy left-hand spin to it, like the spin of diseased blood. On the other hand, when a positive thought exits our mind, studies with the random light generator reveal the thought wave/particle has a healthy, or right-hand spin to it. So regardless of what is going on around us, we need to give thanks for all things, and think on whatever things are good, pure, kind, gentle, etc. It's more healthy to do so.

It seems that when a happy thought comes out of our mind with a healthy right-hand spin, it affects the pineal and pituitary glands and cycles through the cerebrum into the cerebral spinal fluid, down the spine, bathes the pericardium of the heart, unites with the oxygen, nutritional and mineralization content of the blood in the heart, and is thereby transformed from an electromagnetic pulse to physical reality, from whence it is established emotionally in the pelvic cradle in the bowels, grounded to 7.83 Hertz (the Schumann oscillating frequency of the earth and of all *"healers"* in mode) and then radiates up and out through the body, into the countenance/aura/electromagnetic field. The 7.8-Hertz frequency is the frequency of the parasympathetic nervous system, too. Truly, as a man thinketh so he is, biologically/physically, mentally/emotionally, and electromagnetically. Imbedded within us is the negative natural emotional reaction to physical and psychological pain. It is therefore true that an ultimate sign of discipline and maturity in an individual is bringing every thought captive and not allowing any negative emotions (followed by unlawful actions), and also rigorously controlling what one eats (natural foods with proper food combining). It's a body, mind, spirit and soul integration.

Emotion has to do with the complicated circuitry which interconnects the neuron network and the pattern of the nerve impulses which travel among them. Negative emotions, such as fear, are caused by negative interpretation of events, which have hit the sensory receptors in the retina of the eye. This photographic-type electromagnetic signal is instantly translated to chemical signals which race to the brain. Different parts of the lymphatic system (critical to the health of the immune system) and higher brain centers debate and interpret the significance of the event. Signals sent by the hypothalamus to the pituitary gland trigger a flood of hormones, alerting various parts of the body to the possibility of danger and producing a *"flight or fight"* response. Rapid pulse, rising blood pressure, dilated pupils and other physiological shifts prepare a person for action when the emotion of fear, for example, settles in. (Perfect love casts out fear.)

Hormone signals are carried through the blood at a much slower rate than on the nerve pathways. So even after the perceived danger which caused the fear is past, it takes a few minutes for the individual to again "settle down" and stabilize. "Settling down" is the process of allowing the body's energy to drift back down below the waist into the grounded, magnetic, red energy reservoir. People who are "up" all the time, "high," exhaust themselves.

Emotions in the brain are located in the limbic system. It's interesting to note that people who eat junk food and dead, processed food operate almost exclusively in this primitive brain center, the limbic system, the area of the "natural man." These folks are therefore, by definition, consistently irrational and emotional. They do not have the enzymes, vitamins, minerals, calcium, etc., to think rationally. They cannot detoxify. They cannot build up the bowel, which is the basis for sound physical, mental and spiritual health. Men who race their minds constantly are likewise afflicted. They need to cool their heels working in a garden, in the red earth.

I tend not to trust pure intellectuals. They are not grounded, literally. I generally feel much better about people who work with their hands and/or with plants and animals, as well as with their head. They are more settled, balanced and generally carry their energy lower in the body. (Does this imply that cities are unhealthy? Yes.)

I like garlic and onion, radishes, beets, cayenne and other root crops, llamas, horses, goats, cleaning llama and horse stalls, bicycling, gardening and power walking. It's good for my bowels! It helps keep me grounded.

People who suffer from Irritable Bowel Syndrome (IBS) are usually subject to depression, anxiety and cancer, and have a history of frequent illness. They have a strong tendency to suppress negative emotions. Emotional stress and ineffective ways of dealing with it play a major role in IBS. So IBS sufferers endure a double whammy. First, they mentally process their emotions incorrectly. Then they suppress them by burying them in the bowel. The end result is dis-ease. They get physically out of sync.

Dr. Jeffrey Blumberg, at the Human Nutrition Research Center on Aging, reported, *"We know now that the major age-old killers - heart disease, cancer, stroke and infections - are greatly affected by diet."*

Dr. Delane Kitzman of Duke University at Durham, North Carolina, speaking at the American College of Cardiology meeting, declared, *"A healthy lifestyle with plenty of exercise could stall the effects of age."*

Until our diets changed from natural foods, and until stress entered our society around 1900, people did not die of diseases of the heart and blood vessels, of hypertension, tumors or cancer of the respiratory tract. These diseases were all but nonexistent back in the early 1900s. Dr. Donald B. Ardell has documented that five of the ten leading causes of death are diet-related - heart disease, cerebrovascular disease, cirrhosis of the liver, diabetes mellitus and arteriosclerosis.

Dr. Lester Roloff of Corpus Christi, Texas, who operated the most successful youth reform school ever, made nutrition and home-grown organic food the basis of his program. Until the nutritional aspect was added to the equation, it didn't matter how much Roloff loved, disciplined, taught or scolded the youth. They had no physical basis so the instruction could "take." Buchsbaum has further demonstrated that schizophrenics and manic-depressives have low glucose levels and less frontal lobe activity.

Take steps to prevent osteoporosis

The best way to manage osteoporosis is to prevent it from developing. Since osteoporosis develops silently over many years, proper diet and exercise, throughout your life, are extremely important.

• Adequate calcium. The daily diet should include foods that are high in calcium like dairy products (including milk, cheese, and yogurt), dark green leafy vegetables (like collards, turnip greens, spinach and broccoli), salmon, sardines, oysters, and tofu.

• Adequate vitamin D. Vitamin-fortified milk, cereals, saltwater fish, liver and daily sunshine are good sources of this vitamin.

• Adequate manganese. Manganese is an important mineral found in whole-grain products, fruits (especially bananas), vegetables (especially legumes), eggs, liver and other organ meats.

• Adequate exercise. Walking, jogging, dancing, bicycling, aerobics, rowing, hiking, rope jumping, tennis and other exercise in which the bones have to support body weight, helps promote bone growth.

• With your doctor, consider estrogen replacement therapy during menopause. When estrogen replacement therapy is started right after women stop menstruating, hip and wrist fractures can be reduced as much as 60 percent.

• Avoid smoking, alcoholic beverages, drinks containing caffeine, soft drinks, meat, and high protein foods.

Source: National Institutes of Health and *Stand Tall* by Notelovitz **and Wars** — JMF

* * * * *

Brain researcher and psychologist Robert Ornstein and his co-author, Dr. David Sobel, in their book, *Healthy Pleasures*, say that the most important thing we can do for our health is have fun. *"For most of us, living a happy life is much more important to our health than all the regimes we could undertake."* In other words, *"Put on a Happy Face and a Trusting Heart."*

Electromagnetic Health

When we realize that the Kaznacheyev experiments in the former Soviet Union proved that any cellular death or disease pattern can be induced in cells electromagnetically, it becomes increasingly crucial that we control what we think, believe, and eat, and thereby support our immune systems. The Kaznacheyev experiments were duplicated in Germany and at the University of Sidney. In Sidney, this experiment was accomplished at 100 meters distance.

Imagine what the Russians are doing in this area of psychic/electromagnetic warfare. Psychic warfare is nothing more than a scientific radionic application of what religiously is called voodoo. The Russians used the 5-28 MHz Woodpecker signal to upset people in Salem, Oregon in 1978. The 1987 Dr. Robert East-land and Atlantic Richfield Oil weather engineering patent is along these lines, a phased-array over-the-horizon radar. Shades of Tesla and Tom Bearden.

In 1984, the U.S. Navy demonstrated that ELF (Extra Low Frequency) waves could alter cell behavior, body tissues, organs, hormone levels, cell chemistry, reaction time, inhibit or enhance bone growth, alter cell differentiation, RNA synthesis, DNA transcription, entrain brain waves, slow aging, cure certain diseases, alter time perception, affect the immune process, increase fetus mortality, cause sterility, produce non-invasive genetic engineering and trigger defects and alterations in embryos. And, of course, on a much cruder level, high power lines have been shown to cause cancer and decreased immune response (Denver).

But, there's a positive side to this whole electromagnetic nature of thoughts and wavelengths. The Antoine Priore machine in France in the 1960s and 1970s proved conclusively that electromagnetics can be used to cure diseases such as cancer, leukemia, sleeping sicknesses, and also to positively boost the immune system. It has to do with charging an organ electromagnetically at its healthy resonant frequency. Antoine Priore was initially championed by the prestigious French Academy of Sciences. Skilling and Rapsomanikis have achieved similar results in this country. They have been persecuted and harassed, too. But so too were their predecessors - Dr. Albert Abrams and Lakhovsky.

This is along the same line as the work performed by Dr. Royal Rife in the '40s and '50s in this country. Using his Rife microscope, Dr. Royal Rife proved that living entities are composed of structured electricity. These electro-magnetic bugs, literally living electricity, which are at work in and around viruses and bacteria, can be killed by methods similar to scalar electromagnetic energy, using color and frequency. This is further confirmation of Darius Din-shah's work with color healing, performed with Dr. Kate Baldwin, chief of surgery for 20 years at Women's Hospital in Philadelphia. Rife was so successful at treating cancer and other maladies that the AMA came in and shut him down. Rife even got thrown in jail. Which reminds me, the very best and the very worst of men are in prison these days. The U.S. rates right up there along side the former Soviet Union and South Africa in the percentage of its people it throws in jail, political prisoners. Birds of a feather... (For more reading I recommend *The Royal R. Rife Report*, available from Borderland Sciences, P.O. Box 429, Garberville, CA 95440-0429.)

The April 1986 *Discover* magazine featured the work of Swedish radiologist Bjorn Nordenstrom. Dr. Nordenstrom established the equivalent of electric circuits in the human body. He successfully treated both lung and breast cancer electrically. *"The biological circuits are driven by the accumulated charges,...which oscillate between positive and negative. The larger vessels act as insulated cables, blood plasma as the conductor. In the permeable tissue, the fluid between cells conducts ions. A key component of the circuit: the natural electrodes in the capillary walls."*

Warner Enterprises (P.O. Box 690573, Tulsa, OK 74169-0573, phone 918/663-3832) manufactures a device called the *"Snake Doctor."* The *"Snake Doctor"* emits 25,000 volts of DC at less than 1 Ma. When applied to snake, spider, ant or tick bites, or wasp, scorpion or bee stings, it allegedly neutralizes the venom. The *"Snake Doctor"* has been written up in the medical journal *Lancet*, by Dr. Lawrence K. Alterman in *The New York Times*, and by research teams in Germany and at Michigan State University. The electrical current supposedly rearranges the venom's molecular structure into a non-lethal substance.

The reality of electromagnetic medicine should really come as no surprise. The earth is a big electromagnet. The ionosphere is electrical. We bounce radio waves off of it. If we oscillate the ionosphere at 8 times per second, we can release usable energy from it (Source: *Omni*). The magnetosphere and its Van Allen belts produce many kinds of electromagnetic radiation. The earth is a big magnet with a north and south pole. The earth, a magnet, rotates within the ionosphere's electrical field. Plus, we are bombarded by solar charged electromagnetic particles emitted by the sun. Bingo: Electromagnetic reality! The magnetic field of the sun is 8 Hertz. The harmonics are that the human body operates at .08 millivolts and healers heal at 8 Hertz and the earth oscillates at 8 (7.83) Hertz. Dr. Bernard J. Eastland holds patent #4,686,605 whereby artificial lightning can be generated. Given all this evidence, why does the United States allow 10,000 times more electromagnetic pollution than the former Soviet Union or Western Europe?

(For more reading see Richard Gerber, M.D.'s book, *Vibrational Medicine*, John Evans' book, *Mind, Body & Electromagnetism*, *The Dark Side of the Brain* by Harry Oldfield and Roger Coghill, *The Body Electric* by Robert O. Becker, M.D. and *Biocircuits* by Leslie Patten.)

Simple kinesiology (muscle testing) has become a lot more sophisticated. Touch for Health, point holding, chelation, healing with magnets and crystals, the Accupath 1000, the Super Pro Resonator, the Intercro - what's next?

The essence of man's spirit (mind field) is electromagnetic. This is what man's electromagnetic field/countenance/aura is all about, as proven by Heisenberg, Abrams, Eccles, Beck, McKenna, Ludwig, Pribrem, Bohm, Talbot, Kirlian, Voll and others. Research at UCLA (Hunt) has confirmed that if you remove the electrical portion of the electromagnetic spectrum from people, they become sad and weep; if it is increased, subjects become joyful and experience mystical spiritual phenomenon. If the magnetic end of the electromagnetic spectrum is removed from an individual, he loses muscular coordination; if it is increased, physical coordination increases (proven with football teams). The electromagnetic spectrum harmonizes with the color spectrum, with violet on one end (electrical) and red on the other (magnetic). Medical instruments measure both electrical and magnetic signals around the head with an EEG and an EMG respectively. Physicist Gottfried Mayer-Kress of Los Alamos National Laboratory's Center for Nonlinear Studies has worked with the EEG as people shift behavior. He has developed a mathematical model showing how changes in patterns of electrical activity in the brain are linked to changes in behavioral state.

Dr. Phil Callahan, working at Gainesville, Florida and with the USDA has proven that the healthiest of food has an electromagnetic charge, the electrical charge coming from the inorganic mineralization of the paramagnetic rock structure of the soil, the magnetic segment arising from the organic content of the soil which feeds the food-producing plant.

Dr. Jonathan Tennebaum, director of the Fusion Energy Forum of Germany, declared in a speech, *"We have abundant evidence that the biosphere is organized as an electromagnetic system in which various processes are very precisely 'tuned' to each other."* Question: If we are "tuned" to each other, then shouldn't our efforts be cooperative and gentle rather than hostile and destructive?

Wesley Rogers, president of Electronic Development, Inc., has demonstrated that ham radios in automobiles can sterilize men because of improper grounding. Dr. William Adey, a cancer researcher, has proven that cells whisper together in a private and very faint language, and that a block in these signals created by electromagnetic smog can produce tumors and undermine the body's disease-fighting ability. Dr. Robert Becker, author of the important book, *The Body Electric*, and a research director in a firm which specializes in biomagnetics, declares that the pineal gland, the gland which controls the release of certain brain chemicals, is confused by abnormal magnetic fields, leading to chronic stress and aberrant behavior. So, for good or evil, the present-day equivalent of the French Death Whistle, which the French used against the Germans in World War II to explode their organs internally, is with us. So far, evil rather than good has been the primary direction taken by the Establishment in this area.

Inner Workings

People have to first live within themselves. Literally, the kingdom of God is within and patterned without. Dr. Edmound Burgler, M.D. declared, *"Change of scene has no effect upon unconscious conflicts."* Environmental determinism does not cut it. Indeed, methods of healing now being taught in seminars at Stanford work with discovering a person's psychological conflict in order to produce the physical healing response. Physical posture can bring to mind negatively handled emotions and violations of God's law which are stored (and are potentially disease-producing) in the body's muscles, organs, bones and other tissues. A teaching nurse informed me that the skill of "laying on of hands" is regularly taught now nationwide.

The conscious mind operates at its own level and talks to itself to try to find answers. But the conscious mind has a limited amount of memory and creative circuitry, because it deals with everyday issues, not deeper issues. Therefore, introspection on the conscious level does not always work. However, when one learns to relax, listen to music or stand still and know God (meditate), one literally enters the alpha state and then is in touch with the unconscious mind and creativity, according to Alan Rogers of Mind Corporation. This is where intuition, hunches and gut feelings come from.

The alpha brain frequency is ten cycles per second. When the brain reaches this frequency level and is also conscious, individuals literally have the ability to program their brain or other consciousness and then to achieve many goals on the conscious level. The human mind normally oscillates between 13 and 30 Hertz. (I might also again mention that all healers measured worldwide with sophisticated equipment operate at 7.83 Hertz, the oscillating rate of the earth, when they are in their healing mode.)

Researchers are using the same radio waves which broadcast the Golden Oldies on the AM dial to treat patients with uncontrolled rapid heartbeats, according to Dr. Jonathan Lamberg of the University of California, San Francisco.

If you want to get really way out, as in the movie *"Ghost Busters,"* use geiger counters and infrared film to locate ghosts/spirits/demons. Such evil spirits only have access to man through defects in the electromagnetic countenance/aura, which in turn reflects unhealthy organs in the twelve primary frequencies of the color spectrum. Incorrect mental and emotional processing (error/sin) plus genetic defects (the sins of the father are visited upon the sons in the chemical make-up of RNA/DNA) cause the defect. Resistance results and impedes energy flow as biological thought crystals are established in the human body (reflexology, for example). This weakness is reflected in the countenance.

If both parents are fat, an individual's chances of becoming fat are about 80%. If neither parent is fat, the chances of an individual becoming fat are only 10%, according to Kenneth E. Warner, M.D., chief medical examiner of the State of Alabama, and Dr. Dale M. Atrans in their book, *Don't Diet.* The sins (mistakes) of the father (and mother) are visited upon the sons and daughters through the RNA/DNA structure.

Robert Burton, in his book, *The Anatomy of Melancholy,* demonstrated that idleness is deathly. We know this from watching career military officers who have been active all of their lives, who then retire. Many quickly die within two or three years, particularly if they become sedentary and depressed. In order to be healthy, people need to do work they love, to work hard, to sweat physically, to eat right, sleep right, think right, and be actively involved with other people. Hypochondriacs are classically people who believe they are relatively powerless, such as children with an overprotective mother, an insecure wife, an unimportant steel worker, or a typical American today at the mercy of the federal government.

Susan Baur, author of *Hypochondria: Willful Imaginations*, demonstrated that people can literally worry themselves sick, particularly if they are preoccupied with every little ache and pain and view it as a harbinger of some oncoming fatal disease. As a man thinketh so he is. Put on a happy face and a trusting heart.

In and Out

The health of the immune system is critical to overall health. The immune system is the garbage collection system of the body. Diet, thought processes, emotions, lifestyle, rest and exercise (or lack thereof) all impact the immune system. A positive outlook is vital to the health of the immune system. Dr. Carolyn Coulan of Methodist Hospital in Indianapolis, Indiana has proven that 40% of all women diagnosed as infertile simply suffer from too aggressive or too lax an immune system, which causes miscarriages before the women are even aware that they are pregnant.

The idea of *"putting on a happy face"* was popularized by Norman Cousins, whose studies have demonstrated that laughing boosts the immune system. Psychologist Kathleen Dillon at Western New England College showed that laughter decreases the level of cortisol, an immune suppressor in the body. The work of Dr. Suzanne Kobasa was discussed in a book, *Who Get Sick*, by Blair Justice, Ph.D. The bottom line, according to Justice, is that people with positive attitudes and the ability to get along with others have a low frequency of illness. They see change as an opportunity for growth and have a sense of control over their own lives. They are also committed and interested in work activities. A positive mental attitude, thinking on whatever things are good and pure, working in line with one's God-given calling, being productive, and serving other people are keys to good health.

Exercise is also important. It increases the oxygenation of the cells, which allows the cells to discharge waste products and debris. (Cancer can only grow in a deoxygenated, toxic, debris-filled environment, beginning at the cellular level.) Exercise also makes sugar more readily available to the brain, which helps it to function better. Rest allows the body to rebuild.

AMA Away?

So what about the modern medical monopoly? Why is the U.S. rated so low overall globally in health care? Has any union, such as the AMA, which has been granted an effective medical monopoly by the government, ever best served the needs of the consumer? Economists tell us unequivocally no. Certainly M.D.s, surgeons, other specialists, anesthetics (magnets may be better, or acupuncture), miracle drugs and antibiotics have an important place in modern medicine, particularly in emergencies and to save lives. But the practice of medicine is different from health. Thomas A. Edison once commented, *"The doctor of the future will give no medicine, but will interest his patients in the care of the human frame, in diet, and in the cause and prevention of disease."*

This is in fact the direction the world is taking. It is the direction leading M.D.s are taking. Eric R. Braverman, M.D. and the late Carl C. Pfeiffer, M.D., authors of *The Healing Nutrients Within*, have achieved startling results at the Brain Bio Center in Rocky Hill, N.J. Also, H. Ray Evers, M.D., has achieved unusual results at the Evers Health Center in Cottonwood, Ala., as has Dr. Fuller Royal, M.D., at the Nevada Clinic for Preventative Medicine in Las Vegas.

According to Kathleen Bloomquist, Ph.D., an assistant professor of nursing at the University of Texas and the University of Kentucky, one out of ten hospital stays is unnecessary. This study was released by the Inspector General of the Department of Health and Human Services. Eugene Robin, M.D., Stanford professor of medicine, declared, *"Unless you absolutely need them, doctors are good people to stay away from and hospitals are very good places to stay out of."* The director of nursing at California State University, Fullerton, California, declared, *"Health has become a laughing matter. Good humor is an integral part of wellness and health."* Put on a happy face! Have a trusting heart!

Stress and Health

Insight Magazine reported in its February 6, 1989 issue that individuals vulnerable to physical and psychological stress are more likely to succumb to chronic fatigue syndrome and the Epstein Barr virus (EBV). Anger and depression may trigger EBV, according to the National Institute of Allergy and Infectious Diseases. Put on a happy face! Work at UCLA (Hunt) has confirmed that neither schizophrenics nor women with EBV have any energy below the waists, in their emotional/bowel area. They are literally not grounded. They have no red magnetic energy. They have burned up the mineralization of their bowel and their emotional reserve. They need to "settle down." Ever wonder why a drunk seldom gets hurt in a car wreck? Because the drunk is relaxed and offers no resistance to the impact. The energy simply passes through him. EBV people are more likely to develop Hodgkin's disease, a cancer of the lymph nodes. People who get at least 400 units of Vitamin D a day are half as likely to get colon cancer as those who get less, according to Dr. Cedric Garland, of the University of California School of Medicine at San Diego. Heavenly sunshine. Put on a happy face.

The April 1989 issue of *Psychology Today* featured an article entitled, *"The Mindset of Health,"* by Ellen J. Langer. Langer wrote a book entitled *Mindfulness.* *"State of mind shapes state of body...The emotional context, our interpretation of the events around us, could thus be the first link in the chain leading to serious illness."*

The December 1988 issue of *Psychology Today* reported, *"There are two classes of diseases - bodily and mental. Each arises from the other, and neither exists without the other. Mental disorders arise from physical ones, and likewise physical disorders arise from mental ones."* This was a direct quote from Mahabharata, an Indian physician of 4000 years ago. What goes around comes around. Human nature is constant, not evolving. What does this say for our isolated, lonely, rush hour, office complex lifestyle? It is literally sick.

The Heart of the Matter

Hans J. Euisenck, Ph.D., M.D., one of the world's most cited psychologists, works at the Institute of Psychiatry, University of London. He declared, *"There is less cancer and coronary heart disease where there is a therapy group. The type of personality often ascribed to the cancer-prone individual combines two major features. One is the inability to express emotions, such as anger, fear and anxiety; the other is an inability to cope with stress and a tendency to develop feelings of hopelessness, helplessness and finally depression."* ...Put on a happy face, stemming from a happy and trusting heart.

"Coronary heart disease has also been linked to certain personality types, most often to the so-called 'Type A' personality or behavior pattern,... The only components that seem to stand up to the test are tendencies toward anger, hostility and aggression."

The February 1989 issue of *Psychology Today*, in an article by T. George Harris entitled *"Heart and Soul,"* reported that spiritual need may be the underlying crisis among Type-A people prone to heart attacks, according to research by cardiologist Meyer Friedman. Another researcher, Ray Rosenman, focused on deep-seated anxiety among the truly coronary-prone. The deep-seated anxiety was the result of trying to support a presented self that does not harmonize with the real self. This facade causes heart disease. Dean Ornish, a University of California, San Francisco physician, has found among heart patients that loneliness, which leads them to seek intimacy by pretending to be someone they are not, aggravates heart disease. Dallas, Texas, are you listening? Dallas historian Green says that if in Dallas, Texas you lose your money you become a non-person. This is unhealthy! (Source: *US News & World Report)*

University of Maryland psychologist James Lynch found that blood pressure goes up when we talk, even for those who use sign language. Blood pressure goes down, however, when we listen.

"I think the mind is where heart disease begins for many people," according to heart specialist Dean Ornish. Another researcher, Redford Williams, M.D. is a behavioral medicine specialist at the Duke University Medical Center. He has written a book entitled, *The Trusting Heart: Great News About Type-A Behavior*. Williams reported that cynical attitudes and hostile emotions cause biological responses which lead to coronary disease. *"It is now pretty clear that only the hostility and anger associated with Type A behavior actually contribute to heart disease....Children who don't get unconditional parental love and care and lots of physical contact are*

more likely to be mistrusting, easy-to-anger adults... " Like children left in government-run day care centers.

Thoughts and feelings which cause injury to the coronary arteries attract patches of cholesterol that block blood flow and bring on heart attacks. *"You can begin to see why healthy thoughts and a healthy diet are an essential part of a heart-healthy lifestyle. The cynical life is often a short one. Hostility and cynical mistrust are now regarded as the lethal elements of Type-A behavior by several researchers,"* according to Dr. Williams. Also, a research team at Bowman-Gray School of Medicine in North Carolina demonstrated that psychological stress affects the biology of heart disease, particularly the repeated stress of trying to dominate another individual. This is what bureaucrats, politicians, judges and business tycoons attempt to do all the time - dominate other individuals and control their lives. It is the "Big Brother" syndrome. It is unhealthy.

Martin G. Groder, Ph.D. found that macho men tend to wind up physically crippled or dead at an early age from hypertension and coronary artery disease. Macho types suffer physically from denying their feelings of vulnerability, from stifling their emotions and not networking.

The 61-degree angle is the angle of fermentation. It is 22 Hertz (11 Hertz is a harmonic). This is the frequency of anger. It is what the ancients called the inner fire which consumes an individual. It eats up the gall bladder in people. When the gall bladder memory bank is full, the heart tries to compensate. When the heart is overloaded, bingo, heart attack!

The gall bladder meridian runs the length of the right side of the body. When a person is angry, he consumes the emotional red energy of the bowel, which runs along this meridian, through the gall bladder, and exits at two points on either side of the top of the head. These two red energy spirals exiting the head were originally depicted by artists as the horns of a red, angry devil!

The April 1989 issue of *Psychology Today* had another article entitled, *"Type-A: Healing the Spirit."* Thirty years of research by cardiologist Meyer Friedman discovered that Type-A behavior and heart disease go hand in hand. *"The impatience, hostility and all-consuming trying for results that typify Type-A men and women produce a one-dimensional personality, one with a profound and deadly absence of spiritual life. There is an absence of a basic concern with human relations and other interests that enrich life. Without the spirituality, changing diet and exercise habits to lower cholesterol levels and improve health overall isn't enough to protect Type-A's heart.*

"You could call Type-A behavior a medical problem, an emotional condition or a spiritual disease. All three labels are accurate...."

Cancer prevention tips

- Avoid drinking or cooking with chlorinated water
- Avoid using talcum powder in the genital areas
- Avoid drinking coffee, either regular or decaffeinated
- Avoid contact with asbestos
- Avoid excessive exposure to the sun
- Avoid fried foods
- Avoid cured meats and processed foods containing carcinogenic addi tives such as nitrates
- Avoid barrier forms of contraception
- Eat foods rich in vitamin D, calcium, molybdenum, and selenium, such as fish, whole grain foods, wheat germ, and beans
- Include lysine, an amino acid found in skim milk and other dairy products, in your diet
- Eat crunchy, yellow and dark-green leafy vegetables
- Reduce sodium and increase potassium in your diet
- Eat foods rich in dietary fiber
- Avoid cigarettes
- Avoid excessive amounts of alcohol

(Source - *Natural Health and Wellness Encyclopedia*, FC&A Publishing, 1988.)

Having a Prayer

Herbert Benson, a Harvard cardiologist, found that secular society suffers pains and disease for lack of prayer. Dr. Benson works with the Society for Scientific Study of Religions.

The March 1989 issue of *Psychology Today* reported that when researchers played tapes with an encouraging message to surgical patients under anesthesia, almost all experienced better than expected recoveries.

Prayer is the most powerful form of homeopathy. From the Christian perspective (88% of the U.S. population), Jesus Christ, as the Great Physician, voluntarily shed His magnetically perfect red blood to ground man and remove the flaw/error of nature. He also thus made the shift from electromagnetic to magnetoelectric to reunite the Newtonian, fallen, death-based natural world back with the all-in-all holographic supernatural world of the quantum. Only perfect blood could accomplish this Creator/creation reunion. As such, the blood of Jesus Christ is the basic vital homeopathic remedy turning the switch from death to life, from temporal to eternal. This is also why so many occult religions demand a blood sacrifice.

Ronald Grossarth-Maticek, a well-know Yugoslav psychologist working in Heidelberg, Germany, also demonstrated that personality attributes lead to cancer and heart disease. As a man thinketh, so he is physically. Put on a happy face! Have a trusting heart!

Others Orientation

Dr. Barry Grieff, a psychiatrist who has taught at Harvard, says to live successfully, an individual must: (1) have the capacity to love; (2) the capacity to learn; (3) the capacity to labor; (4) the capacity to laugh; (5) the capacity to leave. How do we as Americans measure up? These healthy pursuits were the foundation of what made America great.

Psychologist Larry Scherwitz at the University of California, San Francisco found that people who overuse the pronouns *"I," "me," "mine"* or other self-centered pronouns are twice as likely to have heart attacks. His solution to this problem is to *"fall in love."* When we love, we listen, we are empathetic, we give, we serve, we are others-oriented.

To have a more trusting heart requires an individual to: (1) reduce his cynical mistrust of the motives of others; (2) reduce frequency and intensity with which that individual experiences anger, irritation, frustration and rage; (3) treat others with kindness and consideration and use assertive skills only for unavoidable situations.

No one has the right to be angry until they have first communicated their problem to others causing the perceived distress. (Emotions are subjective internal reactions to external situations.) The problem can be communicated not by attacking the other person, but by using a sentence structure somewhat like this, *"I feel violated when such-and-such occurs, because..."*

Americans need to learn to forgive others who have mistreated them or angered them, to let go of resentment, to not be negative, to not try to get even, to avoid litigation, to live one day at a time while planning for the future, to learn to listen, to be thankful, to be empathetic and put themselves in other peoples' shoes, to learn to laugh at themselves and not to be so proud and arrogant, but instead be humble and quiet. Americans need to monitor their cynical thoughts, not judge others, confess their errors, relax and be more trusting. Americans need to talk to each other on the street and aboard airplanes, and also to their neighbors. Americans need to be anxious about nothing. Give other people enough rope to either build a bridge or to hang themselves. Accept the risk of pain short-term on the hope that a meaningful relationship can be built long-term.

The March/April 1989 issue of *Hippocrates* reported that terror in the mind sometimes triggers violent electrical storms in the heart. The result can be fatal. There are far too many electrical storms in the hearts of Americans today.

According to Shelley Taylor, a psychologist at UCLA, exaggerated optimism and a sense of control gives folks the strength and confidence to cope

with problems and be productive. A positive view about oneself is more bene-
ficial to one's mental well-being than seeing one's faults as others truly do.
According to Taylor, the three critical rules of success are: Always be positive.
Always be positive. Always be positive.

Dr. Richard Heslien of Purdue University in his work, *All About Touching:
Different Objectives*, has compiled studies which show that babies who are deprived of the touch and handling which signifies human bonding fall into depression, withdrawal and apathy that can even lead to death. In other words, babies
and small children need their mothers at home. Day care centers, particularly those
run by bureaucrats, are unhealthy! We need a touching society, not a distant, void,
hostile, alienated, bureaucratic one. We each need at least seven hugs a day. As
iron sharpens iron, so does a man strengthen the countenance of a friend.

People are homeopathic. Birds of a feather flock together. Like attracts
like. The longer a couple live together, the more their health habits and psychological perceptions converge, with each partner gradually influencing the
other. These couples have almost identical cholesterol and blood pressure levels. Both tend to be similarly overweight or underweight, or just about right.
Both feel about equally satisfied with life, according to researcher Dee Ed-
ington, of the University of Michigan Fitness Research Center. Each influences
the other partner's electromagnetic field/aura/countenance.

Do men who carry a lot of energy and intensity (particularly of the negative sort) above their waists and in their heads radiate an electromagnetic umbrella which draws from their wives' energy reserves, depressing their feminine
immune systems, making them vulnerable to EBV? Women are the weaker
vessel. Is the reason some men have prostate problems, IBS, and colon cancer
because they carry their energy too high in the body?

So, what we think, say and do influences our health, the health of those
around us, plus much, much more. Put on a happy face. Have a trusting heart!
The unhealthy consequences of not doing so are far too high. We're not
wealthy unless we're healthy! None of us are immune.

* * * * *

*"The world pharmaceutical industry is, like conventional medicine, suffering a
crisis of confidence. The old systems whereby the family doctor acted as bedside com-
forter to his patient are steadily being replaced by waiting rooms crowded with people
more likely to have a mental than a physical complaint, to be tranquillized or energized
by drugs whose action may ultimately be more pernicious than curative. Whereas the
pressures of demand and the structures of public health services are being severely
overstrained and underfunded, the pharmaceutical conglomerates by contrast move
from strength to international strength, and, swollen by profit, spend millions on research into developing new product lines with which they can subsequently hold health
authorities to oligopolistic ransom, and keep their corporate structures intact."* —
Harry Oldfield and Roger Coghill in — *The Dark Side of the Brain*

* * * * *

"The only way to keep your health is to eat what you don't want, drink what you don't like, and do what you'd rather not." — Mark Twain

* * * * *

"A smile is a smile wherever you go - at least in terms of the physiological changes it creates in people." — Paul Ekman, Psychologist —U. of California, San Francisco

* * * * *

Caution: Do not initiate any change in lifestyle, diet, exercise or medical treatment without first consulting your physician and/or counselor.

* * * * *

THE POWER OF THOUGHT TO INFLUENCE THE SUN

Turning Point for Humanity?

The Academy for Peace Research

A four year study has just been completed by the Academy for Peace Research to test whether or not humans can alter solar and geomagnetic activity by meditating, visualizing, or praying.

Preliminary analysis of the data indicates that this is possible. If so, the implications are awesome!

Why influence the Sun? Research by Professor Raymond Wheeler (deceased) at the University of Kansas uncovered the fact that international battles wax and wane at nearly regular intervals of about 11 years. Wheeler's data extended back 2,500 years and was extensively analyzed by Edward Dewey, who founded the Foundation for the Study of Cycles now located at the University of California, Irvine. Buryl Payne, a physicist/psychologist who directs the Academy for Peace Research, was able to correlate the onset of international battles with sunspot peaks for the past 200 years. Prior to that, sunspot data is not available, but presumably humans have been responding to this influence indefinitely into the past.

Crimes, riots, accidents, psychotic episodes, many types of illness, and just plain grouchiness have all been found to increase at times of solar activity and/or geomagnetic disturbances. This is not a theory; diverse studies by many researchers in different countries over many years have supported the same general conclusion.

The link appears to be: Solar flare - solar winds (sprays of electrons and protons) - disturbances to Earth's magnetic field - hormone changes - mood changes.

Men may be more affected than women, since warring behavior appears to be a male activity and Buryl hypothesizes (no experimental evidence as yet) that testosterone production in males increases at times of certain types of magnetic disturbances. Increased production of testosterone in males under 40 is known to produce irritability and aggressiveness. Buryl calls this: MMS or Male Macho Syndrome and suggests that warring behavior be considered a new type of social disease.

When people learned of this research they proposed that peace meditations could have a beneficial and calming effect on solar activity. Edgar Cayce had said this would be possible many years ago. The hypothesis was formalized in the design of an experiment called: **THE GLOBAL MEDITATION PROJECT.** People were invited to meditate at six dates each year (the Solstices, Equinoxes, etc.). A 3-1/2 year study culminated in June 1988 with the alignment of six planets close to the Galactic Center. Normally such an alignment would have been expected to trigger a large increase in solar activity, and an increase in international battles. Although there was an increase in solar activity there was actually a dip around the time of the largest peace meditations. (There were few world upsets and a number of positive international steps taken towards peace in June, a wonderful turning point may have occurred.) Such dips were also observed during the first two years of the experiment, the only times that the data has been analyzed so far. On the average the effects of several million people meditating appears to have resulted in a decrease in solar activity of 30% for a period of 7 to 10 days following the meditations.

This remarkable result, if it proves to have occurred during the other times of the meditations, and can be shown to stand up under careful mathematical analysis, will help unify science and religion and perhaps provide a humankind with a new way to maintain peaceful conditions.

How people can possibly influence the magnetic field of Earth or the Sun is a big scientific mystery. However, one possible link might be related to a biological energy field which Buryl discovered how to detect and measure. This energy field, which has been discovered and rediscovered in the past, is not magnetic, but it varies with variations in Earth's field. It could be considered a type of spin force and if it were magnetic it would be more than one million times as large as the body's intrinsic magnetic field and about 100 times as large as the Earth's magnetic field strength. When people calm down, this field also quiets. Perhaps when enough people meditate they quiet down Earth's field by some unknown resonance mechanism. The Earth in turn, could be in resonance with the Sun and hence a quiet Earth could result in a quieter Sun.

The device which detects and measures this field is inexpensive and easy to build. Details as well as research data, have been published in a book by Buryl Payne called **"THE BODY MAGNETIC."** The book is $10 and may be purchased from the Academy for Peace Research....

The Journal of Borderland Research May-June 1989

Stress Reduction

In the past, after a challenging and chaotic time, I'd return home, where I was raised, kick back and sleep a couple of days, and eat some homemade ice cream. Then, by the third day, I could finally fully relax. But, this is no longer necessary. Modern technology has come to my rescue. I now use a stress reduction device named *"Baby BETAR."* (BETAR means Bio-Energetic Transduction Aided Resonance.) I can lay down on the *"Baby BETAR"* for 30 minutes to an hour, listen to the music of my choice, totally relax, and often fall into a deep sleep. I usually awaken within the hour amazingly refreshed. In fact, the *"Baby BETAR"* has cut my night's sleep requirement by a full third.

Frankly, I wouldn't have believed a relaxation device could have been this effective if I hadn't experienced it personally. So strongly do I believe in the *"Baby BETAR"* I have plunked down my cold, hard cash and purchased a second one. This way, when I want it personally (in a family of eight), I have it available to me. I just can't say enough nice things about what a god-send this *"Baby BETAR"* has been for our family at a time when we have been under tremendous stress.

My reading in quantum mechanics of late has convinced me that the physical body is really nothing more than layered energy patterns which are stacked on top of each other in a gigantic grid and slowed down below the speed of light into a dense form. This is what we call matter, or more appropriately, flesh. As we go through life, we tend to armor ourselves defensively with energy patterns to protect ourselves against more of the same pain and hurt we have received over time. But the Catch-22 of it all is that this armor, these stress patterns, act as antennae and end up attracting what we least desire. So when I'm on the *"Baby BETAR"* and experience a thought which dissipates commensurate with the departure of an energy stress pattern, I truly rejoice.

This experience has brought new meaning to the importance of forgiving, forgetting, letting go, enduring all things, giving thanks for all things, and focusing on whatever things are good, kind, positive, etc. In short, scientifically the *"Baby BETAR"* makes real these long-stated religious truths. But that's not all. Medical research is increasingly confirming that 70% of all disease is stress-related. Disease is caused first by a breakdown in the flow of energy (often stress-induced) in the body. After the breakdown of the energy flow, the tissue then becomes dis-eased. The Shealy Institute for Comprehensive Health Care and Pain Management in Springfield, Missouri, under the direction of researcher Dr. C. Norman Shealy, has experienced very positive results with the *"BETAR,"* working with a sample of 800 patients. Shealy reported on having cut medical expenses 80%-85%, with pain intensity reduced an average of 70%. The *"Baby BETAR,"* which I fondly call the *"stress buster,"* is also being used for additional research at Children's Hospital in St. Petersburg, Florida, at Michigan State University, and at the University of Washington. Dr. Arthur Harvey, who helped develop a new program to study the effects of music on health at the University of Louisville School of Medicine, stated, *"Sound vibrations have the potential to change neurological, molecular or cellular activity in the body."*

One of the neat things about the *"BETARs"* is that there are no electrodes that have to be attached to the body. In the case of the *"Baby BETAR,"* one only has to put on a set of earphones and adjust the sound to one's desired enjoyment level while lying on the *"bed."* Both *"BETARs"* access and use energy/sound as information to bring about relaxation and help people recover from depression. Plus, I think I have experienced true long-term healing. I have noticed stubborn stress patterns, which repeatedly had to be worked out by massage therapists or a chiropractor, are no longer reappearing. They have literally disappeared since I've had the *"Baby BETAR."*

I flew to Georgia personally to spend three days researching the *"BETAR"* and the *"Baby BETAR."* This was after I had done research in Dallas, Texas; Boulder, Colorado; and Santa Fe, New Mexico. One unexpected benefit of the visit to Georgia was that I was able to interact face to face with a professional sound engineer who designs sound speakers for a living. This sound professional plunked down $45,000 to personally invest in a *"BETAR."* Needless to say, I pay close attention when competing professionals in a field put their money on the line.

For more information on the *"BETAR"* and the *"Baby BETAR,"* contact Dimensional Sciences, Inc., P.O. Box 167, Lakemont, GA 30552, 1-800-33BE-TAR. (404) 782-2524.

* * * * *

A Smile

A smile costs nothing, but gives much.

It enriches those who receive, without

making poorer those who give.

It takes but a moment, but the memory of it

sometimes lasts forever.

None is so rich or mighty that he can get

along without it, and none is so poor but

that he can be made rich by it.

A smile creates happiness in the home,

fosters good will in business, and is the

countersign of friendship.

It brings rest to the weary, cheer to the

discouraged, sunshine to the sad, and it is

nature's best antidote for trouble.

Yet it cannot be bought, begged, borrowed,

or stolen, for it is something that is of no

value to anyone until it is given away.

Some people are too tired to give you a smile.

Give them one of yours, as none

needs a smile so much as he who has

no more to give.

When a fetus agrees with the father and mother that the problem is its fault and an abortion is needed, the fetal hostility is fed back into the mother psychosomatically, who passes it on to subsequent children in the form of over-reactive anger, rage, convulsions, migraine — Dr. Lowell Ward, — Stressologist, Long Beach California

* * * * *

By age 18, the average American will have seen 250,000 acts of violence and 40,000 attempted murders on TV alone. The numbers become staggering when acts of violence portrayed in films are added to these TV statistics. We have now reached the point in the United States where the risk of being a violent crime victim is greater than becoming involved in an automobile accident. Over the past 30 years, violent crime has grown 12 times faster than the U.S. population.

* * * * *

To motivate your children and be in touch with them: (1) Encourage your children to read biographies of the people with careers they are interested in; (2) use specific examples of positive traits; (3) be specific with praise; (4) build your child's self-worth; (5) ask open-ended questions; (6) realize that experience is ten times more effective than words; (7) establish rapport with your child by seeing things from a child's perspective, see hear and feel things the way a child/teenager does.

* * * * *

"Hugging is healthy. It helps the body's immune system; it cures depression, reduces stress, and induces sleep. It is invigorating, rejuvenating, and it has no unpleasant side effects. Hugging is nothing less that a miracle drug. It's all natural. It's organic and naturally sweet. It contains no pesticides, no preservatives, no artificial ingredients and is 100% wholesome.

"Hugging is practically perfect. There are no moveable parts to loose, no batteries to wear out, and no periodic checkouts. Hugs require little energy yet yield high energy. They're inflation proof, have no insurance requirements. Hugs are theft proof, non-taxable, non-polluting, and of course, are fully returnable." - Dr. David Kritzman, *Interdimensional News*, June 1992

LIGHT MAN

July 1, 1990

Heavenly Fireworks

On June 12, 1991, the largest solar flare in at least two years hit Planet Earth. The National Oceanic and Atmospheric Administration (NOAA) reported that the geomagnetic field was mostly active due to these solar flares, and that storm conditions were possible.

On June 8, 1991, Mount Unzen exploded in Japan, and Mount Pinatubo blew its top in the Philippines. These two volcanoes became active for the first time in 200 years and 600 years, respectively. Mount Pinatubo shot sulfur dioxide gas into the stratosphere 21 miles high. Volcanic debris in the upper atmosphere in significant amounts blocks sunlight and plays havoc with crop production. An El Nino resulted, and 1992 saw roaring bull markets in *"protein gold"* and a coffee freeze in Brazil. The upside was that the California drought ended.

The heavenlies are churning. Graviton waves, put out by nova stars, are going bonkers. A full solar eclipse hit July 11, 1991. The full moon of July 26, 1991 recorded a lunar eclipse. The bright planets of Venus, Jupiter and Mars appeared to rendezvous in the evening sky on the summer solstice of June 21, 1991. Love and war were at it. These three planets were within three degrees of each other. The last time they were this close was December 23, 1769, when the American colonists were arguing with King George over taxes. This massing of planets again found Americans grim-faced over taxes. The hit movie was *Robin Hood: Prince of Thieves.* Robin Hood stole from the government to give to the people. Globally, governments everywhere (except Singapore) were shaky.

Electromagnetic Man

Upset in the heavens causes turmoil in the earth and distress among the nations. After all, the earth is just a big electromagnet that creates an energy grid around itself. Peter Kelly of Interdimensional Sciences tells me the last time the earth's magnetic field went through such a radical shift was at the time of Jesus Christ. History records that during such times supernatural manifestations proliferate. Given Hollywood's emphasis in this area, we should expect such an outbreak.

In a sense, we human beings are living electromagnetic units also. Medically, we are measured with an EEG (electrically) and an EMG (magnetically). We say that some folks have their heads in the clouds, where others have their feet on the ground. Some people are called air-heads, others are well grounded. If someone is *"losing ground,"* he is in trouble. These sayings speak to this electromagnetic continuum, too.

Kirlian photography measures the energy field/countenance/aura emanating from the human body. This field is still intact even if a physical limb is missing. Light is taken in through the human eye and is processed through the retina to the optic nerve connected to the brain from whence it feeds the pineal, pituitary and hypothalamus. On the other end of the electromagnetic spectrum, African tribes partially bury men in paramagnetically charged iron-rich red earth to cure them of skin disease and other illnesses. Stateside, a famous major medical school has used the work of Albert Davis and Walter Rawls, Jr. and affected a 90% cure rate of cancer using magnets (north pole, I suspect). Human blood carries a magnetic charge. Magnetic therapy is in widespread use in India and France. Healing results.

As human beings, we are holographic, compressed energy patterns, slowed down below the speed of light, held together by an electromagnetic field. We are human photocells, frozen, compressed light. This is why physicians of various specialties around the earth can analyze a particular part of the human body and from it obtain a picture of the whole. We are holographic; each part reflects the whole. A reflexologist can analyze a foot. Lines in the hands or in the face provide clues to the system's health. An acupuncturist can evaluate an ear. An Indian doctor can analyze the urine, a medical doctor the tongue or the blood, an iridologist the eye, and so it goes. Each holographic part contains within it the picture of the entire living, holographic, electromagnetic unit. So it should come as no surprise that as go the heavens, so goes the earth, and man individually and collectively.

Scattered Light

Leading physicians today state that at least 80% of all disease has an emotional base. The thing is, when we emotionally fail to handle the challenges of life properly, our emotions slow down below the speed of light and in our bodies become living crystals, biological resistors which impede light/energy flow, shutting down geometric and holographic electromagnetic connections which vent and feed from the heavens through the head down to the feet, grounding in the earth. The greater our number of bio-resistors the less functional we are.

Of course, we all come into this world with excess baggage, bio-resistors already built in which have been passed down to us genetically via our ancestors' RNA/DNA. So, we all have these inherited light/energy bio-resistors to contend with, as well as our own creations. The more biological resistors, the darker the shadow we cast, the less light there is in our bio-system. If our ancestral and/or personal error/sin creates too many biological resistors, particularly where they start to shut down the holographic circuitry in the 695 key acupuncture points of intense luminosity (confirmed by Kirlian photography), then we really are headed for trouble. We start to get sick in many ways, perhaps emotionally, mentally, and/or physically, and we make increasingly poor judgments. We are literally in bondage. The heart is of course key in all this as it not only pumps life (oxygen, cellular food), but also controls the endocrine system which affects everything else. Plus, the heart is the spiritual/mental/emotional/physical integration organ between the conscious and subconscious.

Yes, the likes of homeopathy, Rolfing, stressology, point holding, colonics, massage, reflexology and chiropractic can clear some of the circuits short term. But unless the spirit, heart, soul and mental software programming is changed, particularly down into the theta region of the subconscious, the same old patterns may reemerge, maybe worse, perhaps seven times worse.

An Electromagnetic Biblical Perspective

Old Adam had it good (perfect environment) before ambitious Eve was deceived into playing god, and Adam let the woman dominate him. All of Adam's circuits were originally on line. He was perfectly electromagnetically connected, both supernaturally and naturally, in touch with both heaven and earth. All twelve of his key organ systems manifested through his skin and cranium the perfect piezoelectric charge, carried there without resistance along the twelve acupuncture meridians, handled superconductively by the central and governing meridians. Adam's system was superconductive before his self-will entered a bio-resistor into the system and began shutting him down.

Later on, Moses, the most humble man on the face of the earth, had to ground out by taking his shoes off in the presence of the Burning Bush. Whoever touched the Ark of the Covenant (in part a capacitor) in ancient Israel was electrocuted. The high priest of ancient Israel was required to wear a breastplate of twelve gemstones, representing not only the twelve tribes of Israel, but also the twelve organ systems in his own body. These twelve gemstones provided each of the high priest's individual key organs a piezoelectric colored crystal crutch, as it were, so that he could come on line electromagnetically and directly access the throne room of God from earth. It is no accident that in Revelation the twelve gemstones in the heavenly city are identical to those which were worn by the high priest of Israel.

THE Light Man

When God in the fullness of His historic chosen time became matter through the personalized energetic work of the Holy Spirit, He created the earthly representative of Himself in the person of Jesus Christ. Because, according to God's Newtonian-realm law, the sins of the father are visited upon the sons, Jesus Christ had to avoid the inherited baggage and biological resistors which come down the pike for all the rest of us. He escaped the blown circuits by way of the immaculate conception. None of the rest of us had the Holy Spirit working on behalf of God the Father. So Jesus Christ came in clean, with all systems go, all twelve acupuncture meridians perfectly on line, superconductive, central and governing meridians a go, perfectly pH balanced, fully mineralized, complete enzymes, etc., void of any biological sin/error resistors, the 695 key acupuncture points operating at maximum luminosity, with all the rest of the points operational, too. The total holographic light network was intact.

As God and man, Jesus could operate both supernaturally and naturally, in the quantum realm and in the Newtonian realm, crossing the Einsteinian relativity bridge without a problem. He had perfect access to both extremes (and everything in between) of the electromagnetic spectrum. He was Alpha and Omega. He was the second Adam. Jesus was on earth humanly as Adam was initially, before the first Adam violated God's law and set into play the downward dark death spiral, as biological resistors entered his system. But there was still a catch. Jesus had to walk through his entire life on earth without making a mistake (sin). It was only by perfectly keeping God's law that He could keep from introducing error/sin/biological resistors into His own system, and thereby prevent the short-circuiting of His perfect electromagnetic connection.

If we possessed perfect electromagnetic connections, or perhaps even partially good ones, and strengthening faith, even the equivalent of a mustard seed, we'd be able to say to a mulberry tree, *"Be uprooted and planted in the ocean,"* and it would happen. Neat, huh? Christ said, *"Greater things than I have done you shall do."*

As Creator, Law-giver, and godly establisher of religious protocol, Jesus Christ was the personalization of government as religion applied to economics, the $E=mc^2$ of human action. Thus, it was no accident that Satan's three Gospel-recorded temptations of Jesus were governmental (kingdoms of the world), religious (cast yourself down) and economic (stones into bread). Because God is basically covenantal (Old Covenant/New Covenant), to keep the faith and restore the rift in the heaven/earth electromagnetic connection, Jesus Christ made the voluntary decision to take on all the world's error/sin/biological resistors on the cross. He thereby laid the covenantal basis for His people to clear their systems in time on earth. The eternal connection was first reestablished by the work of Christ Himself. How could the earth/grave/death hold someone who had no personal or ancestral death in His system? The Father of Lights would not permit it. Justice prevailed.

The proof of the eternal connection for saved man was to be manifest in time through his works on the earth as he progressively moved from darkness to light, clearing his system of darkness, increasingly filing it with light through obedience to God's commandments until physical death. This *"magnetic"* activity was joined on the *"living electrical"* end of the spectrum by faith and the work of the Holy Spirit.

Biblically, man, by attaching through God-given faith to His perfect holographic model, Jesus Christ, and the laser plumbline of His blood, could establish himself spiritually in both the electrical and magnetic ends of the spectrum, heaven and earth, the supernatural and the natural, quantum and Newtonian. By walking out his life on earth in faith through increasing perfect obedience to God's moral law and supernatural guidance, man further clears, grounds, and establishes both the electrical and magnetic ends of the spectrum within himself - harmless as a dove yet wise as a serpent, manifesting the fruit of the Spirit and obeying the law of God, spirit and truth, faith and works, becoming in time what he had already established by faith abstractly and conceptually in the spiritual realm eternally. Man is required to ground out what he believes to be true eternally, to prove all things, to complete the connection. (The kingdom of God is within before it can be externalized.) In such a fashion, the electromagnetic and magnetoelectric scalar interferometry is established. The ultimate goal is an integrated, holographic, electromagnetic, linear and cyclical, personal and spiritual, supernatural and natural, energetic and physical perfect living photocell. The creation groans, eagerly awaiting the revealing of the sons of God.

What A Man Believes He Sees

So yes, Martha, signs in the heavens, geophysical upset on earth, and turmoil among mankind is joined by war in the spirit realm. (Planetary angles in the infrared emit frequencies which affect specific human organ systems and trigger emotional responses in the natural man.) And true enough, some people don't believe what they can't see. But they might consider what historical evidence has confirmed with regard to the spiritual realm, and what we can now measure with advanced instrumentation, Ghostbusters-style. After all, we humans only see 5% of the entire light spectrum, from 0.4-0.7 micrometers. Yet we live at 10 micrometers in the infrared range. Therefore, all demons/ghosts/spirits have to do is move in and out of this narrow light spectrum to be seen or unseen by our extremely limited eye camera. Those (medicine men, hippies) who have fooled around with drugs like LSD and moved outside of this limited 0.4-0.7 micrometer light spectrum, along with those researchers and religious leaders who have delved into exploring the infrared ranged (the arena of dark light), know all too well of the existence of the demonic.

For me, a good case of contrary opinion applies. I want to stay grounded, settled down, keep my feet on the ground, stay in my body, and walk by faith not by sight, according to God's edicts. With the earth's magnetic field weakening, the crowd wants to be lawless, being their own gods by doing what is right in their own eyes, emotionally based, stripping their protective grounding flesh from their souls, getting out of their bodies, free of the bounds of earth, so they can manifest ungodly, ungrounded, quantum realm supernatural power which sure as hell will burn them out. They're ungrounded. I intend to go the other way. It's the garden, the mountains, and the Tree of Life for me, thank you. If you want to go up, you have to get down first. Scalar interferometry proves this scriptural principle. We also get back what we give off. And we reap what we sow. That's electromagnetic, quantum and Newtonian in combination. It's not either/or, it's both. Everything is alive in a sense, and has a *"spirit,"* even stones.

This is the unvarnished man. Notice how almost insignificant the *"ALL VISIBLE LIGHT"* spectrum is? That's all we see. Look at all the rest of the spectrum that bombards us. Think of the technology, for good or evil, which could (and has) harnessed all this light/energy.

Light Man

Now here's another work I'd like to introduce: Bruce L. Cathie's *The Energy Grid: Harmonic 695: The Pulse of the Universe* (American West Publishers, P.O. Box 3300, Bozeman, MT 59772, $13.95, ISBN 0-922356-20-3, Phone 406/585-0700). Chapter 17 of Cathie's latest book is entitled, *"The Harmonics of Humans."* Cathie writes, *"The unified equations tell us that the whole universe is manifested by the harmonic geometric matrix of light itself. The whole of reality is light. Therefore, it follows, that we as human beings must consist of nothing more than a geometric collection of the harmonic waveforms of light - guided by intelligence...*

"As each day forms a part of our geometric time cycle it seems reasonable to assume that perfection would be more likely to result from a gestation period of: 269.44 days.

"This would tune the body directly with the harmonic value derived from the unified equation: 26944...

"I would predict that the temperature at which the human body performs most efficiently, both physically and mentally, is 98.80412 degrees F.

"98.80412 degrees fahrenheit - 37.1134 degrees centigrade - The harmonic reciprocal of 371134 = 269444.

"If the unified harmonic is built into the body at birth, then the temperature at which it functions appears to be at a level which would set up the harmonic reciprocal, causing a reaction, and life.

"A third clue is evident in the nodal points in the human body where our bio-energetic processes are most prevalent. These are the major points used in the science of acupuncture...

"At Alma-Ata, the Leningrad surgeon, Dr. M.K. Geykin, was experimenting with Kirlian Photography. He had spent some time in China, where he worked on acupuncture. Fascinated by Kirlian's method, he decided to visit him in Krasnodar and induce him to build a gadget that could help physicians find the points of acupuncture on the human body. Kirlian listened to him with great interest. He had already discovered long before that the 695 points on the human body considered to be the points for acupuncture coincided with the points of intense luminosity brought out by Kirlian Photography.

"The number of acupuncture points: 695.

"The reciprocal harmonic of the speed of light at the Earth's surface. Again it appears that the body's bio-energy system is tuned to react to the harmonic of light. "...

Man was created in the image of the Father of Lights.

Gridlock

Now, let's turn our attention to the earth's electromagnetic grid system, its energy grid. The earth as a big spinning electromagnet, winds energy lines around it, called ley lines, much in the same manner a baseball is constructed with the strands crisscrossing each other.

The technology exists to tap this earth energy, providing the world with an endless supply of free energy. Tesla proved this in New York earlier in this century. Also, when the earth's magnetic field weakens and/or solar storms rage, these gridlines weaken, allowing more earthquakes and volcanic eruptions. Additionally, during times of ley line distortions, the dividing line between the natural and the supernatural blurs.

Nearly all of the early churches in Europe, England, Ireland and North America were located at *"power points"* on these ley lines, vortexes and the like. Map readers in Japan, China (Feng Shui), and in Egypt going back to the pyramids considered the electromagnetic *"ley of the land"* in computing where and how to place buildings. Present-day petroleum geology, utility companies and water dowsers are bringing this work into the modern scientific world. Research at Utah State University has advanced the science.

Earth Sick

The June, 1989 *East-West* Magazine featured an article by Richard Leviton entitled, *"Can the Earth's Stress Spots Make You Sick?"* The answer is yes. The beds of people who died from cancer were found to be consistently located above noxious radiation emanating from the earth's faults in Vilsbiburg, a small Bavarian community in southern Germany.

In the town of Stettin, 5,438 cancer deaths over 21 years were found in each case to have a subterranean water vein under the house. This work was accomplished by Baron Gustav Freiherr von Pohl's colleague, Dr. Hager, back in the 1920s. Later, in the 1940s, a German physician, Manfred Curry, M.D., discovered the Curry Network Screen, a grid which girds the planet. German Ernest Hartmann, M.D., director of the Research Circle for Geobiology, formulated the Hartmann Grid. It runs diagonally to the Curry Grid. The intersections of these grids are found to be harmful to plants, animals and humans, particularly the intersection of grid lines of similar electrical charge.

In 1972, in Austria, Kathe Vachler, a mathematics teacher commissioned by the Pedagogical Institute in Salzburg, found 95% of slow-learners' beds were situated on either water veins or Curry Grid crossings.

Ludger Mersmann, M.D. contends that the cause of geopathic stress is localized magnetic anomalies that upset human health. It is Mersmann who invented the Geo-Magnetometer and Data Logger which can take precise readings in a suspected geopathic zone and get a three-dimensional computer graphic of the disturbed field. Says Mersmann, *"Geopathic stress consists of several factors, but the main factor is a disturbed magnetic field. Here the natural homo-*

geneous magnetic field meets with or turns into a nonhomogeneous field, resulting in a disturbed zone."

The earth oscillates at the resonant frequency of 7.83 Hertz. The earth's natural magnetic field usually averages about 0.5 gauss. However, regularly occurring anomalies and sudden field shifts often range up to three times as high. So with all the solar, geophysical and geomagnetic field upset we are experiencing presently, we should expect people to increasingly become ill. Says Leviton, *"For two decades scientists have been gathering evidence of the deleterious effects on humans of extremely weak magnetic fields, and it all supports Mersmann's hypothesis. The human body has composite and individual organ fields as low as 1×10^{-9} gauss, or about one-billionth of the earth's field. Recent studies in New York and Colorado have linked exposure to low-frequency, weak electromagnetic fields (for example, from high voltage power lines) and cancer, particularly childhood leukemia."*

Helmut Ziehe, president of the International Institute of Baubiologie and Ecology in Clearwater, Florida, has found a dozen physiological changes scientists have observed in people who live within geopathic zones. These include electrocardiogram and pulse changes, changes in blood sedimentation, pH, electrical cell polarity, and alterations in immune function. Dr. Hans Nieper of the Sibersee Hospital in Hanover, Germany maintains that 75% of his multiple sclerosis patients *"spend too much time in a geopathogenic zone,"* and at least 92% of all his cancer patients have remained for long periods in geopathogenic zones.

Underground water and magnetic field anomalies are consistently the main problems. In Germany, approximately 50% of all physicians are aware of the geopathic factor. How many U.S. M.D.s are conscious of it? However, there is some emerging consciousness in the United States. In Seattle, Washington, a group of architects, artists and the like, called the Geo Group, have mapped the ley lines of Seattle.

In understanding how these subtle earth energies cause illness, it is helpful to remember that we are well when we are at *"ease,"* when all our bodies' systems are oscillating at their correct resonant frequencies. When we are emotionally upset, ungrounded, not settled down, or under stress we are *"diseased."* This is also why we are to think on whatever things are true, noble, just, pure, lovely and of good report. As a man thinketh so he is. We should ground out by eating fresh, live, non-toxic foods, too, drink plenty of pure water, breathe correctly, and exercise appropriately.

Fly the Leys

There is another interesting aspect to these ley lines or energy grid lines of the earth. They have long been the tracks on which the purported UFOs have run. Now, flying saucers, or anti-gravity devices, are well documented. The Nazis had flying saucers. The U.S. had them as early as 1942, as reported by the April 7, 1950 *U.S. News & World Report*. Press reports on them went underground in the mid-1950s, following a North Carolina confab.

Studies at Michigan State University have confirmed the connection between magnetism, levitation and gyroscopic motion. This is anti-gravity device material.

The July/August 1989 issue of *The Journal of Borderland Research* featured an article by Michael Potter, *"UFOs: We have the Technology."* Wrote Potter, *"UFOs are aerodynamic...This half-lens shape - like a frisbee - is an aerofoil and when flown it will create lift.*

"However, unlike a frisbee, the UFO glider does not need to be spun to fly. UFOs have never been observed to spin, although energy has been seen spinning around them...

"Circular aircraft are certainly not new. Before the 1947 UFO flap there was a round airplane called a 'U.S. Flying Flapjack' and the Russians experimented with a similar craft. What was different about these airplanes is that they had propellers, tails and elevators...

"A UFO glider's center of gravity - the coin - is its means of guidance. The saucer 'follows' the weight of the falling coin. If the coin is shifted to the center of the lower dome the UFO glider will descend vertically.

"Now a magnet replaces the rim coin with an internal mechanical ballast. In fact, a shifting ballast is a method blimps use to navigate. However, unlike a blimp, any part of the saucer's rim can be a front. If the ballast is quickly moved around the saucer's rim 90 degrees, the gliding saucer will execute a right-angle turn as it follows the falling ballast...

"The elliptical-hull airship designed by the Spacial Company in Mexico is a circular rigid blimp. This helium aircraft comes very close to fulfilling our UFO theory...

"Now imagine a saucer that combines the asymmetrical lenticular shape of the UFO glider, the structural strength of the Spacial airship and the hot air lift of a Cameron airship. Here we have an entirely new aircraft capable of vertical takeoff and landing, rapid horizontal flight and right-angle turns."

If gravity is a wave, if the wave of gravity is offset through the correct harmonic frequency, then a saucer could literally fall into a vacuum in any direction also.

Anti-Gravity and the World Grid, by D.H. Childress, points out that Australia has a permanent diamagnetic levitation vortex at Alice Springs, Australia. Alice Springs is located in the middle of Australia. It is where an infamous longtime U.S. super-secret military installation is located, known as Pine Gap. Pine Gap is as hush-hush as Area 51 in Nevada. Nevada? UFO sightings are common in an area known as S-4, located about 7 miles south of the western border of Area 51. This region is also known as *"Dreamland."*

A Space Hoax?

I suspect by 2001, and for sure by 2010, all this technology that's been with us since at least the early 1950s, will be sprung on us in an attempt to *"wow"* mankind into accepting a New World Order, complete with a one world government, a one world currency, a one world central bank. The point is, it won't be anything new. I have personally visited with many of the men who have developed this fascinating technology. Put differently, there is not a natural problem I know of we face on this earth which has not already been solved technologically if the present establishment would get out of the way politically, financially and legally, and special interests be damned.

Levitate Your Friends

The book, *Anti-Gravity and the World Grid*, also presents an interesting section subtitled, *"Human Diamagnetism Gravity Antenna Levitation."* This section shows how any group of people, anywhere, as a party activity, can levitate anyone else. The step-by-step directions, along with the easy-to-understand theory, is all presented there.

Levitation is not necessarily magic or an occult activity. It's more times than not technology which has been hidden from us. The ancients had it. Bruce Cathie documented how Tibetan monks used sound waves to create an anti-gravitational effect (offsetting the frequency of gravity) to levitate stones. This was confirmed by Dr. Jarl, a Swedish doctor (who studied at Oxford) on behalf of the English Scientific Society. One wonders if this is one of the reasons why the Red Chinese have shut off Tibet from the rest of the world, perhaps at the behest of the proponents of the New World Order. Could they not want all of this fantastic knowledge released just yet? These Tibetan monks functionally understood the laws governing the structure of matter. And the TM meditators, with their *"soft landing"* pillow? Their chanted mantras reach the point where they harmonically oscillate all their body's cells at a frequency which offsets gravity. And in nature? Water moves up the trunk of a tree. Anti-gravity!

All of the above, while possibly somewhat shocking to some of you, and undoubtedly mind-blowing to the American general public, has become over time matter-of-fact to this writer. It is pretty much demonstrable, verifiable, and repeatable. Among the global scientists, it is all taken for granted as common working knowledge. But then again, the federal government persecutes the independent avant garde global scientists the same way it does the Franklin Sanders-type moneychangers, and the American patriot tax protestor/honest money movement. The Dark Ages did not occur in the Middle Ages. The Dark Ages are now. Let there be light! This, then, is my contribution to *"a thousand points of light."* Quite frankly, I'd settle personally for 695 bright ones. I have no desire to be a heavyweight, but rather a Light Man.

QUALITY OF LIFE
June 7, 1990

Quality of life has its basis in both conception and reality. *"As a man thinks, so he is." "Don't worry about things that are beyond your control." "The glass is half empty; the glass is half full."* In other words, the quantum filters down to the Newtonian, and the Newtonian percolates up to the quantum. It's a two-way street.

Conception and reality are constantly interacting and interrelating. Each has its own set of fundamental laws which relate to its position in life's hologram. Hopefully, as we walk through life, the concrete world of facts correctly alters our conceptions. Simultaneously, the more correct our conceptions, the more accurately we view reality, and the clearer our thinking, the more common our sense, the greater we are in touch with the real world, both seen and unseen. The greater we are in touch and able to respond to reality, the healthier we tend to be physically, the more perceptive, and the more sensitive. And finally, the clearer and more grounded our head is, the more we can accurately perceive opportunity and profit from it. So for all the above reasons, what follows in this *"Quality of Life"* chapter are summaries gleaned from my extensive reading. These insights should help us all better respond, cope and adapt to the challenges we face over the upcoming difficult years.

* * * * *

Researchers at the American Heart Association have documented that hormones relay feelings straight from the heart. The human heart is an intelligent organ that communicates regularly with other parts of the anatomy, and sometimes gives advice to the brain. Atrial natriuretic factor is a family of hormones manufactured in the heart that sends messages to organs throughout the body. And as we know, the cerebral spinal fluid of the head bathes the pericardium of the heart. So the mental and emotional integration of the head and heart trigger hormones in the endocrine system which in turn affect the health of the other parts of the body and determine its *"organ"* -ization. As a man thinks in his heart, so he is.

* * * * *

The human body is a glandular mechanism. Every organ is under the control of certain ductless glands, which activate and energize it by their secretions. Disturbances in the organs are traced to glandular origins or deficiencies of activating hormones. The ductless glands are the centers of mineral metabolism. Each extracts from the blood certain organic minerals obtained from assimilated foods.

* * * * *

The nervous system also controls the human body. A fundamental model of how the nervous system functions and adapts is by the production of dominant patterns. Energy and matter are interchangeable. Therefore, the energy patterns produced by the nervous system in turn produce mental, emotional and biochemical reactions, altering physiology. So, in a sense, sickness or disease is a dominant behavior pattern expressed by an energy pattern laid down by the nervous system of the body. Healing thus requires a recovery or unwinding/breaking of the psychologically dominant patterns. Therefore, recovery is structural, organizational, biochemical, electrical, emotional, and mental. It is also conscious and subconscious, sympathetic and parasympathetic.

* * * * *

To enhance immunity, one must love oneself, express feelings instead of keeping them locked up inside, laugh, and talk to oneself with nurturing and uplifting words. Also, one must assert oneself in stressful situations to bring about change. Additionally helpful to strengthen the immune system is rest, exercise, a nutritious diet, prayer and meditation, deep relaxation, personal growth, service to others, and surrounding oneself with supportive people while being supportive of others. Source: Victoria Moran, from her book *Compassion, the Ultimate Ethic*

* * * * *

Angry Type A people are best served by exercising, making relaxation a habit, and working at developing their creative right brain by doing such things as reading worthwhile books, listening to music, and enjoying people. Type A's also benefit from engineering the day to get rid of trash events, learning to enjoy traffic, getting the spiritual element back into their lives, enjoying pets and plants, learning that the trivial errors of others need not be one's total preoccupation, and knowing that harmful Type A behavior, such as anger, irritation, aggravation and impatience, can in fact be changed.

* * * * *

Fifteen percent of those who scored high on unresolved anger on a personality test at age 25 had died by age 50. Only 2% who scored low on the test died in the same period, according to Dr. Redford Williams of Duke University.

* * * * *

Words influence physical health. For example, words of embarrassment cause blushing. A psychological spark ignites a physiological fire.

* * * * *

The progression of physical pain normally involves a seven-step process: (1) brain lateralization in response to a perceived danger; (2) disrupted electrical potential, resulting in selectively weak areas throughout the body; (3) heightened tension in those parts of the body that are opposite to the already weakened areas; (4) sodium invasion of tissue cells in the constricted body parts; (5) potassium loss at the cellular level; (6) inability of the involved cells to take up oxygen; (7) pain. All this eventually leads to chronic degenerative diseases in the physical body. When in physical discomfort, taking drugs or pain pills is like shutting off a fire alarm that's sounding because of a fire in the basement.

Shutting off the alarm has nothing to do with the cause, and only masks the real issue. The function of pain is to warn, protect and remind us that we are not *"organ"*-ized.

* * * * *

Happy Hour is an oxymoron, because alcohol is a depressant. The use of recreational drugs is a willful decision to escape reality. The use of prescription drugs for pain is a willful decision to suppress symptoms of the dis-ease and not deal with the underlying cause.

* * * * *

Daily beer drinkers' risk of colon cancer is 12 times greater than that of teetotalers.

* * * * *

Fetal exposure to alcohol is the leading cause of mental retardation.

* * * * *

Long-term use of cocaine by men leads to infertility.

* * * * *

Eighty percent of cancers are potentially preventable. Tobacco is responsible for 30% of cancers, dietary factors 35%, radon, X-rays and other radiation, chemical exposures, medication, alcohol and overexposure to the sun account for most of the remaining cancers.

* * * * *

Physicians have long known that drugs alter behavior because of their biochemical reactions. For the same reason diet alters behavior.

* * * * *

The greatest alchemist in the world is the human body.

* * * * *

According to Dr. Kay Tte Katwe of Cambridge, an additional serving of fruit or vegetables may help reduce the risk of stroke-related death by as much as 40%. Fruits and vegetables are generally high in potassium. A high dietary intake of potassium has been shown to reduce fatal strokes.

* * * * *

According to Dr. Maurizio Trevisan, of State University of New York's School of Medicine, olive oil is good for the heart. Olive oil is linked with low blood cholesterol, blood pressure and blood sugar.

* * * * *

The average person who walks one mile a day expends the same number of calories as a jogger, according to Lawrence T.P. Sitfler, Ph.D., president of Health Management Resources.

* * * * *

According to Dr. Herman Frankel, manager/director of the Portland Oregon based Health Institute, and chairman of the board of the Obesity Foundation, a little weight gain over the years may actually help an individual live longer, provided that individual is healthy. Gradual, modest weight gain seems to go along with a lower mortality rate.

Dr. Albert Stunkard of the University of Pennsylvania, writing in *The New England Journal of Medicine*, found that when it comes to gaining weight, genes make more difference than anything else in determining whether a person is fat, thin or in between.

* * * * *

In the brain, beta waves, from 16 to 13 hertz, have to do with the conscious level of the brain. Beta waves involve thinking and vigilance, attention externally directed, an alert mind. From 13 to 8 hertz is the alpha level. This is the emotional level. Alpha waves are detached awareness, the mind not actively engaged, and a state of relaxation. From 7 down to 4 hertz is the theta level. This is the mental/subconscious level. Theta waves are associated with meditation, profound relaxation, drowsiness, memory and creative thought. Then there are delta waves, which are common during sleep and related to empathy and compassion while awake.

* * * * *

According to Dr. Harold Saxton Burr, anatomy professor at the Yale University School of Medicine, the magnetic field around the heart was measured at 0.000001 gauss, while the brain measured at 0.000000001 gauss. The magnetic intensity of the earth is 0.50 gauss. The earth, with the greater intensity, has a tremendous influence on the human body.

* * * * *

"We do have scientifically repeatable proof of measurable changes in electromagnetic forces that take place on the surface of the skin which correspond to the loci of the ancient acupuncture points." - Albert S. Anderson, M.D.

* * * * *

At least six mechanisms by which magnetic fields affect the body have been identified: (1) Increasing blood flow to treated areas; (2) enabling the blood to carry more oxygen; (3) increasing enzyme action; (4) increasing cell division; (5) altering the acid-base balance of the tissues; and (6) affecting the endocrine system. Everything in the universe has a magnetic field, from the tiniest electrons to the greatest galaxies.

* * * * *

Magnetic energy is influenced by brain action. The voluntary motion of lifting a finger in response to a signal results from magnetic activity in the motor cortex of the brain just prior to the action. Additionally, there's a magnetic field surrounding a living organism which controls the development and functioning of that living system. Any electromagnetic energy directed to a life system affects the protein, amino acids and enzymes of that system, according to researchers Albert Roy Davis and Walter C. Rawls.

* * * * *

Researcher Lilly Kolisko demonstrated that the seeds of fruits, grains and vegetables sown in the ground just 48 hours prior to the full moon were more bountiful than the seeds sown during any other period of the lunar cycle. Plants were healthier and yields more bountiful in every case. Tomato seeds sown two days prior to the full moon produced 60% more tomatoes than seeds sown during the new moon. Beans and peas showed even greater yields when compared to new moon plantings. When maize was sown under full moon conditions, it was plentiful and sweet. When maize was sown under new moon conditions, it was sick, spindly and unappetizing. ...Also, planting in harmony with the earth's magnetic field, from north to south, has been shown to have benefits by way of increased yields.

* * * * *

The book, *Healing Music*, by Andrew Watson and Neville Drury, discussed how emotions are triggered by music, and therefore how hormonal changes in the heart create alterations in the endocrine system, which in turn affect the entire physical body. Emotions exist in their own right as potential energy patterns in the nervous system, which are triggered by music in addition to other outside stimuli. The musical expression of joy, sadness or love requires not only a certain spacing of time and pitch, but also the amplitudes of the music follow appropriate form. The more precise the form is realized in the musical composition, the greater its impact on the listener. This makes it easier for the person to feel or experience emotion with repetition of the music. There are standard cycles of emotion. The cycle consists of seven emotions: anger, hate, grief, love, sex, joy and reverence. Each emotion has a span of expression ranging from 4.8 seconds (anger) to 9.8 seconds (reverence).

The resonant frequency of the seven notes in an octave correspond to both emotions and colors. Specifically, C equals red; D equals orange; E equals yellow; F equals green; G equals blue; A equals indigo; and B equals violet. As one moves from red and orange to indigo and violet, one moves from action to introspection.

Today, 50-75% of all illnesses are stress related. Soothing music has been shown to lower the heart rate, blood pressure and the amount of free fatty acids in the blood.

* * * * *

Dr. Sue Chapman of New York City Hospital has found that premature infants benefitted from the playing of the orchestral string version of Brahms' Lullaby. The preemies who listened to the music gained weight faster, had fewer complications, and were released from the hospital an average of one week earlier than babies who did not listen to this music. In Bulgaria, Dr. Lozanov found that when listening to Bach's music, alpha activity in the brain increased. This was associated with relaxation.

* * * * *

In Red China, folk music is used to make chickens more productive (lay more eggs and grow faster). In the northern U.S., rock music is used to drive ducks and geese away from polluted ponds.

* * * * *

The basic moral virtue is humility. However, a person must be grounded and have a root in themselves to be humble. People with low self-worth/self esteem are so vulnerable that even the smallest embarrassment or criticism is viewed as threatening. Admitting their mistakes is nearly impossible; helping others is a blow to their ego. Feeling and acting helpless also comes from low self-worth/self-esteem. Such folks become victims by choice. They need to stop blaming others and view themselves as victims. They need to choose to be responsible for their own lives, actions, and reactions. They need to take control of their lives. So humility, self-worth, being responsible, and having the capability to serve are all inescapably interrelated.

* * * * *

Creativity stems from tension, passion and conflict. When we're totally truthful with ourselves about what's really going on, we can then grow. If our experience is too far out of line with our belief system, then we will change our beliefs. This is the linking up of the abstract with the concrete, the temporal with the eternal, of principles with facts. It is easier to work ourselves into a better mode of thinking than it is to think ourselves into a better mode of working/acting.

* * * * *

To be happy: (1) Live one day at a time; (2) take advantage of what you already have; (3) have a sense of humor; (4) set some priorities; (5) make a change and stick to it; (6) forgive and forget; and (7) count your blessings.

* * * * *

R.S. Elliott, in his book *Is It Worth Dying For?*, stated, *"Stress is only a burden when you respond to it with a feeling that you have lost control."* People become stressed primarily because of perfectionism, unrealistic self-image, being unwilling to delegate, and excessive need for approval. Other causes of stress are believing only in oneself, worrying about the future, pursuing happiness, and wanting to handle things alone. Problems become stressful if an individual does not handle them positively and productively.

* * * * *

Traits necessary for success: (1) Having and maintaining focus; (2) being involved in something the individual wants to do; (3) developing competence;

(4) having efficient and effective time management; (5) possessing persistence in the face of obstacles; (6) focusing on the task at hand; (7) being in the right place at the right time, and knowing its importance; and (8) having the ability to recognize and seize opportunities.

* * * * *

To sell an idea an individual needs to: (1) prove the need; (2) develop possible alternatives; (3) select the most practical ideas; (4) consider the politics; (5) document the evidence; (6) enlist allies; (7) defuse disagreement; (8) add emotional appeal while describing the benefits; and (9) prepare an action plan for implementing the idea.

* * * * *

Nancy Tober, editor of *Bride's*, declares that there are five brands of marriage: (1) Total marriages - this is one where the couple lives and works together and are totally involved with each other. (2) Vital marriages - this is a marriage where two people do entirely different things, have different occupations, but are both very involved with each other's lives. They spend time together, communicate well together, and stay together. (3) Passive congenial marriages - here is where two people get along, but are on clearly separate tracks. (4) Devitalized marriages - this is where the man comes home from work too late to talk to his wife, and they never have anything in common. A lot of marriages in Hollywood end up this way. The two people drift apart, and eventually the marriage splits. (5) Conflict oriented marriages - this is where the marriage is a dog and cat fight all the time, and where violence breaks out. These marriages usually end in divorce.

* * * * *

In marriage, three rules apply: No expectation, no blame and no judgment.

* * * * *

With regard to rearing well-balanced children: (1) Set a positive example; (2) communicate clear expectations; (3) emphasize the positive; (4) discuss consequences; and (5) encourage children to make amends and restitution for the wrong they do.

* * * * *

Wealth is achieved and enjoyed as a byproduct of doing things correctly. Wealth sought purely for wealth's sake does not bring happiness. In other words, when people indulge in self-gratification, inevitably ten new desires will spring up, creating unhappiness. There is no end to this process. Further, because people attract what they give off, misery loves company. Such people choose to be associated with those who further allow them to remain unhappy. The way out of this trap is service. Service is the easiest way to train the mind. Ask: What good deeds can one perform with no expectation, only to serve? How can one help one's fellow man? Reject self-pity; feel love for those who are troubled. Be absolutely certain before accusing another person of wrong-doing. When one gets angry, it sets back upon them.

Our purpose in life is to serve, so we should not be overly concerned, and definitely not be worried, about discomfort. But we should also take care of ourselves, eat properly, exercise properly, rest properly and pray properly. We need to be patient and tolerant of others. It is most constructive to go out of our way to express positive things to other people. Serve, smile, laugh, love. Humor is the best medicine. Stay focused on the positive.

* * * * *

In 1900, there were 22 homeopathic colleges in the United States, and one of every six practicing physicians (M.D.s) was a homeopath. It was at that time that the AMA strengthened its alliance with the pharmaceutical industry, and the drug companies flooded the market with vast quantities of medications whose names and contents were protected by law.

* * * * *

Sweden's Director of Chemical Inspection has recommended to the Swedish government that dental amalgam be banned, since mercury appears on their list of hazardous chemicals. Mercury has been found to be damaging to the fetus of a pregnant woman if it's found in her teeth. In 1987, the Swedish National Board of Health and Welfare found that amalgam is toxicologically an unsuitable dental material.

Back in 1840, organized dentistry in the United States formed the American Society of Dental Surgeons. Members were required to sign pledges promising not to use mercury in the fillings of teeth. Several members were suspended from the society in New York City in 1848 for *"malpractice for using silver mercury fillings."*

* * * * *

"If you wish to glimpse inside a human soul and get to know a man, don't bother analyzing his ways of being silent, of talking, of weeping, or seeing how much he is moved by a noble idea; you'll get better results if you watch him laugh. If he laughs well, he's a good man...All I claim to know is that laughter is the most reliable gauge of human nature." - Fyodor Dostoyevsky, from his novel, *The Adolescent*

* * * * *

Humanity is a renewable resource. When men's thinking, hearts and diets individually are changed, then human institutions will be changed. When human institutions are altered, then the earth will be restored.

* * * * *

"The healthiest environment by far is found at higher altitude. That's why the healthy people of the world live at Hunzaland, the Vicabamba of Ecuador, and Georgia in the Soviet Union. These areas are virtually disease free. Bacteria and viruses cannot survive very long in high electron, negative ion envi-

ronments. Throughout history, plagues have survived in the lowlands that are not abundant in electrons and negative ions. There has never been a plague in the mountains." — Patrick Flanagan, Ph.D., *Acres U.S.A.*, March 1992

* * * * *

By the year 2000, it is estimated that 80% of Americans will live within 100 miles of the coasts.

CONCLUSION

GETTING GROUNDED
IN AN OPEN SYSTEM

June 2, 1993

The Issue

If there is one perspective that captures the essence of these times it is this: All of our established institutions operate via the closed system of conflict, chance, cycles, shortages, misery, negativity, poverty and death. These institutions are dying. They are locked into a trend which is topping out. By contrast, the abstract philosophical and scientific basis for institutions founded upon an open system of love, life, light, liberty, law, laughter and a long-term view is emerging in the new uptrend. We are caught up in the throes of this transition.

The Oppression

The old ways, the established institutions, fighting for their lives as they must, are doing everything they can to prevent this new emergence. Thus, the Gestapo tactics, the oppression and persecution of human life, freedom, creativity, free energy, non-drug based free market medicine, honest money, self-government, supernatural law, free enterprise, positivity, nuclear heterosexual families, decentralization, local government, free choice in education, an armed militia, a national sales tax versus the income tax, an open and free media, balance, the U.S. Constitution, contract, common law, and on and on.

The Police State

A social order is always either moving toward self-government or a police state. A social order is either operating with a win-win-win system anchored in supernatural law, or it is moving toward bankruptcy in a statist natural system. The United States is clearly moving toward the latter, a fascist, occult, Nazi-type police state. The uncovered/ungrounded New Age feministic spirit which is guiding (sic) these chaotic times will most probably find its grounding in a polarity reversal come 1996. The inevitable masculine compensation will be in the form of a Caesar, a Ross Perot or his equivalent, if you will. This is precisely what happened in Nazi Germany. The feministic New Age spirit there found its grounding in Hitler, who was eventually worse than the feministic, ungrounded extreme at the other end of the spectrum. There was no feminine-masculine balance in pre-Hitler Germany, no male grounding authority. Nor is there one in the United States today. Thus, it is no accident that Ross Perot, who has a classic Napoleon complex, is seen favorably today by 64% of Americans. Perot represents the masculine authority and self-discipline that Americans today lack individually. Americans are ready to give up their few remaining freedoms to a responsibility-assuming police state.

Given the present closed system, what choice do we have? Government is eventually the ultimate power in every natural earth-based system. Government is in reality a parasite, a religious and economic parasite. It draws its ideas for its laws from the religious realm of right and wrong, good and evil, and morality. It draws its economic sustenance from taxes extracted from its subjects. But today the parasite, civil government, has consumed the host. It has wrapped itself up like a cat in a ball of twine with excessive laws which have rendered the system not only noncompetitive, ineffective and cumbersome, but unintelligible, irrational, and gridlocked. On the economic end of the spectrum, by 1995-96, the federal government will have sucked so much economic sustenance from its subjects, that the compounding effect of the interest on the debt alone will consume the host, *"we the people."* The civil government has destroyed its former religious base, primarily the Ten Commandments and English common law, the Founding Fathers' Constitution, and courageous individuals like George Washington and Christopher Columbus. It has also consumed its economic base, having destroyed the dollar, first by removing its gold and silver backing, and now even removing what little confidence remains in a fiat currency that has been depreciated 95% since the turn of the century.

True to the death spiral that exists in outmoded institutions (and also in individuals) the federal government is doing exactly the wrong thing at the wrong time, biting off more than it can chew, which ensures its destruction. It should be backing off. It is exhausted and bankrupt, spiritually and economically. Getting U.S. troops involved in wars all over the world, telling Japan what to do to get its house in order, attempting to regulate all areas of life stateside, propagating endless domestic programs - it is suicidal.

The Elitists

What is really ironic is that this frozen core of government elitists represent a mere 1% exercising controlling power over the other 99%. The hard core of the Clintonistas are homosexuals, or so biased, which represent 1% of the U.S. population. Add to that the media, the feminazis, radical environmentalists and minorities, and far less than 20% of the population is in power. This violates the basic *"80-20 rule"* bell-shaped curve rule for social stability. It is made possible by a Hollywood-based media, *"holly wood"* being the wood of witches who worship Mother Earth. Its heroes are people who spend their lives in illusion - games, entertainment and witchcraft. Its mindless bureaucrats just take their orders and follow them, no different than did the Nazi bureaucracy.

Louis Beam, an accredited reporter for the *Jubilee* newspaper, was banned from BATF news conferences in Waco, Texas after he asked the question about whether or not the tactics of the ATF resembled those of a police state. When Beam tried to attend another ATF news conference, he was arrested for *"criminal trespass."* His simple question was, *"Are we seeing the emergence of a police state in the United States?"* Dan Conroy, ATF spokesman, refused to answer. What the government denies, it affirms. Other establishment reporters congratulated Beam. They said they were not *"allowed"* to ask such questions. We are living in a Disneyland Dictatorship of the Media, disguising our police state.

A Wake-Up Call

The general public is receiving its *"wake-up call."* The needless murder of the Branch Davidians in Waco, Texas by the federal government, coupled with the price explosion upward by gold and silver, captured the hearts, minds and pocketbooks of middle America. Clintonphoria flipped to Clintonphobia. As mentioned above, the 64% approval rating now enjoyed by a likely upcoming Caesar, Ross Perot, is just one example. *USA Today* reported on April 30, 1993, *"A poll of 1200 moviegoers nationwide, commissioned by the Indianapolis-based Heartland Film Festival, found that 77% do not feel Hollywood portrays their values, and that even PG films have too much violence, bad language and sex."* Seventy-nine percent of Americans said the most important thing in their families growing up was *"discipline when you did something wrong."* Eighty percent of Americans disapproved of the Supreme Court's ruling that banned prayer at school functions. There's that *"80-20 Rule"* again. (The *"80-20 Rule"* provides stability just off the first standard deviation of the bell-shaped curve.) The University of Chicago's National Opinion Research Center found, in a 1993 survey of 19,000 people in 20 countries with a Judeo-Christian tradition, that 90% of Americans believe in God.

The public is also realizing that the Clinton White House is run by ungrounded secular elitists, or as former Republican drug czar William Bennett put it, the White House reminds him of *"the law school dorm of an Ivy League university."* *"...Yale, Yale, the gang's all here."* ...A new *Washington Post*/ABC News poll showed that seven of ten voters believe the nation is headed down the wrong path. More than 50% believe the Clintonistas are doing too little to change things. Fully 45% of the Army surveyed stated it would rather quit than serve with gays. So effectively, democracy in the United States today is a farce. The common people are disenfranchised, and the American public knows it. So the only way the government can maintain power is through Force, Brow-beating and Intimidation, i.e. through the FBI, the police state.

Four No-No's

Moneychanger writer Franklin Sanders states that there are three questions that cannot be asked openly in this country any more, particularly in court. They are: *"1) If we have a constitutional right to gold and silver money, why are we using the notes of a private corporation, i.e. the Federal Reserve System? 2) What statute makes any individual liable for an income tax? 3) If we have a constitutional republic, why is an oligarchy running it?"* And I would add one other: *"How can there truly be equal rights in a country if minorities have special privileges, and our elected representatives are immune from the laws they pass?"* ...A dark, closed, death-based system has to oppress and persecute an open, living system. A lit candle illuminates a dark room. This is why my work for the President of Guatemala was overthrown in 1983.

Revolutionary Times

These are clearly revolutionary times. Ideally, there would be a peaceful, nonviolent repentance, revival, renewal, reformation, restoration and reconstruction in this country to turn things around. But the history of a natural order in a closed system such as ours argues, sadly, for violence. (There is always that blood sacrifice and the operative second law of thermodynamics.) There is something very sinister about the fact that over 500 gang members from all around the country met in Kansas City, Missouri on April 29, 1993, just prior to the high day of witchcraft, the anniversary of the birth of both the Illuminati and the Bolshevik revolution, under the guise of the National Urban Peace and Justice Summit. You just get the sense that the cities are getting ready to be torched and that the earth changes are about to break wide open.

Man/Earth

I have talked about *"man"* and the *"earth"* being the two basic parts of the economic equation, and that as goes man so goes the earth, and vice versa. I want to clarify. People who adhere to the tenets of natural order in a closed death-based system, the *"natural man"* if you will, inescapably are environmentally influenced. As goes the earth, so goes such a man. This is the case in the United States today. The EPA was just promoted to the Cabinet level. No accident. By contrast, what used to exist somewhat in the early history of this country, at least up until the War of Northern Aggression (called by modern historians the U.S. Civil War), was a faith based in an open system of law, which came supernaturally (the Ten Commandments, etc.). This gave man an abstract base to withstand natural earth changes. Thus, as went man, so went the earth in early American history to a degree. Man had dominion over the earth rather than being a slave to it. Where the U.S. missed the boat was by not building on the masculine foundation of supernatural law so that legalism and materialism could have been overcome by a masculine-based spiritualism and stewardship, kinder and gentler in nature, love based, satisfying to the feminine gender, where men are more *"response-able"* (responsible).

(The R. Buckminster Fuller dome is 20 equilateral triangles put together to enclose a space. These 20 triangles create a balance of the overall electromagnetic field/countenance/aura of an individual who has a frequency like that of a perfect spiritual master, Jesus. It projects a <u>masculine</u> feeling, is <u>yang</u>, <u>positive</u>, and balances <u>male</u> gender impulses.)

Scientifically, man is tied to the earth, given the connecting commonality of the piezoelectric charge and his carbon/mineralized base. But mankind is also inescapably religious. He will either posit his faith increasingly in the creation, the earth, and see it as sacred, which locks him into the second law of thermodynamics and the death spiral of a closed system, or he will posit it in a source from outside of nature, a supernatural God and His laws, if you will, which provides the faith and following institutions for an open system with all the hope that brings. Today the faith is clearly in the creature creation (the earth) versus the Creator, rabidly so by the ruling elite. Thus, the unchallengeable witchcraft-based environmentalism which is moving anew to control food and farming and eliminate hunting and grazing on all public lands. The Clintonistas now see agriculture as the primary pollutant of U.S. rivers (64%) and public lands as a wilderness, not a potential garden. The masses have been deceived into buying the idea that government can solve all of man's problems and can clean up the earth, despite the history of the U.S. and the U.S.S.R. to the contrary. Therefore, we are told, people are the problem. None other than one of our Nobel Prize winners in economics, Milton Friedman, has described this issue clearly: *"So long as the attitude in society is that people are responsible for themselves, but that nature inevitably will limit what we can have, there is a chance that the discontent people feel will be directed at nature. But when we take the attitude that government is all-powerful, that it's only because somebody didn't pass the right law that we're in a bad way, the discontent will be directed at people."* There you have it, the contrast in philosophies, and the contradiction of an ungrounded, polluting, parasitic government serving as the ultimate Smokey Bear environmentalist. Dr. Friedman also makes apparent that personal responsibility focuses on redeeming a niggardly earth, while a focus on government results in godlike demands.

The federal government today wrongfully sees itself as an unrestrained god/goddess, locking up and prohibiting man's access to *"Mother Earth,"* which is viewed as the sacred source of life. This is, again, in sharp contrast to our Western Hebrew-Christian heritage which sees the earth as under man's dominion (masculine), over which he had stewardship (feminine). This is an irreconcilable conflict in philosophies. Men's thinking will inescapably stem ultimately from one of these two faiths, an evolutionary one or a creationist one, and the results of this faith will work out over time.

Law

Recall in American history a phrase which long existed regarding our law: *"Ignorance of the law is no excuse."* This phrase did not arise from so-called evolutionary or natural law (a contradiction in terms). Instead it stemmed from the fact that up until relatively recently, everyone knew the law of God, the Ten Commandments. They were posted on the walls of the public schools and taught to the children. After all, government is always religion applied to economics (human action). Education is such an indoctrination.

What I have found truly incredible is that even now, after a century of conditioning, still in keeping with the *"80-20 rule"* of stability, *Time* magazine reluctantly admits that 80% of Americans in the 46-64 age group agree that the Bible is the *"totally accurate"* word of God. In the younger 25-45 age bracket, *Time* found that 73% agree that the Bible is the *"totally accurate"* word of God. We have to have laws that come from outside of a closed, earth-based system - supernatural laws - in order to have true self-government and freedom.

After all, the source of law is the god of any society, because laws are legislated religious ideas which frame the arena of human action (economics). Only ruling supernatural law can relegate the federal government to the status of an institution like any other - the family, the church, the school, business, the military, the federal government, etc. The federal government has a limited function when supernatural law is the basis of a society, because the civil government cannot play the role of god.

What I have also found exciting in our evolutionary, closed system, secular humanistic society is a study done by the Century III Foundation of Oak Brook, Illinois. The Century III Foundation has held numerous seminars made up of people of all races, religions, and age groups, from all economic strata in the U.S., and had them logically and rationally formulate a series of laws to govern society on which they could agree. Remarkably, there was over 80% consensus among these seminar attendees that the Ten Commandments met their criteria for justice, equality and uniformity in society. How's that for grounding and an open system opportunity?

Science, Religion and Law

Let's take this one step further. I just read an interesting book by one of the world's leading scientists, a Jew, Peter M. Rothschild, M.D., entitled, *"The Scientific Background of the Ten Commandments."* Stated Dr. Rothschild, *"As Quantum Physics, the most advanced discipline, demonstrated beyond the slightest doubt - the ultimate mechanisms of the Universe cannot be explained without this concept of God, or whatever the term you care to use to refer to a supreme Maker.*

"Unquestionably, the complex laws that govern the behavior of all forms of energy and their interactions with all matter - which are but expressions of energies - necessarily had to precede the material processes of Creation, which we describe as our Universe.

"Creation is an ever-open process. And so is, for that matter, intelligence." ...There it is, the open system! Dr. Rothschild continues, *"...[R]ecent discoveries made in Quantum Physics - the stoutest pillar of modern science - reveal that indeed everything that exists stems from a central source, God, without whose acts the entire Creation would not have occurred."*

Dr. Rothschild concluded, *"Love is the most essential ingredient in the entire Creation. It is love that secures the delicate balance of opposing forces - good and bad; positive and negative - and ensures the stability of the Universe. The Ten Commandments contain the complete formula of love. The first Ten Commandments are the original vectors which began all the energies necessary to generate and perceive the magnificence of love."* ...And yet our death-based, closed system of federal government has ruled the Ten Commandments not only out of court, but out of our schools, and out of our lives. No wonder there is so little love in our society; no wonder there are over 40 wars on the planet today. We have a death wish in our closed system. No wonder we are the world's leading debtor (death) country, the world's leading arms exporter (death), the world's financier of the global drug trade (death), the U.N.'s military strong arm (death), the leader in abortion (death), allow those infected with AIDS, TB and hepatitis to roam freely (death), and the leading exporter of violence billed as entertainment (death).

The Sabbath

I found particularly fascinating Dr. Rothschild's comments concerning the Fourth Commandment, the keeping of the Sabbath day, taking one day out of seven for rest. Such used to be standard practice in this country. Dr. Rothschild writes, *"The six-plus-one day concept is perfectly compatible with the postulates of Quantum Physics for the simple notion that reveals that nothing can progress as long as its existence is subject to an unvaried, uninterrupted routine. The 6:1 proposition is one of the most dynamic factors in the progressive processes of the Universe. Without periodic interruptions, harmonics deteriorate, progress comes to a standstill, and after a brief period of stagnation, the Universe reverts to chaos. The ideal rhythm to interrupt harmonics in order to prevent there becoming a routine is represented by the proposition 6:1. Indeed, Quantum Physics establishes that beyond doubt none of the energies that exist in the Cosmos are generated in continuous emissions, but in variable packets, that is, partial transmissions.*

"Remarkably, the time-lapse required for the transmission of a quantum is exactly six times longer than the intervals that separate each transmission from the next one."

Where is our Sabbath rest today? Where is the 6:1 break that allows us to progress? Where is routine worshipped? Where is initiative, creativity, and innovation thwarted? In the brain-dead big bureaucracies. There is the open versus the closed system in a nutshell, life versus death, freedom versus slavery, prosperity versus poverty, peace versus conflict, creativity versus bureaucratic rules and regulations, and on and on. This sent me scurrying back to Proverbs 19:16, *"He who keeps the commandments keeps his soul, but he who is careless of his ways will die."* Also Proverbs 8:36, *"But he who sins against me wrongs his own soul; all those who hate me love death."*

Our Spiritual Essence

We must keep our perspective. We are spiritual beings, having a physical experience, biochemically activated and emotionally charged. We are made in the image of God, but formed from the dust of the earth.

At a time when the earth is losing its magnetic charge and everything is becoming ungrounded, when the line between the natural and supernatural is being blurred, the compensation is that scalar energy (left brain/right brain interaction across the corpus callosum) is becoming more powerful. Thus, it is critical now as never before that we control all of our thoughts and E-motions to keep us *"at ease"* so that we don't become *"dis-eased."* But for this to occur, our thoughts and E-motions have to be grounded in eternal values and principles, such as the Ten Commandments and the Second Great Commandment. Moreover, in the positive-negative, masculine-feminine balanced perspective, we must think on whatever things are true, just and noble (masculine), and whatever things are pure, lovely and of good report (feminine). We must think primarily of those things which are praiseworthy and virtuous. This must be the focus of our balanced meditations. To perform well at anything we must be *"at ease"*, not *"dis-eased."*

Our Physical Essence

In addition to our spiritual grounding, we must ground ourselves physically, with a good nutritional base. Our physical plant then has to be balanced and correctly nutritionally nourished. I will never forget what I learned when I lived in Corpus Christi, Texas. There I visited with the staff of the Lester Roloff school for wayward girls. I was told that regardless what was done with these girls, regardless what they were taught, how they were disciplined, how much they were loved, worked, exercised and rested, nothing worked, nothing stuck, until these girls first received the right nutritional grounding physically so that the psychological, emotional, mental and spiritual change desired could be anchored, take root and flourish. (Of course exercise, rest and sunlight are important, too.)

Today, 70-80% of *"dis-ease"* is traced to bad emotions, emotional problems, confirmed by the exciting new establishment medical field of psychoneuroimmunology. (A related book on the subject of E-motion and *"dis-ease"* is Louise L. Hay's HEAL YOUR BODY.) And over 70% of *"dis-ease,"* according to Dr. Robert Kaplan, can be traced to nutritional deficiencies. Negative E-motion burns up the nutritional grounding. We can therefore conclude that if we are emotionally and nutritionally correct, that is spiritually and physically correct, we stand a good chance of being *"at ease,"* rather than *"dis-eased."* So I hope it is with you. We all want to soar, to be loving personally, grounded physically, and obedient spiritually. By so doing we can be in good health and prosper long-term, and be more *"response-able"* (responsible).

THE GREAT E-MOTION
June 30, 1993

As Dr. Gary Martin, Ph.D., of the Biological Immunity Research Institute of Scottsdale, Arizona puts it, man is a spiritual being, having a physical experience, biochemically activated, and emotionally charged. ...Just think what this world would be like if we became more interested primarily in our spiritual development than in our physical acquisitions, in open systems rather than in closed ones. After all, we are eternal. We're not wealthy unless we're healthy, physically and E-motionally. It is the highly charged issue of E-motion, Energy-In-Motion, that I want to deal with here. E-motional stability is basic to grounding, health, and prosperity. Disciplined E-motions are as important as a disciplined mind and body.

Minding the Earth

E-motions, like fire, are fearful masters but wonderful servants. E-motions, properly placed, are a choice, not a reaction. Harnessing E-motion, staying grounded with values stemming from faith, allows one to stay calm, cool and collected under all circumstances in life. This is critical now as never before. Why? Because life is becoming increasingly ungrounded. As the earth loses its magnetic charge, the compensating power is flowing to the mind of a man by way of scalar energy. This means the left-brain/right-brain scalar transmitters, pulsating simultaneously opposite each other across the corpus callosum, are increasing in strength. Moreover, the human mind extends to all its bodily satellite stations wherein memory is stored, in the organ systems and every cell of the body. If this mind field, this energy field, is not rooted in solid, supernatural values that support a faith, mentality, and E-motion which enable an individual to constructively handle the circumstances of life, he will self-destruct. The essence of our age is self-destruction and madness. As the earth loses its magnetic charge and the mind becomes more powerful, the chaotic E-motion is chewing up nutritional grounding regardless of how solid it may be.

My old friend Peter Kelly at Interdimensional Sciences, whose equipment has been used by a chiropractic college to measure the electrical discharge from a chiropractic adjustment, and who has designed wonderful BETAR and Baby BETAR musical relaxation systems (1-800-33BETAR), has confirmed what I have just written. The mind of man is becoming stronger, more scalar and spiritual, as the earth magnetically becomes weaker. Thus, with all this energy flowing upward, it will take much more conscious effort to stay grounded.

Light Man

What this means practically is that the Clintonista New Agers have it 180 degrees out of phase again. They are E-motionally out of control, angry, power hungry, insecure, fearful. Some attempt to get grounded by focusing selfishly on their bodies, being self-absorbed about getting in shape and eating right. But spirit is more important than flesh, indeed it determines flesh. To paraphrase Jesus, it's not what a man eats that is most important, but what comes out of his mouth (his heart) that is significant.

Dr. Robert O. Becker, M.D., in his books, *The Body Electric* and *Cross Currents*, has confirmed that the electrical field of man is the determinant of what occurs in the physical body. Dr. Harold Saxton Burr, M.D., in his 1972 book, *Blueprint for Immortality*, established that the L-field, the electrodynamic field, reveals the physical and mental conditions of the body and makes it possible for M.D.'s to diagnose illnesses before the usual symptoms develop and are manifest in the physical body itself. Dr. Burr, for 43 years a faculty member of the Yale University School of Medicine as professor of anatomy and neuro-anatomy, compiled 40 years of documentation to confirm that all living things - plants, animals and humans - are controlled by an electrodynamic field, which can be measured and mapped with standard modern volt-meters. From another perspective, Dr. Stanley Keleman, in his book, *Your Body Speaks Its Mind*, establishes the same thing. The physical human body is a reflection of its mental and emotional processes. A chiropractor in California, Dr. Lowell Ward, and his son, working with Loma Linda there, have over thirty years of documentation, in conjunction with German physicians, in mapping out with computers how the body reflects what is going on in the mind and E-motions. Two x-rays taken from the back, one standing, one sitting, and two more from the side, the results run through a computer with mathematical and geometric analyses, confirm what E-motional software programming an individual brought into this world from his forefathers. Dr. Lowell Ward has effectively demonstrated that the errors of the father (and mother) are passed on to the sons and daughters for at least four generations. Ward's work was recently featured on early-morning CBS.

In France, physicians have over 800,000 documented cases gathered over a twelve-year period, showing that with Kirlian photographic pattern recognition, the energy field of the body can actually predict what *"dis-ease"* will appear in the body 3, 6, 9, 12 months or more down the road. Dr. Samuel C. West, a Utah naturopath, has demonstrated that the fourteen acupuncture meridian systems of the human body and the lymphatic system are effectively identical. Both the meridian system and the lymphatic system are electrical. This means they (we) are effectively spiritual living energy - light men! The lymphatic system has a greater fluid content than blood in the body. The lymphatic system is key to health. So literally, as a man thinks, so he is physically.

Louise L. Hay's book, *Heal Your Body*, lists the supposed E-motional basis of *"dis-ease."* Dr. Valerie V. Hunt, formerly of UCLA, has successfully demonstrated that the human mind is an energy-information field and is the true source of all health problems.

D-E-R

If we stop and think about it, we know that over 80% of dis-ease these days is caused by stress, by not processing life correctly E-motionally. In other words, over 80% of dis-ease these days stems from energy in motion, dysfunction, negative energy. Ponder three key words: *"dis-ease," E-motion," "response-ability."* If we are able to process our *"E-motion"* constructively, we will be *"at ease"* and not be subject to *"dis-ease."* We will then be better equipped to process and respond to life, or be *"response-able"* (responsible). People who are able to respond to life, to be "response-able," are free. Freedom and responsibility run hand in hand. Bureaucrats - corporate, military, charitable, educational, religious and governmental - seem almost inhuman sometimes. Why? Obviously, they are not free, nor, are they responsible. Vast, geographically dispersed vertical bureaucracies are dehumanizing.

Roots

E-motion (energy in motion), both positive and negative, stems from values (and their following thoughts) which have either been confirmed or violated. To be comprehensively healthy, we need a value system which is eternal, which is by definition supernatural/quantum if we are to stay steady and grounded in our ever-changing world of flux, our Newtonian, natural world, subject to the second law of Thermodynamics of entropy and death. We want to home in on an open system rather than a closed one in establishing our value base. This is why the supernaturally given Ten Commandments and the Second Great Commandment (the Golden Rule) are so important. Their implementation on earth has resulted in freedom and unequaled prosperity wherever they were applied historically. People have been *"able to respond."*

To become E-motionally correct, and at peace rather than chaotic, we need to establish this value system, which is a supernatural/eternal/quantum-based open system, so that light, life, love, liberty, law, laughter and a long-term view consistently govern our lives. This brings into balance the masculine and feminine, the linear and cyclical, the yin and the yang, the one and the many, in a yet structured holographic authority relationship. We also need to learn the techniques necessary to process negative E-motions, and particularly clean up the chaotic and destructive E-motion (energy in motion) in our subconscious, bringing it up to the level of consciousness where we can deal with it and release it, so it is no longer destructive to our system.

There are only three things we can do with E-motion: 1) express it; 2) suppress it; or 3) confess it/release it. We always want to do the latter, confess/release it. When we express negative E-motion we do harm to ourselves and to others which results in damage control later on. When we suppress negative E-motion we do damage to ourselves. What we need to do instead is to confess/release it, to cancel it, to forgive.

Airheads

We all know that life is breath. Every time we experience a negative E-motion we literally shorten our breath and therefore, effectively shorten our lives. We lock the memory and destructive force of that negative E-motion into our bodies' systems. It continues to work below the level of consciousness to our detriment. Thus, we always want to breathe deeply, under all circumstances, particularly through negative E-motional experiences. Hale Dwoskin of The Sedona Institute in Phoenix places primary emphasis on feeling the negative E-motions in the diaphragm/solar plexus area where the breath is shortened, then using an effective release technique, allowing the release of apathy, grief, fear, anger, lust, pride and all their negative sub-categories which are stored up in the body. Could we, would we, let such negative E-motions go? Sure. When? Now!

Three Amigas

If we go back to our initial human experience, our consciousness in the womb, we find it is the closest natural thing on earth we will experience to a perfect environment. So, we naturally in life keep attempting to recreate it. There, in the womb, most of us felt secure, loved (approved of), and in control. These three needs, which we try to reestablish over and over again in life, stem from our initial feminine womb connection. We have a primal need for control, approval, and security, not to mention the ego's (pride's) need to be *"right."* If we don't get them, we tend to scream.

If we live to satisfy these primal natural E-motions, we err. This is why if we are to move from milk to meat, from immaturity to maturity, eventually we have to become grounded and move from the ungrounded feminine to the grounded masculine hierarchical perspective, while simultaneously maintaining a balance between the masculine and the feminine. Ideally both the feminine and the masculine (of both sexes) need to be held in a dialectic co-equal balance, but the authority relationship is simultaneously masculine covering and grounds the feminine - justice tempered with mercy if you will. The offset is that mercy is preferred to justice.

If we look to establish security (feminine) as a primary motive, drive and goal, we will incorrectly perceive actuality in establishing our own subjective perception of reality. In life, to be true, we often have to do the opposite to reach the desired end. For example, good leaders serve. We have to take risks if we want to be secure. Risk assumption is primarily a masculine trait. How many risk-averse investors have we seen lose fortunes by playing it safe and secure? There is profit only where risk exists! ...If we want approval (feminine), we have to give to others what they want, both in the tangible and intangible realms. This means our own E-motion has to be subordinated first for us to be empathetic with the needs of others. We have to possess the humility to recognize and align with the highest and best in others, and be response-able to meet their needs empathically and with a sense of duty. ...Finally, if we seek control (feminine) in life, it inevitably eludes us. (The natural tendency is for men to be response-unable and women to be dominant.) We all have limited time, limited resources, limited knowledge, limited ability, limited power, limited mobility, and limited energy. Total control is beyond us, even of ourselves, much less others. About the only thing we can control successfully is ourselves, keeping in mind, we are only invulnerable where we are without defenses. (The need to control is secondarily masculine - liver/gall bladder/left brain. The need for acceptance/approval is also secondarily feminine - heart/spleen/right brain.)

Faith

We all know that as we get older, life - energy in motion (E-motion) - takes its toll on our bodies if we don't handle it correctly. We want to be *"E-motionally correct."* As we get older, we either get *"bitter"* or we get *"better."* Stated differently, as we grow older, we either live more by *"faith,"* or by *"fear"* (feminine - masculine anger masks underlying fear.) Faith is risk-based (masculine) because it involves hope in something which does not yet exist in the tangible world, but instead exists in the mind and heart of man, in the intangible and abstract. Faith is sightless. Faith is also futuristic. Faith is thus the essence of growth and progress, the antithesis of uniform control, retrenching fear, security craving, and group approval, which lead to stagnation, decay and death. How many football teams have we seen attempt to sit on (control) a lead only to blow it? Fear, security, control, being comfortable in the approval of the status quo - all lead to failure. Life, E-motion (energy in motion), is dynamic. It is never stagnant. Any time we're coasting, we're going downhill, and we do that naturally, according to Newtonian physics and the second law of thermodynamics, the law of decay and death.

We've already established the importance of grounding ourselves in values arising from supernatural law, law from outside of nature, coming from a Source Who exists in the open system, at the zero crossover point of the sine wave, integrating linear with cyclical time, so that our own natural E-motion and chaotically flawed values, stemming from our ancestry and culture, don't lead us into error. But what about techniques to confess/release the negative E-motion which is locked up in our genetic pool (which can and does change), and our subconscious? Well, for better than 90% of us the belief system exists to establish such a release. Our biblical heritage teaches us to be anxious about nothing, to bring every thought into captivity to obedience to Christ, to give thanks in all things, to renew our minds, that all things work together for good, that we're to overcome evil with good, that we're to bless our enemies, that we're to think on whatever things are good, noble, and just (masculine), and whatever things are pure, lovely, and of good report (feminine), and to meditate on whatever things are praiseworthy and virtuous. As we do this and grow in grace (power), our E-motions become increasingly still, quiet, at peace. Joy takes over. We are better able to live in the present moment, to be fully conscious in the *"now,"* and then be *"response-able"* (responsible). The intangible things such as love, freedom, joy and health become more manifest in our being. We become more relaxed, more *"at ease."* We become more *"thought-full"* (thoughtful) as we become more *"faith-full"* (faithful), and less *"fear-full"* (fearful). The more feminine traits of compassion, kindness, gentleness, and mercy become manifest. We become overall more loving. And love is the primary characteristic of the supernatural Law-Giver, covering both ends of the spectrum, that base which establishes the foundation/grounding which makes life-giving E-motion possible. After all, The Most High God is the great eternal E-MOTION (ENERGY IN MOTION).

Recommendation

You know, to *"feel"* is both physical and emotional. There is the basic psychosomatic connection. Accordingly, over the past year I have worked through three different systems, all of which have proven beneficial. I have used these three constructive techniques to begin cleaning out at the conscious and subconscious levels, the head and the heart, negative and destructive E-motion (energy in motion). I recommend ALL three of these courses on E-motional processing to you, from teenagers on up. My preference is the following order:

1. First we put our heads on straight. We understand. Dr. Michael Ryce's series *"Why Is This Happening to Me...Again?!"* is great for this. Dr. Ryce teaches us why the same thing happens to us over and over again, and why we react the same way over and over again, and how to clear it out and change things for good. Order from Robert Fridenstine, New Horizons Trust, 800-755-6360, 53166 St. Rt. 681, Reedsville, OH 45772).

2. Next, to link the heart and E-motions up with breath, the body, and the subconscious, the Sedona Institute's Sedona Method is a long-standing, highly appreciated technique. Phone (602) 553-3770; fax (602) 553-3790; or write 2701 E. Camelback Rd., #500, Phoenix, AZ 85016. The Sedona Method includes eight videotapes, a master E-motion chart (invaluable), five workbooks to use with the videotapes, including three special workbooks on your appearance, health and well-being, your relationships, and your financial freedom.

3. For detailed, specific and precise scientific integration of the E-motional with the physical, Dr. Gary Martin's Biological Immunity Research Institute is on the cutting edge. Phone 800-654-3734; fax (602) 948-8150; or write to 13402 N. Scottsdale Rd., Suite B-170, Scottsdale, AZ 85254. Dr. Martin works with the *"dragons"* within each of us which emit chaotic negative E-motion, literally destructive radiation, which attracts our repeating problems and frustrate our life's purpose. We get back what we give off. Dr. Martin confirms negative E-motion on the biochemical end with saliva and urine tests, leading to the suggested nutritional support. It's incredible to watch how an individual's saliva and urine test results change once their E-motional pattern changes and they become more calm and at peace. For counseling on literally slaying your own *"dragons,"* contact Dr. Gary Martin at Biological Immunity Research Institute.

Whew

Well, there you have it. I feel like this chapter and the one on the open system are an important high point for which I've been striving in my writings all these 17 years. I really believe/think/feel that with what you now have available to you as presented in these two chapters, and specifically in this chapter regarding these three emotional processing systems, you have basics for your holistic well-being for the challenges soon forthcoming. We shall overcome the closed natural death-based Newtonian system in whose grip we reside today. We shall overcome by 2008-2012, maybe sooner.

Let me conclude with one of my favorite verses from the Old Testament of the Bible. It speaks to the importance of the mind/E-motion energy field which surrounds the body, the aura, the countenance. *"The Lord bless you and keep you; The Lord make his face shine upon you, and be gracious unto you; The Lord lift up His countenance upon you, and give you peace."*

* * * * *

Regarding emotion, for the exclusively investment-oriented among you, I wanted you to know that this emotional training has made a substantial beneficial contribution to my personal investment and trading efforts. Why? Because in today's society, inescapably so, money is tied directly to emotion. Money is the means to the end of physical survival in our social order. Specifically, I have noticed the following benefits: Trading the markets is less stressful because I do not have the emotional tie-in that I had previously, either by way of fear or greed, or by way of exhilaration or remorse. This has made me more objective, with the byproduct being increased psychological reserves, the ability to carry more positions simultaneously, and an enhanced, keener and broader perception of the markets than what previously existed. In short, the above-discussed emotional training has made me a better investor because I have become more astute, more aware, and gleaned more insight because my own emotional issues don't get in the way. I am stronger, I am more grounded. I see more clearly, and I act more readily. This was the delightful, unexpected byproduct to all this emotional work. It was worth it.

You know, we all go through a good part of our lives seeing things primarily one way and responding accordingly, based upon our genetic programming, our parental, social, and peer group programming, etc. Then all of a sudden, these emotional processing techniques come along and open up an entirely new way of perceiving and dealing with the world in which we live. The result is new, varied and more productive options in both thinking and behavioral response to opportunities and challenges as they present themselves. It's great.